INDIA DEVELOPMENT REPORT
2011

INDIA DEVELOPMENT REPORT
2011

edited by

D.M. NACHANE

OXFORD
UNIVERSITY PRESS

OXFORD
UNIVERSITY PRESS

YMCA Library Building, Jai Singh Road, New Delhi 110 001

Oxford University Press is a department of the University of Oxford. It furthers
the University's objective of excellence in research, scholarship, and education by
publishing worldwide in

Oxford New York
Auckland Cape Town Dar es Salaam Hong Kong Karachi
Kuala Lumpur Madrid Melbourne Mexico City Nairobi
New Delhi Shanghai Taipei Toronto

With offices in
Argentina Austria Brazil Chile Czech Republic France Greece
Guatemala Hungary Italy Japan Poland Portugal Singapore
South Korea Switzerland Thailand Turkey Ukraine Vietnam

Oxford is a registered trademark of Oxford University Press
in the UK and in certain other countries

Published in India
by Oxford University Press, New Delhi

ISBN-13: 978-0-19-807153-2
ISBN-10: 0-19-807153-1

Typeset in Minion 10.5/12.7
by BeSpoke Integrated Solutions, Puducherry, India 605 008
Printed by De Unique, New Delhi 110018
Published by Oxford University Press
YMCA Library Building, Jai Singh Road, New Delhi 110 001

Preface

The Indian economy has experienced significant changes in the two decades of the reform period which started in 1991. In the post-reform period, India has done well according to some indicators such as economic growth, exports, balance of payments, significant accumulation of foreign exchange, resilience to external shocks, service sector growth, revolution in IT sector, stock market boom, and so on. Thus, one broad conclusion is that the economic reforms have contributed greatly to macroeconomic stability and growth. GDP growth was around 8 to 9 per cent per annum in the period 2004–5 to 2007–8. India is a 1.6 trillion dollar economy. Investment and savings rates have been quite high in recent years at 32 to 36 per cent. In spite of the global financial crises, India's GDP growth rate has not declined significantly. Having witnessed a slowdown in growth in the wake of the crises, India's growth rate picked up to 8 per cent in 2009–10 from 6.7 per cent a year ago. The economy expanded by 8.9 per cent in the first half of the current fiscal year (2010–11), making it one of the fastest growing economies in the world. GDP growth rate is expected to reach more than 8.5 per cent in the next financial year (2011–12) despite the uncertain global scenario. In the last two decades, India has also managed the inflation rate within limits although the problem of rise in food prices has been a worry in recent years.

However, despite high growth, there have been concerns on low agriculture growth, low-quality employment growth, low human development, rural–urban divides, gender and social inequalities, and regional disparities. Rightly, the government has emphasized on the need for inclusive growth during the Eleventh Plan period and beyond. It is, however, yet to be seen whether the country has moved towards achieving inclusive growth.

The *IDR* series provides an independent assessment of the Indian economy including contemporary problems, issues, and policies. The *IDR 2011* (sixth in the series) examines the experiences of Indian economy during the two decades of structural reforms in India. Among other things, it discusses the long-term perspective on the *sustainability* of the general strategy of development adopted in the post-reform period. Three types of sustainability viz. economic, social, and ecological are analysed. The report covers a whole range of topics: macroeconomic policies, crisis in agriculture, food security, industrial sector, role of auditors, telecommunications, capital inflows, export sector, poverty, inter-regional inequality, employment and industrial relations, banking services, disasters, energy sector, and environment sustainability.

The publication of this report has provided us an opportunity to bring the research insights of Indira Gandhi Institute of Development Research (IGIDR) scholars to a wider audience. Most of the papers are written by IGIDR faculty. Few scholars from other institutes have also contributed papers to this volume. The views expressed in this report are those of the individual authors.

I am grateful to Prof. D.M. Nachane for editing this volume and writing the overview. Thanks are also due to all the contributors to this volume and the Economic and Political Weekly Research Foundation (EPWRF) for the statistical appendices. I thank Mahesh Mohan for ably coordinating the production of the chapters and the Oxford University Press team for editorial support and help in bringing out the report.

S. MAHENDRA DEV
DIRECTOR, IGIDR

Contents

Tables

Figures

Boxes

A Statistical Profile

Abbreviations

AIDIS	All India Debt and Investment Survey
APL	above poverty line
BIS	Bank of International Settlements
BPL	below poverty line
BSE	Bombay Stock Exchange
BSNL	Bharat Sanchar Nigam Limited
CAC	capital account convertibility
CAD	current account deficit
CDMA	Code Division Multiple Access
CPCB	Central Pollution Control Board
CPI	consumer price index
CRR	cash reserve ratio
CSO	Central Statistical Organisation
DoT	Department of Telecommunications
ECB	external commercial borrowing
EM	emerging market
ESI	export similarity index
FDI	foreign direct investment
FII	foreign investment institution
FPI	foreign portfolio investment
FRBM	Fiscal Responsibility and Budget Management
GDP	gross domestic product
GFCF	gross fixed capital formation
GoI	Government of India
GSDP	gross state domestic product
GSM	Global System for Mobile Communications
HCR	head count ratio
HDI	Human Development Indicator
HPI	Human Poverty Index
IEA	International Energy Agency
IIP	index of industrial production
IMF	International Monetary Fund
INR	Indian rupee
IT	information technology
MDG	Millennium Development Goal
MoEF	Ministry of Environment and Forests
MPCE	monthly per capita expenditure
MRP	mixed recall period
MSP	minimum support prices
MSS	market stabilization scheme

MTNL	Mahanagar Telephone Nigam Limited
NCAER	National Council of Applied Economic Research
NEP	National Environment Policy
NGO	non-governmental organization
NREGS	National Rural Employment Guarantee Scheme
NSDP	net state domestic product
NSS	National Sample Survey
NSSO	National Sample Survey Organisation
NTB	non-tariff barrier
OBC	other backward class
PCC	Pollution Control Committee
PDS	public distribution system
PGR	poverty gap ratio
PPP	purchasing power parity
QOI	quality overlap index
R&D	research and development
RBI	Reserve Bank of India
SC	Scheduled Caste
SDP	state domestic product
SEBI	Securities and Exchange Board of India
SEC	Securities and Exchange Commission
SHG	self-help group
SPCB	State Pollution Control Board
ST	Scheduled Tribe
TE	triennium ending
TRAI	Telecom Regulatory Authority of India
UN	United Nations
UNDP	United Nations Development Programme
UPA	United Progressive Alliance
URP	uniform recall period
WPI	wholesale price index

Contributors

Debashish Bhattacherjee	Professor, Indian Institute of Management, Calcutta
S. Chandrasekhar	Associate Professor, Indira Gandhi Institute of Development Research, Mumbai
Errol D'Souza	Professor, Indian Institute of Management, Ahmedabad
Ashima Goyal	Professor, Indira Gandhi Institute of Development Research, Mumbai
Sunil Mani	Planning Commission Chair Professor, Centre for Development Studies, Thiruvananthapuram
Srijit Mishra	Associate Professor, Indira Gandhi Institute of Development Research, Mumbai
Sripad Motiram	Associate Professor, Indira Gandhi Institute of Development Research, Mumbai
D.M. Nachane	Professor Emeritus and Former Director, Indira Gandhi Institute of Development Research, Mumbai
R. Nagaraj	Professor, Indira Gandhi Institute of Development Research, Mumbai
Hippu Salk Kristle Nathan	PhD Scholar, Indira Gandhi Institute of Development Research, Mumbai
Rupayan Pal	Associate Professor, Indira Gandhi Institute of Development Research, Mumbai
K.V. Ramaswamy	Professor, Indira Gandhi Institute of Development Research, Mumbai
D. Narasimha Reddy	Visiting Professor, Institute for Human Development, New Delhi
B. Sudhakara Reddy	Professor, Indira Gandhi Institute of Development Research, Mumbai
Gordhan K. Saini	Assistant Professor, Tata Institute of Social Sciences, Mumbai
Jayati Sarkar	Associate Professor, Indira Gandhi Institute of Development Research, Mumbai
Subrata Sarkar	Professor, Indira Gandhi Institute of Development Research, Mumbai
Nirmal Sengupta	Professor, Indira Gandhi Institute of Development Research, Mumbai
Vinod Kumar Sharma	Professor, Indira Gandhi Institute of Development Research, Mumbai
M.H. Suryanarayana	Professor, Indira Gandhi Institute of Development Research, Mumbai
Rajendra R. Vaidya	Professor, Indira Gandhi Institute of Development Research, Mumbai
Vamsi Vakulabharanam	Lecturer, University of Hyderabad, Hyderabad
C. Veeramani	Assistant Professor, Indira Gandhi Institute of Development Research, Mumbai

Overview

Two Decades of Structural Reforms: A Balance Sheet

*D.M. Nachane**

INTRODUCTION

By many of the externally visible signs, the Indian reforms story has been a remarkable success. As Table 1.1 shows, after a long period of stagnation in the years following Independence, growth rates shifted into high gear sometime during the 1980s and in the last decade accelerated sharply, reaching undreamt of stratospheric heights. Further (see Table 1.2), India's recent growth record has been bettered among the Asian countries only by China (Mainland). This growth resurgence has enabled India to move up in the world per capita (PPP-corrected) GDP rankings from 93 (out of a total of 109 countries) in the mid-1970s to 58 by 2004 (Basu and Maertens 2007). On several other macroeconomic indicators, the country has been doing equally well. Investment as a proportion of GDP, for example, rose from about 10 per cent in the 1950s to about 23 per cent in the early 1980s and to about 35 per cent currently. Similarly, India today qualifies as an 'open economy' with exports (as a percentage of GDP) amounting to nearly 20 per cent, as compared to less than 5 per cent in the mid-1960s. And finally on the forex front, we have transited

from a perennially shortage situation to one that can only be described as an 'embarrassment of riches'. Inflation, always a serious concern in the Indian context, was sharply reined in, in the late 1990s, and even though it has once again shown signs of strong revival in the last year, it is not clear as to what extent it poses a serious threat to the overall success story. All these trends seem to have generated a great deal of optimism about India's future, especially in sections of the Western media, an optimism that sometimes borders on the euphoric.

And yet, as always in the past, India continues to baffle and defy any facile analysis, with its stark contrasts. For even the spectacularly rosy growth picture cannot fail to hide embarrassing (and one may add, even ugly) scars and warts. According to a recent estimate (Polaski et al. 2008), 792 million Indians (constituting around 73 per cent of the population) survive on less than $1 per day, while 94 per cent of the population live on less than $2 per day.[1] This dismal aspect, along with other alarming signals (to be discussed below), foretell that somehow 'all is not well in the

* I am extremely grateful to Prof. S. Mahendra Dev, Director, Indira Gandhi Institute of Development Research (IGIDR), for his valuable comments on an earlier draft of this chapter. The views expressed are the author's sole responsibility and may not necessarily reflect those of IGIDR.

[1] If one goes by the national poverty line, then in 2004–5 the proportion of people below the poverty line was 28.3 per cent for the rural areas and 25.7 per cent for urban areas (NSSO 2005). For the same year, as per the NCEUS (2007), about 77 per cent of the population had an income below Rs 20 per diem (twice the official poverty line), which is approximately 45 US cents at the current exchange rate.

Table 1.1 Growth Rates in India over Successive Plan Periods

Plan Period	Annual Growth Rate of GDP (Factor Cost) %	Average Annual Gross Domestic Capital Formation (as % of GDP at Factor Cost)
I. 1951–6	3.6	10.3
II. 1956–61	4.2	15.4
III. 1961–6	2.8	15.6
IV. 1969–74	3.3	17
V. 1974–9	4.8	20.2
VI. 1980–5	5.6	21.9
VII. 1985–90	6.0	25.2
VIII. 1992–7	6.7	25.4
IX. 1997–2002	5.5	25.9
X. 2002–7	7.6	27.51
2005–6	9.5	34.2
2006–7	9.7	35.8
2007–8	9.2	38.2
2008–9	6.7	34.9

Source: Basu and Maertens (2007); RBI (2010a).

Table 1.2 Growth Rates (%) for Select Countries in Asia, 1981–2008

Country	1981–90	1991–7	1998–2003	2004–8
India	5.6 (5.4)	5.3 (5.7)	5.7 (5.5)	8.1 (8.3)
China (Mainland)	8.9 (8.8)	10.3 (10.2)	8.0 (7.8)	10.7 (10.5)
China (Hong Kong)	6.3 (6.2)	5.5 (5.3)	2.2 (2.4)	6.1 (6.6)
Singapore	6.9 (7.5)	8.4 (8.2)	2.7 (2.2)	6.5 (7.5)
Bangladesh	3.9 (4.0)	4.5 (4.5)	5.0 (5.0)	6.1 (6.1)
Indonesia	5.3 (5.4)	6.7 (6.8)	4.0 (3.9)	5.6 (5.6)
Korea	8.3 (8.3)	6.7 (6.8)	3.9 (5.4)	4.1 (3.9)
Malaysia	5.8 (6.2)	8.8 (9.0)	2.7 (3.4)	5.6 (5.7)
Thailand	7.6 (7.3)	6.5 (7.6)	4.7 (4.9)	4.6 (4.8)
Pakistan	6.0 (6.0)	4.1 (4.2)	3.5 (3.3)	6.4 (6.3)
Sri Lanka	4.2 (4.3)	5.1 (5.1)	3.8 (4.6)	6.3 (6.3)

Source: International Financial Statistics, IMF.

Note: The figures in brackets represent the winsorized growth rates (i.e., calculated by omitting the highest and lowest observations over each sub-period).

Kingdom of Denmark'. Under such circumstances, it is no surprise that there seems to be a growing perception in the common mind, that at least a part of the social and political unrest now threatening to become endemic in specific regions of the country, could be attributable to fault lines in the economic growth and distribution strategy that has underpinned the Indian reforms process.

Considering that it is now nearly two decades since we broke so decisively with the past, the time seems to be propitious for Indian academics and policymakers alike to probe a little deeper below the outwardly benign surface of the market-oriented reforms strategy, in a dispassionate manner, bereft of ideological barnacles, instead of oscillating between the fixed points of antipodal dogmas.

It was thought that this *India Development Report* could address itself to the ambitious task of a critical assessment of some of the important aspects that the two decades of structural reforms have brought home. It need hardly be said that the issues span several dimensions, not all of which can be encompassed within the scope of a single report. We have, therefore, concentrated in this report on a cross-section of selected issues, which are deemed to be of cardinal significance. The report thus lays no claims to being a full critique of the reforms process; nevertheless it is hoped that the insights and findings of this report will serve to throw light on the extent to which the achievements of the reforms process are genuine and whether the glitter of *India shining* is 24-carat gold or just gold-plated nickel.

The development strategy initiated in India in the early post-Independence years was focused on four key elements (i) an emphasis on the development of basic and heavy industries, (ii) a system of centralized investment planning, (iii) an overarching role for the public sector, and (iv) national self-reliance via import-substitution coupled with 'export pessimism'. While there is a tendency nowadays to underplay the achievements of this 'Nehruvian' development strategy, it cannot be denied that this strategy laid the basis for a modern industrial economy, and kept the macro-economy on a moderate inflation path in spite of several droughts, international oil price shocks, and at least three major military conflagrations. However, in the late 1960s, the system was stretched in several directions, resulting in a highly bureaucratic and over-regulated economy. Some of the undesirable consequences of this *License Permit Raj* were (i) a high-cost domestic industry protected from foreign competition via tariffs and quotas, (ii) artificially low nominal interest rates (financial repression) combined with high inflation resulting in extremely low (often negative) real interest rates, in turn contributing to the adoption of undue capital-intensive techniques in manufacturing, and (iii) fiscal dominance over monetary policy, leading to a tendency towards fiscal profligacy.

The initial hesitant steps in the direction of liberalization were taken in the 1980s but the reforms story really begins with the balance of payments crisis of 1991, which forced the country to approach the IMF for assistance. Partly in response to the urgings of the IMF and partly owing to the general disillusionment with existing policies that inevitably accompanies a crisis, the government made a distinct historical break with the past and launched an ambitious reforms programme spanning several areas. Considering that several comprehensive accounts of the reforms measures abound in the literature (see, for example, Panagariya 2008), we do not go into a detailed recounting of all the measures.

It may be convenient in evaluating India's reforms story to distinguish the long-term issues of sustainability from the short and medium-term issues of macroeconomic stabilization. Without denying the importance of the latter, it is necessary to emphasize that governments facing the continual prospect of imminent elections are prone to be concerned overwhelmingly with macroeconomic stabilization to the neglect of longer-term issues of sustainability. As we shall see this seems to have been, to some extent, the case in India too.

MACROECONOMIC PERFORMANCE

The two major dimensions of macroeconomic performance are growth and inflation and we discuss each of these in turn.

Growth Trajectory

One of the issues which has attracted a great deal of attention from 'India watchers' revolves around the timing of the *growth miracle*. This is not of mere statistical interest, for if the vital structural break is located in the 1990s then a major role in the growth spurt could be assigned to the reforms, whereas earlier breaks would, in some measure, emasculate their contribution. Econometrically speaking, the most dependable study seems to be Wallack (2003), which locates the sole significant break in Indian GDP as early as 1980.[2] However, even if the growth acceleration does date back to the 1980s, as is well known, the growth impulses during this decade proved fragile. A number of explanations have been advanced about the transitory nature of this growth phase. A popular explanation (especially favoured by the liberalization advocates of the 1990s) is the view emphasized by DeLong (2001) and Panagariya (2004) that the growth impulse of the 1980s was fragile and unsustainable, because the reforms undertaken lacked depth and did not go far enough. A more plausible explanation runs in terms of a constellation of unfavourable circumstances emerging at the end of the 1980s, including the poor agricultural performance in two successive years (1986–7 and 1987–8), fiscal slippage (gross fiscal deficits in excess of 7 per cent from 1984–5 to 1990–1), an over-valued exchange rate, and a current account deficit which coursed through the 3 per cent (of GDP) barrier in 1990–1, leading to the well-known currency crisis of 1991.[3]

Table 1.1 affords a quick overview of the growth rate over successive plans. It can be seen that the quinquennial averages have been steadily increasing since the Fifth Plan

[2] A later break (1992–3) is discerned for two important components of the GDP viz. (i) trade, transport, storage, and communications and (ii) public administration, defence, and other services

[3] The debate on the timing of the *take-off* still remains an open issue. Sen (2007), for example, dates the break to the mid-1970s, when private capital investment increased noticeably, driven by the impetus of financial deepening, public investment, and the declining relative price of machinery.

period (1974–9). In the immediate wake of the reforms—if one omits the year 1991–2 itself, which witnessed a meagre growth rate of 1.3 per cent as being a year of adjustment—the growth rate picked up sharply over the five-year period 1992–7. Deceleration set in with the domestic political uncertainty of 1997, coupled with the Asian crisis, which also erupted simultaneously. However the growth momentum was more than restored beginning 2003 onwards, with the successive years 2005–6 to 2007–8 all posting rates above 9 per cent. Perhaps the greatest challenge that Indian macroeconomic management faced was the global financial crisis of 2008–9. Contrary to popular expectations, the Indian economy weathered the storm fairly well, at least so far as the growth rate was concerned (which remained comfortably at 6.7 per cent, though of course sharply lower than the record growth of the previous three years).[4]

Stabilization of Inflation

Considerable success was also achieved in the post-reforms decades in stabilizing inflation as well as inflationary expectations. The 1950s was a decade of low but volatile inflation with a decadal average of 1.7 per cent (see RBI 2006: 70). Inflation shot up sharply (as measured by the WPI) in the 1960s and accelerated further in the 1970s, moderating somewhat in the 1980s (averaging 6.4 per cent, 9.0 per cent, and 8.0 per cent in the three successive decades). This rise was in tandem with similar global and regional trends emanating from the collapse of the Smithsonian agreement, the oil price shocks of 1974, 1979, and 1987, fiscal profligacy coupled with loose monetary policies in the advanced economies (especially in the 1970s), and several other factors. The 1990s is often called the decade of *great moderation* as the advanced economies started streamlining their monetary policies and improving fiscal–monetary coordination, which resulted in a significant deceleration of inflation. However in India, the first half of the 1990s witnessed an upsurge of inflationary pressure while distinct signs of moderation did not become visible till 1996–7. A major reason for this moderation was undoubtedly the process of fiscal consolidation underway. Fiscal dominance over monetary policy was sought to be alleviated by phasing out the system of *ad hoc* Treasury Bills in April 1997 (and their replacement by a more transparent system of Ways & Means Advances), thereby precluding automatic monetization of the fiscal deficit. Further, possibly the biggest step in the direction of curbing possible fiscal profligacy was taken via the enactment of the Fiscal Responsibility and Budget Management Act 2003. Other reasons for this turnaround could be the pricing of government securities on a market-related basis (thus lending more edge to the RBI's open-market operations), a deceleration in M_3 growth rate, as well as an easing of domestic food supply imbalances and the global moderation, already alluded to.

The years 1996–7 to 2008–9 thus marked a period of unprecedented price stability, a happy trend which has been rudely interrupted by the sustained upward movement in the inflation trajectory beginning October 2009. Inflation, especially food inflation, is now emerging as a very serious threat to India's growth story.[5]

The first serious challenge of macroeconomic management that confronted Indian policymakers in the post-reforms period was the Asian crisis of 1997–9. As is now well known, through some extremely deft manoeuvring by the RBI on the monetary policy and exchange rate fronts, contagion was substantially contained (see, for example, Bhalla and Nachane 1998). An even greater challenge was posed by the recent global crisis. How some of the more serious fall-outs of this crisis were averted by a series of measures on the fiscal and monetary fronts forms the subject matter of Chandrasekhar's paper in this report (Chapter 2).

According to Chandrasekhar, a number of factors allowed India (and China) to remain *decoupled* from the global turmoil during the recent crisis. First, India's relative insularity is a key part of this explanation. India's low share in world exports meant that the slump in global demand did not affect Indian economy to any appreciable extent. Second, and probably fortuitously, the implementation of the recommendations of the Sixth Central Pay Commission gave a boost to domestic demand thereby contributing to growth.[6] Third, the nationwide implementation of the National Rural Employment Guarantee Scheme also had a salutary effect. Fourth, the Government of India rolled out the fiscal stimulus packages fairly rapidly and, finally, on the monetary policy front, the RBI carefully calibrated its response to the worldwide crisis, by reducing the cash reserve ratio and important policy rates.

Thus, by and large, India's record on macroeconomic stability in the two post-reform decades, while not exactly impeccable, could still be viewed with a sense of satisfaction.

ECONOMIC SUSTAINABILITY OF REFORMS

We now turn to a longer-term perspective on the *sustainability* of the general strategy of development adopted in the post-reforms period, which has been one based on the

---

[4] This is, of course, not say that the crisis left no marks on the Indian economy or that macro-management was totally flawless (see Nachane 2009 and Rakshit 2009).

[5] Addressing the chief secretaries (4 February 2011), the Prime Minister expressed serious concern about inflation posing a 'serious threat to growth momentum'.

[6] It is estimated that over 4.5 million central government employees and 3.8 million pensioners benefited in terms of higher incomes.

cardinal principles of marketization, export orientation, domestic and external financial liberalization, and a slew of industrial policies aimed at encouraging big ticket foreign and domestic investments in manufacturing, services, and infrastructure. Even though an enormous literature exists on *sustainable development*, a precise definition of *sustainability* is hard to come by. However, following Bartelmus (1999), we may in a broad fashion distinguish between three types of sustainability viz. *economic*, *social*, and *ecological* (concerned respectively with the maintenance of *economic/manufactured*, *social*, and *natural* capital).[7] We try to examine each of these in turn here, and begin with a discussion of economic sustainability.

A widely accepted definition of *economic sustainability* is maintenance of *manufactured* capital and closely corresponds to Hick's (1946) definition of income. In our context, we can define it as a growth rate which can be sustained without detriment to the long-term prospects of the economy.

The first and most important dimension to the issue of *economic sustainability* comes from an examination of the sources of economic growth and the sectoral composition of this growth. In particular, it is necessary to discuss the oft-posed question as to whether services-led growth (which may, for short be referred to as the Indian model of growth in the post-reforms period) can be sustainable. Special sectoral problems in the agricultural and manufacturing sectors can also impinge significantly on the issue of sustainability. Financial sector reforms represent a common theme running through all the sectors of the economy and their pace and design also crucially impinges on the overall issue of long-term price and financial stability. Finally, external sector imbalances can seriously threaten economic and political stability as was brought home to us on several occasions in the past[8] and most recently and with telling effect in 1991.

Sources of Economic Growth

An important dimension of the medium-term sustainability of the growth momentum pertains to the sources and composition of economic growth. Let us first delve into the sources of economic growth. If the growth acceleration is attributable primarily to a resources shift from the relatively low productivity agriculture sector to higher productivity manufacturing and services sectors then, in some sense, this acceleration is merely a reflection of a shift in development strategy (such as occurred in the Second Five Year Plan period) and not of the greater market orientation in the economy. Marked rises in total factor productivity (TFP) growth on the contrary indicate a crucial role for markets and/or openness of trade policies. Unfortunately, empirical evidence on this issue is mixed. Goldar (2004), for example, records a decline in the TFP growth rates from 0.92 per cent (1982–1991) to 0.65 per cent (1992–2000). Using slightly different methods, Bosworth et al. (2006) attribute an important role to resource allocation shifts but note a significant increase in the contribution of TFP to services growth in the post-reforms period (1993–2004) as compared to the decade (1983–93), while for the manufacturing sector an exactly opposite trend is in evidence. Of the other major studies, the conclusions of Sivasubramonian (2004) are broadly in agreement with those of Bosworth et al. (2006) and Goldar (2004), while Sengupta's (2005) study attributes a major role to the foreign trade effect in explaining the high post-reforms growth. Overall, most studies seem to explain the high growth momentum via the twin factors of (i) a shift in resources towards the services sector and (ii) the relatively faster TFP growth in services as compared to manufacturing and agriculture.[9]

Agricultural Sector

As a source of employment for about 75 per cent of the county's population and as a means of livelihood to an even greater percentage, the importance of agriculture for a country like India need hardly be gainsaid. That high growth rates of overall GDP, such as witnessed in the last decade, can only be secured by a robust agricultural sector, has been recognized by successive Indian governments since Independence. In recent years, a 4 per cent growth rate target for agriculture has been repeatedly affirmed at several official fora and, most importantly, has been emphatically delineated in all Plan documents since the Ninth Plan.

---

[7] Even though it is convenient for the purpose of analysis to maintain the distinction between various types of sustainability, significant overlaps can render the distinction fuzzy. To take only two examples: (i) financial sector reforms also influence the availability of credit to the poor and hence have important consequences for *social sustainability*, even though here we have listed them as an important determinant of *economic sustainability*; (ii) health and education are important determinants of economic growth and their role has been emphasized as such in the endogenous growth theory literature (see, for example, Salvadori 2003); but in the Indian context their role in the alleviation of poverty seems far more immediate and significant. Hence there is a stronger case for classifying expenditure on social infrastructure under the general rubric of *social sustainability*. We follow the general convention of persisting with these distinctions, always keeping in mind their somewhat ambivalent character.

[8] One may recall the balance of payments crisis of 1956, the rupee devaluation of 1966, the oil price shocks of 1974 and 1979, etc.

[9] Goldar and Mitra (2010) enter the important caveat that part of the TFP growth in services could be due to purely accounting reasons (such as the downsizing in public administration in the aftermath of deregulation).

However, the target has proved remarkably elusive, with the decadal average growth rate for 2000–1 to 2008–9 at 2.4 per cent, several notches lower than the decadal averages of about 3 per cent and 3.3 per cent obtained in the 1980s and 1990s respectively.

The constraints on agriculture and the dilemmas confronting official policy have both been the subject of extensive analyses (Polaski et al. 2008, Chand 2010, among others). Of the many constraints identified in the literature, seven seem to be particularly endemic (see Chand Ibid.): (i) paucity of institutional credit, (ii) erratic and inadequate power supply coupled with inefficient use of power, (iii) overall scarcity of high quality certified seeds, (iv) shortages of fertilizers and pesticides, (v) serious shortfall of state level extension services, (vi) increasing non-availability of agricultural labour, and (vii) rudimentary market infrastructure, affording middlemen space for an exploitative role in the supply chain from producer to consumer.

The lackadaisical performance in the agricultural sector has, in recent years, accentuated two perennial structural problems of the Indian economy. The first of these pertains to food insecurity. In a major initiative, the Government of India switched over to a targeted public distribution system (TPDS) in 1997, largely in the hope that the problem of food insecurity could be alleviated by a more focused and targeted approach to food distribution. By and large, the TPDS achievements have fallen considerably short of expectations.

Food security, of course, is a wider term than equitable food distribution, and M.H. Suryanarayana in his paper (Chapter 3) addresses certain methodological flaws in the Eleventh Five Year Plan's approach to the issue of food security. The Plan interprets the food security dimensions and health outcomes of the deprived sections with reference to estimates of mean-based averages for the past two decades, while disregarding the lags between inputs and outcomes. This methodological limitation, according to him, can have serious consequences in terms of interpretations and policy recommendations. His paper profiles income, food consumption, nutritional intake, and health outcomes for the past two decades by disaggregated decile groups at the national level and verifies the maintained hypotheses underlying the recent policy formulations of the *reform era*, that of the Eleventh Plan in particular. The disaggregated empirical profiles provide little evidence in favour of the maintained hypotheses underlying policy formulations. There is scope for revising the parameters used and assessment made of the situation on food and nutrition security in India. Finally, there is a need to distinguish between health inputs (income/energy intake) and outcomes (underweight children) and recognize the lags before comparing contemporary estimates and making policy related inferences.

Unless this is done, recommended policies will not deliver the results desired.

Another set of serious problems afflicting the production side of the agricultural sector is subsumed under the general term *agrarian distress*, whose extreme manifestation is the large-scale incidence of farmers' suicides. Mishra and Reddy (Chapter 4) analyse the entire gamut of issues surrounding agrarian distress (bordering on crisis) and attempt to suggest a framework for redressal based on technological and institutional initiatives. They recognize two dimensions to the agrarian crisis—a livelihood crisis that threatens the very basis of survival for the vast majority of the agriculturally dependent population and an agricultural developmental crisis that lies at the heart of the neglect of the sector arising out of poor design of programmes and inadequate allocation of resources. They trace the roots of the twin crises to several interrelated phenomena including the deceleration of agricultural production and productivity for almost all crops from the mid-1990s, the dependence of large sections of the population on agriculture, limited opportunities for non-farm employment, increasing marginalization of holdings, a decline of public investments in irrigation and other related infrastructure, the failure of research and extension for crops and regions under rain-fed or dry land conditions (which account for nearly three-fifths of the net sown area), inadequate supply of credit from formal sources to the agricultural sector leading to greater reliance on informal sources (with higher interest burden), and finally the rapidly changing technology and market conditions that expose the farmer to increasing uncertainties in the product as well as factor markets.

They also document that between 1995 and 2007, more than 200,000 farmers have committed suicides, more than four-fifths of these being males. The suicide mortality rate (SMR, suicide death for 100,000 persons) for male farmers has nearly doubled from little more than 10 to around 19 whereas that of male non-farmers has more or less remained around 13. The major states with SMR for male farmers greater than the all-India average are Kerala, Maharashtra, Chhattishgarh, Karnataka, Andhra Pradesh, Tamil Nadu and West Bengal.

Industrial Sector[10]

Industrial liberalization in India has proceeded via two routes viz. deregulation (relaxation of licensing and investment

---

[10] There is no fundamental difference from the point of view of economic parlance between *industry* and *manufacturing*. However, in India, a distinction is made with *industry* consisting of three components, viz. 'mining and quarrying', 'manufacturing', and 'electricity'. Manufacturing accounts for the lion's share (around 80 per cent) in this classification.

restrictions) and disinvestment in public sector enterprises (PSEs), that is, selling of government stakes usually between 1 to 49 per cent. In the pre-reform period, eighteen industries were reserved exclusively for the public sector,[11] which has now been brought down to three (defence, aircrafts and warships, railways, and atomic energy generation). Similarly, the list of 800 items reserved exclusively for the small-scale sector has been progressively pruned to about 230 currently. Two of the cardinal points of industrial policy in the pre-reforms era had been the MRTP Act 1969 (which subjected investment by large industrial houses to several restrictive provisions) and the FERA 1973 (which imposed strict limits on foreign exchange transactions on the current as well as capital account). Both now stand replaced by much more liberal versions viz. the Competition Act 2002[12] and the FEMA 1999. Further, several liberalization measures for attracting foreign direct investment (FDI) were introduced in the wake of the reforms in 1991, while foreign portfolio investment (FPI) was also selectively liberalized from 1995–6 onwards.

In spite of this extensive liberalization, manufacturing did not surge ahead in the first decade after reforms, though it did register significant progress. A detailed empirical study by Gupta et al. (2008), for example, indicates that the value added in Indian manufacturing grew at only a marginally higher rate (about 0.5 per cent) in the period 1992–2003 than the 6 per cent growth rate registered over the period 1973–92. Since 2004–5, however, manufacturing growth seems to have gone into top gear, clocking an average of 9.76 per cent growth over the period 2004–5 to 2009–10.[13]

However, there has been a great deal of discussion in recent years regarding the long-term structural constraints on manufacturing growth. While there is a near unanimity about the constraints posed by transport and power supply bottlenecks, the role of other factors is not clear. One issue in particular, which is extremely contentious, is the role of labour market reforms (see the section 'Unemployment' in this chapter for a detailed discussion on this issue). Among the other factors that have been listed as constraints, mention must be made of external finance for small and medium enterprises (Banerjee and Duflo 2003; McKinsey & Co. 2006,

etc.), shortage of skilled labour, the failure of the MRTP Act to curb restrictive trade practices and foster competition, legal weaknesses,[14] etc.

The paper by Nagaraj (Chapter 6) offers a comprehensive overview of India's recent industrial experience offering interesting comparisons with China. His detailed empirical analysis is mainly with respect to manufacturing that accounts for 80 per cent of industry value-added. He focuses on both output and labour market outcomes, in the organized as well as the unorganized sectors. His analysis of the output and employment effects of the reforms, both in the organized and unorganized sectors, leads him to questions such as: why have the reforms not delivered the promised outcomes? Is it because of poor or half-hearted implementation, or is it the design of reforms that is to be blamed? Was the diagnosis of reforms agenda correct in the first place? In other words, are the theoretical underpinnings of the reforms correct? He feels that such a questioning of the premises of the reforms is now warranted and the time seems to be ripe for redesigning industrial policies that can deliver faster output and employment growth.

A major issue that had lain implicit in India's corporate structure, but whose importance has now been explicitly acknowledged is the issue of corporate governance. Traditionally the Indian corporate sector has suffered from a number of structural problems (see Chakrabarti et al. 2008) such as (i) undue exercise of managerial control by promoters with very little equity investment of their own; (ii) pyramiding and tunnelling of funds among group companies; (iii) irregularities in share transfers and registrations; (iv) frequent resort to non-voting preference shares; (v) non-compliance with disclosure norms; (vi) ineffectiveness of the board of directors in monitoring the actions of management, etc.

Driven by the imperatives of globalization and the consequent drive towards harmonization of corporate and financial practices,[15] several initiatives on the corporate governance front emerged. The establishment of SEBI in 1992, of the NSE in 1993, and the CCIL in 2001 were important landmarks, as one of the key considerations in the design of these organizations was to improve corporate governance in the country. Thinking on the modalities of corporate governance was crystallized by two committees appointed by the SEBI—the Kumar Mangalam Birla Committee (2000) and the Naryana Murthy Committee (2003). Most of the

---

[11] Among the major industries in this category were iron and steel, minerals, telecommunications, oil, mining, air transport, and electricity generation and distribution.

[12] Some doubts are being raised about loopholes in the Competition Act and its effectiveness in dealing with *appreciable adverse effects on competition* (see Ghosh and Ross 2008; Bhattacharjea 2010).

[13] Further confirmatory evidence on India's industrial progress comes from the fact that as per UNIDO (2010), India now ranks 9th globally in terms of aggregate industrial production. India is also fast emerging as a global manufacturing hub (for Yamaha deluxe bikes, Volvo Eicher commercial vehicles, vaccines, etc.)

[14] According to the IFC–World Bank (2009) Report, India ranks 122 out of 181 countries for the ease of doing business. Most notably the country is almost at the bottom in terms of contract enforcement.

[15] As suggested by Goswami (2002), the move towards corporate governance could also be a reflection of the several scams that broke out in the early 1990s, with the Harshad Mehta scandal topping the list.

recommendations of these committees were accepted by the SEBI leading to the enactment of Clause 49 of the Listing agreements. But while considerable progress has been made in the domain of corporate governance (especially in the areas of minority shareholders' rights, disclosure norms for IPOs, responsibilities of Audit committees, etc.), important lacunae[16] continue to persist.

Sarkar and Sarkar (Chapter 8) address the important role of external auditors and audit committees as mechanisms for ensuring good governance of companies. These mechanisms ensure that a company produces relevant, adequate, and credible information that investors and independent observers can use to monitor the company's performance. Poor information quality coupled with weak governance mechanisms can adversely affect the reliability of financial statements for investors, weaken the link between earnings and firm valuation, and increase transaction costs in the capital market. The external auditor and the audit committee certify both the quantity and the quality of the information produced by a company. It is, therefore, not surprising to find that regulations all over the world have placed a major emphasis on the structure, role, and powers of the external auditor and the functioning of the audit committee. The authors review the governance reforms done in India with respect to auditor and audit committee independence and compare them with existing regulations in the US. They suggest various governance reforms that may be put on the anvil to further strengthen auditor independence and strengthen the functioning of audit committees in India.

Services Sector

One of the most remarkable features of India's recent growth experience relates to the spectacular showing by its services sector.[17] During the last decade and a half (1995–6 to 2009–10), this sector has recorded an average annual rate of growth of 7.55 per cent much in excess of those recorded in the agricultural sector (2.63 per cent) and the industrial sector (5.66 per cent). Today, the share of the services sector in

India's GDP is around 64 per cent with much of this increase being at the expense of the agriculture sector's share.

Opinion on the long-term prospects of such service-led growth differs sharply. Critics of the *services-led growth* thesis in India have included Mazumdar (1995), Arunachalam and Kumar (2002), and most notably Acharya (2004). The criticism focuses on three special aspects of services growth viz. (i) its dependence on growth in the other sectors (especially manufacturing), (ii) its low employment potential, and (iii) its concentration in a few selected sub-sectors (construction, hotels and restaurants, communication, finance, insurance, real estate, and business services).[18] Sastry et al. (2003) and Hansda (2002) (who use an input–output framework) probably represent the most systematic analyses of service-led growth sustainability in the Indian context. Their results have been somewhat updated by the RBI (2010a: Box II.2, p.18). Based on the *Leontief Inverse*, the RBI report finds substantial forward linkages of the services sector with the rest of the economy, though the backward linkages are weak for agriculture and only moderate for the industrial sector.[19] The strong forward linkages reflect the crucial dependence of sustained growth in the services sector on the rest of the economy (especially manufacturing) growing in tandem.[20] Hence, it is difficult to believe that the service sector, of itself, can be an engine of economic growth.

Optimism on service sector growth is essentially centred on an ever expanding role for foreign demand (induced by global trade liberalization) (Sengupta 2005; Ghani 2010). But global trade liberalization faces several hurdles—for the developed countries service trade liberalization often means liberalization of Modes 1–3, whereas the relative advantage of emerging market economies (EMEs) like India is located in Mode 4, on whose liberalization the developed world has been slow-pedalling.[21] Besides, granted the intense

---

[16] These include (i) lack of shareholder activism, (ii) absence of director professionalism, (iii) overlapping responsibilities of the SEBI, Stock Exchanges, and Department of Company Affairs (DCA) in the supervision of listed companies, (iv) trades through dummy entities, which is rampant in regional exchanges, and (v) inability of SEBI's investigation process to get to the root of fraudulent practices.

[17] To avoid confusion, it may be useful here to list the major components of the industry and services sector. Industry comprises (i) mining and quarrying, (ii) manufacturing, and (iii) electricity, gas, and water supply. Services comprise (i) construction, (ii) trade, (iii) hotels and restaurants, (iv) transport (railways and other), (v) storage, (vi) communication, (vii) finance, insurance, real estate, and business services, and (viii) community, social, and personal services.

[18] In addition there is a fourth aspect which does not seem to have attracted much attention in the Indian context viz. that increasing tertiarization can trigger an aggregate productivity slowdown in the economy, due to what Baumol (1967) has termed the 'cost disease' effect, whereby productivity lags wages in the services sector. Evidence in support of this phenomenon for the US economy is reported in Triplet and Bosworth (2000).

[19] As is well known, these concepts were introduced into the development literature by Hirschman (1958). Backward linkages reflect the demand for inputs of a given activity, while forward linkages reflect output utilization (i.e., the extent to which outputs from a given activity will be used as inputs in other activities). See Drejer (2002).

[20] This conclusion is more in conformity with the view expressed by Acharya (2002) and others above, rather than the contrary view espoused in OECD (2000) that it is manufacturing activity that flows to countries with adequate services infrastructure.

[21] GATS defines four ways in which a service can be traded—(i) Mode 1: *Cross Border Supply* (service supplied from one country to another), for example, international telephone calls, (ii) Mode 2: *Consumption*

competition that India now experiences from China, some other Asian countries and Eastern Europe in its major service export (viz. IT), it is difficult to believe that the terms of trade will not deteriorate in the long run—the so-called Baumol effect (see Baumol 1967).

Infrastructure (Physical)

In a comprehensive sense, infrastructure includes both physical and social infrastructure. As clarified earlier, physical infrastructure is being viewed as a critical binding constraint on growth and hence a determinant of economic sustainability, while social infrastructure, an equally important long-term determinant of economic and social sustainability, is proposed to be discussed later in the social sustainability context.

The Indian (physical) infrastructure sector suffers from a huge backlog, in part inherited from the pre-reform years, when the typical approach vis-à-vis infrastructure was a *bottleneck approach*, that is, one in which specific bottlenecks were identified and sought to be removed as and when they started cutting into the growth process. What was essentially missing was a *forward looking* approach in which infrastructure was built up ahead of projected demand. The strategy of the current government (especially since 2004) partakes to a large extent of this forward looking approach to the infrastructure sector.

The task on the physical infrastructure front is daunting, to say the least. At a modest estimate, if the Indian growth rate is to be maintained around the targeted rate of 9 per cent, then the investment in physical infrastructure will have to be stepped up from its modest level of 5 per cent of GDP (as obtains now) to a figure comparable to that of China, which currently invests about 9 per cent of its GDP in infrastructure. The Deepak Parekh Committee Report (Ministry of Finance 2007), estimated an investment of US$ 320 billion (at 2005–6) prices for maintaining growth rates around a high of 9 per cent or so. The Committee stresses the public–private partnership (PPP) model as the most suitable for generation of funds on this scale, with a major role assigned to foreign institutional investors (FIIs). While PPPs certainly appear attractive in the blueprint and have now become a favourite in both official and private sector circles, international experience is accumulating pointing to several deficiencies in their operationalization, especially when compared to more traditional models of private

sector involvement such as government procurement or concessions.[22]

A number of noteworthy initiatives have been launched officially in recent years to overcome the capacity constraints in the power and transport sector. The Ministry of Power (at the Chief Ministers' Conference held in May 2007) has identified seven core issues for priority attention, including most importantly rural electrification, reduction of aggregate transmission and commercial (ATC) losses to less than 15 per cent by the end of the Eleventh Plan, energy conservation, demand management, and a revamping of the Accelerated Power Development and Reform Programme (APDRP). In the transport sector the government is keen to put in place an integrated transport policy covering all four essential segments of the sector viz. railways, roads, civil aviation, and coastal shipping.

There is one aspect of infrastructure, however, which can be flouted as an Indian success story viz. the telecom sector. This sector is almost playing the role of what some of the neo-Schumpeterian growth theories (see Lipsey et al. 2005) call a general purpose technology (GPT).

Mani (Chapter 10) details the successful story of India's telecommunications industry. His main thesis is that technological changes and reasonably well-executed regulatory policies have actually contributed to the success of the industry. Both these factors have, by reducing the steepness of entry barriers to the industry, made it extremely competitive. The result has been rapid diffusion of new technologies in the provision of telecom services, accompanied by significant reductions in prices. The author traces the evolution of India's telecom services industry and then attempts to assess the role that policy measures have played in shaping its growth trajectory. He concludes by indicating two areas where policy measures still have a role to play in improving the state of affairs— first, in bridging the *digital divide*[23] and, second, in enhancing the diffusion of Internet within the economy.

---

[22] Of the several difficulties noted with the implementation of PPPs in OECD and Latin American countries, three in particular stand out. First, PPPs entail an inherent ambiguity in the contractual obligations of the private party as most PPP arrangements span long periods and it is difficult to envisage and provide for all the unforeseen contingencies that may occur over its long tenure. Second, we have the phenomenon much in evidence in Latin America of 'hidden rent backloading' (see Engel et al. 2006). Finally, there is evidence that PPPs result in higher prices for the services of the utility than comparable traditional modes of involving the private sector in infrastructure projects (see Blanc-Brude et al. 2006, who cite several examples of road construction in France).

[23] The *digital divide* refers to the fact of telecom services being strongly concentrated in urban centres with much of the rural areas excluded.

Abroad (for example, tourism), (iii) Mode 3: *Commercial Presence* (company from one country setting up subsidiaries or branches to provide services in another country), and (iv) Mode 4: *Movement of Natural Persons* (individuals travelling from their own country to supply services in another).

Financial Sector Reforms and Macroeconomic Stability

The financial sectors in the various economies of South Asia prior to the initiation of structural reforms in the 1990s, constituted typical examples of what McKinnon (1973) and Shaw (1973) had dubbed as 'financial repression'.[24] The process of financial liberalization is usually viewed as encompassing four dimensions: (i) Financial Deregulation, (ii) Financial Innovation, (iii) Market Making, and (iv) Re-orientation of Financial Supervision.[25]

In India, financial liberalization has proceeded apace with considerable impetus since the 1990s and the financial sector roadmap has been extensively redrawn.[26] Financial liberalization was viewed as an integral component of overall liberalization, in the twin beliefs that (i) liberalization in the real sector could not proceed satisfactorily in the absence of financial liberalization and (ii) financial liberalization was an 'enabling condition' of faster economic growth, as it increases competition, transfer of know-how, and transparency. However, it is becoming increasingly clear that financial liberalization is at best a double-edged weapon. On the one hand, there does seem to exist a positive association between financial liberalization, savings (domestic plus foreign) investment, and growth (though the causal nexus seems to run both ways). On the other hand, financial liberalization poses several problems for monetary and fiscal policy and increases the vulnerability of developing economies to banking and currency crises.

The relationship between financial liberalization and economic growth has been extensively debated in the academic literature as well as in policy circles and the empirical evidence can at best be described as *mixed*.[27] The only conclusion to emerge robustly from the various studies is the important role of conditioning factors in determining the differential effects of financial liberalization across countries.[28]

The challenges posed by financial liberalization to the autonomy of domestic monetary policy have been by now well documented in the literature as a trilemma (see Bernanke [2005] for a recent discussion).[29] In the Indian context, the problems confronting monetary policy in the wake of capital inflows (and financial liberalization generally) have been discussed extensively in Rangarajan (2000), Reddy (2005), Nachane and Raje (2007), BIS (2009), and so on. There is in evidence a general movement away from a heavily managed exchange rate system of the 1980s and early 1990s towards a more flexible policy of letting the exchange rate gravitate towards its equilibrium value (as determined by market fundamentals) with the concerns over exchange rate management limited to short-term considerations such as the need to smoothen out excessive volatility and foreclose the emergence of destabilizing speculative activities.

One of the key ingredients of the financial liberalization process has been a progressive dismantling of capital controls, which were widely prevalent in the developed world and almost universal in the developing countries in the two decades following the Smithsonian agreement. Advocacy of open capital accounts is based on the neo-liberal view that free global capital markets enable EMEs and least developed countries (LDCs) to get cheaper access to international credit, thereby promoting growth and stability. This view, always of dubious theoretical merit (see Arteta et al. 2003, Nachane 2010, DeLong 2009) has been further discredited

---

[24] The *financial repression* thesis maintained that governmental restrictions on the financial sector, by reducing the quantum as well as the quality of investment, had a retarding effect on a country's economic growth prospects.

[25] As financial liberalization proceeds, it is expected that the central bank (and other regulators, if any) will move away from direct intervention in financial markets to indirect measures (such as provisioning norms, capital adequacy, etc.).

[26] In the banking sector, the administered interest rate structure was gradually phased out with both lending and deposit rates freely determined by market forces. There was a move in the direction of more operational autonomy to public sector banks, while simultaneously allowing them to broad-base their ownership by allowing them to raise equity capital up to 49 per cent of their total paid-up capital. The Indian banking system was sought to be made more transparent and prudent by introducing global standards (as encapsulated in the two successive Basle Accords) relating to adequate capitalization, risk management, asset classification, and provisioning norms. Transparent guidelines were also laid down for establishment of new private sector and foreign banks. A number of far-reaching reforms were simultaneously introduced in the money, forex, and capital markets.

[27] Some studies have uncovered a beneficial association between financial liberalization and growth (Levine 2001; Bonfiglioli and Mendicino 2004; Bekaert et al. 2006), others have found the effect to be detrimental (Eichengreen and Leblang 2003), while still others find no association at all (see Rodrick 1998; Grilli and Milesi-Ferretti 1995)

[28] Two sets of factors have been broadly distinguished. On the one hand, there are the country-specific factors such as local conditions, internal policies, size of the government, the structure of the legal system, levels of education, and other human capital variables (La Porta et al. 1998) and, on the other hand, there are factors which are outside the control of individual countries such as the diversification potential of the local equity market for world investors, regional trading and investing agreements, etc. (Bekaert et al. 2006).

[29] The *trilemma* in question refers to the impossibility of maintaining in simultaneous operation (for a given country) all three of the following policy regimes: (i) an open capital account, (ii) a fixed exchange rate, and (iii) an independent domestic monetary policy. Of course, in practice, concepts like 'openness', 'fixity', or 'independence' are not absolute, but relative or even fuzzy. Hence the *trilemma* needs to be interpreted as a move in one direction having to be compensated by a countervailing move along another dimension.

with the recent experience of currency crises (see Ocampo and Stiglitz 2008). The received theoretical literature, as well as empirical evidence (see BIS 2009) are broadly pointing to a consensus on three issues: (i) the benefits of capital account liberalization are vastly overstated by their advocates, (ii) they (benefits) are circumscribed by too many conditionalities that are unlikely of fulfilment in many EMEs and LDCs, and (iii) controls over capital inflows can effectively reduce the vulnerability of economies to financial crises.

The problem has been accentuated in the last three years, following the eruption of the global financial crisis in 2008. As the developed world struggles with a tepid industrial recovery, weak financial systems, burgeoning fiscal deficits, and unsustainable debt–GDP ratios, it is becoming increasingly clear that part of the burden of the painful adjustment to global imbalances is likely to fall upon EMEs. The low interest rates, quantitative easing of credit and frequent bailouts in the US and Europe are all injecting massive amounts of global liquidity which is wending its way inexorably to EMEs, driven by the search for greater returns and the relatively sound macroeconomic fundamentals of the latter. India seems to be a particularly favourite destination—as between April to October of this year, about US$ 80.0 billion has flown in (of which FDI flows accounted for $ 13.5 billion, FIIs for $ 51.0 billion, and ECBs for $10.6 billion) (RBI 2010b). Confronted with capital flow upsurges, several EMEs have imposed some form of capital restrictions (most notably Brazil, Venezuela, Thailand, Indonesia, South Korea, and Taiwan). India remains a notable exception, with official pronouncements repeatedly reaffirming commitments to further capital account liberalization.

Goyal (Chapter 11) in her contribution takes stock of the various policy choices which were available to the government with respect to liberalization of the capital account, and assesses the kind of capital inflows which resulted as a consequence of the 'middle path' adopted by the government. She also assesses the positive contributions of the inflows together with the kind of constraints they impose on policy. In her opinion, by and large the government strategy has justified itself as capital inflows did contribute to the trend rate of growth and India escaped the worst consequences of the both the Asian crisis as well as the recent global crisis. She however cautions on the need for debate on issues such as flexibility of exchange rates, reserve accumulation in response to volatile inflows, graded restrictions on the capital account, market development with counter-cyclical prudential regulations, etc. Her emphasis is on the need for strengthening domestic institutions as well as reform of the international financial architecture. She expresses the hope that greater representation of EMEs in the G-20 could fructify in real improvements, and lower the risks of opening the capital account.

External Sector Liberalization

One of the key pillars of reforms has been the extensive liberalization of international trade and investment.[30] As a result of these measures, India's share in world exports of goods and services rose from about 1 per cent in 1990 to about 4 per cent in 2007, with the share of exports in GDP rising from 19 per cent to 49 over the same period (see De 2009). But apart from the rapid rise in exports (as well as imports), there has also been a marked rise in trade diversification as measured by the *(absolute) trade entropy index* (Ibid.: 4).[31] However, from a long-term point of view certain constraints are becoming evident. First, the stagnation in the WTO Doha Round has meant that certain measures considered very crucial from the developing world point of view, such as the *special safeguard measures* in agriculture, are not making headway. Second, in the aftermath of the recent global crisis there has been a strong revival of protectionist sentiments in the developed world (in spite of the impressive rhetoric to the contrary at the successive G-20 Summits). Third, there has been a substantial escalation in *trade costs*[32] in recent years as documented, for example, in De (2008) and Brooks and Hummels (2009). Finally, in the Indian context the absence of a strong *trade facilitating* infrastructure[33] is increasingly emerging as a binding constraint.

---

[30] Indian trade policy prior to reforms was characterized by (i) high tariffs as well as quantitative restrictions (QRs) on import of capital goods and raw materials. There was also a more or less comprehensive ban on imports of manufactured final consumer goods and agricultural products. In 1993, import licences were abolished and capital goods and raw materials became freely importable. There was noticeable success in reducing high tariff rates. The weighted average import duty was reduced from 72.5 per cent in 1991–2 to about 29 per cent in 2002–3, while simultaneously the peak customs duty was reduced from 150 per cent in 1991–2 to 30.8 per cent in 2002–3. The tariff rates structure was simplified with the number of basic duty rates reduced from 22 in 1991–2 to 4 in 2002–3, while QRs on final consumer goods and agricultural products were finally removed much later on 1 April 2001. Immediately after liberalization, the external parity of the rupee was sharply reduced via two successive depreciations and gradually a transition was effected from the earlier regime of a fixed parity for the Indian rupee (vis-à-vis a fixed currency basket) to a managed but flexible exchange rate mechanism.

[31] For a definition of the *trade entropy index*, see Marwah and Klein (1995).

[32] *Trade costs* include all costs incurred in getting a good to a final user (apart from the actual production costs) such as transportation costs, inventory and storage costs, information costs, contract enforcement costs, and legal and regulatory costs. Tariffs and non-tariff barriers are also sometimes included in trade costs but from the analytical point of view it may be desirable to consider them separately.

[33] Trade facilitation measures refer to mitigation measures in respect of transaction costs associated with enforcement, regulation, and administration of trade policies.

Veeramani (Chapter 16) analyses the relative *sophistication* of India's exports of manufactures during the pre- and post-liberalization periods. The significance of this issue arises from the fact that trade liberalization can lead to intra-industry reallocation of resources in two possible ways. First, market shares might be reallocated from the least productive to the most productive firms within a given industry. Second, firms are forced to focus on their *core competencies* by dropping the product lines that are inconsistent with their comparative advantages. An important outcome of these adjustments is the potential improvement in the *sophistication* level of the country's export basket. He also compares the Indian experience with those of other 17 comparable developing countries, and finds that there has been considerable increase in sophistication of Indian exports as measured by the export similarity index (ESI).[34]

ISSUES OF SOCIAL SUSTAINABILITY

If growth is not broad based, if it has little impact on poverty, and if the benefits of growth are increasingly cornered by a minuscule section of the population, the consequent social tensions and political instability will inevitably frustrate the growth process. This brings us to our second dimension of sustainability viz. *social sustainability*.[35] In recent years, the phrase *inclusive growth* has become ubiquitous in Indian official policy pronouncements. But if the phrase has to transcend the purely rhetorical plane, then concrete results need to be evident in terms of poverty reduction as well as moderation of interpersonal and inter-regional inequality. Poverty and inequality are distinct but highly interconnected phenomena, whose incidence is an outcome of the general growth strategy adopted and its implications for wage levels and unemployment, as well as the specific policy interventions for promoting social infrastructure and financial inclusion.

Incidence of Poverty

The ultimate touchstone of reforms will be the success they have in making a dent on the deeply entrenched poverty in India. The standard concept of poverty is the per cent of population below a threshold (poverty line), usually based on a minimum level of nutrition in a benchmark year with

allowance for some non-food expenditure and deflated by an appropriate cost of living index. Poverty estimates in India are based on the consumer expenditure surveys carried out by the National Sample Survey Organisation (NSSO).[36] After the reforms, three quinquennial surveys have been carried out viz. the 50th NSS Round (1993–4), 55th NSS Round (1999–2000), and 61st NSS Round (2004–5). As a benchmark pre-reform comparison point, we use the results from the 43rd NSS Round (1987–8). Results are presented in Table 1.3.[37]

Table 1.3   Poverty Measurement: Head Count Ratio (HCR)

	1987–8	1993–4	1999–2000	2004–5
Rural	39.1%	37.3%	27.1%	22%
Urban	38.2%	32.4%	23.6%	21.6%
All-India	38.9%	36%	26.1%	28%

Sources: Sen and Himanshu (2004); Tendulkar (2006); Radhakrishna and Panda (2006).

The fact that the all-India poverty ratio has increased between 1999–2000 and 2004–5 is largely a reflection of the fact that the results of the 55th NSS Round are not comparable with the results of the 50th Round. The methodology of the 61st Round is however comparable to that of the 50th Round (and hence not with that of the 55th Round). Thus the dent on poverty is nowhere comparable in the post-reforms period to what reforms enthusiasts were prone to claim earlier. Instead of declining by nearly 10 per cent over a six-year span, it has actually declined only by 8 per cent over an eleven-year span. Thus the average annual decline in the poverty ratio is a meagre 0.7 per cent, and not 1.6 per cent as thought before.[38] Poverty in India has also been consistently higher than that in South Asia

---

[34] The ESI is predicated on the assumption that the sophistication level of a country's exports improves as its export basket becomes more similar to that of the high-income OECD countries.

[35] As mentioned earlier, *social sustainability* pertains to the maintenance of *social capital*. This variety of capital refers to the investments that create and maintain the social framework. Such capital lowers the cost of working together (transaction costs) and facilitates cooperation by promoting trust (see Daly 1999).

[36] These include both the annual surveys based on a *thin* sample of four households per village/urban block, as also the quinquennial surveys based on a *thick* sample of eight to ten households per village/urban block.

[37] The poverty line used in the Table is as per the recommendations of an Expert Group set up by the Planning Commission in 1993. It uses a base poverty line of per capita consumption of Rs 49 per month (rural) and Rs 57 per month (urban), based on the recommended daily intake of 2,400 calories (rural) and 2,100 calories (urban). Adjustments are made to this base by using the CPI for agricultural workers in case of the rural line and the CPI for industrial workers for the urban poverty line

[38] Chen and Ravallion (2004) in their well-known comparative study on world poverty, using the international poverty line definition ($1.08 a day per person at 1993 PPP), obtain significantly higher estimates for the HCR than shown in Table 1.3 (for the year 2001, for example, their HCR was 34.7 per cent).

generally, whether measured by the HCR or by Poverty Gap Indices.[39]

The aggregative measures of poverty do not enlighten us about important issues such as the following:

1. The intensity of poverty (as captured by poverty gap index and squared poverty gap index)
2. Its concentration in particular regions
3. Its distribution by occupation, sex, caste, and religion

Only very detailed studies can throw light on such issues which are fraught with tremendous social and political consequences. Attempts to deal with these aspects are only now commencing (for example, Radhakrishna and Ray 2005; and Radhakrishna and Panda 2006).

There is an influential section of academic opinion which maintains that *economic growth does accelerate poverty reduction* (see, for example, Kraay 2005; Friedman 2005).[40] However this proposition can hardly be characterized as generally held. A more nuanced statement viz. that growth is essential for poverty reduction, under the assumption that *the distribution of income remains constant* (Deininger and Squire (1998), Dollar and Kraay (2002) etc.), seems to hold greater appeal. As a matter of fact, as shown by Chen and Ravallion (2004) (also Bourguignon 2003), rapid poverty reduction will be hard to achieve, even in the face of high growth rates, if initial income inequality is substantial, or if the growth process itself aggravates inequality. Thus the main leg in the 'poverty–growth–inequality triangle' (a concept due to Bourguignon 2004) is that connecting growth and inequality.

Interpersonal Inequality

Inequality is possibly one of the most neglected and least emphasized dimensions of the liberalization programme in most LDCs. It becomes a crucial factor determining long-term sustainability of the reforms programme, because of several reasons, of which the two most important seem to be the following:

1. First, as we have seen above, the impact of growth on poverty alleviation is likely to be critically dependent on the level of initial inequality in a society.

2. Second, high levels of inequality are inhibitive of the development and survival of democratic norms in a society. Inequality undermines good public policy, by eroding collective decision-making processes and social institutions essential to a healthy functioning of democracy (the so-called 'vanishing middle class' syndrome as discussed in Birdsall 2005).

The relationship between inequality and economic growth is a more contentious issue on which at least two major schools of thought are apparent. The early work in this area was heavily influenced by Kuznets (1955), wherein an inverted U-shaped curve was posited (and empirically sustained) between inequality and economic growth. As is well known, Kuznet's explanation ran in terms of physical investment as the main driver of growth in the early stages, with investment in human capital assuming importance as the economy matured. While it is not clear what is the exact direction of causation envisaged in the Kuznets curve, modern analysts have tended to view the degree of inequality, if not exactly as a *political datum*, at least as something which is difficult to derive from purely economic considerations. This leads them to focus on how inequality affects growth rather than the other way around.

There is a vast theoretical literature, the bulk of which predicates a growth-retarding role for inequality, typically focusing on the ideal rate of taxation for different individuals (Alesina and Rodrik 1994; Persson and Tabellini 1994; Bertola 1993).[41] By and large, the empirical work in this area also tends to be supportive of the detrimental role of inequality vis-à-vis growth (Persson and Tabellini 1994; Birdsall et al. 1995, Benabou 1996; Deininger and Squire 1998), a view also emerging robustly in Friedamn's (2005) detailed historical evaluations.

Motiram and Vakulabharanam (Chapter 5) have undertaken a highly disaggregated analysis of poverty and inequality and generated considerable new insights. They note substantial variation across states in poverty as well as poverty reduction rates. In a majority of the states, both in rural and urban areas, the rate of poverty reduction was much higher in the pre-reform (as compared to the post-reform) period. There is also considerable differential in the incidence of poverty across various social groups (such as STs, SCs, Muslims, non-SC Hindus, etc.). Motiram and Vakulabharanam also go into a class-wise decomposition of rural poverty and find that even though poverty rates have declined across all classes,

---

[39] The Poverty Gap Index refers to the proportionate shortfall of income of all the poor from the poverty line as expressed in per capita terms (for the entire population).

[40] 'It is clear that over time economic growth, in the familiar sense of a rising per capita income, enables ever more citizens of a developing country to escape the sorry conditions that make up the everyday burdens and genuine miseries of poverty' (Friedman 2005: 357).

[41] Typically the argument runs as follows. The higher the income that an individual derives from capital, the greater his preferences for lower tax rates on capital (which favour growth). The more equitable the societal income distribution, the higher the *median voter's* capital endowment, thus (by the *median voter theorem*) favouring growth enhancing policies.

only in the case of large farmers has the decline in the post-reform period been higher than in the pre-reform period. They also demonstrate that inequality along all the three dimensions of consumption expenditure, wealth, and income has increased perceptibly in the post-reforms period (1993–4 to 2004–5) after remaining constant over the pre-reforms decade (1983 to 1993–4). Overall their conclusions point to post-reforms growth having a much muted *trickle down* effect, while simultaneously aggravating inequality, whether measured in terms of income, consumption, or wealth. They are thus inclined to hold the reforms strategy adopted as at least partly responsible for the prevailing rural distress and make out a strong case for reorienting this strategy to encompass measures that support small farmers (for example, the revival of cooperatives, design of appropriate trade regimes, strengthening the National Rural Employment Guarantee Scheme [NREGS], protective insurance mechanisms, etc.) as well as the urban poor (for example, by encouraging low skill labour-intensive employment schemes).

Inter-regional Inequality

In a federal set-up such as India's, lack of attention to inequality among states has the potential to generate strong centrifugal political tendencies. It is not surprising, therefore, that regional inequality has received a great deal of attention from policymakers as well as academicians in India. The fact that regional inequality has, in fact, increased significantly in the post-reforms period is borne out by a long list of studies including Noorbaksh (2003), Bhattacharya and Sakthivel (2004), and Dev and Ravi (2007). The inequality is reflected not only in per capita net state domestic product but also in broader social indicators such as Human Development Index (HDI), under-five mortality rates, percentage of population below poverty line, and adult literacy rates.[42] As to the reasons for the accentuation of regional inequality in the post-reforms period, a number of explanatory factors have been advanced in the literature most notably population growth, governance, and lack of public investment (Bhattacharya and Sakthivel 2004), urbanization and infrastructure development (Wu 2008), human capital, R&D, and proximity to the technology frontier (Aghion et al. 2006), and the locational preferences of foreign investors with respect to FDI (Nunnenkamp and Stracke 2007; Mukim and Nunnenkamp 2010).

The paper by Ramaswamy (Chapter 7) begins by investigating whether there has been a tendency for convergence

of manufacturing activity across Indian states in the post-reforms period (based on the registered manufacturing sector in fourteen major states of India) . His empirical analysis suggests a weak evidence for convergence in the post-reform period (1993–4 to 2004–5)—weaker than even in the pre-reform decade (1980–1 to 1990–1). Using an index of manufacturing activity dispersion, he further finds that inter-state disparities have increased in the post-reforms era. A significant part of the explanation could be located in two key proximate determinants of growth, viz. physical and human capital. The share of high-income states in the distribution of private corporate investment (as measured by loans given by All-India Financial Institutions) is observed to be disproportionately high. Similarly, the high-income states are found to have higher than average per capita capital expenditures (proxy for public investment). Higher public investment in richer states actually *crowds in* private investment, reflecting the complementarity between the two types of investment. Additionally, available data on the number of investment proposals and the amount of FDI approved clearly indicate the concentration of FDI inflows in a few states.[43] This confirms the strengthening of unequal tendencies in the distribution of investment in the post-reform period. Further, the stock of human capital (the schooling attainment) is positively related to per capita manufacturing product. In brief, the author finds that initial differences in manufacturing capacity, human capital, and infrastructure (especially power) seem to be the key factors behind the observed inter-state disparities in manufacturing development.

Unemployment

Closely juxtaposed with the issue of poverty is that of unemployment. In the early debates on reforms, proponents of liberalization typically contended that although new technology displaces labour, it also lowers costs and prices, and hence expands the demand for labour in the long run.[44]

Empirical analysis of unemployment in India is beset both by data problems as well as a multiplicity of measurement concepts. At least four concepts are currently in use viz. usual principal status (UPS), usual principal and

---

[42] Formal econometric studies support the contention that there is no convergence among states in the post-reforms period. Wu (2008), for example, notes that there is substantial divergence both on the sigma-convergence and beta-convergence criteria.

[43] Six states, namely, Maharashtra, Tamil Nadu, Karnataka, Delhi, Andhra Pradesh, and West Bengal accounted for over 86 per cent of the total FDI amount approved during 1991–2002. Their share in total number of approvals was found to be over 75 per cent.

[44] As later analyses have recognized, the key flaw in this argument is that with each successive wave of technology, the new demand is for increasingly skilled workers. In the absence of a suitable education and training policy, the already displaced labour cannot be absorbed—only a skill-job mismatch situation develops with an excess demand for highly skilled workers co-existing with a vast army of the long-term unemployed.

Table 1.4   Unemployment Rates in India

	Rural						Urban					
	Male			Female			Male			Female		
	UP	CWS	CDS	UP	CWS	CDS	UP	CWS	CDS	UP	CWS	CDS
1993–4	20	30	56	14	30	56	45	52	67	83	84	105
2004	24	47	90	22	45	93	46	57	81	89	90	117

Notes: (i) The unemployment rates are shown as number of persons unemployed per 1,000 persons. (ii) UP—usual principal status; CWS—current weekly status; CDS—current daily status. (iii) Data for 1993–4 is from NSSO 50th Round and for 2004 it is from NSSO 60th Round.

Table 1.5(a)   Sector-wise Employment Growth Rates (per cent) (CDS Basis)

	Organized		Unorganized	
Sector	1983–94	1994–2000	1983–94	1994–2000
1. Agriculture, Forestry, and Fishing	0.02	−1.00	2.23	0.02
2. Mining and Quarrying	−1.91	−1.30	3.68	−1.91
3. Manufacturing	2.58	0.87	2.26	2.58
4. Electricity, Gas, and Water Supply	−3.55	0.51	5.31	−3.55
5. Construction	5.21	−0.69	4.18	5.21
6. Trade, Hotels, and Restaurants	5.72	1.43	3.80	5.72
7. Transport, Storage, and Communications	5.53	0.21	3.35	5.53
8. Finance, Insurance, Real Estate, and Business Services	5.40	1.27	4.60	5.40
9. Community, Social, and Personal Services	−2.08	0.8	3.85	−2.07
All Sectors	**1.07**	**0.56**	**2.67**	**1.06**

Source: Planning Commission (2002); Hansda and Ray (2006).

Table 1.5(b)   Sector-wise Employment Growth Rates (per cent) (UPSS Basis)

Sector	1993–4 to 1999–2000	1999–2000 to 2004–5
1. Agriculture, Forestry, and Fishing	−0.33	2.4
2. Mining and Quarrying	−2.80	3.83
3. Manufacturing	2.05	2.19
4. Electricity, Gas, and Water Supply	−0.88	1.37
5. Construction	7.09	7.76
6. Trade, Hotels, and Restaurants	5.04	4.76
7. Transport, Storage, and Communications	6.09	3.42
8. Finance, Insurance, Real Estate, and Business Services	6.20	6.32
9. Community, Social, and Personal Services	0.55	1.43
All Sectors	**0.98**	**2.89**

Source: Rangarajan et al. (2007).

subsidiary status (UPSS), current weekly status (CWS), and current daily status (CDS).[45] The unemployment rates are presented in Table 1.4, which present a somewhat depressing picture and underscore the failure of the Indian

reforms process to tackle the unemployment issue with much success. The unemployment rate (all-India) shows an appreciable rise over the post-reforms period (1993–4 to 2003–4). The conclusion applies with similar force to the rural employment rates, and also (but with considerably less force) in the urban case.

The sectoral story, which is displayed in Tables 1.5(a) and 1.5(b), however, conveys a more nuanced message.

[45] For detailed explanations of the various concepts involved, see Hansda and Ray (2006).

Table 1.6 Sector-wise Employment Elasticities (UPSS)

Sector	Share of Employ-ment (1999–2000) (%)	Pre-reform Period 1983–4 to 1993–4	Post-reform Period I 1993–4 to 1999–2000	Post-reform Period II 1999–2000 to 2004–5
1. Agriculture	56.7	0.50	0.00	1.52
2. Mining and Quarrying	0.67	0.69	0.00	0.82
3. Manufacturing	12.11	0.33	0.26	0.34
4. Electricity, Gas, and Water Supply	0.34	0.52	0.00	0.33
5. Construction	4.44	1.00	1.00	0.88
6. Trade, Hotels, and Restaurants	11.15	0.63	0.55	0.59
7. Transport, Storage, and Communications	4.05	0.49	0.69	0.27
8. Finance, Insurance, Real Estate, and Business Services	1.38	0.92	0.73	0.94
9. Community, Social, and Personal Services	9.16	0.50	0.07	0.28
All Sectors	100	0.41	0.15	0.48

Source: Planning Commission (2002) and Rangarajan et al. (2007).

Table 1.5(a) is a comparison of sectoral employment growth rates of the immediate post-reforms period (1994–2000) with the pre-reforms decade (1983–94), using the CDS definition of employment and mirrors the broad pattern exhibited by the aggregate unemployment rates. Employment growth (in both the organized and unorganized sectors) has decelerated sharply in the immediate aftermath of reforms. As in the decade prior to reforms, the unorganized sector continued to grow faster than the organized sector in the early post-reforms period.[46] This growth was also accompanied by an increasing *casualization* of labour (see Pais 2002; Ghosh 2004). However, the data emerging from the 61st NSSO Round (2006) seems to offer some solace. Table 1.5(b), which compares sectoral employment growth rates over two successive post-reforms quinquenniums 1993–4 to 1999–2000 and 1999–2000 to 2004–5, shows a distinct turnaround in the sectoral employment growth rates.

From a futuristic perspective, an important parameter is the employment elasticity of growth across sectors. The sectoral employment elasticities given in Table 1.6 replicate the V-shape observed earlier (for employment growth rates) viz. a steep fall in the employment elasticity in the early post-reform years, followed by a modest recovery in the later period across all sectors except transport, storage and communications, and construction.

The above set of results needs careful interpretation. First, the results in Tables 1.5(a) and 1.5(b) are not strictly comparable, being based on two distinct measures of employment. Second, even allowing for the possible differences in the two measures, the rate of employment growth in the period 1999–2000 to 2004–5 is significantly lower than in the pre-reform period 1983–94, for at least two sectors viz. manufacturing and community, social, and personal services (which together account for a sizeable section—about 22 per cent—of the total employment). A somewhat similar pattern is observed for the sectoral elasticities in five sectors (viz. electricity, gas, and water supply; construction; trade, hotels, and restaurants; transport, storage, and communications; and community, social, and personal services) accounting for nearly 30 per cent of the total employment. Finally, the sectoral results presented in Tables 1.5(b) and 1.6 (based on the UPSS), which indicate a distinct improvement in the employment scenario over the decade 1994–2004, seem to be in conflict with the aggregate picture presented in Table 1.4 (based on the three other measures of employment viz. UP, CDS, and CWS), which shows a distinct deterioration over the corresponding period. Thus considerable further research is necessary before concluding that the era of 'jobless growth' is now passe.

There is an influential strand of thinking (see, for example, Panagariya 2008) that locates the source of the employment problem in India in the labour market rigidities and the various legislations effected in the past to safeguard workers' interests (such as the Minimum Wages Act, Contract Labour Act, Industrial Disputes Act, etc.). It is argued that such safeguards (which typically apply for enterprises above a threshold scale and mainly in the organized sector) act as a disincentive for exploiting scale economies. Further by pushing up labour costs they discourage the use of labour-intensive techniques. While analytically appealing,

[46] According to one estimate, the unorganized sector accounted for 91.66 per cent of the total employed labour force in 1999–2000.

this genre of arguments has several weaknesses. Labour laws are only one of a series of factors affecting aggregate employment, and possibly of a much lower order of importance than other factors such as infrastructural facilities, credit availability to MSMEs, social security, and the overall macroeconomic strategy (in particular whether employment generation is an explicit macroeconomic policy objective or whether it is simply some kind of a residual outcome from policies addressed primarily to other objectives).[47] As pointed out by Ghosh (2004), the macroeconomic policies adopted in the post-reforms period have systematically operated to the disadvantage of small-scale producers via a host of factors including reduction of priority sector lending, removal of export subsidies, monopolization of distribution networks by large-scale enterprises, and the inability of small-scale producers to match the import competition from large MNCs with their huge advertising budgets. But what is most objectionable about the arguments for abolishing the *tyranny of labour market regulations* is that they are contrary in spirit to well-accepted international principles regarding the fundamental rights of workers (as enshrined, for example, in the ILO 1998).[48]

A laudable policy initiative to meet the unemployment problem headlong has been the introduction of the Mahatma Gandhi National Rural Employment Guarantee Scheme (NREGS for short) in February 2006. This ambitious scheme is addressed to guaranteeing a minimum of 100 days of wage employment every year to all rural households on asset creation projects.[49] In spite of several shortcomings which have emerged in the operationalization of the scheme,[50] overall the initiative merits praise for making a significant dent in the rural underemployment problem.

D'Souza and Bhattacherjee (Chapter 9) uncover two opposite tendencies characterizing the labour market in post-liberalization India viz. participation and exclusion—a growth in employment in the unorganized sector of the economy, co-existing with a decline in the organized sector's ability to generate productive employment. This absorption of surplus labour in the unorganized sector and the shift towards increased productivity, associated with more skill-intensive production in the organized sector, has also resulted in a widening differential between skilled and unskilled wage rates as well as between incomes in the organized and unorganized sectors. Thus liberalization seems to have been associated not only with income inequality due to a skill bias but also with a sectoral bias of greater labour income inequality.

The authors also analyse the effects of economic liberalization on trade unions and industrial relations. First, they find that *union density* continues to be very low compared to other large emerging economies, with trade unions unable to make a dent outside the formal manufacturing sector. Second, the structural character of industrial conflict has changed since liberalization in the 1990s although its regional concentration (West Bengal and Kerela accounting for nearly 70 per cent of days lost) continues as before. Industrial strife seems to be reflecting a shift in countervailing power in favour of employers vis-à-vis trade unions.[51] Finally, to reform the highly complex Indian industrial relations system, the Second National Commission on Labour (Ministry of Labour 2002) recommended the need for fruitful labour–management partnerships in order to generate commitment to both quality and productivity, keeping in mind the fundamental rights as enshrined in the Indian constitution.[52] While the recommendations of the Commission (in the view of the authors) could lead to the encouragement of unionization in erstwhile non-unionized activities, the authors point out that in the ultimate analysis, the persisting inequalities in the labour markets can only be effectively addressed by active state intervention, for example, through a comprehensive social security system for unorganized workers as well as through the tying of minimum wage increases to the cost of living for industrial workers.

---

[47] For example in the World Bank–ICRIER survey mentioned by Gupta et al. (2008), labour regulations as a restriction were mentioned by only 4 per cent of the respondents as a primary obstacle, tailing well below other causes such as infrastructure, tax issues, governance, and finance.

[48] The Second National Labour Commission (Ministry of Labour 2002) also strongly endorses the ILO vision.

[49] The scheme has several in-built safeguards such as unemployment allowance (payable by the state to an applicant if he cannot be offered employment within a fortnight of application), guaranteed labour component in each project, guaranteed share of female employment, and minimum wage rate stipulations. The scheme now covers all the 593 districts of the country and involved an annual outlay of Rs 39,100 crore in 2009.

[50] The major shortcomings identified (see Dreze 2009; Ambasta et al. 2008) include (i) lack of timely devolution of funds, (ii) violating the stipulations on the relative share of women; (iii) lack of provision of on-site crèches, (iv) evasion of payment of unemployment allowances in certain states, and (v) arbitrary de-registration of seasonal workers.

[51] The number of days lost due to employer-imposed lockouts far exceeded those lost due to worker/union-led strikes since the mid-1990s, as opposed to the earlier decades of the 1970s and 1980s when strikes dominated industrial conflict.

[52] The Commission recommended important changes with respect to trade union recognition and explicitly expressed its preference for decentralized bargaining structures. On the issue of downsizing, it recommends that prior state permission is no more necessary with respect to layoffs and retrenchment in an establishment of any employment size and in its stead argues that workers should be given a two-months notice or pay in lieu of notice, in case of retrenchment.

Social Infrastructure

The crucial importance of social infrastructure in determining the social sustainability of the reforms momentum is now universally recognized. In India, the emphasis on building up a social infrastructure base to upgrade human capital pre-dates the reforms period. The two most important dimensions to social infrastructure are education and health and we discuss each of these in turn.

The benevolent causal linkages from education to a wide range of developmental issues is well documented in the theoretical literature (see Jones et al. 2010) as well as empirically borne out by the experience of several countries especially in the East Asian region. Universal primary education is also listed as one of the major goals in the Millennium Development Goals (MDGs) manifesto (2000). In all fairness, the Government of India cannot be accused of inaction on this front. In particular, the passage of the *Right of Children to Free and Compulsory Education Act 2009* is widely regarded as a landmark achievement. However, the difficulties ingrained at all tiers of the education system still defy solution. While the net enrolment ratio (NER) at the primary level was placed at 94.5 per cent by the NCERT survey (2002) and more or less reaffirmed by independent surveys such as the SRI-IMRB[53] survey (Ministry of Human Resources Development 2009), and may afford some room for satisfaction, there are a multitude of problems which aggregate statistics fail to reveal. The long list of problems (see Taneja 2010) plaguing the primary education sector comprises, among others, (i) low rates of retention (especially for girls in rural areas), (ii) high pupils–teacher ratios (PTRs)—much higher in several states than the 30:1 norm laid down in the Right To Education Act 2009, (iii) low quality of teachers, and (iv) poor school amenities (with about 22 per cent schools without access to drinking water, 46 per cent without a separate toilet for girls, and a whopping 64 per cent without electricity).

Enrolment at the secondary school stage is constrained by an overall shortage of secondary schools. Only 65 per cent of total villages at the all-India level have a secondary school within a radial distance of 5 km, and there is considerable regional variation in this figure.[54] Additionally there is a 10 per cent gap in secondary enrolment between boys and girls, with female enrolment in rural areas being barely 32 per cent (see World Bank 2009).[55]

Adult literacy, especially female adult literacy, is also considerably lower than that in comparable developing countries. The UNDP *Human Development Report 2009* indicates India's rank at a low 149 out of 180 countries. The latest available NSSO (2010) data for the year 2007–8 places the adult literacy figure (that is, population of fifteen years and above) at 76.7 per cent for men and 54.9 per cent for women.[56] One characteristic feature to emerge prominently across all levels of education is the pronounced incidence of discrimination by caste, gender, and community status.

The problems ailing the education sector are not located in resource allocation alone, though resources to this sector have always been some kind of a residual and subordinate charge on both the central and state governments' expenditure commitments. The total expenditure on education as a proportion of GDP which has in recent years been about 3.5 per cent of GDP is only slightly more than half the norm (6 per cent of GDP) suggested by the Kothari Commission nearly half a century ago.

The situation on the other major dimension of social infrastructure viz. health is even more dismal. Once again the government cannot be accused of wholly neglecting the issue. Major health sector reforms were initiated in the Eighth Five Year Plan (1992–7) and were broadly organized around four principles viz. (i) levy of user charges for people above the poverty line for access to medical services in public health institutions, (ii) introduction of health insurance and other cover mechanisms, (iii) greater private sector participation, and (iv) increasing reliance on decentralization of health services at the district levels via the involvement of Panchayati Raj Institutions and civil society organizations (CSOs).

In alignment with the MDGs (Nos 4 to 6), the thrust of official policy has been on reducing infant and maternal mortality, maternal health care, and combating communicable diseases (especially malaria, tuberculosis, and HIV/AIDS). But in spite of several laudable initiatives in recent years (most notably the Janani Suraksha Yojana [2005], National Vector Borne Disease Control Programme [2004]),[57] outcomes continue to be discouraging. The under-five child mortality rate, for example, has decreased from 116 (per 1,000 live births) in 1990 to 69 in 2009, but this rate of

---

[53] The full forms of SRI and IMRB are Social and Rural Research Institute and Indian Market Research Bureau respectively.

[54] The figures for Bihar (46 per cent) and Jharkhand (36 per cent), for example, are much lower than the national average.

[55] The problems of the higher education sector have been analysed in detail in the *India Development Report 2008* (see chapter by S.R. Hashim) and are not revisited here.

[56] As expected, rural–urban differences as well as gender differences are substantial. The overall literacy rates for the urban and rural population are respectively 82 per cent and 59.7 per cent, while the figure for rural females and males is respectively 47.55 per cent and 71.8 per cent.

[57] In addition the government is also actively continuing a number of programmes launched earlier such as National AIDS Control Programme (1987), Revised National TB Control Programme (1993), and Integrated Child Development Services Programme (1975).

decline is insufficient to hit the target of 39 deaths (per 1,000 live births) by 2015, set forth in MDG (No. 4). On communicable diseases, the situation is a real cause for alarm, as the incidence of second generation drug-resistant communicable diseases (such as malaria, TB, and HIV/AIDS) continues to rise unabated. Once again inadequate resource allocation is an important causal factor—at 1.5 per cent of GDP in 2008–9, it is not only way short of international norms[58] but also of the Indian government's own announced commitment to raise it to 3 per cent of GDP. However, other structural causes also need to be addressed on a priority basis, including most notably the shortage of health workers (especially skilled birth attendants), geographical inaccessibility of maternity hospitals and maternal health care centres, city-centric orientation of the provision of health services (including doctors, nurses, and mid-wives), and recognition of social rights of HIV/AIDS patients.

Financial Inclusion

Financial inclusion, in the sense of ensuring timely access to a wide range of financial services for the economically and socially disadvantaged sections of the population, has always been recognized as a key pillar of successive governments' poverty alleviation strategies. Beginning with the thrust on widening and strengthening the cooperative banking structure in the 1950s, followed by nationalization of a major segment of commercial banking activity in the late 1960s, the setting up of the regional rural bank (RRB) network in the 1970s, and a detailed programme of directed credit allocation throughout the 1970s and 1980s, state-directed financial inclusion had been a perennial concern of Indian policymakers in the pre-reforms era. This concern lay somewhat dormant in the first one and a half decades of the reforms phase, but then in a welcome *volte face* was suddenly revived around 2005, but with a greater emphasis on grass-roots participation involving self-help groups (SHGs), non-governmental organizations (NGOs), and micro-finance institutions (MFIs). Simultaneously the earlier exclusive focus on credit has been broadened to include a variety of other financial services including those related to insurance, pension, remittances and payment, and risk mitigation.

The extent of the financial exclusion problem in India can hardly be overstated. The Rangarajan Committee on Financial Inclusion (Ministry of Finance 2008), for example, notes that of total farm households around 73 per cent have no access to formal sources of credit, whereas 55 per cent of marginal farmer households have access neither to formal nor informal finance sources. Financial exclusion also varies across states as shown in the contribution by Pal and Vaidya (Chapter 12) to this volume. They uncover wide variation in the outreach of banking services across Indian states over time. By constructing an index of outreach of banking services, they examine the tendency of convergence of these services among the states of India over the period 1981–2007. Interestingly they find evidence supportive of unconditional β-convergence of the outreach during the pre-reform period (1981–90), but strong evidence for divergence in the post-reform period (1996–2007). The study thus adduces further evidence for aggravation of regional imbalance (discussed earlier) as an unintended consequence of the reform process.

Financial exclusion also varies across social and occupational groups (as noted in both the Rangarajan Committee and the Raghuram Rajan Committee on Financial Sector Reforms [2007]). The two high-level committees, aforementioned, have suggested a slew of measures to consolidate the various existing financial inclusion programmes. Key suggestions include (i) further extension of the SHG–Bank Linkage programme, (ii) introduction of joint liability group (JLG) lending to cover landless, sharecropping, and oral lease households, (iii) funding support to RRBs, (iv) assigning key roles to business facilitators (BFs) and business correspondents (BCs) in microfinance, (v) capacity building of government functionaries, (vi) extending NABARD support for microfinance in urban areas, and (vii) combination of micro-credit and micro-insurance provisions. Several of these measures are under active consideration of the government (see RBI 2010b). Recently, a spate of farmer suicides and attacks on some microfinance institutions in protest against alleged high interest rates and arbitrary loan recovery methods in Andhra Pradesh has drawn attention to some key outstanding problems of the microfinance sector, especially the *for profit* MFI segment (see Panagariya 2010). Partly as a response to these developments, the RBI set up the Malegam Committee, which submitted its report in January 2011 (see RBI 2011). It is widely expected that the government will act on several of the Committee's key recommendations.[59] However, several concerns have been raised in the context of this report, including, most importantly, that it will raise the operating costs of MFIs and thus affect their viability (see, for example, Subramanian 2011).

---

[58] The OECD average for public health expenditure as a percentage of GDP stood at 8.5 per cent in 2007 (see UNDP *Human Development Report 2007*).

[59] The main recommendations of the Malegam Committee relate to (i) capping MFI lending rates at 24 per cent, (ii) MFIs to ensure that the borrower's household income is less than Rs 50, 000 per annum, (iii) MFIS to verify that the borrower is a member of only one SHG, and (iv) MFIs to monitor and supervise the borrower to ensure that not more than 25 per cent of the loan is used for non-income generation purposes, among others.

ENVIRONMENTAL SUSTAINABILITY

The third dimension of sustainability (ecological)[60] is critically dependent on whether sufficient attention is paid in the development process to long-term issues such as energy, environment, and natural resources.

While the environmental implications of economic growth have been widely noted in the engineering and economic literature for at least the past fifty years or even more (see, for example, Pigou 1932; Forrester 1970; Mesarovic and Pestel 1974), global concerns relating to energy and environmental conservation, climate change, and ecosystems in general became crystallized after the Earth Summit held in Rio de Janeiro in 1992. This summit held under the auspices of the United Nations Conference on Trade and Environment (UNCED), put forth an international treaty—United Nations Framework Convention on Climate Change (UNFCC)—aimed at limiting greenhouse gas (GHG) emissions on a global basis. The provisions of the treaty (purely voluntary at the time of its promulgation in March 1994) acquired a binding status at the Kyoto conference (1997) with a roadmap for *mitigation commitments* laid out a decade later at the Bali Conference (2007). The most controversial provision of the UNFCC (maintained under the successive protocols at Kyoto, Bali, Copenhagen, etc.) is the provision relating to exemption of developing countries (most prominently China and India) from *mitigation commitments*. This position is strongly opposed by many developed nations (including most prominently the US). The international initiatives have also been supplemented by several national initiatives such as the Waxman-Markey Act (2009) in the US and the EU 20:20:20 Plan (2007). We now turn to the situation in India.

Energy Sector Issues

One of the key determinants of economic, social, and environmental sustainability is the evolution of the energy sector. While an equally strong case could be made out for including a discussion of energy-related issues under each of the three categories of sustainability, we follow standard practice in discussing it specifically in the environmental sustainability context, especially in view of energy being at the heart of climate change.[61]

In India, energy has already emerged as a significant bottleneck to the official targets of a *high and inclusive growth.*

The successful overcoming of this bottleneck would require massive investments in both the energy as well as the transport sectors. Sengupta (2010) concisely summarizes the three emerging challenges for the Indian energy sector viz.

1. To meet the substantially accelerating energy needs of agriculture, manufacturing, and services (most notably transport services which are a major consumer of primary commercial energy)
2. To remove *energy poverty*[62]
3. To reduce the local and global externalities due to pollution and the environmental degradation stemming from pollution as well as natural resource-intensive uses of energy

The Report of the Expert Working Group on an Integrated Energy Policy (Planning Commission 2006) went into several alternative feasible scenarios based on considerations such as variations of fuel-mix for power generation, increased fuel efficiency in the transport sector, greater development of renewable energy systems, and demand management strategies. The report does indicate some room for cautious optimism. As compared to the business-as-usual (BAU) scenario, the optimal scenario (that is, one derived from a *maximum achievable combination* of the various factors) can generate an economy of about 20 per cent in total energy requirement, with an associated reduction in CO_2 emissions of the order of 35 per cent (see Sengupta 2010: 182–3).

In recent years the issue of energy security has increasingly come to dominate the discourse on energy issues. The International Energy Agency (IEA) defines *energy insecurity* as 'the loss of welfare that may occur as a result of a change in the price or availability of energy' (IEA 2007: 32).

Reddy and Nathan (Chapter 14) discuss the broad contours of issues related to energy security on the supply as well as demand side. Supply side energy security involves an examination of different energy sources (coal, oil, gas, and renewables), intermediate means (electricity, refineries), and transportation modes (grids, pipelines, ports, ships). All of these have risks of supply interruptions or failures, challenging the security of undisturbed energy supply. Demand-side energy security involves measures to provide access to quality energy carriers to the needy and improving the quality, reliability, and affordability of energy services. Their study raises four main strategic issues mandating

---

[60] Environmental sustainability is aimed at promoting human welfare by conserving *natural capital*, which includes water, land, air, minerals, and the ecosystem generally (see Daly 1999).

[61] I have already remarked about the somewhat fuzzy boundaries separating the various sustainability categories.

[62] 'Energy poverty' essentially refers to the low per capita consumption of modern commercial energy and an excessive reliance on inefficient non-commercial modes of energy such as fuel wood, dungcake, and other biomass sources (see Birol 2007). According to the NSSO (2007), 84 per cent of rural households and 23 per cent of urban households in India depend on biomass sources for cooking.

coordinated action viz. (i) supply security, (ii) demand security, (iii) energy sustainability, and (iv) institutional framework for regulatory policy cooperation. The authors also emphasize the need for energy security policies of the country to be oriented with sustainable development as the primary goal and climate mitigation as its by-product.

Environment and Climate Change

Vinod Kumar Sharma (Chapter 13) in his contribution analyses the key questions relating to the type of reorientation in development strategies necessary to address the issues of environmental conservation and climate change. He laments the fact that in spite of a long history of environmentalism, with the passage and codification of various Acts (some even before the reforms period), none of the official initiatives on environmental conservation and climate change seem to have had much success in their avowed objectives. Several factors seem to be responsible for this state of affairs including predominantly the lack of coordination between the Centre, states, and local governments; systematic corruption; and a reluctance or lack of capacity of official bodies to accommodate the viewpoints of CSOs and local groups (occasionally leading to serious transgressions of the right to livelihood of local disadvantaged groups). He reviews the state of major sub-sectors of environment in India and examines the effectiveness of policy and other measures adapted to improve their condition. According to him, while the country's contribution to global environmental problems such as global warming and ozone depletion may be lower than other transitional economies, the local problems related to air, water, land, etc., within the country, are quite disturbing. Environmental challenges of development strategies are multidimensional and transcend national boundaries. Thus, to deal with these multidimensional and multinational problems, appropriate policies and striking a balance between environmental care and economic development are necessary at international, national, and local levels.

An important fallout of global climate change is the likelihood of increasing recurrence of natural disasters whose severity is often aggravated by corruption and other governance failures. Sengupta (Chapter 16) distinguishes between disasters due to primarily natural phenomena (like earthquakes, tsunami, drought, cyclones, heat and cold waves, landslides, avalanches, epidemics, etc.), and those that are man-made (for example, large-scale chemical spills, air and water poisoning, collapse of buildings and structures, transport disasters, and terrorist acts). He examines trends in natural and man-made disasters in India in the recent years and estimates the economic loss thereof. He advocates a series of measures to limit the collateral damage of such

calamities, with a particular emphasis on their financial implications.

CONCLUSION

A future historian writing of our times would most likely describe the closing decades of the twentieth century as marking the complete intellectual triumph of the trinity of liberalization, privatization, and globalization. The *neo-liberal* ideology, which underpinned the liberalization wave of the 1980s in LDCs and EMEs and has underlain many of the recommendations of the IMF and World Bank on structural adjustments (the so-called Washington Consensus), derives in large measure from the tenets of neo-classical economics. It is necessary to emphasize the well-known (but much neglected) fact that as of date, no economic doctrine (not even neo-classical economics) has theoretically proved markets as the best mechanism for static (leave alone dynamic) resource allocation. As to *w*hether freer markets will promote growth or otherwise is not a forgone conclusion but is essentially an empirical issue, circumscribed by a number of country-specific features including demographic structures, levels of literacy and general education, as well as other institutional features. It is against this backdrop, that we have attempted the task of providing a balance sheet of the Indian reforms experiment, with some prognostication about the face of the future, in this report.

The overall assessment of reforms emerging from the various contributions to this report, is like the proverbial curate's egg, 'good in parts'. On the growth front, reforms have indeed delivered beyond expectations, while simultaneously macroeconomic stability has been more or less successfully maintained. But the resultant growth and stability has had a fairly limited impact on poverty and seems to have aggravated both interpersonal and inter-regional inequality. The growth has also had an extremely low employment generation potential. On the agricultural front, stagnation seems to be setting in, while agrarian distress is increasingly becoming an important cause of social concern. While large industry has made considerable progress, there is evidence of growing concentration scale-wise and location-wise; as far as the medium- and small-scale sector is concerned it is encountering several bottlenecks not only in the infrastructure sector but also in access to credit. Services of course are the star performer in the Indian context, but serious doubts attach to the sustainability of a services-led growth momentum. Looking at the face of the future, especially on issues of the social and environmental sectors, which are critical to the fate of the vast majority of the population as well as future cohorts, while good intentions on the part of the government are very much in evidence especially since 2005, the actual achievements are falling considerably short of government targets (leave alone MDGs and international norms) in fields such as primary and secondary education, health, and financial inclusion.[63] On longer-term issues such as food and energy security, bio-diversity, ecosystem conservation, water and waste management, and climate change, little has been done beyond rhetoric.

Apart from these issues, there is a wider set of issues related to the reforms process such as corruption,[64] the degree of 'autonomy' of domestic policy, the freedom of the press from vested interests, and the quality of public opinion and socio-political unrest. However, without denying the importance of these broader issues, they have been kept outside the purview of the present report.

In conclusion, one may say that the reforms strategy, which seemed to be on a gradual track in the early years of the reforms process (1991–6), was suddenly shifted into high gear around 1996 with a distinct thrust in favour of large-scale industry and foreign investment, while several precautionary regulations on the financial sector were removed in undue haste. The fault lines, so evident in the reforms strategy now, are essentially an outcome of this latter epoch which stretched for a decade or so. Since 2005, however, the government seems to be seriously concerned with the 'human face' aspects of the reforms and has initiated a number of laudable initiatives. But clearly far more needs to be done on this front, and it is important to highlight that, as long as the reforms strategy continues in its present form, these measures will essentially be of a supplementary nature.

As an epilogue, one may add that while the reforms story, thus far, has provided India Inc. plenty of reason for celebration, from the perspective of the *aam admi* (who seems to have, through no fault of his, become the rallying point of all political parties) the story can at best draw a feeble half-cheer.

---

[63] Apologists of the official reforms strategy often put forth the defence that these problems have plagued Indian society for ages, so why blame the reforms in particular? This is, of course, an argument of sorts (shades of Dr Pangloss here!), but flies seriously in the face of the several findings in this report (and elsewhere) that on many fronts, the situation with respect to several social and environmental indicators has actually deteriorated in the post-reforms era. Even where improvements have occurred, these have often been on a significantly lower scale than corresponding improvements in the immediate pre-reforms decade.

[64] Corruption has been an endemic feature of the Indian polity. However, contrary to the pious expectations of the reform advocates, corruption has not diminished with the move towards markets and has actually become more deeply entrenched (see Nachane 2011).

REFERENCES

Acharya, S. (2002), 'Services not the Real Saviour', *The Economic Times*, 9 September.

——— (2004), 'India's Growth Prospects Revisited', *Economic and Political Weekly*, 9 October, pp. 4537–42.

Aghion, P., R. Burgess, S.J. Redding, and F. Zilibotti (2006), 'The Unequal Effects of Liberalization: Evidence from Dismantling the License Raj in India', Discussion Paper No. 5492, CEPR, London.

Alesina, A. and D. Rodrik (1994) 'Distributive Politics and Economic Growth', *Quarterly Journal of Economics*, 109(2): 465–90.

Ambasta, P., P. Vijay Shankar, and M. Shah (2008), 'Two Years of NREGA: The Road Ahead', *Economic and Political Weekly*, 43(8): 41–50.

Anderson, J.E. and E. van Wincoop (2004), 'Trade Costs', *Journal of Economic Literature*, 42(3): 691–751.

Arteta, C., B. Eichengreen, and C. Wyplosz (2003), 'When does Capital Account Liberalization Help More than It Hurts?', in E. Helpman and E. Sadka (eds), *Economic Policy in the International Economy: Essays in Honour of Assaf Razin*. Cambridge University Press.

Arunachalam, R. and N.K. Kumar (2002), 'Inter-temporal Comparison of Inter-industrial Linkages in the Indian Economy (1968–69 to 1988–83)', *Reserve Bank of India Occasional Papers*, 15(1): 1–30.

Banerjee, A. and E. Duflo (2003), 'Do Firms want to Borrow More? Testing Credit Constraints using a Directed Lending Program', BREAD WP 2003-5.

Bartelmus, P. (1999), 'Economic Growth and Patterns of Sustainability', Wuppertal Institut für Klima, Umwelt, Energie, Paper No. 98.

Basu, K. and A. Maertens (2007), 'The Pattern and Causes of Economic Growth in India', *Oxford Review of Economic Policy*, 23(2): 143–67.

Baumol, W.J. (1967), 'Macroeconomics of Unbalanced Growth: The Anatomy of Urban Crisis', *American Economic Review*, 57(3): 415–26.

Bekaert, G., C.R. Harvey, and C. Lundblad (2006), 'Growth Volatility and Financial Liberalization', *Journal of International Money and Finance*, 25(3): 370–403.

Benabou, R. (1996), 'Inequality and Growth', in B. Bernanke and J. Rotemberg (eds), *NBER Macroeconomics Annual 1996*. Cambridge, MA: MIT Press.

Bernanke, B. (2005), 'Monetary Policy in a World of Mobile Capital', *Cato Journal*, 25(1): 1–12.

Bertola, G. (1993), 'Factor Shares and Savings in Endogenous Growth', *American Economic Review*, 83: 1184–98.

Bhalla, A. and D. Nachane (1998), 'Asian Eclipse: India and China in the Penumbra?', *Economic and Political Weekly*, 5–12 September, pp. 2357–78.

Bhattacharjea, A. (2010), 'Of Omissions and Commissions: India's Competition Laws', *Economic and Political Weekly*, XLV(35): 31–7.

Bhattacharya, B.B. and S. Sakthivel (2004), 'Regional Growth and Disparity in India: Comparison of Pre- and Post-reform Decades', *Economic and Political Weekly*, 6 March, pp. 1071–7.

Birdsall, N. (2005), 'Why Inequality Matters in a Globalizing World', WIDER Annual Lecture.

Birdsall, N., D.R. Ross, and R. Sabot (1995), 'Inequality and Growth Reconsidered: Lessons from East Asia', *World Bank Economic Review*, 9(3): 477–508.

Birol, F (2007), 'Energy Economics: A Place for Energy Poverty in the Agenda?', *The Energy Journal*, 28(3): 1–6.

BIS (Committee on the Global Financial System) (2009), 'Capital Flows and Emerging Market Economies', CGFS Papers No. 33 (Chairman: R. Mohan).

Blanc-Brude, F., H. Goldsmith, and T. Välilä (2006), *Ex-Ante Construcion Costs in the Eurpean Road Sector: A Comparison of Public Private Partnerships and Traditional Procurement*, European Investment Bank, Economic & Financial Reports, 2006/01.

Bonfiglioli, A. and C. Mendicino (2004), 'Financial Liberalization, Banking Crises and Growth : Assessing the Links', Department of Economics & Business, Universitat Pompeu Fabra, Economics Working Paper No. 946.

Bosworth, B., S.Collins, and A. Virmani (2006), 'Sources of Growth in the Indian Economy', paper presented at The India Policy Forum, New Delhi.

Bourguignon, F. (2003), 'The Growth Elasticity of Poverty Reduction: Explaining Heterogeneity across Countries and Time Periods', in T. Eicher and S.Turnovsky (eds), *Inequality and Growth: Theory and Policy Implications*. Cambridge: MIT Press.

——— (2004), 'The Poverty–Growth–Inequality Triangle', paper presented at ICRIER Conference, 4 February.

Brooks, D. and D. Hummels (2009), *Infrastructure's Role in Lowering Asia's Trade Costs: Building for Trade*. Cheltenham, UK: Edward Elgar.

Chakrabarti, R., W. Megginson, and P.K. Yadav (2008), 'Corporate Governance in India', *Journal of Applied Corporate Finance*, 20(19): 59–72.

Chand, R. (2010), 'Achieving 4 per cent Growth Rate in Agriculture during the Eleventh Five Year Plan: Feasibility and Constraints', in P. Nayak, B. Goldar, and P.Agrawal (eds), *India's Economy and Growth: Essays in Honour of V.K.R.V. Rao*, pp. 69–86. New Delhi: Sage Publications.

Chen, S. and M. Ravallion (2004), 'How Have The World's Poorest Fared since the Early 1980s?', Development Research Group, World Bank, Washington DC.

Daly, H.E. (1999), *Ecological Economics and the Ecology of Economics*. Cheltenham, UK: Edward Elgar.

De, P. (2008), 'Empirical Estimates of Trade Costs for Asia', in D. Brooks and J. Menon (eds), *Infrastructure and Trade in Asia*. Cheltenham, UK: Edward Elgar.

——— (2009), 'Global Economic and Financial Crisis: India's Trade Potential and Future Prospects', Asia-Pacific Research and Training Network on Trade, Working Paper Series No. 64.

Deininger, K. and L. Squire (1998), 'New Ways of Looking at Old Issues: Inequality and Growth', *Journal of Development Economics*, 57(2): 259–87.

DeLong, J.B. (2001), 'India since Independence: An Analytical Growth Narrative'. Available at http//www.Delong@Econ.Berkeley.Edu

Delong, J.B. (2009), 'What has Happened to Milton Friedman's Chicago School?', 6th Singapore Economic Review Public Lecture, 7 January.

Department of Industrial Policy and Promotion (2002), *Report on Reforming Investment Approvals and Implementation Procedures* (Govindarajan Committee Report). New Delhi: Government of India.

Dev, S.M. and C. Ravi (2007), 'Poverty and Inequality: All-India and States, 1983–2005', *Economic and Political Weekly*, February, pp. 509–21.

Dollar, D. and A. Kraay (2002), 'Growth is Good for the Poor', *Journal of Economic Growth*, 7(3): 195–225.

Drejer, I. (2002), *Input–Output Based Measures of Interindustry Linkages Revisited—A Survey and Discussion*. Copenhagen: Centre for Economic and Business Research, Ministry of Economic and Business Affairs (Denmark).

Dreze, J. (2009), 'Operational Framework of NREGA Needs Overhaul', *The Times of India*, 30 March.

Eichengreen, B. and D. Leblang (2003), 'Capital Account Liberalization and Growth: Was Mr. Mahathir Right?', *International Journal of Finance and Economics*, 8(3): 205–24.

Engel, E., R. Fischer, and A. Gelatovic (2006), 'Renegotiation without Holdup: Anticipating Spending and Infrastructure Concessions', Cowles Foundation Discussion Paper No. 1567.

Forrester, J.W. (1970), *World Dynamics*. Portland, Oregon: Productivity Press.

Friedman, B.M. (2005), *The Moral Consequences of Economic Growth*. New York: Alfred Knopf.

Ghani, E. (ed.) (2010), *The Service Revolution in South Asia*. New Delhi: Oxford University Press.

Ghosh, J. (2004), 'Macroeconomic Reforms in a Labour Policy Framework for India', ILO Employment Strategy Papers No. 2004/1.

Ghosh, S. and T.W. Ross (2008), 'The Competition (Amendment) Bill 2007: A Review and Critique', *Economic and Political Weekly*, XLIII(51): , 35–40.

Goldar, B. (2004), 'Indian Manufacturing: Productivity Trends in Pre- and Post-reform Periods', *Economic and Political Weekly*, 20 November, pp. 5033–43.

Goldar, B. and A. Mitra (2010), 'Productivity Increase and Changing Sectoral Composition: Contribution to Economic Growth in India', in P. Nayak, B. Goldar, and P. Agrawal (eds), *India's Economy and Growth: Essays in Honour of V.K.R.V. Rao*, pp. 35–68. New Delhi: Sage Publications.

Goswami, O. (2002), 'Corporate Governance in India', in *Taking Action against Corruption in Asia and the Pacific*. Manila: Asian Development Bank.

Grilli, V. and G.M. Milesi-Ferretti (1995), 'Economic Effects and Structural Determinants of Capital Controls', *IMF Staff Papers*, 42(3): 54–88.

Gupta, P., R. Hasan, and U. Kumar (2008), 'What Constrains Indian Manufacturing?', ICRIER Working Paper No. 211.

Hansda, S. and P. Ray (2006), 'Employment and Poverty in India during the 1990s: Is There a Diverging Trend?', *Economic and Political Weekly*, 8 July, pp. 3014–23.

Hansda, S.K. (2002), *Sustainability of Services-led Growth: An Input–Output Analysis of Indian Economy, Staff Studies (DEAP)* No. 1/2002, Reserve Bank of India.

Hashim. S.R. (2008), 'State of Higher Education in India', chapter 5 in R. Radhakrishna (ed.), *India Development Report 2008*. New Delhi: Oxford University Press.

Hicks, J.R. (1946), 'Income', chapter XIV in *Value and Capital* (2nd edition). Oxford: Clarendon Press.

Hirschman, A. (1958), *The Strategy of Economic Development*. New Haven, Connecticut, USA: Yale University Press.

IFC–World Bank (2009), *Doing Business in India 2009: Reforms Promote Competitiveness and Growth in Indian Cities*. New Delhi and Washington DC: World Bank.

International Energy Agency (IEA) (2007), *Energy Security and Climate Change: Assessing Interaction*. Paris: IEA/OECD.

International Labour Organization (ILO) (1998), *Declaration on Fundamental Principles and Rights at Work*.

Jones, P., D. Selby, and S. Sterling (2010), *Sustainability Education: Perspectives And Practices across Higher Education*. Ottawa, Canada: Renouf Pub. Co. Ltd.

Kraay, A. (2005), 'When is Growth Pro-poor? Evidence from a Panel of Countries', *Journal of Development Economics*, 80(1): 198–227.

Kuznets, S. (1955), 'Economic Growth and Income Inequality', *American Economic Review,* 45: 1–28.

La Porta, R., F. Lopez-de-Silanes, A. Shleifer, and R.W. Vishny (1998), 'Law and Finance', *Journal of Political Economy*, 106: 1113–55.

Levine, R. (2001), 'International Financial Liberalization and Economic Growth', *Review of International Economics*, 9(4): 688–702.

Lipsey, R.G., K. Carlaw, and C. Bekar (2005), *Economic Transformations: General Purpose Technologies and Long-Term Economic Growth*. Oxford, UK: Oxford University Press.

Marwah, K. and L.R. Klein (1995), 'The Possibility of Nesting South Asia in Asia-Pacific Integration', *Journal of Asian Economics*, 6(1): 1–27.

Mazumdar, K. (1995), 'Disproportional Growth of Service Sector in India: 1960–1990', *The Indian Economic Journal*, 43(2): 835–64.

McKinnon, R.I. (1973), *Money and Capital in Economic Development*. Washington DC: Brookings Institution.

McKinsey & Co. (2001), *India—The Growth Imperative: Understanding the Barriers to Rapid Growth and Employment Creation*. New Delhi: McKinsey & Co.

——— (2006), *Accelerating India's Economic Growth through Financial System Reform*. San Francisco: McKinsey Global Institute, McKinsey & Co.

——— (2009), *Environmental and Energy Sustainability: An Approach for India*. Magnum Custom Publishing. Available at http://www.mckinsey.com/clientsservice/cssi/pdf/India_Environmental_Energy_Sustainability_final.pdf

Mesarovic, M. and E. Pestel (1974), *Mankind at the Turning Point, Second Report to the Club of Rome*. Boston: Dutton Pub. Co.

Ministry of Finance (2007), *Report of the Committee on Infrastructure Financing* (Chairman: Deepak Parekh). New Delhi: Government of India.

——— (2008), *Report of the Committee on Financial Inclusion* (Chairman: C. Rangarajan). New Delhi: Government of India.

Ministry of Human Resources Development (2009), *Survey of Out of School Children* (SRI-IMRB Survey). New Delhi: Government of India.

Ministry of Labour (2002), *Report of the Second National Labour Commission* (Chairman: R. Varma). New Delhi: Government of India.

Mukim, M. and P. Nunnenkamp (2010), 'The Location Choices of Foreign Investors: A District-Level Analysis in India', Kiel Working Paper No. 1628.

Nachane, D.M. (2009), 'The Fate of India Unincorporated', in *Global Economic and Financial Crisis: Essays from the Economic and Political Weekly*, pp. 191–212. Delhi: Orient Longman Publishers.

——— (2010), 'Capital Management Techniques for Financial Stability and Growth', *Economic and Political Weekly*, 45(46): 36–9.

——— (2011), 'Liberalization, Globalization and the Dynamics of Democracy in India', *International Journal of Development and Conflict* (forthcoming).

Nachane, D.M. and N. Raje (2007), 'Financial Liberalization and Monetary Policy', *Margin: The Journal of Applied Economic Research*, 1(1): 47–83.

National Commission for Enterprises in the Unorganized Sector (NCEUS) (2007), *Report on Conditions of Work and Promotion of Livelihoods in the Unorganised Sector* (Chairman: A. Sengupta). New Delhi: Government of India.

National Sample Survey Organisation (NSSO) (2005), *Household Consumption Expenditure and Employment–Unemployment Situation in India* (NSS 59th Round). New Delhi: Government of India.

——— (2006), *Employment and Unemployment Situation in India, July 2004–June 2005 (*NSS 61st Round*).* New Delhi: Government of India.

——— (2007), *Energy Sources of Indian Households for Cooking and Lighting, 2004–05* (NSS 61st Round). New Delhi: Government of India.

——— (2010), *Education in India 2007–08: Participation and Expenditure* (NSS 64th Round), Report No. 532.

NCERT (2002), *Seventh All-India School Education Survey*.

Noorbaksh, F. (2003), 'Human Development and Regional Disparities in India', Department of Economics, University of Glasgow, Discussion Paper No. 2003-12.

Nunnenkamp, P. and R. Stracke (2007), 'Foreign Direct Investment in Post-Reform India: Likely to Work Wonders for Regional Development?', Kiel Working Paper No. 1375.

Ocampo, J.A. and J.E. Stiglitz (2008), *Capital Market Liberalization and Development*. New York: Oxford University Press.

OECD (2000), *A Report on Business and Industry*. Paris: Policy Forum.

Pais, J. (2002), 'Casualization of the Urban Labour Force: An Appraisal of Recent Trends in Manufacturing', *Economic and Political Weekly*, 37(7): 631–52.

Panagariya, A. (2004), 'Growth and Reforms during 1980s and 1990s', *Economic and Political Weekly*, 39(25): 2581–94.

——— (2008), *India: The Emerging Giant*. New Delhi: Oxford University Press.

——— (2010), 'MFIs: Confusion Still Reigns', *The Economic Times*, 29 December.

Persson, T. and G. Tabellini (1994), 'Is Inequality Harmful for Growth?', *American Economic Review*, 84(3): 600–21.

Pigou, A.C. (1932), *The Economics of Welfare*. London: Macmillan & Co.

Planning Commission (2002), *Report of the Special Group on Targeting Ten Million Employment Opportunities per Year over the 10th Plan* (Chairman: S.P.Gupta). New Delhi: Government of India.

——— (2006), *Integrated Energy Policy: Report of the Expert Committee*. New Delhi: Government of India.

——— (2007), *A Hundred Small Steps: Report of the Committee on Financial Sector Reforms* (Chairman: Raghuram Rajan). New Delhi: Government of India.

Polaski, S., M. Panda, and A. Ganesh-Kumar (2008), 'Policy Dilemmas in India: The Impact of Changes in Agricultural Prices on Rural and Urban Poverty', IGIDR Working Paper No. 2008-012.

Radhakrishna, R. and M. Panda (2006), *Macroeconomics of Poverty Reduction: Indian Case Study* (study carried out for the Asia-Pacific Regional Programme on the Macroeconomics of Poverty Reduction), UNDP.

Radhakrishna, R. and S. Ray (eds) (2005), *Handbook of Poverty in India: Perspectives, Policies and Programs*. New Delhi: Oxford University Press.

Rakshit, M. (2009), 'India amidst the Global Crisis', in *Global Economic and Financial Crisis: Essays from the Economic and Political Weekly*, pp. 137–70. Delhi: Orient Longman Publishers.

Rangarajan, C. (2000), 'Capital Flows: Another Look', *Economic and Political Weekly*, 9 December, pp. 4421–7.

Rangarajan, C., P. Iyer Kaul, and Seema (2007), 'Revisiting Employment and Growth', *Money and Finance, ICRA Bulletin*, September.

Reddy, Y.V. (2005), 'Overcoming Challenges in a Globalising Economy: Managing India's External Sector', Lecture at the India Programme of the Foreign Policy Center, London, 23 June.

Reserve Bank of India (RBI) (2006), *Handbook of Monetary Statistics of India*.

——— (2010a), *Annual Report 2010*.

——— (2010b), *Second Quarter Review of Monetary Policy 2010–11*.

——— (2011), *Report of the Sub-committee of the Central Board of Directors of the RBI to Study Issues and Concerns in the MFI Sector* (Chairman: Y. Malegam).

Rodrick, D. (1998), *Who Needs Capital Account Convertibility?* Harvard University (mimeo).

Salvadori, N. (ed.) (2003), *Old and New Growth Theories*. Cheltenham, UK: Edward Elgar.

Sastry, D.V.S., B. Singh, K. Bhattacharya, and N. Unnikrishnan (2003), 'Sectoral Linkages and Growth Prospects: Some Reflections on the Indian Economy', *Economic and Political Weekly*, XXXVIII(24): 2390–7.

SEBI (2000), *Report of the SEBI Committee on Corporate Governance* (Chairman: Kumar Mangalam Birla).

——— (2003), *Report of the SEBI Committee on Corporate Governance* (Chairman: N.R. Narayana Murthy).

Sen, A. and Himanshu (2004), 'Poverty and Inequality in India: I & II', *Economic and Political Weekly*, 18 September, pp. 4247–63 and 25 September, pp. 4361–75.

Sen, K. (2007), 'Why Did the Elephant Start to Trot? India's Growth Acceleration Re-examined', *Economic and Political Weekly*, XLII(43): 37–47.

Sengupta, J. (2005), *India's Economic Growth: A Strategy for the New Economy*. New York: Palgrave McMillan.

Sengupta, R. (2010), 'Inclusive Economic Growth and Sustainable Energy Development of India', in P. Nayak, B. Goldar, and P. Agrawal (eds), *India's Economy and Growth: Essays in Honour of V.K.R.V. Rao*, pp. 155–90. New Delhi: Sage Publications.

Shaw, E.S. (1973), *Financial Deepening in Economic Development*. New York: Oxford University Press.

Sivasubramonian, S. (2004), *The Sources of Economic Growth in India 1950–1951 to 1999–2000*. New Delhi: Oxford University Press.

Sridhar, A. (2006), *Environmental Governance Reforms, Rephrasing the Reform Process*. New Delhi: International Institute for Environment and Development.

Subramanian, K. (2011), 'Malegam Report to Hurt Microfinance', *The Economic Times*, 8 February.

Taneja, A. (2010), 'GOAL 2: Achieve Universal Primary Education', in *Millennium Development Goals in India: A Civil Society Report*. New Delhi: Wada Na Todo Abhiyan.

Tendulkar, S. (2006), 'Post Reform Trends in Poverty and Inequality in India', Symposium held in Mumbai, Indian Liberal Group, 29 June.

Triplet, J.E. and B.P. Bosworth (2000), *Productivity in the Service Sector*. Washington DC: Brookings Institution.

UNDP (2007), *Human Development Report 2007*.

——— (2009), *Human Development Report 2009*.

UNIDO (2010), *Yearbook of Industrial Statistics 2010*.

Wallack, J.S. (2003), 'Structural Breaks in Indian Macroeconomic Data', *Economic and Political Weekly*, 11 October, pp. 4312–15.

World Bank (2004), *India: Investment Climate Assessment 2004, Improving Manufacturing Competitiveness*. Washington DC: World Bank.

——— (Human Development Unit) (2009), *Secondary Education in India—Universalizing Opportunity*. New Delhi: World Bank.

Wu, Y. (2008), 'Comparing Regional Development in China and India', UNU-WIDER Research Paper No. 2008/13.

2

Macroeconomic Overview

S. Chandrasekhar

INTRODUCTION

Decoupling of emerging economies from the developed countries has been a hotly contested conjecture since the onset of the financial crisis in the US. The final word is yet to be written on this issue. Nor is the issue likely to die down in the immediate future. Proponents of the decoupling hypothesis would argue that since emerging markets have made considerable progress in reducing external imbalances and have grown on the strength of domestic demand, they are likely to be less affected by shocks emanating from developed countries. However, critics debunk this notion by arguing that in an era of globalization, economies have become more interconnected through trade and finance. Hence, the business cycles of developed and developing countries would get synchronized.

In their recent work, Kose et al. (2008) attempted to examine this issue empirically. They found evidence of 'business cycle convergence' within industrial countries and emerging market economies but 'divergence (or decoupling) between them'. In their study, India and China were grouped under emerging market economies. Their finding is unlikely to settle the issue one way or the other. After all, the results of such studies are sensitive to the grouping of countries, the time period of the study, and the techniques used for the analysis.

The experience of India and China is often advanced as evidence in favour of the decoupling hypothesis since these two countries were relatively less affected by the decline in growth rates in advanced economies and developments

in the financial markets in the US. At a time when world output increased by 0.5 per cent in the advanced economies in 2008 and then shrunk by 0.8 per cent in 2009, China and India grew at 8.7 per cent and 5.6 per cent respectively in 2009. As per the advance estimates, the Indian economy grew at 7.2 per cent during 2009–10. It is projected that India and China will continue to grow well above the projected growth rate of world output of 4.3 per cent in 2011 (Table 2.1).

India was shielded from the slump in global output on account of a couple of factors. First, India's current share in world exports is 1.1 per cent. This is miniscule compared to China, which accounted for nearly 9 per cent of world's exports in 2008 (Government of India 2010a). Hence, the slump in global demand did not affect Indian economy

Table 2.1 The World Economy

	2008	2009	2010	2011
World output	3	−0.8	3.9	4.3
Advanced economies[*]	0.5	−3.2	2.1	2.4
United States	0.4	−2.5	2.7	2.4
Euro area	0.6	−3.9	1	1.6
China	9.6	8.7	10	9.7
India	7.3	5.6	7.7	7.8

Source: World Economic Outlook Update, January 2010, International Monetary Fund.

Note: [*] Includes the US and Euro area.

Table 2.2 Rate of Growth at Factor Cost at 2004–5 Prices (per cent)

	2005–6	2006–7	2007–8	2008–9	2009–10
Agriculture, Forestry, and Fishing	5.2	3.7	4.7	1.6	−0.2
Mining and Quarrying	1.3	8.7	3.9	1.6	8.7
Manufacturing	9.6	14.9	10.3	3.2	8.9
Electricity, Gas, and Water Supply	6.6	10	8.5	3.9	8.2
Construction	12.4	10.6	10	5.9	6.5
Trade, Hotels, and Restaurants	12.4	11.2	9.5	5.3	8.3*
Transport, Storage, and Communication	11.5	12.6	13	11.6	
Financing, Insurance, Real Estate, and Business Services	12.8	14.5	13.2	10.1	9.9
Community, Social, and Personal Services	7.6	2.6	6.7	13.9	8.2
GDP at Factor Cost	9.5	9.7	9.2	6.7	7.2

Source: *Economic Survey 2009–10*, Government of India.

Note: *Transport and communication included for 2009–10 in trade, hotels, and restaurants.

as much as it would have had were India's share in world trade higher. Second, and probably fortuitously, the implementation of the recommendations of the sixth Central Pay Commission gave a boost to domestic demand, thereby contributing to growth. It is estimated that over 4.5 million central government employees and 3.8 million pensioners benefitted in terms of higher incomes. The nationwide roll-out of the National Rural Employment Guarantee Scheme also had a salutary effect. In addition, the Government of India rolled out the fiscal stimulus packages fairly rapidly. On the monetary policy front, the Reserve Bank of India (RBI) carefully calibrated its response to the worldwide crisis. The central bank followed an easy money policy by reducing the cash reserve ratio and important policy rates.

MACROECONOMIC DEVELOPMENTS

India became a trillion dollar economy in 2007. Its gross domestic product (GDP) increased by 1.4 times from $293.1 billion in 1988 to $416.3 billion in 1998. In the next ten years, the GDP increased by 2.82 times to $1,176.9 billion in 2007.[1] The fact that India's GDP almost trebled could be attributed to high growth rates over the period 2004–5 to 2007–8. The GDP (at factor cost 2004–5 prices) grew at well over 9 per cent per annum in each of those years. The crisis emanating from the US acted as a dampener and GDP grew at 6.7 per cent in 2008–9 and 7.2 per cent in 2009–10. In the coming years, the objective of policymakers is to achieve a growth rate upwards of 9 per cent per annum.

India has always maintained a healthy savings rate. The savings rate increased from 32.2 per cent of GDP in 2004–5 to 36.4 per cent of GDP in 2007–8, and then declined to

32.9 per cent of GDP in 2008–9. The decline in 2008–9 was on account of a decline in savings by the public sector. The capital formation rate mirrored the savings rate. It was 32.7 per cent of GDP in 2004–5 and 34.9 per cent in 2008–9 (Government of India 2010a).

In 2008–9, there was a decline in the rate of growth of every sector of the economy, barring community, social, and personal services (Table 2.2). The decline in the growth rate of agriculture, forestry, and fishing cannot be attributed to external developments. All other sectors have smartly bounced back in 2009–10. The share of agriculture, forestry, and fishing in the GDP (at 2004–5 prices) in 2009 was 15 per cent and that of manufacturing was 16 per cent (Figure 2.1). In the medium term, it is expected that the share of the construction sector will increase beyond the current level of 8 per cent. Construction is a labour-intensive sector and its growth bodes well for employment. However, the absence of growth in non-farm employment

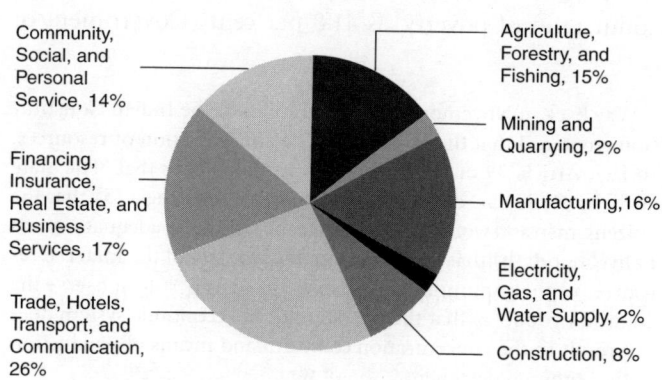

Source: Calculated from Government of India (2010c).

Figure 2.1 Components of Gross Domestic Product (at 2004–5 prices) in 2009

[1] http://devdata.worldbank.org/AAG/ind_aag.pdf

in rural India and the lack of movement of people out of agriculture to other occupations are causes of concern. This has implications for incidence of poverty and rural–urban disparities.

The last edition of the *India Development Report* clearly brought out the point that the impressive growth rate India has achieved since the mid-1990s has not translated into a faster rate of reduction in poverty in the period. Among the issues that were flagged as areas of concern included increase in inter-state, inter-district, and urban–rural disparities. The recent increase in Naxalite activity is often attributed to the failure of the growth and development process in being inclusive and high levels of poverty and malnutrition in certain districts of India.[2] It is estimated that the Naxalite movement is spread over 12 states and active in 125 districts (Government of India 2008). The report of the Expert Group on Development Challenges in Extremist Affected Areas stated, 'There is no denying that what goes in the name of "naxalism" is to a large extent a product of collective failure to assure to different segments of society their basic entitlements under the Constitution and other protective legislation' (Government of India 2008: 83). The ongoing national rural employment guarantee scheme and the proposed Food Security Act will go a long way in alleviating the economic conditions in the backward districts and Naxalite-affected districts in India.

But these are not permanent solutions. The Expert Group on Development Challenges in Extremist Affected Areas made specific recommendations including: effective implementation of protective legislation, land-related measures including recommendations relating to land acquisition and rehabilitation and resettlement, livelihood security, universalizing basic social services to standards, and strengthening the planning system. Another expert group, constituted with the objective of examining the issue of the count of number of poor in India, submitted its report in November 2009. The expert group revised the estimate of poverty in India. For 2004–5, it estimates that the all-India rural head count ratio of poverty[3] is 41.8 per cent (Government of

India 2009a). This is in contrast to the official estimate of 28.3 per cent. A higher estimate of poverty has budgetary implications. The government will have to increase its social expenditure in line with the number of individuals living below the poverty line.

AGRICULTURE

Economic reforms were expected to give a fillip to agriculture. However, in reality, this has not proved to be the case. Bhalla and Singh (2009) establish that in the post-reform era (1993–2006), annual compound growth rate of value of output was 1.73 per cent as against 3.37 per cent in the pre-reform era (1983–93). The growth in output was driven by yields. Not surprisingly, the pattern of annual compound growth rate of yields is similar to that of output. The growth rate of yields was lower in the post-reform era than in the pre-reform era. Bhalla and Singh attribute the decline in rate of growth of yield and output to declining public investment in irrigation and water management and scientific research. The continued lacklustre performance of Indian agriculture has been a source of concern. In 2007–8, agriculture and allied sectors grew at 4.7 per cent. In 2008–9, the sector grew only at 1.6 per cent, and in 2009–10 the sector shrunk by 0.2 per cent. (Government of India 2010a)

The question foremost on people's mind is what or where would be the next breakthrough in Indian agriculture. For a long time it has been pointed out that the eastern region has immense potential and this needs to be exploited. Finally, in the Union Budget for 2010–11, there is mention of a strategy to 'extend the green revolution to the eastern region of the country comprising Bihar, Chhattisgarh, Jharkhand, Eastern UP, West Bengal and Orissa'.

In the absence of improvements in water management practices, Indian agriculture continues to be exposed to the vagaries of the monsoon. In the decade 2001–10, some region in India has been affected by drought every year.[4] The two major drought years since 2001 occurred in 2002–3 and 2008–9. Deficiency in rainfall in the south-west monsoon season affected agricultural output in 2009. In order to reduce the impact of weather shocks, the often repeated

---

[2] Way back in November 1949, the framers of the Indian Constitution envisaged that there should not be concentration of resources. In fact, Article 39 of the Indian Constitution states that 'The State shall, in particular, direct its policy towards securing—(a) that the citizens, men and women equally, have the right to an adequate means of livelihood; (b) that the ownership and control of the material resources of the community are so distributed as best to subserve the common good; (c) that the operation of the economic system does not result in the concentration of wealth and means of production to the common detriment.'

[3] In 2005, the Government of India had appointed an Expert Group to Review the Methodology for Estimation for Poverty. In their report, they start with the premise that the official estimate of head

count ratio (HCR) of urban poverty of 25.7 per cent for 2004–5 is less controversial. They 'recommend MRP-equivalent of urban PLB corresponding to 25.7 per cent urban headcount ratio as the new reference PLB to be provided to rural as well as urban population in all the states after adjusting it for within-state urban-relative-to-rural and rural and urban state-relative-to-all-India price differentials' (http://planningcommission.gov.in/reports/genrep/rep_pov.pdf).

[4] http://www.agricoop.nic.in/DroughtMgmt/Finance%20Comm25609.pdf

promise of making Indian agriculture drought-proof needs to be translated into reality.

The recent spike in food prices clearly brought into focus the role of the government's minimum support price programme and buffer stocking operations. Concerns have been raised in the context of specific commodities. For instance, the *Economic Survey 2009–10* highlighted the issue of production and low yields of oilseeds and pulses. Bhalla and Singh (2009) point to the fact that farmers who diversified into cotton and oilseeds are exposed to the shocks emanating from international price movements. Particularly in case of pulses, the *Economic Survey* states that the ability to import is greatly limited given that very few countries in the world grow pulses. What is of concern is that the share of pulses in total gross cropped area in India has declined from 14.4 per cent in 1990–3 to 12 per cent in 2003–6. The share of pulses in total value of output similarly declined from 6.8 per cent to 5.8 per cent. The Union Budget 2010–11 has announced a measure to organize 60,000 'pulses and oilseed villages' in rain-fed areas.

It remains to be seen whether the government would encourage higher production of pulses via the minimum support price programme. Currently, the minimum support price programme is working effectively in case of rice, wheat, and sugarcane, and is most effective only in Punjab, Haryana, and parts of Uttar Pradesh. In 2009–10, over 72 per cent of the rice procured was from Haryana and Punjab. If we include Uttar Pradesh and Andhra Pradesh, then nearly 87 per cent of the rice procurement is from four states (Government of India 2010b). There is a need to expand the procurement machinery to other states given the proposal to extend 'green revolution to the eastern region' of the country.

In addition to food price inflation, the other issue dominating policy discourse is flow of credit to agriculture. A piquant situation has developed in Indian agriculture with the declining share of small and marginal farmers in total credit despite their increase in total agricultural production. It is estimated that the share of farmers with a holding of less than 2 hectares in production of rice increased from 43 per cent in 1981 to 52 per cent in 2001, and from 31 per cent to 43 per cent in case of wheat. Their share in pulses, sugarcane, and oilseeds increased by 10, 14, and 10 percentage points, respectively (Singh et al. 2002; Mehrotra 2010).

However, the share of small farms in credit from formal sector declined from over 30 per cent in 1990–1 to less than 25 per cent in 2006–7 (Figure 2.2). Their share in number of accounts too declined from 48 per cent to less than 42 per cent (Figure 2.3). Notice that over the period 2004–7, the share of large farms in number of accounts has increased. What is of concern is that this was the period when the Government of India sought to double the flow of credit

to agriculture. During this period, the loans per account sharply increased in case of the large farmers (Figure 2.4). Thus, it appears that during the phase of doubling of credit, it is the large farmers who benefitted. What is of concern is that the doubling of credit phase did not necessarily lead

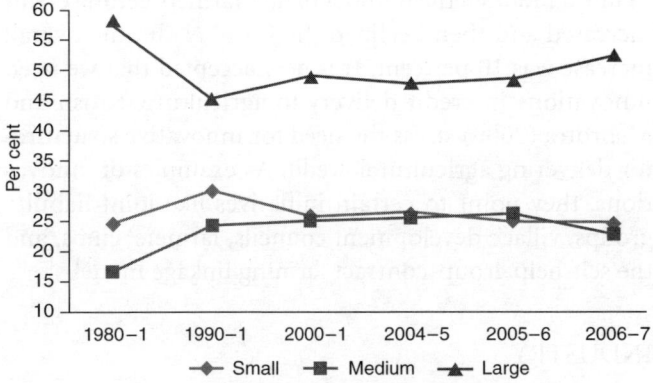

Source: RBI Database on Indian Economy.

Figure 2.2 Distribution of Quantum of Loans Disbursed by Scheduled Commercial Banks by Size of Landholdings

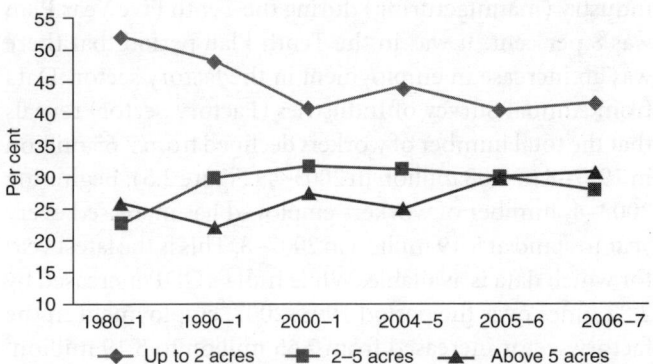

Source: RBI Database on Indian Economy.

Figure 2.3 Distribution of Number of Loan Accounts with Scheduled Commercial Banks by Size of Landholdings

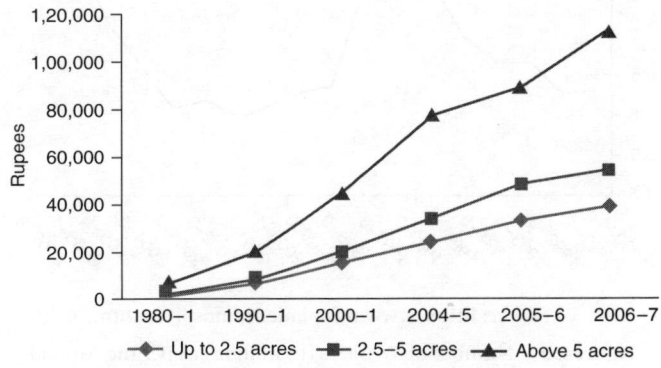

Source: RBI Database on Indian Economy.

Figure 2.4 Average Loan per Account Disbursed by Scheduled Commercial Banks by Size of Landholdings

to new farmers getting credit. The pattern differs across Maharashtra, Madhya Pradesh, Rajasthan, Tamil Nadu, and Uttar Pradesh (College of Agricultural Banking 2009). In Maharashtra, there was an increase in number of new farmers every year. In Rajasthan and Uttar Pradesh, the number of new farmers getting access to credit declined. In Madhya Pradesh, the number of new farmers getting credit increased and then declined. In Tamil Nadu, the overall increase was 10 per cent. It is now accepted that we need innovations in credit delivery to agriculture. Satish and Mehrotra (2009) stress the need for innovative structures for delivering agricultural credit. As examples of innovations, they point to certain initiatives like joint liability groups, village development councils, farmers' clubs, and the self-help group-contract farming linkage model.

INDUSTRY

If the agricultural sector was a laggard, the situation was different in case of Indian industry. The phase of jobless growth seems a thing of the past; at least since the Tenth Five Year Plan period. The compound annual growth rate of Indian industry (manufacturing) during the Tenth Five Year Plan was 8 per cent. It was in the Tenth Plan period that there was an increase in employment in the factory sector. Data from Annual Survey of Industries (Factory Sector) reveals that the total number of workers declined from 7.65 million in 1997–8 to 6.08 million in 2003–4 (Figure 2.5). Beginning 2003–4, number of workers employed has increased every year to stand at 8.19 million in 2007–8. This is the latest year for which data is available. While India's GDP increased by 2.82 times over the period 1998–2007, employment in the factory sector increased from 7.65 million to 8.19 million, a paltry increase of 0.54 million.[5]

Focussing on the period 2007–8 onwards, it is clear that there was a steady decline in the growth of index of industrial production (IIP) and its components (Table 2.3). The growth rate was lowest in the fourth quarter of 2008–9. In this quarter, the IIP grew by 0.5 per cent. Since then there have been signs of recovery, beginning with the first quarter of 2009–10. The recovery is evident in case of manufacturing. The growth rate of manufacturing sector is still below the 12.5 per cent achieved in 2006–7. In 2006–7 the mining and quarrying sector grew at 5.3 per cent and the electricity sector at 7.3 per cent. The growth rate of the electricity sector is a cause for concern. In 2007–8 and 2008–9 the addition in capacity was to the extent of 9,263 MW and 3,454 MW respectively. Many parts of the country are experiencing power cuts since supply is not keeping pace with demand. The Index of Infrastructure Industries, reflecting the performance of six core industries, increased to 275.1 in January 2010. This reflects a growth of 9.4 per cent over January 2009. In fact, this is the highest recorded growth rate since August 2007 (Figure 2.6). Table 2.4 presents the growth in core industries and infrastructure sector. The slowdown is evident in 2008–9 compared to 2007–8.

Turning to the recent time period, we find that IIP grew by 17.6 per cent in December 2009, 16.7 per cent in January 2010, and 15.1 per cent in February 2010. In the Monetary Policy Statement 2010–11, the RBI takes note of the fact that the recovery is broad-based with '14 out of 17 groups recording accelerated growth during April 2009–February 2010'. The RBI also points to the revival of investment activity since September 2009, given the double-digit growth of the capital goods sector.

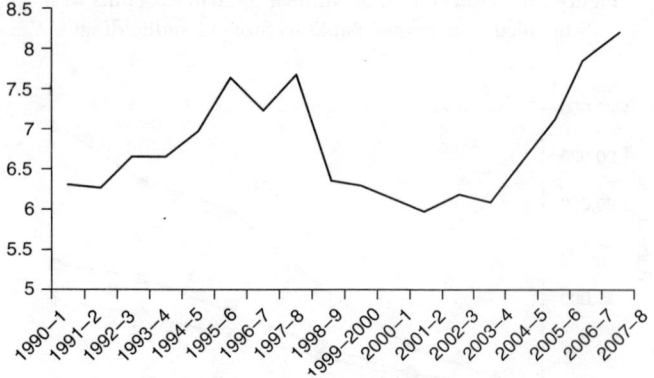

Source: http://www.mospi.nic.in/mospi_asi.htm.

Figure 2.5   Number of Workers (in million) as per the Annual Survey of Industries (Factory Sector)

[5]   http://mospi.nic.in/asi_result_2007-08tab1_1june10.pdf

Table 2.3   Growth in Index of Industrial Production (IIP) and Its Major Components (per cent)

	Mining	Manufacturing	Electricity	IIP
Q1 2007–8	2.7	11.1	8.3	10.3
Q2 2007–8	7.4	8.9	7.1	8.7
Q3 2007–8	5.5	8.9	4.6	8.3
Q4 2007–8	5.2	7.3	5.5	7
Q1 2008–9	4	5.8	2	5.3
Q2 2008–9	3.8	4.9	3.2	4.7
Q3 2008–9	2	0.5	2.9	0.8
Q4 2008–9	0.9	0.3	3	0.5
Q1 2009–10	6.8	3.4	6	3.8
Q2 2009–10	9	9.3	7.5	9.1
Oct–Nov 2009	9.5	11.9	4	11

Source: *Economic Survey 2009–10*, Government of India.

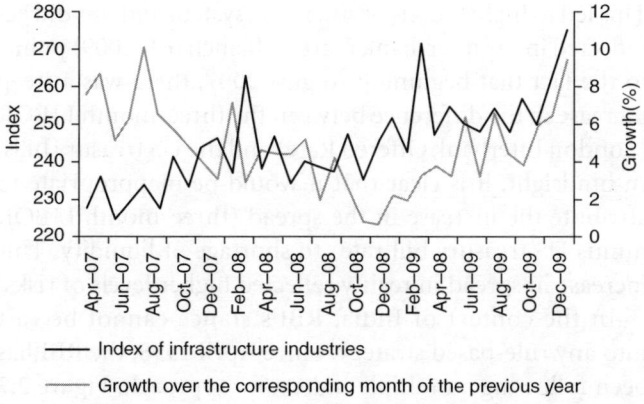

Source: http://www.epwrf.res.in/upload/MER/mer1100204.pdf

Figure 2.6   Index of Infrastructure Industries, Growth over the Corresponding Month of the Previous Year

SERVICES

The lack of sufficient progress in implementation of recommendations of the National Statistical Commission with regard to national income accounts has hampered the precise estimation of national income of India in general, and the service sector in particular. In the context of financial sector, concerns have been expressed on how the output of the financial sector is actually calculated. Among the components of the financial sector for which reliable information is available are commercial banks, banking department of RBI, public non-banking financial corporations, insurance sector, post office saving, and employees' provident fund. However, database on non-government non-banking financial companies, cooperative credit societies, and unorganized financial services is inadequate (Kolli et al. 2010).

The organized segment of the services sector includes construction, tourism, information technology (IT) and IT-enabled services (ITeS), and financial services. The share of construction sector in India's GDP is nearly 8 per cent. The contribution of the travel and tourism economy to GDP is lower at less than 6 per cent. The worldwide average share of travel and tourism economy in GDP is 10.7 per cent. This suggests that there is substantial scope to increase employment and output of the travel and tourism sector. The share of the sector consisting of finance, insurance, and real estate business services in India's GDP was 16.5 per cent (see Figure 2.1).

The construction industry grew at well over 10 per cent over the period 2005–6 to 2007–8. In 2009–10, this sector grew at 6.5 per cent. In the coming years, it is expected that this sector will exhibit double-digit growth. The sector will grow on the back of a significant increase in government expenditure on physical infrastructure. There is a proposal in the Union Budget for 2010–11 to spend Rs 48,000 crore on upgrading rural infrastructure. The government is also planning on adding 20 km of national highways every day. This works out to 7,300 km of new roads during this fiscal. One would need to go back to 2003–4 when there was a comparable increase in road length. The length of the national highways increased from 58,112 km in 2003 to 65,569 km in 2004 (Government of India 2010a). Construction of roads and upgradation of rural infrastructure should boost the growth of the construction sector.

IT and ITeS sector is one of India's largest foreign exchange earners. Total export revenues earned by this sector grew at a compound rate of 32 per cent over the period 2001–2 to 2006–7 (Government of India 2010a). Given that the US and the UK are the major markets for this sector, the slowdown in these economies would have had an impact in 2009–10. In order to sustain the growth prospects of this sector, it is important to ensure the availability of skilled workforce. It is projected that the total manpower requirements of this sector will be to the tune of 2.72 million people in 2012.

MONETARY POLICY AND FISCAL POLICY

Since 2008, the stance of monetary and fiscal policy across the world has been dictated by developments in the US. In

Table 2.4   Growth in Core Industries and Infrastructure Services (per cent)

	2007–8	2008–9		2007–8	2008–9
Power	6.3	2.7	Cement	7.8	7.5
Coal	6	8.1	Crude Oil	0.4	−1.8
Finished Steel	6.8	0.6	Refinery	6.5	3
Railway Revenue-earning Freight Traffic	9	4.9	Natural Gas	2.1	1.4
Cargo Handled at Major Ports	12	2.1	Air Export Cargo		7.5
Telephone Connections	83.7	10.1	Air Import Cargo	19.7	−5.7
Cell Phone Connections	38.3	44.8	Passengers at International Terminals	11.9	3.8
Fertilizers	−8.6	−2.5	Passengers at Domestic Terminals	20.6	−12.1

Source: Economic Survey 2009–10, Government of India.

this section, we do not describe how the crisis unfolded and how its effects were transmitted through the world, since there are many articles on this subject (see, for example, Blanchard 2009).

We focus on a narrower issue, viz., the debate over the decision by Federal Reserve to keep interest rates low in the US economy. One way of making a judgement call on what constitutes as low interest rate is by using the Taylor Rule. The Taylor Rule stipulates nominal interest as a function of two variables: difference between the actual inflation rate and the target rate, and the difference between the actual output and potential output. Critics of the interest rate policy followed by the Federal Reserve point to the fact that the interest rate was lower than that implied by the Taylor Rule.

The relevance of the Taylor Rule and its possible variants is now currently the subject of intense debate. The Chairman of the Federal Reserve, Ben S. Bernanke, in his address at the annual meeting of the American Economic Association in 2010 took the following position: 'Which version of the Taylor rule—the standard version, that uses current values of inflation, or the alternative version, that employs inflation forecasts—is the more reliable guide? I have explained my preference for using inflation forecasts[6] rather than actual inflation in the policy rule: Monetary policy works with a lag, and therefore policy decisions must be forward look-ing' (Bernanke 2010). In his address, he also disputed the conjecture that the low interest rate policy fuelled the growth of credit to housing markets. He attributed the growth in housing loans to 'the increasing use of more exotic types of mortgages and the associated decline of underwriting standards'. As an explanation for the rising house prices, he proffered capital inflows from emerging economies as a pos-sible explanation. However, it appears that Thomas Hoenig, President of Federal Reserve Bank of Kansas City, had a slightly different perspective than Bernanke. In a speech in January 2010, Hoenig said, 'Over the past decade, we chan-nelled too many resources into residential construction and financial activities. During this period, real interest rates—nominal rates adjusted for inflation—remained at negative levels for approximately 40 percent of the time.'

As things played out, the collapse of the housing markets and higher level of foreclosures affected the balance sheets of the lenders.[7] This led to the recapitalization of banks in the US.

In the low interest environment, the players in the finan-cial markets took excessive risks in search of higher yields.

This led to higher levels of risk in the system and this did get reflected in the inter-bank market. Blanchard (2009) points to the fact that beginning August 2007, there was a steep increase in the difference between the three-month LIBOR (London Interbank Offered Rate) and the US treasury bills. In hindsight, it is clear that it would be inappropriate to attribute the increase in the spread (three-month LIBOR minus US treasury bill rate) to shortage of liquidity. This increase in spread in reality reflected higher levels of risks.

In the context of India, RBI's stance cannot be cast into any rule-based strategy. Since April 1998, the RBI has been following a multiple indicators approach. Figure 2.7 provides a description of the multiple indicators approach. Notice the absence of a pre-defined anchor in this approach. In his assessment of the multiple indicators approach, Mohanty (2010) concludes that 'the period 1998–99 to 2008–09 reveals that actual outcome of GDP growth has been generally higher than the projections indicated in the monetary policy statements, while it has generally been lower in case of inflation'.

Notwithstanding the debate on the relevance of Taylor Rule as a guiding principle, consensus is emerg-ing on other critical issues in order to avoid a redux of the events in the recent past. First, the need to monitor the build-up of systemic risk is accepted. Regulating the level of systemic risk needs to be one of the objectives of the regulator or the central bank. Second, the regulator needs to monitor the level of leverage. Third, from the perspective of introduction of new financial instruments, they should be priced in a transparent fashion and traded

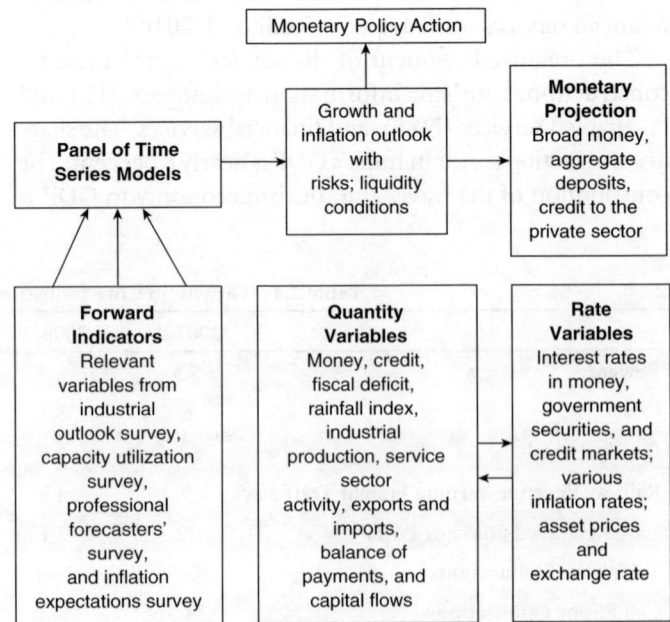

Source: Mohanty (2010).

Figure 2.7 Augmented Multiple Indicators Approach

---

[6] In response to the suggestion by Bernanke, valid concerns can be raised over the appropriate measure of inflationary expectation.

[7] Blanchard (2009) points out that it was only in the fall of 2008 that realization dawned that under-capitalization was actually the issue.

in an exchange. In return for higher level of oversight and regulation, the central bank in turn could provide liquidity to avoid any runs on the financial system. As is evident, from the measures that are being contemplated, the role of the central bank would extend beyond monetary policy to also include ensuring stability of financial markets as an objective.

Monetary Policy

In 2008, in India, the objective of the package rolled out by the RBI was to ease liquidity constraints. The RBI decreased the repo rate and reverse repo rate, and cut the cash reserve ratio (Figure 2.8). A slew of measures were announced. These included: relaxation of provisioning norms for housing loans and capital market exposures, relaxation of external commercial borrowing norms, easing of export credit norms, and the increase in interest rate ceiling on FCNR (Foreign Currency Non-resident) deposits. Steps were also taken to augment availability of credit to mutual funds and non-bank finance companies in order to ensure that they did not face any liquidity problems. At the same time, certain institution-specific measures were also taken. The Export Import Bank of India, Small Industries Development Bank of India (SIDBI), and National Housing Bank (NHB) were given refinance facilities to the order of Rs 5,000 crore, Rs 7,000 crore, and Rs 4,000 crore respectively.

The measures taken by RBI were in sync with measures taken by other central banks. With the world economy beginning to show signs of recovery, the roll back of the easy money policy began in October–December 2009. It started with the Reserve Bank of Australia increasing the cash rate by 25 basis points to 3.25 per cent in October 2009. Since then it gradually increased the cash rate in increments of 25

basis points to 4.25 per cent by April 2010.[8] The rationale for this steady increase is the improved prospects for the world economy in 2010. The statement issued by the Reserve Bank of Australia on 6 October 2009 said, 'Growth in China has been very strong, which is having a significant impact on other economies in the region and on commodity markets.'[9] Following the hike in interest rates in Australia, it was only a matter of time before central banks in Asia swung into action. In order to rein in lending by banks, China's central bank increased the bank reserve ratio by 50 basis points each in January 2010 and February 2010 to 16.5 per cent for large banks and 14.5 per cent for smaller banks. In March 2010, the Central Bank of Malaysia increased the overnight policy rate to 2.25 per cent.

Turning to the case of India, RBI's quarterly Industrial Outlook Survey suggested an improvement in business expectations for the third quarter of the financial year 2009–10. A clear improvement in various indicators, including the Business Expectation Index, was visible. The RBI concluded that the recovery was robust and pointed to the 'continuing consolidation of business confidence' (Reserve Bank of India 2010a).

In addition, inflation was emerging as a serious concern. The year-on-year inflation rate has exhibited considerable volatility since 2008. There was a sharp increase in the wholesale price index (WPI) from February 2008 onwards for a period of eight months, following which the WPI began to exhibit a decline from October 2008–March 2009 onwards. Hence, the inflation as measured by year-on-year change in WPI was not a concern over the period October 2008–March 2009. Since the beginning of April 2009, the WPI has steadily increased, and the year-on-year inflation increased to 9.89 per cent by February 2010. The steady increase in inflation rate can be partially attributed to the base effect. The base effect is only one aspect of the story since current evidence points to an increase in the prices of various goods, in particular food products. The year-on-year (January 2009–January 2010) increase in the prices of food articles was 17.9 per cent as against 7.6 per cent in the corresponding period in 2008–9. It was expected that there would be a failure of the kharif crop. This led to the build up of inflationary expectations and probably set off the upward movement of price indices. Given the higher weight to food items in consumer price index (CPI) as compared to WPI, April 2008 onwards there was a divergence in the year-on-year inflation as measured by CPI and WPI (Figure 2.9). It is expected that a good rabi crop will soften food prices and the year-on-year inflation rate based on CPI and WPI will exhibit co-movement.

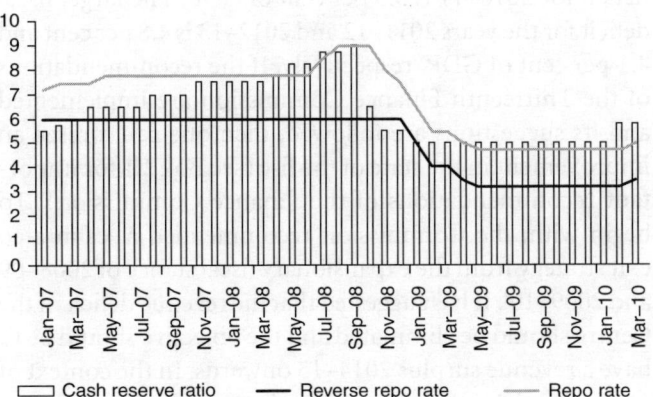

Figure 2.8 Cash Reserve Ratio, Reverse Repo Rate, and Repo Rate over the Period January 2007–April 2010

[8] http://www.rba.gov.au/statistics/cash-rate.html
[9] See http://www.rba.gov.au/media-releases/2009/mr-09-23.html

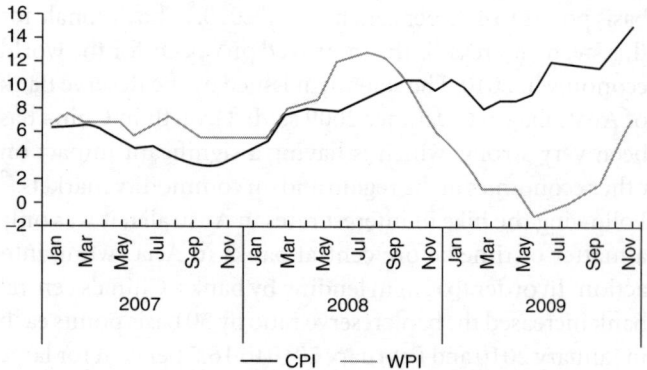

Source: RBI Database on Indian Economy.

Figure 2.9 Year-on-Year Inflation based on CPI and WPI

Given the signs of recovery as evidenced from RBI's quarterly Industrial Outlook Survey and persistence of inflation, RBI swung into action in February 2010 when it raised the cash reserve ratio in two stages of 50 basis points and 25 basis points to 5.75 per cent. The central bank's strategy appeared to be one of extracting liquidity from the system. It followed this up with a 25 basis point increase in repo rate and reverse repo to 5 per cent and 3.5 per cent respectively. The decision to increase the interest rates was probably necessitated by an increase in prices of manufactured goods and the concern that inflation was going to be increasingly demand-led. The contribution of food prices to overall inflation declined. As discussed earlier, the divergence between inflation measured by CPI and WPI was no longer the pattern. One began to observe co-movement of inflation as reflected by WPI and CPI. In April 2010, RBI further increased the cash reserve ratio, repo rate, and reverse repo rate by 25 basis points each to 6 per cent, 5.25 per cent, and 3.75 per cent respectively.

Fiscal Policy

As part of the fiscal stimulus package, the central government extended the cut in central value added tax, cut the service tax, provided support to states for purchase of buses, committed to additional plan expenditure to the tune of Rs 20,000 crore, took steps to address the concerns of exports and importers, and stepped up expenditure on specific programmes like Indira Awas Yojana. The impact of the stimulus package is evident when one examines the growth in consumption demand and investment demand. During the Tenth Five Year plan period, the Indian economy witnessed investment-led growth since the contribution of gross capital formation was higher than consumption. Beginning 2007–8, the growth was driven by consumption. This pattern continued on

account of the stimulus package whose objective was to boost private and government consumption (Government of India 2009b).

The Union Budget for 2010–11 was presented amidst signs of economic recovery. In line with expectations, the finance minister began the process of rolling back the stimulus package by increasing the central excise duties. The budget did not propose any changes with regard to income tax rates, which have been unchanged since 1997–8. The income tax rates continue to be at 10 per cent, 20 per cent, and 30 per cent for the three income slabs. One of the measures announced in the Union Budget was the revision of the three slabs from the existing Rs 1.6–Rs 3 lakh, Rs 3 lakh–Rs 5 lakh, and above Rs 5 lakh to Rs 1.6 lakh–Rs 5 lakh, Rs 5 lakh–Rs 8 lakh, and above Rs 8 lakh respectively. On the issue of tax reforms, the finance minister mentioned that he expected that the Direct Tax Code would be implemented from 1 April 2011. The objective of the Direct Tax Code is to 'build a simple tax system with minimum exemptions and low rates'. The most important development in the case of indirect taxes was the introduction of goods and services tax, and it is expected that it will be rolled out by April 2011. In order to make the roll out of goods and services tax palatable to state governments, the Commission has recommended a grant of Rs 50,000 crore to offset the losses of state governments stemming from implementation of goods and services tax. The share of every state in all shareable taxes as suggested by the Commission is given in Table 2.5.

The health of the central government's finance did deteriorate on account of the stimulus package. In the years following the enactment of the Fiscal Responsibility Budget Management Act, the fiscal deficit declined from 4.5 per cent of GDP in 2003–4 to 2.6 per cent in 2007–8. In 2009–10, the fiscal deficit was 6.9 per cent (revised estimates). This increase could be partially attributed to the fiscal stimulus package of the Government of India. The projected fiscal deficit for 2010–11 is 5.5 per cent of GDP. The target fiscal deficit for the years 2011–12 and 2012–13 is 4.8 per cent and 4.1 per cent of GDP, respectively. If the recommendations of the Thirteenth Finance Commission are implemented and its suggestions are followed, then one can foresee an improvement in the state of the fisc (see Box 2.1 for important recommendations of the Finance Commission). To begin with, the Commission recommended a 'calibrated exit strategy from the expansionary fiscal stance of 2008–09 and 2009–10'. It has suggested that the revenue deficit of the Centre should be eliminated and the objective should be to have a revenue surplus 2014–15 onwards. In the context of combined debt of the Centre and states, the Commission has suggested a target of 68 per cent of GDP to be achieved by 2014–15.

Table 2.5 Inter se Shares of States

	Share of all Shareable Taxes* (per cent)	Share of Service Tax (per cent)		Share of All Shareable Taxes* (per cent)	Share of Service Tax (per cent)
Andhra Pradesh	6.937	7.047	Maharashtra	5.199	5.281
Arunachal Pradesh	0.328	0.332	Manipur	0.451	0.458
Assam	3.628	3.685	Meghalaya	0.408	0.415
Bihar	10.917	11.089	Mizoram	0.269	0.273
Chhattisgarh	2.47	2.509	Nagaland	0.314	0.318
Goa	0.266	0.27	Orissa	4.779	4.855
Gujarat	3.041	3.089	Punjab	1.389	1.411
Haryana	1.048	1.064	Rajasthan	5.853	5.945
Himachal Pradesh	0.781	0.793	Sikkim	0.239	0.243
Jammu and Kashmir	1.551	Nil	Tamil Nadu	4.969	5.047
Jharkhand	2.802	2.846	Tripura	0.511	0.519
Karnataka	4.328	4.397	Uttar Pradesh	19.677	19.987
Kerala	2.341	2.378	Uttarakhand	1.12	1.138
Madhya Pradesh	7.12	7.232	West Bengal	7.264	7.379

Source: Report of Thirteenth Finance Commission, Government of India 2010.

Note: *Excludes service tax.

Box 2.1 Recommendations of the Thirteenth Finance Commission

The following are some of the key recommendations of the Thirteenth Finance Commission:

- The share of States in net proceeds of shareable Central taxes shall be 32 per cent every year for the period of the award.
- Revenue accruing to a State is to be protected to the levels that would have accrued to it had service tax been a part of the shareable Central taxes, if the 88th Amendment to Constitution is notified and followed up by a legislation enabling States to levy service tax.
- Centre is to review the levy of cesses and surcharges with a view to reducing their share in its gross tax revenue.
- The indicative ceiling on overall transfers to States on revenue account may be set at 39.5 per cent of gross revenue receipts of the Centre.
- The Medium Term Fiscal Plan (MTFP) should be a statement of commitment rather than intent.
- New disclosures have been specified for the Budget/MTFP including on tax expenditure, public–private partnership liabilities and the details of variables underlying receipts and expenditure projections.
- The Fiscal Responsibility and Budget Management (FRBM) Act needs to specify the nature of shocks that would require relaxation of the targets thereunder.
- States are expected to be able to get back to their fiscal correction path by 2011–12 and amend their FRBM Acts to the effect.
- State Governments are to be eligible for the general performance and special area performance grants only if they comply with the prescribed stipulation in terms of grants to local bodies.
- The National Calamity Contingency Fund (NCCF) should be merged with the National Disaster Response Fund (NDRF) and the Calamity Relief Fund (CRF) with the State Disaster Response Funds (SDRFs) of the respective States.
- A total non-Plan revenue grant of Rs 51,800 crore is recommended over the award period for eight States. A performance grant of Rs 1,500 crore is recommended for three special category States that have graduated from a non-Plan revenue deficit situation.
- An amount of Rs 19,930 crore has been recommended as grant for maintenance of roads and bridges for four years (2011–12 to 2014–15).
- An amount of Rs 24,068 crore has been recommended as grant for elementary education.
- An amount of Rs 27,945 crore has been recommended for State-specific needs.
- Amounts of Rs 5,000 crore each as forest, renewable energy, and water sector-management grants have been recommended.
- A total sum of Rs 3,18,581 crore has been recommended for the award period as grants-in-aid to States.

Source: Economic Survey 2009–10.

FINANCIAL MARKETS

There have been many interesting developments in the financial markets since 2007. We focus on two developments, viz., changes in reporting requirements for banks and companies, and introduction of new instruments in financial and commodity markets. There has been a significant change in the way banks and companies are filing their returns with RBI and the stock exchanges respectively, following the decision to adopt eXtensible Business Reporting Language (XBRL), 'an open source, royalty free information reporting standard'. Among developing countries, India has taken the lead in introducing the XBRL standard (see Box 2.2). The adoption of XBRL standard leads to standardization of information concepts and the attributes of every data element are carried wherever the data is used. Since data validations take place when the data is captured, this ensures accuracy of data. This standard has been known to result in greater transparency since every data element and notes can be linked. The use of XBRL provides information at a disaggregated level and this would help in flagging potential frauds.

Trading in currency futures and interest rate futures commenced in 2008. In August 2008, the National Stock Exchange was first off the blocks by offering trading in currency futures. The Bombay Stock Exchange and the Multi Commodity Exchange Stock Exchange are now also offering trading in currency derivatives. The introduction of this instrument has allowed market participants to hedge their currency risks. In January 2010, currency futures were also allowed in the following pairs: Euro–Indian Rupee, Pound Sterling–Indian Rupee, and Japanese Yen–Indian Rupee.

In the period January–December 2009, in the currency futures segment, the total number of contracts traded on the National Stock Exchange was 226 million and that on Multi Commodity Exchange Stock Exchange was 224 million. Since August 2009, interest rate futures contract on ten-year notional coupon bearing Government of India security rate futures has been traded on the National Stock Exchange. There is now a proposal to introduce interest rate futures on five-year and two-year notional coupon bearing securities and 91-day Treasury Bills. The introduction of currency futures and interest rate futures helps plug important gaps in instruments that help in managing risk.

There has been a lot of action in commodity markets. In 2010, futures trading is permitted in sixty-six commodities. The commodities in which futures trading is permitted can be grouped under the following categories: fibres, spices, edible oil, oilseeds and oil cake, pulses, energy products, metals and bullions, vegetables and grains, and others. Trading in commodity futures, particularly in case of food grains, has been controversial at a time of rising food prices. The government banned futures trading in tur and urad (January 2007); rice and wheat (February 2007); gram, soy oil, potato, and rubber (June 2007); and sugar (May 2009). Since then, the ban has been lifted from some of the commodities, including wheat and potato.

EXTERNAL ENVIRONMENT

Unlike other crises in the twentieth century, the current economic crisis was not triggered by imbalances in balance of payments or precarious debt situation of one or more developing countries. The fact that the Indian economy

---

Box 2.2   XBRL—The New Reporting Standard

A significant change has occurred in the way commercial banks submit their returns to RBI. The RBI has adopted the eXtensible Business Reporting Language (XBRL) as a standard for reporting Basel II returns. It is envisaged that banks will be required to submit all their returns in XBRL standard within a three-year timeframe. The Bombay Stock Exchange and National Stock Exchange have adopted XBRL-based filings following the decision by Securities and Exchange Board of India (SEBI) to mandate this system for the top 100 companies. SEBI is extending this to all companies in a stage-wise manner; and also extending to other asset classes (starting with mutual funds). The Ministry of Company Affairs in India is building a roadmap for adoption of XBRL to enable all companies to submit financial accounts to the Registrar of Companies in XBRL.

According to RBI, 'This open standard offers cost savings, greater efficiency and improved accuracy and reliability to all those involved in supplying or using financial data. XBRL enhances the usability and transparency of financial information reported under existing accounting standards, simplifies disclosure, and allows users to communicate financial information more readily and accurately.' The potential offered by XBRL has been exploited by the Dutch Water Board, the state of Nevada in the US for debt collection and tracking accounts receivable and grants, and by the Ministry of Economy in Spain for financial data across the centre and states, and local budget and finance disbursement data at the local body level including municipalities.

Source:

1. Reserve Bank of India (2008), 'RBI Moving Towards XBRL Standards: RBI Reduces the Number of Returns to 223 from 291'.
2. Government of India (2009), 'Reinventing a Ministry', available at http://www.mca.gov.in/Ministry/latestnews/Supp_Minister_Corporate_Affairs_30mar2009.pdf

managed to weather the current storm is testimony to its resilience to external shocks. The resilience can be attributed to a host of factors. The country's foreign exchange reserves increased from $141.5 billion in March 2005 to $283.5 billion in December 2009. The prevailing level of reserves is sufficient to cover over twelve months of imports. It is estimated that in 2009, the ratio of reserves to imports of goods and services was 81.1 as compared to 53.6 for developing countries (excluding India and China) in Asia.

It is well known that the RBI and the Government of India have a track record of being hawkish on running up external debt, and short-term debt in particular. After all, in 1990–1, the ratio of short-term debt to foreign exchange reserves was 146.5 (Table 2.6). Since then, India's external debt position has improved over the years despite a 3 percentage point increase in the ratio of total external debt to GDP in the recent years, that is, over the period 2006–7 to 2008–9. India's external debt stood at less than $243 billion in September 2009. In terms of composition of debt, the share of the government declined from 40.6 per cent in March 2004 to 27.1 per cent in September 2009. The debt service ratio declined marginally in 2008–9. The ratio of short-term debt to foreign exchange reserves too declined as did the ratio of short-term debt to total debt.

To put India's external debt situation in perspective, it would be useful to compare a couple of key indicators with other developing countries. In 2007, India was the fifth most indebted country, in terms of stock of external debt. However, as a percentage of gross national income, it was the sixth lowest indebted country. The countries with a more favourable external debt to gross national income ratio were the following: China (11.6), South Africa (15.8), Mexico (17.7), Brazil (18.7), and Venezuela (18.7). In 2007, the ratio of short-term debt to total debt varied from 5.1 per cent in case of Mexico to 54.5 per cent in case of China. In case of India, it is below the

developing country average of 24.5 per cent (Government of India 2010a). In terms of foreign exchange reserves as a percentage of external debt, India (125.2) compares favourably with Brazil (75.9), Russia (129.1), and South Africa (75.9).

Indian exports were indeed affected in line with the downturn in international trade. In 2009, there was a 12.3 per cent decline in quantum of world trade. Imports by advanced countries declined by 12.2 per cent while that of emerging and developing economies declined by 13.5 per cent. After growing at nearly 29 per cent in 2007–8, Indian exports grew by only 13.7 per cent in 2008–9. A comparison of 2008 and 2009 reveals that Indian exports and imports grew by 48.1 per cent and 51 per cent respectively in April–September 2008; they declined by 27 per cent and 20.6 per cent respectively in the corresponding period in 2009. If India aims to increase its share in world's exports from the current level of just over 1 per cent, then Indian companies across all sectors of the economy have to not only increase their shares in world exports but also need to export to new markets. India accounts for 18 per cent of world's exports of computer and information services. In all other sectors, India has miniscule share in world exports. Over 60 per cent of India's exports are to 15 countries, and this pattern has not changed in the recent years. Within these 15 countries, the export to import ratio is 0.5, implying that India's imports from these countries are twice the value of India's exports to these countries (Government of India 2010a). The last edition of the *India Development Report* stressed the need to expand trade with the Asian countries and that India's GDP could grow by an additional 1 per cent per year (Panda 2008). However, not enough has been done in the context of India's economic integration with Asian countries. In 2010 and 2011, the International Monetary Fund (IMF) forecasts that world trade will grow by 5.8 per cent and 6.3 per cent respectively (Table 2.7). The exchange rate will have a bearing on the

Table 2.6   India's External Debt: Important Indicators

Year	External Debt (US$ billion)	Ratio of Total External Debt to GDP	Debt–Service Ratio	Ratio of Foreign Exchange Reserves to Total External Debt	Ratio of Concessional Debt to Total External Debt	Ratio of Short-term Debt to Foreign Exchange Reserves	Ratio of Short-term Debt to Total Debt
1990–1	83.8	28.7	35.3	7	45.9	146.5	10.2
2001–2	98.8	21.1	13.7	54.7	35.9	5.1	2.8
2006–7[*]	172.4	17.5	4.7	115.6	23	14.1	16.3
2007–8[*]	224.4	18.1	4.8	138	19.7	14.8	20.4
2008–9[+]	224.6	20.5	4.4	112.1	18.7	17.2	19.3
End-September 2009 QE	242.8			115.8	18.4	15.1	17.5

Source: *Economic Survey 2009–10*, Government of India.

Notes: [*]Revised estimates, [+]Partially revised estimates.

Debt–service ratio is the proportion of gross debt service payments to external current receipts (net of official transfers).

Table 2.7   World Economic Outlook Projections on World Trade (per cent)

	2008	2009	2010	2011
World Trade Volume (Goods and Services)	2.8	−12.3	5.8	6.3
Imports				
Advanced Economies	0.5	−12.2	5.5	5.5
Emerging and Developing Economies	8.9	−13.5	6.5	7.7
Exports				
Advanced Economies	1.8	−12.1	5.9	5.6
Emerging and Developing Economies	4.4	−11.7	5.4	7.8

Source: WEO Update, January 2010, International Monetary Fund.

competitiveness of India's exports. The value of the rupee, as reflected by the six-country real effective exchange rate, appreciated by 15.5 per cent over the period April 2009–February 2010 (Reserve Bank of India 2010b). It remains to be seen whether this appreciation reflects a decision by RBI of not actively intervening when the rupee appreciated.

Despite the financial crisis worldwide, quantum of FDI inflows into India increased from $25.1 billion in 2007 to $41.5 billion in 2008. There has been a 5.5-fold increase in quantum of FDI inflows over the period 2005–8. The magnitude of increase is higher in case of outward FDI from $2.9 billion in 2005 to $17.6 billion in 2008. India still lags behind China, which received $108.3 billion as FDI inflows in 2008. The outward FDI in case of China was $52.1 billion. In terms of FDI stocks, inward FDI constituted 9.9 per cent of GDP and outward FDI constituted 5 per cent of GDP in 2008 (Figure 2.10). Indian companies have been acquiring assets abroad. According to the World Investment Report of the United Nations Conference on Trade and Development (UNCTAD), the two Indian companies among the top 100 non-financial transnational corporations from developing countries ranked by foreign assets in 2007 were Tata Steel Ltd and Oil and Natural Gas Corporation. A few more Indian companies can be expected to make it to this list during the coming decade. In light of scarcity of raw materials and higher demand for energy, it is perhaps appropriate to encourage both public and private sector firms to acquire assets abroad. China has a head start and has already invested heavily in the African continent. A conscious decision needs to be taken to provide Indian firms with adequate long-term finance at competitive rates of interest in order to acquire strategic assets abroad.

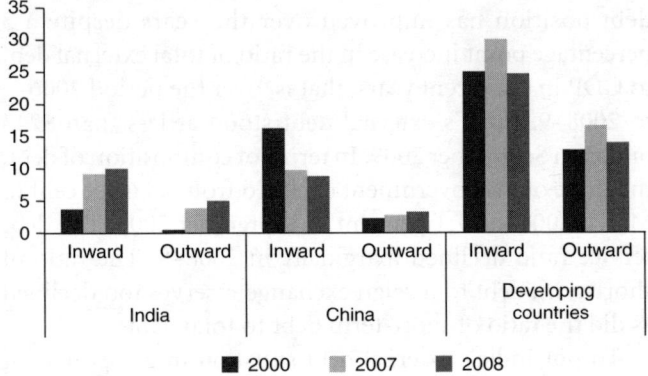

Source: UNCTAD (2010).

Figure 2.10   Foreign Direct Investment Stocks as Percentage of GDP

CONCLUSION

The Indian economy is now a trillion-dollar economy; yet, in terms of per capita income its worldwide ranking is very low. Of 109 countries, for which information is available on purchasing power parity corrected GDP per capita, India was ranked 89th in 1984, 80th in 1994, and 75th in 2004 (Government of India 2010a). Increasing per capita income

and translating the slogan of 'inclusive growth' into reality will be the challenges for Indian policymakers in the coming years. Ideally, double-digit rate of growth should be driven by growth in employment and also result in acceleration in the rate of poverty reduction. The rate of poverty reduction becomes important in light of the upward revision of the number of poor by the Expert Group to Review the Methodology for Estimation for Poverty. These revised estimates have budgetary implications to the extent that allocation for programmes targeted at poor households will increase. The scope of the Food Security Bill currently under discussion will also affect the finances of the central government. At the same time, the Thirteenth Finance Commission has outlined the path towards reducing the combined debt of the Centre and the state governments and elimination of revenue deficit by 2014–15. Hence, improving the state of the fiscal without slashing social sector expenditure is the challenge facing the government.

In its report, the Thirteenth Finance Commission stressed the importance of a carefully calibrated roll back of the stimulus package. On the monetary front, the roll-back was hastened by the concern over the inflationary pressures experienced by the economy and the observation that housing prices and the stock market had recovered to their pre-crisis levels. In addition to food price inflation, there was an increase in the prices of manufactured goods. Beginning January 2010, RBI tightened money supply by increasing the cash reserve ratio. In March and April it followed this up by increasing the repo rate and reverse repo rate. The government began a partial roll-back in the Union Budget for 2010–11. On account of the stimulus package, the government's finance worsened, as reflected by the increase in fiscal deficit. The stimulus package did boost consumption demand and assisted in moderating the decline in growth rate of the Indian economy. During the recovery process, it is important to ensure that there is a smart recovery in private investment as reflected by change in gross fixed capital formation. The *Economic Survey 2009–10* points to the fact that the growth in gross fixed capital formation in 2009–10 was 5.2 per cent in comparison to over 14 per cent in the years 2004–8.

There are specific concerns pertaining to every sector. In the case of agriculture, it is attaining food security, drought-proofing agriculture, and increase in capital formation. In the context of rural India, the challenge is expansion of rural non-farm employment. In order to sustain the growth rate of industry and services, it is important to ensure the availability of skilled manpower. A broad-based upturn in the world economy across the developed and developing economies is integral to the recovery process. At the same time, Indian companies need to explore new markets and the Government of India needs to have a clearly enunciated policy for Indian multinationals.

REFERENCES

Bernanke, Ben S. (2010), 'Monetary Policy and the Housing Bubble', speech at the Annual Meeting of the American Economic Association, Atlanta, Georgia, 3 January 2010. Available at http://www.federalreserve.gov/newsevents/speech/bernanke20100103a.htm

Bhalla, G.S. and Gurmail Singh (2009), 'Economic Liberalisation and Indian Agriculture: A Statewise Analysis', *Economic and Political Weekly*, Vol. 44, No. 52, 26 December 2009–1 January 2010, pp. 34–44.

Blanchard, Olivier J. (2009), 'The Crisis: Basic Mechanisms, and Appropriate Policies', International Monetary Fund, Working Paper WP/09/80. Available at http://www.imf.org/external/pubs/ft/wp/2009/wp0980.pdf

College of Agricultural Banking (2009), A Study Report on the Doubling of Agricultural Credit Programme (2004–05 to 2006–07): A Brief Summary, CAB Calling, October–December, pp. 62–7.

Government of India (2010a), *Economic Survey 2009–10*. New Delhi: Government of India.

———(2010b), *Annual Report of Department of Food and Public Distribution*, Ministry of Consumer Affairs, Food and Public Distribution. New Delhi: Government of India.

———(2010c), 'Revised Estimates of Annual National Income, 2009–10 and Quarterly Estimates of Gross Domestic Product,

2009–10', Press Note, 31 May 2010, Press Information Bureau, Government of India.

———(2009a), *Report of the Expert Group to Review the Methodology for Estimation of Poverty, November*. New Delhi: Planning Commission, Government of India.

———(2009b), *Economic Survey 2008–09*. New Delhi: Government of India.

———(2008), Development Challenges in Extremist Affected Areas: Report of an Expert Group to Planning Commission, April 2008, Government of India, New Delhi.

Hoenig, Thomas M. (2010), 'The 2010 Outlook and the Path Back to Stability', Speech Delivered at The Central Exchange, Kansas City, Missouri. Available at http://www.kansascityfed.org/SpeechBio/HoenigPDF/Hoenig.01.07.10.pdf

Indira Gandhi Institute of Development Research (2008), *India Development Report 2008*. New Delhi: Oxford University Press.

Kolli, Ramesh, J.S. Venkateswarlu, and S.S. Jakhar (2010), 'Data Base in Financial Sector—A National Accounts Perspective', paper presented at the Seminar on Data Base Issues in the Financial Sector, organized by IGIDR–EPWRF, Mumbai, 13 March.

Kose M.A., A. Otrok, and E.S. Prasad (2008), 'Global Business Cycles: Convergence or Decoupling?', NBER Working Paper 14292.

Mehrotra, Nirupam (2010), 'Emerging Patterns in Share of Small Farms in Production and Credit: Implications for Policy Formulation', paper presented at Annual Money and Finance Conference, organized by Indira Gandhi Institute of Development Research, Mumbai, 11–12 March.

Mohanty, D. (2010), 'Monetary Policy Framework in India—Experience with Multiple-Indicators Approach', Speech at the Conference of the Orissa Economic Association, Baripada, Orissa, 21 February. Available at http://www.bis.org/review/r100304e.pdf

Panda, Manoj (2008), 'Macroeconomic Overview', in R. Radhakrishna (ed.), *India Development Report*. New Delhi: Oxford University Press, pp. 20–39.

Reserve Bank of India (2010a), Macroeconomic Quarterly Industrial Outlook Survey: July–September 2009 (47th Round), *RBI Monthly Bulletin*, January.

———(2010b), Macroeconomic and Monetary Developments in 2009–10. Available at http://rbidocs.rbi.org.in/rdocs/Publications/PDFs/MMDAP190410F.pdf

Satish, P. and N. Mehrotra (2009), 'Credit Markets for Small Farms: Role for Institutional Innovations', paper presented at the International Conference '111 EAAE–IAAE Seminar "Small Farms: Decline or Persistence"', 26–27 June 2010, organized by the University of Kent, Canterbury, UK.

Singh, R.B., P. Kumar, and T. Woodhead (2002), 'Smallholder Farmers in India: Food Security and Agricultural Policy', FAO. Available at ftp://ftp.fao.org/docrep/fao/005/ac484e/ac484e00.pdf

UNCTAD (2010), *World Investment Report 2010: Investing in a Low-carbon Economy*, United Nations Conference on Trade and Development. Available at http://www.unctad.org/en/docs/wir2010_en.pdf

3

Food Security

Beyond the Eleventh Plan Fiction

M.H. Suryanarayana

INTRODUCTION

To be effective, policies should be based on sound evidence and an appreciation of the nature, profile, and magnitude of the issue being addressed. This is one area that calls for serious attention in India today. For instance, the Eleventh Plan review on food security presents a disturbing report and recommends wide-ranging policy options for the public distribution system (PDS) (Government of India 2008). Possibly in pursuit of the Food Security Act, the Planning Commission has even set up a committee to redefine the poverty line and revise poverty estimates, which are more than the estimates based on the current official approach (Siddhanta 2009). But the fact is that the Plan has cared for neither evidence nor method. It suffers from a very simple methodological limitation that it interprets, comments, and recommends policies on issues concerned with food deprivation of the poor with reference to estimates of mean-based averages and not distributional profiles. As is well known, mean is not a robust estimator of average for skewed distributions, and hence would largely represent changes in the upper percentiles for the case under review. As a result, the Plan document ends up presenting a fictionalized account of the food insecurity of the poor. It recommends an extent of calorie provision much more than what is called for, as reflected in observed behavioural patterns across decile groups of the Indian population. As regards revisiting methodology for poverty estimation, one is not sure if this effort is worthwhile, given the inadequacies of the information base.

Food security is an area that has received wide attention in the wake of the recent food inflation across the world. Hence, this chapter seeks to highlight inadequacies in the Plan review of and recommendation on food insecurity of the poor, with reference to the same data source as that used in the Eleventh Plan.[1] The chapter is organized as follows: the next section provides a brief profile of the Eleventh Plan discussion on food security and health status based on estimates of food grain consumption and calorie intake. The third section reviews the Plan assessment and presents factual evidence. The final section presents the conclusions.

PLAN PERSPECTIVE ON FOOD SECURITY

The Plan recognizes the importance of food security in order to improve, inter alia, what it calls 'nutritional outcomes' for the poor and to facilitate quick recovery from illness

[1] This chapter reviews only the empirical evidence on food consumption and calorie intake though the Plan document touches upon related dimensions of malnutrition.

(Government of India [GoI] 2008: 128–48). The issue under review is all the more important if the following Plan perceptions are true: (i) per capita cereal production has declined, and (ii) income levels of the poor have been stagnant. The document cites empirical details on nutritional outcome measures like low birth weight of newborn babies and weights and heights of adults, and explains in terms of, inter alia, deficit in energy intake. It presents evidence to show that malnutrition as reflected in estimates of underweight children did not decline between 1998–9 and 2004–5, though the economy was growing at the rate of 6 per cent per annum during that period. Hence, the Plan calls for a review of issues relating to food security not simply in terms of cereal production and consumption but also in terms of scope for improving nutritional outcome for the poor. While one may appreciate the Plan emphasis on assessing the situation with an integrated perspective on outcomes, it is also important to make factually correct assessments of food deprivation from a distributional perspective, for the poor in particular, given its bearings on policy choice and design.

The Plan observations on changes in cereal consumption, consumption patterns, and calorie intake since 1972–3 are as follows:

(i) Cereals are a major source of energy intake for the Indian population. Average per capita cereal consumption has declined in both rural and urban areas. Consumption of non-cereals has not increased to make up for this decline.

(ii) Reasons for this decline are stagnant incomes and declining budget shares for food. Between 1972–3, 1987–8, and 2004–5, food share declined from 73 per cent to 64 per cent and finally to 55 per cent in rural India and from 65 per cent to 56 per cent and to 43 per cent in urban India (GoI 2008: 131).

(iii) In rural India, though the shares of other food items like milk and milk products, fish, egg and meat, and fruits and nuts increased, the increase has not been sufficient to make up for the loss in calories due to decline in cereal consumption. In urban India, the share in expenditure of other food items like milk and milk products, edible oils, and sugar has declined.

(iv) As a result, average per capita calorie intake per diem decreased from 2,221 kcals (1983) to 2,153 (1993–4), 2,149 (1999–2000), and to 2,047 (2004–5) in rural India, that is, by 8 per cent between 1983 and 2004–5; the corresponding estimates for urban India are 2,089, 2,071, 2,156, and 2,020, involving a reduction of 3.3 per cent in calorie intake.

(v) Average calorie intake in rural as well as urban areas has fallen increasingly short of the corresponding calorie norms for official poverty lines (2,400 kcals for the rural and 2,100 kcals for the urban sector).

The Plan recommends that, given the prevailing inequities in distribution, average calorie availability in the country should be at 'least 20% higher than the per capita requirement (i.e. 2100 calories for urban and 2400 calories for rural areas)' (GoI 2008: 132). As regards policies, the Plan goes on to evaluate the PDS and concludes that the 'PDS seems to have failed in serving the second objective of making food grains available to the poor. If it had, the consumption levels of cereals should not have fallen on average—as it has consistently over the last two decades' (GoI 2008: 135). Observing that purchasing power is a serious constraint on household food security, the Plan review assesses the PDS in terms of rupees transferred as given by the difference between average market price and the PDS price, and concludes that what matters is possession of ration card and its type and not economic status of the household.

Such interpretations and policy recommendations raise several issues. How valid are the observations about stagnant real incomes of the poor during the sample period under review? How meaningful are the interpretations of estimates of consumption budget shares at current prices? What do the estimates of cereal quantities consumed for different population groups suggest? How valid is the interpretation that the PDS failure to deliver to the poor has accounted for the decline in cereal consumption on average? How valid are the exogenous norms for threshold levels of calorie intake worked out in the 1950s and 1960s, that is, almost half a century ago since when the economy has experienced structural and technological change and improvements? What have been the temporal changes in calorie intake across different decile groups? How far the self-perception of the population with reference to adequacy of food consumption corroborates such findings? How robust is the information base for policy decisions relating to the poor? The following section examines these issues.

REVIEW

Real Incomes and Budget Share Estimates

One important explanation put forward by the Eleventh Plan for the decline in average cereal consumption and, hence, calorie intake of the population is stagnant real incomes. It states: 'Low and stagnating incomes among the poor has meant that low purchasing power remains a serious constraint to household food and nutritional security, even if food production picks up as a result of interventions in agriculture and creation of total infrastructure' (GoI 2008: 128). But real incomes, as reflected in estimates of consumption at constant prices (using fractile group-specific deflators), were not really stagnant during the sample period

Table 3.1   Monthly Per Capita Consumer Expenditure (at 1972–3 Prices) by Select Decile Groups: Rural and Urban India

Decile Group	1972–3	1977–8	1983	1987–8	1993–4	1999–2000	2004–5	Increase (%) between 1972–3 and 2004–5	Increase (%) between 1993–4 and 2004–5
				Rural All-India					
0–10	16.26	16.92	19.18	22.05	22.69	26.45	25.76	58.41	13.51
10–20	22.70	23.97	26.46	29.36	30.26	34.13	33.59	47.97	11.01
20–30	26.90	28.89	31.47	34.39	34.69	39.32	38.65	43.68	11.41
30–40	30.86	31.83	34.83	38.28	39.34	44.21	43.61	41.33	10.87
40–50	35.56	36.80	40.65	42.71	43.82	48.86	48.58	36.61	10.85
0–100	44.17	48.90	50.67	55.09	54.98	59.69	63.08	42.80	14.72
				Urban All-India					
0–10	21.90	21.00	23.38	24.30	25.93	30.22	28.45	29.91	9.74
10–20	29.90	29.80	32.03	32.92	35.82	40.57	38.78	29.70	8.28
20–30	36.11	35.73	38.03	38.57	42.68	48.41	46.84	29.71	9.75
30–40	38.39	40.92	46.04	44.01	48.76	56.14	54.90	43.01	12.59
40–50	48.51	46.75	49.03	51.08	56.33	64.66	64.36	32.68	14.25
0–100	63.33	65.26	68.55	71.41	77.02	89.07	92.44	45.96	20.02

Source: Author's estimates based on corresponding NSS estimates at current prices (GoI 1979, 1986a, 1986b, 1991, 1996a, 2001a, 2006b) and deflators implicit in the official poverty lines. Poverty lines from 1977–8 till 2004–5 are GoI estimates, and corresponding estimates for 1972–3 are from Tendulkar et al. 1993.

under review. In rural India, the poorest three decile groups experienced higher (in percentage terms) increases in consumer expenditure than the whole population during the period 1970–1 and 1988–9. The consumption expenditure (at constant prices) for the rural population as a whole increased by 18.88 per cent; it increased by 32.02 per cent for the poorest and by 28.05 per cent for the second poorest decile group. As regards the urban sector, the profile of increases in per capita consumer expenditure for different decile groups was similar to that obtained for the rural one (Suryanarayana 1995a). This is only a subset of the period under review in the Eleventh Plan.

Table 3.1 provides estimates of decile group-wise per capita consumer expenditure for rural and urban India for the different years cited in the Plan document.[2] Unlike the estimates cited in the preceding paragraph, estimates at 1972–3 prices in Table 3.1 are obtained using common deflators (implicit in the poverty lines for the corresponding years) for all the decile groups in rural and urban India separately. The estimates of averages for both rural and urban India show that real per capita consumption levels

have increased by more than 40 per cent since 1972–3. The increases have been progressive in rural India in the sense that the poorest three decile groups enjoyed greater percentage increases in their real consumption than the population as a whole and, hence, than the relatively better off. However, the increases in real consumption in urban India have been regressive.

The Plan attributes the decline in calorie intake largely to changes in consumption patterns involving a decline in budget shares for cereals and other essential food items. The estimates of budget shares are at current prices for the total population by sector. Such estimates at current prices could reflect changes in relative prices rather than consumption patterns. Further, mean-based averages reveal little about the status of the poor. Commodity-wise monthly per capita consumer expenditures at current as well as at constant prices for different population decile groups for the period 1972–3 to 1988–9 show that the former exaggerate the extent of decline in the budget shares of cereals (Suryanarayana 1995a). As regards budget shares for other food groups, the extent and direction differed depending upon the changes in relative price structures. These estimates at constant prices, though careful, do not exhaust the entire period under review. Hence, one option could be to examine changes in terms of cereal consumption (expenditure as well as quantities consumed) and calorie intakes.

[2] This is also because the National Sample Survey (NSS) consumption estimates for the post-1970s are reasonably comparable (Suryanarayana 1995a).

Cereal Consumption

Consistent with the observed increases in per capita total consumer expenditures at constant prices, given the generally low levels of consumption, one would expect increases in cereal consumption expenditure to be a priority. However, cereal expenditure declined for all but the poorest decile group in both rural and urban India. Generally, the percentage decrease in cereal expenditure was higher for the richer decile groups in both the sectors (Suryanarayana 2009a). This would call into the question the Plan observation that low purchasing power is a constraint on household food security and with limited purchasing power households could not diversify their consumption basket.

Relative prices have changed. Though prices have increased, coarse cereals continue to be the cheapest among cereal grains (Suryanarayana 2009a). Still, both the poor and the rich have reduced their consumption of coarse cereals, with the difference that the poorer decile groups in both rural and urban India have substituted coarse cereals by superior cereals. The net result is that only the poorest decile group enjoyed an increase (above 10 per cent) in total cereal consumption in rural and urban India (Table 3.2). Accordingly, estimates of average per capita cereal quantities consumed for the total population show a decline in both rural and urban India during the sample period under consideration (Suryanarayana 2009a). A profile across decile groups of population shows that the decline in average per

Table 3.2 Cereal Consumption Basket across Decile Groups: Rural and Urban India

Decile Group	Per Capita Cereal Consumption (kg per month)								Increase (%) between 1972–3 and 2004–5			
	1972–3				2004–5							
	Rice	Wheat	Coarse Cereals	Total	Rice	Wheat	Coarse Cereals	Total	Rice	Wheat	Coarse Cereals	Total
Rural All-India												
0–10	3.79	1.42	3.88	9.09	6.10	3.00	1.32	10.41	61.13	110.92	−66.08	14.59
10–20	5.06	2.25	4.72	12.03	6.33	3.56	1.46	11.35	25.02	58.56	−69.09	−5.64
20–30	5.75	2.59	4.99	13.33	6.37	3.97	1.39	11.73	10.92	53.15	−72.20	−12.00
30–40	6.33	3.03	4.99	14.35	6.41	4.08	1.52	12.00	1.20	34.51	−69.62	−16.39
40–50	6.83	3.41	4.92	15.16	6.59	4.14	1.45	12.18	−3.41	21.43	−70.58	−19.62
50–60	7.10	3.62	4.88	15.60	6.59	4.46	1.36	12.41	−7.19	23.20	−72.16	−20.46
60–70	7.68	4.24	5.15	17.07	6.72	4.55	1.38	12.65	−12.49	7.19	−73.20	−25.93
70–80	7.90	4.58	5.28	17.75	7.00	4.65	1.16	12.81	−11.38	1.50	−77.96	−27.87
80–90	8.01	5.44	5.51	18.96	6.66	5.00	1.10	12.76	−16.84	−8.10	−80.08	−32.71
90–100	7.47	8.22	5.57	21.26	6.72	5.54	0.94	13.20	−9.99	−32.67	−83.08	−37.92
All	6.59	3.88	4.99	15.46	6.55	4.29	1.31	12.15	−0.62	10.64	−73.81	−21.42
Urban All-India												
0–10	3.48	3.17	2.10	8.75	4.52	4.40	0.74	9.66	29.96	38.72	−64.64	10.46
10–20	4.47	3.93	2.12	10.52	5.08	4.36	0.67	10.11	13.63	10.94	−68.24	−3.89
20–30	4.90	4.38	1.95	11.23	5.06	4.63	0.57	10.26	3.35	5.63	−70.63	−8.59
30–40	5.02	4.56	1.88	11.46	5.18	4.43	0.54	10.16	3.25	−2.77	−71.09	−11.34
40–50	5.16	5.01	1.67	11.84	4.95	4.81	0.53	10.28	−4.14	−4.03	−68.32	−13.16
50–60	5.22	5.07	1.61	11.90	4.91	4.81	0.41	10.13	−6.06	−5.10	−74.57	−14.91
60–70	5.48	5.32	1.35	12.15	4.84	4.90	0.40	10.13	−11.75	−7.97	−70.16	−16.59
70–80	5.47	5.41	1.22	12.09	4.94	4.69	0.39	10.03	−9.58	−13.26	−67.68	−17.09
80–90	5.34	5.56	0.93	11.84	4.72	4.65	0.32	9.69	−11.73	−16.34	−65.32	−18.12
90–100	4.86	5.79	0.77	11.43	4.34	4.78	0.25	9.37	−10.73	−17.42	−67.58	−17.96
All	4.94	4.82	1.56	11.32	4.85	4.65	0.48	9.98	−1.76	−3.61	−68.97	−11.81

Source: Author's estimates based on GoI (1979, 2006b).

Table 3.3 Estimates of Energy Intake: Rural and Urban All-India (kilocalories per capita per diem)

Decile Group	Rural All-India						Urban All-India					
	1972–3	1983	1993–4	1999–2000	2004–5	Change (%)**	1972–3	1983	1993–4	1999–2000	2004–5	Change (%)**
0–10	1,192.09	1,356.31	1,460.12	1,491.48	1,480.52	24.20	1,298.70	1,331.76	1,443.50	1,520.88	1,510.50	16.31
10–20	1,591.90	1,681.80	1,731.32	1,730.52	1,681.42	5.62	1,575.94	1,588.29	1,702.40	1,731.16	1,687.67	7.09
20–30	1,783.40	1,847.86	1,850.00	1,865.30	1,800.00	0.93	1,745.94	1,724.00	1,803.48	1,912.56	1,833.00	4.99
30–40	1,944.00	1,952.00	1,971.66	1,955.22	1,882.45	−3.17	1,802.18	1,861.19	1,896.79	1,970.46	1,856.41	3.01
40–50	2,115.04	2,111.53	2,056.48	2,049.15	1,958.95	−7.38	1,980.00	1,912.41	1,992.81	2,092.92	1,944.62	−1.79
50–60	2,210.00	2,229.56	2,156.34	2,170.62	2,044.32	−7.50	2,035.48	2,046.00	2,074.64	2,189.89	2,024.00	−0.56
60–70	2,451.41	2,322.00	2,275.17	2,287.78	2,158.00	−11.97	2,266.00	2,221.13	2,186.00	2,297.00	2,111.12	−6.83
70–80	2,581.40	2,506.92	2,410.00	2,403.00	2,290.00	−11.29	2,382.13	2,294.20	2,296.74	2,467.69	2,209.00	−7.27
80–90	2,929.00	2,779.53	2,584.72	2,582.54	2,376.40	−18.87	2,658.75	2,500.71	2,470.50	2,536.00	2,343.04	−11.87
90–100	3,861.77	3,422.49	3,034.19	2,954.39	2,797.94	−27.55	3,324.88	3,410.30	2,843.14	2,841.53	2,680.64	−19.38
All	2,266.00	2,221.00	2,153.00	2,149.00	2,047.00	−9.66	2,107.00	2,089.00	2,071.00	2,156.00	2,020.00	−4.13

Source: Author's estimates based on GoI (1983, 1989a, 1989b, 1996b, 2001b, 2007b).

Note: **Changes refer to the period between 1972–3 and 2004–5.

capita cereal consumption for the total rural and urban population has largely been due to a pronounced decline in cereal consumption of the top decile groups. At a time when the PDS meets the households' cereal requirements only to a partial extent and the open market prices, levels as well as spread across space or seasons, themselves are determined substantially by state interventions (Suryanarayana 1995b), the Plan estimates and interpretation of income transfers through the PDS (to promote food security) in terms of differences between open market and PDS prices would make little sense.

Changes in the composition of the consumption basket mentioned earlier could partly reflect changing tastes, consumer responses to changing relative prices, and their substitution effects on consumer choices, but largely changing production and supply conditions. Under the new agricultural growth strategy, benefiting largely wheat and rice, crop composition of food grains has changed considerably in favour of superior cereals. Structural changes in the rural economy involving a decline in coarse cereal availability and changes in labour markets could have accounted for some decline in total cereal consumption of the rural population groups.[3] In sum, the share of wheat in the cereal basket increased and that of coarse cereals decreased in both rural and urban sectors. Thus, there have been some qualitative improvements in the consumption patterns of the population.

[3] For further empirical details, see Suryanarayana (1995a).

Calorie Intake

With the decline in average cereal consumption, a decline in average calorie intake would follow, unless accompanied by compensating increases in non-cereal consumption. Though cereal consumption increased only for the poorest decile group (Table 3.2), per capita calorie intake has generally increased for the bottom two decile groups in rural India and bottom three decile groups in urban India (Table 3.3). This would suggest that there have been compensating increases in non-cereal consumption for the bottom two/three decile groups of the rural/urban population. Still, their calorie intakes fall short of the norms used for defining the poverty lines. The poor seem to have opted for some diversification in consumption, providing a more nutritious diet though not adequate energy (Suryanarayana 1995a). On the other hand, top decile groups have reduced their cereal consumption and, hence, calorie intake. The decline in the calorie intake of the richer sections could be explained in terms of changing consumption patterns in favour of non-calorie food and non-food items at the expense of calorie intake. The combined impact of these two diverse patterns of changes across decile groups is that estimates of incidence of calorie deficiency by the conventional calorie norms for the total (rural and urban combined) population turn out to be higher for about 80 per cent for India.

The calorie norms cited earlier have been worked out in the 1950s/1960s, and hence may be outdated and irrelevant with improvements in modes of production and standard of living. This could be the reason for voluntary reductions in cereal consumption and calorie intake of the richer decile groups. This would raise a question on the relevance of the calorie norms for food security estimates.

In sum, the NSS estimates of consumer expenditure, cereal consumption, and calorie intake by decile groups provide little evidence to corroborate the hypothesis that 'low and stagnant incomes' have proved a constraint on household food and nutritional security. Instead, they call into question (i) the relevance of calorie norms proposed half a century back for a scenario when modes of production were very dissimilar to those obtaining at present and (ii) the policy recommendation of the Plan to increase average calorie intake by 20 per cent. If the calorie norms are still valid, then they call for consumer education to guide choice of nutritious diets and healthy consumption habits among the non-poor.

Household Perception on Food Adequacy

Since its 38th round (1983), the National Sample Survey Organisation has periodically asked what are called probing questions, like whether the household gets two square meals a day throughout the year. Such questions were asked during the 38th (1983–4), 50th (1993–4), and the 61st (2004–5) rounds. Till the 55th round (1999–2000), the investigator asked direct questions to the household. In 1983, 81 per cent of the rural households reported adequate food consumption (two square meals a day); this percentage increased to 95 in 1993–4, 96 in 1999–2000, and 97 in 2004–5 (Suryanarayana 2009a). In the urban sector, the corresponding numbers increased from 93 per cent in 1983 to 99 per cent in 1999–2000 and 2004–5. In sum, this piece of evidence corroborates the perception that the general population is well fed.

Perceptions on Food Security and Morbidity

Given the Plan emphasis on an integrated perspective on food security and health outcomes, one may review the available evidence (Suryanarayana 2009a). Cross-sectional evidence on rural household perceptions on adequate food consumption varies inversely with estimates of per capita calorie intake across states, while the association is observed to be positive for the urban sector. Consistent with this finding, household perception on food adequacy bears significant positive association with incidence of calorie deficiency (with reference to alternative norms) in the rural sector and simple negative association in the urban sector. The only sensible estimate of association pertains to that between calorie intake and incidence of calorie deficiency in both rural and urban sectors. Other measures of association between subjective and objective measures of food security and alternative measure of morbidity/health consciousness are insignificant for the rural sector. As regards the urban sector, either they are insignificant or do not make any sense. For instance, association between incidence of calorie efficiency and infant mortality is significant and inverse, implying that higher the incidence of calorie deprivation, lower is incidence of infant mortality, which is absurd.

While food security per se is important to promote good health outcomes, the latter depend crucially on other important factors like biology, choice, and environment. Most important is to recognize the prevalence of morbidity rates across states, which definitely would affect the utilization of nutrients consumed. In this context, programmes to reform the health sector in India, which included inter alia user charges for services in public health facilities to the non-poor in particular since the early 1990s (GoI 2007c: 221) might have also adversely affected health outcomes.

Therefore, it is important to distinguish between input and outcome measures. The process is not instantaneous to generate contemporaneous correlations; instead, there would be lags also. There is limited scope for cross-sectional/time series comparisons between incomes/growth rates, malnutrition, and health outcomes. It is important to take a holistic perspective on this issue.

Reliability of Information Base

While the Plan document is at fault in its description of the food security status of the poor, it is casual in its review of the policy options, the PDS in particular. It recognizes the errors, both Type I and Type II, in implementing the targeted PDS (below poverty line [BPL] or Antyodaya cards), which benefited about 29 per cent of the rural and 13 per cent of the urban population by providing food grains at concessional prices. Among the beneficiaries of this targeted PDS, 70 per cent in the rural and 43 per cent in the urban sector were non-poor (Suryanarayana 2009b).

However, the Planning Commission does not seem to have bothered about authenticating the information. The NSS has its own explanation for the Type II errors: 'It should be mentioned here that the monthly per capita expenditure (MPCE) of a household is based on its consumption expenditure during the last 30 days. A poor household that bought a durable good during the 30 days prior to the date of survey might conceivably be placed in a higher MPCE class than the class in which its usual MPCE lies' (GoI 2007a: 16; Footnote 3).

If this explanation were valid, it would mean that even by the current methodology, estimate of poverty would have to be revised upwards by 20 percentage points for rural India and 5.35 percentage points for urban India. That is, actual estimates of poverty even by the current methodology should be 48.3 per cent for rural India and 31 per cent for urban India.

Most important is to note that the explanation provided by this important department of the government is casual and not based on evidence since about 75 per cent of the population above the poverty line with BPL cards did not incur any expenditure on durables during the reference period (Suryanarayana 2009b). In other words, it is the sound institutional capacity for (i) information generation and (ii) its review that is a prerequisite for an appropriate pro-poor policy choice and design. This is the need of the hour today.

SUMMING UP

This chapter examines the veracity of the Eleventh Five Year Plan assessment of and recommendation for food security in India. The Plan perspective on distributional dimension of changes in food security is based on estimates of averages only. As per the Plan review, food security of the poor as measured by estimates of average cereal consumption and calorie intake has worsened in India during the past couple of decades due to stagnant incomes and perverse changes in consumption patterns.

Average does not measure the status of the poor. Therefore, this study reviews the basis for such assessments in terms of disaggregate analysis of changes in consumer expenditures and consumption patterns by decile groups in rural and urban India. The study brings out that real consumption expenditure of all the decile groups, the bottom three decile groups in particular, increased since the mid-1970s. Per capita cereal expenditures of the bottom decile groups in rural India increased. However, this was not accompanied by corresponding increases in quantities of cereal consumption because of structural changes in the food economy. With casualization and, hence, monetization of the labour market, there has been a progressive increase in the dependence of the poor households, landless labour in particular, on the commodity market. With changes in cereal production patterns and hence availability in favour of superior cereals, these households had to shift their consumption in favour of superior but costlier rice and wheat, which are inferior to coarse cereals in terms of calorie content. As a result, cereal consumption and, hence, calorie intake have not increased to a commensurate extent. On the other hand, with changes in infrastructure and technology, average energy requirements seem to have declined, calling for reduced calorie intake. This could be one major reason for the observed trend decline in average calorie intake of the richer decile groups in rural and urban India. Therefore, estimates of incidence of calorie deficiency with reference to outdated norms show a trend increase.

On the other hand, NSS findings show that the percentage number of rural and urban households reporting adequate food consumption throughout the year has increased since 1983, and has reached almost 98 per cent. This would raise the question regarding an appropriate norm and strategy for food security. Should one measure it in terms of objective estimates of calorie intake with reference to an exogenous norm or subjective perceptions on adequate food consumption? The limited evidence in terms of bivariate correlations between subjective and objective estimates of food consumption, and measures of health status do not provide any unambiguous answer. The estimates are either weak or perverse, which could be because of the lags and simultaneous interaction of a host of variables in determining these outcomes. Hence, there is a need to revisit the calorie norms for minimum subsistence and poverty line, and their implications for policy for food security. The most important issue is the adequacy and reliability of the information base, which appears suspect because of misleading findings and explanations.

REFERENCES

Government of India (1979), 'Survey Results: Consumer Expenditure, NSS 27th Round (October 1972–September 1973)', *Sarvekshana*, II(3): S287–S436.

——— (1983), 'A Note on Per Capita Per Diem Intake of Calories, Protein and Fat based on the Data Collected in the Household Survey on Consumer Expenditure, NSS 27th Round (October 1972–September 1973)', *Sarvekshana*, VI(3–4): 1–10.

——— (1986a), 'Some Results on the Second Quinquennial Survey on Consumer Expenditure, NSS 32nd Round (July 1977–June 1978)', *Sarvekshana*, IX(3): S51–S184.

——— (1986b), 'A Report on the Third Quinquennial Survey on Consumer Expenditure, NSS 38th Round (January–December 1983)', *Sarvekshana*, IX(4): S1–S102.

——— (1989a), 'Results on Per Capita Consumption of Cereals for Various Sections of Population, NSS 38th Round (1983)', *Sarvekshana*, XIII(2): S1–S176.

——— (1989b), 'Results on Per Capita and Per Consumer Unit Per Diem Intake of Calorie, Protein and Fat and Perceptions of the People on Adequacy of Food', *Sarvekshana*, XIII(2): S177–S258.

——— (1991), 'Results of the Fourth Quinquennial Survey on Consumer Expenditure (sub-sample 1), NSS 43rd Round (July 1987–June 1988)', *Sarvekshana*, XV(1): S1–S473.

——— (1996a), *Level and Pattern of Consumer Expenditure. 5th Quinquennial Survey 1993–94*, Report No. 402, National Sample Survey Organisation, Department of Statistics, New Delhi.

——— (1996b), *Nutritional Intake in India, NSS 50th Round, July 1993–June 1994, Fifth Quinquennial Survey on Consumer Expenditure*, Report No. 405, National Sample Survey Organisation, Department of Statistics, New Delhi.

——— (2001a), *Level and Pattern of Consumer Expenditure in India 1999–2000, NSS 55th Round, July 1999–June 2000*,

Report No. 457 (55/1.0/3), National Sample Survey Organisation, Ministry of Statistics and Programme Implementation, New Delhi.

————— (2001b), *Nutritional Intake in India 1999–2000, NSS 55th Round (July 1999–June 2000)*, Report No. 471(55/1.0/9), National Sample Survey Organisation, Ministry of Statistics and Programme Implementation, New Delhi.

————— (2006a), *Morbidity, Health Care and the Condition of the Aged, NSS 60th Round (January–June 2004)*, Report No. 507(60/25.0/1), National Sample Survey Organisation, Ministry of Statistics and Programme Implementation, New Delhi.

————— (2006b), *Level and Pattern of Consumer Expenditure, 2004–2005, NSS 61st Round (July 2004–June 2005)*, NSS Report No. 508(61/1.0)/1), National Sample Survey Organisation, Ministry of Statistics and Programme Implementation, New Delhi.

————— (2007a), *Poverty Estimates for 2004–05*, Press Information Bureau, New Delhi.

————— (2007b), *Nutritional Intake in India 2004–2005, NSS 61st Round (July 2004–June 2005)*, Report No. 513(61/1.0/6), National Sample Survey Organisation, Ministry of Statistics and Programme Implementation, New Delhi.

————— (2007c), *Economic Survey 2006–2007*, Ministry of Finance, New Delhi.

————— (2008), *Eleventh Five Year Plan 2007–12, Volume II, Social Sector*, Planning Commission. New Delhi: Oxford University Press.

Siddhanta, Priyadarshi (2009), 'Poverty Line Fluctuates with Conflicting Data', *The Indian Express*, 20 August, p. 21.

Suryanarayana, M.H. (1995a), 'Growth, Poverty and Levels of Living: Hypotheses, Methods and Policies', *Journal of Indian School of Political Economy*, 7(2): 203–55.

————— (1995b), 'PDS: Beyond Implicit Subsidy and Urban Bias', *Food Policy*, 20(4): 259–78.

————— (2009a), 'Food Security: Beyond the Eleventh Plan Fiction', revised version of the paper presented at the 'International Conference on Health and Development', organized by the School of Development Studies, Department of Economics, Kannur University, Thalassery, and sponsored by the Indian Council of Medical Research, New Delhi, at Thalassery, 22–23 October 2008.

————— (2009b), 'What Ails Our Public Policies for the Poor?', revised version of the paper presented at the 'Fourth Annual International Conference on Public Policy and Management', Centre for Public Policy, Indian Institute of Management, Bengaluru, 9–12 August.

Tendulkar, S.D., K. Sundaram, and L.R. Jain (1993), 'Poverty in India, 1970–71 to 1988–89', ARTEP Working Papers, International Labour Organization, Asian Regional Team for Employment Promotion, New Delhi.

4

Persistence of Crisis in Indian Agriculture
Need for Technological and Institutional Alternatives

Srijit Mishra and D. Narasimha Reddy

INTRODUCTION

Agriculture is conventionally looked at in a narrow technical way, but needs to be seen in a larger context where not only production but also producers are equally important. Today, both are in crisis. These are two dimensions to the current crisis in Indian agriculture—the agricultural and the agrarian. The former is a developmental crisis that lies in the neglect of the sector arising out of poor design of programmes and inadequate allocation of resources. The latter is a livelihood crisis threatening the very basis of survival for the vast majority of the population dependent on agriculture (Government of India 2007; Reddy and Mishra 2009). On the one hand, there is a neglect of farming, and on the other hand, there is a neglect of the farmer. In the developmental discourse these would be contextualized with the displacement of ideology and the displacement of people, respectively (Bhaduri 2008). The two dimensions are inter-related in the sense that the problem at the larger structural context cannot be separated from the problem that the individual farmer faces. What is worrying is that this crisis in agriculture, which has been there for nearly two decades now, is taking place at a time when the overall Indian economy, except during the recent global financial crisis, has been witnessing a high growth.

Some aspects of the agricultural crisis are the following. Compared to the 1980s, agricultural production, productivity, and value of output have decelerated for almost all crops

from the early 1990s. The state, instead of facilitating the risk-taking farmers, has been withdrawing. There has been a decline of public investment in irrigation and related infrastructure. An increase in private investments on borewells/tube wells in some parts of the country led to a tragedy of the commons through declining water tables. Inadequate access to formal sources of credit led to increasing dependence on informal sources of credit with a greater interest burden. Waning link between research and extension and farming increased reliance on the input provider for advice bringing about supplier-induced demand.

With changing technology and market conditions, the farmer is increasingly being exposed to the uncertainties of the product as well as factor markets. The farmer faces multiple risks, vagaries of weather, price shocks, and spurious inputs, among others, further compromising on his already lower returns. This takes us to the agrarian crisis, and on which we discuss the following. Growth of the agriculture sector has been lower than that of the overall economy, but what is worrying is the deceleration in agriculture in the 1990s than in the 1980s. In 2004–5, the share of agriculture in national income was around one-fifth, but this sector still continues to employ nearly three-fifths of the workers. For the same year, after taking a reduced norm, the incidence of calorie poor is much higher than the incidence of expenditure poor. What is worrying is that the incidences are much higher for agricultural labourers and households with marginal and

Table 4.1   Growth Rate of Area, Production, and Yield of Major Crops in India, TE 1981–2 to 1993–4 and TE 1994–5 to TE 2007–8

Crops	TE 1981–2 to TE 1993–4				TE 1994–5 to TE 2007–8			
	Area	Production	Yield	Value	Area	Production	Yield	Value
Food Grains	−0.3*	3.0*	3.3*	3.0*	−0.2*	1.1*#	1.3*#	1.0*#
Total Cereals	−0.3*	3.2*	3.5*	3.2*	−0.2*	1.2*#	1.4*#	1.1*#
Rice	0.7*	3.7*	3.1*	3.7*	0.1#	1.0*#	0.9*#	1.0*#
Wheat	0.8*	4.1*	3.3*	4.1*	0.7*	1.6*#	0.8*#	1.6*#
Coarse Cereals	−2.1*	0.4	2.5*	0.5	−1.3*#	0.7*	2.0*	0.4
Total Pulses	−0.2	1.4*	1.6*	1.4*	−0.2	0.0#	0.2#	0.3#
Gram	−0.8	0.8	1.6*	1.1	0.2	0.8	0.6*#	0.9*
Tur	1.6*	0.7	−0.8*	0.8*	−0.2#	−0.1	0.1	0.1
Total Oilseeds$	3.4*	6.2*	2.9*	5.8*	0.0#	1.2*#	1.3*#	0.9#
Groundnut	1.4*	2.9*	1.4*	3.3*	−2.4*#	−1.6*#	0.9*	−1.5*#
Rapeseed and Mustard	4.4*	8.1*	3.6*	7.3*	0.0#	1.2*#	1.2*#	1.5*#
Soyabean†	16.9*	20.1*	3.1*	20.5*	5.3*#	6.2*#	0.9*#	6.3*#
Sugarcane	2.2*	4.0*	1.8*	3.4*	1.4*	1.2*#	−0.2#	1.9*
Cotton‡	0.2	3.2*	3.0*	3.4*	1.1*	3.1*	2.0*	2.9*
Jute	−0.8	1.8*	2.6*	1.8*	0.7	2.0*	1.3*#	2.1*
Mesta	−4.0*	−2.3*	1.7*	−2.6*	−2.8*#	−1.5*	1.3*	−1.0*
Coconut	3.7*	6.6*	2.9*	6.4*	1.6*#	1.5*#	−0.1#	1.7*#
Potato	3.2*	5.1*	1.8*	5.2*	2.2*#	3.0*#	0.7*#	3.1*#
Tobacco	−0.6	1.6*	2.3*	1.5*	−0.9	−0.5	0.4#	−0.5

Sources: Government of India (2009); *National Accounts Statistics* (including back series), Ministry of Statistics and Programme Implementation, Government of India, various years. All were accessed at http://www.mospi.gov.in/mospi_cso_rept_pubn.htm (on 28 September 2009).

Notes: Growth rates have been calculated using a kinked exponential curve $\ln(Y_t) = a + b(t_1) + c(t_2)$; Y = Area, Production, and Yield; $t = 0$ for TE 1981–2 and 26 for TE 2007–8, with TE indicating triennium ending; $t_1 = (dt + (1-d)k)$ and $t_2 = (1-d)(t-k)$, where d = 1 for the first period (TE 1981–2 to TE 1993–4) and $d = 0$ for the second period (TE 1994–5 to TE 2007–8), and $k = 12$ representing TE 1993–4; b and c are growth rates for the first and second periods, respectively.

* indicates that the growth rates are significantly different from zero at 95 per cent confidence interval (CI).

\# indicates that the growth rates between the two periods are significantly different from each other at 95 per cent CI.

‡ cotton, potato, and tobacco, data are available till TE 2006–7.

$ comprises of nine major oilseeds.

† value of soyabean available from 1980–1, and hence for $t = 0$, it is a two-year average.

small holdings. There has been an increase in marginalization of holdings. In 2001, from the total operational holdings, more than three-fifths were with less than 1 hectare of land and for nearly one-fifth the land size was between 1 and 2 hectares. Farmers' suicides, which, like indebtedness, are symptomatic of the larger crisis, have been showing an increasing incidence and continue to remain much higher than those by non-farmers.

There is need for institutional structures to organize the farmers to help them address their concerns and problems. Concurrently, unlike the green revolution technology that began with large farmers in resource-rich areas, community-managed sustainable agriculture focusing on marginal and small farmers in resource-poor dry and drought-prone areas needs to be promoted.

AGRICULTURAL CRISIS

Production and Productivity

Coming to agricultural production and productivity, using Boyce (1986) we analyse the kinked exponential growth rate for two periods—triennium ending (TE) 1981–2 to TE 1993–4 and TE 1994–5 to TE 2007–8 with regard to area, production, and yield across major crops (Table 4.1).

In the 1980s, growth in area was significantly negative for coarse cereals and mesta, and not significantly negative for some others. But what is important is that production and yield were significantly positive for almost all crops, except for mesta in production and tur in yield. In more recent years, the significantly negative growth in area continued for coarse cereals and mesta, and to these was added groundnut. With regard to production and yield, significantly negative growths were limited to groundnut and mesta for production. But what is worrying is that the growth rate of production as also the yield has been significantly lower for most crops/crop groups when compared with the 1980s.

Growth rate for value of output was also lower in recent years when compared to the 1980s for all major crops/crop groups, and the difference was significant for cereals, pulses, oilseeds, coconut, and potato. If we take all the major crops/crop groups together, then the growth rate per annum for the two periods is 3.4 per cent (CI: 2.9, 3.9) and 1.3 per cent (CI: 0.9, 1.7), respectively. For other crops largely comprising indigo and dyes, drugs excluding tobacco, condiment and spices, fruit and vegetables excluding potato, and by-products, among others, the per annum growth rate for the first period at 1.7 per cent (CI: 1.3, 2.0) was significantly lower than that for the second period at 4.0 per cent (CI: 3.7, 4.3). The latter group of crops constitutes more than two-fifths of the value of output in agriculture, but a rough estimate shows that it comprises less than 15 per cent of the area under cultivation (gross cropped area plus area under miscellaneous trees and groves less area under major crops/crop groups). The cultivation of these being relatively less labour-intensive, the number of man-days spent by cultivators and agricultural labourers in these activities will have a lower proportion than the share of area under these crops.

What is even more alarming is that the growth rate in production of cereals and oilseeds at 1.2 per cent per annum in recent years has been lower than the growth rate of population at 1.9 per cent per annum from 1991 to 2001. There has been no growth in the production of pulses. Overall, deceleration is evident in production, productivity, and value of output of almost all major crops/crop groups.

The share of value of agricultural output across crop groups indicates the following (Table 4.2). The share of cereals declined from the mid-1990s, and that of pulses from the 1980s. The reliance on by-products and kitchen garden seems to be on the decline. As against these, the share of fruits and vegetables has been increasing. Oilseeds show an increase in the 1980s, followed by a decline from mid-1990s and again an increase in recent years. Among oilseeds, soyabean has been showing an increase from the 1980s. Sugars have been showing a consistent increase but the share of sugarcane, its biggest component, decreased during the 1990s. Fibres (largely cotton) decreased during the 1990s, the period that saw an increasing incidence of suicides, particularly among cotton farmers. Drugs show a decrease in the 1980s and an increase in the 1990s. Condiment and spices show an increase in the 1980s and 1990s, and some decline in recent years.

Risks and Vulnerability

For the current agricultural season of 2009–10, paucity of rain in the initial period led to drought-like conditions and abundance of rain later in the period led to flood-like situation in some parts. In monsoon India, this has been a continuing problem. The vagaries of nature, it seems, are likely to increase because of global climate change. Besides weather, pests, diseases of plants, and spurious quality or

Table 4.2   Share of Value of Agricultural Output across Crop Groups, TE 1981–2 and TE 2007–8

Crop Groups	1981–2	1993–4	2004–5	2007–8
Cereals	35.3	36.8	31.8	31.2
Pulses	6.3	5.6	4.7	4.4
Oilseeds	6.8	9.3	7.9	8.3
Sugars	4.4	4.6	5.5	5.8
Fibres	4.0	4.0	3.8	5.2
Drugs	2.4	2.3	2.6	2.6
Condiment and Spices	3.1	3.6	4.7	4.5
Fruits and Vegetables	18.6	18.8	24.1	24.3
Others	8.7	6.2	7.9	7.1
By-products	9.7	8.1	6.4	6.0
Kitchen Garden	0.8	0.6	0.6	0.5
All	100.0	100.0	100.0	100.0

Source: *National Accounts Statistics* (including back series), Ministry of Statistics and Programme Implementation, Government of India, various years. Available at http://www.mospi.gov.in/mospi_cso_rept_pubn.htm (accessed on 28 September 2009).

Note: The figures have been rounded off.

inappropriate usage of inputs would bring about productivity and production loss. This affects food security of farmer households. Conventionally, prices largely depended on local demand and supply conditions; its variation did not affect overall returns much. Integration with the global market has increased price volatility and the farmer can face output and price shocks, together resulting in substantial reductions in income (Reserve Bank of India 2006; Mishra 2008; World Bank 2007).

Moreover, international prices are distorted because of huge farm subsidies by the developed countries. At the same time, tariff on agricultural imports in India is low. The cushion from minimum support prices (MSP) to farmers is only possible for select commodities and in regions with easy access to designated centres/market yards where one can sell the produce. In any case, the increase in MSP was low. Keeping 1997–8 as benchmark, the percentage increase by 2007 was 55 per cent for paddy, 67 per cent for other cereals, 72 per cent for maize and tur, 58 per cent for groundnut-in-shell, 51 per cent for sunflower seed, 36 per cent for soyabean black, 35 per cent for cotton medium staple, and 47 per cent for wheat (Table 4.3). If one controls for inflation, then these seem to have decreased during a period when the economy boomed. The farmer household has been having difficulties in providing for normal activities like education of wards, health care of family members, and other social obligations.

At a time when returns to cultivation have been decreasing, there is an increasing dependence on the market for inputs. The failure of research and extension service, which is striking in case of crops/cultivation in rain-fed/dry land areas, has resulted in reliance on the unregulated input seller, leading to supplier-induced demand. This is concurrently happening along with deskilling—new technology and new methods of cultivation make the accumulated knowledge of social capital on cultivation redundant. From 1990–1 to 2006–7, per annum growth in net area under irrigation was negative for canals (–1.3 per cent) and tanks (–3.5 per cent), and positive for tube wells and other wells (2.3 per cent) and other sources (4.7 per cent). In 2006–7, nearly 60 per cent of area under irrigation was through wells/borewells. In 1999–2000 prices, public gross fixed capital formation (GFCF) in agriculture as a per cent of agricultural gross domestic product (GDP) declined from 5.3 per cent in Sixth Plan (1980–1 to 1984–5) to 2.1 per cent in the Ninth Plan (1997–8 to 2001–2), and then increased to 3.0 per cent in the Tenth Plan (2002–3 to 2006–7) (Government of India 2009). Despite revival in recent years, inadequate public investment in infrastructure, like canals, led to private investments in borewells and along with it a tragedy of the commons (particularly in Andhra Pradesh), having implications on indebtedness.

With regard to credit, some of the difficulties that a farmer household faces are the following. Credit from formal sources is not available at the appropriate time, leading to greater reliance on informal sources with a higher interest burden, particularly for small and marginal farmers. The All-India Debt and Investment Survey (AIDIS) of 2003 indicates that for all the outstanding debt from non-institutional sources at the end of June 2002, three-fourths carried interest of more than 20 per cent per annum; of these, more than half carried interest of more than 30 per cent per annum. There is difficulty in repayment during crop loss or price shock, but

Table 4.3 Increase in Minimum Support Price (MSP) of Selected Crops in India, 1997–8 to 2008

Crops	1997–8	2007	2008	Absolute Increase (Rs)		Percentage Increase	
		(Rs)		2007 over 1997–8	2008 over 2007	2007 over 1997–8	2008 over 2007
Paddy Common	415	645	850	230	205	55	32
Coarse Cereals	360	600	840	240	240	67	40
Maize	360	620	840	260	220	72	35
Arhar (Tur)	900	1,550	2,000	650	450	72	29
Groundnut-in-shell	980	1,550	2,100	570	550	58	35
Sunflower Seed	1,000	1,510	2,215	510	705	51	47
Soyabean Black	670	910	1,350	240	440	36	48
Nigerseed	800	1,240	2,405	440	1,165	55	94
Cotton (F-414/ Medium Staple)	1,330	1,800	2,500	470	700	35	39
Wheat (Rabi Crop)	510	750	1,000	240	250	47	33

Source: Directorate of Economics and Statistics, Department of Agriculture and Cooperation, Ministry of Agriculture, Government of India, various years (for recent years, see http://dacnet.nic.in/eands/MSP.htm).

there is no system to address such exigencies through credit guarantee or some such scheme. The more recent debt waiver of 2008 is basically a book-keeping exercise that would clear the non-performing assets of the banks. As a result of this waiver, farmers do not have a loan burden and can avail fresh loans. This was preceded by a doubling of credit, but these just address the symptom and not the problem of poor returns to cultivation. Moreover, such solutions, instead of drawing the farmers out of credit, draws them into a vortex of debt. The problem is further compounded because of market-induced consumerism (Reserve Bank of India 2006; Mishra 2008).

During the 1990s and till a few years ago (about 2004), there were important changes in the banking structure. The number of rural branches declined from 32,981 (51 per cent of total) in March 1996 to 31,967 (46 per cent of total) in March 2005. The number of agricultural borrowal accounts declined from 277.4 lakh in March 1992 to 198.4 lakh in March 2001. Agricultural credit as percentage of net bank credit declined from 18 per cent at the end of the 1980s to 11 per cent in 2004. There was a shift to activities that would give greater returns to banks. Between 1981–2 and 2002–3, distribution of credit disbursed and area operated across size-class of holdings indicate that the ratio of proportion of credit disbursed to proportion of area operated decreased for marginal holdings from 2.41 to 0.98 whereas that of semi-medium and higher holdings increased from 0.72 to 0.93. Concurrently, the share of number of credit accounts to share of number of operational holdings decreased for marginal holdings from 0.90 to 0.56, and increased for small holdings from 1.28 to 1.85 and for semi-medium and higher from 1.0 to 2.19. This means that for marginal holdings, when the share of area and the share of number of holdings are increasing, the share of credit disbursed and the share of number of accounts have been decreasing (Government of India 2007; Shetty 2009).

AGRARIAN CRISIS

Agricultural GSDP

Growth of gross (state) domestic product (GDP/GSDP) was higher than growth in agricultural GDP/GSDP in all the periods given in Table 4.4, except for Gujarat in 2000s. At the all-India level, the differences between the two have always been statistically significant.

With faster growth rate of overall GDP and India as one of the front-running emerging market economies, the gap between overall growth rate and growth of agricultural GDP is bound to increase, and with it the share of agricultural GDP in the national product is bound to decrease. This process may mimic the development path of all developed market economies except that those eking out their livelihood from agriculture constitute a large workforce and most of them are increasingly small-marginal farmers and agricultural labourers with severe constraints on earnings and in meeting their basic consumption needs, including food.

From 1993–4 to 2004–5, the share of agriculture and allied activities in GDP at current prices (1999–2000 series) decreased from 30 per cent to 20 per cent, whereas persons working in the usual principal and subsidiary status in this sector decreased from 64 per cent to 57 per cent (Government of India 2007). Three-fifths of the workforce is still dependent on this sector. For the same period, using shares of GDP and workforce available across the nine categories of economic activity (agriculture and allied; mining and quarrying; manufacturing; electricity, water, and gas, construction; trade, hotel, and restaurant; transport and communication; finance and banking; and community and other services), one computes Gini coefficient and observes that inequality has increased from 0.43 to 0.48.

As mentioned earlier, agriculture and allied category is the only economic activity whose share in GDP is continuously on the decline and the gap between GDP share and workforce share is continuously on the increase.

Poor in Rural India

Rural poverty is strongly associated with the state of agriculture. The overall diminution of the place of agriculture in the national economic performance and the multitudes of problems faced by this sector, pushing it to serious crisis, also reflect in the distress and deprivation of consumption to fulfil basic energy requirements.

The per capita per annum net availability (excludes seed, feed and wastage, and exports, includes imports, and also accounts for change in stock) of food grains has reduced from 177 kg in TE 1992 to 159 kg in TE 2007; the growth rate for the period being negative at –0.67 per cent per annum (CI: –0.91, –0.44). Growth rates of production of milk, egg, and fish are positive. Per capita per annum availability of these was around 90 litres of milk, 45 eggs, and 6.1 kg of fish in 2006–7 (Government of India 2009). Are these enough? How much of these are available in rural India? We will try to discuss this indirectly. From 1993–4 to 2004–5, per consumer unit consumption of calorie (2,683 to 2,540 kcal) and protein (75 to 71 grams) decreased and that of fat (39 to 44 grams) increased in rural India (NSSO 1996, 2007). Across food groups, the decline in calorie (maximal fall to least fall) was in cereals, sugar and honey, pulses, nuts and oilseeds, and milk and milk products; whereas increase in calorie (minimum to highest) was in fish, egg and meat, fruits and vegetables, roots and fibre, miscellaneous items that include beverages and snacks, and oil and fats. The decline in pulses as also milk and milk products and the increase in miscellaneous items and oil and fats are matters of concern from the health perspective.

Table 4.4   Growth Rate of Gross State Domestic Product (GSDP) and Agricultural GSDP across States

States	1980s (1983–4 to 1993–4) 1980–1 prices		1990s (1993–4 to 2004–5) 1993–4 prices		2000s (1999–2000 to 2008–9) 1999–2000 prices	
	GSDP	AgrGSDP	GSDP	AgrGSDP	GSDP	AgrGSDP
Andhra Pradesh	4.5*	3.0*	5.7*	2.6*#	7.0*§	5.0*
Assam	3.5*	2.4*	3.2*	0.7*#§	5.1*§	0.7*#
Bihar (undivided)	2.7*	−1.0#	4.5*§	2.7*§	6.7	2.3#
Bihar			4.5*	2.0	6.8*	3.0
Chhattisgarh			3.8*	−2.4#	7.1*§	6.4*§
Gujarat	4.9*	0.6	6.0*	1.7	8.5*	10.2*§
Haryana	6.0*	4.7*	6.0*	2.0*#§	8.9*§	3.2*#
Himachal Pradesh	5.7*	2.9*#	6.4*	3.0*#	7.1*	5.8*
Jharkhand			4.6*	4.4*	6.4*	0.0#§
Karnataka	5.7*	3.6*#	6.7*	0.9#	6.5*	0.1#
Kerala	5.2*	4.6*	5.6*	−2.5*#§	7.7*§	2.2*#§
Madhya Pradesh (undivided)	5.1*	3.4*	3.9*	0.0#	4.7	4.0
Madhya Pradesh			3.9*	0.6#	3.9*	3.2
Maharashtra	7.8*	5.4*	5.2*§	0.8#§	7.0*	4.7*§
Orissa	3.3*	−0.8#	4.4*	0.0#	7.6*§	3.3*#
Punjab	5.0*	4.6*	4.3*§	2.1*#§	4.8*	2.5*#
Rajasthan	6.0*	3.4	5.5*	1.9	5.8*§	4.7*
Tamil Nadu	5.6*	4.1*	4.8*	−0.9#§	6.5*	1.6#
Uttar Pradesh (undivided)	4.6*	2.8*#	4.0*	2.1*#	4.7	1.4*#
Uttar Pradesh			3.9*	2.1*#	5.0*	1.9*#
Uttarakhand			5.4*	1.8*#	8.7*§	2.6*#
West Bengal	4.8*	4.3*	6.8*§	3.1*#	6.1*	2.1*#
India	5.2*	3.1*#	5.9*§	2.2*#	7.1*§	2.8*#

Source: State Domestic Product (State Series) and National Accounts Statistics, Ministry of Statistics and Programme Implementation, Government of India, http://www.mospi.gov.in/mospi_cso_rept_pubn.htm (accessed on 1 September 2009).

Notes: GSDP is gross state domestic product and AgrGSDP is agricultural GSDP. Growth rate calculated using linear trend, $\ln(Y_t) = a + bt + et$; b is the growth rate. In 2000s, data for Gujarat and Uttar Pradesh (undivided) are till 2006–7. For Andhra Pradesh, Himachal Pradesh, Kerala, Madhya Pradesh (undivided), Maharashtra, and West Bengal, they are till 2007–8; and for the remaining they are till 2008–9.

* denotes growth rate is significantly different from zero at 95% Confidence Interval (CI).

# denotes growth rate of AgrGSDP is significantly different from GSDP at 95% CI.

$ denotes growth rate of 1990s is significantly different from 1980s at 95% CI.

§ denotes growth rate of 2000s (which also includes the latter part of the 1990s series) is significantly different from 1990s at 95% CI.

We make use of household unit level data from the consumption expenditure schedule of the 61st round of the National Sample Survey (NSS) in 2004–5 to compute incidences of expenditure and calorie poor across states in rural India (Figure 4.1). Incidence of expenditure poor is the number of persons in households with monthly per capita expenditure below the poverty line provided by the Planning Commission. Poverty lines, first calculated for 1973–4, were used to define the per capita daily calorie requirements of people: 2,400 calories in rural and 2,100 calories in urban areas (after adjusting for age and sex composition, it was considered as equivalent to per consumer unit calorie norm of 3,000 in rural and 2,600 in urban areas). There are discussions that the calorie norm needs a downward revision because of increasingly sedentary lifestyles and better health and hygiene. In the absence of any guidelines, we use a consumer unit norm to the existing benchmark of 2,400 calorie for rural areas. This could

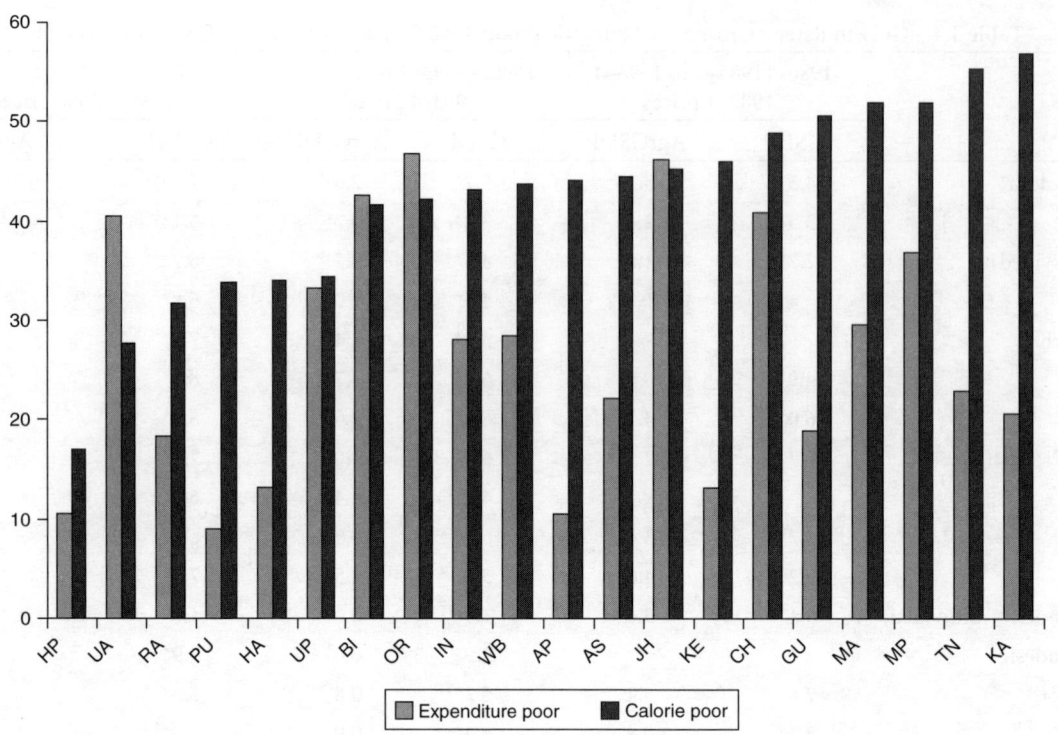

Source: Calculated from unit level data using Schedule 1.0, 61st Round, National Sample Survey, Government of India.

Notes: AP = Andhra Pradesh, AS = Assam, BI = Bihar, CH = Chhattisgarh, GU = Gujarat, HA = Haryana, HP = Himachal Pradesh, IN = India, JH = Jharkhand, KA = Karnataka, KE = Kerala, MA= Maharashtra, MP = Madhya Pradesh, OR = Orissa, PU = Punjab, RA = Rajasthan, TN = Tamil Nada, UP = Uttar Pradesh, UA = Uttarkhand, WB = West Bengal. Expenditure poor are based on poverty line for states given by the Planning Commission, and calories poor are based on per consumer unit calorie norm of 2,400 (this is a reduced norm and is just indicative).

Figure 4.1   Incidences of Expenditure Poor and Calorie Poor across States in Rural India, 2004–5

be on the lower side, leading to an underestimation of poor, particularly for groups that continue to put in hard labour. In spite of this self-imposed reduced norm, our incidences of calorie poor (43 per cent) are much higher than the incidences of expenditure poor (28 per cent) for rural India.

Among major states, those with incidences of calorie poor higher than the all-India average (from high to low) are Karnataka (57 per cent), Tamil Nadu (55 per cent), Madhya Pradesh (52 per cent), Maharashtra (52 per cent), Gujarat (51 per cent), Chhattisgarh (49 per cent), Kerala (46 per cent), Jharkhand 45 per cent), Assam (45 per cent), Andhra Pradesh (44 per cent), and West Bengal (44 per cent). The states of Uttarakhand, Orissa, Jharkhand, and Bihar have incidences of calorie poor that are lower than their incidences of expenditure poor. Uttarakhand has relatively higher share of calories coming from milk and milk products (10.5 per cent; it is 6.4 per cent for rural India) and sugar and honey (7.6 per cent; it is 4.8 per cent for rural India). What is surprising is that all the other three states are among those having the highest incidences of expenditure poor. This anomaly is because of a relatively

higher share of cereals (mostly rice) in their consumption basket (80 per cent for Orissa, 75 per cent for Jharkhand, and 74 per cent for Bihar). In addition, the average protein and fat intake for these three states is among the lowest. These states also spent a larger share of their expenditure on food (62 per cent for Orissa and Jharkhand, and 65 per cent for Bihar; it is 55 per cent for rural India). Moreover, these three states are perhaps less sedentary and their health conditions are not as improved as in other parts. This is suggestive that, while there is a need to revise the calorie norms downwards, this need not be uniform across states. More importantly, nutritional deprivation has to go beyond just calories.

Incidences of poor are higher for agricultural labourers (44 per cent for expenditure poor, 58 per cent for calorie poor) from household type and marginal holdings (32 per cent for expenditure poor, 47 per cent for calorie poor) from size-class of land possessed. A matter of concern is that 70 per cent of the rural population is from households with marginal holdings (0–1 hectare), and half of them are near landless (less than 0.1 hectares of land). Another 15 per cent of the population is from households with small holdings

(1–2 hectares). These are households where the working members would be putting in hard labour, and hence, using a common norm will underestimate the incidences of calorie poor. To reiterate, our estimates using a lower calorie norm is only indicative to suggest that in spite of this, incidences of calorie poor are quite high. This is also to suggest that calorie norms need regular updating. But while doing the same, one should take into consideration the differences in the sex and age composition, occupational patterns, and state-specific conditions, among others factors. There should also be norms to take us beyond calories to identify protein, micronutrient, or other food-based deprivations.

Small and Marginal Farmers

Agricultural census from 1970–1 to 2000–1 show that the distribution of operational holdings across size-classes of land possessed has increased from 51 per cent to 63 per cent for marginal holdings (0–1 hectare), has remained around 19 per cent for small holdings (1–2 hectares), and has decreased for all the other size-class of holdings. In 2000–1, semi-medium holdings (2–4 hectares) constituted 12 per cent, medium holdings (4–10 hectares) 5 per cent, and large holdings (more than 10 hectares) at 1 per cent of the number of operational holdings. With these shifts, inequality with regard to distribution of landholdings decreased from 0.64 to 0.56. Recall that this was happening when inequality in the economy was increasing because of decreasing share of agriculture in the GDP while its share in employment continued to remain high. What is worrying is that most people depended on this sector are largely from households of agricultural labourers and the marginal and small farmers.

The situation assessment survey of 2003 indicated that the average monthly income for a farmer household is lower than its expenditure in case of households with holdings that are marginal (Rs 1,659 and Rs 2,482), small (Rs 2,493 and Rs 3,148), and semi-medium (Rs 3,589 and Rs 3,685); it is higher for households with holdings that are medium (Rs 5,681 and Rs 4,626) and large (Rs 9,667 and Rs 6,418). The latter two constitute less than 5 per cent of farmer households, and even for a large farmer household, average income per month is less than Rs 10,000. The average per hectare returns from cultivation was Rs 6,756 in kharif and Rs 9,290 in rabi. Across states, one observes relatively lower returns per hectare and greater share of expenses in Andhra Pradesh, Gujarat, Haryana, Karnataka, Maharashtra, Madhya Pradesh, Orissa, Rajasthan, and Tamil Nadu during kharif. This could be indicative of high costs or crop failure. The share of expenses in the value of output is less than 30 per cent in most of the hill states (Himachal Pradesh, Jammu and Kashmir, Jharkhand, and Uttarakhand) and the north-eastern states, indicating relatively less dependence on market-based inputs (Mishra 2007).

In 2002–3, the average returns from cultivation were Rs 11,259 per annum per household. If one increases this by one-third (which is on the higher side) to account for the drought of 2002–3, per capita per day returns to farmer households is less than Rs 8. Other sources become important, but only 60 per cent and 10 per cent of farmer households take to farm animals and non-farm business, respectively. The average monthly returns per farmer household from these two activities are Rs 85 and Rs 236, respectively. This reiterates that non-farm opportunities are limited and income of 83 per cent (94 per cent if one includes the semi-medium holdings also) of farmer households hardly suffices to meet their day-to-day requirements. Forty per cent of farmers indicated that they do not like farming as a profession. Of these, the most important reason given by more than two-thirds was its non-profitability and another two-fifths considered it risky (Mishra 2007).

Farmers' Suicides

Between 1995 and 2007, more than 200,000 farmers committed suicides, 83 per cent of them males. The suicide mortality rate (SMR, suicide death for 100,000 persons) for male farmers increased from 10.5 in 1995 to 18.2 in 2007, and that for male non-farmers increased from 12.4 to 14.1 (Figure 4.2).

An average for 2005–7 shows that the major states with male farmers' SMR higher than the national average of 18 are Kerala (275), Maharashtra (60), Chhattisgarh (54), Andhra Pradesh (38), Karnataka (34), West Bengal (22), and Tamil Nadu (21). Except for some recent media stories, high incidence of farmers' suicides in Chhattisgarh has remained outside the purview of public policy. What is much more

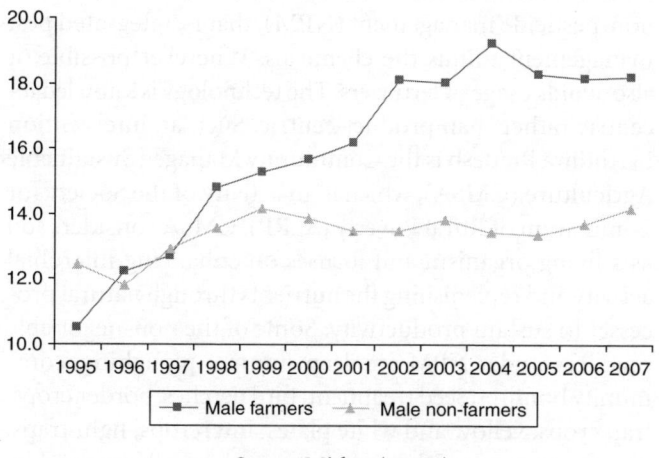

Source: Mishra (2009a).

Figure 4.2 Suicide Mortality Rate (SMR) for Male Farmers and Male Non-farmers in India, 1995–2007

important from the perspective of Chhattisgarh, as also a large part of central India, now under a Maoist–Security imbroglio, is the poor returns and absence of quality life for a vast majority. It is to be reiterated that suicide is a symptom of the larger crisis, and its absence does not in any way indicate the absence of a crisis. The increasing incidence of farmers' suicides is symptomatic of the agrarian crisis, but it is also a manifestation of the agricultural crisis. It indicates that for every farmer committing suicide, there are hundred thousands more in crisis. Further, the larger malaise or the agrarian/agricultural crisis is not just limited to regions reporting higher suicides. It is much more widespread (Mishra 2009a).

TECHNOLOGY AND INSTITUTIONAL ALTERNATIVES

One of the features of the current agrarian crisis is poor returns to cultivation. Technological interventions such as the green revolution meant for increasing production were neutral to land size in terms of output, but were not neutral in terms of resources, making it a costly imperative for marginal and small farmers. In recent years, a number of financial products too were introduced to address uncertainties, but more often than not, they ended up adding to rather than reducing risks (Mishra 2008, 2009b). The need of the hour is reducing costs.

Alternative Technology

Choice of technique, a la Sen (1960), refers to interventions that are either output-enhancing or input-saving. Farmers in many parts of world, including India, have been trying out or need to explore alternatives that reduce usage of input-intensive cultivation, and in the process, reduce costs and risks (World Bank 2007; McIntyre et al. 2009). One of this is non-pesticide management (NPM), that is, integrated pest management minus the chemicals. Wherever possible, it also avoids usage of fertilizers. The technology is knowledge-centric rather than product-centric. Such an intervention in Andhra Pradesh is the Community Managed Sustainable Agriculture (CMSA), which is an activity of the Society for Elimination of Rural Poverty (SERP). CMSA considers soil as a living organism and focuses on enhancing microbial activity and replenishing the nutrients through natural processes to sustain productivity. Some of the non-negotiable practices under NPM are deep summer ploughing, community bonfires, seed treatment, bird perches, border crops, trap crops, yellow and white plates, intercrops, light traps, pheromone traps, delta traps in groundnut, alleys in paddy, and cutting of the tips in paddy at the time of transplantation. Botanical extracts are applied as a last resort.

Under CMSA, a group of 15 to 20 farmers is organized to form farmer field schools. The group meets once every week for field-level observation, practice, and training ingrained in the understanding of ecological systems. The farmers learn the life cycle of pests as also predators, and develop a pest calendar. Pest management as also the problem of nitrogen fixation or other soil nutrient deficiencies are addressed through locally available resources that involve minimal expenditure, except for labour. Besides, efforts are made to encourage community seed banks, promote appropriate cropping and crop rotation, improve soil health through tank silt application, biomass plantation, encouraging local unemployed youth to start micro-enterprises for preparing inputs based on local resources, developing marketing networks, among others (SERP 2010).

Institutional Imperative

It is becoming increasingly clear that to successfully replicate such experiments among the large mass of marginal and small farmers requires, among other things, institutional arrangements. CMSA of SERP is showing the promise of replication: beginning with 400 acres in 2004–5, it covered 18.15 lakh acres of agricultural land in 2009–10, and aims to further increase its scale to 300 lakh acres in 2010–11 (SERP 2010). This has been possible because of the existing institutional structure—federation of self-help groups (SHGs) and the facilitating structure of SERP.

Personal interaction during field visits suggest that to begin with, SHGs were formed with about 15 women members, all the SHGs in the villages were federated to a village organization (VO), and these were further federated to *mandal smakhyas* (at the block level) and *zilla smakhyas* (at the district level). The organizational structure of the SERP had professionals based at the state, district, block, and village levels, helping in the facilitation of empowerment. The professionals were given autonomy while working under the aegis of the government. As most of the poor households came from agricultural backgrounds, the demand from the SHGs and the federated structure led to interventions in the form of community-managed sustainable agriculture. There are plans of forming farmer groups (field schools or farmers SHGs with a woman and a man as members from a household) at the village, mandal, and zilla levels that would work in tandem with the SHG federation structure.

Some of the lessons from this, as also other successful experiments like the Grameen Bank experience in Bangladesh and the Peoples Participation Programme of the Food and Agriculture Organization (FAO) particularly through the involvement of agriculture extension services in Sri Lanka, Thailand, and Zambia among others, are the following. The number of members in each group should be small (10–15 in SHGs or 20–25 in farmer groups). Members should be from homogenous backgrounds with common interests and similar resource base so as to reduce internal conflicts and enable them to function better compared to groups with heterogeneous membership. Groups should focus on solving common problems faced in the local conditions, instead of those identified by outsiders. The outside promoters like non-governmental organizations should take low-key presence and should enable the members of the group to take over soon. Developing sustainable small–marginal farmer groups that are also federated is a long-term process; there is need for a minimum of four to five years of training and capacity building. The use of specially trained resident farmer group organizers is fundamental to sustainable organizational structure. Formation of groups at the village level is only a first step. Building a sound organizational structure by federating groups from the village level upwards to block and district levels is fundamental to successful functioning of small–marginal and tenant farmers. Once the institutional structure is firmed up and capacity augmented, these organizations become self-sustaining and may diversify into other functions serving the small–marginal farming community (Rouse 1996; Reddy 2009).

While discussing the institutional imperative, it is worth pointing out six principles for successful bottom-up collectives, discussed by Agarwal (2010). These are: voluntary membership (there should be no coercion or compulsion); small size (around 15–20 members per group); socioeconomic homogeneity or social affinity among members; participatory decision making in production, decision, and management; checks and penalties for containing free riding and ensuring accountability; and group control of the returns and a fair distribution that has been transparently decided by the members. These principles also ascribe to the human rights approach to development. The SHG-based CMSA of SERP has been following some of these principles and is one of the many successful experiments. We have been citing this because of their proposed plans of scaling up the successes to cover 30 lakh acres in 2010–11.

CONCLUDING REMARKS

The persistence of distress in Indian agriculture has two intertwined dimensions—the agricultural and the agrarian. On the one hand, there is an agricultural developmental crisis arising out of poor designing of programmes and inadequate allocation of resources. This has adversely affected the production and productivity. Withdrawal of the state, manifested in insufficient public investments, poor availability of credit, and the failure of research and extension to address the needs of dry land/rain-fed agriculture, increased the risk and vulnerability in farming. On the other hand, there is an agrarian crisis threatening the mass of small–marginal farmers and agricultural labourers. The ratio of share of employment in agriculture to share of agricultural GDP is increasing. Incidence of calorie poor is higher than expenditure poor among cultivators and agricultural labourers, and the average calorie and protein consumption among farmers and agricultural labourers has been decreasing. The irony is that the hands that produce food do not get adequate amounts to consume. A symptom of the larger crisis is the increasing incidence of farmers' suicides.

To revive farming as also the farmer, it is necessary to have alternative technology and institutional structures. There is a need to do away with input-intensive cultivation in favour of cost-reducing knowledge-centric technology that builds on local resources and further strengthens the existing social capital. The latter is possible through structures that empower the farmers at the grassroots and organize them into federations so that they can aggregate different things at different levels. In short, the need of the hour is innovation in institutions (like federation of SHGs), government structure that facilitates empowerment (not the current line departments that have become burdened under their own weight), and technologies that reduce costs/risks (not the input-intensive production practices) if we have to revive farming and save farmers. And the successful experiments indicate that this is possible.

REFERENCES

Agarwal, Bina (2010), 'Rethinking Agricultural Production Collectives', *Economic and Political Weekly*, 45(9): 64–78.

Bhaduri, Amit (2008), 'Predatory Growth', *Economic and Political Weekly*, 43(16): 10–14.

Boyce, James K. (1986), 'Kinked Exponential Models for Growth Rate Estimation', *Oxford Bulletin of Economics and Statistics*, 48(4): 385–91.

Government of India (2007), *Report of the Expert Group on Agricultural Indebtedness*, Ministry of Finance, New Delhi.

——— (2009), *Compendium of Selected Indicators of Indian Economy, Special Issue of Time Series Data—Volume I, Economic Sector*, Ministry of Statistics and Programme Implementation, New Delhi.

McIntyre, Beverly D., Hans R. Herren, Judi Wakhungu, and Robert T. Watson (eds) (2009), *Agriculture at Crossroads: Global Report*. Washington D.C.: International Assessment of Agricultural Knowledge, Science and Technology for Development (IAAKSTD).

Mishra, Srijit (2007), 'Agrarian Scenario in Post-reform India: A Story of Distress, Despair and Death', *Orissa Economic Journal*, 39(1&2): 53–84.

——— (2008), 'Risks, Farmers' Suicides and Agrarian Crisis in India: Is There a Way Out?', *Indian Journal of Agricultural Economics*, 63(1): 38–54.

————— (2009a), 'Farmers' Suicides in India: Some Trends and Patterns', paper presented at the International Seminar on 'Multi Disciplinary Perspectives on Suicide: The Experience of SAARC Countries', 9–10 January, Centre for Economic and Social Studies, Hyderabad.

————— (2009b), 'Agrarian Crisis and Farmers' Suicides in India', revised version of paper presented at a one-day international seminar, 'Environmental Degradation and Food Crisis—Lessons for India', 24 October 2008, India International Centre, New Delhi, Greenpeace India.

National Sample Survey Organisation (NSSO) (1996), *Nutritional Intake in India, NSS 50th Round (July 1993–June 1994)*, Report No. 405. New Delhi: Department of Statistics, Government of India.

————— (2007), *Nutritional Intake in India, NSS 61st Round (July 2004–June 2005)*, Report No. 513 (61/1.0/6). New Delhi: Ministry of Statistics and Programme Inmplementation, Government of India.

Reddy, D. Narasimha (2009), 'Initiatives in Group Based Approaches to Strengthen the Economy of Small and Marginal Farmers in Andhra Pradesh', mimeo.

Reddy, D. Narasimha and Srijit Mishra (eds) (2009), *Agrarian Crisis in India*. New Delhi: Oxford University Press.

Reserve Bank of India (2006), *Report of the Working Group to Suggest Measures to Assist Distressed Farmers*, Rural Planning and Credit Department, Mumbai.

Rouse, Jon (1996), 'Organising for Extension: FAO Experiences in Small Farmer Group Development', Sustainable Development Department, Food and Agriculture Organization, Rome.

Sen, A.K. (1960), *Choice of Techniques: An Aspect of the Theory of Planned Economic Development*. Oxford: Basil Blackwell.

SERP (Society for Elimination of Rural Poverty) (2010), 'Brief Note about Community Managed Sustainable Agriculture', SERP, Hyderabad. Available at http://www.serp.ap.gov.in/CMSA/aboutus.jsp (accessed on 19 November 2010).

Shetty, S.L. (2009), 'Agricultural Credit and Indebtedness: Ground Realities and Policy Perspectives', in D. Narasimha Reddy and Srijit Mishra (eds), *Agrarian Crisis in India*. New Delhi: Oxford University Press, pp. 61–86.

World Bank (2007), *World Development Report 2008: Agriculture for Development*. Washington D.C.: World Bank.

5

Poverty and Inequality in the Age of Economic Liberalization

Sripad Motiram and Vamsi Vakulabharanam

INTRODUCTION

For many social scientists and intelligent lay observers, a defining aspect of the world today is the emergence of India (along with China) as a powerful entity. This perception is largely shaped by the huge size of the Indian economy and the high growth rates that it has been witnessing in recent times. There is considerable debate about when the Indian economy really took off, the causes behind this growth, and the role played by the economic reforms initiated in 1990–1.[1] However, there is no doubt that compared to international standards and its own historical experience, India has been growing at impressive rates since the mid-1980s.[2]

In this chapter, we understand this growth process by focusing on two aspects, namely, poverty and inequality.

Our focus on poverty reduction, we believe, needs no justification. However, it is worthwhile to point out that poverty reduction played an important role in motivating these reforms. In fact, poverty reduction has been an important factor behind most major policy initiatives in India, and has been a touchstone for evaluating them. Our focus on poverty reduction is to a certain extent motivated by these observations. Our focus on inequality is dictated both by a belief that inequality is not only intrinsically important (especially in its ethical dimensions), but could also have functional implications, for example, by affecting further growth or poverty alleviation. We are not alone in this perspective towards distributional considerations in the Indian context—these two views towards inequality have played an important role in shaping policies since independence (Chakravarty 1987, chapter 2).

In the following discussion, we document and analyse changes in poverty and inequality in roughly the past two-and-half decades, primarily by using the National Sample Survey (NSS) data. Although we cannot (and therefore do not) provide causal linkages, we do suggest some mechanisms through which economic liberalization might have led to the patterns in poverty and inequality that we document. We also briefly discuss the policy implications of our findings. Given the importance of these issues, considerable

---

[1] See Sen (2007) for a discussion of the various positions in this debate.

[2] In terms of gross domestic product (GDP) at purchasing power parity (PPP), India ranked fifth in the world in 1980 and fourth in the world (behind US, China, and Japan) in 2003. Among large economies (above $100 billion 2001 PPP), in terms of growth of GDP, India ranked twelfth in the period 1991–5 and fourth in the period 1996–2001. These figures are from Bery and Singh (2007) and are based upon the World Development Indicators CD ROM. In the 1990s, Indian per capita GDP grew at the rate of 4.1 per cent per annum, which was somewhat higher than the same in the 1980s (3.3 per cent) but substantially higher than the same in the 1950s (1.7 per cent), 1960s (1.2 per cent), and the 1970s (1.1 per cent) (Dreze and Sen 2002: 316).

literature has already accumulated on poverty and inequality in India since economic liberalization. We attempt to both synthesize this literature and to provide a new perspective based upon our analysis.

Our main conclusion is that poverty reduction has occurred since the onset of economic reforms, but poverty continues to be high, and the rate of reduction was much higher in the 1980s (i.e., before the liberalization policies were introduced on a grand scale), when growth rates were comparable. Moreover, the qualitative features of poverty have not seen a significant change. This could be due to the fact that although growth has occurred since the reforms, it has been accompanied by an increase in disparities on several dimensions—the growth process has been uneven and disequalizing.

The remaining part of the chapter is divided into three sections. The next section analyses poverty, the third section analyses inequality, and the final section concludes with a discussion of the findings.

POVERTY—ESTIMATES AND CHARACTERISTICS

In this section, we will describe the changes that have occurred in poverty over the past two decades. We will first provide quantitative estimates of poverty and changes in these. We will then present a more detailed profile of poverty by examining poverty among various socio-economic groups, classes, and occupational categories. Finally, we will look at the issue of growth vis-à-vis poverty reduction.

To compute estimates of poverty, we use data from the 38th, 50th, and 61st rounds of the NSS consumption expenditure surveys conducted in 1983, 1993–4, and 2004–5, respectively. The choice of these rounds is dictated by the consideration that this will give us an opportunity to examine poverty roughly a decade before and after the economic reforms. Fortunately, the Uniform Recall Period (URP)[3] consumption data from the 61st round is comparable to data from the previous rounds, and therefore we do not need to address the issues raised in the literature on the comparability of surveys (for references, see Sen and Himanshu 2004a, 2004b). Table 5.1 presents the Head Count Ratio (HCR) and the Poverty Gap Ratio (PGR)[4]

for rural and urban areas for major states and at the all-India level.[5]

As we can observe from Table 5.1, poverty continues to be high, but after the economic reforms it has declined in both rural and urban areas, both at the all-India level and for most of the major states. However, this is not a new phenomenon—poverty has been declining since the 1970s after increasing earlier (Dreze and Sen 2002, Table A6). So, what is relevant for our purposes is how the rate of poverty reduction during the period of economic reforms compares to the same in the previous period. We can compute the rate of poverty reduction in a simple manner, by dividing the change in HCR during a given period by the length of the period.[6] Using this method, we can see that the rates of rural (urban) poverty reduction for the periods 1983 to 1993–4 and 1993–4 to 2004–5 are 0.95 per cent (0.98 per cent) and 0.81 per cent (0.64 per cent), respectively. We can note that both in rural and urban areas, the rate of poverty reduction was lower in the latter period. Given the unprecedented growth that India experienced in this period, one would have expected and liked to see a higher rate of poverty reduction (more on this in the following).

While the aforementioned presents an all-India picture, to get a better insight into poverty, we need a disaggregated view. Considering different states, we can note that there is substantial variation in poverty and poverty reduction rates. However, in a majority of the states, both in rural and urban areas, the rate of poverty reduction was much higher in the pre-reform period. States that have done remarkably well in poverty reduction in the post-reform period are Assam, Himachal Pradesh, Haryana, and Bihar in rural areas and Tamil Nadu, Gujarat, and Andhra Pradesh in urban areas.

Continuing on the theme of disaggregation, Table 5.2 presents poverty measures for various social groups and occupational categories. In the 38th and the 50th rounds we have information only on whether a household belongs to Scheduled Caste (SC), Scheduled Tribe (ST), or others, whereas in the 61st round, Other Backward Classes (OBCs)

---

[3] The URP data is based upon a uniform 30-day recall period for all the items. On the contrary, Mixed Recall Period (MRP) data is based upon a 365-day recall period for five infrequently consumed non-food items (clothing, footwear, durable goods, education, and institutional medical expenses) and a 30-day recall period for the other items.

[4] We do not present estimates of higher order Foster–Greer–Thorbeck (FGT) measures to keep matters simple. They are available upon request from the authors.

[5] After the writing of this chapter, the expert group appointed to review the methodology for estimating poverty submitted its report, which is available at http://www.planningcommission.gov.in/eg_poverty.htm. According to these revised estimates, in 2004–5, rural and urban poverty stood at 41.8 per cent and 25.7 per cent, respectively. The corresponding figures for 1993–4 are 50.1 per cent and 31.8 per cent, respectively. We can observe that in rural areas, the revised estimates are higher than our estimates (reported in Table 5.1). However, our estimates and these revised estimates reveal the same (decreasing) trend between 1993–4 and 2004–5. Moreover, the quantum of decrease, and therefore the rate of poverty reduction, are roughly the same.

[6] This is consistent with the literature (e.g., Himanshu 2007). An implicit assumption here is that poverty changes uniformly.

are also enumerated. To make the comparison consistent, for the 61st round, we adopt the same classification as in the other rounds. We can observe that at the all-India level for rural areas, STs are the poorest group in terms of incidence of poverty. They also have the lowest average monthly per capita expenditure (MPCE). They are followed by the SCs, non-SC/ST Muslims, non-SC/ST Hindus, and others. It is worth noting that in all the periods, in both rural and urban India, Muslims are poorer than both other Hindus and others, which is consistent with the findings of the Sachar Committee

on the status of Muslims in India. While poverty has reduced for all groups, poverty rates continue to be high, especially for the STs and SCs. It is also worthwhile to point out that except for Muslims in rural areas and SCs in urban areas, the rates of poverty reduction were higher in the pre-reform period.

To understand the relationship between poverty and agrarian class position, we divide people in rural areas into eight classes—large farmers, medium farmers, small farmers, marginal farmers, agricultural labourers, self-employed in non-agriculture, other labourers, and others. The results

Table 5.1 Poverty and Poverty Reduction Rates

	HCR			PGR			Rate 1	Rate 2
	1983	1993–4	2004–5	1983	1993–4	2004–5		
Rural								
Andhra Pradesh	26.8	15.9	10.5	5.9	2.9	1.9	−1.09	−0.49
Assam	43.3	45.2	22.1	8.4	8.3	3.6	0.19	−2.10
Bihar	64.9	58	42.6	20.2	14.7	8.1	−0.69	−1.33
Chhattisgarh			40.8			9.2		
Gujarat	29.4	22.2	18.9	6.2	4.1	3.3	−0.72	−0.30
Haryana	22.4	28.3	13.2	4.9	5.6	2.3	0.59	−1.37
Himachal Pradesh	17.8	30.4	10.5	4.5	5.6	1.6	1.26	−1.81
Jammu and Kashmir	27.4	18.2	4.3	5	3.2	0.6	−0.92	−1.26
Jharkhand			46.2			9.9		
Karnataka	36.2	30.1	20.7	9.8	6.3	2.9	−0.61	−0.85
Kerala	39.8	25.4	13.2	10.2	5.6	2.8	−1.44	−1.11
Madhya Pradesh	49.7	40.7	36.8	13.7	9.5	8	−0.90	−0.25
Maharashtra	46	37.9	29.6	12.1	9.3	6.3	−0.81	−0.75
Orissa	68.4	49.8	46.9	22.7	12	12.1	−1.86	−0.26
Punjab	14.4	11.7	9	3.3	1.9	1.2	−0.27	−0.25
Rajasthan	38.6	26.4	18.3	14.6	5.2	3	−1.22	−0.74
Tamil Nadu	56.7	32.9	23	20.9	7.3	3.8	−2.38	−0.90
Uttarakhand			40.6			7.8		
Uttar Pradesh	47.2	42.3	33.3	12.5	10.4	6.3	−0.49	−0.79
West Bengal	63.8	41.2	28.4	21.2	8.3	5.3	−2.26	−1.16
All-India	46.7	37.2	28.3	13.4	8.5	5.7	−0.95	−0.81
Urban								
Andhra Pradesh	38	38.8	27.4	10.1	9.3	5.7	0.08	−1.04
Assam	22.1	7.9	3.6	4.4	0.9	0.5	−1.42	−0.39
Bihar	48.9	34.8	36.1	13.6	7.9	7.4	−1.41	0.12
Chhattisgarh			42.2			12.3		
Gujarat	41.4	28.3	13.3	10.1	6.2	2.4	−1.31	−1.36
Haryana	28.1	16.5	14.5	6	3	3.3	−1.16	−0.18
Himachal Pradesh	12.6	9.3	3.2	3.8	1.2	0.9	−0.33	−0.55
Jammu and Kashmir	17.5	5.1	7.4	3.3	1	1.7	−1.24	0.21
Jharkhand			20.3			4.3		

(Continued)

Table 5.1 *Continued*

	HCR			PGR			Rate 1	Rate 2
	1983	1993–4	2004–5	1983	1993–4	2004–5		
Karnataka	43	39.9	32.6	13.4	11.4	8.7	−0.31	−0.66
Kerala	45.7	24.3	20	13.8	5.5	4.5	−2.14	−0.39
Madhya Pradesh	53.7	48.1	42.7	15	13.4	12.1	−0.56	−0.50
Maharashtra	41	35	32.1	12.2	10.1	9.1	−0.60	−0.26
Orissa	49.7	40.6	44.7	13.8	11.4	13.4	−0.91	0.37
Punjab	23.5	10.9	6.3	6.5	1.7	0.7	−1.26	−0.42
Rajasthan	38.5	31	32.3	11.1	7	7.2	−0.75	0.12
Tamil Nadu	50.8	39.9	22.5	15.5	10.2	4.7	−1.09	−1.58
Uttarakhand			36.5			8.5		
Uttar Pradesh	51.1	35.1	30.1	14.4	9	7.1	−1.60	−0.42
West Bengal	33.4	22.9	13.5	8.8	4.5	2.5	−1.05	−0.85
All-India	42.4	32.6	25.6	11.9	8	6.1	−0.98	−0.64

Source: Authors' calculations.

Notes: (i) HCR: Head Count Ratio; PGR: Poverty Gap Ratio. Both these are in percentages.

(ii) State-level HCR and PGR are calculated based upon state-wise poverty lines set by the Planning Commission. All-India HCR and PGR are calculated based upon the all-India poverty line. The URL: http://planningcommission.nic.in/reports/genrep/nhdrep/nhdtstatapx.pdf lists poverty lines for 1983 and 1993–4. The 2004–5 poverty lines can be found at: http://planningcommission.nic.in/news/prmar07.pdf (both URLs accessed on 27 June 2009).

(iii) Rate 1: (HCR in 1993–4 – HCR in 1983)/10—Rate of poverty reduction in the period 1983 to 1993–4.

Rate 2: (HCR in 2004–5 – HCR in 1993–94)/11—Rate of poverty reduction in the period 1993–4 to 2004–5.

Both rates are expressed as percentage points per year.

Jharkhand, Chhattisgarh, and Uttarakhand were carved out of Bihar, Madhya Pradesh, and Uttar Pradesh, respectively after 1993–4. Hence, to compute Rate 2 for Bihar, we recalculated the HCR in 2004–5 for Bihar after including Jharkhand and used this figure. A similar procedure was used for Madhya Pradesh and Uttar Pradesh.

are quite intuitive—in general, poverty rates increase as we move down the class hierarchy (i.e., from large farmers to agricultural labourers). Those self-employed in non-agricultural occupations are generally better off than those at the lower rungs of agrarian class hierarchy (marginal farmers and agricultural labourers). Non-agricultural labourers are better off than their counterparts in agriculture. For all rural classes, poverty has declined, but only for large farmers is the rate of poverty reduction higher post-reforms. This is consistent both with the story of a rural distress that has enveloped India since the economic reforms (most dramatically reflected by the suicides of thousands of farmers) and the idea that large farmers were able (at least to a certain extent) to protect themselves from its effects.[7]

For urban areas, we do not adopt an elaborate classification similar to the one in rural areas. Instead, we stick with the employment categories provided in the NSS surveys.[8]

Doing so, and ignoring the residual category (i.e., others), we can observe that poverty is highest among casual labourers, followed by the self-employed and then by the salaried group. It is worth noting that the self-employed in urban areas could include professionals (doctors, lawyers, etc.) and those working in the urban informal sector. Hence, to shed more light on this, we examine poverty rates among various occupational categories using the National Classification of Occupations (NCO). For the 61st Round, poverty (at 43.9 per cent) is highest among Group 9 ('Elementary Occupations', e.g., street food vendors, garbage collectors, and porters) and lowest (at 7.4 per cent) among Group 1 ('legislators, senior officials, and managers').

From Tables 5.1 and 5.2, we can see that although poverty has decreased over time, the rankings of various socio-economic groups and classes have been preserved. In other words, certain groups (STs, SCs, landless agricultural labourers in rural areas, and casual labourers in urban areas) continue to share the brunt of poverty. We now come to the crucial issue of the relationship between growth and poverty reduction. Given the high growth rates that India has been experiencing since the initiation of economic reforms, optimism was expressed that this growth would somehow 'trickle down'.

[7] We have explored these issues in detail in an earlier paper, Vakulabharanam and Motiram (2011).

[8] In the 38th round, there were only two categories in urban areas —self-employed and the others. So, we do not present results for this round, or compare it with the other rounds.

Table 5.2 Poverty, Poverty Reduction Rates, and MPCE for Various Groups

	HCR			MPCE			Rate 1	Rate 2
	1983	1993–4	2004–5	1983	1993–4	2004–5		
Rural								
Social Group								
ST	64.5	52.0	47.6	86.61	234.37	426.29	−1.2	−0.4
SC	59.2	48.3	36.8	93.23	238.91	474.72	−1.1	−1.0
Hindu (Non-ST/SC)	41.0	30.5	22.1	118.88	302.17	599.32	−1.0	−0.8
Muslim (Non-ST/SC)	47.9	41.2	29.2	105.87	266.96	546.06	−0.7	−1.1
Others	25.9	14.5	6.0	157.24	426.81	1,006.95	−1.1	−0.8
Class								
Large Farmer	19.1	15.0	7.0	156.93	392.29	870.12	−0.4	−0.7
Medium Farmer	33.9	24.2	16.3	130.94	325.93	635.56	−1.0	−0.7
Small Farmer	41.7	31.2	22.4	112.90	288.65	565.51	−1.1	−0.8
Marginal Farmer	46.0	33.6	25.6	109.16	281.11	544.23	−1.2	−0.7
Agricultural Labourer	65.9	56.6	46.3	85.07	217.95	415.81	−0.9	−0.9
Non-agricultural Self-employed	44.1	32.2	23.5	112.72	295.24	604.41	−1.2	−0.8
Non-agricultural Labourer	48.5	39.7	30.4	110.21	266.74	519.81	−0.9	−0.8
Others	29.5	17.6	14.0	142.81	384.20	818.36	−1.2	−0.3
Urban								
Social Group								
ST	53.3	40.7	33.9	135.37	380.54	857.46	−1.3	−0.6
SC	56.9	49.8	39.8	127.06	342.18	758.38	−0.7	−0.9
Hindu (Non-ST/SC)	36.5	25.8	18.7	175.56	498.43	1,172.19	−1.1	−0.6
Muslim (Non-ST/SC)	58.2	49.2	41.4	126.02	349.88	776.41	−0.9	−0.7
Others	27.4	13.6	5.9	212.76	668.96	1,628.68	−1.4	−0.7
Occupation								
Self-employed		36.2	27.7		427.96	982.35		−0.8%
Regular Wage		20.9	15.3		531.68	1,212.65		−0.5%
Casual Labour		62.6	57.0		276.99	579.63		−0.5%
Others		26.5	16.1		535.48	1,444.97		−0.9%

Source: Authors' calculations.

Notes: (i) HCR in percentages. Nominal MPCE in Rs Rate 1 and Rate 2 as in Table 5.1.

(ii) Definitions: Large farmers (self-employed in agriculture, land possessed >10 hectares); medium farmers (self-employed in agriculture, land possessed between 2 and 10 hectares); small farmers (self-employed in agriculture, land possessed between 1 and 2 hectares); marginal farmers (self-employed in agriculture, land possessed between 0 and 1 hectare); agricultural labourers (self-employed in agriculture with no land or who define themselves as agricultural labourers).

(iii) In the 38th Round of NSS (1983), in urban areas, there were only two categories: self-employed and others. So, we do not present poverty rates and rate of poverty reduction involving this round for urban areas.

To get a perspective on this issue, we look at the relationship between the rate of growth of per capita real net state domestic product (NSDP) for various states and their rates of poverty reduction. Figures 5.1 (a) and (b) presents the relevant scatter plots. For rural poverty rates, we can observe that there is almost no relationship (correlation coefficient of –0.08) and for urban poverty rates, there is a weak relationship (correlation coefficient of 0.51). When we look at the relationship between growth rate of real MPCE and rate of

poverty reduction, the correlations are somewhat better, but still quite moderate: 0.57 and 0.52, for rural and urban areas, respectively.[9] While these figures do not conclusively establish

[9] Real MPCE is at 2006–7 values. In rural areas, we computed this by using the Consumer Price Index for Agricultural Labourers (CPIAL), and for urban areas we used the Consumer Price Index for Industrial Workers (CPIW). CPIAL and CPIW values were obtained from the Reserve Bank of India data base on the Indian economy on 25 July 2009.

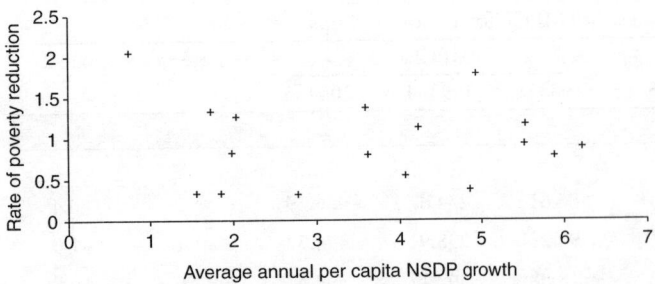

Figure 5.1(a) Relationship between Growth and Poverty Reduction (Rural)

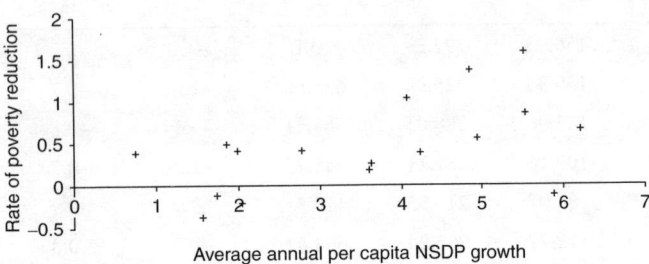

Notes: The real per capita NSDP data (at 1993–4 prices) was taken from the EPW Research Foundation on 25 July 2009. Data is available for all states till 1999–2000, so we compute the growth rate between 1993 and 2000.

Figure 5.1(b) Relationship between Growth and Poverty Reduction (Urban)

that growth did not trickle down, they do suggest that the links between growth and poverty reduction are somewhat weak.

Overall, one can argue that since the economic reforms, poverty has decreased, although it continues to be at a high level. Moreover, the rate of poverty reduction is lower than that in the 1980s. Different sections (caste groups, classes, etc.) of the Indian society have fared differently. The qualitative nature of poverty has not witnessed a transformation, that is, the relative positions of various sections (caste groups, classes, rural–urban, etc.) have roughly remained the same. If we locate this in the context of the growth experience of India in the 1990s, achievements on the poverty reduction front seem at best modest.[10] A simple explanation suggests itself for this—although growth has occurred, it has disproportionately benefited some sections of the society. This is an issue that we address in the following.

[10] In the interests of space, we have not discussed nutrition and access to food in the post-reform period. According to NSS (2007), between the periods 1993–4 and 2004–5, average intake of calories dropped by 4.9 per cent from 2,153 to 2,047 kcal/day in rural India and by 2.5 per cent from 2,071 to 2,020 kcal/day in urban India. Moreover, the intake of many nutrients (fats being an exception) has also seen a decrease. On the face of it, these figures suggest that malnutrition has increased. However, this question is far from settled. See Deaton and Dreze (2008) for a detailed discussion of the debate and the issues involved.

THE MANY DIMENSIONS OF INEQUALITY

In this section, we will look at the changes that have taken place in inequality as measured on several dimensions. At the outset, it is worthwhile to point out that researchers face certain limitations while using NSS surveys (which we will continue to rely on) to analyse inequality. Some of these have been discussed in Jayadev et al. (2007a, 2007b) in the context of wealth inequality, but are applicable to inequality in general. Essentially, the rich/wealthy are likely to be under-represented in the sample and/or are likely to undervalue their expenditure, wealth, etc. The NSS survey design does not adequately address these issues. Since the distributions of most economic variables of interest (e.g., income, expenditure, and wealth) are usually unequal, a systematic under-representation or undervaluation of the upper tail of the distribution will lead to an underestimation of inequality. Moreover, when we are interested in analysing changes in inequality, we do not know in which direction the bias might lie since inequality is underestimated in both the initial and final periods. This is not as severe a problem with poverty measurement (which focuses on the lower tail of the distribution) or in the computation of averages, where we could use the median (which is less sensitive to the presence or absence of outliers). This has to be kept in mind while interpreting the results that follow.

We will first examine inequality in MPCE. Vakulabharanam (2010) analyses this issue and we reproduce findings from his study in the following. Table 5.3 presents inequality in MPCE for major states and at an all-India level for both rural and urban areas. We can observe that for most states, inequality was decreasing between 1983 and 1993–4, although the decrease was slight. However, this trend was reversed between 1993–4 and 2004–5. At the all-India level, the rural, urban, and total Gini coefficients roughly remained the same between 1983 and 1993–4. On the contrary, between the periods 1993–4 and 2004–5, there was a perceptible increase in the total Gini, mostly driven by changes in urban inequality.

An examination of expenditure deciles is more insightful. In 1983, the average person in the poorest decile had a consumption of 56.64 per cent of the median and this figure increased to 56.67 per cent in 1993–4. This increasing trend was reversed in 2004–5, when the figure fell to 56.32 per cent. At the upper tail of the distribution, the ratio of the 90th percentile to the median decreased from 215.66 per cent in 1983 to 212.63 per cent in 1993–4, but then increased to 235.20 per cent in 2004–5.

The modest changes in inequality that are revealed by the Gini could hide more interesting patterns, which can be revealed by a decomposition exercise. The most commonly used measures for decomposition are the mean log

Table 5.3   Gini Index of MPCE in India

	1983			1993–4			2004–5		
	Rural	Urban	Total	Rural	Urban	Total	Rural	Urban	Total
Andhra Pradesh	0.31	0.36	0.33	0.29	0.32	0.31	0.29	0.38	0.35
Assam	0.23	0.31	0.25	0.18	0.29	0.22	0.20	0.32	0.24
Bihar	0.26	0.31	0.27	0.22	0.31	0.25	0.21	0.33	0.24
Chhattisgarh							0.30	0.44	0.37
Gujarat	0.26	0.28	0.28	0.24	0.29	0.28	0.27	0.31	0.33
Haryana	0.29	0.29	0.29	0.31	0.28	0.31	0.34	0.37	0.36
Himachal Pradesh	0.27	0.29	0.28	0.28	0.46	0.32	0.31	0.32	0.33
Jammu and Kashmir	0.30	0.28	0.30	0.24	0.29	0.27	0.25	0.25	0.26
Jharkhand							0.23	0.36	0.31
Karnataka	0.30	0.34	0.33	0.27	0.32	0.31	0.27	0.37	0.36
Kerala	0.32	0.37	0.33	0.30	0.34	0.32	0.38	0.41	0.39
Madhya Pradesh	0.29	0.33	0.32	0.28	0.33	0.32	0.27	0.40	0.35
Maharashtra	0.31	0.35	0.36	0.31	0.36	0.38	0.31	0.38	0.39
Orissa	0.27	0.31	0.29	0.25	0.31	0.28	0.29	0.35	0.32
Punjab	0.30	0.29	0.30	0.28	0.28	0.29	0.29	0.40	0.35
Rajasthan	0.32	0.35	0.33	0.27	0.29	0.28	0.25	0.37	0.30
Tamil Nadu	0.33	0.36	0.36	0.31	0.35	0.34	0.32	0.36	0.38
Uttarakhand							0.29	0.33	0.31
Uttar Pradesh	0.29	0.34	0.31	0.28	0.33	0.30	0.29	0.37	0.33
West Bengal	0.26	0.35	0.31	0.25	0.34	0.31	0.27	0.38	0.35
All-India	0.30	0.35	0.33	0.29	0.34	0.33	0.30	0.38	0.36

Source: Authors' calculations.

deviation and the Theil, both of which belong to the single parameter entropy family of inequality measures.[11] Using these measures, if we decompose inequality based upon the sub-groups of the population that we are interested in (e.g., caste groups, states, and gender), we obtain 'within' and 'between' components. The former is a weighted average of the inequalities within sub-groups, whereas the latter is the inequality between (or among) sub-groups. For example, if we consider decomposition on the basis of rural and urban sectors, total inequality is the sum of two components: (i) a weighted average of the inequality within rural and urban areas and (ii) inequality between rural and urban areas. Decomposition using the Gini is more complicated since the 'within' component involves overlapping indices for each sub-group, which measure the extent to which the distribution of a sub-group lies within

the distribution of the population.[12] Both the 'between' and 'within' components are interesting since they can both contribute to changes in inequality. However, we focus on the former because we are interested in changes in inequality between (or among) sub-groups—an increase in this component in absolute terms implies that inequality between sub-groups has increased, and vice-versa. An increase in the contribution of this component to overall inequality implies that inequality between sub-groups has become more important.

Decomposing mean log deviation and Theil for MPCE on the basis of sectors (rural and urban) and states indicates that the between component has grown in importance in the post-reform period on both these dimensions. Decomposing the Gini on the rural–urban axis, we can note that the percentage of total inequality that is contributed by inequality between rural and urban areas has been

[11] For a detailed discussion of these and an application, see Shorrocks and Wan (2004).

[12] See Frick et al. (2006) for a detailed discussion of Gini decomposition and an explanation of these components.

increasing since 1983, and there has been a sharp jump in the period 1993–4 to 2004–5. A similar phenomenon can be observed when we decompose using states as sub-groups.[13] These results are consistent with the view from casual empiricism, media reports, and scholarly work that disparities of various kinds have been accentuated in recent times. We have explored the issue of an increase in rural–urban inequality in detail elsewhere (Vakulabharanam and Motiram 2011), but it is worthwhile to present some figures here. The ratio of urban to rural mean MPCE increased from 1.47 in 1983 to 1.63 in 1993–4, and further increased to 1.88 in 2004–5.

We now turn to another dimension, namely, wealth, on which disparities have manifested themselves, in fact in a more dramatic fashion. Jayadev et al. (2007a, 2007b) present a comprehensive analysis of wealth and changes in wealth inequality in the period of economic reforms using the NSS AIDIS (All-India Debt and Investment Survey) for 1991 and 2002. They use two notions of wealth: total assets per capita and net worth (the difference between assets and liabilities) per capita. Using either of these measures, there has been an increase in wealth in both rural and urban areas during 1991–2002. Median rural (urban) real per capita net worth increased from Rs 9,988 (Rs 10,991) in 1991 to Rs 12,720 (Rs 14,569) in 2002, the implied annual growth rate being 2.5 per cent (2.9 per cent). Median rural (urban) real per capita total assets increased from Rs 10,251 (Rs 11,348) in 1991 to Rs 13,184 (Rs 15,233) in 2002, the implied annual growth rate being 2.6 per cent (3.0 per cent).

Wealth inequality (as measured by both per capita net worth and per capita total assets) increased between 1991 and 2002. The Gini coefficient for per capita total net worth increased from 0.64 in 1991 to 0.66 in 2002. The corresponding figures for per capita total assets are 0.64 and 0.65, respectively. The Lorenz curves for per capita net worth reveal that between 1991 and 2002, there has been a small but perceptible decrease in the shares of wealth held by all quantiles (e.g., quintiles, deciles, percentiles), revealing that there has been an unambiguous increase in wealth inequality. An examination of wealth quantiles reveals a more dramatic picture. In 1991, the per capita total assets held by the 90th, 95th, and 99th percentiles as a percentage of the median were 479 per cent, 758 per cent, and 1851 per cent, respectively. In 2002, these already high values increased to 515 per cent, 814 per cent, and 1958 per cent, respectively. A similar picture is revealed by examining per capita net worth. The corresponding figures for per capita net worth are 482 per cent, 766 per cent, and

1886 per cent in 1991 and 522 per cent, 824 per cent, and 2012 per cent in 2002. Motiram et al. (2008) present a decomposition exercise on the basis of sector (rural vis-à-vis urban), caste, and state using three different measures of inequality (log mean deviation, Theil, and Gini). The main finding is that the between component of inequality has increased during 1991–2002 on all these dimensions, although it is small compared to total inequality.

Finally, we examine inequality in income using the Indian Human Development Survey conducted by the National Council of Applied Economic Research (NCAER) in 1994 and 2004–5. The 1994 survey focused only on rural India whereas the 2004–5 survey covered both rural and urban India. The Gini of per capita income was 0.43 in rural India in 1994 (Shariff 1999), but it increased to 0.50 in 2004–5 (Singh 2009). In 2004–5, the urban and total Ginis stood at 0.47 and 0.51, respectively. The ratio of the income of the average person in the 10th percentile to the median is 38.89 per cent whereas the ratio of the income of the average person in the 90th percentile to the median is 347.60 per cent.

Table 5.4 presents all the aforementioned results together. Overall, data of various kinds (consumption expenditure, wealth, and income) indicate that when we examine complete measures of inequality like the Gini, there has been a small increase in inequality, whereas focusing on the relative expenditure/wealth/income held by the upper or lower tail of the distribution indicates a much larger increase in inequality. Moreover, inequality on several dimensions (e.g., rural–urban, state, and caste) has also grown. Given the limitations of the survey design that we talked about earlier, we strongly believe that both the inequality estimates and the changes in inequality are underestimates of their true values. This has to be also seen in the context of other evidence that has accumulated regarding the uneven nature of the growth process in India. For example, Dreze and Sen (2002, chapter 9) discuss differential performance of the various sectors (agricultural, industrial, and service) since the reforms. They also present evidence for inter-state disparities in growth rates (p. 319).

DISCUSSION AND CONCLUSIONS

Writing in the late 1980s, a few years before the economic reforms were initiated, Chakaravarty (1987) offerd an incisive analysis of the successes and limitations of the Indian policy framework that was in place since independence. In his opinion, poverty reduction did not meet the expectations of policymakers. According to him, stepping into the 1990s, a key problem that India had on its hands concerned the viability of small farms (Ibid., p. 87). It is ironic that roughly two decades later, these issues are still confronting Indian policymakers—in fact they have become more pressing.

[13] The contributions of rural–urban inequality to total inequality in 1983, 1993–4, and 2004–5 were 10.46 per cent, 13.75 per cent, and 19.85 per cent, respectively. The corresponding figures for inter-state inequality were 8.29 per cent, 10.54 per cent, and 14.04 per cent.

Table 5.4 A Summary of Inequality Comparisons

	MPCE			Wealth		Income	
	1983	1993–4	2004–5	1991	2002	1994	2004–5
Rural Gini	0.30	0.29	0.3	0.61	0.62	0.43	0.50
Urban Gini	0.35	0.34	0.38	0.7	0.69		0.47
Total Gini	0.33	0.33	0.36	0.64	0.66		0.51
P10/p50	56.64%	56.67 %	56.32%				38.89%
P90/p50	215.66%	212.63%	235.20%	482.00%	522.00%		347.60%

Source: Authors' calculations.

Notes: MPCE figures are from Vakulabharanam (2010). Wealth is per capita net worth, and these figures are from Jayadev et al. (2007a, 2007b). Income figures for 1994 and 2004–5 are from Shariff (1999) and Singh (2009), respectively.

We have seen that poverty rates are still high, and rates of poverty reduction have been lower post-reforms. This is particularly true in rural areas, which are sustained largely by a small-peasant-based economy. The fight against poverty reduction has seen a setback in the rural areas. As mentioned earlier, rural India has been going through severe distress, with thousands of small and marginal farmers committing suicides. Reforms have played a direct role in this distress in a few ways. Other contributions in this report and our previous work (Vakulabharanam and Motiram 2011) explain this in detail, so we will be brief. On the output side, due to the reforms, farmers have been linked to global markets without adequate support against risks faced in these markets. On the input side, costs have increased due to the rollback of the state in certain key areas. A crucial input where this has happened is credit—institutional credit has always been inadequate for small and marginal farmers, but since the reforms and the demise of social banking that accompanied it, dependence on informal sources of credit (e.g, money-lenders) at high interest rates has increased further.

What are the policies that need to be adopted to quicken the pace of poverty reduction in rural areas? This is not an easy question to answer, but one can argue that the paradigm needed is different from the one adopted as a part of the economic reforms. In particular, measures that support small farmers (e.g., the revival of cooperatives, design of appropriate trade regimes, and insurance mechanisms that protect them) can potentially work, and should therefore be considered. In this context, we consider the National Rural Employment Guarantee Scheme (NREGS), if implemented properly, as a step in the right direction.

The preceding focus on rural poverty does not, of course, imply that urban poverty should be relegated to a secondary status. In fact, rural and urban poverty are inextricably linked—many of the urban poor live in slums and are migrants from rural areas, who are either thrown out by rural distress or lured to the city by hopes of a better life.[14]

Measures to promote labour-intensive manufacturing, which can absorb unskilled labour, may be able to quicken poverty reduction in urban areas.

On the issue of inequality, as noted earlier, it has increased on several dimensions after economic reforms. One comforting answer that economists have in this regard is in the form of the Kuznets' hypothesis, which would predict that inequality would eventually reduce, so that one need not worry about its consequences. However, in the Indian context, previous studies (e.g., Virmani 2006) have found no evidence for a Kuznets type of relationship. The literature on inequality suggests several channels (e.g., savings, political pressure for redistribution, socio-political instability, and crime) through which inequality can hurt (Weil 2005). Given this, should one be concerned about rising inequality in India, and if so, through which channel might it affect outcomes? This is a difficult question to answer, and needs further research. However, apart from considerations of equity, a case can be made for addressing distributional concerns on the basis that there is an intimate connection between these and poverty reduction. This point is elaborated in Dreze and Sen (2002, chapter 9), but to put it briefly using an example, some groups/regions that are lagging behind are those that depend predominantly upon agriculture—so reduction in rural poverty goes along with reducing disparities.

REFERENCES

Bery, Suman and Kanhaiya Singh (2007), 'India's Growth Experience', in Wanda Tseng and David Cowen (eds), *India's and China's Recent Experience with Reform and Growth*. London: Palgrave Macmillan, pp. 23–58.

Chakravarty, Sukhamoy (1987), *Development Planning: The Indian Experience*. New Delhi: Oxford University Press.

Davis, Mike (2007), *Planet of Slums*. London: Verso.

Deaton, Angus and Jean Dreze (2008), 'Nutrition in India: Facts and Interpretations', Working Paper 1075, Princeton University, Woodrow Wilson School of Public and International Affairs, Center for Health and Wellbeing.

[14] On the issue of slums and urbanization, see Davis (2007).

Dreze, Jean and Amartya K. Sen (2002), *India: Development and Participation*. New Delhi: Oxford University Press.

Frick, Joachim, Jan Goebel, Edna Schechtman, Gert G. Wagner, and Shlomo Yitzhaki (2006), 'Using Analysis of Gini (ANOGI) for Detecting Whether Two Subsamples Represent the Same Universe: The German Socio-Economic Panel Study (SOEP) Experience', *Sociological Methods & Research*, 34(4): 427–68.

Himanshu (2007), 'Recent Trends in Poverty and Inequality: Some Preliminary Results', *Economic and Political Weekly*, 42(6): 497–508.

Jayadev, Arjun, Sripad Motiram, and Vamsi Vakulabharanam (2007a), 'Patterns of Wealth Disparities in India during the Era of Liberalization', *Economic and Political Weekly*, 42(39): 3853–63.

_____ (2007b), 'Imagined Problems in Computing Wealth Inequalities', *Economic and Political Weekly*, 42(51): 69–71.

National Sample Survey (NSS) (2007), 'Nutritional Intake in India, 2004–05, NSS 61st Round', Ministry of Statistics and Programme Implementation, Government of India, New Delhi.

Motiram, Sripad, Vamsi Vakulabharanam, and Arjun Jayadev (2008), 'Indian Wealth Inequalities in the Era of Liberalization: A Detailed Decomposition Analysis', paper presented at the Annual Conference of the Indian Econometric Society, Hyderabad, 3–5 January 2009.

Sen, Abhijit and Himanshu (2004a), 'Poverty and Inequality in India—I', *Economic and Political Weekly*, 39(38): 4247–63.

_____ (2004b), 'Poverty and Inequality in India—Growing Disparities in the 1990s', *Economic and Political Weekly*, 39(38): 4361–75.

Sen, Kunal (2007), 'Why Did the Elephant Start to Trot? India's Growth Acceleration Re-examined', *Economic and Political Weekly*, 42(43): 37–47.

Shariff, Abusaleh (1999), *India Human Development Report: A Profile of Indian States in the 1990s*. New Delhi: Oxford University Press.

Shorrocks, Anthony and Guanghua Wan (2004), 'Spatial Decomposition of Inequality', WIDER Discussion Paper No. 2004/01.

Singh, Ashish (2009), *Essays on Inequality of Opportunity in India*, mimeo, Indira Gandhi Institute of Development Research, Mumbai.

Vakulabharanam, Vamsi (2010), 'Class Structure and Worsening Inequality in India after Economic Reforms', *Economic and Political Weekly*, 45(29): 67–76.

Vakulabharanam, Vamsi and Sripad Motiram (2011), 'Political Economy of Agrarian Distress in India since the 1990s', in Sanjay Ruparelia, Sanjay Reddy, John Harriss, and Stuart Corbridge (eds), *Great Transformation: Understanding India's New Political Economy*. London: Taylor and Francis.

Virmani, Arvind (2006), 'Poverty and Hunger: What is Needed to Eliminate Them?' Planning Commission Working Paper No. 1/2006-PC.

Weil, David (2005), *Economic Growth*. New York: Addison Wesley.

6

Industrial Performance, 1991–2008

A Review[*]

R. Nagaraj

INTRODUCTION

In 1990–1, industry (manufacturing) contributed 26 per cent of India's gross domestic product (GDP) (15 per cent), employing 15 per cent (12 per cent) of the workforce and using 39 per cent (24 per cent) of the economy's net renewable capital stock.[1] In the 1980s, industry was the economy's 'leading' sector, growing annually at over 6 per cent, while the domestic output grew annually at around 5.5 per cent and exports (two-third of which were manufactures) at 8.5 per cent (in current dollar terms). The decade witnessed modernization of the production structure with a step up in infrastructure, de-licensing of investment and output controls, and a shift in trade policy from quotas to tariff. However, in 1991, the economy faced a liquidity crisis on account of (a) the Gulf war (leading to the drying up of inward remittances and project exports), (b) collapse of the Soviet Union (then India's largest trading partner), and (c) the domestic political uncertainty, paralysing policymaking.

Encouraged by the industrial and export boom of the 1980s, the orthodox economic reforms initiated in 1991

sought to (i) make a bonfire of the remaining output and investment controls that are said to have throttled private initiative; (ii) cut back public investment as it is believed to have 'crowded out' private investment; (iii) undermine the protective and promotional measures for small-scale industries that are claimed to have bred inefficiency and failed to expand labour-intensive manufactures; and (iv) sell minority equity holding in public sector enterprises (called 'disinvestments') to reduce government's fiscal deficit. Policymakers apparently perceived an opportunity in the crisis to quickly undo India's state-led, inward-oriented industrialization strategy, as it is claimed to have delivered neither adequate growth nor measurable equity—unlike in East Asia and China that have succeeded in export-oriented industrialization following market-friendly policies.

Surely, disenchantment with the regulatory mechanism in India had been growing for quite a while. Starting with R.K. Hazari's evaluation of the industrial licensing system in the mid-1960s to the Dagli Committee report (1979) on controls and subsidies in the late 1970s, there was compelling official evidence against the dysfunctional and discretionary policies, buttressing the critique of India's industrialization strategy, starting with Bhagwati and Desai's (1970) contribution.

There was, however, an equally persuasive scepticism of the virtues of unbridled play of market forces in a large, diverse, and unequal agrarian economy. Liberal trade and

[*] I am grateful to K.L. Krishna, K.V. Ramaswamy, and C. Veeramani for their comments and suggestions on an earlier draft of the chapter.
[1] Industry includes mining, manufacturing, electricity, gas and water, and construction. Unless otherwise mentioned, all growth rates reported in this chapter are at constant prices, estimated using long-linear trend equation.

investment regime could be a recipe for a flood of imports, decimating domestic enterprise and retrenching workers; domination of foreign capital resulting in de-industrialization, compelling the nation to revert to exporting primary products that face cyclical fluctuations and adverse terms of trade in the long run. Serious apprehensions were also expressed that the reforms could undermine the domestic market–driven independent path of industrialization, denting the long-term growth prospects—as had happened in much of Latin America and Africa after the debt crisis in the 1980s. In other words, while the market-oriented reforms were espoused on the promise of faster and labour-intensive (hence equitable) growth, critics feared debt, deflation, and de-industrialization.

After nearly two decades of the reforms, it is perhaps an opportune moment to ask: how does the industrial performance measure up against these expectations and apprehensions? This chapter offers a brief answer, mostly using the official aggregate statistics. Excluding the introduction and conclusion, the chapter has three sections: the next section describes the industrial performance. The section that follows it makes a critical assessment of the competing perspectives on the reforms, and the section thereafter outlines possible policy options.

INDUSTRIAL PERFORMANCE AFTER 1991–2

Figure 6.1 plots the annual growth rates in industrial output as measured by (i) the index of industrial production (IIP) and (ii) GDP in industry since 1990–1; both the indices show the same trend. After an expected dip in 1991–2 on account of the crisis and adjustment, output boomed for four years,

peaking in 1995–6 at 13 per cent—following the predicted 'J' curve, vindicating the reform stance. For a variety of reasons, however, the boom petered out quickly, followed by a steep deceleration for seven years until 2002–3. The next boom lasted for five years, from 2003–4 to 2007–8.

So, the average of annual growth rate over the 17-year period since 1991–2 is 6.6 per cent. During this period, consumer durables grew the fastest at 8.1 per cent per year (weight in the index in 1993–4, 2.6 per cent), followed by capital goods at 7.4 per cent per year (weight 16.4 per cent) (Table 6.1). By two-digit industry groups, beverages (National Industrial Classification [NIC 22]) recorded the fastest growth at 12 per cent per year (Table 6.2). However, capital goods, hurt by the sharp reduction in tariffs, stagnated during the first boom but bloomed in the next one, growing annually at nearly 15 per cent during 2003–8, led by transport equipment (NIC 37).

How does the industrial growth after the reforms reported above compare with the 1980s? Table 6.3 reports the trend growth rates for two-digit industry groups for total manufacturing GDP using the National Accounts Statistics. In the aggregate, there is hardly any difference in growth rate in the two periods. However, electrical machinery (NIC 31 and 32) grew faster in the 1980s at 12.7 per cent per year, while transport equipment fared better after the reforms of 1991.

How does the forgoing performance measure up against the alternative perspectives discussed earlier? In spite of the dismantling of the much criticized 'permit licence raj', industrial growth rate has not accelerated, nor has the growth rate of labour-intensive consumer goods gone up; but there has been no de-industrialization either, as the critics feared: the

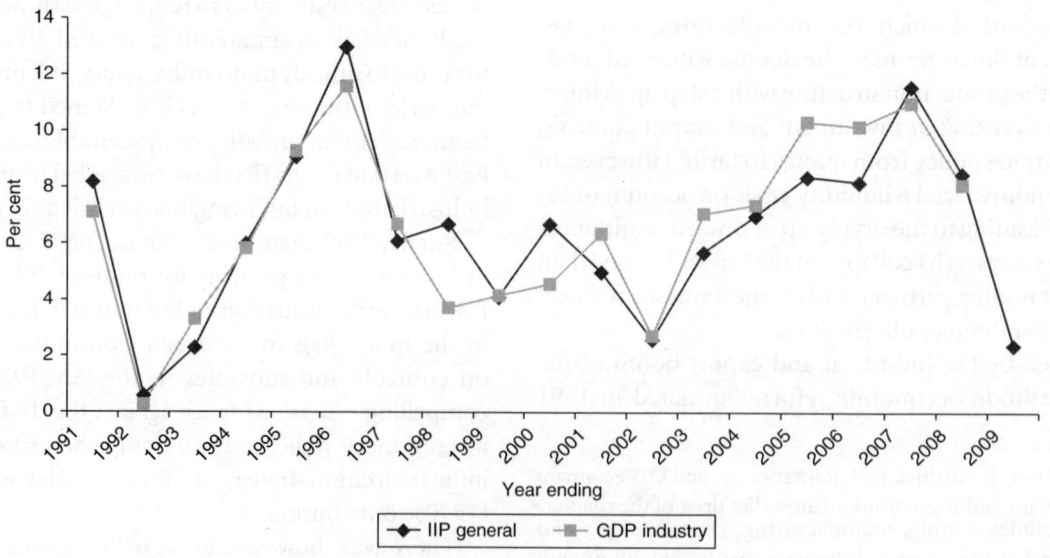

Source: *Economic Survey* and *National Accounts Statistics*, various issues.

Figure 6.1   Industrial Growth, 1991–2009

Table 6.1   Industrial Output Growth, 1991–2 to 2007–8 (Average of annual growth rates)

	IIP General	IIP-Manufacturing	Use-based Classification of IIP				Consumer Goods	
			Basic	Capital	Intermediate	Consumer Goods	CDs	CNDs
1992–6	6.2	6.1	7.8	0.3	8.0	12.8	7.3	3.7
1997–2002	5.2	5.6	3.9	5.8	6.2	5.6	9.6	4.3
2003–8	8.2	8.9	6.5	14.8	6.6	9.0	7.2	9.7
1992–2008	**6.6**	**6.9**	**5.9**	**7.4**	**6.8**	**7.7**	**8.1**	**6.0**

Source: *Economic Survey*, various issues.

Note: CDs: Consumer durables; CNDs: Consumer non-durables.

Table 6.2   Industrial Output Growth by Two-Digit Industry Groups, 1991–2 to 2007–8 (Average of annual percentage growth rates)

NIC	Industry Group	1992–6	1997–2002	2003–8	1992–2008
20–21	Food	4.6	2.7	4.5	3.9
22	Beverages	9.2	11.6	14.3	11.9
23	Cotton Textiles	6.8	2.4	4.9	4.6
24	Silk and Wool Textiles	10.7	9.0	4.3	7.8
25	Jute	1.3	−0.2	4.3	1.8
26	Textile Products	0.6	3.8	10.3	5.2
27	Wood	5.0	−4.3	7.2	2.5
28	Paper	7.4	5.4	7.3	6.6
29	Leather	1.2	8.3	1.2	3.7
30	Rubber	3.4	6.7	6.4	5.6
31	Chemicals	6.6	8.0	9.2	8.0
32	Non-metallic Minerals	8.9	9.0	6.6	8.1
33	Basic Metals	13.6	3.0	12.4	9.4
34	Metal Products	−2.2	6.4	3.4	2.8
35–36	Electrical and Non-electric Machinery	3.0	6.4	12.1	7.4
37	Transport Equipment	8.0	7.6	11.0	8.9
38	Other Manufacturing	3.5	4.8	13.2	7.4
2–3	**Manufacturing**	**6.1**	**5.6**	**8.9**	**6.9**

Source: *Economic Survey*, various issues.

Table 6.3   Comparing Industrial Growth, 1981–91 and 1992–2008

NIC-98	Industry Description	Growth Rate	
		1981–91	1992–2008
151–154	Food Products	6.6	5.2
155+16	Beverages and Tobacco	4.4	8
171–173+181+014505	Textiles	4.6	5.2
182+19	Leather and Fur	3.4	4.4
20+361	Wood	−2.7	−1.5
21+22	Paper and Printing	9.1	3.9
23+25	Rubber and Petroleum	13.6	5.8
24	Chemicals	9.3	8.3

Table 6.3 *Continued*

NIC-98	Industry Description	Growth Rate	
		1981–91	1992–2008
26	Non-metallic Mineral Products	8.7	7.3
271+272+2731+2732	Basic Metals	5.8	7.9
28+29+30	Metal Products and Machinery	6	5.6
31+32	Electrical Machinery	12.7	10.3
33+369	Other Manufacturing	10.6	8.5
34+35	Transport Equipment	5.5	8.6
	GDP manufacturing	**6.3**	**6.5**

Source: *Economic Survey*, various issues.

shares of industrial employment and output in the total have not declined (as had happened in Latin America and Africa after the debt crisis in the 1980s) (Figure 6.2 and Table 6.4). The structural transformation of workforce has continued at the same pace after the reforms, though the workforce has gone into the services, not manufacturing (Table 6.4). Within industry, the incremental workforce has gone into construction (not shown here). Measured by investment, the reforms were not a setback for industrialization, as the manufacturing sector's share in total fixed investment (gross fixed capital formation) has gone up from around 27 per cent in the 1980s to about 40 per cent in the current decade (Figure 6.3).

The proponents and the critics of the reforms alike expected the share of capital goods in output and

Source: *National Accounts Statistics*, various issues.

Figure 6.2 Shares of Industry and Manufacturing in GDP

Table 6.4 Employment and Output Share of Principal Sectors, 1983 to 2004–5 (per cent)

	Employment			GDP		
	1983	1993–4	2004–5	1983	1993–4	2004–5
1. Agriculture	68.5	64.0	56.5	37.1	30.0	20.2
2. Industry	13.8	15.0	18.7	24.3	25.2	26.2
2.1 Manufacturing	10.7	10.6	12.2	14.5	14.5	15.1
3. Services	17.6	21.1	24.8	38.6	44.8	53.6

Sources: *National Accounts Statistics*, various issues; NSS *Employment and Unemployment Surveys*, various rounds.

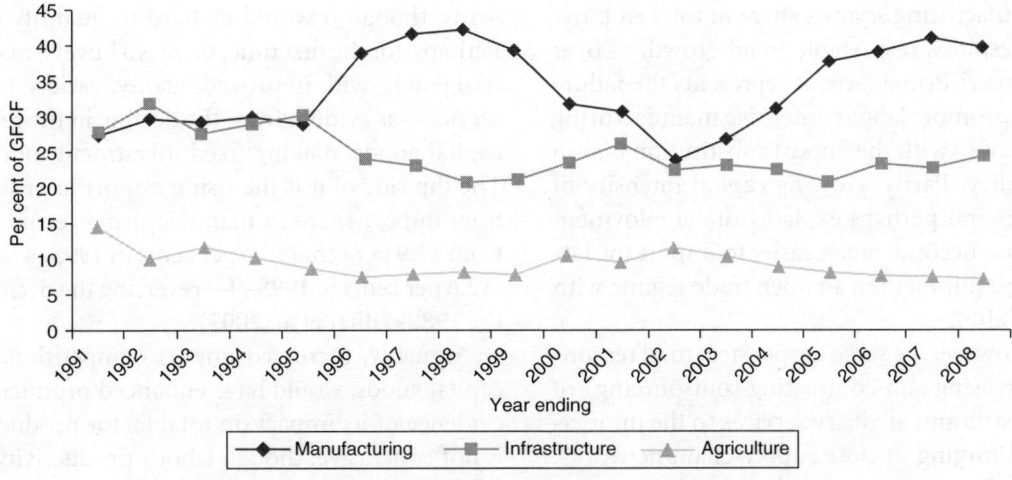

Source: *National Accounts Statistics*, various issues.

Figure 6.3   Investment Shares, 1991–2008

investment to fall, as it was considered emblematic of the state-led import substitution industrialization. But its growth rate went up modestly after the reforms (mainly in the automotive industry in the current decade).

India's export basket has got diversified after the reforms, mainly into services—surprising the proponents and critics of the reforms alike. This is perhaps an unintended outcome of India's sustained investments in capital goods and high-technology industries made earlier on, along with the nurturing of scientific and technical education. However, within merchandise exports, the share of manufactures has fallen from 80 per cent in the 1990s to 64 per cent in 2007–8 as primary exports (mainly iron ore) also boomed in the current decade (Figure 6.4).

While the foregoing account represents a broad picture of continuity with change, on a closer look, however, there are some causes of concern. While there is no de-industrialization, industry or manufacturing sector's share in domestic output has practically stagnated and its export share has declined; by implication, primary sector's shares in merchandise exports has risen (Figure 6.4). Arguably, the rising share of primary exports is almost entirely due to iron ore exports to China (propelled largely by the Beijing Olympics–related construction), as India rode the commodity boom, perhaps out of the necessity to finance burgeoning petroleum imports. This was perhaps avoidable, if the much-anticipated expansion of labour-intensive manufacturing was realized.

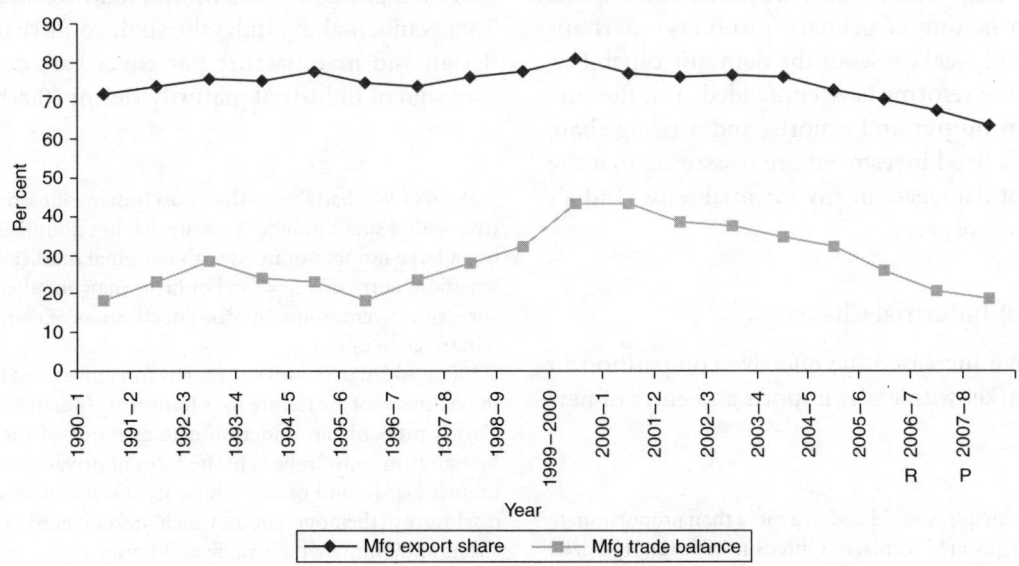

Source: *Economic Survey* and *National Accounts Statistics*, various issues.

Figure 6.4   India's Trade Balance, 1991–2008

Why did manufacturing sector's share in total employment stagnate, despite a respectable trend growth of over 6.5 per cent per year? Prima facie, it represents the failure of the reforms to promote labour-intensive manufacturing in spite of doing away with the import substitution bias in the industrial policy. Partly, growing capital intensity of production in general perhaps explains the employment stagnation, as it has become much easier to import the latest labour-saving equipment in an open trade regime with modest tariffs (if any).

There could, however, be some deeper structural reasons as well, with increasing sub-contracting (outsourcing) of manufacture of parts and auxiliary services to the unorganized sector, and forging of close supply-chain networks. Such an organization of production is quite the opposite of the vertically integrated production structures that were common in the early years of industrialization. After the reforms, with increased competitive pressure, under the liberalized rules of resource use, and with lax enforcement of labour laws, firms have apparently restructured their production processes by shedding labour. Conceivably, some of the employment lost in the organized sector would have reappeared in the unorganized sector, though no direct evidence for it is available.[2] Therefore, while the stagnation of the industrial employment share is a cause for concern, it perhaps represents an outcome of the changing market conditions, organization of production, and technology in an open labour-surplus economy.

Thus, what emerges from the foregoing (mainly) statistical account is a nuanced picture of industrial change. While India has managed to avert de-industrialization, its output growth rate has not accelerated. Manufacturing sector's share in GDP has stagnated; its share in merchandise exports has declined in favour of primary products—perhaps suggesting signs of weaknesses of the domestic capability, as the critics of the reforms have contended. Yet, the sustained growth in output and exports, and a rising share in the economy's fixed investment are reassuring that the reforms have not damaged, in any essential sense, India's industrialization prospects.

Other Aspects of Industrial Change

The reforms have increased the effective competition in the domestic market with easier imports and entry of new firms, though it would be hard to quantify these effects.[3] Perhaps, for the first time, there is a buyers' market in industrial goods, with improved quality, variety, and after-sales service—as evident from the decline in the relative price of capital goods, making fixed investment more productive. The flip side of it is the rising import intensity of production: import share in manufacturing (economy) went up from 12.9 per cent (10.5 per cent) in 1993–4 to 16.8 per cent (12.6 per cent) in 1998–9—reversing the declining trend up the 1980s (Bhat et al. 2007).

Arguably, increased import competition, especially in capital goods, would have enhanced productivity. Yet, the evidence of its impact on total factor productivity growth is not conclusive, though labour productivity has climbed steadily (Balakrishnan et al. 2000).

With the reduction in the entry barriers for foreign-owned firms, their share in manufacturing GDP has gone up from 5 per cent in 1991 to about 8 per cent in 2007—probably an underestimate.[4] With the decline in public investment, the share of public sector enterprises in total manufacturing GDP has halved to 8 per cent between 1991 and 2008 (Figure 6.5).

In the 1990s, the manufacturing sector underwent painful restructuring—plant closures, sell offs of productive assets and relocations, and unprecedented lay offs and retrenchments—that is yet to be adequately documented. In the end, however, it has apparently improved production efficiency to face the increased competition, especially from China. Although research and development (R&D) investments have contracted as a proportion of the domestic output, the restructuring and competitive pressure seem to have spurred innovation and product development—perhaps best exemplified by Tata Indica, followed more recently by Tata Nano, making India the sixth country in the world to design and manufacture passenger cars domestically—a sure sign of industrial maturity (Mani 2009).[5]

---

[2] Such a shift, in principle, should lead to a more than proportionate rise in employment, given higher labour intensity in the unorganized sector. But as the length of the working day is generally longer and intensity of supervision greater, such an employment expansion may not materialize.

[3] Desai (1985) had shown that most Indian industries were competitive, with a small number of firms having dominant market shares but a large number of firms with marginal market shares. In such a situation, entry of a few foreign firms may not alter the usual measures of concentration, but the effectiveness of competition is likely to have gone up.

[4] Value added in manufacturing by foreign-owned firms is based on the estimates of the Centre for Monitoring Indian Economy (CMIE). This is probably an underestimate as much of the recent entry of foreign firms into India is in the form of private limited companies, branch plants, and offices whose legal status does not warrant full disclosure of their operations, which makes it hard to get their balance sheets and estimate their value addition.

[5] Ashok Parthasarathy, a careful observer of industrial technology, recently stated, 'If we are talking of "technological innovation", I would put India ahead of both China and Brazil' (Parthasarathy 2009).

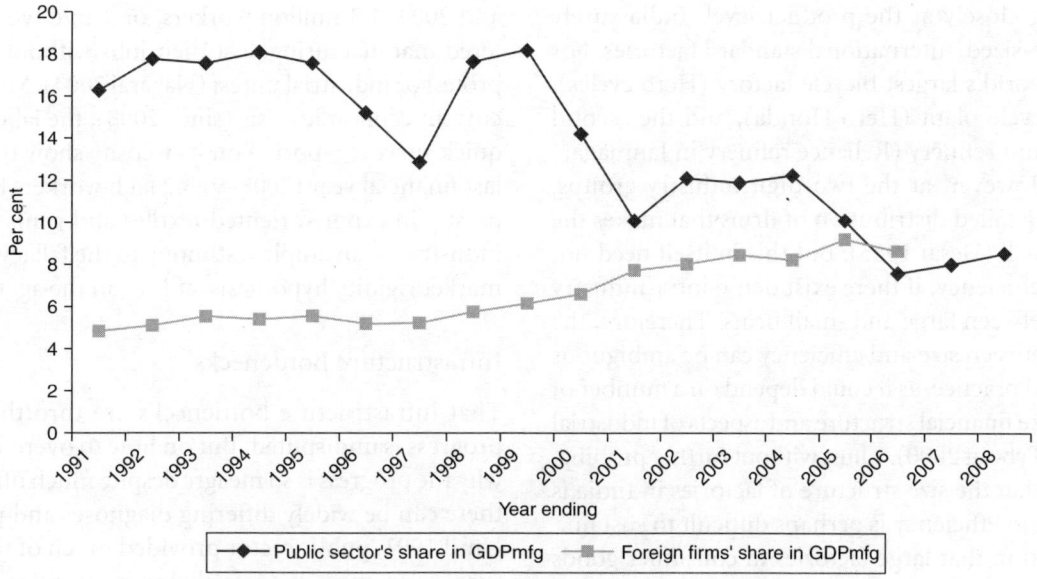

Source: National Accounts Statistics; Corporate Sector, CMIE, various issues.

Figure 6.5 Public Sector's and Foreign Firms' Share in GDPmfg

The growing strength and stature of Indian industry and enterprise are also evident from their ability to acquire and manage factories and firms in developed economies in relatively advanced manufacturing industries. For instance, Tata group's exports apparently account for 15–20 per cent of its sales, and (as per the group's website)[6] it earned 61 per cent of its annual revenue from international operations. Moreover, the growing outward foreign direct investment (FDI) by large private Indian firms in the recent boom, estimated at $17.6 billion cumulative stock as in 2008 (UN 2009)—to leverage their domestic manufacturing capability and use it as a short-cut to acquire technology—is yet another testimony of the coming of age of Indian business (Nagaraj 2006a; Nayyar 2008).

WHY DID THE REFORMS FAIL TO DELIVER THE EXPECTED RESULTS?

Still, the principal question remains unanswered: why did the speeding up of the reforms after 1991 not yield faster output, employment, and labour-intensive growth? The protagonists would contend that the reforms have remained incomplete, with the persistence of the labour market rigidities (lack of entrepreneurial freedom to hire and fire workers at will), infrastructure bottlenecks, and incomplete financial integration, including full convertibility of the currency (Kocchar et al. 2006; Panagariya 2008; Krueger 2009, among others).

Based on cross-country analysis, Kocchar et al. argue that India has followed idiosyncratic policies in promoting

skill-intensive industries, discouraging labour-intensive manufactures—a pattern that has not changed after the reforms because of the labour market rigidities. These scholars also contend that on average Indian firms tend to be small because workers cannot be fired, preventing them from reaping the advantages of economies of scale in production. But, since skilled workers and professionals are outside the purview of trade unions, India has specialized in skill-intensive industries.

Following I.M.D. Little (1987), Anne Krueger (2009), on the other hand, has argued the opposite: industrial productivity is low in India because of the dominance of large-sized factories in manufacturing industries, representing vestiges of inward-looking state-dominated industrialization. Krueger believes that Indian factories are either too large (employing 1,000 or more workers) or too small (less than 10 workers, in the unregistered sector), both of which are said to be inefficient, while the middle-sized factories (100–500) are the most efficient. She has also identified poor agricultural productivity growth, inadequate infrastructure, and labour market rigidities as the other reasons for poor industrial growth.

What then are the facts of the matter? The average factory size in registered manufacturing in 2004–5 was 35 workers per factory, declining steadily over the last half century from over 140 workers (Nagaraj 1985). Krueger's observation was correct for the 1950s but not any more, with the growth of factories in the intermediate-sized classes. At the other end of the scale, household manufacturing has become marginal with the expansion of smaller-sized workshops and factories. These are long-term trends of industrial change, unaffected by the reforms.

[6] http://www.tata.co.in (accessed on 14 October 2009)

But looking closely at the product level, India surely has many large-sized, international standard factories. For instance, the world's largest bicycle factory (Hero cycles), largest motorcycle plant (Hero Honda), and the second largest petroleum refinery (Reliance refinery in Jamnagar) are all here. However, at the two-digit industry groups, India has a long tailed distribution of firms that makes the average size small (Desai 1985). But this in itself need not be a sign of inefficiency, if there exist dense intra-industry transactions between large and small firms. Therefore, the relationship between size and efficiency can be ambiguous in principle and practice, as it could depend on a number of other factors like financial structure and aspects of industrial organization (Tybout 2000). Thus, without further probing, the argument that the size structure of factories in India is per se inimical to efficiency is perhaps difficult to sustain.

The contention that large factories in consumer goods industries in China (like textile weaving or knitting) represent efficient production scale is debatable. Historically, in light manufactures, the average factory size usually tended to be small, with dense inter-firm relationship in small geographical locations. For example, in Japan in early twentieth century, or in Taiwan more recently, a lot of light manufactures were produced in small and household enterprises, but were sold world over by large trading houses (especially the Japanese *Sogo-Soshos*), which provided them with credit, technical assistance, and marketing expertise. Such an industrial organization is predicated on reasonably well-functioning product and credit markets.

But in China, perhaps because of inadequate development of these market-based relationships, firms have often sought to internalize their functions in vertically integrated plants. So, the large-sized factories in China are probably not a sign of a superior or more efficient production organization but perhaps a symptom of its weakness (Nagaraj 2007b). Therefore, to hold up China as the model to follow and to find fault with India on this count is perhaps an incorrect reading of the comparative experience.

Labour Market Rigidity Hypothesis

The reformists believe that India's labour laws are the most protective of the organized labour, which makes firing of workers almost impossible, rendering labour a quasi-fixed capital, leading to substitution of capital for labour, yielding little employment growth. Such a reading of the labour law is perhaps facile as it overlooks the 'fine print' of exemptions and loopholes that are built into them. By now, there is abundant evidence to question such a simplistic view.[7] Perhaps it is suffice to present the telling evidence that between 1997

and 2004, 1.3 million workers, or 1 in 6 workers in registered manufacturing, lost their jobs without a murmur of protest or industrial unrest (Nagaraj 2004). Moreover, in the current economic crisis (since 2008), the labour ministry's quick surveys reported on its website show that during the last financial year (2008–9) 3.7 lakh workers lost their jobs, mostly in export-oriented textiles and gems and jewellery industries—an ample testimony to the fallacy of the labour market rigidity hypothesis, at least in the aggregate.[8]

Infrastructure Bottlenecks

That infrastructure bottlenecks are throttling industrial progress is undisputed. But on how to overcome them and why the progress is so meagre despite much official rhetoric, there can be widely differing diagnoses and prescriptions. Until 1991, public sector provided much of the infrastructure, as in most industrializing economies. But its poor supply was often blamed on lack of resources, enormous cost and time overruns in project completion, and poor public management in general.

Attributing these problems to public ownership, the reforms have encouraged entry of private and foreign capital in these industries. Infrastructure services, by definition, have a long gestation period and are capital intensive, with low rates of return spread over a long period. They are often networked industries, where efficiency of an individual plant or a firm depends on the performance of the entire network, and financial returns depend on output pricing, which are public policy decisions. In such industries, foreign investment is fraught with risk, as evidence world over can testify (Wells and Gleason 1995). Closer home, the nation has paid dearly for the misadventures like the Enron's Dabhol power project, but policymakers seem to have learnt few lessons from it (Mehta 1999).[9]

WHAT SHOULD BE DONE NOW?

If the foregoing critique is valid, what then is the alternative? The reforms implicitly assume that the policy-induced restrictions on supply are holding back output growth.

---

[7] For a review of the relevant literature, see Bhattacharjea (2006) and Nagaraj (2007a).

[8] As the job losses reported seem to refer only to the organized sector, they could be much higher in the unorganized sector, which accounts for an increasingly larger share of consumer goods and labour-intensive exports.

[9] During the first United Progressive Alliance (UPA) government (2004–9), there were serious shortfalls in the targets for additions to electricity-generating capacity and road construction (after a reasonably successful record in laying the Golden quadrilateral in the preceding five years), despite the much advertised 'Bharat Nirman' programme. Why? One suspects that this was because of the policy of public–private partnership, of introduction of private partners, and development of private markets.

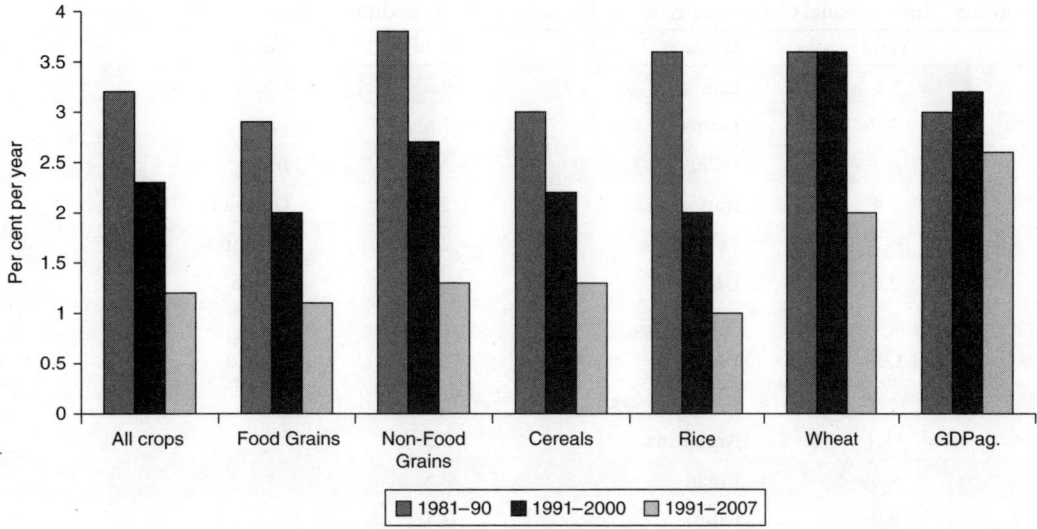

Source: Economic Survey, various issues.

Figure 6.6   Trends in Agriculture Production, 1981–2007

Surely, there is some truth in this, as industrial regulation had degenerated into an inefficient and dysfunctional system. But were these the binding constraints on long-term growth, as the reformists claim? Probably not.

The reforms, in our view, failed to deliver because they ignored the demand factors. Careful analytical work and econometric evidence have suggested that long-term industrial growth in India is constrained by supply as well as demand factors, which, it seems, runs on the twin engines of public investment and agriculture productivity (Chakravarty 1979; Storm 1993). Moreover, in a large agrarian economy, public investment removes constraints on productivity growth in agriculture, creating demand for industrial goods—a crucial insight that the writings on the reforms have inadequately appreciated—a view also endorsed by Krueger (2009). Surely, the creative function of competitive industrial structure is to spur efficiency, but it need not necessarily translate into faster and labour-intensive growth, as argued in the mainstream economic literature. As the experience of the 1980s has demonstrated, gradual deregulation of industrial markets, along with stepping up of public infrastructure investment and rising agriculture productivity perhaps provided the right demand and supply conditions for industrial turnaround.

Arthur Lewis famously said that if a nation wants to industrialize, it should enrich its farmers. But farmers have got impoverished after the reforms as the growth rate of crop production has decelerated (Figure 6.6). This seems to get reflected in the widespread phenomenon of farmers committing suicide (under debt burden), which is not just a crisis of production but also a serious humanitarian

problem. The agrarian distress has also manifested itself in a political crisis, fuelling rural violence, as evident from the spread of left-wing radical movements, engulfing nearly one-third of the districts in the country.

Proponents of the reforms would probably contend that agriculture has lost the capacity to absorb labour and, in any case, India is saddled with excess food stocks. Both are probably half-truths, as best. As Table 6.5 shows, India's land productivity in all major crops is a modest fraction of the world average, so the argument that agriculture has little scope for absorbing labour to increase productivity is simply incorrect. As is widely acknowledged, overflowing food stocks are not a measure of food self-sufficiency when a large proportion of the poor cannot demand food for lack of purchasing power. So, the argument that agriculture cannot absorb labour is patently false. If we believe that the pace of workforce transformation depends on agriculture productivity to sustain non-agricultural employment, then poor agricultural growth is surely retarding industrial progress.

The other extreme view—of agrarianism and anti-industrialization mainly emanating from the recent West Bengal experience—that agriculture alone can cure all the ills of unemployment and underemployment is perhaps equally false, as the 'excess' growth of agriculture can choke industrialization via rising wages in the industrial sector and lack of industrial inputs in agriculture.[10] Therefore, what is needed, as Lewis argued long ago, is *balanced*

[10] Political difficulties faced in West Bengal to acquire agriculture land for large industrial projects like Tata Motor's car plant has given rise to intellectual arguments against modern industrialization as a means of long-term economic development.

Table 6.5   International Comparisons of Yield in Selected Commodities in 2004–5 (Metric tonnes/hectare)

Rice/Paddy	Yield	Wheat	Yield	Maize	Yield
Egypt	9.8	China	4.3	USA	9.2
India	*2.9*	France	7.6	France	7.6
Japan	6.4	*India*	*2.7*	*India*	*1.2*
Myanmar	2.4	Iran	2.1	Germany	6.7
Korea	6.7	Pakistan	2.4	Philippines	2.1
Thailand	2.6	UK	7.8	China	4.9
USA	7.8	Australia	1.6		
World	**3.96**	**World**	**2.9**	**World**	**3.38**
Cotton	Yield	Major Oilseeds	Yield		
China	11.1	Argentina	2.5		
USA	9.6	Brazil	2.5		
Uzbekistan	8.0	China	2.1		
India	*4.6*	*India*	*0.9*		
Brazil	11.0	Germany	4.1		
Pakistan	7.6	USA	2.6		
World	**7.3**	**World**	**1.0**		

Source: *Economic Survey 2008–9*, Ministry of Finance, Government of India, New Delhi.

growth.[11] Surely, rising demand from rural economy can boost industrial output, but unless industry modernizes to augment exports, economy may face external imbalance. Therefore, what is also required after reaching a certain level of economic development, as Kaldor (1967) argued, is growing exports of manufactures to meet finance import requirements. As India has more or less completed import substitution phase, what it now needs to vigorously pursue is export of labour-intensive goods to finance its burgeoning import requirements (especially of oil) to lubricate the engine of domestic market-led growth. This requires modern infrastructure and long-term credit at reasonable interest rates.

But we are now in a peculiar situation: even after steady improvement in the financial performance of public sector enterprises (PSEs) over the last two decades (Nagaraj 2006b), rising tax–GDP ratio, and a steep increase in

domestic saving rate (Nagaraj 2008), policymakers continue to favour private sector over public sector in infrastructure development due to fiscal orthodoxy. It is true that in the period after the mid-1960s to 1980, excessive and discretionary regulation stifled private initiative. However, it is equally true that leaving infrastructure to private initiative after the reforms did not lead to faster investment and output growth. Therefore, what is needed, as Hazari (1985) insightfully noted, is a judicious rebalancing between the *babu* and *bania*, to achieve the national goals—a balance that needs to be pragmatically reassessed from time to time.

CONCLUSIONS

Ending the strategic role of the state-led import-substituting industrialization, the two decades of industry and trade policy reforms have dismantled the output and investments controls. Many lines of manufacture have become more competitive with a marginal rise in India's share in world merchandise trade to 1 per cent in 2005 (*Economic Survey 2007–08*). Quality and variety of goods produced have improved; relative price of capital goods has declined (enhancing the productivity of fixed investment), although the import content in domestic production has risen. The unintended boom in the export of information technology and related services can be clearly seen as a consequence of investments early on in heavy industry and scientific and

---

[11] To quote Lewis, 'If we assume that the subsistence sector is producing more food, while we escape the Scylla of adverse terms of trade we may be caught by the Charybdis of real wages rising because the subsistence sector is more productive. We escape both Scylla and Charybdis if rising productivity in the subsistence sector is more than off set by improving terms of trade. However, if the subsistence sector is producing food the elasticity of demand for which is less than unity, increase in productivity will be more than off set by reduction in prices' (1954: 174).

technical education. A growing number of Indian firms have gained technical expertise to run factories and firms across the globe, leveraging their domestic competence and, in turn, to acquire technology to enhance their domestic capabilities.

Yet, these achievements have not translated into faster and labour-intensive industrial growth or growth in industrial exports, as compared to the 1980s. As a result, the services sector has replaced manufacturing as the economy's leading sector. Though India did not witness de-industrialization, as the critics of the reforms apprehended, industry's share of domestic output and employment has stagnated; its share in merchandise export has declined, with rising exports of primary exports (mainly of iron ore). Why did the reforms fail to deliver a faster and equitable industrial growth? In other words, why did the reforms fail to promote labour-intensive growth and manufactured exports, as in East Asia and China?

Mainstream economists point to the remaining distortions, mainly the alleged rigidities in the labour market, inadequate infrastructure, and the incomplete financial sector reforms. Labour market rigidities hypothesis does not hold water, with over a million manufacturing jobs lost during 1997–2004 and unprecedented job losses during the current downturn, without a murmur of protest.

There is, however, a great unanimity on the need for stepping up infrastructure investment, but not on how to achieve it. With the rising tax revenue and domestic saving as proportions of the domestic output, and with a steady improvement in public sector's physical and financial performance, lack of resources and organization are no longer the binding constraints on augmenting infrastructure. The real stumbling block, therefore, appears to be the policymakers' commitment to (i) fiscal orthodoxy and (ii) encourage private and foreign investment in infrastructure provision. Such persistence to the means rather than the ends seems galling, even in the face of the disaster with Enron's Dabhol power project in the 1990s and worldwide experience in large infrastructure investment.

The principle drawback of the reforms is its exclusive focus on removing supply constraints at the neglect of demand. There is a growing consensus on the need to raise agriculture productivity to find markets for industrial goods, but the view has no serious takers as (i) there are enough buffer stocks to ward off any emergency and to maintain price stability, and (ii) there is a growing belief that agriculture has lost the capacity to absorb labour. Both the arguments are fallacious since the nation's food needs are far from fulfilled (though enough to meet demand) and the agriculture productivity in most crops is only a modest fraction of the world average.

REFERENCES

Balakrishnan, Pulapre, K. Pushpangadan, and M. Suresh Babu (2000), 'Trade Liberalisation and Productivity Growth in Manufacturing', *Economic and Political Weekly*, 35(41).

Bhagwati, Jagdish and Padma Desai (1970), *India: Industrialisation*. Delhi: Oxford University Press.

Bhat, T.P., Atulan Guha, Mahua Paul, and Partha Pratim Sahu (2007), 'Estimation of Import Intensity in India's Manufacturing Sector: Recent Trends and Dimensions', Institute for Studies in Industrial Development (ISID) Working Paper No. 2007/8.

Bhattacharjea, Aditya (2006), 'Labour Market Regulation and Industrial Performance in India: A Critical Review of the Empirical Evidence', *The Indian Journal of Labour Economics*, 49(2): 211–32. Available at http://ssrn.com/abstract=954908

Chakravarty, S. (1979), 'Keynes, "Classics", and the Development Economics', in C.H. Hanumantha Rao and P.C. Joshi (eds), *Reflections on Economic Development and Social Change*. Delhi: Allied Publishers, pp. 75–89.

Dagli Committee (1979), *Report of the Committee on Controls and Subsidies*, Ministry of Finance, Government of India.

Desai, Ashok (1985), 'Market Structure and Technology: Their Interdependence in Indian Industry', *Research Policy*, Vol. 14.

Hazari, R.K. (1985), 'Rents of Misdelivery: A Case for Modernisation of Industrial Planning' (Review Article), *Economic and Political Weekly*, 20(28): 1177–84.

Kaldor, Nicholas (1967), *Strategic Factors in Economic Development*. Ithaca, New York: Cornell University.

Kocchar, Kalpana, Utsav Kumar, Raghuram Rajan, Arvind Subramanian, and Ioannis Tokatlidis (2006), 'India's Pattern of Development: What Happened and What Follows?', *Journal of Monetary Economics*, 53(5): 981–1019.

Krueger, Anne (2009), 'The Missing Middle', ICRIER, New Delhi, Working Paper No. 230.

Lewis, William Arthur (1954), 'Economic Development with Unlimited Supply of Labour', *Manchester School of Economic Studies*, May, reprinted in A.N. Agarwala and S.P. Singh (eds) (1963), *The Economics of Underdevelopment*. Delhi: Oxford University Press, pp. 400–49.

Little, I.M.D (1987), 'Small Manufacturing Enterprises in Developing Countries', *The World Bank Economic Review*, 1(2): 203–35.

Mani, Sunil (2009), 'Is India Becoming More Innovative since 1991?', mimeo, Centre for Development Studies, Thiruvananthpuram.

Mehta, Abay (1999), *Power Play: A Study of the Enron Project*. Hyderabad: Orient Longman.

Nagaraj, R. (1985), 'Fall in Organised Manufacturing Employment: A Brief Note', *Economic and Political Weekly*, 20(8): M26–M32.

——— (2004), 'Fall in Organised Manufacturing Employment: A Brief Note', *Economic and Political Weekly*, 39(30): 3387–90.

——— (2006a), 'Indian Investments Abroad: What Explains the Boom?', *Economic and Political Weekly*, 41(46): 4716–18.

————— (2006b), 'Public Sector Performance since 1950: A Closer Look', *Economic and Political Weekly*, 41(25): 2551–7.

————— (2007a), 'Are Labour Regulations Holding up India's Growth and Exports? A Review of Analysis and Evidence', paper prepared for National Commission for Unorganised Sector Enterprises.

————— (2007b), 'Industrial Growth in China and India: A Preliminary Comparison', in K.L. Krishna and A. Vaidyanathan (eds), *Institutions and Markets in India's Development, Essays for K.N. Raj*. New Delhi: Oxford University Press, chapter 9, pp. 178–204.

————— (2008), 'India's Recent Economic Growth: A Closer Look', *Economic and Political Weekly*, 43(15): 55–61.

Nayyar, Deepak (2008), 'The Internationalization of Firms from India: Investment, Mergers and Acquisitions', *Oxford Development Studies*, 36(1): 111–31.

Panagariya, Arvind (2008), *India: The Emerging Giant*. New Delhi: Oxford University Press.

Parthasarathy, Ashok (2009), 'Who Says We Have Not Innovated?', *Business Standard*, 18 March.

Storm, Servaas (1993), *Macroeconomic Considerations in the Choice of an Agricultural Policy: A Study into Sectoral Interdependence with Reference to India*. Aldershot: Avebury.

Tybout, James (2000), 'Manufacturing Firms in Developing Countries: How Well Do They Do, and Why?', *Journal of Economic Literature*, 38(1): 11–44.

United Nations (UN) (2009), *World Investment Report 2009*. Geneva: UNCTAD.

Wells, Louis T. and Eric S. Gleason (1995), 'Is Foreign Direct Investment Still Too Risky?', *Harvard Business Review*, September–October, pp. 44–55.

7

Regional Disparities in Manufacturing Growth in India

K.V. Ramaswamy

INTRODUCTION

Regional differences in economic performance have begun to receive greater policy consideration as instances of unequal benefits of growth (reduction of poverty and income inequality) emerged in many countries, including India and China.[1] The uneven growth across sub-national units (states or provinces) in an economy suggests that the growth processes have created differential economic opportunities across regions. In India, some states have forged ahead (Gujarat and Haryana) seriously leaving behind others (Bihar and Uttar Pradesh). The growth rate of per capita state domestic product (SDP) of Gujarat (8.1 per cent) stands in sharp contrast to that of Uttar Pradesh (2.1 per cent) during 2000–5.[2] If one looks at the differences in levels of income, then one finds that the per capita SDP of Goa was 2.5 times that of West Bengal in 2005–6. Structural changes within states have been broadly similar, with the income share of agriculture falling (20 per cent), moderate rise in the share of industry (27 per cent), and substantial rise in the share of services (50 per cent) by 2005–6 (EPWRF 2009: chapter 8). Closer observation reveals large inter-state disparities in growth and change within individual sectors like services and manufacturing. Disparities in economic growth across regions and differences in growth within sectors have brought back the issue of regional equity in development policy debate. The key questions have been the following. What are the sources of this disparate growth? How have economic reforms since 1991 impacted growth across states relative to the pre-reform period? Is there a tendency for geographic concentration of economic activity leading to greater disparities? What are the factors that help or hinder such tendencies? Is there a role for regional policy in an environment of market-driven industrialization? Admittedly, there are no easy answers. In this chapter we focus on the registered manufacturing sector and bring out certain features of inter-state differences in growth and regional concentration of industries.[3] The natural question that arises is why registered manufacturing?

First, registered manufacturing has been the sector most subjected to economic policy reform and at the forefront of India's industrial licensing, trade, and foreign investment liberalization since 1991. Second, studies have found a significant role for registered manufacturing in explaining variations in inter-state growth rates. The simple correlation between per capita net state domestic product (NSDP)

---

[1] See, among others, Chaudhuri and Ravallion (2006).

[2] At 1999–2000 prices.

[3] Registered manufacturing refers to all factories with more than 10 workers using power, or more than 20 workers without using power, registered under the Factories Act (1948).

and the share of registered manufacturing in output was found to be negative in the 1970s but significantly positive in the 1980s. The share of registered manufacturing sector is reported to be significant in explaining per capita NSDP growth rate of states in the 1990s (Rodrik and Subramanian 2004). This is consistent with the idea of the key role assigned to manufacturing productivity in growth and structural change in developing countries. Understanding the drivers of spatial differences in registered manufacturing growth in India is crucial for investment and fiscal policy.

ECONOMIC REFORMS AND INDUSTRIAL LOCATION POLICY

Economic reforms relaxed the entry restrictions on domestic and foreign firms. They liberalized access to intermediate inputs, capital goods, and technology. The location restrictions on industries were removed. It is useful to summarize the policy reform to put the discussion in perspective.

Industry, Trade, and Foreign Investment Policy

The foremost instrument of industrial policy was the industrial licensing for private entrepreneurs based on Industrial Regulation Act of 1956. The new industrial policy of 1991 abolished industrial licensing except in eighteen industries. The major areas of trade reform included reduction of average tariff rates, the removal of licensing and other non-tariff barriers (NTBs) on all imports of intermediate and capital goods, the elimination of trade monopolies of the state trading agencies, and the simplification of the trading regime. The mean tariff was reduced from 128 per cent before July 1991 to 35 per cent by 1997–8, and later it was reduced to 30 per cent in 2001. Ninety-five per cent of the tariff lines were freed from NTBs in 2001. Restrictions on foreign direct investment (FDI) were relaxed in 1991. In the years prior to 1991, FDI was permitted only up to 40 per cent in certain industries, known as 'Appendix I Industries', subject to the discretionary approval by the government. In 1991, FDI was allowed up to 51 per cent equity in these industries under the 'automatic route'. This was later liberalized in 1997 to enable setting up of 100 per cent subsidiaries in the manufacturing sector. The list of products reserved for exclusive manufacture by small-scale industries has been progressively removed from the reservation list, enabling large domestic and foreign firms to enter those product lines.

Industrial Location Policy

The concern for regional disparity was expressed very early in India in the Industrial Policy Statement of 1956. Multiple instruments were brought into use during the 1970s and 1980s in order to achieve the desired objective of industrial dispersal.[4] They may be fall broadly into two types:[5] (i) policies that influenced inter-regional distribution of industry and (ii) policies that impacted intra-regional distribution of industries. Industrial licensing to direct investment into backward or 'no industry' districts and prohibiting heavy industry from metropolitan areas, the location of public sector plants in backward states (Bihar, Madhya Pradesh, and Orissa), and pricing and distribution policy for intermediate inputs fall under the first category. Applications for setting up units in backward areas were favoured and this showed up in the higher share of letters of intent and total licences. The most powerful was the control of distribution and pricing of intermediate inputs like coal, cement, and steel. This policy was implemented through the operation of freight equalization policy. This policy equalized the prices of coal, steel, and cement nation-wide. As a consequence, states in the eastern region rich in these resources lost their natural competitive advantages. Other states in the northern and western regions that were not producers of these commodities were the beneficiaries. Later, this policy was discontinued, beginning with the decontrol of the cement industry in 1989.

Within or intra-state distribution of industries was influenced by another set of policies that included the central government capital subsidy schemes, transport subsidy for industries in hilly backward areas, income tax concessions for new industrial units in backward districts that permitted 20 per cent deduction of profits in the computation of taxable income, and financial assistance at below normal lending rates by financial institutions. The latter is reported to be quite successful as the share of backward areas in the financial assistance sanctioned and disbursed by the All-India Financial Institutions is found to be between 40 per cent and 50 per cent since the mid-1970s. Further, the industrial licensing system was used to restrict the location of new industrial units within certain limits of large metropolitan cities. The Industrial Policy Statement of 1977 prohibited the location of new industrial units above a certain size in all cities with a population of more than 500,000. All these policy rules clearly suggest a serious intention on the part of government's industrial policy to induce industries to locate away from existing locations with high degree of industrial concentration.

The Industrial Policy Statement of 1991 that liberalized industrial regulatory rules by de-licensing of industries removed all restrictions regarding location of industries. It retained the licensing requirement for setting up an industry within 25 km of cities with population more than 1 million in 1991. Environmental, pollution,

---

[4] This section is based on Sekhar (1983) and Mohan (1993).
[5] See Sekhar (1983) for an early detailed discussion of these policies.

and other local use restrictions have been continued. All other incentives, except income tax concessions for backward districts, were withdrawn. Later in 2001, the Parthasarathy Shome committee on tax policy for the Tenth Plan advised the abolition of income tax concessions for regional industrial development. The approach of the central government during the era of economic reforms is that provision of infrastructure is more important than income tax concessions for encouraging economic activity in backward regions. The state governments on their part have continued many fiscal incentives, like sales tax exemption, to attract domestic and foreign investment to their states.

The emphasis and speed of economic reforms at the state level have been rather mixed. An early attempt to classify Indian states in terms of reform orientation suggested the following classification (Bajpai and Sachs 1999): (a) Reform-oriented: Andhra Pradesh, Gujarat, Karnataka, Maharashtra, and Tamil Nadu; (b) Intermediate Reformers: Haryana, Orissa, and West Bengal; (c) Lagging Reformers: Bihar, Kerala, Madhya Pradesh, Punjab, Rajasthan, and Uttar Pradesh. This classification took into consideration reform of the power sector through tariff reform and power distribution, public finance reform to reduce fiscal deficit, and clear-cut incentives for industrial investment, among others. This classification is purely indicative and need not bear any relationship with investment climate and subsequent growth. Similarly, another recent study (Iarossi 2009) ranked Indian states in terms of investment climate based on interview responses of businessmen and entrepreneurs. Three factors that influence investment, namely, cost of inputs, reliability of infrastructure, and institutions are included in the investment climate index. The four top-ranked states were Karnataka, Kerala, Gujarat, and Andhra Pradesh. West Bengal was ranked above Tamil Nadu. A useful point that emerges from this survey is that infrastructure comes up as a particularly binding constraint in currently low-investment states, while institutional factors like corruption and tax regulations impact both high- (currently) and low-investment states equally. The relationship between investment climate measured in one particular year and the subsequent investment and growth has not been well established. In this context, let us analyse the empirical evidence on inter-state disparities in post-reform years.

INTER-STATE DISPARITIES IN REGISTERED MANUFACTURING

A number of studies have investigated inter-state differences in growth rates and levels of per capita incomes (per capita SDP) in India.[6] Recent studies are much influenced by the modelling of cross-country difference in growth and levels of per capita income (Hall and Jones 1999). This is not surprising as these studies investigated why growth rates differ between countries. Why do some countries produce greater output per worker than others? These questions have much relevance for analysis of inter-state differences in per capita SDP in India.

Growth and Divergence

We confine ourselves to fourteen major states of India, as listed in Table 7.1.[7] This will help maintain comparability with other recent studies of regional income disparities (see Ahluwalia (2000), Sachs et al. (2002), and Singh and Srinivasan (2002), among others). These fourteen states have large populations and together share more than 93 per cent of India's population. Their share in India's registered manufacturing GDP was 79 per cent in 2004–5. We have divided the period 1980 to 2004 into two sub-periods. The years 1980–1 to 1990–1 constitute the pre-reform period and the years 1993–4 to 2004–5 are considered as the post-reform period.[8] We have used the database created by the Economic and Political Weekly Research Foundation (EPWRF 2009), which provides time series data on domestic product of states of India.

The average annual growth rate of registered manufacturing gross state domestic product (GSDP) in the fourteen selected states improved in the post-reform period relative to the pre-reform period (5.4 per cent against 4.2 per cent). State-wise growth rates in Table 7.1 reveal that the range (minimum to maximum) of growth rates in the pre-reform period (2.6 per cent to 12 per cent) is much higher than the range in the post-reform years (3.2 per cent to 8.2 per cent). The growth rate decelerated in ten out of fourteen states. An interesting fact emerges from Table 7.1 as the states are arranged in the descending order of their per capita GSDP in 1993–4. Of the five top states, four states (Punjab, Maharashtra, Gujarat, and Tamil Nadu) experienced deceleration in growth rate in the post-reform period. Two states, the low-income Uttar Pradesh (4.2 per cent from 12 per cent) and the high-income Punjab

---

[6] See Krishna (2004) for a useful survey and Nayyar (2008) for the most recent econometric analysis.

[7] Data for three states—Madhya Pradesh, Bihar, and Uttar Pradesh—includes the data on newly carved out states in 2000: Chhattisgarh, Jharkhand, and Uttarakhand respectively.

[8] The year 1991–2 was a crisis year in which there was a sharp fall in industrial activity in India. It may be reasonable to drop the immediately following year, 1992–3. This is also justified by the introduction of new series of national accounts with 1993–4 as the base year.

Table 7.1 Growth Rates of Registered Manufacturing GSDP for Fourteen Major States (per cent)

States*	1980–90**		1993–2004***	
	Average Annual Growth Rate	Coefficient of Variation	Average Annual Growth Rate	Coefficient of Variation
Punjab	9.0	56	3.3	104
Maharashtra	6.8	100	4.2	224
Haryana	7.5	44	7.8	27
Gujarat	8.4	123	7.6	125
Tamil Nadu	6.5	157	3.2	222
Kerala	2.6	605	4.6	158
Karnataka	8.5	104	8.2	130
Andhra Pradesh	7.0	54	5.6	67
West Bengal	2.7	120	5.1	61
Madhya Pradesh	7.9	132	4.7	173
Rajasthan	9.9	125	7.9	236
Uttar Pradesh	12.0	91	4.2	311
Orissa	6.3	426	7.5	219
Bihar	7.8	194	5.8	533
Above 14 States	4.2	69	5.4	102

Source: Estimates based on EPWRF (2009).

Note: *States in descending order of per capita GSDP in 1993–4.
**At constant 1980–1 prices.
***At constant 1993–4 prices.

(3.3 per cent from 9 per cent) experienced the steepest fall in growth rates. The growth rate did not change much in Haryana and Karnataka. Three relatively low-income states—West Bengal, Kerala, and Orissa—improved their growth performance in the post-reform period. These preliminary facts apparently suggest a tendency for convergence with the slowing down of growth in rich states and some acceleration in low- and middle-income states. This may or may not imply any reduction of inter-state disparities in Indian manufacturing.

It is pertinent to draw attention to the two concepts of convergence in the growth literature (Barro and Sala-i-Martin 1995). First is Beta convergence. Assuming all economies have access to the same technology and diminishing marginal returns to capital, poor economies have a tendency to grow faster (they have lower levels of physical capital stock, and therefore higher marginal productivity of capital) than rich economies. It follows that a negative relationship between initial level of income and subsequent growth rates can be postulated. The Beta convergence is said to take place when a low-income country tends to catch up with a high-income country in terms of per capita product. If all countries in the world or regions within a

country have the same technology and preferences, then all economies converge to the same steady state level of per capita income in the long run. This stronger version is called absolute convergence.[9] A simple econometric test of Beta convergence is to carry out a regression exercise. Regress the average growth rate of per capita income of a sample of countries (both rich and poor) on their initial level of per capita income. If the coefficient (called the convergence coefficient) is found to be negative and significant then this is taken as evidence in favour of Beta convergence.

The second concept is Sigma convergence that refers to a situation when the dispersion of per capita product across a group of countries or states within a country declines over time. Sigma convergence is a very appealing concept as it

[9] If we permit 'other' factors like technology, saving rates, and population growth rates to differ, then we get the concept of 'conditional convergence'. Under this, each country converges to its own steady state determined by country-specific features. Consequently, the steady state per capita income level of a country would be different from another country. Each state may be converging to a different level of income. We do not attempt to test conditional convergence in this chapter.

essentially looks at development distance between economic units (countries or states). We should note that Beta convergence is necessary but not sufficient for Sigma convergence.[10] It is possible that on average high (low) income states grow slower (faster) but the variance in income across states does not narrow over time. In other words, even if initially poor states grow faster, the gap between rich and poor states may not disappear as the process of Beta convergence could be offset by unexpected shocks or disturbances that tend to increase dispersion (Barro and Sala-i-Martin 1995). Therefore, the test of Sigma convergence is of critical importance in this context. If one observes an increasing dispersion of per capita product over time, then it implies Sigma divergence.

Do poor states tend to catch up with rich ones? If they do, then it is possible to predict convergence in per capita SDP over time. In our context of particular sector, that is manufacturing, we may like to know whether per capita manufacturing product of different states in India exhibits a tendency to converge to similar levels. Is it likely that opening up of the economy has weakened the convergence tendency? What are the possible factors that contribute to inter-state differences in SDP in manufacturing and perhaps slow down the pace of convergence or strengthen divergence tendency?

We have carried out some simple regressions similar to that found in the growth convergence literature. Our main objective is modest and hopes to throw light on some recent tendencies in cross-state differences in Indian manufacturing. We do attempt to get a broader understanding of determinants of cross-state differences in registered manufacturing growth in the pre-reform and post-reform periods.[11] We begin by assuming that all firms across states have access to the same technology in the manufacturing sector. There are no other inter-state differences in endowments like human capital, institutions like rule of law, etc. This is much more plausible as we are looking at a single sector within a country.[12] We then regress the average growth rate of each state in each period on the log of initial per capita manufacturing GSDP. For the pre-reform period, growth rates of per capita GSDP (1980–91) are regressed on the initial level of per capita product (1980–1).[13] Similarly, for the post-reform period. This is done using the sample fourteen states mentioned earlier. We get a statistically significant negative coefficient for both the periods. The convergence coefficient turns out to be –0.12 (pre-reform) and –0.04 (post-reform). Two inferences may be made. First, the evidence for convergence in the post-reform period is very weak as the numerical value of the convergence coefficient is not strongly negative. Second, the comparison of estimates of convergence coefficient in the two periods suggests that the convergence tendency has actually weakened in the post-reform period. Notice that the numerical magnitude of the convergence coefficient has decreased (less negative) in the post-reform period. This is consistent with the pattern of growth rates of GSDP in the fourteen states presented in Table 7.1. As we observed earlier, Sigma convergence is perhaps of greater interest as it reveals whether the gap (economic distance) that separates states in manufacturing is declining over time. This need not happen even in the presence of a tendency for Beta convergence. In other words, whether the dispersion of per capita manufacturing product has decreased in the post-reform period is the critical question. If the dispersion is not found to have declined, then the industrial growth process in India is leaving behind some states.

A widely used measure of dispersion is the standard deviation of logarithm of real per capita manufacturing GSDP. This measure is estimated for a cross-section of fourteen states, covering the period from 1980–1 to 2004–5 (Figure 7.1). It shows a lot of fluctuations but, on the average, a clear systematic rise in the post-reform period. The dispersion declined in the first half of the 1980s from 0.58 in 1980–1 to 0.53 in 1984–5, and then rose in the next two years to reach 0.59 in 1986–7. Then it fell continuously till 1989–90. The post-reform years show a sharp rise in the dispersion. The peak level of 0.65 is in 1996–7 and reflects the adverse effects of collapse of the manufacturing growth and investment in that year. It declined in the next four years to reach 0.55 in 1999–2000. The next peak level of dispersion is in 2001–2, another year of significant fall in industrial growth in India. Thereafter, it has shown a declining trend but the level of dispersion is much higher than the average in the pre-reform

---

[10] Absolute convergence implies convergence in income levels assuming that there are no random shocks that benefit or hurt states with high or low incomes. Sharp rise in energy prices will affect more those states with high share of energy-intensive industries. Similarly, import liberalization of machinery will affect more those states with higher share of import-competing machinery industries.

[11] There are alternative methods of testing the convergence hypothesis with varying levels of rigour. Our analysis is not to be construed as a serious econometric testing of convergence hypothesis that is a long-term trend. This is a preliminary approach, subject to further verification.

[12] Absolute convergence in this framework of single-sector analysis within a country can be argued to approximate conditional convergence due to similarity of technology and other conditions across

states within a country. This is not necessarily true as we observe large inter-state differences in resource endowments, institutions, and work culture in a large country like India.

[13] Actually, we estimate a modified version of the regression equation stated in the text. We regress the end period level of per capita GSDP on the beginning period GSDP and recover the convergence coefficient as $(1 + \beta) - 1$. See Nayyar (2008).

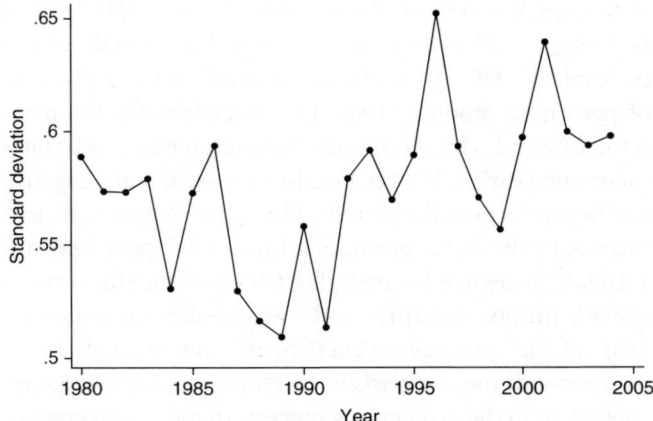

Figure 7.1 Standard Deviation of Log Per Capita Output in Manufacturing

years, as evident from Figure 7.1. This finding is in favour of the hypothesis of Sigma divergence.[14] Inter-state disparities in registered manufacturing growth in India have increased in the recent years of economic reforms.

Determinants of Inter-state Differences

What are the key factors that could help us someway in understanding the lack of convergence and increasing regional disparities in Indian manufacturing? In this section we focus on explaining inter-state differences in levels of manufacturing per capita.[15] A significant argument would be that inter-state differences largely reflect differences in two key proximate determinants of growth, namely, physical and human capital. An important earlier study that examined convergence in per capita SDP in India found per capita private investment and per capita public investment as the two critical determinants of steady state income levels across states (Nayyar 2008). A natural question to ask is: what are the determinants of private and public investment? More broadly, what drives greater physical investment into particular states in India relative to other states? The share of high-income states in the distribution of private corporate investment in India measured by loan given by All-India Financial Institutions is observed to be disproportionately high. Similarly, the high-income states are found to have higher than average per capita capital expenditures (proxy for public investment). Higher public investment in richer states actually 'crowds in' private investment, indicating

complementarities between the two types of investment. It is equally likely that differences in manufacturing sector are being driven by large differences in investment (gross fixed capital formation) between states in the reform period. We found the share of top three states in our set of fourteen states, namely, Maharashtra, Gujarat, and Tamil Nadu, in manufacturing investment to be more than 49 per cent in 2005–6. This share was 48 per cent in 1993–4 and less than 40 per cent in 1980–1. The post-reform period also facilitated the flow of FDI into India. Available data on the number of investment proposals and the amount of FDI approved clearly indicates concentration of FDI inflows in a few states. Five states—Maharashtra, Tamil Nadu, Karnataka, Andhra Pradesh, and West Bengal—and the Union Territory of Delhi accounted for over 86 per cent of the total FDI amount approved during 1991–2001. Their share in total number of approvals was found to be over 75 per cent.[16] This confirms the strengthening of unequal tendencies in the distribution of investment in the post-reform period. One needs to answer what drives FDI and domestic investment into particular states. There is some evidence to believe that similar factors influence the location decisions of both domestic and foreign firms.

Differences in physical capital stocks and investment flows are an outcome of differential perception of firms' and corporate entities' production–location decisions. Location decisions are driven by potential access to material inputs and cost economies. The level of urbanization of a state is used here as an index of economic diversity. Urbanization economies arise as a result of diversity of economic activities in a location and access to diverse inputs, infrastructure, and labour skills. The study by Sachs et al. (2002) found that differences in initial urbanization (percentage of urban population in a state) alone explained 82 per cent of cross-state variation in per capita growth rates over the period 1980 to 1998. They showed that FDI flowed mainly to the urbanized states and to those states with large mining sectors as per cent of GSDP. Following this reasoning, we can expect that urbanization is a key factor that influences both domestic and foreign investment flows. Initial differences in urbanization could partly explain inter-state differences in the depth of manufacturing activity.

Another source of the lack of convergence outcome would be the initial differences in human capital stock and infrastructure like power. As noted in the literature on growth and human capital (Barro 2001; Krueger and

---

[14] Different Indian states are perhaps converging to different steady state level of manufacturing product per capita.

[15] Understanding level differences is perhaps more important as growth rates differences could be largely transitory (Hall and Jones 1999).

[16] Based on the data provided by the Secretariat of Industrial Approvals (SIA), Ministry of Commerce and Industry, Government of India, in *SIA Newsletter* (Annual Issue 2001).

Table 7.2   Determinants of Inter-state Differences in Per Capita Manufacturing GSDP, 2004–5

Dependent Variable: Log of Per Capita Registered Manufacturing GSDP in 2004–5

Urban—1991	0.06*** (5.99)					0.04*** (3.89)
Schooling Attainment 1992		3.74*** (5.49)				
GER—Secondary Education 1991			0.05*** (4.71)			
Literacy Rate 1991				0.03*** (4.45)		0.02*** (5.57)
Power Infrastructure Index 1995					0.01** (2.72)	
Constant	5.5 (18.3)	5.48 (15.5)	5.75 (19.6)	5.14 (1.7)	6.17 (17.4)	4.99 (21.9)
R^2	0.59	0.46	0.47	0.52	0.30	0.72
No. of Observations	14	14	14	14	14	14

Notes: GER is Gross enrolment ratio.

**Significant at 5% level.

***Significant at 10% level.

Figures in parentheses are robust '*t*' values.

Lindahl 2001), initial schooling levels can impact subsequent growth, particularly in poor countries. Given the level of GDP, a higher initial stock of human capital implies a higher ratio of human to physical capital. It is argued that higher ratio of human to physical capital can generate higher growth in two ways. First, greater human capital helps absorption and adaptation of received technology. Second, its ability to absorb physical capital is higher when human capital and physical capital are complementary. Given initial GDP per capita, countries with greater human capital are likely to grow faster, generating conditional divergence. Cross-country studies have emphasized the importance of initial stock of human capital, like average years of schooling completed, and initial investment in human capital, like school enrolment ratios. Data on school enrolment is considered less reliable as school dropout rates are equally high in developing countries.[17]

We have reported the results of some simple regression models in Table 7.2 that form the basis for our arguments to emphasize initial differences in urbanization and human capital (educational enrolment and attainment) as important factors contributing to regional disparities in manufacturing in India.[18] The reason for their importance as determinants is based on the finding that they are found to be key drivers of FDI and, therefore, presumably domestic investment. A positive and statistically significant association was observed between average per capita FDI approvals (1991 to 2001—cumulative value of approved investment) and urbanization in the fourteen states. Similarly, a positive and highly significant association was observed between per capita FDI and the two measures of human capital, namely, literacy rate in 1991 and the average schooling attainment in each state in 1992. The data on average schooling attainment refers to the proportion of 15–19 year olds who have completed education till at least Class VIII.[19] In other words, states with greater initial human capital are likely to have received relatively more FDI inflows. This is consistent with the earlier finding of per capita SDP and literacy positively impacting loans advanced by financial institutions (Nayyar 2008).

As evident from Table 7.2, initial urbanization measured by percentage of urban population is positively related to per capita manufacturing GSDP. This strongly supports the earlier finding from econometric cost functions that

---

[17] In cross-section growth models, differences in per capita income levels are attributed to differences in physical capital stock per worker, human capital stock per worker, and productivity (technology).

[18] Literacy rates are taken from *National Human Development Report 2001*, Planning Commission, Government of India, New Delhi.

[19] Schooling attainment estimates for each state are based on *National Family Health Survey 1992–3*, estimated by Filmer and Pritchett (1998).

Table 7.3 Distribution of Manufacturing GSDP by State

States*	1980–1	1993–4	2004–5
Punjab	2.9	3.9	2.8
Maharashtra	27.7	24.0	22.5
Haryana	3.1	3.5	6.2
Gujarat	10.4	11.7	15.2
Tamil Nadu	10.5	12.1	9.3
Kerala	3.0	2.0	2.0
Karnataka	5.3	5.6	7.5
Andhra Pradesh	4.7	7.0	7.0
West Bengal	11.4	5.8	4.2
Madhya Pradesh	5.5	6.0	5.7
Rajasthan	2.3	2.6	3.2
Uttar Pradesh	6.2	8.8	7.6
Orissa	1.9	1.9	2.3
Bihar	5.1	5.1	4.6
Above 14 States	100	100	100

Source: Estimates based on EPWRF (2009).

Note: *States in descending order of per capita GSDP in 1993–4.

economic diversity of a state yields significant external economies (Lall and Chakravorty 2005). Similarly, the three alternative measures of human capital—literacy, schooling attainment, and gross enrolment ratio (GER) in secondary education[20] are highly significant and positive. Modern manufacturing activity emphasizes training and on-the-job learning that requires educated workers. In this context, the significance of GER in secondary education clearly underlines the importance of investment in human capital. Consistent with the education and growth literature, the stock of human capital (the schooling attainment) emerges with highly significant positive coefficient. What is surprising is the significance of initial literacy even in the presence of variable urbanization. This result has the following interpretation. Holding constant the level of urbanization in different states, states with higher initial literacy levels will have higher per capita manufacturing GSDP. The development of power infrastructure is found to be a significant factor contributing to inter-state disparities. The power infrastructure index encompasses four aspects of power sector, namely, (a) installed capacity per capita; (b) net generation per capita; (c) electricity availability per capita; and (d) transmission and distribution lines per 100 sq km in the area. The power index reflects the relative position of different states in terms of cost disability that states suffer in providing public services because of their underdeveloped infrastructure. It is centred at the all-India value at 100. A state's index value measures the distance of that state from the all-India average level for the power sector.[21] In brief, initial differences in human capital and power seem to be the key factors behind the observed inter-state disparities in manufacturing development. It is important to emphasize that we have used initial values on the right hand side to minimize the possibility of reverse causation.[22]

SPATIAL CONCENTRATION OF MANUFACTURING IN INDIA

The flip side of industrial growth in India is the spatial concentration of industries. In the beginning of the 1980s the top three states in terms of their share in GSDP were Maharashtra, West Bengal, and Tamil Nadu (Table 7.3). These three states had received 56 per cent of the industrial licences issued between 1953 and 1961.[23] In 1970–1, their combined share

---

[20] Data on GER in secondary education in 1991 are taken from Rani (2007).

[21] The power index is taken from a study on state infrastructure done for the Twelfth Finance Commission by Nirmal Mohanty, available at http:// financeindia.nic.in (accessed on 17 July 2009).

[22] We have also considered the average of log per capita product over the period 1993–2004 as the right-hand side variable with similar results.

[23] Estimated by Chakravorty and Lall (2007).

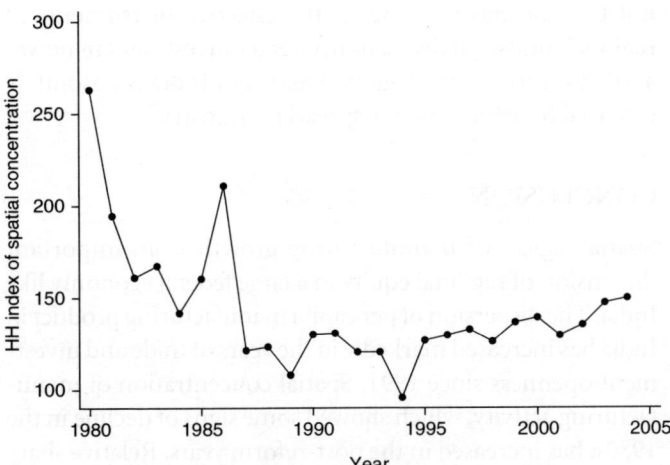

Figure 7.2   Spatial Concentration of Registered
Manufacturing in India

of value added in registered manufacturing was 48 per cent. Between 1970 and 1980 there was little redistribution of value added except for the fall in the share of West Bengal (Mohan 1993). The share of these three states in total registered manufacturing was higher than their share in total NSDP in the 1970s. In other words, the spatial inequality of registered manufacturing was probably increasing in the 1970s.[24] It started declining in the 1980s (Figure 7.2). Our measure of

regional inequality is the spatial Herfindhal–Hirschman index (HH index) of concentration, defined as follows:

$$HH \text{ index} = \Sigma \, (s_i - x_i)^2$$

where s_i is the output share of the ith state in manufacturing and x_i is the state's share in total GDP of the country. The HH index is a relative index that measures the extent to which an individual sector (manufacturing in our case) is spatially concentrated within a country. It compares a given state's share in manufacturing output relative to its share in total economy output. The estimates of HH index for the period 1980–1 to 2004–5 are shown in Figure 7.2.

It is evident that spatial concentration of manufacturing was declining in the 1980s. The years after 1990 do not show the kind of steep falls except in 1994–5. Spatial concentration in Indian manufacturing clearly shows an increasing trend, particularly after 1995–6. On this basis we may argue that spatial concentration is increasing in the post-reform years. The decline in the 1980s is an outcome of industrial decline of West Bengal in particular and stagnation of the eastern states of Bihar and Orissa. The rise in concentration may be attributed to the superior industrial performance of Gujarat, Karnataka, and Haryana, and the continuing dominance of Maharashtra. An indirect way of supporting spatial concentration is to examine the distribution of cumulative gross fixed capital formation (GFCF) over the

Table 7.4   Distribution of Investment by State, 1980–2005*

State	1980–91	1993–2005	2002–6
Andhra Pradesh	7.5	5.4	6.5
Bihar	5.5	4.1	3.5
Gujarat	10.5	18.3	16.8
Haryana	2.8	1.5	4.4
Karnataka	4.1	7.6	8.2
Kerala	2.1	1.6	1.1
Madhya Pradesh	8.8	6.8	5.3
Maharashtra	19.4	18.9	18.9
Orissa	4.1	3.3	4.0
Punjab	4.6	3.0	3.1
Rajasthan	3.9	2.5	2.6
Tamil Nadu	9.7	11.4	13.4
Uttar Pradesh	9.8	9.8	8.8
West Bengal	7.0	5.9	3.2

Sources: EPWRF (2002).

Note: *Cumulative gross fixed capital formation over the respective years.

[24] We say probably because we have not estimated the index of spatial inequality for the 1970s.

same period (Table 7.4). The emergence of Gujarat and Karnataka with higher shares is obvious. The third column is particularly informative as it shows the shares over the period 2002–3 to 2005–6, the years of industrial recovery and faster growth of exports in India. In the recovery phase, the four states that lead the investment shares are Gujarat, Haryana, Tamil Nadu, and to some extent Karnataka. Maharashtra maintains its leadership.

What are the forces behind this trend of increasing concentration of manufacturing? One could argue that in the post-reform period private entrepreneurs gravitated towards states with relatively better infrastructure and agglomeration advantages (Lall and Chakravorty 2005). This is facilitated by the liberalization of entry of domestic and foreign firms since 1991. Such states are invariably states that have already achieved higher levels of industrialization, production experience, and industrial diversity. History of industry in a state seems to matter more than geography. With India's greater integration with the world economy since the 1990s, new investment was favourable to states with greater access to coastal areas. We found a significant positive relationship between investment shares of states in 2004–5 and an index of coastal access.[25] Haryana is an exception that is driven by the emergence of automobile industry in Gurgaon district and proximity to Delhi.

What can be done to break the tendency for regional concentration of industries? In the new economics of geography, uneven development is an outcome of relative strengths of forces of agglomeration (centripetal forces) and forces of dispersion (centrifugal forces). Flow of more investment into few states like Gujarat and Tamil Nadu and the continuing dominance of Maharashtra suggest that agglomeration benefits outweigh costs associated with agglomeration like rising costs of non-traded goods like power, housing for labour, congestion, and competition for skilled labour. In the years of trade protection and import substituting industrialization, the forces of agglomeration were forward linkages like proximity to final consumers (access to large domestic markets in cities) and backward linkages like access to intermediate inputs. This situation was reinforced by higher transport costs and the underdevelopment of transport infrastructure. The importance of market access as a determinant of production location has declined in recent years of economic reforms with improved transport and communication infrastructure, reduction of transport costs, and trade liberalization. Access to (or the lack of) power (quality plus quantity) and human capital have become critical determinants of manufacturing investment decisions. In the absence of these two—power and educated people—regionally targeted financial–fiscal incentives will

not be (and have not been) the effective instruments of regional industrial dispersion. Greater investment in power and education in the lagging regions of India is absolutely essential to achieve better spread of industry.

CONCLUSION

Spatial aspect of manufacturing growth is an important dimension of regional equity in a large federal economy like India. The dispersion of per capita manufacturing product in India has increased markedly in the years of trade and investment openness since 1991. Spatial concentration of manufacturing activity, which showed some signs of decline in the 1980s, has increased in the post-reform years. Relative share of investment in the period of recovery (2002–5) has largely favoured Gujarat, Haryana, and Tamil Nadu. Maharashtra, the state with the initially well-developed industrial structure and production experience, continues to enjoy its comparative advantage. In brief, agglomeration tendencies have not diminished with improved potential market access. Location advantages of availability of quantity and quality of power and labour skills (human capital) have emerged as critical determinants of spatial disparities in manufacturing growth. Greater investments in these two areas in the lagging states, perhaps through public–private partnerships, appear to be the only way to strengthen the convergence forces in India.

REFERENCES

Ahluwalia, M.S. (2000), 'Economic Performance of States in Post-Reforms Period', *Economic and Political Weekly*, 35(19): 1637–48.

Bajpai, N. and J.D. Sachs (1999), 'The Progress of Policy Reform and Variations in Performance at the Sub-National Level in India', Harvard Institute for International Development, Development Discussion, Paper No. 730, Harvard University.

Barro, R.J. (2001), 'Human Capital and Growth', *The American Economic Review*, 91(2): 12–17.

Barro, R.J. and X. Sala-i-Martin (1995), *Economic Growth*. Boston MA: McGraw-Hill.

Chakravorty, S. and S. Lall (2007), *Made in India: The Economic Geography and Political Economy of Industrialization*. New Delhi: Oxford University Press.

Chaudhuri, S. and M. Ravallion (2006), 'Partially Awakened Giants: Growth in China and India', The World Bank Policy Research Working Paper No. 4069, Washington DC.

Economic and Political Weekly Research Foundation (EPWRF) (2002), Annual Survey of Indian Industries 1973–74 to 2003–04, A database of the Industrial Sector in India, Mumbai.

——— (2009), Domestic Product of States of India 1960–61 to 2006–07. Second updated edition, Mumbai.

Filmer, D. and L. Pritchett (1998), 'Estimating Wealth Effects without Expenditure Data or Tears', The World Bank Policy Research Working Paper No. 1994, Washington DC.

---

[25] This index is the percentage of population within 100 km of coast (Sachs et al. 2002).

Hall, E.R. and C.I. Jones (1999), 'Why Do Some Countries Produce So Much More Output per Worker Than Others', *The Quarterly Journal of Economics*, 114(1): 83–116.

Iarossi, G. (2009), 'The Investment Climate in 16 Indian States', World Bank Policy Research Working Paper No. 4817, Washington DC.

Krishna, K.L. (2004), 'Patterns and Determinants of Economic Growth in Indian States', Working Paper No. 144, ICRIER, New Delhi.

Krueger, A. and M. Lindahl (2001), 'Education for Growth: Why and For Whom', *Journal of Economic Literature*, 39(4): 1101–36.

Lall, S. and S. Chakravorty (2005), 'Industrial Location and Spatial Inequality: Theory and Evidence from India', *Review of Development Economics*, 9(1): 47–68.

Mohan, R. (1993), 'Industrial Location Policies and Their Implications for India', Paper No. 9, Studies in Industrial Development, Ministry of Industry, New Delhi.

Nayyar, G. (2008), 'Economic Growth and Regional Inequality in India', *Economic and Political Weekly*, 43(6): 58–67.

Rani, G. (2007), 'Secondary Education in India: Determinants of Development and Performance', Working Paper, NIEPA, New Delhi. Available at http:\www.esocialsciences.com (accessed on 10 July 2009).

Rodrik, D. and A. Subramanian (2004), 'The Mystery of Indian Growth Transition', NBER Working Paper No. 10376. Available at http://www.nber.org/papers/w10376

Sekhar, A.U. (1983), 'Industrial Location Policy: The Indian Experience', World Bank Working Paper No. 620, Washington DC.

Sachs, J., N. Bajpai, and A. Ramiah (2002), 'Understanding Regional Economic Growth in India', Working Paper No. 88, Center for International Development, Harvard University.

Singh, N. and T.N. Srinivasan (2002), 'Indian Federalism, Economic Reform and Globalization', UC Santa Cruz Center for International Economics Working Paper No. 02-13. Available at SSRN: http://ssrn.com/abstract=315968

8

The Role of Auditor and Audit Committee in Governance

Jayati Sarkar and Subrata Sarkar

INTRODUCTION

External auditors and audit committees are two important governance mechanisms designed to ensure that a company produces relevant, adequate, and credible information that investors and independent observers can use to monitor the company's performance. Poor information quality coupled with weak governance mechanisms can adversely affect the reliability of financial statements for investors, weaken the link between earnings and firm valuation, and increase transaction costs in the capital market. The external auditor and the audit committee certify both the quantity and the quality of the information produced by a company. It is therefore not surprising to find regulations all over the world to have placed a major emphasis on the structure, role, and powers of the external auditor and the functioning of the audit committee.

The Sarbanes-Oxley Act of 2002 (SOX hereafter) that came into force in the US within one year of the Enron debacle has set in motion far-reaching changes in the regulations governing auditor independence and audit committee across the world. In India, the onset of the liberalization measures and the accompanying governance reforms that began in 1991 have put great emphasis on the role of the external auditor and the audit committee. The Clause 49 Regulations (SEBI 2004) that were made part of the Listing Agreement by the Securities Exchange Board of India (SEBI) in 2001 required every listed company to have an audit committee, and specified detailed guidelines regarding its composition, role, and power. The Naresh Chandra Committee (NCC hereafter) (NCC 2004) that was constituted in August 2002 produced an exhaustive report on auditor–company relationship and functioning of the audit committee. Many of these recommendations have been incorporated in the Companies Bill, 2009,[1] which is currently waiting for legislative approval. When enacted into law, the regulations will be at par with the best international practices and will lead to fundamental changes in the way auditors and audit committees have been functioning in India.

This chapter reviews the governance reforms undertaken in India with respect to auditor and audit committee independence. In doing so, it critically compares them with the regulations existing in the US. This is followed by a discussion of the existing research on the effectiveness of audit committees and audit independence in corporate governance. The chapter concludes by suggesting some governance reforms that may be considered to further strengthen auditor independence and the functioning of audit committees in India.

AUDITOR INDEPENDENCE

Wikipedia defines audit as 'an evaluation of a person, organization, system, process, enterprise, project or product,

---

[1] The Companies Bill, 2009, http://www.mca.gov.in/Ministry/actsbills/pdf/Companies_Bill_2009_24 Aug2009.pdf

on a test basis, to ascertain the validity and reliability of information and to provide an assessment of a system's internal control. … In the case of financial audits, a set of financial statements are said to be true and fair when they are free of material misstatements—a concept influenced by both quantitative and qualitative factors'.[2]

Auditors are the lead actors in the auditing process and provide independent oversight to the financial reporting by companies. Modern-day corporations are huge and their operations are complex. While accounting standards and norms are specified by the regulators for proper accounting, preparation of proper financial reports requires an evaluation of the judgements and assumptions made by the management and justification of the choice made by it from among several alternative accounting principles. Consistency of applications in preparing accounts and coverage of all relevant financial aspects are required. Auditors scrutinize and verify the accounts and certify that the financial statements are prepared in accordance with the prescribed principles and that the accounts are free from material misstatements. It is therefore expected that the law in all countries would put enormous responsibility on the auditors to ensure that the accounts give a true and fair view of the operations of a company. In the US, the SOX has put great emphasis on auditor independence, and following the Act, the US Securities and Exchange Commission (SEC)[3] has made specific rules to put the provisions of the Act into operation. At home, the NCC has given a series of recommendations that have been incorporated in the Companies Bill, 2009, and are awaiting Parliament's approval.

The rules and regulations regarding auditor's independence framed by regulators are predicated on some fundamental principles. The NCC lists two fundamental principles behind auditor's independence: (i) independence of mind—which permits arriving at an informed and reasoned opinion without being affected by factors that compromise integrity, professional scepticism, and objectivity of judgement; and (ii) independence in appearance—which requires avoiding facts, circumstances, and instances where an informed third party could reasonably conclude that integrity, objectivity, and professionalism have, or may have, been compromised (NCC 2004: 36). As the NCC rightly points out, 'For the public to have confidence in the quality of audit, it is essential that auditors should always be—and be seen to be—independent of the companies that they are auditing' (Ibid. 37). Thus, when situations of potential conflicts arise, the law in general has taken a sceptical view and erred on the side of caution by putting the interest of the general public before the interest of the auditor.

Similar principles are enshrined in the Code of Ethics for Professional Accountants, prescribed by the International Federation of Accountants (IFAC), which identifies five types of potential threats to an auditor's independence:

(i) *Self-interest threats*, which occur when an auditing firm, its partner, or associate could benefit from a financial interest in an audit client.

(ii) *Self-review threats*, which occur during a review of any judgement or conclusion reached in a previous audit or non-audit engagement, or when a member of the audit team was previously a director or senior employee of the client.

(iii) *Advocacy threats*, which occur when the auditor promotes, or is perceived to promote, a client's opinion to a point where people may believe that objectivity is getting compromised.

(iv) *Familiarity threats* are self-evident, and occur when auditors form relationships with the client where they end up being too sympathetic to the client's interests.

(v) *Intimidation threats*, which occur when auditors are deterred from acting objectively with an adequate degree of professional scepticism because of threat of replacement.

Building on these five fundamental principles, both the NCC and the SOX have put in place a number of regulations/recommendations regarding the qualification of auditors for engaging in statutory audit, the type of non-audit services that they can render, the need for rotating members of the audit engagement team, and restrictions on the extent of non-audit fees that an auditing firm can get from an audit engagement. The single purpose of these efforts has been to ensure auditor independence.

Key Aspects of Auditor Independence

The three key aspects of auditor independence that all regulations try to address are: (a) potential conflicts of interest that arise from employment, financial interest, and other relationships between the auditing firm and the audit client; (b) types of non-audit services rendered by the auditing firm; and (c) audit partner rotation. The NCC has deliberated extensively on these three aspects and come up with recommendations that are in line with the best international practices and that closely follow the provisions under the SOX Act.

Disqualification for Audit Assignments

Conflict of interest is one primary concern of the regulators for ensuring auditor independence. The NCC recommended that an auditing firm will be disqualified from being

---

[2] http://en.wikipedia.org/wiki/Audit.
[3] Sarbanes-Oxley Rulemaking and Reports, http://www.sec.gov/spotlight/sarbanes-oxley.htm

appointed as the statutory external auditor if the audit firm, its partners, or members of the engagement team as well as their 'direct relatives' (i) had any financial interest in the audit client, (ii) received any loans and guarantees from the audit client, (iii) had any business relationship with the audit client, and (iv) had any personal relationships with the key officers of the audit client, that is, any whole time director, CEO, CFO, company secretary, senior management belonging to the top two managerial levels, and the officer who is in default. The NCC also recommended to have a (v) cooling period of two years before any partner or member of the auditing firm can join the audit client, or any key officer of the audit client can join the auditing firm, and (vi) prohibition on undue dependence under which an audit firm was disqualified from auditing if the fees from the audit client exceeded 25 per cent of the total revenues of the audit firm. The recommendations were tight in that they included all the affiliates and the subsidiaries of the both the audit client and the audit firm in the determination of independence. Section 124 of the Companies Bill, 2009, incorporated the first four recommendations of the NCC report. The recommendations regarding undue dependence and, more strikingly, the recommendation regarding the cooling period were not incorporated in the Companies Bill, 2009.

The recommendation regarding undue dependence had attracted some debate as this may affect the survival of small firms. The NCC has been sympathetic to this argument and specified that its recommendation with respect to undue dependence was not applicable to audit firms for the first five years from the date of commencement of their activities, and for firms whose total annual revenues were less than Rs 15 lakh per year. The principle of 'intimidation treat', which is likely to operate on the audit firm when it is reliant on a few clients for its survival, may have prompted the committee to make this recommendation. Equally arguable of course is the reverse viewpoint that if regulatory action for wrongdoing is credible, then the audit firm is likely to work even more diligently when it has only a few clients. Coupled with this, the audit committee that is envisaged to play a critical role in ensuring that the external auditor is protected from the pulls and pressures of the management, may have prompted the Companies Bill, 2009, to not include this recommendation for enactment. Similar regulation on undue dependence, however, does not exist in the SOX Act.

The more striking omission from the Companies Bill, 2009, is the NCC recommendation of providing a cooling off period before a member of the audit engagement team can join the audit client or a key officer of the audit client can join the audit firm. This recommendation comes from the basic concern that a member of the audit engagement team who has only recently been a key officer of the audit client poses significant 'self-review' threat as this person will be less inclined to detect errors that he/she may have committed in his/her capacity as a key officer of the audit client. Simultaneously, a key officer of the audit client who has only recently been a member of the auditing firm can significantly influence the auditor's incentive, ability, and inclination to detect potential accounting and financial errors by the audit client. The recommendation views passage of time to be essential in reducing the possibility of influencing the policies of the accounting firm and the resultant perceived loss of independence.

The provision of the cooling period is one of the major concerns under the SOX Act. Section 206 of the SOX Act specifies that an accounting firm cannot perform an audit of a company '[i]f a chief executive officer, controller, chief financial officer, chief accounting officer, or any person serving in an equivalent position for the issuer, was employed by that registered independent public accounting firm and participated in any capacity in the audit of that issuer during the 1-year period preceding the date of the initiation of the audit'.[4] The SEC, while framing its Rule on 'Conflicts of Interest Resulting from Employment Relationships' for implementing these provisions of the SOX Act, expanded the coverage of the cooling off period from the four specified key officers named in the Act to any person in a 'financial reporting oversight role'. However, recognizing the over-reaching nature of the laws, it narrowed down the application of the cooling period to only the lead partner, concurring partner, and any other member of the audit engagement team body who provided ten or more hours of audit, review, and attestation services (SEC Rules 208-2).

There are some notable differences between the SEC Rules and the recommendations of the NCC. Under the NCC recommendations, the cooling off period applies to not only the audit partners but to all members of the audit engagement team. In contrast, the SEC Rules are applicable to the lead partner, concurring partner, and to only those members rendering ten or more hours of audit services, the assumption being that some minimum amount of participation is required for a member to have significant interaction with the management during the audit process. Second, under the NCC recommendation, the cooling off period is applicable irrespective of the employment position which the former audit firm member takes up in the audit client and not restricted to positions with financial reporting and oversight role, as it is under the SEC Rules. Third, the NCC recommendations apply not only to members of the audit firm taking up positions in the audit client, but also to employees of the audit client taking up positions in the audit

---

[4] http://www.sec.gov/rules/final/33-8183.htm

firm. Finally, the cooling off period under the NCC is two years while it is one year under the SEC Rules. Perhaps the first two recommendations of the NCC are too broad in their applicability and can be narrowed down to some extent. The major criterion in determining the applicability of the law should be the ability and the incentive of the members of the audit firm and the audit client to influence the effectiveness of the audit process. Unlike the SEC, the NCC recommendations that require the cooling off period to also apply to employees of audit client while joining the audit firm is a well thought out move and recognizes the reverse influence that former employees of the audit client can exercise when they are part of the audit engagement team. However, in this case too, the scope of the recommendation can be narrowed down by making the law applicable only to key officers of the audit client joining key positions in the audit firm. Thus, the ideal rule would be one that provides for a cooling period before the lead, concurring, or any significant member of the audit engagement team takes up a financial reporting oversight role in the audit client, or a person in a financial reporting oversight role in the audit client becomes a lead, concurring, or a significant member of the audit firm. The

terms 'significant audit member' could be defined based on the nature and duration of services by the audit member. The extent of the cooling period could be left to be decided based on norms and practice in other countries.

Prohibited Non-audit Services

Provision of non-audit services is another major concern to the regulator in ensuring auditor independence as rendering many of these services puts the independence of the auditor standard at significant risk. Auditing firms have incentives to perform non-audit services to augment their income because of the informational advantage that they gain during the auditing process about the financial status of the audit client. Accordingly, laws in various countries list a number of services that an auditing firm is prohibited from rendering to its audit clients. The prohibition of non-audit services comes from the two principles, namely, self-review threat, and advocacy threat, outlined earlier. Similar principles are highlighted by the SEC when it mentions that 'the Commission's principles of independence with respect to services provided by auditors are largely predicated on

---

Box 8.1   List of Prohibited Non-audit Services by the NCC and the SEC

List of Prohibited Non-audit Services under NCC (Recommendation 2.2)

1. Accounting and book-keeping services, related to the accounting records or financial statements of the audit client
2. Internal audit services
3. Financial information systems design and implementation, including services related to IT systems for preparing financial or management accounts and information flows of a company
4. Actuarial services
5. Broker, dealer, investment adviser, or investment banking services
6. Outsourced financial services
7. Management functions, including the provision of temporary staff to audit clients
8. Any form of staff recruitment, and particularly hiring of senior management staff for the audit client
9. Valuation services and fairness opinion

Note: The Companies Bill, 2009, includes the first seven recommendations of the NCC.

List of Non-audit Services Prohibited by the SEC

1. Book-keeping or other services related to the Accounting records or financial statements of the audit client
2. Financial information systems design and implementation
3. Appraisal or valuation services, fairness opinions, or contribution-in-kind reports
4. Actuarial services
5. Internal audit outsourcing
6. Management functions
7. Human resources
8. Broker–Dealer, investment adviser, or investment banking services
9. Legal services
10. Expert services

three basic principles, violations of which would impair the auditor's independence: (1) an auditor cannot function in the role of management, (2) an auditor cannot audit his or her own work, and (3) an auditor cannot serve in an advocacy role for his or her client'.[5]

The NCC recommended nine types of services that an audit firm should be prohibited from rendering to its audit client. The list of services mimics those prohibited under the SEC, except for legal services and expert services which are prohibited under the SEC but not recommended for prohibition by the NCC (Box 8.1). The SEC puts forward purposeful arguments built on the principle of 'advocacy threat' for including these two services in the prohibited list but the NCC does not cite any reasons for excluding them in its recommendations. Further, under the SEC Rules (208-6), the lead, concurring, and audit partner cannot receive compensation based on selling engagements other than audit, review, and attestation services as rendering these services can hamper an accountant's objectivity and shift the focus from audit to non-audit works. Other members of the audit engagement team, however, can receive compensation for rendering non-audit services, provided that those are not in the prohibited list and are approved by the audit committee. No such rule exits in the Companies Bill, 2009, nor is it recommended by the NCC.

Section 127 of the Companies Bill, 2009, incorporated the first seven recommendations of the NCC (see Box 8.1)[6] but did not include the recommendations relating to (i) any form of staff recruitment, and particularly hiring of senior management staff for the audit client, and (ii) valuation services and fairness opinion in the list of prohibited services. Under the SEC, both (i) appraisal or valuation services, fairness opinions, or contribution-in-kind reports as well as (ii) human resources services are strictly prohibited. As the SEC recognizes in its discussion of Rules, when an auditor actively assists the management to recruit, train, and evaluate employees for the audit client, especially in senior management positions, the accountant would be reluctant to suggest the possibility that those employees failed to perform their jobs appropriately, or at least reasonable investors might perceive the accountant to be reluctant, because doing so would require the accountant to acknowledge shortcomings in its human resource service'.[7]

With respect to valuation services and fairness opinions, the SOX Act recognizes that undertaking these services may put the accountant under the self-review threat of having to review his/her own work as these services often require the auditing firm to make key assumptions, projections, and valuations of a company's assets, cash flow, and other relevant financial variables that can become the subject of audit later. Also, valuation services being fairness opinions that are offered mostly for judging the sufficiency of consideration in a financial transaction are likely to be based on an aggressive assessment of risk assessment as opposed to the conservative assessment that is expected of auditors when auditing the company's accounts in public interest.

It is apparent that an expanded list of prohibited services is not in the interest of the auditing firms. Rendering valuations services, fairness opinion, and human services can provide significant opportunities of augmenting the revenue of audit firms, especially when the fees from audit services is low. Thus, restricting these services can significantly hamper the survival of the audit firms, and especially the smaller ones. Yet, the survival of auditing firms has to be balanced against the interest of the public at large to ensure that the integrity of the auditing process is not jeopardized. If survival is the reason for not enacting these two provisions into law, then it puts the independence issue into serious question because audit firms are more likely to stand by their assessment as doing otherwise puts them at the risk of losing these non-audit services. On the other hand, if these services account for an insignificant proportion of the revenue of the audit firms, then there is a great point in including them in the prohibited list as doing so does not materially affect the auditing firm but increases the public's confidence in the audit process.

Compulsory Audit Partner Rotation

Rotation of audit firms as a means of safeguarding auditor independence has been a subject of intense debate for many years. Proponents of compulsory audit firm rotation advance two arguments: (i) decline in audit quality and competence in the absence of audit firm rotation and (ii) loss of independence due to long association (Hoyle 1978). With respect to the former, these proponents point to the laxity in standards and the decline in creativity that occur when working for an audit client for a long period, and argue that mandatory auditor rotation is necessary for a fresh look. In addition, mandatory rotation is expected to lead to better audit quality by increasing competition among audit firms, reducing the dependence on a single client, and increasing audit effort as incumbent firms are likely to work harder when they are aware that their work will be reviewed shortly by another auditor. With respect to

---

[5] See 'Strengthening the Commission's Requirements Regarding Auditor Independence', Section II.B, available at http://www.sec.gov/rules/final/33-8183.htm

[6] The Companies Bill, 2009, broke up the investment adviser or investment banking services separately into investment adviser services and investment banking services.

[7] See 'Strengthening the Commission's Requirements Regarding Auditor Independence', Section II.B, available at http://www.sec.gov/rules/final/33-8183.htm

the latter, these proponents point to the significant familiarity threat that occurs with long association, causing the auditor to develop friendly ties and to endorse the views of the management.

Opponents of mandatory auditor rotation point out that modern-day corporations that have complex financial operations cutting across national borders demand auditors who are well versed in accounting standards and auditing rules specified by the laws and regulations of each country. Accordingly, these proponents argue that mandatory audit firm rotation can pose even greater threat to audit quality by resulting in loss of continuity and reducing audit competence. In addition, they point to the increase in training costs by audit firms, which are eventually likely to be passed on to the audit clients. It is not that those who do not support mandatory audit firm rotation do not acknowledge the potential problems that can arise out of long-term association of the auditor with the client; what they disagree with is that rotating the audit firm is the best way to solve the problem, given the potential cost that mandatory rotation involves. Instead, they suggest that improving the regulatory framework governing the appointment and functioning of the auditor, enhancing accounting and reporting standards, and making auditors responsible for their oversight role would be safer and better ways of ensuring audit independence.

Given the equally persuasive arguments of both sides, regulators in various countries have tried to strike a balance between the need for a fresh look with concerns about loss of continuity and decline in audit quality and competence, by requiring audit partner rotation instead of rotation of the audit firm itself. In India, the NCC recommended that all partners and at least half of the audit engagement team (excluding article clerks) be rotated after five years. The recommendation also provided for a cooling period of five years before rotated members could join the audit engagement team for the particular audit client. In the US, the SEC Rules (208-4) require the lead partner and the concurring partner to rotate after every five years, and specify a five-year time-out period before they can return to the audit engagement team. The Rules also define 'audit partners' as those who played a significant part in the auditing process, and require them to rotate after seven years of engagement and subject to a two-year time-out period before joining the audit engagement team.

In the US, until the enactment of the SOX Act, rotation rules were very lax. The SOX Act made sweeping changes. In India, there are no formal rules regarding auditor or audit partner rotations, and the recommendations of the NCC represent the first attempts to formalize the norms in this respect. In general, the NCC recommendations regarding auditor rotation are very similar to those specified under the SOX regulations, but these have not been adopted in the Companies Bill, 2009. Mandatory rotation exists for government firms but not for private listed companies. This omission needs urgent rethinking, especially in light of the Satyam failure which brought into focus the importance of having vigilant auditors and audit committees in corporate governance.

Powers, Responsibility, and Accountability of Auditors

Given the enormous importance of auditors in ensuring the integrity of the financial reporting process, the law gives adequate powers to the auditors to help them discharge their functions effectively, and at the same time requires that auditors follow prescribed auditing standards and take responsibility for their actions. Section 126 of the Companies Bill, 2009, gives the auditors the right to access all information relevant for the audit from any place in India, and in case of a holding company, gives the auditors the power to access the records of all its subsidiaries that it deems necessary for preparing consolidated accounts. The last provision is particularly important, given the presence of business groups that have listed companies with multiple subsidiaries and for which proper consolidated accounts are required to judge the financial health of the companies. The Bill also makes unilateral replacement of the auditor difficult by requiring a Special Resolution to be passed by shareholders before an auditor can be removed from office before the expiry of its term. However, the NCC recommendation that a Special Resolution be passed in case a retiring auditor who is otherwise qualified for re-appointment is replaced has not been included in the Companies Bill, 2009.

In terms of ensuring auditor responsibility, the Companies Bill, 2009, requires the auditors to prepare and sign an auditors' report that has to be read to the shareholders in the annual general meeting, with the report being available for inspection by any shareholder. The auditor's report must state whether the auditor obtained all the information that was relevant to the audit, that all internal controls are in place and proper books of accounts have been kept, and that the financial statements have been prepared in accordance with the accounting and auditing standards specified by the National Advisory Committee on Accounting and Auditing Standards[8] and give a true and fair view of the state

---

[8] Accounting and auditing standards in India are notified by the central government based on the recommendations of the National Advisory Committee on Accounting and Auditing Standards. The Advisory Committee prepares its recommendations in consultation with the Institute of Chartered Accountants of India. In cases where accounting standards for certain items are yet to be notified by the central government, the standards specified by the Institute of Chartered Accountants of India are deemed to be the auditing standards.

of affairs of the company at the end of the financial year. The Bill requires the auditors to point out qualified opinion, reservation, or adverse remark relating to the maintenance of accounts; in case a qualified opinion is passed, the auditor's report has to state the reasons behind it. The NCC recommendation that the audit firm should send a copy of the qualified report to the Registrar of Companies (ROC), the SEBI, and the relevant stock exchange, and inform the management about the same has not been incorporated in the Companies Bill, 2009.

It has often been said that even when rules and regulations are adequate, the penalty levels for contravention of rules are so low that they fail to act as effective deterrents to their contravention. In the existing Companies Act of 1956, the penalty on companies and the relevant officers is Rs 500 and that on the auditor is Rs 1,000, and that too for only wilful default (Sections 232 and 233). The Companies Bill, 2009, addresses this issue by mandating much stricter punishment for any violation of the rules governing the audit process. It provides not only monetary penalties but also imprisonment. Under Section 130 of the Bill, any contravention of the auditing rules by the company attracts fines ranging from Rs 25,000 to Rs 5 lakh. If an officer is in default, the fines range between Rs 10,000 and Rs 1 lakh and imprisonment up to one year. Penalties for auditor range between Rs 25,000 and Rs 5 lakh, and for wilful contravention, the penalties could be as high as Rs 25 lakh with up to one year in imprisonment. In addition, the auditors are required to refund the remuneration received and, more importantly, pay for damages to the company or to any other persons for loss arising out of incorrect or misleading statements in the audit report.

Independent Oversight of the Auditors

The SOX Act has set up the Public Companies Accounting Oversight Board (PCAOB) 'to oversee the audit of listed companies in order to protect investors' and public interest in matters relating to the preparation of audited financial statements'.[9] The SOX Act empowers the PCAOB to register all audit firms, establish auditing rules, conduct periodic inspection of audit firms, carry out investigation and disciplinary proceedings against errant firms, and ensure compliance with all the accounting and auditing rules specified under the Act and the SEC Rules. The NCC reviewed the necessity of establishing a Public Oversight Board in line with the PCAOB, but ultimately did not recommend its establishment, largely keeping in view that its establishment requires the consolidation of powers, which are now

distributed among the various regulatory authorities like the Department of Company Affairs (DCA), the SEBI, and the Reserve Bank of India (RBI), into a single regulatory body, which is impractical. Instead, the NCC recommended the establishment of independent Quality Review Boards (QRBs) 'to periodically examine and review the quality of audit, secretarial and cost accounting firms, and pass judgment and comments on the quality and sufficiency of systems, infrastructure and practices' (NCC 2004: 52). The main objective behind the recommendations was to speed up the investigation and adjudication process of complaints received against errant member firms, while ensuring that the process did not come in conflict with the provisions of the existing Acts. To this extent, the Committee recommended an elaborate institutional structure consisting of a Prosecution Directorate, Disciplinary Committee, and an Appellate Body which were to be responsible for timely disposal and resolution of the various stages of the disciplinary process. It is hoped that the QRBs would further strengthen the integrity of the financial reporting process by requiring auditors to be more vigilant in the discharge of their functions.

AUDIT COMMITTEE

The audit committee plays a vital role in ensuring the independence of the audit process. Auditing the operations of modern corporations is a complex process requiring understanding of the rules and judgements made by the management in preparing the financial statements. For verification of these financial statements, the auditor requires access to all necessary documents and a truthful explanation of all procedures. It is unlikely that this can be expected from the inside management whose very actions are the subject of the auditing process. Even if it is assumed that the management is truthful, there is a need to insulate the verification process from the influence of the inside management so that outsiders perceive the audit process as independent because they cannot directly observe the managers' truthfulness. If auditors are hired by the management and the scope of auditing services and auditors' compensation are decided by it, then the audit process is unlikely to be perceived as independent. The audit committee has been formed to act both as a conduit of information supplied by the management to the auditors, and at the same time to insulate the auditor from the pulls and pressures of the management. The audit committee is therefore required to be 'independent' of the management and has the responsibility of deciding the scope of work, including the fixation of audit fees and determination of the extent of non-audit services. The basic idea is to not make the auditor dependent on the inside management, either it terms of discharge of its functions or in terms of its survival.

---

[9] http://www.sec.gov/rules/final/33-8183.htm

Size and Composition of Audit Committee

Constitution of audit committees is now mandatory for listed companies both under the Companies Bill, 2009, as well as under Clause 49 (SEBI 2004). Section 158 of the Companies Bill, 2009, requires all listed companies to have an audit committee with a minimum of three directors, with independent directors forming a majority and at least one director having knowledge of financial management, audit, or accounts. The chairman of the audit committee has to be an independent director. The company is required to disclose the composition of the audit committee in its Director's Report. Under Clause 49, all listed companies are required to have an audit committee of at least three directors of which two-thirds should be independent. The chairman of the audit committee is required to be an independent director. Clause 49 requires the audit committee to meet at least four times a year, with the gap between two successive meetings not exceeding four months. The regulation tries to ensure the quality of audit committee by requiring all audit committee members to be 'financially literate', with at least one member having 'accounting or related financial management expertise'.

The regulations regarding size, composition, and expertise under Clause 49 mirror the NYSE regulations in many respects, but there are two important differences. Like Clause 49, Section 303A.07 (NYSE Listed Manual) of the NYSE regulations also requires the audit committee to be have a minimum of three members. But under the NYSE regulations, the audit committee is to be constituted entirely of independent directors, unlike the two-thirds rule under Clause 49. Second, the NYSE regulations, actively discourage audit committee members to serve in more than three audit committees and require that the company make an affirmative determination of the ability of an audit committee member to effectively discharge his/her responsibilities in case he/she serves in more than three audit committees. The company is required to disclose the basis of such determination in its proxy statement or annual report. No such affirmative determination is required under Clause 49.

The NCC expressly pointed to the considerable amount of additional time that an audit committee requires 'to successfully discharge its obligations in letter and in spirit.' This observation acquires special significance due to the high incidence of multiple directorships in India (Sarkar and Sarkar 2009) and the fact that many companies belonging to business groups have multiple subsidiaries that demand significant amount of time by audit committee members to oversee the preparation of consolidated accounts. Section 146 of the Companies Bill, 2009, does limit the number of directorships to fifteen, and Clause 49 does restrict the number of committee memberships to ten and the number

of chairmanship to five that directors can have in public limited companies, but no separate restrictions exist for directors serving on audit committees. Indeed, even the aforementioned restrictions are considered to be liberal to allow the directors to fully discharge their functions and responsibilities.

Another area that needs tightening in Clause 49 is the definition of 'financially literate' and the conditions under which a member will be considered to have 'accounting or related financial management expertise'. Currently, these are too broad and open-ended. As the NCC points out, 'While one member of the committee may be positioned as the one having "financial and accounting knowledge", it is worth asking how deep that knowledge is, especially given the new accounting standards and complexities' (NCC 2004: 70). To be fair, even the NYSE regulations that also have the same requirements do not define these terms but instead give the board the ultimate power to determine if in its business judgement, the qualification of a person is satisfactory enough to induct him/her as an audit committee member. A much tighter definition of financial expertise comes from the S-K Regulations in the US, which require all companies filing financial statements with the SEC to declare if their audit committees contain an 'audit committee financial expert'. The regulations specify five attributes that a person must possess to qualify as an 'audit committee financial expert', and list five alternative ways in which these attributes must have been acquired by such a person[10] (Box 8.2). The Clause 49 regulations, moving a step forward from the NYSE regulations, have put some guidelines that define what qualifies a member as having 'accounting or related financial management expertise', but these are well short of the S-K definition.

One argument for not adopting a stricter definition of financial expertise could be the concern that there may not be enough persons who can qualify as having 'accounting or related financial management expertise'. This is likely to make it difficult for companies, especially the smaller companies, to comply with the regulations. Academic research has shown that independent audit committees increase the quality of financial reporting when the audit committee members are financially qualified. Put in this context, future regulation must make an attempt to increase the financial expertise of the audit committee. The SEC approach which requires companies to disclose, but not require, if their audit committees have a financial expert may be a way of leaving it to the company to decide the quality of its audit committee for the time being. With full disclosure, investors would value these companies based on the attributes of the audit

[10] http://www.sec.gov/rules/final/33-8177.htm

Box 8.2 Definition of 'Audit Committee Financial Expert' under S-K Regulations

The SEC Rules (Item 401 of S-K Regulations) define an 'audit committee financial expert' as a person who has the following attributes:

(1) An understanding of generally accepted accounting principles and financial statements
(2) The ability to assess the general application of such principles in connection with the accounting for estimates, accruals, and reserves
(3) Experience preparing, auditing, analysing, or evaluating financial statements that present a breadth and level of complexity of accounting issues that are generally comparable to the breadth and complexity of issues that can reasonably be expected to be raised by the registrant's financial statements, or experience actively supervising one or more persons engaged in such activities
(4) An understanding of internal controls over financial reporting
(5) An understanding of audit committee functions

A person shall have acquired such attributes through:

(1) education and experience as a principal financial officer, principal accounting officer, controller, public accountant, or auditor, or experience in one or more positions that involve the performance of similar functions;
(2) experience actively supervising a principal financial officer, principal accounting officer, controller, public accountant, auditor, or person performing similar functions
(3) experience overseeing or assessing the performance of companies or public accountants with respect to the preparation, auditing, or evaluation of financial statements; or
(4) other relevant experience.

committee members, which in turn might incentivize these companies to decide on the optimal composition.

Role and Power of the Audit Committee

In addition to the size, composition, and the expertise of the audit committee members, Clause 49 specifies detailed guidelines regarding the role and powers of the audit committee. These regulations are mirrored in Section 158 of the Companies Bill, 2009. Under Clause 49, the role of the audit committee is to provide oversight of the company's financial reporting process and ensure the credibility, correctness, and the sufficiency of the disclosure that are required under the Companies Act of 1956 and the various stipulations specified under the Listing Agreement drafted by SEBI. The audit committee is also responsible for recommending to the Board of Directors regarding the appointment, re-appointment, and, if required, the removal of the statutory auditor and the fixation of the audit fees. The audit committee also has the responsibility of approving all non-audit activities of the statutory auditors and the fixation of the non-audit fees. In addition, the audit committee is required to review with the management the annual financial statements before submission to the Board for approval, especially with respect to changes in accounting policies, audit qualifications, significant adjustments arising out of auditor findings, major accounting entries based on judgements made by management, disclosure of related party transactions, and audit qualifications. Clause 49 also gives powers to the

audit committee to investigate any matter that is included in its terms of reference, seek any information from any employee, and to obtain external legal or professional advice that it considers necessary.

A significant number of proactive regulations have been enacted in India since the 1990s. For the first time, the Companies Amendment Bill of 2000 made the formation of audit committees mandatory for all companies with paid up capital of Rs 5 crore. Clause 49, which was first notified in February 2000, reiterated this requirement for all listed companies. It required the formation of an audit committee and specified its roles and functions. The amended version of Clause 49, which was notified in October 2004, detailed the role, power, and functions of the audit committee. The Companies Bill, 2009, has also listed down the power and functions of the audit committee, which were not specified under the Companies Act of 1956. But two aspects that require further attention are the composition of the audit committee and its authority to implement its decisions. These two aspects together affect the independence of the audit committee and its effectiveness in ensuring the integrity of the financial reporting process.

A review of the sequence of regulations shows that there has been a steady dilution of the independence requirement with respect to the audit committee. The original Clause 49 regulations required the audit committee to have a minimum size of three and to be constituted entirely of non-executive directors, with majority of them being independent (SEBI 2000). The revised Clause 49 (SEBI 2004) removed the non-executive director requirement and instead specified that the audit committee should have a minimum of three members with two-thirds of them being independent. Given the specification of a minimum of three members, the move from the majority to the two-thirds rule did not impose any extra independence burden.[11] The only effect of the revised Clause 49 regulations was that management directors could now be part of the audit committee. The Companies Bill, 2009, follows the revised Clause 49 regulations by not insisting that the audit committee comprise only of non-executive directors but reverts to the majority rule from the two-thirds rule.[12] If the idea of allowing management presence in the audit committee is to get management input into the financial reporting process, then the same can be easily obtained as elsewhere Clause 49 empowers the audit committee to invite any of the executives, as it considers appropriate, to be present at the meetings of the audit committee. The overwhelming objective of the regulations with respect to the audit committee should be to ensure that the audit committee is truly independent of the management. Seeking management input should be a discretionary choice of the committee and not mandated by law. The NCC in its report, while applauding the existing Clause 49 regulations on the audit committee, pointed out that one area that needed improvement and tightening was the composition of the audit committee, and recommended that if the audit committee is perceived to be independent, then it should consist only of independent directors. Unfortunately, this has not been incorporated in the Companies Bill, 2009. In a situation where regulations all over the world are trying hard to increase investor confidence in the financial reporting process by envisaging an audit committee that is perceived as a body independent of the management, the regulations in India seem to be falling behind.

The lower independence requirement regarding the composition of the audit committee has to be seen in context of the fact that the audit committee's recommendations relating to hiring, oversight, compensation, and firing of the outside auditor are not binding on the Board. While Clause 49 is silent on this matter, Section 158(9) of the Companies Bill, 2009 (and currently under Section 292-A of the Companies (Amendment) Act, 2000 states that if the Board does not accept the recommendations of the audit committee, reasons should be communicated to shareholders.[13] This is quite in contrast to the regulation in the US where under the SOX Act of 2002, and implemented by SEC under Rule 10A-3, the audit committee is 'directly responsible for the appointment, compensation, retention and oversight' of the statutory auditor and each such statutory auditor 'must report directly to the audit committee'.

The power of the Board to overrule the decision or recommendations of the audit committee has to be also seen in the context of the current Clause 49 regulations governing Board independence. Clause 49 allows the Board to have only one-third independent directors in case of a non-executive chairman. Allowing the Board to overrule the recommendations of the audit committee brings in the possibility of management overrule as the Board will be dominated by insiders in this case. Even in the case of an executive chairman where Clause 49 regulations require independent directors to comprise at least 50 per cent of the audit committee, the strength of the inside directors is evenly poised with that of the independent directors and possibly tilted towards the management as the chairman is an insider. Under the Companies Bill, 2009, this problem will be further aggravated as the proposed regulation with respect to board composition requires companies to have only a minimum of one-third of the board to consist of independent directors and does not make any distinction between companies with executive and non-executive status of the chairman.[14]

Ensuring the integrity of the financial reporting process by providing independent oversight by the audit committee is paramount for governance. The SOX regulations try to ensure this by requiring the audit committee to consist entirely of independent directors and giving it the sole authority to discharge all audit-related functions. The SOX

---

[11] For an audit committee size of three, four, and six, the two requirements are effectively the same. For size five, only the modified Clause would require four independent directors as opposed to three under the previous regulations. For audit committees of size seven or more, the modified regulations would require more independent directors, but very few companies have audit committees with seven or more members.

[12] Section 158(2) of the Companies Bill, 2009, specifies that 'The Audit Committee shall consist of a minimum of three directors with independent directors forming a majority and at least one director having knowledge of financial management, audit or accounts.'

[13] Recommendation 4.7(11) of the Sanjeev Reddy Report on Corporate Excellence (Task Force on Corporate Excellence 2000) commissioned by the Department of Company Affairs, which forms the basis of the 2000 Amendment, states that the audit committee being the creature of the Board 'should be subordinate to the authority of the Board. The Board should have the authority to override any decisions of the Committee. In the interests of the professionalism and transparency, where the Board disagrees with any material decision of the Audit Committee, there should be a disclosure requirement in the annual reports to set out any such instances together with the reasoning of the Board for such decisions.' Similar recommendations are found in the J.J. Irani Committee Report on Company Law (Expert Committee on Company Law 2004), which forms the basis of the Companies Bill, 2009, which states that 'The recommendation of the Audit Committee if overruled by the Board, should be disclosed in the Directors' Report with the reasons for overruling.'

[14] Section 132(3) of the Companies Bill, 2009.

has no role for independent directors apart from serving in the audit committee. The NYSE regulations provide for a majority independent Board to oversee the overall running of the company. Together, they provide an environment for more independent reporting of the numbers. In India, in contrast, the audit committee is much more subjected to the influence of the management. The power of the Board to overrule the recommendations of the audit committee and the current regulations governing Board composition make audit committees in India less powerful and more subject to the influence of the management than is the case in the US.

Also, while Clause 49 has detailed specifications regarding the powers, role, and reviews of the audit committee, it does not formally require the preparation of an audit committee report, as required under the SEC regulations. The Quarterly Compliance Report stipulated under Clause 49 only requires the company to report the compliance status (yes or no) with respect to the various aspects of audit committee functioning, which amounts to tick-box regulation. The suggested items for inclusion in the Annual Corporate Governance Report with respect to audit committees only require the company to give a brief description of the terms of reference, composition, including names of members and chairperson, and meetings and attendance of the audit committee during the year. The NCC recommended that the role and functions of the audit committee be laid down in an Audit Committee Charter, and also recommended that the chairman certify whether the audit committee discharged all the functions listed in the Audit Committee Charter, which would form the Action Taken Report to Shareholders. The NCC further recommended that the statement of the Chairman should also certify whether the audit committee met with the statutory and internal auditors, without the presence of management, and whether such meetings revealed materially significant issues of risks. The NYSE regulations are clear in specifying that for the audit committee 'to perform its oversight functions most effectively, it must have the benefit of separate sessions with the management, the independent auditors and those responsible for the internal audit function' (Listed Company Manual). Currently, the Clause 49 regulations do not specifically require the audit committee to meet separately the external auditor and the internal auditor without the management to get an independent assessment of the internal audit procedure. Similar requirements are also not included in the Companies Bill, 2009.

The general tone of the SEC regulations is that the audit committee is a body that is independent of the management and works closely with the external auditor to ensure that the management justifies all critical accounting policies and practices that it uses in preparing the financial statements. The NYSE rules specifically state that one of the duties and responsibilities of the audit committee is to 'review with

the independent audit any audit problems or difficulties and management's response' (Listed Company Manual). In contrast, under Clause 49, the audit committee reviews 'with the management' the financial reporting process and evaluates the performance of the internal and external auditors, which gives the notion of a teamwork of which the management, the internal auditors, the audit committee, and the external auditors are equal partners. This probably reflects the philosophy of 'self-governance' and the often made assertion that 'compliance should come from within'. Only time will tell which approach is more justified.

EFFECTIVENESS OF AUDIT COMMITTEES AND AUDITOR INDEPENDENCE—EMPIRICAL EVIDENCE

Audit committee and auditor independence have been important areas of research in the accounting literature. Studies on audit committees have focused on the independence, activity, and the financial expertise of the audit committee members. Research on auditor independence has focused on the extent of non-audit services provided by the external auditor as well audit firm tenure, both of which are generally seen as hindrances to auditor independence. There is renewed interest in these topics in light of the new regulations that were enacted in the wake of the major corporate scandals in the US, especially the collapse of WorldCom and Enron, and the consequent enactment of the SOX regulations. The SOX regulations have been a reference point for similar reforms relating to audit committees and auditor independence, initiated in many other countries. As we have seen earlier, the SOX regulations emphasize not only the independence but also the financial expertise of the audit committees. Similarly, the SOX regulations and the recent provisions of the Companies Bill, 2009, prohibit a number of non-audit services which are conceived to be a hindrance to auditor independence. The extant literature provides strong empirical support that independent audit committees and higher audit independence have a significant beneficial role in enhancing the quality of disclosures, reducing discretionary earnings management, increasing the informativeness of earnings, and, in general, enhancing the value of the firm.

Studies on Earnings Management and Audit Committees

A number of empirical studies have looked at the relation between audit committee independence and earnings management. Earnings management occurs when managers use judgement in financial reporting and in structuring transactions to alter financial reports to either mislead some stakeholders about the underlying economic performance of a company or to influence contractual outcomes that depend on reported accounting numbers (Healy and Wahlen 1999). The study by Klien (2002), which analyses the relation between audit committee and board characteristics and earnings management using a two-year sample of 500 S&P (Standard and Poor's) firms, finds that independent audit committees significantly reduced abnormal accruals, as did an independent boards. Reductions in audit committee independence are accompanied by large increases in abnormal accruals. The effect is most pronounced when the board or the resultant audit committee is comprised of a minority of outside directors, that is, when audit committee changes from majority to minority of independent directors. Carcello et al. (2002), using a sample of a hundred Fortune 500 companies, examine if a more independent audit committee tries to protect its reputation by insisting on differentially higher audit quality. The authors hypothesize that this should lead to the demand for higher audit effort and consequently to the hiring of high-quality auditors. Consistent with this conjecture, the study finds a positive relation between audit fees and audit committee independence, diligence, and expertise. Abbott et al. (2003) address issues relating to auditor–client independence using a sample of 538 companies for the year 2001. Rendering of certain types of non-audit services is perceived by regulators as hampering auditor independence. Independent audit committees may have incentives to limit non-audit services and according non-audit fees to enhance auditor independence in either appearance or fact. The study finds that active and independent audit committees, consisting of fully independent directors and meeting at least four times a year, are associated with significantly lower non-audit fee ratio. The evidence is consistent with the general perception that high level of non-audit fees could act as a hindrance to auditor independence.

Many studies examine whether the financial expertise of the audit committee matters in increasing the quality of accounting disclosures. For example, Yeh and Woidtke (2007) examine the effect of concentrated ownership, independence of the audit committee, and the presence of financial expertise on earnings informativeness. Earnings informativeness measures how stock market returns respond to changes in measures of accounting performance. The study is based on a sample of 450 observations consisting of the largest 150 companies each from Singapore, Hong Kong, and Malaysia. The study finds that concentrated ownership reduces earnings informativeness. However, independent audit committees enhance earnings informativeness only if there are independent directors in the audit committee with financial expertise. In addition, the benefits of having an independent audit committee along with directors having financial expertise

more than offset the detrimental effect that is associated with concentrated ownership. Similarly, Xie et al. (2003), using a sample of 110 firms from the S&P 500 for three years—1992, 1994, and 1996—show that audit committees with members having corporate or financial backgrounds are associated with lower earnings management. Similar results are found for frequency of meetings by the audit committee. The study shows that it is not independence per se but the quality and activity of the audit committee that are important.

Studies on Earnings Management and Auditor Independence

Auditor independence has been another area of intensive research in the accounting literature. Auditor independence has been generally proxied by the ratio of non-audit to audit fees under the assumption that a relatively higher non-audit fee makes the auditor more dependent on the company for its economic survival and hinders and comprises its ability to fully and faithfully discharge its audit-related functions. Accordingly, studies in this genre have looked at the effect of auditor independence on earnings management, earnings informativeness, and other measures of earnings quality. Frankel et al. (2002) examine whether auditor fees are associated with earnings management, and how the market reacts to the disclosure of auditor fees. Using data collected from proxy statements, they find that non-audit fees are positively associated with small earnings surprises and the magnitude of discretionary accruals, while audit fees are negatively associated with these earnings management indicators. They also find evidence that share values of firms that reported higher ratios of non-audit fees to audit fees were lower on the date the fees were disclosed, although the effect is small in economic terms. In related works, Srinidhi and Gul (2007) explored the relation between non-audit fees and accrual quality to analyse if in settings where audit quality is compromised by a loss of auditor independence, managers use accruals more opportunistically and thereby drive down the accrual quality. They also examined if higher audit effort and quality as which are proxied by higher audit fees translate into better accrual quality. Their results show that accrual quality has a significant negative association with the magnitude of non-audit fees and a significant positive association with audit fees. However, not all studies tend to find evidence that non-audit fees are associated with biased financial reporting (Huang et al. 2007). It is difficult to compare findings of studies from different countries as the ratio of non-audit to audit fees is only a proxy of auditor independence, which can also depend significantly on the institutional and legal framework of the respective countries, and in particular on their accounting standards and punitive actions in case of accounting violations.

Studies on Auditor Rotation and Earnings Management

The issue of audit independence and audit firm rotation has been highly debated in the accounting literature. As mentioned earlier, the debate highlights two opposing perspectives, with the proponents emphasizing the need to have a 'fresh look' at periodic intervals to ensure client–auditor independence and auditor efficiency, while the opponents highlight the risk of lower audit quality and higher audit failures that can occur due to the loss in continuity and audit competence created by mandatory audit firm rotation (Hoyle 1978). Academic studies till date have not been able to produce conclusive proofs about the benefits of audit firm rotation while there are good evidences of the risks. For example, Myers et al. (2003) find that earnings quality is actually lower in firms with shorter audit tenure. They interpret their results as suggesting that longer auditor tenure results in auditors placing greater constraints on management decisions in the reporting of financial performance. Other research indicates that a greater proportion of audit failures occur with newly acquired clients (Berton 1991; Petty and Cuganesan 1996) and that auditors' litigation risk is higher in the initial years of audit engagement (Palmrose 1991). One problem with these empirical studies is that they cannot test if rotating auditors will enhance audit quality, as very few companies have in practice rotated auditors since the law does not require then to do so. Most of the empirical findings cited earlier use length of audit tenure in their analysis and then extrapolate their findings to the case of zero tenure, that is, auditor rotation. However, this may not be the correct approach as auditor rotation is a discrete event and may not be predictable from these models which treat tenure as continuous. Notwithstanding the findings of the empirical studies, theoretical arguments imply that there ought to be term limits for auditors or at least the audit engagement team. Surely, longer tenure is better in that the understanding of auditor of the internal workings of the companies increases with it. But longer the tenure, higher is the risk of management influence on the auditor. Thus, there ought to be some point where rotating auditors or audit partners would result in higher net benefits.

CONCLUSIONS

The theoretical arguments and the empirical literature overwhelmingly suggest that auditor and audit committee independence plays an important role in the governance of companies. Currently, auditor independence in India, especially with respect to rendering non-audit services and presence of conflict of interest, is largely dependent on self-regulation. The Companies Act of 1956 has little to offer in this regard. Under the existing regulations, there are many governance issues with respect to auditor and audit committee independence in India. Among these, the most important ones are: (i) no regulation bars an auditor from having family or other close relationship with the audited company or its key management personnel; (ii) there is no cooling-off period for audit partners or staff to join audit clients in a senior management position or for client personnel joining the audit firm; (iii) auditors can provide non-audit services like tax planning, tax representation before tax authorities, due diligence certification, mergers and acquisition; (iv) there is no mandatory audit firm rotation except for government-owned companies, banks, and insurance companies; and (v) inside management can be present in audit committees.

The recommendations of the NCC have plugged many of these loopholes. The committee's recommendations, especially with respect to auditor independence, are in line with the best international practices. The Companies Bill, 2009, has incorporated many of these recommendations. For investors to have confidence in the independence of the auditor, the Companies Bill, 2009, needs to be quickly enacted into law.

However, notwithstanding the passage of the Companies Bill, 2009, some issues that have not been incorporated into the Bill will remain as matters of concern. The most important among these are the independence of the audit committee both in terms of its composition and the power of the Board to overrule its decisions, and the issues related to conflict of interest in auditor–company relationship and audit partner rotation. These issues have to be addressed in future regulation to make the auditing and oversight standards in India comparable to those in the more mature economies. If it is operationally difficult to do further modifications to the statutes in the immediate future, then the respective stock exchanges should explore the possibility of incorporating these additional standards of independence in their Listing Agreement. Since the provisions of the Companies Bill, 2009, can be interpreted as only laying down minimum standards, nothing should prevent the stock exchanges from insisting on higher standards of independence from companies listed under their supervision.

In conclusion, adequate, relevant, and high-quality disclosures are one of the most powerful tools available in the hands of independent directors, shareholders, regulators, and outside investors to monitor the performance of a company. This is particularly important for emerging economies like India where there is insider dominance. To this extent, measures that strengthen auditor independence and enhance the powers, functions, and independence of audit committees will be crucial in the governance of Indian companies. Governance risk is a key determinant of market pricing of listed securities. A high perceived 'independence quotient' of a company's auditing process can be reassuring to outside shareholders can help reduce the risk premium of raising capital, thereby providing a strong business case for strengthening audit independence.

REFERENCES

Abbott, L.J., Susan Parker, Gary F. Peters, and K. Raghunandan (2003), 'An Empirical Investigation of Audit Fees, Non-Audit Fees, and the Audit Committee', *Contemporary Accounting Research*, 20(2): 215–34.

Berton, L. (1991), 'GAO Weighs Auditing Plan for Big Banks', *Wall Street Journal*, 27 March: A3.

Carcello, J.V., D.R. Hermanson, T.L. Neal, and R.A. Riley Jr (2002), 'Board Characteristics and Audit Fees', *Contemporary Accounting Research*, 19(3): 365–84.

Companies Bill (2009), available at http://www.mca.gov.in/ Ministry/actsbills/pdf/ Companies_Bill_2009_24 Aug2009. pdf

Frankel, Richard M., Marilyn F. Johnson, Karen K. Nelson, William R. Kinney Jr, and Robert Libby (2002), 'The Relation between Auditors' Fees for Non-audit Services and Earnings Management', *The Accounting Review*, 77: 71–105.

Healy, P.M. and J.M. Wahlen (1999), 'A Review of the Earnings Management Literature and Its Implications for Standard Setting', *Accounting Horizons*, 13(4): 365–83.

Hoyle, Joe (1978), 'Mandatory Auditor Rotation: The Arguments and an Alternative', *Journal of Accountancy*, 145: 69–78.

Huang, Hua-Wei, Suchismita Mishra, and K. Raghunandan (2007), 'Types of Non-Audit Fees and Financial Reporting Quality', *Auditing*, 26(1): 133–45.

Klein, April (2002), 'Audit Committee, Board of Director Characteristics, and Earnings Management', *Journal of Accounting and Economics*, 33: 375–400.

Myers, James N., Linda A. Myers, and Thomas C. Omer (2003), 'Exploring the Term of the Auditor–Client Relationship

and the Quality of Earnings: A Case for Mandatory Auditor Rotation?', *The Accounting Review*, 78(3): 779–99.

Naresh Chandra Committee Report on Corporate Audit and Governance (2002), available at http://www.nfcgindia.org/ library.htm

New York Stock Exchange, Listed Company Manual, available at http://nysemanual.nyse.com/lcm

Palmrose, Z-V. (1991), 'Trials of Legal Disputes Involving Independent Auditors: Some Empirical Evidence', *Journal of Accounting Research*, 29(Supplement): 149–85.

Petty, R. and S. Cuganesan (1996), 'Auditor Rotation: Framing the Debate', *Australian Accountant* 66(May): 40–1.

Sarbanes-Oxley Act (2002), available at http://www.law.uc.edu/ ccl/soact/toc.html

Sarkar, J. and S. Sarkar (2009), 'Multiple Board Appointments and Firm Performance in Emerging Economies: Evidence from India', *Pacific Basin Finance Journal*, 17: 271–93.

Securities and Exchange Board of India (SEBI) (2000), Clause 49 Regulations, Circular No. SMDRP/POLICY/CIR-10/2000, 21 February, available at http://www.sebi.gov.in

——— (2004), Clause 49 Regulations, Circular No. SEBI/CFD/ DIL/CG/1/2004/12/10, 29 October, available at http://www. sebi.gov.in

Securities and Exchange Commission (SEC), available at http:// www.sec.gov/rules/final/33-8183.htm

Srinidhi, Bin N. and Ferdinand A. Gul (2007), 'The Differential Effects of Auditors' Non-audit and Audit Fees on Accrual Quality', *Contemporary Accounting Research*, 24(2): 595–629.

Xie, Biao, Wallace III Davidson, and Peter J. DaDalt (2003), 'Earnings Management and Corporate Governance: The Role of the Board and the Audit Committee', *Journal of Corporate Finance*, 9: 295–316.

Yeh, Yin-Hua and Traice Woidtke (2007), 'Corporate Governance and the Informativeness of Accounting Earnings: The Role of the Audit Committee', Working Paper, University of Tennessee, Corporate Governance Center.

9

Employment and Industrial Relations in India

Informality and Inequality

Errol D'Souza and Debashish Bhattacherjee

The labour market in India since liberalization has been characterized by a process of participation and exclusion—a growth in employment associated with large underemployment and new jobs being created in the unorganized sector of the economy as the organized sector's ability to generate productive employment has declined. Large numbers of people left the agricultural sector, and employment shifted gradually from the agricultural sector, where productivity was low and declining, towards sectors where labour productivity was higher and increasing. Agriculture, which employed 65.4 per cent of the workforce in 1983, employed 52.1 per cent by 2004–5. Figure 9.1 depicts the sectoral shares of employment and gross domestic product (GDP) for the secondary and tertiary sectors and shows manufacturing to be a sector where some expansion in employment has taken place. However, liberalization has clearly been associated with the tendency for new jobs to be established in the tertiary sector of the economy, with the relative employment share provided by this sector intensifying. The strongest growth in employment took place in the construction sector, which is labour-intensive. Strong growth in employment also took place in those sectors that have been associated with the transformation of the economy—sectors such as transport, storage and communications, and trade, hotels, and restaurants, and to some extent in financial services, insurance, real estate, and business services.

Employment growth by usual (principal plus subsidiary) status was higher during the period from 1983 to 1993–4 (2.01 per cent) as compared to the period from 1993–4 to 2004–5 (1.89 per cent) that is widely identified as the period of liberalization (Mahendra Dev 2008). However, employment growth declined mainly during 1993–4 to 1999–2000 to 1.09 per cent, but revived in both rural and urban areas to 2.86 per cent between 1999–2000 and 2004–5. Despite this pick up in employment growth in the recent past, there was an increase in the unemployment rate in this period for females in rural areas from 1 per cent to 1.8 per cent, and in urban areas from 5.7 per cent to 6.9 per cent. Male unemployment rates, however, declined. The increase in employment growth accompanied by a rise in the unemployment rate for females gets reflected in the rise in the work participation rates.[1] For males in rural and urban areas, work participation rates during 1999–2000 to 2004–5 increased by 2.8 per cent and 6 per cent, respectively, whereas for females they increased by 9.4 per cent and 19.4 per cent respectively (Mahendra Dev 2008). It is well known that female work participation

[1] The growth rate of the work participation rate is the growth in employment times one minus the unemployment rate plus the growth in unemployment times the unemployment rate minus the growth rate of population.

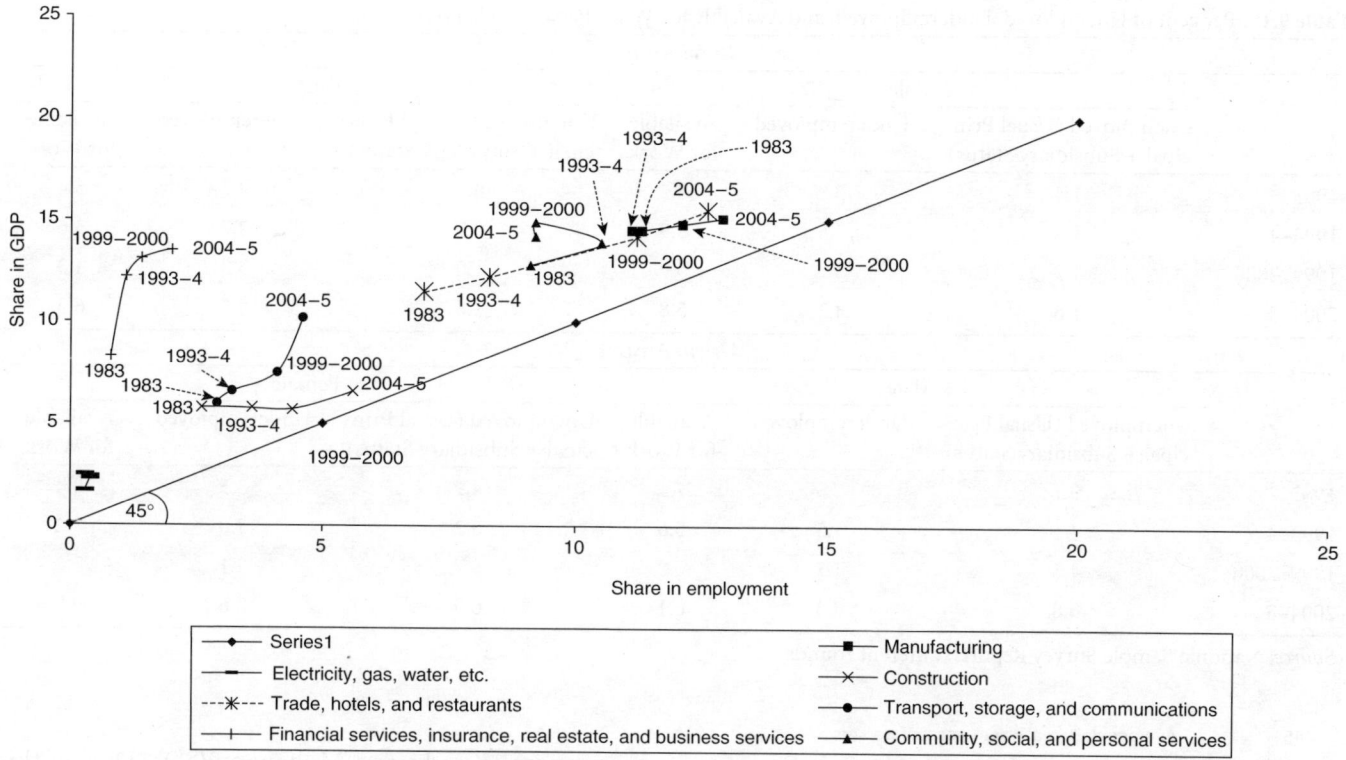

Source: CSO National Accounts Statistics and Planning Commission

Figure 9.1 Sectoral Shares of Employment and GDP

is negatively related to the standard of living and positively to the years of schooling in urban areas (Mahendra Dev 2008). The rise in work participation by females is then a consequence of them being pushed into the labour market to help sustain household incomes when the wages of male heads of households decline. In the recent past, as discussed later, average real wages have marginally declined. For females, the growth in subsidiary employment has also been higher than principal employment in the recent past, reflecting the push of an added worker effect.

It is well known that countries like India have large underemployment and much less unemployment as there is no resort to social security. In the usual status definition, a worker who is engaged in work for the major part of the preceding 365 days is employed. With such a criterion, a person may be unemployed for a large part of the year and yet be counted as employed. A rough measure of underemployment is the difference between the weekly and daily unemployment status. On this measure, underemployment has increased for males as well as females in both rural and urban areas. This underemployment, which had declined from 1983 to 1993–4, shows a steady upward trend from then to 2004–5. If we add the underemployment rate so defined to the unemployment rate, then we obtain a measure of those who are available for work—the unemployed plus the underemployed. Those available for work as a

percentage of the labour force have increased from 1993–4 to 2004–5 for males and females in both urban and rural areas (Table 9.1).

Since employment is negatively related to the real wage[2] and as an increase in those available for work as a percentage of the labour force puts a downward pressure on the wage, we should expect real wage changes to be incremental. The big surprise in the employment situation has been that the real wages for regular workers increased from 1993–4 to 1999–2000 but thereafter they stagnated for males and declined for females (Figure 9.2). Similarly, the real wages for casual workers increased in rural areas but at a slower rate during 1999–2000 to 2004–5 than in the earlier period from 1993–4 to 1999–2000. Real wages for casual workers in urban areas, however, declined during the more recent period (Figure 9.2). Thus, the only increase in real wages has been for casual rural workers, which may be attributable to their absorption in public works and construction projects, as in the National Rural Employment Guarantee

---

[2] This is on the assumption that the economy is on its labour demand curve, implying that for given other inputs, such as the capital stock, a higher level of employment requires a lower real wage. Given that unemployment results from labour demand being on the short side of the labour market and less than labour supply, we expect this situation to prevail.

Table 9.1 Per cent of Unemployed, Underemployed, and Available for Work Persons to Labour Force

	Rural Areas					
	Male			Female		
	Unemployed (Usual Principal + Subsidiary Status)	Underemployed	Available for Work	Unemployed (Usual Principal + Subsidiary Status)	Underemployed	Available for Work
1983	1.4	3.8	5.2	0.7	4.7	5.4
1993–4	1.4	2.5	3.9	0.9	2.7	3.6
1999–2000	1.7	3.3	5.0	1.0	3.3	4.3
2004–5	1.6	4.2	5.8	1.8	4.5	6.3
	Urban Areas					
	Male			Female		
	Unemployed (Usual Principal + Subsidiary Status)	Underemployed	Available for Work	Unemployed (Usual Principal + Subsidiary Status)	Underemployed	Available for Work
1983	5.1	2.5	7.6	4.9	3.5	8.4
1993–4	4.1	1.5	5.6	6.2	2.0	8.2
1999–2000	4.5	1.7	6.2	5.7	2.1	7.8
2004–5	3.8	2.3	6.1	6.9	2.6	9.5

Source: National Sample Survey Reports, different rounds.

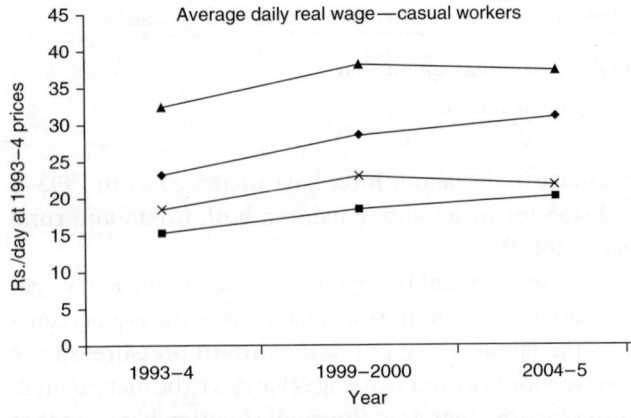

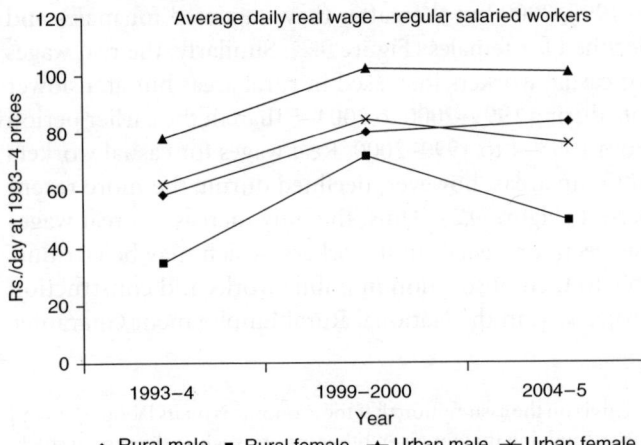

Source: Mahendra Dev (2008: Table 7.8).

Figure 9.2 Average Daily Real Wage of Casual and Regular Salaried Workers

programme (Kundu and Mohanan 2009). During this period, the status of workers also underwent a change. The self-employed as a share of the workforce increased from 53 per cent in 1993–4 to 56.5 per cent in 2004–5, the share of regular workers marginally changed from 15 per cent to 15.2 per cent, and the share of casual workers declined from 32 per cent to 28.3 per cent in the same period (NSS 2005). The increase in employment in the recent past has been mainly in self-employment.

EXPLAINING THE EMERGING EMPLOYMENT SCENARIO

Since the 1980s, a strategic shift in the economic policy regime saw India switch from state controls and import substituting industrialization towards increasing integration with the world economy. Most of the literature identifies the post-1980 period as the time when economic performance improved, and attributes this improvement to various factors such as an attitudinal change away from socialist policies and a pro-business orientation that focused on raising the profitability of incumbent industrial and commercial establishments (Rodrik and Subramanian 2005). The earlier protectionist regime was deemed to be responsible for an inefficient and uncompetitive production system that resulted in the creation of insufficient employment. The reforms that gained pace from the 1990s were justified in terms of the increased efficiency and output and employment growth that would ensue. A very important component of the reforms was the trade reforms that were undertaken with the view to switch production away from import substitutes that were being inefficiently produced and towards production in those commercial units in which India has a comparative advantage. As a result, the economy would specialize in production that more intensively uses factors which it has in abundance, and this would result in a reduction in the capital intensity of production and a rise in employment in the economy.

Accompanying the external liberalization were correlated supporting internal liberalization policies as well. Industrial licensing that included capacity licensing, monopoly control, and small-scale industry reservation, which were principal instruments of control over the private sector, were significantly relaxed. In services too, where public sector presence has been conspicuous in insurance, banking, and telecommunications, considerable private sector participation has been allowed and the financial sector has been significantly liberalized. Increasingly, reforms in the infrastructure sector too have attempted to improve governance by introducing independent regulatory authorities, reforming user fees, and corporatizing or contracting out service provision including public–private partnerships.

The net impact of liberalization has spurred business and commercial units to scale up due to deregulation, the provision of better infrastructure, and a more efficient financial sector. This has also enabled them to reorganize work practices. This reorganization effect of liberalization, we argue, has had significant impacts on employment that have not been sufficiently recognized. Liberalization has been associated in the public discourse more with the reallocation effect, which is the output gain from allocating existing resources as efficiently as possible between alternative uses as the distortions in price are reduced. The reorganization effect of liberalization by contrast induced firms to reorganize their production by economizing in various ways and adopting newer and better techniques of production.[3]

In our understanding, liberalization was associated with attempts to raise productivity and this has had a negative modest impact on employment in the formal sector of the economy. Prior to liberalization, the high entry barriers and the presence of few players due to licensing and the high protection provided by an import substituting industrialization policy resulted in substantial rent sharing between employers and employees. Industry rents were substantial due to licensing and the importance of unions in wage

agreements. With liberalization, firms responded to the increase in competition by upgrading productivity. To generate productivity increases, business enterprises resorted to resizing and cost-cutting. As workers' wages included a rent component and bargaining power was adversely affected by the onset of liberalization, the method of cost-cutting adopted was to resort to a reduction in the wage bill. This involved higher worker earnings for the skilled workforce required to upgrade productivity combined with a substitution of permanent for casual and temporary workers in manufacturing.

Unskilled (including regular unskilled workers) and casual workers bore the brunt of cost-cutting in the form of reduced wages and this enabled enterprises to generate productivity growth without a dent in their profit margins. For instance, in manufacturing, the job creation rate for contract staff in large firms exceeded the job destruction rate, resulting in a net employment increase of 4 per cent a year (Dougherty 2009). In the aggregate, however, including for supervisory staff in large firms, there was a decline in net employment between 1998 and 2004. The rise in employment during this period has been located in small firms employing less than 100 workers where again the new jobs have been growing faster for contract than for other categories of workers. As a result, the share of total labour costs in value added has been declining from 36 per cent in the early 1990s to 29 per cent by 2004 (OECD 2007: 139). In the public sector plants, too, the net contribution to employment has been negative as they sought to reduce overmanning mainly by resorting to the Voluntary Retirement Scheme, which was accepted by workers in this sector as a mutually acceptable mechanism for downsizing. The increased substitution towards contract labour and the increased resort to voluntary retirement schemes with generous severance payments led to the loss of good quality formal sector jobs and resulted in labour increasing its attention to job security and regular employment than to wages, which was its prime concern in the past.

Liberalization is thus associated with a regime where controlling wage costs and raising productivity have been essential parts of enterprise strategy. In the import substitution regime, the focus was on expanding the home market, which was accompanied by a rise in real wages. Job losses in the organized sector as enterprises cut costs by generating productivity growth, generate a search for jobs in the unorganized sector. The increased supply of workers in the unorganized sector generates a pressure for wages to decrease in this sector. Moreover, most of the surplus labour from the organized sector would have a level of educational attainment that makes them overqualified for casual jobs and that pushes them more towards self-employment than towards the casual labour market.

---

[3] We can think of the reallocation effect as a move along the production possibility frontier as distortions in relative prices are removed. The reorganization effect involves an upward shift of the production possibility frontier.

In India, casual wage workers have on average 1.8 years of education, self-employed workers at double this figure have on average 3.7 years of education, and regular workers have on average double the education of the self-employed with 7.8 years (Ghose 2004). We posit elsewhere (D'Souza 2008) that an increased level of human capital has two effects—first, it increases the efficiency with which business opportunities are assessed; second, education raises the wage-earning capacity of the individual as the higher costs incurred in acquiring skills are compensated by higher wages. Increments to human capital after the initial couple of years have a larger impact on the managerial abilities and the capacity to organize by individuals relative to their wage earning capacities and induces them to direct their labour towards self-employment. Self-employment gives a mixed income which is the sum of labour and entrepreneurial income that is higher than the income possibility from seeking casual wage employment. The surplus labour displaced from the organized sector accompanied by the rise in the educational attainment of workers to intermediate levels in the last decade resulted in the increase in self-employment from 53 per cent of the workforce in 1993–4 to 56.5 per cent in 2004–5.

The absorption of surplus labour in the unorganized sector and the shift towards increased productivity associated with more skill-intensive production in the organized sector resulted in a widening differential between skilled and unskilled wage rates as well as a widening differential between incomes in the organized sectors and the unorganized sectors—liberalization has been associated not only with income inequality due to a skill bias but also with a sectoral bias of greater labour income inequality. Kijima (2006) provides empirical evidence that liberalization increased the demand for skilled labour as work practices modernized and that, as a result, wage inequality increased. Narain (2006) shows how wage growth in the 1990s was highly skewed in favour of high-wage earners whereas for most workers wage growth was slower in the 1990s than in the previous decade. Dutta (2005) examines the trend in wages for males aged 15 to 65 years for the period 1983 to 1999–2000, and finds the dispersion in wages for casual (generally unorganized) workers to be much lower than that among regular (organized sector) workers. Inequality amongst regular workers rose from 1983 to 1999 whereas inequality declined for casual workers in this period. Dutta shows that casual workers face flat returns to education and experience, while the return to education is rising along with the increase in the education level for regular workers. The rising gap between graduate and primary education among regular workers is a reflection of the sharp rise in wage inequality during the period of liberalization.

Figure 9.1, depicting the sectoral shares of employment and GDP, reveals that new employment has been generated in sectors whose productivity is higher than the productivity in agriculture. The largest increases in employment have been in services sectors such as trade, hotels, and restaurants; construction; and transport, storage, and communications, and the employment growth in these sectors as well as manufacturing has mitigated the decline in agricultural employment growth as employment has shifted away from agriculture. The largest increase in productivity has been in the financial services, insurance, real estate, and business services sector. In this sector, the share of employment increased from 0.8 per cent in 1983 to 2 per cent in 2004–5, whereas the sector's share of GDP showed a larger increase from 8.3 per cent to 13.5 per cent in the same period. The largest increase in productivity has thus been in a sector that generates producer services that are closely connected with the modernization and reorganization process and require a workforce with high educational attainment.

The other services sectors such as trade, hotels, and restaurants, and transport, storage, and communication are distributive (trade, transport, storage, and communications) and personal (hotels and restaurants) services that require a workforce with relatively lower educational attainments and (apart from communications) are services characterized by low entry barriers as their requirements for capital and technology are not high. In these service sectors, too, where employment has grown significantly, enterprises have been able to generate productivity growth by keeping wages in check due to the moderate skill requirement of workers. The other sector where employment grew is construction but the productivity increase here has been modest. Community, social, and personal services witnessed a reduction in employment as well as productivity. In this sector, community and social services typically require a workforce with high educational levels whereas personal services require one with comparatively lower education levels[4] and have lower barriers to entry. Liberalization has therefore been associated with an increase in employment in the producer, distributive, and personal services as well as in the basic service of construction. Amongst those employed in these sectors, the skilled experienced an increase in wages but those with lower levels of educational attainment experienced stagnancy in wages, culminating in an overall modest decline in wages for regular as well as casual workers.

The reorganization of enterprises and rationalization of employment practices we describe would get accentuated by the spurt in capital inflows to the economy since

---

[4] Amongst services, the stylized fact is that (1) producer services such as financial and business services have the highest education level followed by (2) social services, (3) basic services (electricity, gas, and water supply), (4) distributive services (trade and transport), and finally (5) personal services.

2002. These capital inflows were associated with a growth in investment expenditures (from 25.2 per cent of GDP in 2002–3 to 37.1 per cent of GDP in 2008–9) and aggregate demand as well as a real exchange rate appreciation (till mid-2007, after which there was a reversal of capital flows) (Central Statistical Organisation 2010). An appreciation of the exchange rate is another incentive for the reorganization of enterprise so as to remain competitive in the face of an increase in the supply of imports at more favourable prices. With competition increasingly taking place on a global scale, there is a limitation on the prospects for growth in labour-intensive areas and a pressure on enterprises to choose labour-saving technologies that make more intensive use of human capital. This reduces the opportunities for industrial employment, especially organized employment. Liberalization and increasing global integration of the economy have accordingly been associated with reorganization and improved efficiency in manufacturing and modern services such as financial services, but at the cost of the shift of labour to low-productivity service sectors.

Large numbers of jobs will increasingly come up in the tertiary sector for people with low and intermediate levels of education such as in community and personal services, trade and hotel industry, and business services. This reallocation of employment in the Indian economy has resulted in widening income inequality as the premium on skills in enterprises has increased. Contrary to the standard presumption that liberalization would benefit unskilled labour, which is the country's relatively abundant factor, it is skilled labour that benefits from the importation of skill-intensive technologies and capital inflows. A large component of employment increases has also taken place in low-productivity distributive and personal services sectors where wages have been stagnant. This is indicative of the type of reforms that have been pursued—passive reforms that reduced protection and price distortions—and of the dire need for active reforms in social (and physical) infrastructure that would raise educational attainments in the workforce and contribute to a reduction in income differentials.

LABOUR MARKETS AND INDUSTRIAL RELATIONS

What have been the effects of reforms on industrial and labour relations in general? According to the 2001 Census of India, the workforce consisted of 402 million people, out of which only 7 per cent to 8 per cent (28.14 million) were in the 'organized' sector and the rest were in the 'unorganized' sector. Out of this 7 per cent, 69 per cent (19.4 million) were in the public sector and the rest (31 per cent = 8.7 million) were in the private sector. 'Organized' sector as a percentage of total workforce has remained stationary at 7 per cent to 8 per cent during 1973–2000. In terms of total employment, the census data indicates that the decline in the agricultural sector's share has been matched by an increase in the service sector's share, with the manufacturing sector's share in employment increasing slightly. In 2004–5, the labour force consisted of 430 million workers, growing at 2 per cent annually, with a stable worker–population ratio of 42 per cent (Census of India 2001).

'Organized' does not necessarily mean unionized. In fact, the unionized sector is only a small subset of the 'organized' sector. Union density varies depending on what figure is in the denominator: if it is 'total workforce', then union density is 5.5 per cent (was around 6.5 per cent in 1985); if only 'wage and salary earners', then density is 25 per cent. The percentage of workers covered by collective bargaining is at most between 2 per cent and 3 per cent. However, given that at least around 5.5 million government employees fall under the government's pay commissions and more are covered by constituted wage boards, the low coverage rate underestimates somewhat the number of employees whose wages and working conditions are regulated by some form of legislation (Venkata Ratnam 2006). While employees in the 'organized' sector are covered by labour laws such as the Payment of Wages Act 1936, the Equal Remuneration Act 1976, the Payment of Bonus Act, and the Companies Act 1952 (applicable to managerial and executive compensation), workers in the 'unorganized' sector usually fall under the Minimum Wages Act 1948.

During the initial years after 1991, there were fears that the 'jobless' growth phenomenon in manufacturing of the 1980s would continue into the 1990s and beyond. The central government froze all hiring at lower levels and instituted a 'National Renewal Fund' to take care of voluntary retirement schemes activated in unprofitable public enterprises. According to Nagaraj's (2004) estimate, about 15 per cent of the workforce (1.1 million workers) in the formal sector lost their jobs between 1995–6 and 2000–1. There were several reasons for these losses during the early post-reform years: natural attrition with hiring freezes and existing labour laws being weakly enforced in many states. In the public sector, voluntary retirement schemes with greater than statutory compensation were accepted by workers as a mutually acceptable mechanism for downsizing.

Employers in the private sector changed the compensation package in favour of performance-based pay, with the acquiescence of unions that over time resulted in a decline of factory-level employment (Bhattacherjee 2005). Macro data also reveals this shrinking of average factory size: in the public sector, the average number of workers per factory declined rapidly from 322 in 1990/1 to 193 in 1996/7, and in the private corporate sector the number declined from 129 to 91 during the same period (Datar and Basu

2003). However, many of these losses reappeared as job creation in the informal and self-employed sectors (see earlier section).

What effects have these labour market outcomes in the 1990s and the first half of this decade had on unions and industrial relations in general? During the early 1990s when the state opened up the banking, telecommunications, broadcast media, and the domestic airline sectors to private players, the left unions strongly protested. But now, looking at the empowerment that the large-scale diffusion of mobile phones and the lowering of prices of air travel due to competition has caused, few people are sympathetic with organized labour in these sectors. In fact, many would argue that the introduction of private players has slowly forced service quality improvements in the state-controlled airlines and banks. During the 1990s, thanks no doubt to increased media focus, the ordinary person became acutely aware that organized labour in India represents declining sectional interests and clearly a kind of 'consumer capitalism' ethos has permeated society. More recently, there were debates within the communist parties and their union federations on whether the ever-growing workforce in the information technology (IT) and IT-enabled sectors should be unionized, with major national and foreign employers feeling that unionization in these sectors would surely thwart expansion and employment growth. Unscientific surveys conducted by the print media during this time overwhelmingly found that the largely young employees in these sectors do not want to be part of a union. Interestingly, the reason most cited for the latter is that they value highly their potential for job mobility and feel that a unionized environment would severely curtail this.

In terms of union density, India fares rather badly compared to other large developing countries. According to the International Labour Organization's (ILO's) *World Labour Report* 1997–98,[5] union membership as a percentage of non-agricultural labour force dropped from 6.6 per cent in 1985 to 5.5 per cent in 1995 (the corresponding figure in 1995 for Argentina was 23.4 per cent, for Brazil it was 32.1 per cent, and for Mexico 31 per cent). Union membership as a percentage of formal sector workers in India declined from 26.5 per cent to 22.8 per cent from 1985 to 1995 (the corresponding figure in 1995 for Argentina was 65.6 per cent, for Brazil it was 66 per cent, and for Mexico 72.9 per cent). If these figures are derived from only those registered unions that submit information on their membership, then it is possible that these figures somewhat underestimate union density in India. Again, according to the aforementioned

source, less than 2 per cent of workers in the combined formal and informal sectors in India are covered by collective bargaining agreements. Clearly, a large proportion of workers (certainly those in the formal sector) fall within the ambit of some government labour legislation, even though they may not be covered by a collective agreement.

These low union density figures obviously represent low coverage but hide the fact that a few public sector unions have enormous 'positional' power to impose severe costs and cause inconvenience to ordinary citizens. Indeed, India loses more days annually because of strikes and lockouts than any other country (ILO 1997/98). However, it is true that more days were lost due to employer-imposed lockouts than worker or union-led strikes during the post-reform years. Between 1991 and 2000, roughly 230 million days were lost, out of which 60 per cent was a result of employer-imposed lockouts. While some writers claim that the latter 'indicate an alarming rise in employer militancy during the period of economic reforms' (Badigannavar 2006), this may not be an accurate reading. It could be that employers are left with no choice but to impose lockouts given impending union wildcat action.

The private manufacturing sector accounts for the largest proportion of industrial disputes by sector, and two states—West Bengal and Kerela—accounted for nearly 70 per cent of the loss (Venkata Ratnam 2006). For West Bengal in the 1990s, it was found that a majority of the lockouts ended with a bipartite settlement that inevitably led to the downsizing of the workforce and a retreat of state intervention (Datt 2003). In the overall Indian context, the long-term trend in the 1990s continued the tendencies that were evident from the late 1980s in terms of moving to a more decentralized industrial relations system as workers increasingly preferred to stay away from the politically affiliated central trade union federations, opting instead for plant-level 'independent' unions. While trade unions submitting returns increased in the 1990s, the average membership per union submitting returns declined: while 7,718 unions submitting returns averaged 831 workers each in 1985, the corresponding numbers in 1997 were 9,918 unions and 743 workers (Anant et al. 2006).

Two interesting developments took place on the trade union scenario after the end of the 1980s. The first of these phenomena is the formation of the National Centre for Labour (NCL) in 1995 and the New Trade Union Initiative (NTUI) in 2001 (see Mohanty [2009] for details). The NCL acted as an apex body that brought together various organizations working to organize unorganized labour, and came to represent more than 625,000 workers across ten Indian states. Even though national trade unions had no direct involvement in NCL, it did receive the support of several independent unions in the organized sector. The NTUI was formed in 2001 and consisted of several unaffiliated

---

[5] This is the latest time period for which comparable data is available (ILO 1997/98).

independent unions in both the unorganized and organized sectors under the expectation that the sum of their individual decentralized voices would be more meaningful with a greater collective voice. In March 2006, the founding conference of the NTUI was held that brought together 200 unions, representing roughly 500,000 workers in both the organized and unorganized sectors, ranging from engineering and electrical goods, petroleum, chemicals, pharmaceuticals, ready-made garments, and government employees on the one hand to construction workers, fish workers, agricultural workers, and forest workers on the other.

The other recent phenomenon was when Jet Airways suddenly announced that 800 probationary staff were to be let go with 1,100 to follow (around 15 per cent of the airline's young workforce) as the airlines faced swelling wage bills during the ongoing global aviation crisis (of October 2008). This led to colourful protests by young and attractive Jet Airways employees of both sexes in their bright yellow jackets marching on the streets of our major metros. The news media could not resist extensive coverage of these protests as these employees were a far cry from what we have come to expect from traditional protesting employees. The left unions in Kolkata quickly took up their cause as did the Shiv Sena unions in Mumbai. A laid-off employee said, 'I never took part in any organized protest, but I shall certainly be a trade union member in my next job' (*The Telegraph* 2008: 4). A day or two later, after the civil aviation minister intervened, the owner of the airlines invoking the family metaphor ('As father of the family, the TV images brought tears to my eyes'), re-instated all the laid-off employees (Ibid.). The next day there were victory marches by union officials in both Kolkata and Mumbai but the Jet Airways employees were nowhere in sight. The owner must have figured that a swollen wage bill was preferable in the short run to the potential long-run effects of trade unionism in his airlines.

In a recent study using the 2004–5 National Sample Survey Organisation (NSSO) 61st round of the Employment–Unemployment Survey, Pal (2008) estimated an individual worker's probability of being a union member as a function of several independent variables, considering only the sub-sample of non-agricultural salaried/wage workers based on 'usual principal activity status' in twenty-seven states. His key findings were the following: (i) The reach of communist parties has sizeable predicted effects on an individual's propensity to unionize. In fact, the mere existence of communist parties in a state facilitates unionization significantly. (ii) Both political activism and the unemployment rate have positive and significant effects on an individual's propensity to be a union member. (iii) Predictably, a full-time male worker's probability to join a union is higher than part-time and/or female workers. (iv) Individuals from Scheduled Castes or Scheduled Tribe categories are more inclined to join unions compared to general category individuals, even though minority religion and other backward castes were found to have no relationship to the unionization probability. (v) Finally, an individual's educational attainment positively affects his/her probability to be a union member, except in the case of vocational and technical training.

In terms of the need for reforming the highly complex Indian industrial relations system, especially its plethora of labour legislation, the government appointed the second National Commission on Labour (NCL) in late 1999. Its mandate was 'to suggest rationalization of existing laws relating to labour in the organized sector and secondly, to suggest an "umbrella" legislation for ensuring minimum labour standards for workers in the unorganized sector' (Badigannavar 2006: 212). The Commission submitted its report on 1 June 2002. The NCL recommended the need for fruitful labour-management partnerships in order to generate commitment to both quality and productivity, bearing in mind the fundamental rights as enshrined in the Indian Constitution. It asked employers to invest in multiple skills training to facilitate a flexible and potentially mobile workforce with several employment opportunities. The NCL recommended changes with respect to trade union recognition and the creation of a sole bargaining agent, and it clearly expresses its preference for decentralized bargaining structures (Badigannavar 2006). It also recommended severe penalties against unions that resort to 'illegal' strike action. Finally, on the issue of downsizing, the NCL recommends that 'prior permission (of state authorities) is not necessary in respect of layoff and retrenchment in an establishment of any employment size' (Badigannavar 2006: 212). Instead, workers should be given a two months' notice or pay in lieu of notice in case of retrenchment (Badigannavar 2006).

According to Anant et al. (2006: 266), the recommendations of the second NCL will lead to two types of distortions as regulations are defined in terms of the number of employees. First, the labour force will be fragmented into protected and unprotected segments; second, exempting smaller units from reporting obligations will lead to the lowering of the labour monitoring regime. However, the aforementioned authors agree that the recommendations will enhance the framework for unionization and collective bargaining by encouraging unionization in erstwhile non-unionized activities. Overall though, these authors concur that the NCL's recommendations 'appear to be in the right direction in rationalizing India's labour laws and related institutions'.

Reformists believe that due to rigid labour laws and the resulting lack of flexibility in industrial labour markets, industrial output, export growth, and employment growth in manufacturing have been considerably constrained. However, the evidence does not seem to support such a proposition wholeheartedly, especially given the recent expansion in employment in certain sectors within manufacturing. The latter does not imply that labour markets in industry are working well—far from it. There are wide inequalities embedded in this labour market as reflected in the stark divide between the 'organized' and the 'unorganized' sectors. Trade unions have consistently demanded comprehensive social security legislation for all categories of unorganized workers as well as tying minimum wage increases to rises in the cost of living for industrial workers. There is thus a need to move towards comprehensive income security and only after this can labour laws be rationalized. In this regard, the second NCL recommended the formulation of umbrella legislation for the social security needs of workers in the unorganized sector. The draft bill was prepared in 2003, and in March 2004, implementation of some of the social security provisions was undertaken in fifty selected districts (Anant et al. 2006). More recently, a new bill was proposed that brought workers in the organized sector under this social security purview as well. But Anant et al. (2006) suggest that the effective implementation of this social security system for unorganized workers is several years away.

Employers' associations in the private sector are increasingly demanding that a larger proportion of total pay consist of performance-linked components, and in several instances in the 'organized' manufacturing sector have achieved this with union acquiescence. Unions are confronted with the choice of either agreeing to the latter or facing employment and wage growth freezes. The most glaring aspect of the employment and industrial relations scene is the widening regional disparities in real income and living standards—a phenomenon the government will invariably be confronted with in its economic policy-making sooner than later.

REFERENCES

Anant, T.C.A., R. Hasan, P. Mohapatra, R. Nagaraj, and S.K. Sasikumar (2006), 'Labour Markets in India', in J. Filipe and R. Hasan (eds), *Labour Markets in Asia: Issues and Perspectives*. London: Palgrave Macmillan, pp. 205–300.

Badigannavar, V. (2006), 'Industrial Relations in India', in M.J. Morley, P. Gunnigle, and D.G. Collings (eds), *Global Industrial Relations*, pp.198–217. London: Routledge.

Bhattacherjee, D. (2005), 'The Effects of Group Incentives in an Indian Firm: Evidence from Payroll Data', *Labour: Review of Labour Economics and Industrial Relations*, 19(1): 147–73.

Census of India (2001), New Delhi: Ministry of Home Affairs, Government of India.

Central Statistical Organisation (2010), *Quick Estimates of National Income, Consumption Expenditure, Saving and Capital Formation 2008–09*. New Delhi: Ministry of Statistics and Programme Implementation, Government of India.

Datar, M.K. and P.K. Basu (2003), 'Role of Ownership and Organizational Forms in Labour Market Outcomes: An Explanatory Analysis', *The Indian Journal of Labour Economics*, 46(October–December): 537–47.

Datt, Ruddar (2003), *Lockouts in India*. New Delhi: Manohar.

Dougherty, Sean (2009), 'Labour Regulation and Employment Dynamics at the State Level in India', OECD Economics Department Working Paper.

D'Souza, E. (2008), 'Self Employment and Human Capital', *Indian Journal of Labour Economics*, 51(4): 783–9.

Dutta, P.V. (2005), 'Accounting for Wage Inequality in India', PRUS Working Paper No. 29, University of Sussex, January, mimeo.

Ghose, A.K. (2004), 'The Employment Challenge in India', *Economic and Political Weekly*, 39(48): 5106–16.

International Labour Organization (ILO) (1997/98), *World Employment—National Policies in a Global Context*. Geneva: ILO.

Kijima, Y. (2006), 'Why did Wage Inequality Increase? Evidence from Urban India 1983–99', *Journal of Development Economics*, 81: 97–117.

Kundu, A. and P.C. Mohanan (2009), 'Employment and Inequality Outcomes in India', paper presented at the 'Joint Seminar on Employment and Inequality, organized by the Employment, Labour and Social Affairs Directorate and Development Centre, Paris, 8 April, pp. 1 – 43.

Mahendra Dev, S. (2008), 'Employment: Trends, Issues and Policies', in *Inclusive Growth in India*, pp. 167–200. New Delhi: Oxford University Press.

Mohanty, M. (2009), 'A Note on New Trends in Unionisation in India', Indian Institute of Management Calcutta, Working Paper Series, No. 641, June.

Nagaraj, R. (2004), 'Fall in Organized Manufacturing Employment: A Brief Note', *Economic and Political Weekly*, 39(24): 3387–90.

Narain, A. (2006), 'Wage Trends and Determinants', paper written for 'India: Meeting the Employment Challenge', A Conference on Labour and Employment Issues in India, 27–29 July 2006, India Habitat Centre, New Delhi.

National Sample Survey (NSS) (2005), Report No. 515. New Delhi: Ministry of Statistics and Programme Implementation, Government of India.

OECD (2007), *Economic Surveys: India*. New Delhi: Academic Foundation.

Pal, Rupayan(2008), 'Estimating the Probability of Trade Union Membership in India: Impact of Communist Parties, Personal Attributes and Industrial Characteristics', Indira Gandhi Institute of Development Research, Mumbai, July, WP-2008-015.

Rodrik, D. and A. Subramanian (2005), 'From Hindu Growth to Productivity Surge: The Mystery of the Indian Growth Transition', *IMF Staff Papers*, 52(2): 193–228.

The Telegraph (2008), Calcutta edn, 16 October.

Venkata Ratnam, C.S. (2006), *Industrial Relations*. New Delhi: Oxford University Press.

10

The Performance of India's Telecommunications Industry, 1991–2009[#]

Sunil Mani

INTRODUCTION

India's telecommunications industry is considered to be one of the more successful stories of the Indian liberalization attempt. This is indicated by the fact that the country has one of the cheapest and state-of-the-art telecom services anywhere in the world. The density of telephones in the country has increased from just 0.60 telephones per 100 people in 1991 to about 60 per 100 at the end of August 2010 (Telecom Regulatory Authority of India [TRAI] 2010). Although the access to telecom services has actually increased, it has not been across the board, but concentrated largely in urban centres, leading to a growing 'digital divide' within the country with much of the rural areas being left out of this revolution. Nevertheless, by its sheer size and rate of growth, the industry has become a major contributor to India's gross domestic product (GDP). The market for telecom services is actually giving rise to a large domestic market for telecom equipments and the market for various types of electronic components and semiconductor devices that go into the production of these equipments. In fact, the Indian telecommunications industry is a unique example of a services industry leading to the growth and emergence of a manufacturing industry.

Our argument is that technological changes and reasonably well-implemented policies, relatively speaking, and

especially regulatory policies have actually contributed to the success of the industry. Both these have reduced the height of entry barriers to the industry and made it extremely competitive. The result has been fast diffusion of new technologies in the provision of telecom services and through that process, significant reductions in prices. An interesting outcome of this increased competitiveness of the industry has been that the state-owned incumbent provider has actually improved its performance. The telecom industry thus shows that the performance of public sector enterprises can be improved more, organically, through effective deregulation and through subjecting the incumbent service provider to a modicum of domestic competition.

In the context, the purpose of this chapter will be to trace the performance of India's telecom services industry and then assess the role that policy measures have played in shaping its growth trajectory. In that process, the chapter will also identify those areas where policy measures still have a role to play to improve the state of affairs. Two such areas are: first, the realm of bridging the digital divide; second, enhancing the diffusion of Internet within the economy. The chapter is divided into four sections. The next section maps out the growth and structure of the telecommunications services industry over the last two decades. The second section will identify three substantive issues where public policy still needs to be applied. The third section will distil out the implications of this phenomenal growth in telecommunications services for the domestic manufacturing of telecommunications

[#] This is a revised and updated version of Mani (2008).

equipments within the country. The last section sums up the main findings of this chapter.

GROWTH OF INDIA'S TELECOM SERVICES INDUSTRY

In 1991, India had a total stock of just 5 million telephones. By 2009, this has grown to 562 million phones (see Table 10.1). Consequently, the tele-density has increased from less than 1 per 100 in 1991 to about 41 in 2009. By all accounts, the telecommunications industry has been an astounding success. A striking feature of this growth performance is the ratio of mobile to fixed phones, which has increased from insignificant amounts to about 14. This domination of wireless technology has important implications for the diffusion of Internet in the country. This issue will be analysed in depth in the following.

Monthly Addition to Mobile Subscribers and the Growing Market for Telecom Handsets

As a corollary of the aforementioned, it is seen that there has been a steady increase in the average number of mobile subscribers per month since 2003 (Table 10.2). In 2003, on an average 1.5 million new subscribers were added to the existing stock. This has since increased to approximately 15 million per month in 2009. The very sharp reduction in the number of subscribers in March 2007 was due to a governmental security regulation.

These large increases in the number of mobile handsets have strong positive implications for the telecom equipment industry and specifically the mobile handsets industry, which means that close to 15 million handsets are being bought and sold every month. Consequently, a huge domestic market for telecom equipments has suddenly emerged in the country, spawning the creation of a significant manufacturing base. The south Indian city of Chennai has become a thriving cluster for mobile handsets manufacturing and this has important implications for the downstream industries such as the semiconductor industry.

Increasing Privatization of the Telecom Services Industry

The distribution of telecom services in the country was entirely in the hands of the public sector for a very long time until the middle of the 1990s. The new telecom policy of 1994 changed all this.

Table 10.1   Growth of India's Telecom Services, 1991–2009

Year	Fixed Phones	Growth Rate	Mobile Phones	Growth Rate	Total	Growth Rate	Tele-density	Ratio of Mobile to Fixed
1991	5.07				5.07		0.6	
1992	5.81	14.60			5.81	14.60	0.67	
1993	6.8	17.04			6.8	17.04	0.77	
1994	8.03	18.09			8.03	18.09	0.89	
1995	9.8	22.04			9.8	22.04	1.07	
1996	11.98	22.24			11.98	22.24	1.26	
1997	14.54	21.37	0.34		14.88	24.21	1.56	0.02
1998	17.8	22.42	0.88	158.82	18.68	25.54	1.94	0.05
1999	21.59	21.29	1.2	36.36	22.79	22.00	2.33	0.06
2000	26.51	22.79	1.88	56.67	28.39	24.57	2.86	0.07
2001	32.44	22.37	3.58	90.43	36.02	26.88	3.58	0.11
2002	41.48	27.87	13	263.13	54.48	51.25	4.3	0.31
2003	42.58	2.65	33.58	158.31	76.16	39.79	5.1	0.79
2004	45	5.68	50	48.90	95	24.74	7.04	1.11
2005	49	8.89	76	52	125	31.58	10.66	1.55
2006	40.43	−17.49	149.5	96.71	189.93	51.94	17.16	3.70
2007	39.25	−2.92	233.63	56.27	272.88	43.67	25	5.95
2008	37.9	−3.44	346.89	48.48	384.79	41.01	33.23	9.15
2009	37.06	−2.22	525.15	51.39	562.21	46.11	46.32	14.17

Source: Department of Telecommunications (DoT, 2005) and TRAI (various issues), Press Releases.

Note: Number of subscribers is in million; growth rates are in percentages; tele-density is number of telephones per 100 subscribers.

Table 10.2 Monthly Additions to Mobile Subscribers, 2002–9 (in million)

	2002	2003	2004	2005	2006	2007	2008	2009
January		0.64	1.58	1.76	4.69	6.81	8.77	15.41
February		0.6	1.6	1.67	4.27	6.22	8.53	13.82
March		0.96	1.93	0.78	5.03	3.53	10.1	15.64
April	0.28	0.64	1.37	1.46	3.88	6.11	8.21	11.9
May	0.29	2.26	1.33	1.72	4.25	6.57	8.62	11.59
June	0.35	1.42	1.43	1.97	4.78	7.34	8.81	12.03
July	0.36	2.32	1.74	2.46	5.39	8.06	9.22	14.38
August	0.49	1.79	1.67	2.74	5.9	8.31	9.16	15.08
September	0.37	1.61	1.84	2.48	6.07	7.8	10.07	14.98
October	0.53	1.67	1.51	2.9	6.71	8.05	10.42	16.67
November	0.72	1.9	1.56	3.51	6.8	8.32	10.35	17.05
December	0.8	1.69	1.95	4.46	6.4	8.17	10.81	19.1
Average	**0.46**	**1.46**	**1.63**	**2.33**	**5.35**	**7.11**	**9.42**	**14.85**

Source: TRAI (various issues), Press Releases.

The share of the private sector in the overall telecom industry has been rising (Figure 10.1) and the ratio of private to public sectors actually crossed unity in 2006. This again is due to the fact that the public sector is more dominant in wireline (or fixed) segment and the private sector is dominant in the wireless (mobile) segment (Table 10.3).

This sort of a structure of the industry is largely the product of historical reasons. The two public sector service providers, Bharat Sanchar Nigam Limited (BSNL) and Mahanagar Telephone Nigam Limited (MTNL), dominated the wireline sector, while the private sector was able to dominate the new wireless technology segment. In fact, it was only quite recently that the government allowed the public sector entities to provide wireless communication services.

Given the preponderance of wireless technologies in the total network, over time the telecom services industry in

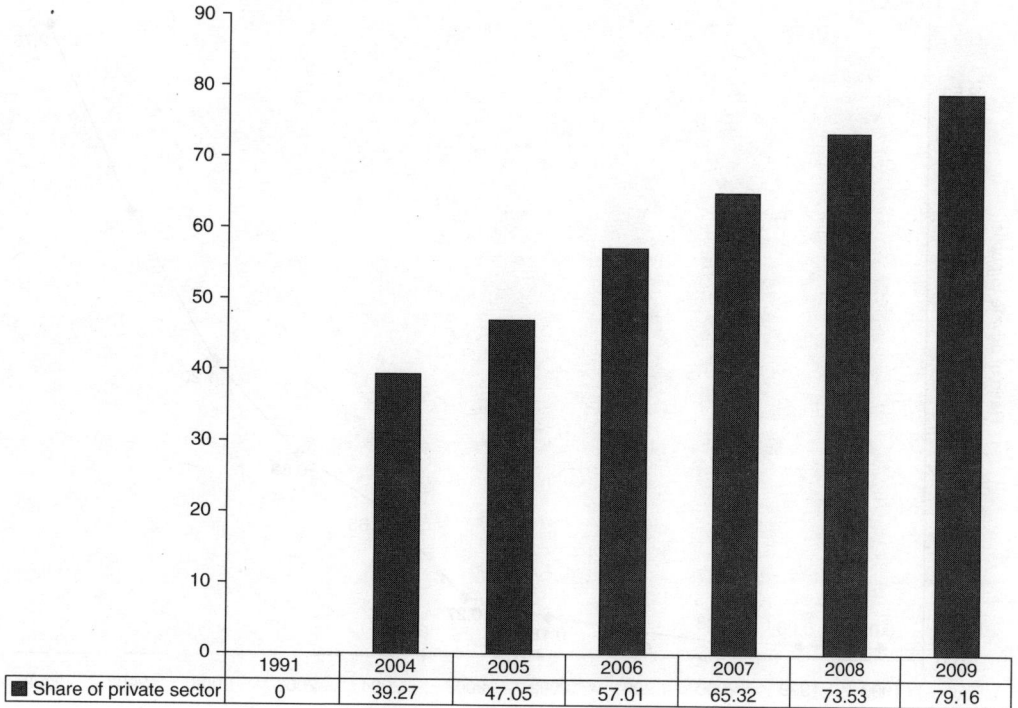

	1991	2004	2005	2006	2007	2008	2009
■ Share of private sector	0	39.27	47.05	57.01	65.32	73.53	79.16

Source: DoT (2009).

Figure 10.1 Rising Privatization of the Telecommunication Services Sector, 1991–2009

Table 10.3   Structure of the Telecommunication Services
Industry according to Ownership

	Wireline	Wireless
Public	91	19.32
Private	9	80.68
Total	100	100

Source: TRAI (various issues), Press Releases.

Note: Percentage shares as on 31 May 2007.

India (both wireline and wireless together) has come to be dominated by the private sector. This growing privatization of the industry is indicated by the ratio of private sector to public sector increasing steadily from 0.05 in 1998 to 2.78 in 2008 (Figure 10.2).

Competition in the Provision of Telecom Services: Fixed vs. Mobile and GSM vs. CDMA

An interesting feature of the industry is that after a very long time, it has suddenly become very competitive. There are three dimensions to this competition. First, it is a competition between two standards or technologies, namely, Global System for Mobile Communications (GSM) and Code Division Multiple Access (CDMA) standards. Second, it is a competition between various service providers, although

this competition was restricted to public policy–designed spaces or markets known as telecom circles. Another dimension is the type of market. There are essentially three types of markets based on the geographic coverage of the service—local telephone market; long-distance or national telecom services; and foreign or the overseas market. We focus on all the three dimensions of competition between the service providers.

Competition in Fixed and Mobile Technologies

The markets for mobile services are much more competitive than the one for fixed line services. In the latter, the incumbent service provider, BSNL, continues to have a lion's share. However, the existence of mobile communication services has made the market for fixed line services contestable and as a result, despite high concentration, prices of fixed telecom services kept falling or were kept under check over the last five years or so. The trends in prices of telecom services will be analysed in detail later. I now analyse competition in the fixed (wireline) and mobile (wireless) technologies separately.

Competition in the Fixed and Mobile Services Industries If one goes by overall summary measures of domestic competition, the market for fixed telephone services is much

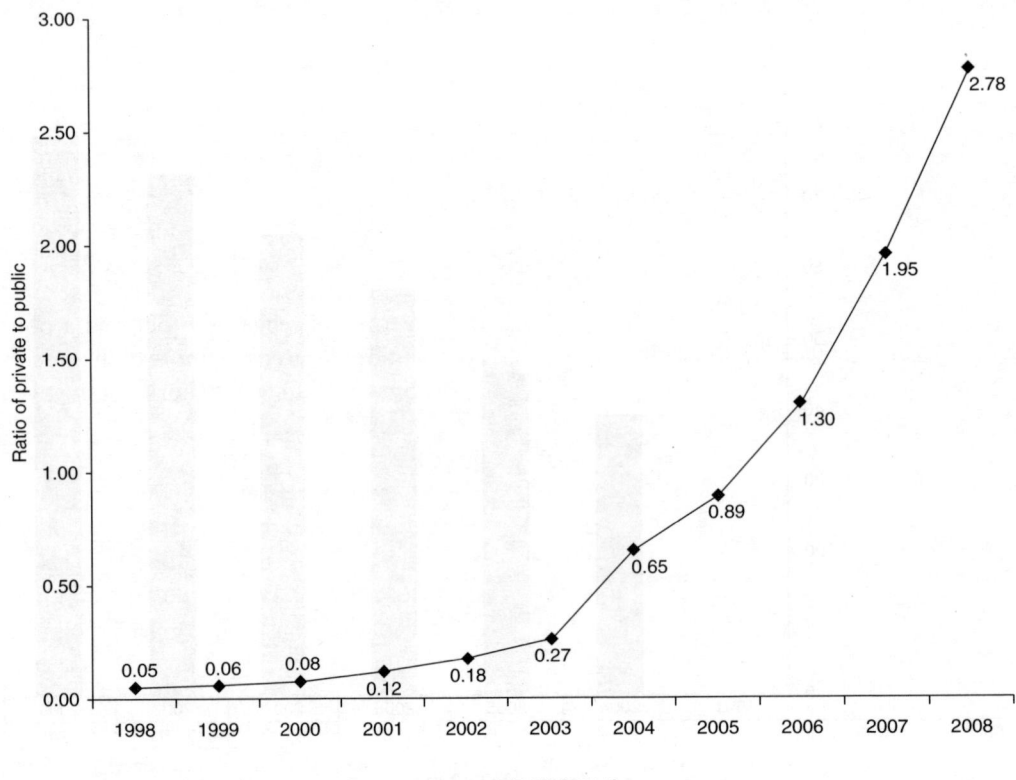

Source: TRAI (2009).

Figure 10.2   Growing Privatization of Telecom Services in India, 1998–2008

more concentrated than the one for mobile services. For instance (as on 31 May 2009), the Herfindahl Index for fixed services for the nation as a whole works out to 0.99 while the one for mobile services works out to 0.21. This national-level picture hides the level of competition that exists at the sub-national level. In order to gauge this, I have computed the structure of the market for fixed telecom services in each of

the twenty-eight telecom circles that the country is divided into. As can be seen from Table 10.4, the market for fixed telecom services is highly concentrated in all the telecom circles, although in eight of them, namely, Andhra Pradesh, Chennai, Chhattisgarh, Delhi-NCR, Karnataka, Madhya Pradesh, Mumbai, and Punjab, the H-Index has a value less than 0.8000. Of course, this does not mean that the market for fixed telecom services is not competitive.

There are two dimensions to this level of competition for fixed services. First, as has been argued earlier, the consumers are increasingly substituting mobile for fixed services, so the fixed service providers face intense competition from mobile services. Second, the existence of a telecom regulator too has acted as a check on the dominant service provider, BSNL, from charging high prices. Instead, what one sees is a significant improvement in the performance of BSNL during this period. First of all, BSNL is one of the leading profit-making central public sector enterprises (PSEs) in the country: in 2005–6 it made a net profit of Rs 89.40 billion, one of the few non-oil PSEs in the top ten profit-making PSEs in the country. Three areas where the firm has made performance improvements are: (a) considerable reductions in the number of consumers on the waiting list for a connection; (b) reductions in the number of faults per subscriber; and (c) number of personnel per 1,000 subscribers. BSNL has made substantial progress on all the three indicators (Department of Telecommunications [DoT] 2007). I argue that this is entirely due to the force of competition leading to efficiency gains for this rather monopolistic firm which had a history of being completely impervious to the demands of consumers.

The history of the mobile services industry can be traced to 1997 or so when GSM cellular services were started. Since then the industry has grown and matured, with another standard, CDMA, being introduced towards the end of 2002. Compared to the fixed services, the mobile services industry has a number of distinguishing features. First, the industry started as one dominated by private sector enterprises and the government religiously followed a policy of 'managed competition' by licensing more than one service provider in a telecom circle. In fact, majority of the twenty-eight circles have at least four services providers, and in a number of cases there are six service providers as well. In short, right through inception, the government envisaged an oligopolistic form of competition. Second, most of these private sector enterprises had some foreign equity holding of sorts. Third, all of them are based on new state-of-the art technologies. Fourth, the conduct of the industry was, relatively speaking, more regulated by the newly created independent regulatory agency, the TRAI. Fifth, it is one of the fastest growing industries in India and it can be safely assumed that it is the growth of this industry that has catapulted the communications sector as one of the major growth-contributing sector of India's economy. Sixth, the mobile communications industry, especially the

Table 10.4   Competition in the Fixed and Mobile Telecommunications Industry

No.	Circle	Mobile	Fixed
1	Andaman and Nicobar Islands	1.00	1.00
2	Andhra Pradesh	0.19	0.76
3	Assam	0.24	1.00
4	Bihar	0.24	0.99
5	Chennai	0.20	0.56
6	Chhattisgarh	1.00	0.67
7	Delhi	0.18	0.47
8	Gujarat	0.21	0.83
9	Himachal Pradesh	0.25	0.98
10	Haryana	0.17	0.92
11	Jammu and Kashmir	0.32	1.00
12	Jharkhand	1.00	1.00
13	Karnataka	0.25	0.63
14	Kerala	0.19	0.94
15	Kolkata	0.20	0.80
16	Madhya Pradesh	0.23	0.67
17	Maharashtra	0.17	0.85
18	Mumbai	0.17	0.53
19	North East-I	0.26	1.00
20	North East-II	1.00	1.00
21	Orissa	0.22	0.98
22	Punjab	0.17	0.68
23	Rajasthan	0.20	0.81
24	Tamil Nadu	0.21	0.85
25	Uttar Pradesh (East)	0.20	0.91
26	Uttar Pradesh (West)	0.18	0.90
27	Uttarakhand	1.00	1.00
28	West Bengal	0.21	0.99

Source: TRAI (various issues), Press Releases.

Note: Based on Herfindahl Indices computed on the basis of market shares in the number of subscribers as on 31 May 2009.

equipment part of the industry, is the second largest in the world (next to China) and has therefore attracted considerable foreign direct investment (FDI) in the manufacture of handsets, leading to the employment of skilled manpower. Seventh, India is supposed to have the cheapest mobile telecom tariffs in the world. The early part of the industry was of course riddled with much controversy pertaining to the terms and conditions under which the licences were issued and the spectrum allocated among various kinds of service providers (Desai 2006). Since all the services providers were new and had the same vintage of technology, their competition was more in terms of price and conditions of sale. Of late, these two aspects are much in public scrutiny, thanks to the timely intervention on various occasions by the regulator.

Most of the service providers have focused on specific regional markets, with the exception of Bharti (the largest mobile service provider). In fact, there are only four service providers who have a presence in at least twenty of the twenty-eight circles. It is also interesting to see that the circles where BSNL has a monopoly position are also those with very low revenue potential. In other words, the private sector providers have positioned themselves in the most revenue-earning circles. Also, it is in the circles with high revenue-earning potential that one sees an increase in the intensity of competition—the metros of Delhi, Mumbai, and Chennai, for instance.

Competition between Mobile Standards

It was discussed earlier that mobile phones were introduced in the country towards the latter half of the 1990s, and specifically in 1997. Ever since that year and until the end of 2002, the market was dominated by just one technology, namely, GSM. But in December 2002, Reliance Infocomm Ltd launched CDMA services across seventeen circles on a country-wide basis. CDMA has since been growing fast at around 75 per cent per annum, although the market is still dominated by the GSM technology (Table 10.5).

Most Indian consumers are unaware of the nitty gritty of the two technologies. So the deciding factor between the two technologies is often based on price and other conditions of offer such as the coverage of the service, ease of obtaining a new connection, and whether a handset is available at a reduced price as part of the deal. Given this sort of a possibility of perfect substitution between the two types of technologies, the existence of the two standards has made the markets for both GSM and CDMA services very competitive. This is especially so when the market for CDMA services is highly concentrated, with just two service providers accounting for almost the entire output (see Table 10.6). This is further indicated by the higher Herfindahl Index for CDMA services. What is being argued here is that despite being highly concentrated, CDMA service providers have to

Table 10.5 Ratio of GSM to CDMA Subscribers, 2001 through 2008 (subscribers in million)

	CDMA	GSM	Ratio of GSM to CDMA
2001			
2002			
2003			
2004	7.54	26.15	3.47
2005	11.15	52.2	4.68
2006	20.95	90.14	4.30
2007	44.64	165.11	3.70
2008	68.37	261.07	3.82

Source: TRAI (various issues), Press Releases.

Table 10.6 Structure of the GSM and CDMA Services Industry

GSM			CDMA
Bharti	0.321	Reliance Infocomm	56.71
Vodafone	0.229	Tata Teleservices	35.58
BSNL	0.1879	BSNL	6.7
Idea	0.1246	HFCL	0.44
Aircel	0.0551	MTNL	0.41
Reliance	0.0364	Shyam Telelink	0.16
Spice	0.0218		
MTNL	0.0168		
BPL	0.0087		
Herfindahl Index	**0.211508**	**Herfindahl Index**	**0.452724**

Note: Market shares as on 31 March 2009.

compete with GSM service providers, and this has prevented the former from wielding any excessive market power.

One of the most important institutional requirements for competition to emerge and sustain is the introduction of mobile number portability (MNP). MNP allows a customer to move from one mobile service to another within GSM, and also between GSM and CDMA, while retaining the same number. In March 2006, TRAI had recommended to DoT that MNP be introduced by April 2007. According to this recommendation, a subscriber would be able to avail the service by making a one-time payment of Rs 200 that would enable the operator to recover in three to five years its investment cost involved in introducing portability. It appears that DoT has not accepted this recommendation, citing technical reasons such as non-availability of dual-technology handsets that can handle both GSM and CDMA technologies.[1]

---

[1] Subsequent to the writing of this chapter, MNP was first launched in Haryana on 25 November 2010. A pan-India launch is scheduled for 20 January 2011.

It is generally held that major opposition to MNP came from GSM service providers, while the CDMA providers welcomed it with the hope that it would allow them to expand their market share.

Price of Telecom Services

One of the more direct effects of this competition is lower prices. Before the deregulation of the telecom services industry, and indeed the entry of mobile service providers, telecom consumers were periodically subjected to increases in tariff. This has now been effectively checked. Although it is not easy to talk about the price of telecom services, it basically follows a two-part tariff, both in the case of fixed and mobile services: first an activation charge followed by a charge for each type of call. For mobile communication consumers, there is a variation in the cost of calls depending on whether it is a post-paid or a prepaid connection. Based on estimates made by TRAI (2006), I have obtained the minimum effective charge derived out of an outgoing usage of 250 minutes per month per quarter during 2003 through 2005. This is plotted for both fixed and mobile services. Although charges for calls in both the cases have come down, a higher reduction is noticed in the case of mobile services. In fact, India now has one of the cheapest mobile tariffs in the world (Table 10.7) and this can give an additional fillip to the growth of the information and communications technology (ICT) industry in the country. If one were to plot the price of telecom services and the number of subscribers, one can see an inverse relationship in the case of mobile services, although in the case of fixed services such an inverse relationship is not visible. This is because of the relative advantages that mobile technology can bestow on its user.

The two state-owned service providers, BSNL and MTNL, launched 'One India Plan' with effect from 1 March 2006. Under this, a three-minute local call and a one-minute national long-distance call (referred to as STD call) will cost only Re 1. The 'One India' plan also, for the first time, takes away the distinction between the fixed line tariff and the cellular tariff, and thus makes the tariff 'technology independent'. A similar plan has also been introduced for the customers of post-paid and prepaid mobile services of BSNL and MTNL.

Institutional Support

An interesting feature of the growth of the telecommunications industry in the 1990s and beyond compared to the earlier period is the strong public policy support that the industry has received. It manifested in the form of the following policies:

- National Telecom Policy of 1994
- Telecom Regulatory Authority Act of 1997
- New Telecom Policy of 1999
- Broadband Policy of 2004

Other policies having an indirect effect are the FDI policy, the Electronic Hardware Policy of 2003, and the Semiconductor Policy of 2007.

Of the four main policies, in my view, the most important piece of legislation that is determining the growth performance of the industry is the establishment of a regulatory agency, the TRAI.

The ten-year history of telecommunications regulation in India can be divided into two phases: the first covering the period 1997–2000 when TRAI was established for the first time; the second covering the period 2000 onwards, when considerable amendments were made to the original TRAI Act. On the whole, TRAI's functioning has been marred by a number of bitter disputes between the regulatory authority, the DoT, and the service providers, although in more recent times (especially since 2001) it has been rather effective in

Table 10.7   Cost of Mobile Calls in India Compared to Other Countries (June 2004)

Country	Call Charges per Minute (US$)	Minutes of Usage per Subscriber per Month	Average Revenue per User (US$)	Termination Rates per Minute Mobile (US$)
Australia	0.24	159	43	0.152 (0.016)**
Brazil	0.11	92	11	0.080 (0.020)
China	0.04	261	10	0.025 (0.010)
Switzerland	0.45	119	59	0.163 (0.017)
Japan	0.33	156	63	0.130 (0.022)
India	0.03*	309	11	0.007 (0.007)

Source: TRAI (2006).

Note: * refers to 2005 rates; ** figures in parentheses indicate the termination rates per minute for fixed telephones.

shaping the conduct of the industry in terms of pricing behaviour and indeed in quality of service. In this subsection, I do not attempt to provide a detailed review of TRAI's operations since its inception, but a quick survey of its place in telecom regulation in India. The purpose is essentially to illustrate the need for a more independent regulator that can effectively oversee the functioning of now an almost completely deregulated industry. The actual benefits that the consumers have received from this regulation have been discussed in detail elsewhere in the chapter in terms of increased easy access to telecom services, considerable improvements in both the price and quality of services, and there being an ever-present watchdog of the industry.

TRAI's functions can be broadly categorized into two: recommendatory and mandatory. It is seen that in most of the important conduct variables such as the promotion of competition, pricing, technology, and quality of service, and in the efficient use of spectrum, the pronouncements of TRAI are merely recommendatory and the final decision is taken by the government. The mandatory powers of TRAI are restricted to a number of technical issues such as fixing the terms and conditions of interconnectivity between the service providers, laying down the standards of quality of service and ensuring that these conditions are actually met by the service providers, and ensuring the effective compliance of Universal Service Obligation. This shows that the effective space that is available for TRAI in terms of asserting its real power is very limited. The fact that TRAI's decision on most matters are only recommendatory in nature reduces its power to improve the market conduct of service providers.

After a detailed review of its functioning during the earlier period (1997–2000), Mani (2002) referred to TRAI as a 'muddled regulator'. This is because during this phase, TRAI's functions were poorly articulated and it was generally viewed as driven by the well-organized and vociferous lobby of private phone service operators. TRAI did little to hide its pronounced contempt for the DoT and the state-owned providers, BSNL and MTNL. At the same time, it failed to ensure that private operators adhered to their licence conditions. Its authority and credibility were undermined by court rulings that clearly exposed its lack of power. Its reputation suffered even more when it allowed the private operators to fight its court battles. In short, it would not be incorrect to state that there was 'regulatory capture' during this first and initial phase of its operations.

The governmental admission of the ineffectiveness of TRAI resulted in the cabinet approval of a plan to reinvent the regulator and define its functions more clearly. This takes us to the second phase in TRAI's history. This thinking manifested itself in the form of the issuance of an ordinance to replace TRAI with an appellate tribunal with judicial powers and a reconstituted regulator that lacked one of the most important functions of any telecom regulator, namely, the power to settle disputes between the various stakeholders. This function has been vested with the newly created Telecom Dispute Settlement and Appellate Tribunal (TDSAT). However, this was followed by the strengthening of TRAI's role in a number of other areas. But it can be shown that though the amendment has further clarified the precise role of the regulator by considerably reducing the grey areas, it has effectively reduced the power of the regulator. TRAI's recommendations to the government are binding only with respect to the non-compliance and efficient use of the spectrum. On the crucial issues of timing and licensing of new service providers, its recommendations are not binding. In sum, TRAI has been reduced to a tariff-setting body empowered only to fix tariffs and interconnection charges and to set norms on quality of service. On these two, especially on the tariff issue, TRAI's role is generally considered to be satisfactory.

Growing R&D Outsourcing

It is generally held that India has emerged as a major research and development (R&D) hub. The recently concluded Technology Information and Forecasting Assessment Council (TIFAC) (2007) study has confirmed this commonly held proposition. According to this study, R&D investment worth $1.13 billion has flowed into India during the five-year period 1998–2003. The total receipts on R&D services have doubled from US$ 221 million in 2004–5 to US$ 519 million in 2005–6 (Reserve Bank of India 2006: 1355). Telecom, along with the pharmaceutical industry, is a major recipient of these investments. The innovative performance of this segment can be gauged from the fact the number of US patents issued to inventors from India (including multinational corporations having operations in India) in the area of telecom technologies have increased from just 2 in 2001 to 29 in 2006 (Table 10.8).

THREE SUBSTANTIVE ISSUES

The previous section outlined several dimensions of the growth of the industry. All these were positive features such as the phenomenal growth of the industry, and significant reductions in the waiting time to get a telephone connection and indeed in the price of telecom services. There are, of course, three aspects of the growth of telecom services in India that need some indepth examination. These three aspects are as follows:

1. The decreasing digital divide
2. Increased dependence on imports as far as the equipments are considered
3. The relatively low penetration of Internet in India

Table 10.8 Number of Patents Issued to Indian Inventors in the US, 2001–6

	Multiplexing	Pulse or Digital	Telephonic	Telecommunications	Total
2001	0	1	0	1	2
2002	2	1	0	1	4
2003	3	1	0	1	5
2004	6	2	1	0	9
2005	7	2	1	3	13
2006	14	4	3	8	29

Source: United States Patent and Trademark Office website.

The Reducing Digital Divide

Several commentators, notably Desai (2006), had referred to the growing inequalities in the availability of telephones, especially between states and indeed between the rural and urban areas within a state. This is so severe that the national picture that presented earlier is only representative of the urban areas of some of the states. This growing digital divide, as it is usually referred to, is of course a reflection of the growing divides within the country as far as income and wealth are considered. The ratio of urban to rural tele-density, which kept falling until 2002, started rising again since 2003 and was much higher in 2006 than in 1996 (when the mobile revolution was just about to begin). Thereafter, it has started falling almost every year (Table 10.9). In order to show this decline in the urban–rural availability of telephones, we compute an index of it by taking the ratio of urban to rural tele-density multiplied by 100. The index at its peak in 2006 stood at 1,636, and has since reduced significantly to 588 in 2009 (up to March).

Table 10.9 The Reducing Rural–Urban Divide in Telecommunication Services, 1999–2009

Fiscal Year	Rural	Urban	Total	Digital Divide Index
1999	0.52	6.87	2.33	1321
2000	0.68	8.23	2.86	1210
2001	0.93	10.37	3.58	1115
2002	1.21	12.2	4.29	1008
2003	1.49	14.32	5.11	961
2004	1.55	20.79	7.02	1341
2005	1.73	26.88	8.95	1554
2006	2.34	38.28	12.74	1636
2007	5.89	48.1	18.22	817
2008	9.46	66.39	26.22	702
2009	15.11	88.84	36.98	588

Source: DoT (2010).

Note: 'Rural' and 'urban' specify number of connections per tele-density. 'Total' refers to the arithmetic mean of urban and rural tele-density.

Table 10.10 The Digital Divide within Telecom Circles in India (as on 31 March 2009)

	Overall	Urban	Rural	Digital Divide Index
Andaman & Nicobar Islands	21.24	28.89	16.57	174
Haryana	43.75	75.98	28.1	270
Punjab	58.25	95.85	33.11	289
Gujarat	45.16	75.43	25.21	299
Tamil Nadu	50.46	79.48	25.62	310
Maharashtra	37.9	69.67	21.7	321
Kerala	58.48	125.35	35.43	354
Uttarakhand	11.59	25.97	6.04	430
Himachal Pradesh	55.5	179.81	40.47	444
Jammu & Kashmir	32.76	77.42	16.72	463
West Bengal	22.51	77.86	13.5	577
All-India	**36.98**	**88.84**	**15.11**	**588**
Rajasthan	37.15	102.56	16.71	614
Orissa	23.3	78.09	12.55	622
Andhra Pradesh	39.59	103.38	15.22	679
Karnataka	45.21	98.73	14.36	688
Madhya Pradesh	30.08	80.36	11.07	726
North East-II	9.21	27.36	3.69	741
Uttar Pradesh (East)	24.91	77.76	10.24	759
Jharkhand	4.11	13.02	1.44	904
Chhattisgarh	5.15	16.69	1.81	922
Assam	20.65	86.98	9.36	929
North East-I	44.49	139.1	14.67	948
Bihar	22.18	133	9.17	1450
Uttar Pradesh (West)				
Kolkata	89.68			
Chennai	127.38			
Delhi	140.18			
Mumbai	110.52			

Source: DoT (2010).

Another dimension of the digital divide is the variation in tele-density across the various telecom circles (Table 10.10). Of the twenty-eight telecom circles in the country, we had data for twenty-seven; of these, twelve had a digital divide higher than the national average. Among the states, Kerala and Punjab have one of the highest tele-densities.

This confirms the oft-expressed view that the telecom revolution spearheaded by the mobile phones has remained largely as an urban phenomenon in a number of poorer states. The government is aware of this situation and has put in place an institutional arrangement for bridging the digital divide. Specifically, the National Telecom Policy of 1999 envisaged implementation of the Universal Service Obligation Fund (USO Fund) to provide telecom services in rural, remote, and non-remunerative areas. This fund is raised through a 'universal access levy', which is 5 per cent of the adjusted gross revenue earned by the service providers under various licences. The Universal Service Support Policy for Implementation of USO took effect from 1 April 2002. It is administered by the DoT and has three major components: (i) providing public shared access; (ii) providing individual access; (iii) infrastructure support for mobile service providers. The latter policy (on provision of infrastructure support to mobile service providers) is on the anvil and is yet to take shape. The overall performance of the USO Fund is far from satisfactory as, cumulatively, only about 13 per cent of the funds accumulated have actually been disbursed (Table 10.11).

The service providers, except for the state-owned BSNL, are rather reluctant to provide shared access. However, private providers are keen to participate in the provision of individual access in rural areas as it is more profitable than providing shared access (DoT 2007).

Hitherto, the USO funds have been utilized only for provision of fixed line connections. Given the fact that the future is in mobile communications, it is prudent to involve mobile

service providers too. Some recent amendments made (in 2006) to the utilization of USO Fund have expanded the scope of the funds to include four more items. In specific terms, the following four additional items were included:

- Creation of infrastructure for provision of mobile services in rural and remote areas
- Provision of broadband connectivity to villages in a phased manner
- Creation of general infrastructure in rural and remote areas for development of telecommunication facilities
- Induction of new technological developments in the telecom sector in rural and remote areas

Only the first of the four is in the form of some implementation. However, it makes a lot of sense to extend the USO funds to provide mobile services in rural areas as increasingly much of the growth in mobile communications has emerged from 'B' and 'C' circles. In fact, the four metros have ceased to be the major force behind the growth of the mobile connections in the country. Encouraging the growth of mobile communications to the other circles and the rural areas within the circles can increase the tele-density in the country. But such increases in tele-density through mobile phones have some negative consequences, which are discussed later. There are also various other proposals for bridging the digital divide, and this is an immediate task before the policymakers.

Increasing Import Dependence for Telecom Equipments

The country had assiduously built up a domestic telecom equipment manufacturing industry in all the three segments of the industry, namely, in switching, transmission, and terminal equipments. After independence, manufacturing

Table 10.11 Functioning of the Universal Service Obligation Fund, 2002–3 through 2008–9 (Rs crore)

	Opening Balance	Funds Collected as USL	Funds Allocated and Disbursed	Balance at the End of Year	Disbursement Rate
2002–3	0.00	1,653.61	300	1,353.61	22.16
2003–4	1,353.61	2,143.22	200	3,296.83	6.07
2004–5	3,296.83	3,457.73	1,314.59	5,439.97	24.17
2005–6	5,439.97	3,533.29	1,766.85	7,206.41	24.52
2006–7	7,206.41	4,211.13	1,500.00	9,917.54	15.12
2007–8	9,917.54	5,405.46	1,290.00	14,033	9.19
2008–9	14,033.00	5,759.52	1,600.00	18,192.52	8.79
Cumulative			**7,971.44**	**59,439.88**	**13.41**

Source: DoT (2010).

Note: USL refers to Universal Service Levy.

of telecom equipments was reserved for the public sector. But in 1985, private sector entry was allowed in the manufacture of certain customer premises equipments like the electronic private automatic branch exchanges (EPBAX). In fact, the first PSE established in independent India, ITI, was devoted to the manufacture of telephone switching and terminal equipments. In 1985, the government established the stand-alone laboratory, Centre for Development of Telematics (C-DOT), to develop a family of digital switching technologies, which it licensed to both government and private sector enterprises. Mani (2005) had argued that the C-DOT is credited with the establishment of a modern telecom equipment industry in the country. The government's policy of public technology procurement through the DoT, the only telecom service provider until the late 1980s, also contributed to the emergence and sustenance of a domestic telecom equipment manufacturing industry. This fitted very well with the overall policy of import substitution that was being followed in the country. The deregulation of both the equipment and services industries, the liberalization of the economy, the virtual abandoning of the public technology procurement policy, and, above all, the growth of the mobile communications industry have virtually put a leash on the growth of a domestic manufacturing industry. This is because both the research and production components of the industry focused only on fixed telephone technologies, and with mobile communications becoming very important, the demand for such equipments had to be increasingly met through imports. Box 10.1 presents a summary view of the present scenario.

I have attempted to estimate the net self-sufficiency rate for India's telecom equipment industry during the period 1992–3 through 2004–5. Self-sufficiency rate (SSR) is defined as the ratio of domestic production to total availability, where total availability is the sum of domestic production and net imports. Two variants of the rate, SSR1 and SSR2, have been computed (Figure 10.3). SSR1 is based on net availability data from the World Telecom Indicators 2006 of the International Telecommunications Union; SSR2 is based on data on net availability of telecom equipments developed by us on the basis of data on exports and imports of telecom equipments from India contained in the online database, UN Commodity Trade Statistics (UN Comtrade, http://comtrade.un.org/db/). Although the levels of SSR1 and SSR2 are slightly at variance with each other, the direction of movement is roughly the same; though SSR1 shows a much steeper fall in the self-sufficiency rate. Suffice it to say that the industry, which was more or less sufficient, is now increasingly dependent on equipment imports. However, with the increases in domestic manufacture of telecom equipments, the SSR is bound to increase in the years to come.

The only disquieting feature is that, unlike in the case of China which too is experiencing phenomenal growth in telecommunications services, the domestic manufacturing sector in India is increasingly dominated by multinational corporations (MNCs) and not by local firms. The New Telecom Policy of 1999 had envisaged making the country a leading centre for the manufacture of telecom equipments. But as will be discussed later, this is being achieved by opening up the market to domestic investments by MNCs. Even for information technology (IT) solutions, such as for software requirements, the domestic mobile service providers are depending on foreign vendors. One of the most publicized examples of this is a US$ 700 million contract between

---

Box 10.1   Present Scenario of the Indian Telecommunications Equipment Industry

- Private sector service providers have no compulsion to use equipment manufactured by indigenous companies. Their procurement of equipment is dependent on choice of technology, funding mechanism with long-term low interest credits by foreign suppliers.
- C-DoT and other R&D institutions could not develop new technologies, resulting in the closure of units set up for the manufacture of their earlier products due to decline in demand.
- The government has allowed trading of telecom equipment to foreign companies under 'cash and carry wholesale trading'. Institutional sale is considered under wholesale.
- With the rapid growth of wireless access, GSM and CDMA, the entire demand is being met through import.
- Even companies like ITI have become 'traders', which are importing the equipment and supplying to BSNL/MTNL. In order to take advantages of lower customs duty, a separate procedure of 'high-sea sale' is being followed. Even reservation quotas of PSUs are being used for trading of goods manufactured abroad and without any commitment of transfer of technology.
- Manufacturing is now based on orders from BSNL/MTNL with no commitment to continued supply. These orders are mostly being met by import of finished equipment from abroad.
- Tie-ups with foreign suppliers are also tender-based. It is seen that, in a number of cases, a single foreign supplier will have tie-up with different companies and such suppliers (and their Indian agents) would become L-1, L-2, and even L-3 so that they get bulk of the order. This has also resulted in the closure of those companies that were doing genuine manufacturing through transfer of technology, as they failed to secure orders from BSNL/MTNL and other private operators.

Source: Compiled by the author.

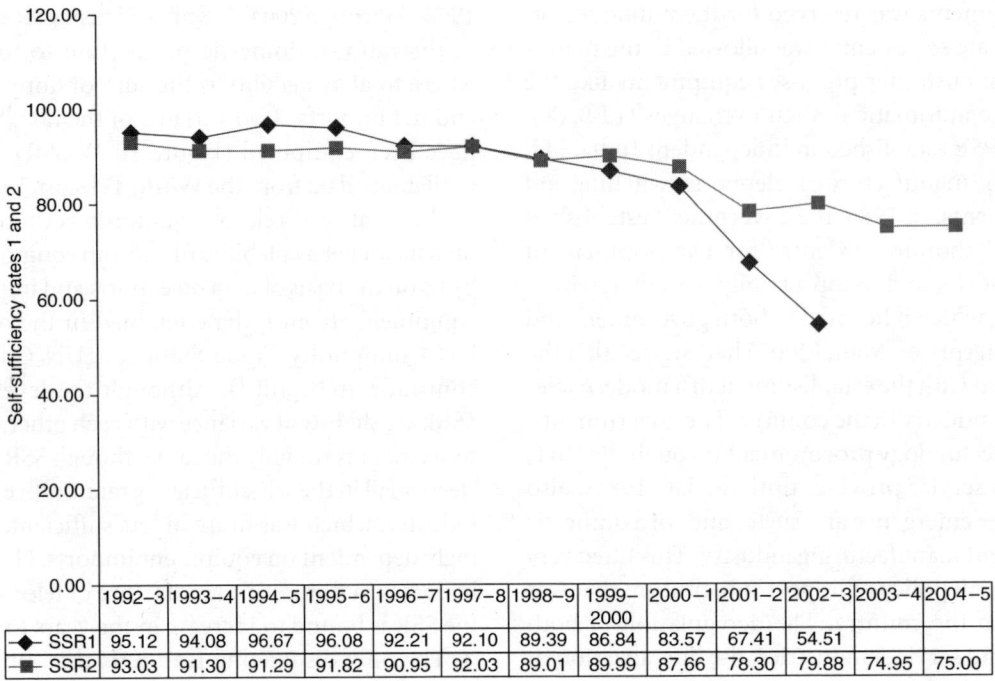

	1992–3	1993–4	1994–5	1995–6	1996–7	1997–8	1998–9	1999–2000	2000–1	2001–2	2002–3	2003–4	2004–5
SSR1	95.12	94.08	96.67	96.08	92.21	92.10	89.39	86.84	83.57	67.41	54.51		
SSR2	93.03	91.30	91.29	91.82	90.95	92.03	89.01	89.99	87.66	78.30	79.88	74.95	75.00

Sources: Computed from International Telecommunications Union (2006) and UN Comtrade.

Figure 10.3   Self-sufficiency Rates of Indian Telecoms Equipment Industry, 1992–3 to 2004–5

Idea Cellular and IBM for consolidating and managing IT infrastructure and applications of the mobile company. Although India is a leading exporter of computer software and indeed telecom software, its own service providers are depending on foreign sources. This is the paradox, if one can call it that way, that is being referred to.

Low Penetration of the Internet

Internet services in India were launched on 16 August 1995 by Videsh Sanchar Nigam Limited (VSNL). During the first three years of VSNL operation, the Internet subscriber base grew slowly. By the end of March 1998, it had barely reached 140,000 subscribers. In November 1998, the government recognized the need to encourage the spread of Internet in the country and opened the sector for provisioning of Internet services by private operators. The licence conditions for providing Internet services were liberal with no entry and licence fee until 31 October 2003; thereafter, a token licence fee of Re 1 per annum. Internet service providers (ISPs) could set their own tariffs and even their own international gateways. There were also restrictions on the number of service providers. To date, there are 389 ISP licensees, but out of this only 135 are operational. Public sector providers dominate with 56 per cent of the market (2006). Five ISPs account for 83 per cent of the market with the top ISP alone accounting

for 42 per cent. The top 20 ISPs cater to 98 per cent of the subscribers, while the remaining 115 ISPs cater only to the remaining 2 per cent of the subscribers. Approximately 60 per cent of the users still use dialup Internet access. Broadband access was introduced in October 2004, but its diffusion is still very low (Table 10.12; TRAI, various issues). It may be pointed out that there is no consensus on the number of Internet and broadband subscribers in the country. There are a plethora of estimates widely diverging from each other. For a detailed account of these various estimates, see Chandrasekhar (2006). Out of 128 ISPs permitted to provide Internet telephony, only 32 have started the service.

The Table 10.12 shows that the rate of growth of the industry has come down over time, and especially since 2002. The number of broad band subscribers among total Internet subscribers is on the increase although currently, as of June 2008, it was only about 37 per cent. According to a recent study on Internet in the country by the Internet and Mobile Association of India (2006), almost 76 per cent of the personal computer (PC) users have Internet connections. This means that the two technical reasons militating against higher Internet diffusion in the country are the lack of ownership of PCs and not having a fixed telephone for accessing the Internet. Although it is possible to access Internet over a mobile phone, the current generation of mobile technology that is common in the

Table 10.12 Diffusion of Internet in India, 1995–2009 (in million)

	No. of Internet Subscribers	No. of Broadband Subscribers	Wireless Internet
August 1995	0.01	n.a.	n.a.
March 1996	0.05	n.a.	n.a.
March 1997	0.09	n.a.	n.a.
March 1998	0.14	n.a.	n.a.
March 1999	0.28	n.a.	n.a.
March 2000	0.95	n.a.	n.a.
March 2001	3.04	n.a.	n.a.
March 2002	3.42	n.a.	n.a.
March 2003	3.64	n.a.	n.a.
March 2004	4.55	0.04	n.a.
March 2005	5.55	0.18	n.a.
March 2006	6.95	1.35	n.a.
March 2007	9.27	2.34	38.02
March 2008	11.10	3.87	65.5
March 2009	13.54	6.22	75.97

Source: TRAI (various issues), Press Releases; Internet and Mobile Association of India (2010).

country is 2G and 2.5G. Recent estimates by TRAI show that approximately 31 million subscribers access Internet through mobile phones. Of course, it is generally held that whenever the country moves over to 3G phones, accessing Internet over mobile phones will be easier. But given the much higher prices of 3G handsets, it is not likely that its diffusion will be high in the initial years. So low Internet diffusion is a direct consequence of the country being too reliant on mobile phones.

IMPLICATIONS FOR THE DOMESTIC MANUFACTURING OF TELECOM EQUIPMENTS

The silver lining is that India is becoming a major manufacturing hub, especially for mobile handsets. This has the potential of increased demand for semiconductor devices, like digital signal processors (DSP). This increased demand can precipitate the domestic manufacturing of semiconductor devices. However, all the players are expected to be MNCs as no local companies are available as of now. The government responded to this prospect by announcing a semiconductor policy on 22 March 2007.

India Emerging as a Manufacturing Hub

The New Telecom Policy of 1999 had envisaged that the country as a major manufacturing and export hub for telecom equipments. But for a long time this sounded more like an empty statement not backed by the reality in

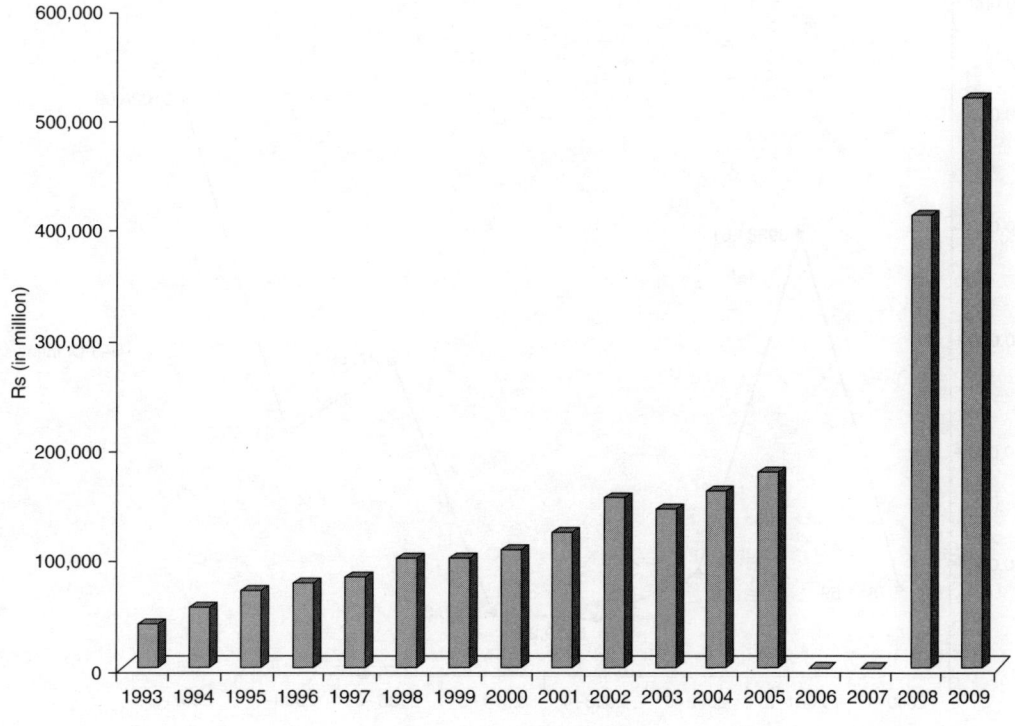

Source: DoT (various years).

Figure 10.4 Domestic Production of Telecom Equipments in India, 1992–3 to 2008–9

which, as noted earlier, the country is dependent heavily on imports. This was reflected in the rates of self-sufficiency, presented earlier, showing a declining trend. However, this situation is changing very rapidly in the last one year, specifically since 2006. The more proximate cause of this change is the large size of the market for mobile communication that is emerging in the country. With a monthly sale of over 5 million pieces since July 2006, India is now the second largest market for mobile handsets in the world. In fact all the major mobile handsets and other equipment manufacturers commenced local manufacturing operations since 2006 (various press releases of TRAI). Domestic output of telecom equipments, although fluctuating, has shown some significant increases over the last two years (Figure 10.4).

This is primarily due to the domestic manufacture of mobile handsets and associated equipments. Although the numbers of data points are few, one can see an almost perfect positive correlation between the growth of the services sector and the equipment sector (Table 10.13). My argument is that this correlation is bound to become more significant in the future, given the present trends.

However, the industry is going to be dominated by affiliates of MNCs. In fact, the telecom industry has been one of the major recipients of FDI in the country since 1991 (Figure 10.5). Although much of these investments (over 50 per cent) are in the services segment, increasingly (since 2001) the equipment sector has received about a quarter of

Table 10.13   Relationship between Growth of the Services and Equipment Segments of the Indian Telecom Industry, 2002–3 to 2005–6 (Rs million)

	Telecom Equipments	Telecom Services
2002–3	144,000	480,000
2003–4	140,000	610,000
2004–5	160,900	800,000
2005–6	178,330	1,000,000

Source: DoT (2010).

Note: The figures indicate the value of output of telecommunication equipments and value of stakes of telecom services.

the total investments. In short, the domestic manufacturing industry will be almost entirely dominated by foreign enterprises (Table 10.14).

Further, the import dependence of the industry will in all probability continue to be high for a few more years as the local manufacturing of mobile equipments is currently based on fully knock down (FKD) and semi knock down (SKD) kits. But as the domestic manufacturing of electronic components and semiconductor devices increases, the import dependence is sure to come down. In this way, the experience on this count will be similar to the Indian automotive industry.

This growth of the mobile equipment manufacturing sector has several spillover effects, besides generating direct

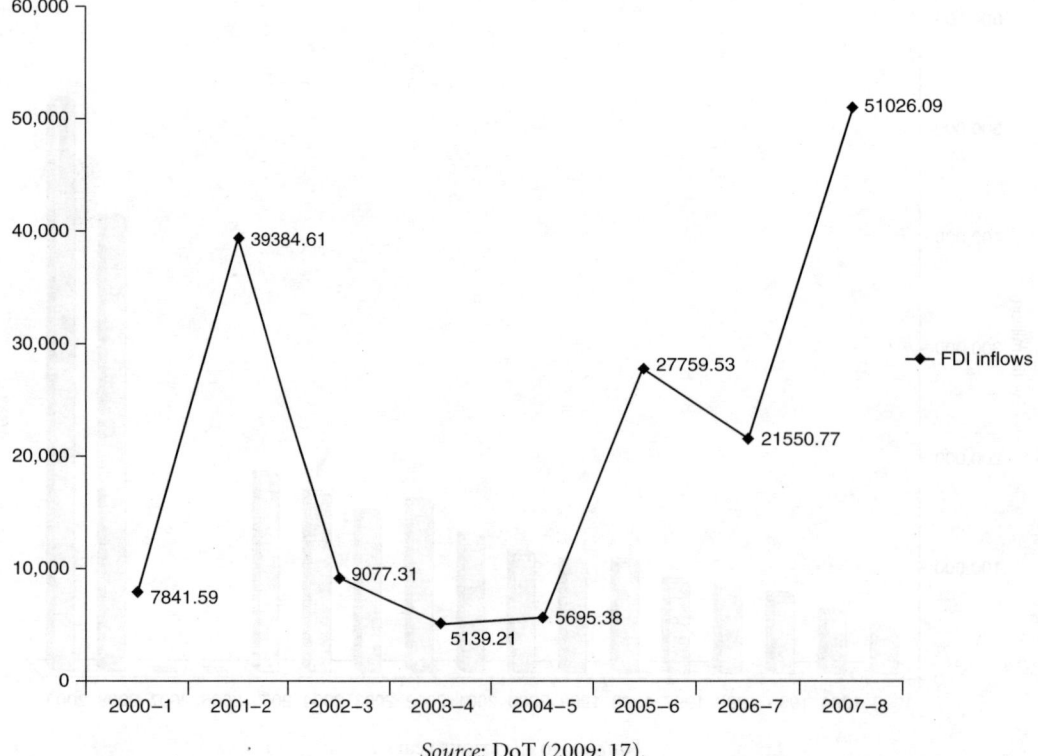

Source: DoT (2009: 17).

Figure 10.5   FDI Inflows to India's Telecommunications Industry, 2000–1 to 2007–8 (Rs million)

Table 10.14   India Emerging as a Manufacturing Hub for Mobile Telecom Equipment (2007)

Manufacturer	Type of Facility with the Location
1. Ericsson	• GSM radio base station facility, Jaipur • R&D centre, Chennai
2. Elcoteq	Contract manufacturer, Bengaluru
3. Nokia	Mobile handsets, Chennai
4. LG Electronics	Mobile handsets, Pune
5. Flextronics	Contract manufacturer, Chennai
6. Foxconn	Contract manufacturer, Chennai
7. Motorola	• Mobile handsets • R&D centres
8. Sony Ericsson	Mobile handsets through Flextronics and Foxconn
9. ITI	• GSM facility with Alcatel at Nainital and Manakapuri, UP • CDMA with ZTE, China, at Bengaluru

Source: TRAI (various issues), Press Releases.

employment. One of the more important of these is an increase in the demand for electronic components, especially semiconductor devices, which are used in the manufacture of these equipments. According to estimates by the newly formed (in 2004) Indian Semiconductor Association (2008), the total available market (after taking into account imports) is bound to increase from $0.91 billion, 2007 to over $16 billion by 2015. Mobile handsets and equipments will be one of the larger markets for these devices. Consequent to this thinking, a semiconductor manufacturing industry is emerging in the southern part of the country:

- SemIndia promoted by Vinod Agarwal, US$ 3 billion (12" Fab), at Hyderabad
- NANO-TECH Silicon India Pvt Ltd (NSTI) promoted by Dr Jun Min, US$ 0.6 billion (8" Fab), at Hyderabad
- Hindustan Semiconductor Manufacturing Co. (HSMC) promoted by Deven Mehta, US$ 4.5 billion (8" Fab), location to be confirmed
- India Electronics Manufacturing Corp (IEMC) promoted by Rajendra Agarwal, US$ 3 billion (12" Fab), location to be confirmed
- A number of chip companies from around the world have established research centres in India. Qualcomm Inc., the largest chip design house by revenue and a major US mobile chip company, has also opened a software and chip development lab in India. The company uses it as a base for R&D as well as a place from which to promote its CDMA, according to its website.
- The state-owned Semiconductor Complex at Chandigarh (which has been taken over by the

Department of Space) is drawing up a roadmap for its new baby. It expects to rejuvenate SCL and put India on the 0.35-micron map in the foreseeable future. Semi-Conductor Laboratory (SCL—formerly known as Semiconductor Complex Limited, established in 1983) is now a society (registered on 8 November 2005 under the Societies Registration Act, 1860, as amended by Punjab Amendment Act, 1957), with the main objective to undertake, aid, promote, guide, and coordinate R&D in the field of semiconductor technology, Micro Electro Mechanical Systems, and process technologies relating to semiconductor processing.

- The Indian Semiconductor Association has close to 100 members as on 1 April 2010.

If all the projects materialize, India will soon be safely in the 'bus' that it had missed several years ago as far as electronic hardware is concerned. The semiconductor industry has based itself on the chip design capabilities which India's IT industry already possesses.

The government responded to these private initiatives by announcing on 21 March 2007 a special financial incentive package to attract investments for setting up semiconductor fabrication and other micro and nanotechnology manufacturing industries in the country. The incentive is in the form of capital subsidies to the tune of 20 per cent of the total investment expenditure incurred by fab or ecosystems units during the first ten years, provided that these units are located within a special economic zone (SEZ), and 25 per cent if they are located outside an SEZ. The units are also exempted from countervailing duties. Further, the units will have to be established before 31 March 2010.

In response to this incentive package, the government is expecting US$ 10 billion worth of investment. It remains to be seen whether this will fructify or not. Such an incentive-induced investment strategy is sometimes criticized as the government is essentially taxing the citizens of a country and passing on the benefits to a few private sector individuals.

Thus, the growth of the telecom services industry is leading to the emergence of not just the telecom equipment industry but also the electronic components and semiconductor devices that are required for the manufacture of these equipments. The Indian telecom industry is therefore an excellent example where the growth of services is leading to the emergence of an attendant manufacturing industry as well.

CONCLUSIONS

Telecommunications services industry is one of the most successful cases of liberalization in India. Here, the liberalization has been opening up areas hitherto reserved for public sector entities to private sector participation. The market conduct of all players, both public and private, was regulated by a reasonably independent regulator. As a result, competition between service providers intensified, leading to significant reduction in prices. This has really improved the access to telephones, first in urban areas but increasingly in rural areas as well. The digital divide is a problem in all the non-metro circles, but it is acute in nearly twelve circles. An examination of these circles shows that these are indeed the lowest developed regions of the country. It must also be argued that the digital divide that is seen in these circles is also a reflection of their low economic growth itself, and therefore these other and more fundamental 'divides' will have to be addressed before some concerted action taken on the telecommunications front.

An interesting observation of the Indian telecommunications industry is that the main public sector provider of telecommunications services, BSNL, has considerably improved its performance after the industry was thrown open to competition from private service providers. Finally, growth of telecommunications services was initially dependent on imported equipment. But now there are signs that India is emerging as a manufacturing hub for telecom equipment exports. Thus, on a number of counts, the Indian telecom industry is a good example of the success of unleashing market forces in a hitherto closed industry, but with effective regulation by the state on the conduct of the market players. To a certain extent, this success was also contributed by the technological changes that were occurring in the industry, which reduced not just the cost of entry but also costs of operations after the firm started its actual operations.

REFERENCES

Chandrasekhar, C.P. (2006), 'India is Online but Most Indians are Not', *Macroscan*, 25 September. Available at http://www.macroscan.com/cur/sep06/cur260906India_Online.htm

Department of Telecommunications (DoT) (2005), *Annual Report 2004–05*. New Delhi: Department of Telecommunications, Government of India.

——— (2006), *Annual Report 2005–06*. New Delhi: Government of India.

——— (2007), *Annual Report 2006–07*. New Delhi: Government of India.

——— (2009), *Annual Report 2008–09*. New Delhi: Government of India.

——— (2010), *Annual Report 2009–10*. New Delhi: Department of Telecommunications, Government of India.

Desai, Ashok (2006), *India's Telecommunications Industry, History, Analysis, Diagnosis*. New Delhi: Sage Publications.

Indian Semiconductor Association (2008), *ISA–IDC Report on Indian Semiconductor and Embedded Design Service Industry (2007–2010)*. Bangalore: Indian Semiconductor Association.

Internet and Mobile Association of India (2006), *Internet in India 2006, Mapping the Indian Internet Space*. New Delhi: IMRB International and IAMAI.

——— (2010), *Report on Mobile VAS in India*. New Delhi: IMRB International and IAMAI.

International Telecommunications Union (2006), *World Telecom Indicators 2006 on CD-ROM*. Geneva: International Telecommunications Union.

Mani, Sunil (2002), 'Private Financing Initiatives in India's Telecom Sector', in Sanford V. Berg, M.G. Pollitt, and Masatsugu Tsuji (eds), *Private Initiatives in Infrastructure*, pp. 118–39. Cheltenham, UK and Northampton, USA: Edward Elgar.

——— (2005), 'Innovation Capability in India's Telecommunications Equipment Industry', in A. Saith and M. Vijayabaskar (eds), *ICTs and Indian Economic Development*, pp. 265–322. New Delhi: Sage Publications.

——— (2008), 'Growth of India's Telecom Services (1991–2007): Can It Lead to Emergence of a Manufacturing Hub?', *Economic and Political Weekly*, XLIII(3): 37–46.

Reserve Bank of India (2006), 'Invisibles in India's Balance of Payments', *Reserve Bank of India Bulletin*, November, pp. 1339–74.

Technology Information and Forecasting Assessment Council (TIFAC) (2007), *FDI in the R&D Sector, Study of Its Pattern 1998–2003*. New Delhi: TIFAC.

Telecom Regulatory Authority of India (TRAI) (2006), *Consultation Paper on the Review of Internet Services, Consultation Paper No: 19/2006*. New Delhi: TRAI.

——— (2009), *Annual Report*. New Delhi: TRAI.

——— (2010), *Press Release No: 53/2010*. New Delhi: TRAI.

——— (various issues), *Annual Report*. New Delhi: TRAI.

——— (various issues), Press Releases. New Delhi: TRAI.

11

Inflows and Policy

Middling Through

Ashima Goyal

INTRODUCTION

There has been a sharp escalation in capital flowing into India following the early 1990s reforms liberalizing entry and exit for private foreign investments[1] (FIs). Inflows were more than just a portfolio rebalancing following permission for entry; there was also a general fall in home bias in asset allocation. Entry barriers were lifted just as technology lowered transaction costs of investing abroad and made restrictions difficult. Lower interest rates in the developed world pushed fund managers to seek higher returns in emerging markets (EMs) even as reforms and higher growth reduced risk. Developed countries, particularly the US, had a comparative advantage in the provision of financial services, and therefore pushed for liberalization, even as it itself turned more towards self-regulation. As a consequence, leverage exploded, magnifying cross-border flows.

Facing inflows is an inevitable part of globalization. The latter has many potential benefits, which can fructify with the correct strategic response. Inflows do make more resources available, demonstrate better organization and technology, and offer a stimulus to local investment, an opportunity for better allocation of world savings, and for better price discovery in markets.

But inflows to EMs are subject to sudden stops or reversals due to infectious panics unrelated to fundamentals. Herd behaviour can cause, or at least magnify, cumulative worsening expectations. These are external shocks facing EMs. The East Asian and the global financial crises interrupted jumps in inflows. Inadequacies in the international financial architecture compound the problems, forcing EMs to adopt costly self-insurance measures. Reserve accumulation occurs also because of limited absorptive capacity. But this and oil surpluses imply a flow from the poor to rich as reserves are invested abroad.

India has a policy strategy in this context and it can be described as 'middling through'. There has been some deregulation to take advantage of the wave, yet protect against the volatility; to develop markets even while restricting foreign participation until they reach full maturity and can handle volatility. Deregulation distinguished between types and direction of flows. Liberalization was much greater for equity compared to debt flows, including bank loans, and for foreign compared to domestic residents. The rationale was equity, in contrast to debt, shares in risk. Therefore, liabilities are reduced in a crisis. For example, as markets fall during outflows, the value remitted is lower. Debt inflows are more difficult to service in difficult times while equity takes a write-down. Inflows have to be allowed to go out if they are to come in, but continuing restrictions on domestic capital outflows can reduce the reserve cover required. Limits on foreign loans prevent excessive borrowing in response to

[1] These include foreign direct investment (FDI), foreign portfolio investment (FPI), and other long- and short-term investment flows.

Table 11.1 Foreign Inflows in India

	FDI (US$ billion)	FPI (US$ billion)	FI Total (US$ billion)	NRI Deposits (US$ billion)	ECBs (US$ billion)	Change in Reserves (Increase) (US$ billion)	Current Account	Capital Account
							% of GDP (Deficit Minus)	
1990–1	0.1	0.01	0.1	2.1	2.3	1.3	−3.0	2.3
1991–2	0.1	0.004	0.1	5.8	1.5	−3.4	−0.3	1.5
1992–3	0.3	0.2	0.6	2.2	−0.4	−0.7	−1.7	1.6
1993–4	0.6	3.6	4.2	1.2	0.7	−8.7	−0.4	3.5
1994–5	1.3	3.8	5.1	1.0	1.1	−4.6	−1.0	2.8
1995–6	2.1	2.8	4.9	1.0	1.3	2.9	−1.6	1.3
1996–7	2.8	3.3	6.1	3.3	2.9	−5.8	−1.2	2.9
1997–8	3.6	1.8	5.4	1.2	4.0	−3.9	−1.4	2.5
1998–9	2.5	−0.1	2.4	1.0	4.4	−3.8	−1.0	2.0
1999–2000	2.2	3.0	5.2	1.5	0.3	−6.1	−1.0	2.5
2000–1	4.0	2.8	6.8	2.3	4.3	−5.8	−0.6	1.9
2001–2	6.1	2.0	8.2	2.7	−1.6	−11.8	0.7	1.8
2002–3	5.0	1.0	6.0	3.0	−1.7	−17.0	1.2	2.1
2003–4	4.3	11.4	15.7	3.6	−2.9	−31.4	2.3	2.9
2004–5	6.1	9.3	15.4	−1.0	5.2	−26.2	−0.4	4.1
2005–6	9.0	12.5	21.5	3.7	2.5	−15.1	−1.2	3.1
2006–7	22.8	7.0	29.8	4.3	16.1	−36.6	−1.1	4.9
2007–8	34.4	29.4	63.8	0.2	22.6	−92.2	−1.5	9.2
2008–9	35.2	−13.9	21.3	4.3	8.2	20.1	−2.4	0.6

Source: Calculated from http://www.rbi.org.in

domestic distortions, even while selective relaxation makes credit available for productive purposes.

We examine the effectiveness of the Indian strategy.[2] While middling through increases tools available with a policymaker, it can give too much discretion. Judgements made under considerable uncertainty can sometimes be lacking. A possible solution is to write more complex rules, closely tailored to the context, thus reducing discretion to the minimum necessary. Such a principled pragmatism implies that although a river is crossed while feeling the stones, knowledge of the riverbed allows one to anticipate some of the stones.

CAPITAL ACCOUNT CONVERTIBILITY: CONSEQUENCES

Table 11.1 shows the rise in different categories of inflows following liberalization. Permitted types of flows vary in their time horizon, volatility, and the arbitrage opportunities they respond to.

There was steady acceleration in both net FDI and FPI.[3] FDI requires stable growth prospects. Even in China, the big jump came about ten years after opening out. For India a big jump came in 2006–7 and higher levels continued despite the global crisis. Gross inflows were even higher, since Indian firms began investing abroad.

FPI shows more fluctuations, turning briefly negative during the East Asian crisis. It peaked at $29.4 billion in 2007–8 but 2008–9 saw outflows of $13.8 billion. Inflows during the period when stock markets were moving up were three times larger than outflows during equivalent movements down,[4] demonstrating the risk-sharing effect (Figure 11.1).

Figure 11.1 shows FPI to be more volatile than the Bombay Stock Exchange (BSE) index with possible mutual

---

[2] The analysis builds upon and expands earlier work. Sources used in this chapter are are available at www.igidr.ac.in/~ashima. Figures quoted, unless otherwise mentioned, are from the Reserve Bank of India (RBI) and Ministry of Finance websites.

[3] After falling to $3 billion in Q4 of the crisis year 2008, foreign investments (FIs) were back at $15 billion in Q1 of the next year. FPI swung from a negative −11.3 billion dollar over April–December 2008, to a positive $23.6 billion over the corresponding period in 2009, while FDI remained steadily positive.

[4] In the two years prior to October 2007, the Bombay Stock Exchange (BSE) stock index rose from 8,000 to 20,000, and FPI inflows were $47 billion. But over the next year, as stock markets fell back to 8,000, outflows were only $15 billion.

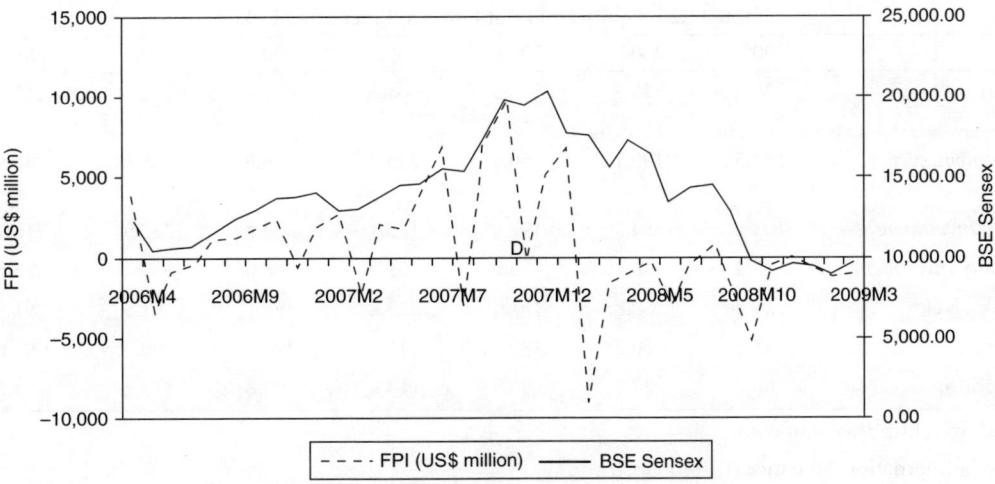

Source: Calculated with data from RBI and BSE.

Note: M refers to the month of the year.

Figure 11.1   FPI and BSE Sensex

causation between the two.[5] The rise in stock indices, or Tobin's q, helps firms raise money. Anticipation of firms' better performance induces more investment. Loans become easier to get and more venture capital enters. The policy studies literature does show that higher equity inflows have been associated with higher level of domestic investment (Henry 2007). India demonstrated this in the high growth period of 2003–8, as the ratio of gross investment to gross domestic product (GDP) rose from 25.2 to 39.1. Firms benefited but households did not. Retail participation shrank after reforms, which raised entry costs for the average investor. Markets remained narrow in many respects, and therefore excessively volatile. Free foreign entry was allowed in mutual funds, which were supposed to give savers more options and develop the financial services industry, taking local skills to international levels. But mutual funds focused on the high end and on firms. Thus, foreign entry is not a panacea. Other conditions also have to be in place. Eventual internationalization of Indian financial services is required as Indian companies go global. But the sequencing has to be correct.

Relaxation of external commercial borrowing (ECB) norms in 2006 aggravated net inflows, despite liberalization also of firms' investment outflows. Since domestic interest rates exceeded foreign interest rates and the exchange rate was expected to appreciate, firms borrowed abroad to finance ambitious investment plans.

Non-Resident Indian (NRI) flows did not show the same amplification. They respond to opportunities for interest rate arbitrage, but NRI deposit rates were capped in the later

years. So NRI inflows were quite low when other types of inflows were booming.

Table 11.1 also shows there was a current account deficit (CAD) during much of the period but it remained limited. Since the positive capital account far exceeded the negative current account, a large part of the capital flows were absorbed as reserves.[6]

The CAD is also the excess of domestic savings over investment. A small CAD implied the contribution of foreign savings to financing the resource gap remained small, although they may have contributed to relieving sectoral financing constraints and to developing markets. Empirical tests have largely found that only countries with strong domestic institutions, markets, and government finances benefit from foreign inflows. These features determine absorptive capacity that reduces volatility and also gives countries the ability to withstand volatility.

Since macroeconomic policy affects the investment–savings gap, the extent of reserve accumulation is a policy decision. The alternative is to allow appreciation, which would increase net imports and the CAD. If temporary capital inflows determine the real exchange rate, it would deviate from equilibrium. Large persistent current account surpluses do require appreciation but not persistent deficits, as in India. Since exports are part of a labour-absorbing development strategy and have to match rising imports, the exchange rate has to be competitive. Even so, there was greater exchange rate flexibility. Some appreciation and two-way movement occurred as the dollar depreciated after 2003.

---

[5] The respective coefficients of variation (the standard deviation divided by the mean) are 5.7 and 0.22. Time series studies confirm the causation.

[6] India's foreign currency reserves peaked at $315.66 billion in June 2008 and had fallen to $262 billion in end-March 2009, when they exceeded India's foreign debt by just $22 billion. Although outflows were only $20 billion, much of the fall was due to valuation effects.

Table 11.2 Equity and Debt Flows to Emerging Markets

Billions of US$	2003	2004	2005	2006	2007	2008	2009f	2010f
Private Flows, Net of which	229.0	330.9	528.3	561.8	887.8	392.3	140.5	373.2
Equity Investment, Net of which	138.5	195.1	250.4	223.8	296.9	185.6	240.9	250.0
Direct Equity Investment, Net	103.2	154.7	197.4	172.1	304.8	277.9	215.4	225.1
Portfolio Equity Investment, Net	35.4	40.4	53.0	51.7	−8.0	−92.3	25.5	24.9
Commercial Banks, Net	29.8	58.8	181.0	223.4	398.1	91.5	−91.9	57.5
Credit Flows, Net	33.4	60.2	180.2	222.0	395.5	90.3	−92.6	56.8
Other Private Creditors, Net	60.7	77.1	96.9	114.6	192.8	115.2	−8.5	65.6

Source: Calculated from http://www.iif.com/

Note: f = Institute of International Finance (IIF) forecast.

Moreover, reserves provide confidence to financial markets. Other ways of absorbing inflows were selective easing of outflows by domestic residents and trade liberalization. Supporting the domestic investment environment, for example, by reducing the gap between domestic and foreign interest rates, also absorbs inflows, but this depends also on deepening markets and reducing administrative interventions—a general rise in absorptive capacity. Given India's higher interest rates, the sterilization[7] of reserve accumulation, to maintain targeted rates of money supply growth, imposed large interest costs borne by the government (explicitly shown in the budget), RBI, and banks.

The sharp rise in inflows after 2003 was also due to external factors. Table 11.2 shows the surge in different types of capital flows into EMs. Post-crisis forecasts do not expect 2007-type of peaks, given deleveraging. To the extent the peak was an aberration due to regulatory weakness in developed countries, self-insurance and restrictions against the surge were the correct policy responses. While equity flows rose, the sharpest rise was in credit flows. India's restrictions on banks[8] and on debt flows protected it from this surge. East European countries that had allowed free entry of foreign banks suffered the most. Large foreign inflows were intermediated through these banks but when they were in trouble, home country rescue packages were not available to the branches.

The International Monetary Fund (IMF) data also shows that private foreign inflows to EMs fell in the period following the East Asian crisis, but more than doubled to an annual average of about $200 billion over 2003–6, peaking at $617.5 billion in 2007.[9] It has been argued that the US monetary policy that kept rates low was responsible for the flood into EMs, seeking higher returns. But US policy interest rates had been held at 1 per cent over June 2003 to June 2004, and were raised after that. So if low US interest rates were driving the flows, they should have been highest in 2003–4 and not in 2007, when the federal fund rate peaked at 5.25 per cent. Leverage enhanced flows in response to profit opportunities.

Nominal amounts outstanding in derivatives grew from $100 trillion in 2002 to $516 trillion in April 2007 (Bank of International Settlements [BIS] 2007). Since 2000, the market for mortgage-backed securities exceeded that for US treasury notes and bonds. Asset-backed securities peaked at $4.1 trillion in 2006 and credit default swaps at $57 trillion in June 2008. Open positions as part of the carry trade facilitated cross-border flows. Although the cost of replacing contracts and the credit exposure are much lower, notional amounts capture the open interest. In 2004, the US securities regulator (Securities and Exchange Commission [SEC]) relaxed the net capital rule or ceiling of twelve times capital on borrowing for investment banks, allowing them to use their own models to determine risk. As a result, leverage shot up; when Lehman Brothers was allowed to fail, its leverage was 30:1 compared to 15:1 for a commercial bank. The 33 per cent compound annual rate of growth in derivatives occurred just over the period the regulations were relaxed.

---

[7] As foreign assets replaced domestic securities in the RBI's balance sheet, its stock of government securities was nearing depletion. A Market Stabilization Scheme (MSS), consisting of 91-day to 1-year government bonds, was introduced in March 2004. The government issued new bonds whose proceeds were sequestered in a special account with the RBI, thus neutralizing the liquidity impact of RBI's foreign exchange (FX) purchase. During capital outflows in 2008 it was possible to buy back MSS securities, which contributed to financing expanded government borrowing requirements because of the fiscal stimulus.

[8] Compulsory reserve requirements (CRR), statutory liquidity requirements (SLR), limits on open positions, securitization, etc., constrain the ability of Indian banks to intermediate foreign borrowing.

[9] The figures are calculated from data available at http://www.imf.org/external/pubs/ft/weo/2009/01/pdf/tables.pdf

Compared to this growth in derivatives, other sources of liquidity were trivial: US broad money supply growth, for example, averaged about $15 trillion with an annual growth rate of about 6 per cent.[10] Modern financial markets have large powers to endogenously create liquidity, and a strong motive to do so in good times. Poor incentive features and the lack of universal regulation increased this procyclicality.

CAPITAL ACCOUNT CONVERTIBILITY: POLITICS

A political economy, overturned by events, underlay the gradual process of capital account convertibility (CAC). Financial interests, and the IMF dominated by these interests, strongly pushed for full capital account liberalization in the 1990s. Since financial reforms were easy to do compared to difficult domestic institutional reform, and there were attractive potential kickbacks, policymakers were also inclined to liberalize. But the East Asian crisis threw a spanner in the works as the costs of CAC ahead of domestic financial reform became clear.

In India, lobbying varied from those who wanted full CAC and a flexible exchange rate, to those who would restrict all types of inflows and control market activity. Apart from extreme pro- and anti-market positions, there were also serious analytical issues. Those who wanted more controls were concerned about crises from volatile flows, fiscal vulnerability, Dutch disease, and appreciation hurting an export-led growth strategy, or inflow-driven asset bubbles in narrow domestic markets (Nachane 2007; Sen, 2007). Those for faster CAC wanted more market-led innovation, an end to financial repression and distortions, and the chance to develop India as a centre for financial services, given its skilled manpower (Rajan 2009).[11]

The first Tarapore Committee (1997) set out macro preconditions for CAC, including improved government finances and current account, and the second (Tarapore 2006) set out the micro-institutional development required in financial markets. But the East Asian crisis overturned the first and the global financial crisis overturned the second committee's recommendations for faster liberalization. Thus, CAC proceeded slowly, as did the task of strengthening domestic markets and policy institutions.[12] There was real progress in the latter, notwithstanding complaints about regulatory speed breakers.

Extreme pro-market positions could not survive the repeated crises, absence of serious reform in the international financial architecture, and excessive leverage due to foreign regulatory lapses. But anti-market forces could not survive the reaction to stifling past controls, the need for financing growth, and pressures to keep up with developments elsewhere. For example, FX futures were allowed in Indian stock exchanges after they were started at the Dubai exchange. Box 11.1 illustrates the development of the Indian FX market.

Box 11.1   Indian FX Markets

Tables 11.3 and 11.4 show both the very low level of Indian FX markets and the extreme rapidity of their development. The average daily turnover in Indian FX markets, which was about US$ 3 billion in 2001, grew to US$ 34 billion in 2007, one of the fastest rates of growth among world markets (Table 11.3).

Deepening shows in the expansion of the turnover relative to trade transactions (Table 11.3), sharp increase in derivative trade, cross-border transactions, and decrease in the share of the RBI[13] transactions (Table 11.4); advent of electronic trading and communication platforms, which reduce transaction costs and risks; falling bid-ask spreads; changing profile of customers from passive price-takers in foreign trade–related services, to foreign investment institutions (FIIs) and to corporates taking ECB loans, or undertaking mergers and acquisitions. Corporates sometimes had treasuries as large and sophisticated as those of banks.

Gradual reforms followed comprehensive blueprints set by various government committees starting in 1995. Earlier policy sought to limit hedging tools to entities with direct underlying FX exposures. However, since a larger set of economic agents now had FX risk, there was a shift to 'economic exposure' (the effect of exchange rates on a firm's value) to allow flexibility in managing FX risk.

Even so, Indian derivative trading remains a small fraction of that in other EMs such as Mexico or South Korea. In futures markets intra-day trades dominate, and often interest that denotes hedging activity is low. Liquidity and robustness of volatility are far from that in the US market. Short-term instruments with maturities of less than one year dominate, and activity is concentrated among a few banks. As elsewhere, FX transactions are mostly over-the-counter structured by banks. The most widely used derivative instruments are the forwards and FX swaps (rupee–dollar). But because of user demand for liquid and transparent exchange traded hedging products, currency futures were started in 2008 and later extended to multiple currencies. Multilateral netting on market platforms saves transaction cost. Guarantees from the trade date reduce FX settlement and counterparty risk.

---

[10] The figures are calculated with data available at http://www.federalreserve.gov/econresdata/default.htm

[11] The macroeconomic section in the report expressed the naïve view that giving capital more freedom in good times would induce it to be more loyal in bad times. But capital is driven by expected returns. Strength attracts it and weakness, or even a hint of weakness, leads to exit.

[12] There were considerable developments in the money, equity, and FX markets, and in strengthening regulatory frameworks.

[13] The low intervention figure for 2006–7 is actually special to that year since there were only purchases and no sales. Purchases more than doubled the next year as inflows rose. Equivalent purchases only in 2001–2 were $23 billion. The share of intervention was 10.4 in 2003–4, but has fallen in recent years.

Table 11.3 FX Turnover Compared to Other Sources of Currency Transactions

US$ Billion	Daily FX Turnover (April)				Merchandise Trade, Daily Average		FX Inflow, Daily Average	
	2001	Per cent of World Total	2007	Per cent of World Total	2000	2007	2000	2007
Australia	52	3.22	170	4.26	0.46	1.05	0.04	0.06
India	3	0.18	34	0.85	0.38	1.17	0.03	0.18

Sources: Calculated from the Bank for International Settlements (BIS 2007, Table E16: 82), available at http://www.bis.org/publ/rpfxf07a.pdf; International Financial Statistics (IMF, various years).

Notes: (i) Foreign inflows are measured as the current account deficit plus reserve gains. (ii) Merchandise trade is calculated as exports plus imports of goods and services (absolute values). (iii) FX turnover is on net-gross basis and includes spot, outright forwards, and swap transactions.

Table 11.4 Aspects of the Indian FX Market

	US$ Billion FCY/INR[a]	2001–2	2006–7
1	Total spot turnover (sales + purchases)	450.16	2085.39
2	Total spot RBI intervention (sales + purchases)	385.81	316.88
3	2 as % of 1	8.57	1.52
4	Share of 1 due to interbank (%)	64.75	67.08
5	Share of 1 due to merchant (%)	35.25	32.91
6	Total forward as % of total spot	20.82	22.94
7	Total swap as % of total spot[b]	149.63	61.01
8	Total spot (for April)[c]	30.38	252.53
9	Share due to RDs (from CB survey) (%)	68.15	78.02
10	Share due to other financial institutions (%)	5.76	10.49
11	Share of non-financial institutions (%)	26.09	11.49
12	Share in total spot of local transactions (%)	95.98	89.86
13	Share in total spot of cross-border transactions (%)	4.02	10.15
14	Total FX derivatives as % of total spot	0.06	226.77

Notes: Items (1) to (7) were calculated from RBI bulletins. The data was collected for all the months in the given years and summed up. Each year is taken from July to June. Items (8) to (14) are figures for the month of April as is available in the Central Bank (CB) Surveys (BIS). Items (9) to (14) are as percentage to (8).

FCY: Foreign currency; INR: Indian rupees; RDs: Reporting dealers.

[a] All transactions involve exposure to more than one currency.

[b] Excluding 'tomorrow/next day' transactions.

[c] A swap is considered to be a single transaction in that the two legs are not counted separately. Including 'tomorrow/next day' transactions.

LIBERALIZATION: SURVIVING CRISES

Did opening out during a period when major global crises occurred benefit India? The presumption in liberalizing reforms was that the country could handle volatility, but the sheer size of global crises was not foreseen. There were benefits, since the trend rate of growth was higher, and there was development of new growth foci so that growth was no longer government-driven. India did not have a financial crisis but growth became volatile. The slowdowns over 1997–2002 and in 2008–9 can be attributed partly to international crises and partly to policy mistakes in handling.

Middling through gives a lot of discretion to policymakers and this can be used with varying degrees of effectiveness. Monetary policy has a challenging task to support inclusive growth, withstand volatile flows of unprecedented magnitude, and prevent asset bubbles in narrow markets, even while deepening and crises-proofing those markets. It succeeded spectacularly in most objectives, but a policy more attuned to context could have reduced volatility and further improved economic performance.

Sharp interest rate rise in response to exchange rate volatility during the East Asian crisis helped trigger the growth slowdown; episodes of tightening in response to repeated supply shocks helped sustain the slowdown. Instead, policy could have focused on the supply side, tackling the problem at its root. Moreover, domestic interest rates that were much higher than international rates created arbitrage gaps for carry trade-driven inflows through gaps in controls.

Reserves, together with the preference for equity over debt liabilities, reduced vulnerability to crises as currency and maturity mismatches were contained. Large reserves held in foreign securities meant gain from currency depreciation, thus lowering its impact. Self-insurance implied costs but the alternative advocated to allow the rupee to float and liberalize debt inflows (Rajan 2009) would have hurt the country badly during the global crisis and deleveraging cycle that followed. EMs that followed such advice were the worst hit. As Calvo (2005) has documented, sudden stops independent of the fundamentals of the country impose large costs on many EMs.

Caballero and Krishnamurthy (2004) show that in shallow markets, domestic firms underinsure reversals. Because of domestic financial market imperfections, they cannot sell insurance to those who need it. Bond issuance (deepening) would allow firms needing external resources to share their revenues with those with access to foreign funds, thus creating more hedging. This is an example of how markets create value by satisfying differentiated needs. Although deeper financial markets and better global governance can provide more efficient forms of insurance, policies such as capital inflow taxation, liquidity requirements, exchange rate, and reserve management are justified in their absence.

Innovative contextual policies are also required. For example, along with the provision of more instruments for hedging, random two-way exchange rate movements, large enough to deliver a substantial loss to one-way bets, are essential to induce hedging or the laying off of currency exposure. In East Asia, relatively fixed exchange rates, with domestic interest rates exceeding international, encouraged unhedged short-term foreign borrowing, which made the system extremely sensitive to interest rate changes.

Moderate two-way movement within an implicit 5 per cent band over 2004–6 was not sufficient to overcome strong expectations of medium-term appreciation, given India's high growth rate. In 2007, market expectations of the rupee–dollar rate had even reached 32. Many corporates borrowed abroad based on such expectations, increasing currency risk. Some had entered into so-called hedging deals, which were actually bets on the value of the Swiss Franc. With the steep rupee depreciation in 2008, many firms lost money. Such deals, where Indian banks were often a front for foreign banks, sometimes sidestepped existing rules that prevented leverage or underlying risk from exceeding export income. Although firms were not allowed to write options, deals

were structured so that firms were in effect doing so. The deals were so complex that some firms did not understand the risks they were taking. The RBI intervened largely to decrease volatility, but creating some volatility would have improved incentives to hedge.

Another post–Asian crisis lesson is the danger of short-term debt. As creditors refused to rollover such debt, the shock to highly leveraged firms and their banks created bankruptcies and intensified the crisis.

India was careful to keep short-term debt low. But with overconfidence from high growth, similar higher domestic interest rates, an appreciating rupee, and more freedom, firms raised their foreign borrowing.[14] Therefore, the liquidity squeeze from outflows, drying up of external credit, and the jump in spreads for EMs,[15] after the fall of Lehman, together with the depreciating rupee, was a severe shock to firms' balance sheets. The Reserve Bank's rapid liquidity provision and the healthy state of Indian banks allowed firms to substitute domestic credit for foreign. Although the fear factor led to a fall in consumer credit demand, credit to firms was maintained. There was only a marginal fall in aggregate credit growth,[16] unlike in the West.

Indian banks were healthy because the RBI had also followed prescient countercyclical macro prudential policies. For example, it increased banks' prudential cover for real estate loans, thus moderating a property boom. However, the finance ministry's relaxation of ECB norms during peak inflows acted in the opposite direction to further fuel the spike in inflows.

But firms need external finance. Although aggregate savings are high, about half of household savings are in a not-readily-available physical form. Indian debt markets have not shown the dynamism of FX, equity, and money markets. Instruments to hedge interest rate risk are missing. Long-term funds for infrastructure are scarce. Financial exclusion is especially high for smaller firms that cannot

[14] External debt had increased to 22 per cent of GDP in 2009, with the share of short-term debt (largely trade credits) at 21.5 per cent (compared to 7 per cent in the late 1990s) and external commerical borrowing (ECBs) at 27.3 per cent. Non-government share of debt rose to 74.6 per cent.

[15] The spread on the Morgan Stanley emerging market bond index (EMBI+) jumped up to 850 in October 2008, from 300 in August. It did not sustain that peak, but began steadily decreasing from March 2009, and in July had reached 400. The index for Asia was the lowest at 330, reflecting the better prospects for this region.

[16] RBI's survey showed credit growth to be 20.5 (March 2009) compared to 23.4 (March 2008) in the top 100 banking centres. The figures for deposit growth were 21 and 25.7. While credit to industry was maintained, personal loan categories showed some fall. In July 2009, annual credit growth of Scheduled Commercial Banks (SCBs) was 16.3 compared to 25 a year ago.

access equity markets and international markets. The first priority must be to bring more households and firms into the financial system. More even access to bank accounts, use of new technology and institutional structures, and data collection including the availability of credit histories, can improve inclusion and intermediation of domestic savings. Until these domestic distortions, including large interest gaps and one-way predictable exchange rate movements, are removed, liberalizing debt inflows has to be done with caution. Unhedged excessive private borrowing abroad, driven by domestic distortions, is dangerous.

LIBERALIZATION: POLICY

Although improvements are possible, and one can debate timing, mix, degree, and direction, some flexibility of exchange rates, reserve accumulation in response to volatile inflows, graded restrictions on the capital account, market development with countercyclical prudential regulations have helped India side-step crises and achieve respectable growth despite financial turbulence. On the whole, regulators exhibited a healthy contrarian attitude, and democratic pulls and pressures resulted in a middling through process. This has a better chance of success in EMs needing development over several fronts to achieve robust diversified growth.

Diversified sources do sustain Indian growth, including domestic demand, agriculture, openness, technology, the demographic profile, the infrastructure cycle, high savings, and having crossed a critical threshold. As a net commodity importer, India gains from lower global prices. Dependence on external demand is low compared to other Asian countries. While foreign capital does not contribute much to aggregate resources, it is useful in financial intermediation. But post-crisis, a sufficient quantity of inflows has revived.

Post-Lehman growth did not collapse as expected by those who believed India's performance to be entirely dependent on foreign largesse. Given our export share of 15 per cent, the trade shock reduced GDP 1 per cent below potential in 2008–9. The health of the financial sector also helped a V-shaped recovery unlike in the West, where financial sector weaknesses and low demand imply persistent weakness.

Monetary and fiscal policy responded rapidly and in a coordinated fashion to the crisis. The global push for individual country governments to provide a demand stimulus allowed us to do what we needed. The post-reform Indian macro policy combination was fiscal loosening and monetary tightening. This has adverse consequences when the structure of the economy is as depicted in Figure 11.2. Frequent supply shocks and

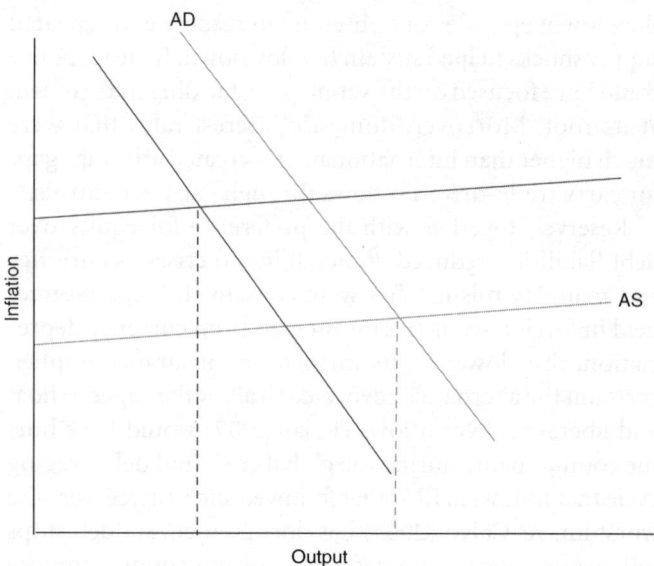

Figure 11.2   Aggregate Demand (AD) and Aggregate Supply (AS)

chronic fiscal waste push up an elastic supply curve as costs rise. It is elastic since output is generally below potential as a large labour force shifts, during a catch-up high growth phase, to more productive occupations. Inflation expectations, fiscal populism, and distortions are other factors pushing up the supply curve. Monetary tightening, in such circumstances, has a high output cost with little effect on inflation as it pushes the demand curve leftwards. Better fiscal rules will make more relaxed monetary policy feasible.

Fiscal Policy

High Indian growth despite high deficits is regarded as a puzzle. But Indian private savings are high enough to cover for some government dissaving, thus preventing a large CAD and potential currency crises. Moreover, high transitional growth in a populous country reduces deficit and debt ratios. To the extent government expenditure helps maintain high growth, it is sustainable.

But there is a tendency for unproductive populist expenditure and waste in a low per capita income democracy. India has seen successful tax reform and elasticity in revenues but reform in expenditure management has been lacking. The Fiscal Responsibility and Budget Management (FRBM) Act adopted in 2003 has been kept in letter rather than spirit. Where necessary, capital expenditure has been cut, and off balance sheet items used to achieve targets. Better incentive features are possible. For example, expenditure caps can improve incentives to comply, while protecting productive expenditure. The composition of public expenditure would then change towards human, social, and physical capital. The Thirteenth Finance Commission has enabled some countercyclical fiscal policy by setting paths for debt reduction. The post-crisis experience has demonstrated the efficacy of a fiscal stimulus when output falls below potential.

Monetary Policy

Operational monetary policy needs to respond to outcomes rather than be tied to nominal money supply targets based on uncertain estimates of rapidly changing potential output. It should gradually move to becoming more forward-looking, responding to forecasts of inflation, so as to more successfully anchor inflation expectations at lower output cost. The aim should be more to reduce costs or shift the supply curve downwards in anticipation of cost shocks. Low interest rates help to facilitate the supply response. Short-term nominal exchange rate flexibility can also contribute. Of all the monetary transmission channels, the lag from the exchange rate to consumer price index (CPI) is the shortest. The higher the weight of imported goods in CPI, the more effective is this channel. This weight rises as border prices begin to affect food prices. Food is still a major component of the average Indian consumption basket. If dependence on oil imports is also high, an inverse movement of the exchange rate in response to commodity price shocks can moderate inflation.

Such a response of the nominal exchange rate to temporary supply shocks also contributes to crises-proofing. The ensuing two-way movement removes an implicit government guarantee and encourages hedging to reduce risk. But it is also necessary to limit excessive volatility, even as homeopathic doses of volatility strengthen thin markets. There is room to surprise markets at times and work with them to achieve targets at others.

A more appreciated nominal rate can help sustain a positive interest rate differential to the extent it leads to expected future depreciation, although with a large interest differential some restrictions on the capital account will be required.

But the real exchange rate must not depart for long from competitive equilibrium levels. Productivity improvements allow a more appreciated non-inflationary equilibrium real exchange rate. The latter is inversely related to real wages—rising average wages require a more appreciated real exchange rate. But a rise in the average wage level cannot occur until surplus labour is absorbed in the modern sector, thus limiting real appreciation. Balassa–Samuelson-type appreciation of the real exchange rate, driven by equality of wages across sectors with varying productivity, comes at a later stage, when the labour transition is complete. If the average real wage is low, nominal appreciation will not lead

to real appreciation since prices will not rise. If conversely, the real exchange rate compatible with the minimum wage is more appreciated than that warranted by labour productivity, a spiral of wage price inflation results. A better alternative to divorcing food prices from border prices through a tariff-food subsidy-procurement barrier is direct income transfers to those below the poverty line. In the longer term, steps must be taken to raise agricultural productivity.

Since domestic interest rates generally exceed international, liberalization gives policy the opportunity to reduce domestic rates, thus closing the arbitrage gap[17] to the extent compatible with the domestic cycle, the inflation differential, any risk premium, and a reasonable return to savings. High spreads also have to be reduced. A lower interest rate stimulates the supply response, maintaining the higher growth feasible in transition economies. It also reduces the cost of government debt. High savings and long-term capital inflows invalidate the argument that developing countries' interest rates have to be higher to reflect the scarcity of capital.

Low interest rates are said to create asset price bubbles in thin markets. But the answer is to use countercyclical prudential regulation and deepen markets, not give up the chance to stimulate capital accumulation.

Monetary policy loses autonomy under a fixed exchange rate and a fully open capital account—to the extent the capital account is not fully open and the exchange rate has some flexibility, monetary policy is effective. This effectiveness is further enhanced by the use of tools such as FX markets intervention, and as markets deepen, signalling to affect the exchange rate, freeing the interest rate for the domestic cycle.

As long as poor global governance and regulation create excess volatility of foreign inflows, EMs must implement different kinds of self and group insurance. The priority must be on strengthening domestic institutions, with capital convertibility to follow only after stringent preconditions are met. One of these is reform of the international financial architecture. Calls for reform after every crisis die down with the crisis. If the greater representation of EMs in the G-20 fructifies in real improvements, risks of openness will be lowered. However, the absence of major change almost two years after Lehman does not bode well.

---

[17] Despite restrictions on debt flows and limits on open positions, international banks found ways to participate in the carry trade, where they borrowed in low-interest currencies such as the yen and lent in high-interest countries. This was one reason for weakness of the low interest rate dollar and yen, prior to the crisis. After the crisis, the carry trade unwound because though the arbitrage gaps continued, credit had frozen. In addition, invisible flows in the current account are correlated to interest differentials. Export payments can be sent earlier and import credit invested locally. NRI loans to relatives can be disguised as transfers—all the more since the purpose does not have to be specified for remittances of less than Rs 5 lakh.

REFERENCES

Bank of International Settlements (BIS) (2007), 'Foreign Exchange and Derivatives Market Activity in 2007', *Triennial Central Bank Survey*, December. Available at http://www.bis.org/publ/rpfxf07t.htm (accessed on 10 November 2008).

Caballero, Ricardo and Arvind Krishnamurthy (2004), 'Smoothing Sudden Stops', *Journal of Economic Theory*, 119(1): 104–27.

Calvo, G. (2005), 'Crises in Emerging Market Economies: A Global Perspective'. Available at http://www.nber.org/papers/w11305.pdf

Henry, Peter Blair (2007), 'Capital Account Liberalisation: Theory, Evidence and Speculation', *Journal of Economic Literature*, 45(4): 887–935.

Nachane, D.M. (2007), 'Liberalization of the Capital Account: Perils and Possible Safeguards', *Economic and Political Weekly*, 8 September, 42(36): 3633–43.

Rajan, R. (2009), *A Hundred Small Steps*, Report of the Committee on Financial Sector Reforms, Planning Commission, Government of India. Delhi: Sage Publications.

Sen, P. (2007), 'Capital Inflows, Financial Repression, and Macroeconomic Policy in India since the Reforms', *Oxford Review of Economic Policy*, 23(2): 292–310.

Tarapore, S.S. (1997), *Report of the Committee on Capital Account Convertibility*. Mumbai: Reserve Bank of India.

——— (2006), *Report of the Committee on Fuller Capital Account Convertibility*. Mumbai: Reserve Bank of India.

12

Outreach of Banking Services across Indian States, 1981–2007

Converging or Diverging?

Rupayan Pal and Rajendra R. Vaidya*

INTRODUCTION

Financial sector reforms in India were undertaken as a corollary to the trade and industrial policy reforms initiated in 1991. Banks, as a group being the most important financial intermediary in the economy, have received special attention in the reform process. There was a realization in both academic and policy circles that the policy of social control of banks had led to a decline in the productivity, profitability, and efficiency of the banking sector. The main objective initially had been to nurse the banks back to health, provide them more operational flexibility, introduce a more competitive environment in the banking sector, and develop a regulatory and supervisory regime wherein depositors' interests are adequately looked after. Whatever the faults of the pre-reform regime, there is little doubt that in this regime a bank network, which improved financial access to India's poor, most of whom resided in the poorer states, was successfully developed. Sen and Vaidya (1997) have demonstrated that there was a distinct tendency towards

equalization in the population per bank branch across states between 1969 and 1994, indicating a rapid shrinkage in inter-state disparities with regard to demographic penetration of banking services. This period saw a substantial increase in the amount of deposits mobilized, essentially due to the positive real rate of return that was available on bank term deposits between 1974 and 1988 due to the fact that these rates were directly administered by the government. In addition, the government put in place a directed credit programme which stipulated that scheduled commercial banks should lend 40 per cent of their net bank credit to the priority sector (agriculture, small-scale industries, and exports).

Moreover, it was required that 25 per cent of the priority sector loans should be made to weaker sections of society. This, without doubt, had led to a higher cost of intermediation (Narasimham Committee 1998). Nevertheless, the importance of these achievements needs to be recognized. The fact that India compared very favourably with other developing countries in the distribution of financial services has been well documented (Basu and Srivastava 2005). This is important for various reasons. It is argued that financial outreach has an impact on poverty reduction (Beck et al. 2004; Honohan 2004). Providing access to finance to the less well-off sections of the population can be seen as a method

*We wish to thank Manoj Panda and Tirthankar Roy for discussions. We are solely responsible for remaining errors.

of making people better off by providing an opportunity for the Schumpeterian process of creative destruction to play a role in generating new sources of income. Lastly, access to financial services can be thought of as a basic need, similar to a clean environment or safe drinking water.

There is a considerable body of evidence (see, for example, Ahluwalia [2000] and Nair [2004]) that suggests that the economic performance of states has diverged considerably after the initiation of reforms. It could thus be expected that banks would mirror this diversion in their deposits, credit, and branch network. This, quite naturally, has given rise to the apprehension that in the post-liberalization period the outreach of banking services could possibly have diverged across states. This chapter attempts to empirically investigate whether this has actually happened over the period 1981 to 2007.

The main difficulty faced here is due to the fact that various aspects of banking operations across states may not necessarily move together over time. For example, the density of branches and per capita deposits and credit may evolve over time quite differently within a state. How then are we to judge how the access to banking services is moving across states and over time? To this end, we propose an index of outreach of banking services and we empirically investigate how this index has evolved over time across states. There are several advantages of an index of outreach of banking services. First, it encapsulates measures of demographic penetration, geographic penetration, and variables signifying the use of banking services in a single number. Second, it is amenable to inter-state comparability as well as to understand the evolution of this index over time. Third, an index of this sort is also relevant from the policy point of view.

We find that there is wide variation in terms of the measures of use of banking services as well as in terms of access to banking services across states and over time. The same is true also in terms of the index of outreach of banking services. The econometric analysis shows unconditional β-convergence of outreach of banking services during the pre-reform period—1981–90. For the post-reform period 1996–2007, we find strong evidence for divergence of states in terms of outreach of banking services.

This chapter makes three important contributions. First, it adds to the evolving literature on financial inclusion. Second, to our knowledge, the chapter is the first to construct an index of outreach of banking services for sub-national economies. Third, it offers an assessment of overall achievement in terms of outreach of banking services across states, its evolution over time, and impact of banking sector reform on it.

The rest of the chapter is organized as follows. The next section provides a brief outline of banking sector reforms in India. The third section describes the data sources and discusses various attributes of outreach of banking services. It also outlines the method of construction of an index of outreach of banking services and illustrates the index. The fourth section presents the methodology followed and the results of the convergence analysis. The final section concludes.

BANKING SECTOR REFORMS IN INDIA: BRIEF OVERVIEW

It is well documented that bank nationalization had a substantial impact on the geographical spread, amount of deposits mobilized, and advances/loans extended. After nationalization, the Reserve Bank of India (RBI) enforced a branch licensing policy, formally in 1977, which restricted banks from opening branches in metropolitan and urban areas. This policy was formulated towards promoting greater access to financial services in a balanced manner across geographical regions in the country. The 1:4 licence rule, which required banks to open four branches in un-banked location(s) in order to open a branch in a location with one or more branches, was a critical ingredient of this strategy. On the deposit mobilization front, the administered interest rates ensured that there was always a good rate of return available on bank fixed deposits so as induce people to hold these deposits. On the credit side, the lead bank scheme initiated in December 1969 went a long way in ensuring that the credit needs of rural and semi-urban districts were adequately looked after. This redistributive nature of banking sector policy made a significant dent on rural poverty by improving access to cheap formal credit for the rural poor (Burgess and Pande 2005).

The reforms relating to the banking sector began in 1992–3 with the abolition of the 1:4 licence rule and interest rate deregulation. This reform was undertaken in stages, and by 1994–5 the interest rate regime had been substantially liberalized, with each bank being free to decide on their deposit and lending rates. At the same time, norms for entry of new private sector banks were liberalized. Banks were, in fact, allowed to close down unprofitable branches. This is likely to have implications both for mobilization of deposits and provision of credit to backward areas.

After 1999–2000, the reforms have concentrated on substantially increasing the operational flexibility that banks have with regard to their credit portfolio. A critical reform that has occurred is the reorientation of the priority sector lending norms. While the norm itself (i.e., 40 per cent of net bank credit [NBC]) has not changed, what counts as priority sectors has undergone a substantial change. The definition of priority sector has been expanded progressively to encompass increasing number of sectors and activities.

Though there are sub-targets like 18 per cent of NBC must go to agriculture and 10 per cent must be allocated to weaker sections, it seems that the statutory need to allocate credit to the priority sector does not effectively constrain a bank's lending programme. More important, in our context this extra flexibility would automatically allow banks to reorient their loan portfolio to more well-off states. Housing loans, loans to the software industry, loans to professionals and self-employed, and even education loans are the categories included in the priority sector, which may have advanced state bias.

The changed rules for branch expansion and priority sector lending seem to have implications for the outreach of banking services across states in the post-reform period. It would thus be important to evaluate whether banking sector reforms have had an adverse impact on outreach of banking services across states.

DATA AND DESCRIPTIVE STATISTICS

For this analysis, we use state-level data on various indicators of outreach of banking services over the period from 1981 to 2007. Clearly, the time horizon of this study is sufficiently long and it includes periods from both the pre-reform and post-reform regimes of banking sector in India, which allows us to examine possible consequences of banking sector reform on outreach of banking services across states. The data includes twenty states and the National Capital Territory, Delhi, of India for which consistent data is available.[1]

Data for this study comes from various sources. First, data on banking is compiled from various issues of Basic Statistical Returns of Scheduled Commercial Banks, Reserve Bank of India. Second, data on per capita net state domestic product (PCNSDP) comes from Central Statistical Organisation (CSO). Third, data of state-wise population and land area is collected from the Census of India.[2]

It is well documented in the literature that better access to financial services does not necessarily correspond to more use of financial services, since high opportunity costs and/or socio-cultural factors might also restrict economic agents to use financial services. Therefore, to assess the level of penetration of financial services in a region, it is necessary to consider both access to financial services and its use in that region (Beck et al. 2007). Following this line of argument, we first construct two sets of measures of outreach of banking services that correspond to different notions of access to and use of banking services, as follows. We report the summary statistics of various measures in Table 12.1.

Measures of access to banking services: We consider (a) geographic penetration, defined as the number of bank offices (branches) per 1,000 sq km land area; and (b) demographic penetration, defined as the number of bank offices per 10 lakh people, as measures of access to banking services. Note that (a) higher geographic penetration of banking services indicates smaller average distance of potential users from the nearest bank branch and thus better access, and (b) higher demographic penetration implies shorter queues in bank branches and thus easier access.[3] It is clear from Table 12.1 that geographic penetration has increased steadily during the period of study. In 1981, there were only about 45 bank offices per 1,000 sq km area, and this number became more than double in 2007. Figure 12.1 depicts the geographic penetration of banking services in India during 1981–2007. However, we observe that the pattern of demographic penetration over the years is very different from that of geographic penetration (see Figure 12.2). Demographic penetration in India increased more or less steadily in the pre-1991 period, but thereafter it started declining. During 1981–91, it grew by 29.16 per cent, which is quite high. In contrast to such phenomenal growth of demographic penetration in the 1980s, it declined by more than 7 per cent during the 1990s and remained almost stagnated after 2000.[4] Therefore, we can say that, though the number of bank branches has increased in both pre- and post-1991 periods, the growth of number of branches has been disproportionately low compared to the growth of population in the post-1991 period.[5]

---

[1] The states are Andhra Pradesh, Arunachal Pradesh, Assam, Bihar, Goa, Gujarat, Haryana, Himachal Pradesh, Karnataka, Kerala, Madhya Pradesh, Maharashtra, Manipur, Orissa, Punjab, Rajasthan, Tamil Nadu, Tripura, Uttar Pradesh, and West Bengal. We club data of Jharkhand, Uttarakhand, and Chhattisgarh with that of Bihar, Uttar Pradesh, and Madhya Pradesh, respectively, for consistency. The remaining states and Union Territories (Jammu and Kashmir, Chandigarh, Sikkim, Nagaland, Mizoram, Meghalaya, Daman and Diu, Dadra and Nagar Haveli, Lakshadweep, Puducherry, and Andaman and Nicobar Islands) are excluded from this analysis because of unavailability of required data.

[2] We interpolate (extrapolate) population data to get population estimates for non-census years and match these estimates with that as provided by www.indiastat.com.

[3] These arguments are based on the assumption that bank branches are uniformly distributed, which may not hold true always.

[4] Demographic penetration of branches increased by a magnitude as small as 1.05 per cent during 2001–7.

[5] We note here that the banking sector has adopted new technologies, such as automated teller machines (ATMs) and core-banking-system, in India very recently, which we do not consider due to unavailability of legitimate data. However, we think that such omission will not affect our analysis significantly. It seems to be likely that these new features of banking services are going to have developed-states-urban bias, which may contribute to accelerate the speed of divergence of states in terms of outreach of banking services in the post-reform period.

Table 12.1 Summary Statistics of Measures of Outreach of Banking Services: Twenty-One States

	1981		1991		1996		2001		2007		1981–2007	
	Mean	SD	Mean	SD	Mean	SD	Mean	SD	Mean	SD	Mean	SD
No. of Bank Offices per 10 Lakh People	66.93	45.86	86.45	39.69	82.34	40.42	80.27	44.87	81.11	50.08	80.9	42.57
No. of Bank Offices per 1,000 sq km	44.89	127.93	63.32	172.63	66.95	182.59	75.67	214.49	91.65	274.2	66.68	186.79
No. of Deposit Accounts per 1,000 People	271.83	269.81	527.06	396.86	537.65	374.11	520.17	376.69	572.04	419.83	458.73	375
No. of Credit Accounts per 1,000 People	33.33	24.51	77.07	36.62	63.77	27.82	57.85	29.73	86.32	53.69	61.79	35.01
Deposit as Percentage of Income	37.46	36.05	48.71	36.02	49.39	33.09	60.81	35.72	94.27	25.61	54.67	42.09
Credit as Percentage of Income	23.28	23.76	27.21	15.43	24.45	20.34	28.04	25.19	57.74	14.1	28.86	25.17
No. of Observations	21		21		21		21		21		567	

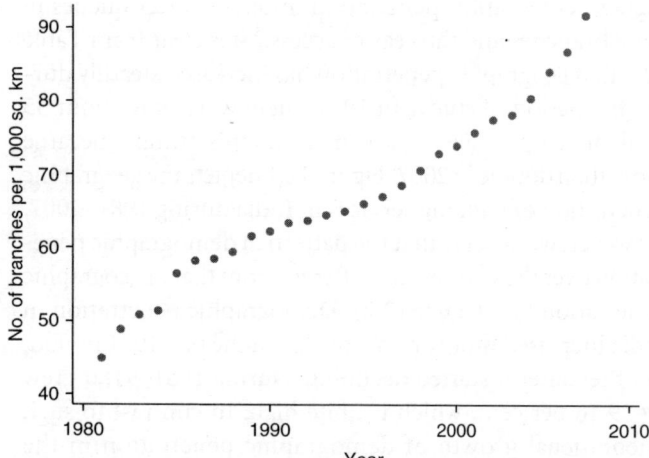

Figure 12.1 Geographic Penetration of Banking Services in India, 1981–2007

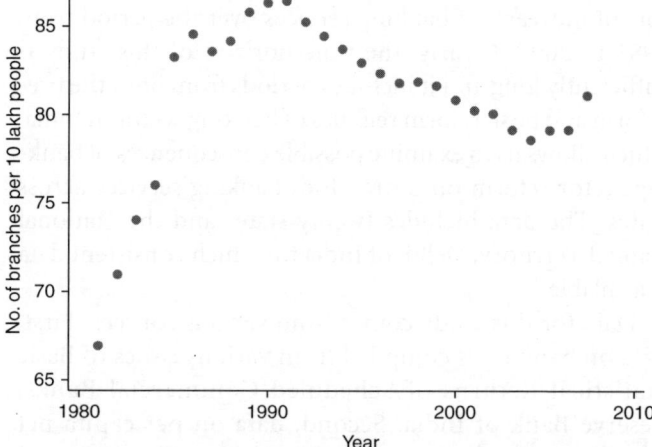

Figure 12.2 Demographic Penetration of Banking Services in India, 1981–2007

Measures of use of banking services: Following Beck et al. (2007), we consider four alternative measures of use of banking services, focusing on two main services offered by banks, deposit and credit: (a) number of deposit accounts per 1,000 people, (b) number of credit accounts per 1,000 people, (c) deposits as percentage of income, and (d) credit as percentage of income.[6] Higher values of these indicators imply better use of banking services.[7]

Table 12.1 shows that in India the number of credit accounts per 1,000 people has remained very low compared to the number of deposit accounts per 1,000 people over the period of study, though both have increased from 33 and 272 in 1981 to 86 and 572 in 2007, respectively. On

since they find negative correlation of these two measures with other measures of access to and use of banking services. However, the argument of Beck et al. (2007) does not appear to be convincing. Moreover, unlike in case of Beck et al.'s (2007) cross-country study, we find that these two indicators are positively correlated with other measures (see Table 12.2), which clearly shows that higher values of these two indicators also reflect better use of banking services in the present context.

[6] (Credits as percentage of income) = 100*(Total credit in a region) / (net domestic product in that region).

[7] We note here that Beck et al. (2007) argued that higher values of (deposits as percentage of income) and (credits as percentage of income) are likely to indicate more limited use of banking services,

Table 12.2   Correlation Matrix

	No. of Branches per 10 Lakh People	No. of Bank Offices per 1,000 sq. km	No. of Deposit Accounts per 1,000 People	No. of Credit Accounts per 1,000 People	Deposit as Percentage of Income	Credit as Percentage of Income
No. of Bank Offices per 10 Lakh People	1					
No. of Bank Offices per 1,000 sq. km	0.2782*	1				
No. of Deposit Accounts per 1,000 People	0.2947*	0.1033	1			
No. of Credit Accounts per 1,000 People	0.4265*	0.1598*	0.1478*	1		
Deposit as % of Income	0.6371*	0.7748*	0.2231*	0.3372*	1	
Credit as % of Income	0.3327*	0.7683*	0.1235*	0.4069*	0.8343*	1
Index of Outreach of Banking Services	0.7438*	0.7356*	0.3209*	0.6464*	0.8803*	0.7830*

Note: *denotes significant at 5 per cent level.

an average, the number of credit accounts was found to be less than 14 per cent of the number of deposit accounts during 1981–2007, whereas the average credit–deposit ratio was about 60 per cent.

Table 12.1 also indicates that the pattern of the aforementioned four indicators over time was very different from each other. For example, the number of deposit (credit) accounts per 1,000 people has decreased from 538 (64) in 1996 to 520 (58) in 2001, but the amount of deposit (credit) as percentage of income has increased from 49.39 per cent (24.45 per cent) in 1996 to 60.81 per cent (28.04 per cent) in 2001. In order to gauge the pattern of these four indicators of usage of banking services, we plot these indicators over time (see Figures 12.3–12.6). It is easy to observe from these figures that the patterns of changes of these indicators over time are quite diverse. We also observe that the measures of use of banking services, as well as the measures of access to banking services, vary widely across states.

Note that though the aforementioned six measures of outreach of banking services are positively correlated with each other (see Table 12.2), most of the correlation coefficients are low (less than 0.5). This is true for measures of the same category, access or use, as well for between category indicators. Scatter plots of the measures also depict that the patterns of changes of these measures over time are quite diverse. Clearly, no single

measure (or pair of measures, one from each category) can be used in isolation for the purpose of this analysis. Moreover, each of these measures captures different aspects of outreach of banking services. So, it is important to construct a composite measure, that is, an index, of outreach of banking services in order to quantify the outreach in a comprehensive manner. An index is also useful to compare outreach of banking services across states and over time.

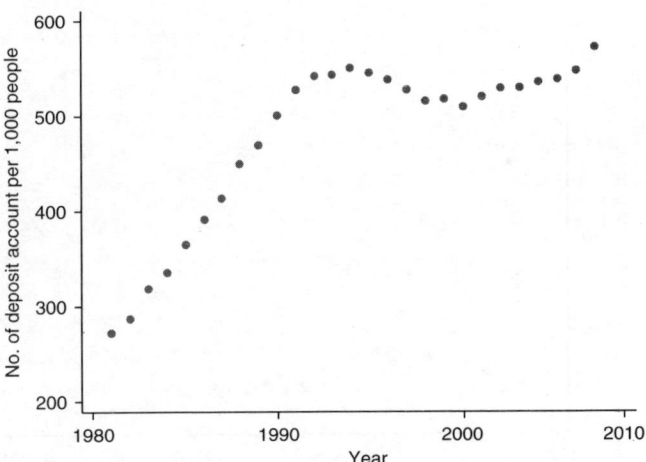

Figure 12.3   Deposit Accounts per 1,000 People in India, 1981–2007

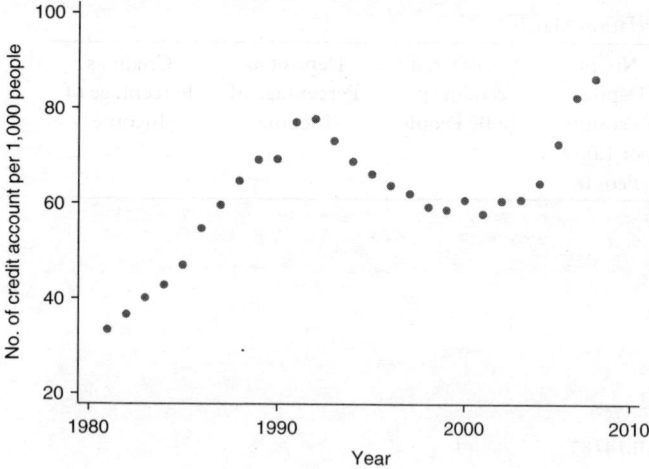

Figure 12.4 Credit Accounts per 1,000 People in India, 1981–2007

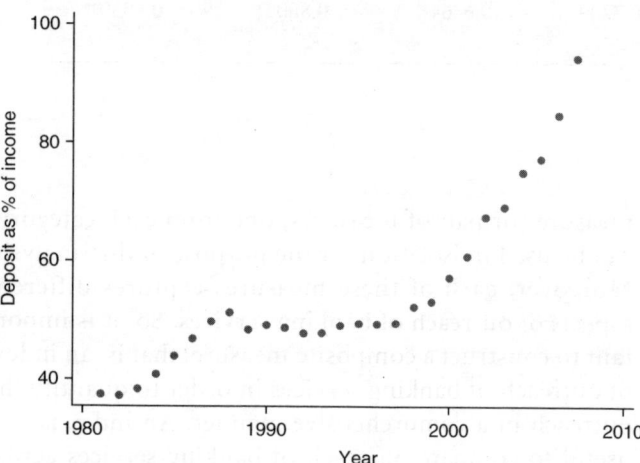

Figure 12.5 Ratio of Deposit to Income in India, 1981–2007

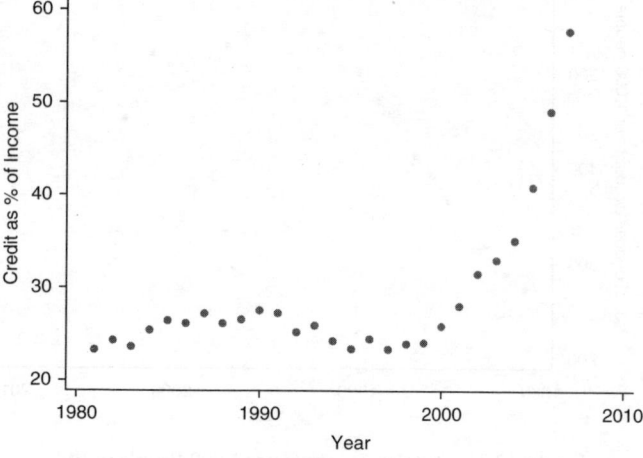

Figure 12.6 Ratio of Credit to Income in India, 1981–2007

Index of Outreach of Banking Services

We now construct the index of outreach of banking services by considering the aforementioned six measures, namely, (a) geographic penetration, (b) demographic penetration, (c) number of deposit accounts per 1,000 people, (d) number of credit accounts per 1,000 people, (e) deposits as percentage of income, and (f) credit as percentage of income.

Let m_{ist} be the value of the ith measure of outreach of banking services in state s in year t. Then the standardized value of m_{ist} is $d_{ist} = \dfrac{m_{ist} - m_i}{M_i - m_i}$, where m_i and M_i are the minimum and maximum values of the ith measure, respectively, over the entire sample, i.e., $m_i = \text{Min}\ \{m_{ist}\}_{s = 1, 2, \ldots, 21;\ t = 1981, 1982, \ldots 2007}$ and $M_i = \text{Max}\ \{m_{ist}\}_{s = 1, 2, \ldots, 21;\ t = 1981, 1982, \ldots 2007}$. Clearly, the standardized values lie in the unit interval: $d_{ist} \in [0, 1]$.

Now, since the higher values of the aforementioned measures indicate better outreach of banking services, we consider the ideal value of each measure to be equal to 1. That is, the ideal point is (1, 1, 1, 1, 1, 1) in the six-dimensional space. Therefore, shorter distance of the observed point, $(d_{1st}, d_{2st}, d_{3st}, d_{4st}, d_{5st}, d_{6st})$ for state s in year t from the ideal point implies better outreach of banking services in state s in year t. Based on this premise, we construct the index of outreach of banking services using the following formula: $Index_{st} = 1 - \dfrac{1}{\sqrt{6}}\sqrt{\displaystyle\sum_{i=1}^{6}(1 - d_{ist})^2}$, where $Index_{st}$ is the index of the outreach of banking services in state s in year t. In other words, the index is the normalized inverse Euclidian distance of the actual point from the ideal point. Sarma (2008) also uses similar formula in the context of cross-country analysis of financial inclusion corresponding to a particular year. Clearly, the value of the index lies in the unit interval, and higher value of the index indicates better outreach of banking services. Note that, since we consider the minimum and maximum values of any measure from the entire sample in order to calculate the standardized value of that measure, the resultant values of the index are comparable across states and over time. Therefore, we can use this index in order to rank the states in terms of outreach of banking services and to trace the growth trajectories of outreach of banking services in various states.[8]

---

[8] We note here that this index does not satisfy the axiom 'Global lower difference in gain at higher levels of attainment difference'. This index attaches equal weight to attainment difference at all levels of attainment. Also, because of its non-linear foundation it cannot be employed to determine the percentage contributions made by different banking services to the overall level of outreach of banking services. Nonetheless, for the purpose of the present analysis, we can use Indexst as a consolidated measure of outreach of banking services.

Table 12.3   Index of Outreach of Banking Services and Ranks of States

States	1981		1991		1996		2001		2007		1981–2007	
	Index	Rank	Index	Rank	Index	Rank	Index	Rank	Index	Rank	Index	Rank
Andhra Pradesh	0.095	8	0.149	8	0.136	9	0.135	8	0.18	9	0.138	8
Arunachal Pradesh	0.027	20	0.078	20	0.079	20	0.082	18	0.09	19	0.071	19
Assam	0.034	19	0.081	19	0.080	19	0.069	20	0.09	20	0.071	20
Bihar	0.047	18	0.106	16	0.102	15	0.081	19	0.11	17	0.089	17
Delhi	0.303	1	0.348	1	0.332	1	0.396	1	0.47	1	0.349	1
Goa	0.237	2	0.28	2	0.245	2	0.259	2	0.32	2	0.273	2
Gujarat	0.076	11	0.124	14	0.107	14	0.112	11	0.13	12	0.109	14
Haryana	0.081	10	0.133	11	0.111	13	0.114	10	0.14	10	0.116	11
Himachal Pradesh	0.095	7	0.165	7	0.146	7	0.157	6	0.18	8	0.15	7
Karnataka	0.117	5	0.18	4	0.160	5	0.159	5	0.23	6	0.167	4
Kerala	0.157	3	0.201	3	0.193	3	0.208	3	0.25	3	0.198	3
Madhya Pradesh	0.047	17	0.103	17	0.089	18	0.084	17	0.1	18	0.085	18
Maharashtra	0.088	9	0.134	10	0.125	10	0.131	9	0.24	4	0.134	9
Manipur	0.022	21	0.054	21	0.059	21	0.043	21	0.05	21	0.046	21
Orissa	0.058	14	0.133	12	0.120	12	0.106	12	0.13	11	0.111	12
Punjab	0.119	4	0.17	5	0.153	6	0.166	4	0.19	7	0.159	6
Rajasthan	0.055	15	0.101	18	0.089	17	0.088	16	0.11	16	0.089	16
Tamil Nadu	0.112	6	0.167	6	0.161	4	0.155	7	0.23	5	0.162	5
Tripura	0.074	12	0.148	9	0.143	8	0.106	14	0.12	14	0.12	10
Uttar Pradesh	0.051	16	0.107	15	0.095	16	0.094	15	0.12	15	0.092	15
West Bengal	0.07	13	0.131	13	0.122	11	0.106	13	0.12	13	0.11	13
All 21 States	0.093		0.147		0.136		0.136		0.17		0.135	

Using the aforementioned formula, we compute the index of outreach of banking services for each of the twenty-one states in each year during 1981–2007. We present the values of the index of states for some years along with the ranks of states in Table 12.3. The minimum value of the index is as low as 0.022 in Manipur in 1981. Whereas, the maximum value of the index is 0.47 in Delhi in 2007, which is also quite less compared to the ideal value of the index (equal to 1). We observe that the outreach of banking services was higher in all the states in 1991 compared to that in 1981, though there are wide variations across states in terms of the level as well as the growth rate of the index. This improvement in outreach of banking services in sub-national regions of India can possibly be attributed to the 'social banking' policy of the government in the pre-1991 period, in which the '1:4 licence rule' was an important component. On the contrary, the outreach of banking services was lower in all the states, except in Arunachal Pradesh and Manipur, in 1996 compared to

that in 1991. The average value of the index, considering all twenty-one states together, has fallen from 0.147 in 1991 to 0.136 in 1996. Such decline of outreach of banking services continued for few subsequent years in most of the states. Out of twenty-one states, in only nine states—Arunachal Pradesh, Delhi, Goa, Gujarat, Haryana, Himachal Pradesh, Kerala, Maharashtra, and Punjab—the outreach of banking services increased in 2001 compared to that in 1996. The increase in outreach of banking services in these nine states exactly compensated the decrease in other states: the average value of the index, considering all twenty-one states together, remained same at 0.136 in 1996 and 2001. However, the outreach of banking services increased in all states in 2007 from that in 2001. Figures 12.7 and 12.8 clearly depict the aforementioned patterns of outreach of banking services over the years in India and across states, respectively.

As far as relative positions of states in terms of outreach of banking services is concerned, on the basis of average

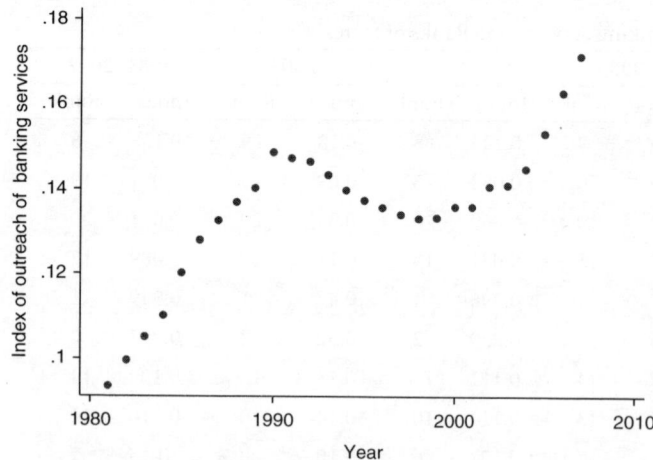

Figure 12.7 Outreach of Banking Services in India, 1981–2007

value of the index over the period from 1981 to 2007, Delhi ranks first, followed by Goa (second), Kerala (third), and Karnataka (fourth). Manipur (rank twenty-one), Assam (rank twenty), Arunachal Pradesh (rank nineteen), and Madhya Pradesh (rank eighteen) had the lowest outreach of banking services, on an average, during 1981–2007. Interestingly, it seems that Delhi, Goa, Kerala, and Manipur have consistently maintained their ranks—first, second, third, and twenty-first, respectively. Nonetheless, there have been some changes in relative positions of states over

time as well. For example, Maharashtra climbed up from the ninth position in 1981 to the fourth position in 2007, but Punjab has slipped from the fourth position in 1981 to the seventh position in 2007.

The annual average growth rate of outreach of banking services in India was as high as 6.74 per cent in the period from 1981 to 1990, whereas the growth rate during the entire period (from 1981 to 2007) was only 3.11 per cent. Moreover, during 1981–90, all states experienced positive growth in terms of outreach of banking services (see Table 12.4). Interestingly, Delhi experienced the lowest annual average growth rate (0.44 per cent) of outreach of banking services in this period, followed by Kerala (2.85 per cent). Note that both these states scored very high in terms of outreach of banking services in the initial year, 1981. On the other hand, Arunachal Pradesh and Tripura fared poorly in the initial year, but experienced phenomenal growth of outreach of banking services (more that 11 per cent average annual growth rate) during 1981–90. It gives some indication of convergence of states in terms of outreach of banking services in 1980s.

In contrast to the pre-1991 period, the average annual growth rate of outreach of banking services in India was as low as 0.99 per cent during the period from 1991 to 2007. Goa, Madhya Pradesh, and Tripura experienced negative growth rate during that period. If we omit the years from 1991 to 1995 and consider the period from 1996 to 2007, the average

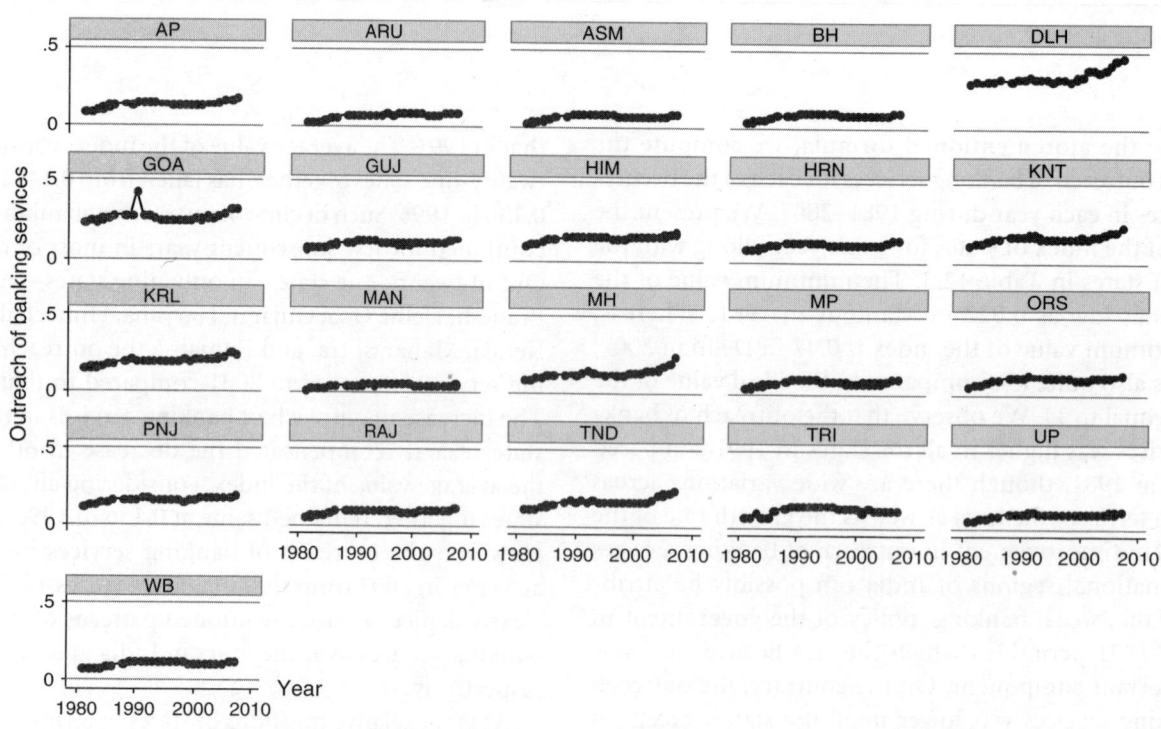

Figure 12.8 Outreach of Banking Services across States in India, 1981–2007

Table 12.4   Growth of Outreach of Banking Services

States	1981–2007		1981–90		1991–2007		1996–2007	
	Annual Avg. Gr. Rate (%)	SD	Annual Avg. Gr. Rate (%)	SD	Annual Avg. Gr. Rate (%)	SD	Annual Avg. Gr. Rate (%)	SD
Andhra Pradesh	2.960	4.700	5.823	5.391	1.276	3.378	2.049	3.575
Arunachal Pradesh	5.831	8.855	12.464	9.177	1.928	6.031	1.298	6.362
Assam	3.780	7.527	9.523	7.912	0.402	4.911	0.393	4.877
Bihar	4.277	8.128	10.753	7.639	0.468	5.735	0.755	6.455
Delhi	1.537	4.351	0.440	2.583	2.183	5.080	3.531	4.958
Goa	1.847	12.473	6.911	15.741	−1.132	9.379	2.090	3.660
Gujarat	2.307	4.310	5.071	3.594	0.680	3.916	1.579	3.878
Haryana	2.488	4.365	5.699	2.863	0.599	4.014	1.629	4.112
Himachal Pradesh	2.797	4.421	6.211	4.436	0.789	3.020	1.331	3.010
Karnataka	3.122	5.117	5.753	4.828	1.574	4.750	2.965	4.742
Kerala	1.844	2.825	2.854	2.566	1.249	2.872	1.929	2.945
Madhya Pradesh	3.068	6.007	8.509	5.098	−0.133	3.825	0.930	3.957
Maharashtra	4.300	7.542	4.181	3.937	4.370	9.148	5.747	7.658
Manipur	3.651	9.278	7.552	9.291	1.357	8.731	−0.325	8.686
Orissa	3.657	6.793	8.969	6.828	0.533	4.555	0.914	4.937
Punjab	2.205	3.599	4.125	3.245	1.076	3.386	1.723	3.391
Rajasthan	3.000	5.354	7.197	4.999	0.531	3.878	1.458	4.207
Tamil Nadu	3.042	4.413	4.550	3.177	2.155	4.869	3.019	5.450
Tripura	3.747	18.381	11.221	27.587	−0.650	8.090	−1.012	9.584
Uttar Pradesh	3.353	5.384	7.091	5.183	1.155	4.256	1.417	3.087
West Bengal	2.586	5.866	6.529	5.190	0.266	5.032	0.270	5.153
No. of Obs.	27		10		17		12	
All 21 States	3.114	7.415	6.735	8.749	0.985	5.496	1.604	5.273
No. of Obs.	567		210		357		252	

annual growth rate of outreach of banking services improves to 1.6 per cent. This is consistent with our earlier observation that in all states, except Arunachal Pradesh and Manipur, the outreach of banking services has been lower in 1996 compared to that in 1991. Moreover, it appears that during the period 1996–2007, states with relatively low levels of outreach of banking services in the initial year, 1996, did not necessarily grow faster than those with relatively high levels of outreach of banking services in 1996. For example, the rate of growth of outreach of banking services during 1996–2007 was only 0.93 per cent in Madhya Pradesh (ranked eighteenth in 1996), whereas the growth rate in Maharashtra (ranked tenth in 1996) was as high as 5.75 per cent during the same period.

CONVERGENCE ANALYSIS

Are the levels of outreach of banking services across states in India converging to the steady state over time? In other words, have states that were initially laggards subsequently grown faster in terms of outreach of banking services? Is there any consequence of banking sector's reform in India on the growth pattern of outreach of banking services across states? It is of paramount importance to answer these questions in order to design appropriate policy to promote balanced growth across sub-national regions and reduce regional disparities in terms of development indicators. However, to the best of our knowledge, the issue of convergence of regions in terms of penetration of financial services, a key factor for growth and development, has not received much attention in the literature so far. In this section, we attempt to fill this gap.

From the discussion in the previous section, it seems that there was a tendency of convergence of states in terms of outreach of banking services in the 1980s; however, in the aftermath of banking sector reform in India, the pattern of growth of outreach of banking services across states might have been reversed. Nonetheless, note that these are casual observations. It calls for more comprehensive and structured analysis of the issue of convergence of states in terms of outreach of banking services.

In the spirit of existing empirical literature on convergence of income across regions, *a la* Barro and Sala-i-Martin (1992, 1995), we consider the following econometric model:

$$(Growth\ of\ Outreach)_{i,\,t_0\,-\,T} = \alpha + \beta\,(Outreach)_{i,\,t_0} + e_i \ldots (12.1)$$

where $(Growth\ of\ Outreach)_{i,\,t_0-\,T}$ is the average annual growth rate of outreach of banking services in state i over the period from the year t_0 to the year T, is the level of outreach of banking services in state i in the initial year t_0, β is the coefficient of the initial level of outreach, α is the constant term, and e_i is identically and independently distributed (IID) error term. Now, if the estimated coefficient of the initial level of outreach of banking services is found to be negative (positive) and significant, we can conclude that states are converging (diverging) over time in terms of outreach of banking services, that is, there is unconditional β-convergence (divergence) across states in India in terms of outreach of banking services during the period $t_0 - T$.

First, we estimate the aforementioned model, for the period 1981–2007, considering all twenty-one states using OLS (robust standard errors) method. Results are reported in Column (1) in Table 12.5. We find that the coefficient of the initial outreach of banking services is negative and significant, suggesting unconditional convergence during the period 1981–2007. The corresponding regression line is shown in Figure 12.9. It also depicts negative relation between initial level of outreach of banking services and its growth. This result of unconditional convergence during the period 1981–2007 remains valid if we estimate the model by considering only fourteen major states[9] following the standard practice of comparing economic performances of states (see, for example, Ahluwalia [2000, 2002]; Nachane et al. [2002]). See column (2) in Table 12.5. We note that the presence of influential data points (which may be outliers and/or high leverage points) may significantly influence the regression results, particularly when the total number of observations is small, as in our case. Upon inspection, we observe that the absolute value of studentized residual of each observation is less than 2. It indicates that there is no outlier in the sample. However, we observe that Delhi and Goa have high leverages (greater

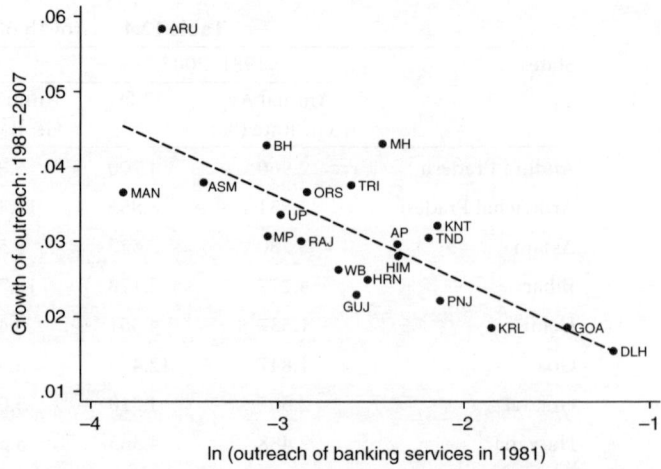

Figure 12.9 Convergence during 1981–2007

than the tolerance level $(2k+2)/21 = 0.190476$), which have potential great influences on regression coefficient estimates.[10] Also, for Delhi and Arunachal Pradesh, (a) the Cook's distance, D—where D_i is a measure of the distance between the coefficient estimates when the ith observation is omitted and when it is not—is found to be greater than the conventional cut-off point $(4/n) = 0.190476$; and (b) the more specific measures of influence, DFBETA, which also assess how each coefficient is changed by deleting the observation, also found to be greater than the cut-off value $(2/\sqrt{n}) = 0.436436$. Therefore, on the basis of regression diagnostics, it seems that Arunachal Pradesh, Delhi, and Goa might have great influences on regression coefficient. In order to address this issue, we estimate the model (1) by dropping these three observations. We find that the result of unconditional convergence during the period 1981–2007 is robust to such alterations (see column (3) in Table 12.5). The estimates of model (1), using the entire sample, indicate that the rate of convergence (unconditional) of states in terms of outreach of banking services is about 10 per cent per year during 1981–2007. At this rate, it would take the states close to seven years to get the half-way towards the steady state level of outreach of banking services.[11]

---

[9] Andhra Pradesh, Bihar, Gujarat, Haryana, Karnataka, Kerala, Madhya Pradesh, Maharashtra, Orissa, Punjab, Rajasthan, Tamil Nadu, Uttar Pradesh, and West Bengal.

[10] Leverage is a measure of how far an independent variable deviates from its mean. To be specific, leverage of a point is given by

$$[(x_i - \overline{x})^2]/[\sum_{j=1}^{21}(x_j - \overline{x})^2].$$

[11] Note that in the neighbourhood of a balanced growth path, we have $\ln y(t) - \ln y^* = [\exp(-bt)][\ln y(0) - \ln y^*]$, where b is the constant rate of growth (see Barro and Salai-i-Martin 1995). Therefore, the half-life, say t^*, of a variable is the solution to $[\exp(-bt^*)] = 0.5$.

Table 12.5   Convergence of States, 1981–2007
Dependent Variable: Growth Rate of Outreach of Banking Services

	Cross-Section			Five-year Panel (1981–2005)		
	(1)	(2)	(3)	(4)	(5)	(6)
Initial Outreach of Banking Services	−0.100 **(0.001)**	−0.118 **(0.009)**	−0.121 **(0.000)**	−0.217 **(0.006)**	−0.536 **(0.041)**	−0.472 **(0.000)**
Constant	0.040 **(0.000)**	0.040 **(0.000)**	0.041 **(0.000)**	0.057 **(0.000)**	0.091 **(0.000)**	0.082 **(0.000)**
Number of Observations	21	14	18	105	70	90
R-Square	0.48	0.29	0.36	0.11	0.25	0.19

Notes: *p*-values are reported in parentheses. Columns (1) and (4) correspond to all 21 states (AP, ARU, ASM, BH, DLH, GOA, GUJ, HRN, HIM, KNT, KRL, MP, MH, MAN, ORS, PNJ, RAJ, TND, TRI, UP, and WB). Columns (2) and (5) correspond to 14 major states (Andhra Pradesh, Bihar, Gujarat, Haryana, Karnataka, Kerala, Madhya Pradesh, Maharashtra, Orissa, Punjab, Rajasthan, Tamil Nadu, Uttar Pradesh, and West Bengal). Columns (3) and (6) correspond to 18 states, excluding Arunachal Pradesh, Delhi, and Goa from the initial 21 states based on regression diagnostics.

Since panel regressions allow for a larger number of observations than the cross-sectional regressions, following Islam (1995), we also estimate the five-year panel versions of model (1) for the period 1981–2005. We present the estimation results considering (a) all twenty-one states, (b) only fourteen major states, and (c) eighteen states selected on the basis of regression diagnostics, in columns (4), (5), and (6), respectively, of Table 12.5. Negative and significant coefficient of the initial level of outreach of banking services in each of these three regressions confirms that states that were initially laggards subsequently grew faster in terms of outreach of banking services during the period 1981–2005. That is, the panel estimates re-confirm that there was a tendency of unconditional convergence of states in terms of outreach of banking services during the period 1981–2005.

Now, as we have noted before, from the descriptive statistics it seems that the tendency of convergence of states in terms of outreach of banking services was present only in the 1980s, not thereafter. Therefore, it is important to examine whether the result of unconditional convergence of states during the period 1981–2007 is due to high influence of observations of some specific sub-periods of analysis. It calls for estimation of model (1) for pre- and post-reform periods separately. Note that the banking sector reform in India started in the early 1990s with the abolition of '1:4 licence rule', and the reform was undertaken in stages, which led to substantial changes by 1994–5, as mentioned in the second section of the chapter. Therefore, it seems reasonable to estimate model (1) considering two sub-periods, 1981–90 and 1996–2007, separately, leaving out the phase of transition (1991–5). These two sub-periods are also sufficiently large to clean out any short-term fluctuation. We also estimate model (1) considering the periods 1997–2007, 1998–2007, 1999–2007, 2000–7, and 2001–7, separately, for robustness checks. We find that the results are not sensitive to such changes in the initial (i.e., the base) year for the convergence analysis for the post-reform period.

Interestingly, we observe that while the regression line for the period 1981–90 is negatively sloped (see Figure 12.10), as expected in case of convergence, the regression line for the period 1996–2007 is positively sloped (see Figure 12.11).

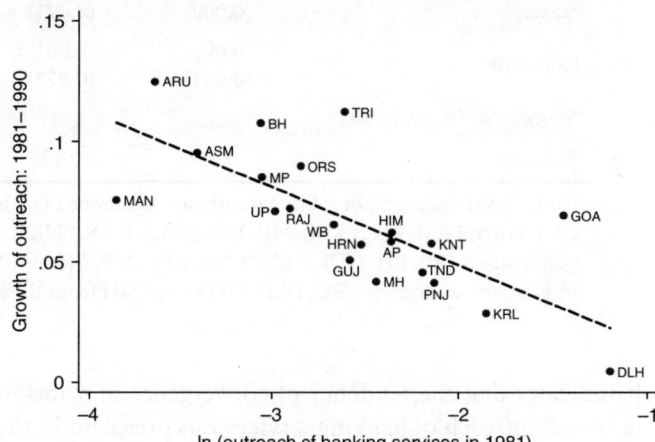

Figure 12.10   Convergence during 1981–90

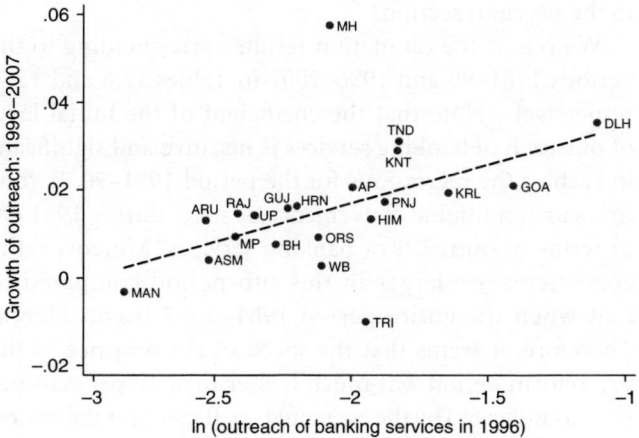

Figure 12.11   Divergence during 1996–2007

Table 12.6 Convergence of States, 1981–90
Dependent Variable: Growth Rate of Outreach of Banking Services

	Cross-Section			Five-year Panel (1981–90)		
	(1)	(2)	(3)	(4)	(5)	(6)
Initial Outreach of Banking Services	−0.287 **(0.002)**	−0.537 **(0.000)**	−0.407 **(0.000)**	−0.336 **(0.003)**	−0.748 **(0.000)**	−0.671 **(0.000)**
Constant	0.094 **(0.000)**	0.109 **(0.000)**	0.085 **(0.000)**	0.105 **(0.000)**	0.138 **(0.000)**	0.128 **(0.000)**
Number of Observations	21	14	17	42	28	34
R-Square	0.47	0.69	0.70	0.28	0.63	0.58

Notes: p-values are reported in parentheses. Columns (1) and (4) correspond to all 21 states (AP, ARU, ASM, BH, DLH, GOA, GUJ, HRN, HIM, KNT, KRL, MP, MH, MAN, ORS, PNJ, RAJ, TND, TRI, UP, and WB). Columns (2) and (5) correspond to 14 major states (Andhra Pradesh, Bihar, Gujarat, Haryana, Karnataka, Kerala, Madhya Pradesh, Maharashtra, Orissa, Punjab, Rajasthan, Tamil Nadu, Uttar Pradesh, and West Bengal). Columns (3) and (6) correspond to 17 states, excluding Arunachal Pradesh, Delhi, Goa and Tripura from the initial 21 states based on regression diagnostics.

Table 12.7 Divergence of States, 1996–2007
Dependent Variable: Growth Rate of Outreach of Banking Services

	Cross-Section			Five-year Panel (1996–2005)		
	(1)	(2)	(3)	(4)	(5)	(6)
Initial Outreach of Banking Services	0.103 **(0.000)**	0.149 **(0.041)**	0.171 **(0.003)**	0.126 **(0.000)**	0.180 **(0.104)**	0.201 **(0.013)**
Constant	0.002 **(0.643)**	0.001 **(0.973)**	−0.006 **(0.264)**	0.010 **(0.091)**	−0.012 **(0.391)**	−0.018 **(0.063)**
Number of Observations	21	14	17	42	28	34
R-Square	0.20	0.12	0.50	0.14	0.06	0.14

Notes: p-values are reported in parentheses. Columns (1) and (4) correspond to all 21 states (AP, ARU, ASM, BH, DLH, GOA, GUJ, HRN, HIM, KNT, KRL, MP, MH, MAN, ORS, PNJ, RAJ, TND, TRI, UP, and WB). Columns (2) and (5) correspond to 14 major states (AP, BH, GUJ, HRN, KNT, KRL, MP, MH, ORS, PNJ, RAJ, TND, UP, and WB). Columns (3) and (6) correspond to 17 states, excluding ARU, DLH, GOA, and MH from the initial 21 states based on regression diagnostics.

It indicates that the tendency of convergence of states in terms of outreach of banking services was prevalent in the pre-reform period (1981–90), but in the post-reform period (1996–2007) the states are actually diverging from each other. These observations are consistent with the discussion in the previous section.

We report the estimation results corresponding to the periods 1981–90 and 1996–2007 in Tables 12.6 and 12.7, respectively. Note that the coefficient of the initial level of outreach of banking services is negative and significant in each of the regressions for the period 1981–90. It confirms unconditional convergence of states during 1981–90 in terms of outreach of banking services. Moreover, the coefficients are larger in this sub-period compared to that when the entire period 1981–2007 is considered. Therefore, it seems that the speed of convergence in the pre-reform period was much higher than 10 per cent per year, as indicated by the estimated coefficient for the period 1981–2007 considering all twenty-one states.

In contrast to the period from 1981 to 1990, we find that the initial level of outreach of banking services in a state has positive and significant impact on its growth rate during the period from 1996–2007 (see Table 12.7). This result holds true if we consider any of the subsequent years, starting from 1997, as the base year (see Table 12.8). Therefore, it seems that during 1996–2007 the states that were initially laggards subsequently grew slower in terms of outreach of banking services.[12] In other words, we have evidence of unconditional divergence among Indian states, in terms of outreach of banking services, during 1996–2007. The OLS estimate of model (1), considering all twenty-one states, indicates that the speed of divergence during this period was about 10 per cent

[12] If we include the phase of transition, that is, if we consider the period 1991–2007, the OLS estimate considering fourteen major states of the coefficient of the initial level of outreach of banking services is also positive and significant. The estimated coefficient and the corresponding p-value are 0.12 and 0.036 respectively.

Table 12.8 Divergence of States, 1997–2007: Considering Different Base Year
Dependent Variable: Growth Rate of Outreach of Banking Services

Base Year	1997	1998	1999	2000	2001
	(1)	(2)	(3)	(4)	(5)
Initial Outreach of Banking Services	0.101 **(0.001)**	0.106 **(0.003)**	0.110 **(0.001)**	0.088 **(0.024)**	0.060 **(0.011)**
Constant	0.005 **(0.335)**	0.008 **(0.211)**	0.011 **(0.081)**	0.017 **(0.024)**	0.024 **(0.000)**
Number of Observations	21	21	21	21	21
R-Square	0.16	0.16	0.16	0.11	0.06

Note: *p*-values are reported in parentheses.

per year. Therefore, it seems that the banking sector reforms in India in the early 1990s might have contributed to the growing distance among states during 1996–2007 in terms of outreach of banking services, which is the reverse of the growth pattern of outreach of banking services across states in the pre-reform period. These results hold true for many subsets of states, categorized on the basis of economic and well as geographical location criteria, as well as alterations in the base year considered for the convergence analysis.[13]

CONCLUSION

In this chapter we analyse the pattern of outreach of banking services across states in India during 1981–2007. We observe that while geographic penetration of banking services in India has increased steadily during the entire period of study, demographic penetration has registered a declining trend in the post-reform period. It indicates that in the post-reform period, the growth of number of branches has been disproportionately low compared to the growth of population. Also, the pattern of changes in measures of use of banking services during the period of study was found to be quite different from each other. In other words, there is wide variation in terms of the measures of use of banking services as well as in terms of the measures of access to banking services across states and over time.

Next, we construct an index of outreach of banking services for sub-national economies in order to assess the overall achievement of states in terms of outreach of banking services. Econometric analysis indicates that there was tendency of unconditional convergence of states in terms of outreach of banking services in the pre-reform period. It indicates that the 'social banking' policy contributed to greater outreach of banking services in a balanced manner. On the contrary, we find that states are actually diverging from each other in terms of outreach of banking services in the aftermath of the banking sector reforms in India. Our results are robust to several alterations in categorizations of states (based on various criterion used to distinguish relatively developed and less-developed states) as well as in the base year considered for the convergence analysis.

It is well documented that the banking sector reforms in India have strengthened the overall balance sheets of banks. Our results indicate that the banking sector reforms have adverse impacts on the outreach of banking services across sub-national economies in a balanced manner. The emergence of this regional imbalance can be considered to be an unintended consequence of the reform process. Given the fact that the outreach of banking services is an important policy objective, there is a need to reorient banking sector reforms to meet this objective. This calls for further research to identify the determinants of outreach of banking services across states in order to design appropriate policy in this regard. Further, it seems to be interesting to extend the present analysis by considering rural and urban areas of each state separately. However, these are beyond the scope of the present chapter. We leave it for future research.

[13] The result of unconditional divergence among states during 1996–2007 holds true if we drop (a) north-eastern states, or (b) BIMARU states, or (c) north-eastern and BIMARU states, (d) states in the last or first quartile in terms of per capita NSDP, or (e) states in the last or first quartile in terms of outreach of banking services measured by the index of outreach. This set of regression results is available upon request.

REFERENCES

Ahluwalia, M.S. (2000), 'Economic Performance of States in Post-Reforms Period', *Economic and Political Weekly*, 35(19): 1637–48.

——— (2002), 'State Level Performance under Economic Reforms in India', in A.O. Krueger (ed.), *Economic Policy*

Reforms and the Indian Economy, pp. 91–122. New Delhi: Oxford University Press.

Barro, R. and X. Sala-i-Martin (1992), 'Convergence', *Journal of Political Economy*, 100(2): 223–51.

——— (1995), *Economic Growth*. New York: McGraw-Hill.

Basu, P. and P. Srivastava (2005), 'Scaling-up Microfinance for India's Rural Poor', World Bank Policy Research Working Paper 3646.

Beck, T., A. Demirguc-Kunt, and R. Levine (2004), 'Finance, Inequality and Poverty', World Bank Policy Research Working Paper 3338.

——— (2007), 'Reaching Out: Access to and Use of Banking Services Across Countries', *Journal of Financial Economics*, 85: 234–66.

Burgess, R. and R. Pande (2005), 'Do Rural Banks Matter? Evidence from the Indian Social Banking Experiment', *American Economic Review*, 95(3): 780–95.

Honohan, P. (2004), 'Financial Development, Growth and Poverty: How Close are the Links?', in Charles Goodhart (ed.),

Financial Development and Economic Growth: Explaining the Links. London: Palgrave, pp. 1–37.

Islam, N. (1995), 'Growth Empirics: A Panel Data Approach', *Quarterly Journal of Economics*, 110(4): 1127–70.

Nachane, D.M., P. Ray, and S. Ghosh (2002), 'Does Monetary Policy have Differential State-Level Effects? An Empirical Evaluation', *Economic and Political Weekly*, 37(47): 4723–8.

Nair, K.R.G. (2004), *Economic Reforms and Regional Disparities in Economic and Social Development in India*. New Delhi: Centre for Policy Research.

Narasimham Committee (1998), *Report of the Committee on Banking Sector Reforms*. New Delhi: Union Ministry of Finance, Government of India.

Sarma, M. (2008), 'Index of Financial Inclusion', Indian Council for Research on International Economic Relations Working Paper No. 215, New Delhi.

Sen, A. and R.R. Vaidya (1997), *The Process of Financial Liberalization in India*. New Delhi: Oxford University Press.

13

Environmental Challenges of Development Strategies in India

Vinod Kumar Sharma

INTRODUCTION

The introduction of the economic reforms in 1990s witnessed a rapid growth in India. While such an accelerated growth is necessary to alleviate widespread poverty in the country, it results in rapid resource depletion and ecological degradation. On one hand, higher targets of economic growth increase pressure on already overburdened natural resources; on the other hand, improved economic conditions of people induce changes in their consumption patterns and lifestyle that often lead to increased environmental stress. In the pre-reforms period, environmental issues were considered external to the economy. But soon it was realized that this approach towards environment might result in an irreversible damage to our ecosystem that would be beyond our control. Probably, this motivated the Government of India to prepare a National Environmental Action Plan in the post-reforms period, aimed at integrating the environmental considerations into the developmental strategies.

Since the beginning of the environmental movement in the early 1970s, India has played a proactive role in framing the relevant policies such as passage and codification of various Acts to safeguard the environment. This produced an exhaustive and stringent environmental legislation in the country. However, implementation and enforcement of various laws and policies have not been very effective, as a result of which an unsustainable use of natural and environmental resources has continued in the country.

There are several reasons for the limited success of environmental policies, such as institutional failure and public apathy. Despite several measures taken by the government, controversies often surround development activities. Until the early 1970s, environmental problems were considered as country-specific because their sources and effects were confined to the national boundaries. But emergence of global warming, ozone depletion, trade of waste, and similar other international issues have made environment a transboundary problem. To deal with these multinational and multidimensional problems, appropriate environmental policies are required at various levels, namely, international, national, and local levels.

Despite stringent regulations, the state of various subecosystems in India is far from being satisfactory. While contribution of India to global environmental problems may be lesser than many other countries, the stress on local resources and environment is much more critical in the country. For example, only about 20 per cent of total sewage generated in the country is treated and the rest is discharged untreated into rivers and other water bodies. Similarly, the number of threatened plant and animal species, known as red list species, has more than doubled from 459 in 2000 to 928 in 2006.[1]

[1] See website of the Ministry of Environment and Forests (http://moef.nic.in/index.php).

In recent times, the Government of India has taken several steps, at all levels, to check further damage to various ecosystems. The country is taking an active part in international negotiations and framing of regulations concerned with climate change, global warming, trade and environment, etc. The Ministry of Environment and Forests (MoEF) is playing a constructive role as the nodal agency for the management of environment and forests in the country. The MoEF frames various laws and policies and implements them through the network of various agencies such as Central and state pollution control boards. The role of the Indian judiciary has also become prominent and Indian courts have fined, and even closed, thousands of industrial units violating the provisions of environmental legislation.

STATE OF ENVIRONMENT

The major areas of environmental concerns in the country may be broadly classified into two categories—local environmental problems and issues of international importance. While the local issues include air pollution, depletion and pollution of water resources, solid waste problem, and land degradation, global issues are focused on climate change, ozone depletion, trade and environment, etc. A brief review of the state of some of these sub-ecosystems is given in the following.

Major Sub-ecosystems

High levels of both indoor and ambient air pollution, particularly in urban areas, have reached a dangerous mark. In general, air pollution levels in cities of southern India such as Chennai, Bengaluru, and Hyderabad are lower than cities in northern India and other metro cities like Delhi, Mumbai, and Kolkata. Though gaseous pollutants are not very harmful, high emission levels of both suspended particulate matter and respirable particulate matter are resulting in various health hazards. Several studies conducted in the rural and urban poor areas, where low-quality fuels such as coal and wood are used for cooking and other household activities, have indicated the presence of high levels of harmful pollutants in the indoor environment. At the same time, industries and various modes of transportation are major anthropogenic sources of ambient air pollution. Similarly, the noise levels in some cities exceed the prescribed standards in all categories, for both day and night, and the situation worsens during festivals and functions.

Depletion and pollution of water resources are crucial issues both in rural and urban areas. Rural India lacks proper water supply infrastructure and people do not have access to safe drinking water. The urban areas, on the other hand, are faced with the problem of inadequate and low quality of water supply services. India has about 20 per cent of the world's population but only about 4 per cent of the world's fresh water resources. The per capita water availability in the country seems to be lower than 1,700 cubic meters—an international benchmark for water-scarce regions. Water contamination is so severe that about 70 per cent of all diseases in India are waterborne and about 73 million workdays are lost each year due to them. The condition of various water bodies like rivers, lakes, and coastal waters is dismal. Further, the growing population, rapid industrialization and large-scale urbanization are increasing the demand for water supply and exerting an enhanced stress on existing water resources.

Solid waste problems are more obvious in the urban rather than in rural areas. They cover many issues such as collection of mixed waste, lack of use of sanitary landfills, dumping of waste in open grounds, and socio-economic problems. The country generates a large amount of municipal solid waste and other types of solid wastes and the quantity generated in major cities and class I towns, due to consumption patterns and higher standard of living, is much more than the class II towns. Delhi and Mumbai generate the highest proportion of municipal solid waste in the country. The daily per capita solid waste generated in small, medium, and large towns in India is around 0.1 kg, 0.3–0.4 kg, and 0.6 kg, respectively, for the year 2006 (Sharma 2007). However, proper scientific management of waste is still lacking.

Degradation of land resources is the result of deficiency in soil nutrients and use of excessive water for irrigation that leads to increased salinity in soils. Water-induced erosion is the major cause for soil erosion and land degradation, which is aggravated by the continuously reducing vegetation cover. Uncontrolled land use change for various purposes to facilitate urban development is responsible for deterioration and degradation of land. Improper disposal of the large quantities of solid waste has also caused significant land degradation. The drive for increased agricultural production has resulted in the loss of genetic diversity in the country.

India's contribution to global environmental problems such as global warming and ozone depletion is much less. Recent estimates indicate that CO_2 emissions, in tonnes per capita per annum for the year 2006, are highest from the US (19.5), followed by Russia (10.7), UK (9.2), China (2.7), Brazil (1.8), and lowest from India (0.9). Similarly, consumption of chlorofluorocarbons, per thousand persons per annum for the year 2006, is 0.08 in the US, 5.70 in Russia, 3.16 in Brazil, 1.61 in China, and 0.04 in India (Sharma 2007). India's coastline includes as many as nine states and many important cities including Mumbai, Chennai, and Kolkata. This obviously is a cause of serious concern as climate change may have severe implications. The coastal regions are agriculturally fertile and sea level rise will make them highly vulnerable to inundation and may increase the soil salinity. Coastal infrastructure, tourist activities, and oil exploration may also be at risk, which may result in huge economic damage. Trade and environment negotiations are often controversial and increase the possibility of international environmental regulations acting as non-tariff trade barriers for developing countries, including India. This may result in reduction in market competitiveness of Indian exports.

To deal with aforementioned and several other problems of environment and development, and to focus on resource conservation and environmental protection, the Government of India has taken several steps such as institutional reforms, framing of laws and policies, and use of economic and other measures.

Institutional Mechanism

The MoEF was created in 1985 and since then it has been the nodal agency in India for all issues related to environment and forests. The MoEF is comprehensive and institutionalized, and has a Union minister and minister of state, two political positions answering directly to the prime minister of India. The MoEF is responsible for all environmental functions such as monitoring, assessments, surveys, enforcement, and promotional work. In December 1993, the MoEF completed its National Environmental Action Plan to integrate the environmental considerations with developmental strategies, which, among other priorities, included industrial pollution reduction. Among the various strategies employed by the MoEF, the implementation of a 'polluter pays' principle was the major one. The ministry provides technical assistance and limited grants to promote common effluent treatment plants, which can be used by a group of small-scale industries. The ministry has also created industrial zones to encourage clusters of similar industries in order to help reduce the cost of providing utilities and environmental services.

The MoEF has empowered the Central Pollution Control Board (CPCB) at Delhi and several State Pollution Control Boards (SPCBs) in various states as well as Pollution Control Committees (PCCs) in the Union Territories to implement and enforce environmental regulations. The CPCB serves as the national board and a sort of technical wing of the MoEF, with oversight powers over the various state boards. It is also the ruling body for the Union Territories. The CPCB may prosecute polluting industries under Section 33 (apprehension of pollution) and Section 44 (violation of conditions of consent order) of the Water Act. In its relationship with the SPCBs, the CPCB serves an advisory role. However, CPCB cannot force a state board to adopt uniform standards or prosecute those cases on which the state board is reluctant. Recent developments indicate more vigilance by government officials towards violators, as Indian courts have fined and even closed thousands of factories, including some multinationals, for violating the provisions of environmental legislations.

The SPCBs also play an important role of conducting plant-level inspections and monitoring and advising the CPCB of problems and trends at the local level. The SPCBs are empowered to provide consent orders regarding new discharges or outlets. The SPCB members have right to access any plant site at any time. In situations wherein a SPCB recommends immediate action to be taken, it has the authority to prevent further discharges and can also apply to a judicial magistrate for a restraining order. In case of an emergency, SPCBs are empowered to take whatever measures they deem necessary. The legislation also sets out specific penalties (prison sentences and fines) for violations of the Environment Act. For example, anyone destroying SPCB property, preventing an SPCB employee from performing his/her duties, knowingly providing false information to the SPCB, and tampering with monitoring devices installed by the SPCB can be imprisoned or fined or both.

Legal Framework

It is worth mentioning that India was the first country to amend its Constitution and empower the state to protect and improve the environment for safeguarding public health, forests, and wildlife. At the Stockholm Conference on Human Environment in June 1972, India attributed the deterioration of environment to the development process and suggested urgent remedial measures for a sustainable development. The 42nd Amendment to the Constitution was adopted in 1976 and came into effect in 1977, focused on these issues. The language of the Directive Principles of State Policy (Article 47) requires not only a projectionist stance by the state but also compels the state to seek the improvement of polluted environments. This allows the government to impose restrictions on potentially harmful entities such as polluting industries.

Although the state governments have clearly delineated lines of authority and jurisdiction, Article 253 of the Indian Constitution provides the central government extensive powers to implement laws for any part of India with regard to the treaties made with other countries or in relation to the decisions made by an international body. For internal environmental matters, the Constitution provides for a distribution of legislative powers between the Union and the states. This was achieved by the creation of three jurisdictional lists—Union, State, and Concurrent. The central government can enact a law for any item on the Union and Concurrent lists, and only in certain cases for an item on the State list, with concurrence of the state legislatures.

The Environment (Protection) Act, 1986, is the umbrella act in India that deals with the overall management of ecosystems in the country. In addition, some of the important national policies are the National Forest Policy, 1988; National Conservation Strategy and Policy Statement on Environment and Development, 1992; Policy Statement on Abatement of Pollution, 1992; National Agriculture Policy, 2000; and National Water Policy, 2002. These policy measures promoted establishment of various organizations or empowered already existing organizations for the management of various sub-sectors of natural resources and environment.

The National Environment Policy 2006 (NEP 2006) was approved by the Union cabinet in May 2006 and adopted by the MoEF. It builds on existing policies and does not replace them. The NEP sets broad guidelines that should be pursued to ensure sustainable development. It is intended to be a guide to action; in regulatory reform, programmes, and projects for environmental conservation; and in review and enactment of legislation by agencies of the central, state, and local governments.

PROBLEMATIC AREAS

Despite several policy measures adopted in the last more than thirty-five years, the problems of excessive resource depletion and environmental pollution still remain critical. Either at implementation or enforcement stage, the effect of the laws and policies has not been translated into reality, resulting in continued deterioration of ecology and environment. Some of the reasons for underperformance of government measures may be indifferent public attitude, insufficient trained manpower, and lack of coordination among authorities. The following examples highlight some of these problematic areas.

- Low level of awareness and education, lack of civic sense, poor willingness, and 'not in my backyard attitude' of people are the crucial problems in the country. People often complain about government measures but hardly contribute to improve the conditions in their neighbourhood. Due to lack of public participation, haphazard vehicle parking, open air defecation, spitting and littering, etc., are common features in the country.
- The subject of environment has been an integral part of the civil engineering discipline since long (Chadderton 1995). As the scope expanded and demand grew, knowledge from some other disciplines such as social sciences and physical sciences has been included. While it is easier to gain knowledge about the issues, finding a solution for the problem requires expertise, which is lacking in the country. Even the government organizations lack expert manpower, and often specialized jobs are outsourced to external experts, making the organizations concerned dependent on others.

- Lack of coordination among various government departments, mismanagement or misappropriation of resources, and sometimes lack of funds may lead to poor implementation and enforcement of regulations and result in widespread non-compliance. While the SPCBs have increased revenues through the 'water cess' over the years, there have been frequent complaints pertaining to the inability of the state governments to adequately return those revenues to the SPCBs. The resulting effect on enforcement and monitoring has been noticeable. Although the SPCBs had filed thousands of cases for prosecution under various Acts, only about 10 per cent of them have been decided.
- Industries are reluctant to submit the environmental audit reports as they fear undue harassment and prosecution by the authorities. They often try to circumvent the law by other means, which could be unfair. In case of a dispute, cumbersome court proceedings and lack of transparency give rise to non-compliance, and at times to corruption, which makes regulations ineffective. Out of hundreds of thousands of industries in India, only few thousands submit environmental audit reports. There is hardly any feedback to the industries that submit these reports as most of the reports are not even checked by authorities.
- Most of the measures are curative in nature and the authorities have hardly focused on preventive measures. It is always better to reduce the environmental load *a priori* rather than handling it after it causes substantial damage. Mere establishing the facilities for environmental protection is not enough and their proper functioning should be ensured by the officers in charge.

CONCLUSIONS AND RECOMMENDATIONS

The state of India's environment has been deteriorating due to large-scale developmental activities and non-compliance of regulations. In order to deal with resource depletion and environmental degradation, an efficient environmental management is necessary in the country. However, it is to be noted that any developmental activity will always cause some damage to the environment. Thus, conflicts between environment and development cannot be eliminated altogether. Therefore, any ameliorative measure should focus on minimizing the negative effects of development process. India has enough legislative and administrative infrastructure to handle environmental problems, but enforcement and compliance are still major challenges.

Although MoEF is the nodal agency in the administrative structure of the government to look after the environmental management programme, there are several other ministries with similar responsibility, for example, Ministry of

Water Resources, Ministry of New and Renewable Energy for Development of Clean Energy, Ministry of Rural Development for Watershed Development, and so on. If more than one organization is involved in performing the same activity, it could lead to misuse of public resources and delays in decision-making. This also confuses the polluters and sufferers who do not know which rules should be followed and which authority to be approached. For avoiding duplication and conflicts among various authorities, it is desirable to strengthen the implementation of the existing pollution laws and increase the coordination among the authorities.

Many environmental problems in the country are the result of lack of education and awareness among the people. At present, people assume that environmental management is solely the responsibility of the government. Environmental education and awareness require significant capacity-building in all the sub-sectors of environment and at all levels, such as schools, colleges, community, and government. People should be educated through awareness and training programmes about the importance of simple measures such as saving water, methods of rainwater harvesting, sustainable use of groundwater resources, and reuse and recycling of wastewater for irrigation and gardening. The authorities concerned should ensure that the concepts of environmental sanitation and personal hygiene are adopted by the masses.

In the future, both due to stringent regulations and higher levels of public awareness, possibility of more litigation on environmental issues is high. Given the present state of the Indian judiciary, it may not be able to handle the load of additional court cases, and hence it is necessary to strengthen the legal institutions. Since most of the environment litigations are connected with the infrastructure sector, delay in deciding court cases may hinder the development process. Therefore, for speedy disposal of environment-related cases, separate courts may be created and expert opinions of environment professionals should be made admissible in the courts of law.

Government authorities should prevent the public from polluting the environment and ensure effective enforcement of legislation. They need to find innovative methods of involving the public in safeguarding the resources. The public, in turn, should reciprocate to the government's efforts by following the rules of health and hygiene and reporting the instances of degradation and pollution of resources. Authorities should find ways to prevent or minimize soil erosion through measures such as preventing the felling of trees and adopting afforestation programmes in the country, particularly in vulnerable areas such as the Western Ghats. Stringent regulation and monitoring of no-development zones and green zones must also be undertaken to prevent further deterioration of land resources.

There is a need to accelerate the ongoing projects and promote new projects on *clean development mechanism* and *ozone deleting substances' phase out* programmes. Proactive role of industry and authorities on issues of trade and environment would benefit the industry and the country and increase the capability to compete in the global market. Using technical and economic measures jointly would immensely benefit the environment. Some measures like fuel-efficient design of automobile engines, recycling of wastewater, and use of low-waste technologies are required to reduce pollution. For example, in most of the conventional irrigation schemes, up to 60 per cent of water is lost on its way from the source to the plant. Another large part is lost in the form of evaporation from the flooded fields. This could be minimized by promoting drip and sprinkler irrigation systems. Similarly, use of cleaner fuels such as compressed natural gas, low sulphur diesel, and biofuel-blended fossil fuels in vehicles help to reduce air pollution. Economic measures such as tradable pollution discharge permits, incentives for achievers of standards, and penalties for defaulters of pollution norms should be promoted further. In addition, proper pricing of resources can minimize their misuse and wasteful use.

REFERENCES

Chadderton, R.A. (1995), 'Should Engineers Counteract Environmental Extremism?', *Journal of Professional Issues in Engineering Education and Practice*, 121(2): 79–83.

Dreyer, Louise, Hauschild Michael, and Schierbeck Jens (2005), 'A Framework for Social Life Cycle Impact Assessment', *International Journal of LCA*, 10(6): 88–97.

EIA (2007), Energy Information Administration of the US, available at http://www.eia.doe.gov/emeu/ cabs/ russenv.html

Fu, H. (2002), 'Life Cycle Assessment on Consumer Environmental Behaviours', Proceedings of the Fifth International Conference on EcoBalance, November, Japan.

Ministry of Environment and Forests (MoEF) (2000), Notification on 'Municipal Solid Wastes (Management and Handling) Rules 2000', Ministry of Environment and Forests, Government of India.

——— (2006), *National Environment Policy, 2006*. Ministry of Environment and Forests, Government of India.

Sharma, Vinod K. and Peiter Van Beukering (1997), 'Environmental and Economic Policy Analysis of Wastepaper Trade and Recycling in India', *Resources, Conservation and Recycling*, 21(1): 55–70.

Sharma, Vinod K. (1998), 'Gaps in Environmental Policy: A Focus on General and Air Pollution Problems', *Environmental Policy and Law*, 28(2): 90–6.

——— (ed.) (2007), 'Institutional Reforms in Environmental Law and Policy in India and Russia', in the Proceedings of the Indo-Russian Seminar on Institutional Reforms and Development Units in Transitional Economies, organized by Russian Academy of Sciences, Indian Council for Social Science Research and Indira Gandhi Institute of Development Research (IGIDR), Mumbai, p. 33.

14

Emerging Energy Insecurity

The Indian Dimension

B. Sudhakara Reddy and Hippu Salk Kristle Nathan

THE CONTEXT

Energy security fulfils a country's energy needs in a sustainable manner. Its role is important since energy is closely linked to economic opportunity, empowerment, and security—both internal and external. The correlation between energy and development suggests a two-way causation. Higher energy use enhances production, promotes economic growth, and improves standard of living—all symbols of development—which in turn leads to greater energy consumption. A strong nexus exists between energy scarcity and poverty. Countries with low per capita energy use have adverse Human Development Indicators (HDI) such as low life expectancy, low literacy, and low per capita income (Reddy 2002). Energy is an essential input in achieving each of the Millennium Development Goals (MDGs) as availability of affordable and sustainable energy services has a multiplier effect on health, education, transport, telecommunications, safe water, and sanitation services, and on investments in and the productivity of income-generating activities in agriculture, industry, and tertiary sectors (Modi et al. 2005). However, consumption and production of energy worldwide play a major role in several sustainability issues such as climate change, depletion of resources, and indoor and local air pollution (Ruijven 2008). In short, for stability—global, national, and internal—and development, the need for energy security is paramount.

Energy security as a policy concept has developed over time. Narrow definitions of energy security are criticized for being only about oil (neglecting other energy carriers), primary fuel (neglecting conversion technologies), imports (neglecting domestic infrastructure), and physical supply (neglecting comparative cost advantages) (Sauter and MacKerron 2008). Belgrave et al. (1987: 2) give an elaborate definition:

Energy security is a state in which consumers and their governments believe, and have reason to believe, that there are adequate reserves and production and distribution facilities available to meet their requirements in the foreseeable future, from sources at home or abroad, at costs which do not put them at a competitive disadvantage or otherwise threaten their well-being.

We conceptualize energy security as both supply-side as well as demand-side security. Supply security for a country means its ability for efficient generation and production of energy from diversified sources, which include renewables. This requires development of new energy sources and ensures ownership or control of such sources within and outside the country. Demand-side energy security means universal provision of energy services, which are accessible and affordable to consumers. Demand security involves equitable and efficient distribution and effective conversion from final to useful energy through appropriate practices and end-use technologies. Both supply and demand security necessitate environmental compliance which otherwise cannot be sustained in the long run.

Energy security has an international character. As a concern, it first surfaced in 1973, with the oil embargo by the Organization of the Petroleum Exporting Countries (OPEC). The initial stage of energy security was linked to the volatile Middle East. However, over time, other issues like regional cooperation and cross-border trade gained prominence. Recently, energy security has drawn high priority policy attention stirred by high oil prices and geopolitical tensions (Kruyt et al. 2009). The incessant spurt in oil prices, until the end of 2008, is due to rapid increase in energy demand in Asia and underinvestment in energy supply and concerns about stability of countries where significant oil and gas reserves are concentrated (Clingendael International Energy Programme [CIEP] 2004). For example, geopolitical tensions such as the Iraq war in 2003 and gas dispute between Russia and Ukraine in 2005–6 led to supply disruptions (Löschel et al. 2010a).

NEED FOR ENERGY SECURITY

Though energy security is a high priority issue on the political and scientific agenda of industrialized and developing economies (Löschel et al. 2010b), it is more of a concern for the latter for the following reasons. First, developing countries account for about two-thirds of increase in energy use and for three-fourths of increase in CO$_2$ emissions during 2003–30 (International Energy Agency [IEA] 2005). Second, the prevailing *energy poverty* in these countries calls for both supply-side and demand-side security. Two billion people from these countries have no or unreliable access to modern energy forms. And for the poor among those who have access, the recent increase in energy prices has put pressure on its affordability (Ruijven 2008). Third, developing countries are a subject of concern worldwide for their high climate-change vulnerability. In the coming decades, it is predicted that billions of people from these regions will face shortages of water and food, and greater risks to health and life as a result of climate change (United Nations Framework Convention on Climate Change [UNFCCC] 2007). Last, but not the least, these countries, being late entrants to the process of industrialization and urbanization, struggle for economic growth to meet the basic needs of the people and fight against poverty (Reddy and Assenza 2009a). Hence, development is the first priority for these countries and so there is no option but to use more energy irrespective of its climate consequences. So, the energy security policy for developing countries needs careful appraisal.

Energy security in India remains a complex and multifaceted challenge, with insecurity at both supply and demand ends. On supply side, India is heavily dependent on world oil markets as more than 70 per cent of the oil consumed in India is imported, indicating a high strain on foreign exchange reserves (British Petroleum [BP] 2008). India also suffers from energy deficit of 12.3 per cent (Central Electricity Authority [CEA] 2006). As per the estimates of IEA (2007a), India will be ranked as the third largest emitter of CO$_2$ in the world by 2015 and the third largest oil importer by 2030, behind China and the US. Nearly 0.4 billion people in India—that is, 45.1 per cent rural and 7.8 per cent urban households—do not have access to electricity (IEA [2007a], National Sample Survey Organisation [NSSO] [2007]). There is an imperative need to reduce dependence on fossil fuel, to secure supply of adequate eco-friendly alternatives, and improve the energy infrastructure to provide quality and reliable energy services to the needy at affordable price.

The present chapter develops a framework for energy security of India. First, it presents the energy supply and demand situation in the country under different scenarios. Then it quantifies energy security for India with the help of different indicators for energy security available in the literature. In the process, it develops a two-dimensional measure to assess energy insecurity. Finally, broad contours to achieve supply- as well as demand-side energy security are discussed. The chapter concludes with specific recommendations on policies to be adopted.

INDIA'S ENERGY SCENE

Recently, IEA (2007a) has studied the energy demand for India under Reference Scenario (RS) and Alternative Policy Scenario (APS).[1] Table 14.1 gives the energy demand, electricity generation, and CO$_2$ emissions under the RS and APS. Table 14.2 gives the data on final energy consumption by fuel types and the sectoral composition under two scenarios.

In the reference scenario, India will remain heavily dependent on coal—produced mostly indigenously—constituting half of the primary energy mix. Coal will dominate electricity generation with around 70 per cent share. Oil will account for one-fourth of India's primary fuel demand in 2030, which is driven mostly by the transportation sector demand that increases its share from 33 per cent in 2005 to 54 per cent in 2030. Natural gas, being a marginal fuel now, registers a

---

[1] The RS assumes that demographic growth, economic development, and energy prices would continue to influence the present patterns of demand and supply. The APS, on the contrary, controls the business as usual growth in the energy demand for reasons of energy security or environmental sustainability, which includes climate-change concerns. APS encompasses the policies and practices that consist of efficiency and emission standardization, use of alternative fuels and clean technologies, and demand-side management options.

Table 14.1 Energy Demand, Electricity Generation, and CO_2 Emissions under Reference Scenario (RS) and Alternative Policy Scenario (APS)

Source	2005	Reference Scenario (RS)			Alternative Policy Scenario (APS)			Change (APS~RS) in 2030 (%)
		2015	2030	AGR*	2015	2030	AGR*	
Total Primary Energy Demand (MTOE)								
Coal	208	330	620	4.5	289	411	2.8	−33.7
Oil	129	188	328	3.8	173	272	3.0	−17.1
Gas	29	48	93	4.8	47	89	4.6	−4.3
Nuclear	5	16	33	8.3	19	47	9.9	41.9
Hydro	9	13	22	3.9	17	32	5.3	42.3
Biomass and Waste	158	171	194	0.8	168	211	1.2	8.5
Other Renewables	1	4	9	11.7	6	21	15.8	145.5
TOTAL	537	770	1,299	3.6	719	1,082	2.8	−16.7
Electricity Generation (TWh)								
Coal	480	889	1,958	5.8	735	1,261	3.9	−35.6
Oil	31	35	31	0.0	33	29	−0.2	−5.6
Gas	62	133	292	6.4	123	246	5.6	−15.6
Nuclear	17	60	128	8.3	71	182	9.9	41.9
Hydro	100	154	258	3.9	200	368	5.3	42.3
Biomass and Waste	2	6	29	11.5	8	79	16	169.8
Wind	6	43	69	10.2	50	124	12.8	79.0
Geothermal	0	0	1	–	0	1	–	–
Solar	0	0	8	35.2	1	15	39	100.7
Tide and Wave	0	0	0	–	0	0	–	–
TOTAL	699	1,322	2,774	5.7	1,221	2,305	4.9	−16.9
CO_2 Emissions (Mt)								
Coal	774	1,226	2,284	4.4	1,069	1,544	2.8	−32.4
Oil	312	475	829	4.0	436	678	3.2	−18.2
Gas	62	104	201	4.8	102	193	4.7	−4.0
TOTAL	1,147	1,804	3,314	4.3	1,607	2,415	3.0	−27.1

Source: IEA (2007a).

Note: *AGR is Average Annual Compounded Growth Rate (in %) during 2005 to 2030.

Table 14.2 Sectoral Consumption under Reference Scenario (RS) and Alternative Policy Scenario (APS)

Source	2005	Reference Scenario (RS)			Alternative Policy Scenario (APS)			Change (APS~RS) in 2030 (%)
		2015	2030	AGR*	2015	2030	AGR*	
Total Final Consumption (MTOE)								
Coal	38	63	119	4.7	58	86	3.4	−27.5
Oil	106	155	287	4.1	142	236	3.2	−17.8
Gas	14	19	38	4.1	19	40	4.4	6.9
Electricity	41	82	181	6.1	79	163	5.7	−10.2
Biomass and Waste	157	168	178	0.5	164	166	0.2	−6.6
Other Renewables	0	0	1	–	1	8	–	–
TOTAL	356	487	804	3.3	463	699	2.7	−13.0

(*Continued*)

Table 14.2 *Continued*

Source	2005	Reference Scenario (RS)			Alternative Policy Scenario (APS)			Change (APS~RS) in 2030 (%)
		2015	2030	AGR*	2015	2030	AGR*	
Industry (MTOE)								
Coal	29	55	111	5.4	50	79	4.0	−28.3
Oil	19	27	38	2.7	25	34	2.3	−10.2
Gas	5	7	10	2.7	7	9	2.4	−7.8
Electricity	18	39	83	6.3	38	78	6.0	−6.2
Biomass and Waste	27	29	30	0.4	30	33	0.8	9.7
Other Renewables	0	0	0	–	0	0	–	–
TOTAL	99	157	271	4.1	149	234	3.5	−13.9
Transport (MTOE)								
Oil	35	63	154	6.1	54	115	4.8	−25.2
Biofuels	0	1	2	22.9	3	8	30.1	–
Other Fuels	2	3	7	5.9	4	13	8.8	95.8
TOTAL	37	66	162	6.1	61	136	5.4	−16.3
Residential, Service, and Agriculture (MTOE)								
Coal	6	6	6	−0.0	5	5	−0.7	−14.9
Oil	27	35	45	2.1	33	39	1.5	−13.0
Gas	1	2	6	8.5	1	5	7.8	−14.3
Electricity	20	39	92	6.3	37	78	5.6	−14.9
Biomass and Waste	130	138	146	0.5	131	125	−0.2	−14.3
Other Renewables	0	0	1	–	1	8	–	–
TOTAL	183	219	295	1.9	210	260	1.4	−12.0
Non-energy Use (MTOE)								
TOTAL	37	45	75	2.9	43	70	2.6	−6.6

Source: IEA (2007a).

Note: *AGR is Average Annual Compounded Growth Rate (in %) during 2005 to 2030.

higher annual average growth rate of 6.4 per cent in power generation and 8.5 per cent in residential, agriculture, and service sectors combined. Among non-fossil sources, nuclear power capacity is projected to increase from 3 GW to 17 GW during 2005–30. This is below the level targeted by the government, which reflects India's difficulties in constructing nuclear power plants and its exclusion from international trade in nuclear power plants and materials (IEA 2007a). Though hydropower output more than doubles, its share in power generation will fall from 14 per cent in 2005 to 9 per cent in 2030 because of the socio-environmental concerns of large dams and resulting displacement. The share of biomass will fall in primary energy demand from 30 per cent to 15 per cent during the same period. Even though biomass fuels presently provide 72 per cent of the domestic energy and 90 per cent of all rural energy needs (The Energy and Resources Institute [TERI] 2006), in future, they get substituted as the

availability and affordability of modern fuels improve in rural areas and among the urban poor. This is evident from the fact that the share of biomass declines from 70 per cent to below 50 per cent. Among the renewable sources, wind registers a significant growth, with its share in electricity generation rising from just under 1 per cent to 2.5 per cent.

In final energy consumption, the transport sector will increase its share from 10 per cent to 20 per cent during 2005–30. This higher consumption in transportation comes from high demand for road mobility, thereby vehicle ownership, by households with increase in income (Asian Development Bank [ADB] 2006). Residential sector has a negative growth in energy share as households continue to switch away from traditional biomass to modern fuels, which are more efficient (IEA 2007a). The industry sector registers a positive growth with greater use of coal and electricity, which will increase their shares in sectoral energy consumption from 30 per cent to 40 per cent and from 18 per cent to 30 per cent, respectively.

Under the alternative policy scenario, there is reduction in demand by about one-sixth for primary energy and electricity generation in 2030 as compared to reference scenario. The corresponding decrease in CO_2 emissions is 27 per cent. There is a reduction in the share of all the conventional fossil fuel resources in primary energy in 2030, with share of coal going down by one-third and so is coal-related CO_2 emission. This is achieved through efficiency improvement of coal-based plants through renovation and modernization and development of new technologies. The electricity supply improves not only because of efficient production but also reduction in transmission and distribution losses. The demand also reduces because of efficiency improvements in appliances and lighting and air-conditioning equipments. Similarly, introduction of emission standards in vehicles and expanded use of biofuels and compressed natural gas (CNG) and improved public transport system bring a reduction of 17 per cent in share of oil. Unlike coal and oil, natural gas increases its share in final energy due to its high quality, convenience of use, and environmental benefits. Among non-fossil fuels, nuclear power is clearly emerging as an option. Both hydro and nuclear energy will command more than 40 per cent increase in demand under APS in 2030 compared to RS. Biomass use increases in industry and transport sector for its use in combined heat and power plants (CHP) and production of biofuels, respectively. The share of other renewable sources, a category that includes wind, solar, geothermal, tidal, and wave energy, will increase in primary energy as a result of policies to control pollution, lower green house gas emissions, and thereby abate climate change. Among solar, bio, and wind-based power generation, solar has the highest average annual growth rate, close to 40 per cent, followed by bio-power and wind power, which will grow at 16 per cent and 13 per cent, respectively.

QUANTIFYING ENERGY SECURITY OF INDIA

In literature, there are multiple measures for energy security, and there is no one ideal indicator. Energy security indicators are highly context-specific and are based on notions of diversity, import dependency, political stability, market liquidity, etc. (Kruyt et al. 2009). Some indicators address just one aspect of security whereas others capture several aspects in a single aggregated index. Here, multiple indicators are considered for broader understanding.

Reserves-to-Production Ratio

The reserves-to-production ratio (R/P) is the ratio of the amount of a resource known to be economically recoverable (proven reserves) to the amount of resource used in

Table 14.3 Reserves to Production Ratio for the Fossil Fuels

Source	Proven Reserves		Production		R/P (years)
	Value (MTOE)	World Share (%)	Value (MTOE)	World Share (%)	
Coal	22150.2	7.1	194.3	5.8	114.0
Oil	747.3	0.5	36.1	0.9	20.7
Natural Gas	979.0	0.6	27.5	1.0	35.6

Source: BP (2009).

one year at the current rate.[2] Table 14.3 gives an account of R/P ratio for coal, oil, and gas in India in 2008 and its world share. Even though India is a major source for coal having 7.1 per cent of the world reserves, it has only 0.5 per cent of oil and 0.6 per cent of gas reserves. This is evident from the low R/P ratios for oil and gas (BP 2009).

Diversity Indicators—Shannon Index and Herfindhal–Hirschman Index

Diversity may primarily relate to diversity in suppliers or fuel types. The indicators, based on notion of diversity, have their share of admirers (Jansen et al. 2004; Asia Pacific Energy Research Centre [APERC] 2007), critics (Stirling 1993; IEA 2007b), and applications (Grubb et al. 2005; Li et al. 2008). The two most commonly used diversity indices are given below.

$$Shannon\ Index\ (SI) = -\sum_f p_f \ln P_f \qquad (14.1)$$

$$Herfindhal–Hirschman\ Index\ (HHI) = \sum_f p_f^2 \qquad (14.2)$$

where p_f is the fuel share of fuel f in total energy mix or the market share of supplier f. The higher the value of SI, or lower the value of HHI, the greater is the diversity. The additive inverse of HHI is used to bring it to the same intuition as SI; that is, higher the value, the better it is. The diversity indices for fuel types in the base year (2005) and the future year (2030) for both RS and APS are shown in Figure 14.1. India's fuel type diversity increases under alternative scenario, whereas in reference case it stagnates or declines.

Import Dependence

Import dependency measures are considered important given the security of external supply in question (Coq and Paltseva 2009; Kruyt et al. 2009). However, in liberalized

---

[2] This is applicable to all natural resources, and most commonly applied to fossil fuels. This indicator is too simplistic as future production is likely to change and there is ambiguity with reserve estimates.

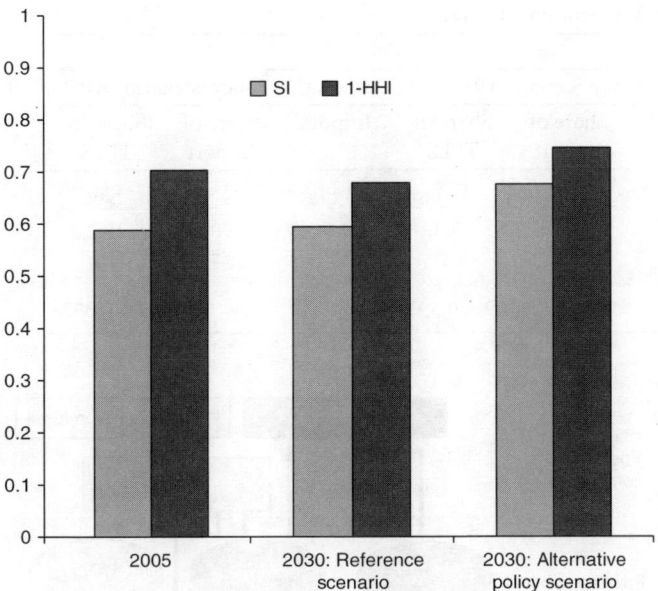

Figure 14.1   Fuel Type Diversity in India: Shannon Index (SI) and Herfindhal-Hirschman Index (HHI)

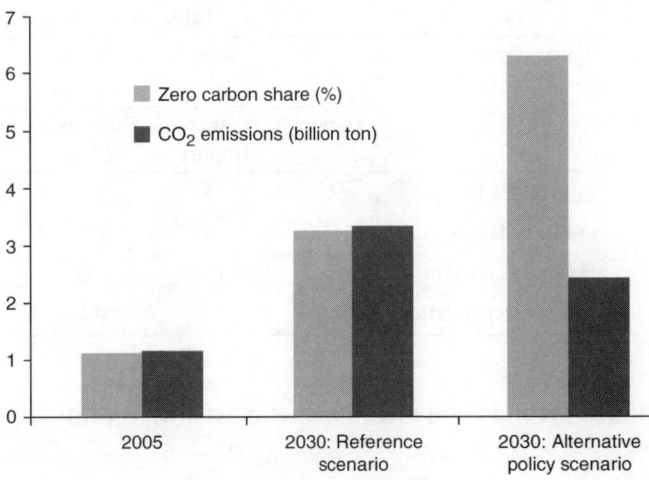

Source: Adapted from IEA (2007a).

Figure 14.2   Zero Carbon Share in Total Primary Energy and CO_2 Emissions

market environments, particularly for coal and oil, the notion of import dependency is considered inappropriate (IEA 2007b). Some examples of application of import dependency are Alhajji and Williams (2003), where the authors have used import of oil relative to its consumption, and APERC (2007), where economy's import dependence is weighted with its fuel diversity. A simple measure of import dependency can be formulated as under

$$Import\ dependence, ID = \sum_f m_f p_f \qquad (14.3)$$

where m_f is the import share of fuel f.

The import dependence of India for RS and APS is calculated for fossil fuels (Table 14.4). It is clear that India will continue to have high import dependency even under APS.

Share of Zero Carbon Fuels

This indicator of energy security is important with regard to climate change. It is calculated as the combined share of renewable and nuclear energies in the total primary energy (APERC 2007). Figure 14.2 shows this indicator along with the CO_2 emission in both the scenarios. It is evident that as the share of zero carbon fuel increases, the CO_2 emissions will decrease.

IEA's Two Energy Security Indices

IEA (2007b) has developed two indicators to measure energy security, namely, price component of energy security

(*Energy Security Index$_{price}$* or *ESI$_{price}$*) and physical availability component of energy security (*Energy Security Index volume* or *ESI$_{volume}$*). *ESI$_{price}$* is given by

$$ESI_{price} = \sum_f \left(ESMC_{pol-f} * \frac{p_f}{TPES} \right) \qquad (14.4)$$

where TPES is total primary energy supply and p_f is the fuel share of fuel f. *ESMC* stands for the Energy Security Market Concentration measure, which is based on Herfindhal–Hirschman Index (HHI),[3] that is expressed as

$$ESMC = \sum_i S_{if}^2 \qquad (14.5)$$

where S_{if} is the share of each supplier i in the market of fuel f defined by its net export potential. To account for political stability of the exporting country, *ESMC* is adjusted as

$$ESMC_{pol} = \sum_i \left(r_i^* S_{if}^2 \right) \qquad (14.6)$$

where r_i is the political risk rating of country i, as measured through World Bank's *Worldwide Governance Indicators* (World Bank 2006).[4]

---

[3] Herfindhal–Hirschman Index (HHI), which is also known as the Simpson diversity index, is a well-established measure of market concentration, which is calculated as the sum of the square of the individual market shares of all the participants. This is an elaborate measure as it takes into account both the number of firms in the market and their respective market shares. HHI is used by governments as a tool to assess market power or concentration.

[4] The Worldwide Governance Indicators devised for over 200 countries were first developed in the late 1990s and have been continually

Table 14.4   Import Dependency for Fossil Fuels

Source	2005			2030					
				Reference Scenario (RS)			Alternative Policy Scenario (APS)		
	Import	Share of Import	Share in TPES	Import	Share of Import	Share in TPES	Import	Share of Import	Share in TPES
Coal (MTCE)	36	12	38.7	247	25	47.7	144	23	38.0
Oil (mb/day)	1.9	70	24.0	6.0	92	25.3	4.9	90	25.1
Natural Gas (bcm)	6	17	5.4	61	55	7.1	56	53	8.2
Import Dependency	$ID = 0.224$			$ID = 0.391$			$ID = 0.357$		

The second component of energy security is expressed as

$$ESI_{volume} = \frac{Pipe\ imp_{(gas)oil\text{-}indexed}}{TPES} \qquad (14.7)$$

where $Pipe\ imp_{(gas)\ oil\text{-}indexed}$ is the net import of gas via pipeline purchased through oil-indexed contracts.[5] The aforementioned method is schematically presented in Figure 14.3.

For India, we have constructed ESI_{price}(Table 14.5).[6] The $ESMC_{pol}$ for coal, oil, and gas in international market is obtained from IEA (2007b), which calculates the same taking the net export potential of five most important participants in the market,[7] and the political risk factor for the same countries. For the reference year, since the whole of the natural gas import is from the Middle East with long-term contracts, the whole of gas can be considered as oil-indexed. It is assumed that by 2030, India will have a 50 per cent share

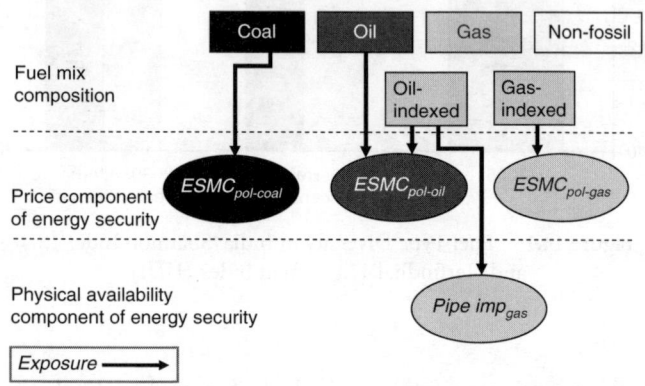

Source: Adapted from IEA (2007a).

Figure 14.3   Components of Energy Security

of liberalized gas market with a 2 per cent annual progressive shift away from long-term oil-indexed contracts to gas-based transactions.[8] The ESI_{price} for India is 3,710 in 2005 and 5,108 and 4,815 in 2030 under RS and APS, respectively.

Demand-side Security Measure

There are multiple approaches to measure energy poverty or deprivation, that is, shortfall from the demand or need.[9] With the goal of universalization of energy services for basic needs, we conceptualize a multidimensional measure of energy insecurity by quantifying deprivations in different dimensions. The two basic needs are identified to be household cooking and lighting.[10] Accordingly, a two-dimensional energy insecurity index (*EII*) has been constructed in Cartesian space with origin *O* as complete

revised and improved. This has six dimensions of governance, namely, voice and accountability, political stability and absence of violence, government effectiveness, regulatory quality, rule of law, control of corruption. 'Political stability and absence of violence' and 'regulatory quality' are taken to formulate r_i.

[5] Natural gas is either priced competitively or indexed to oil. When indexed to oil, it is effectively susceptible to the energy security price risk in the oil market.

[6] Volume-based energy security index is not attempted here because the pipeline-based gas import for India is difficult to estimate as all the three pipeline projects (Iran–Pakistan–India pipeline, Turkmenistan–Afghanistan–Pakistan–India pipeline, and Myanmar–Bangladesh–India pipeline) are full of uncertainties due to the unstable political climate in the linking countries, and the government plan documents do not project any gas supply from this mode in the near future.

[7] We have followed the case where OPEC has been considered as a single participant in the market. Russia follows OPEC in oil export. The last three positions are filled by Norway, Mexico, Kazakhstan, and Angola at different time points between 2005 and 2030. For coal, the five major exporters are Australia, China, Indonesia, South Africa, and Colombia. In the case of gas, the top five positions are filled by the following seven countries at different points of time: Algeria, Qatar, Oman, Malaysia, Nigeria, Norway, and Indonesia.

[8] With diversification of supplier countries and recent instances of India's involvement in spot LNG trades, this seems to be a workable assumption.

[9] For different measures of energy poverty, see Pachauri et al. (2004).

[10] There can be basic needs of energy other than that in cooking and lighting. However, it is reasonable to assume household deprivation of energy as indicative of overall energy poverty. Nevertheless, the current methodology is generic enough to include other dimensions of energy deprivations.

Table 14.5 Energy Security Index (ESI) for India

Source	2005				2030			
					Reference Scenario (RS)		Alternative Policy Scenario (APS)	
	$ESMC_{pol}$	Share in TPES (%)	Exposure (%)	$ESMC_{pol}$	Share in TPES (%)	Exposure	Share in TPES (%)	Exposure
Coal	3015	38.7	38.7	3684	47.7	47.7	38.0	38.0
Oil	8650	24.0	29.4	11439	25.3	28.8	25.1	29.3
Gas	4270	5.4	0	1557	7.1	3.6	8.2	4.1
	$ESI_{price} = 3710$				$ESI_{price} = 5108$		$ESI_{price} = 4815$	

security, that is, no deprivation, and point of complete insecurity, I, where deprivation is maximum. In cooking dimension, deprivation is calculated as share of households deprived from modern fuels, that is, liquefied petroleum gas (LPG), kerosene, biogas, and electricity. In lighting dimension, deprivation is calculated as share of households without access to electricity. EII is calculated using displaced ideal (DI) technique, which is based on the notion of 'closer to ideal being better'.[11] The distance from the ideal (here origin representing complete security is the ideal) can be computed using normalized Minkowski distance from origin.[12] This is in line with Human Poverty Index (HPI) of the United Nations Development Programme (UNDP).[13] For n dimensions, EII can be expressed as:

$$EII = \left(\frac{\sum (w_j x_j)^\alpha}{\sum w_j^\alpha} \right)^{\frac{1}{\alpha}} ; j = 1, \ldots, n \qquad (14.8)$$

where x_j is the deprivation in each dimension j, and w_j is the corresponding weight. α can be termed as 'Benthamite–Rawlsian factor' as with minimum, that is, $\alpha = 1$, (14.8) corresponds to Benthamite or 'average' rule where the energy insecurity is average deprivation across dimensions and with maximum, that is, $\alpha \to \infty$, (14.8) reduces to Rawlsian or 'maximax' rule where the energy insecurity is identified with the dimension having maximum deprivation. Here

$\alpha = 2$ is considered.[14] For the present case $n = 2$, and with equal weights to both dimensions,[15]

$$EII = \sqrt{\frac{(x_1)^2 + (x_2)^2}{2}} \qquad (14.9)$$

The analysis has been done for the seventeen major states.[16] Because of the distinct pattern in energy use in urban and rural areas (Reddy et al. 2009), EII is calculated separately, EII_{urban} and EII_{rural}, and the states are ranked accordingly (see Table 14.6). The composite EII_{compo} for the rural and urban region is calculated by taking population weighted average of both the regions.

$$EII_{compo} = P_{urban} * EII_{urban} + P_{rural} * EII_{rural} \qquad (14.10)$$

where p_{urban} and p_{rural} are population shares of urban and rural areas respectively. The EII_{compo} of India is 0.579 with $EII_{urban} = 0.236$ and $EII_{rural} = 0.711$.

The energy deprivations in cooking and lighting for households for different states are plotted for rural and urban areas in Figures 14.4 and 14.5 respectively. The straight lines represent the overall value for India. Punjab, Haryana, Gujarat, Maharashtra, Andhra Pradesh, and Tamil Nadu are the states having lower deprivation level in cooking and lighting both for rural and urban areas (these states lie in the bottom left quadrant). This is also evident from their lower value of EII and higher ranks (Table 14.6). Similarly, the most deprived states (the top right quadrant) such as Bihar, Orissa, Uttar Pradesh, Jharkhand, West Bengal, and Rajasthan score poorly in EII and occupy lower ranks.

[11] The DI technique was introduced by Zeleny (1974) in connection with multiple criteria analysis. In a recent work, Nathan et al. (2008) and Nathan and Reddy (2010) have applied this technique in the context of Human Development Index and Sustainable Development Indicators respectively.

[12] Subramanian (2004) has used the Minkowski distance function to the Foster et al. (1984) class of poverty measures. In a more recent work, Mishra and Nathan (2008) have used the same function to introduce general class of human development measures.

[13] There are two HPI measures. HPI-1 measures the deprivations in the three dimensions of long and healthy life, knowledge, and decent standard of living. HPI-2 measures deprivations in the same dimensions as HPI-1 and also captures social exclusion (UNDP 2007a).

[14] In HPI calculation, $\alpha = 3$ is used. However, $\alpha = 2$ corresponds to Euclidian distance, that is, common understanding of distance. Plus, $\alpha = 2$ still maintains higher weight to more deprived dimension.

[15] Though cooking is a more energy-intensive than lighting, the latter has been given equal weight as the former because lighting is highly correlated to productive hours in the household, that is, study hours of children and working hours of adults (Reddy et al. 2009).

[16] Major state definition follows the convention of NSSO (2007), which refers to states of India that had a population of 20 million or more as per Census 2001. Together, these states account for 95 per cent of the total population.

Table 14.6   Energy Insecurity Index for Indian States

State	EII_{rural}	Rank (rural)	EII_{urban}	Rank (urban)	Rural–Urban Insecurity Gap	Urban Pop. Share (%)	EII_{compo}	Rank (overall)
Punjab	0.509	1	0.118	1	0.392	33.95	0.376	1
Maharashtra	0.609	7	0.149	3	0.459	42.40	0.414	2
Gujarat	0.574	3	0.172	4	0.402	37.35	0.424	3
Haryana	0.546	2	0.145	2	0.401	29.00	0.430	4
Tamil Nadu	0.602	5	0.210	5	0.393	43.86	0.430	5
Karnataka	0.654	8	0.233	6	0.421	33.98	0.511	6
Andhra Pradesh	0.607	6	0.260	7	0.347	27.08	0.513	7
Kerala	0.591	4	0.395	16	0.196	25.97	0.540	8
Madhya Pradesh	0.709	9	0.300	10	0.409	26.67	0.600	9
Chhattisgarh	0.742	10	0.339	13	0.404	20.08	0.661	10
Rajasthan	0.766	11	0.323	12	0.443	23.38	0.662	11
West Bengal	0.819	12	0.315	11	0.504	28.03	0.678	12
Uttar Pradesh	0.860	15	0.299	9	0.561	20.78	0.744	13
Assam	0.821	13	0.264	8	0.557	12.72	0.750	14
Jharkhand	0.872	16	0.394	15	0.478	22.25	0.765	15
Orissa	0.836	14	0.406	17	0.430	14.97	0.771	16
Bihar	0.941	17	0.358	14	0.582	10.47	0.880	17
All-India	0.711		0.236			27.78	0.579	

Source: NSSO (2007); Census of India (2001).

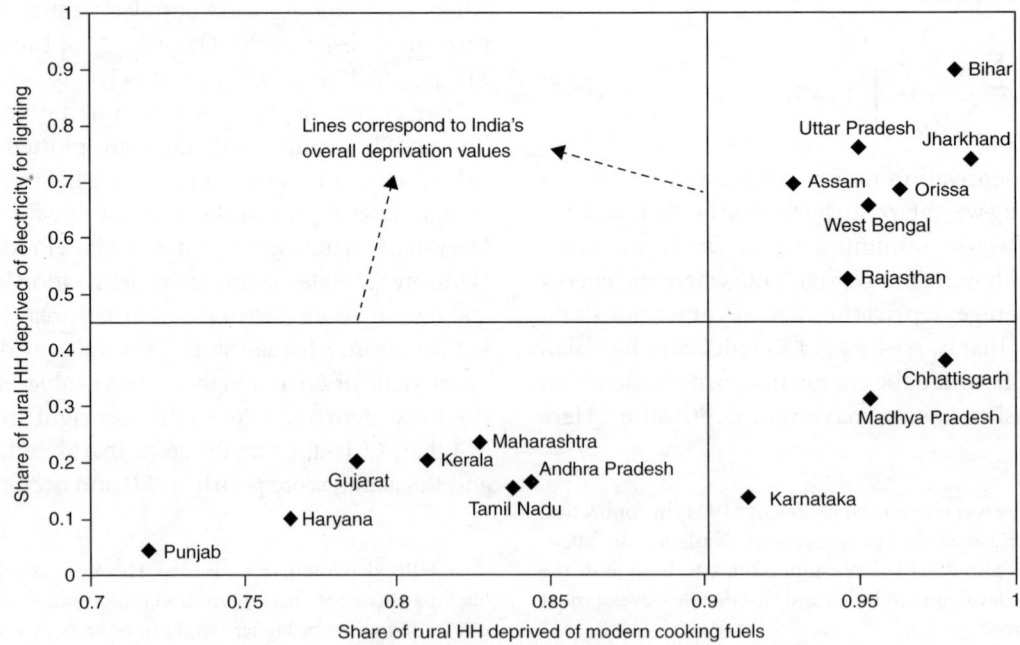

Figure 14.4   Energy Deprivation in Indian States for Rural Areas

Virtually no state in the second quadrant (top left) shows the energy insecurity in cooking as more severe than in lighting. From the positive values of rural–urban insecurity gap, which is expressed as $(EII_{rural} - EII_{urban})$, it is evident that the insecurity is higher in rural areas. Kerala is the only state having energy insecurity in cooking lower than national average in rural areas, but higher in urban areas, symbolizing low urban–rural divide.

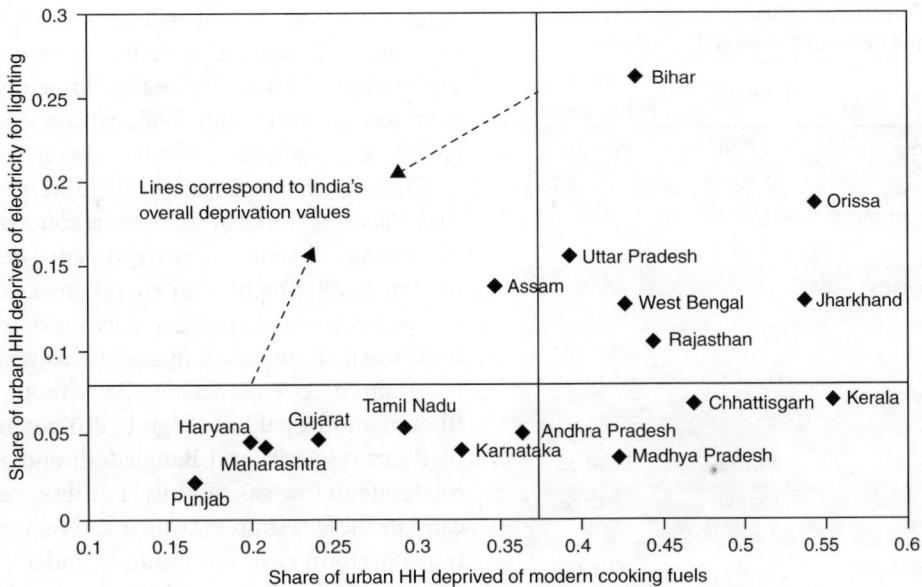

Figure 14.5 Energy Deprivation in Indian States for Urban Areas

The quantification of energy security in both supply and demand shows the need for specific initiatives to attain security on both sides. In comparison to reference scenario, in the alternative policy scenario, India would be better off in terms of cleaner fuel, lower emission, and higher diversity. However, the import dependency indicator and IEA's ESI_{price} show India's continued dependency on the volatile global market. In terms of demand, India has very high insecurity in rural areas compared to its urban counterparts.

ACHIEVING ENERGY SUPPLY SECURITY

Many policymakers seem to equate energy independence with energy security, believing that one will necessarily lead to the other. In a market integrated interdependent world economy, a comprehensive notion of energy security should take into account three principles that supersede the objective of energy independence: energy efficiency, diversity of supply, and global connectedness.

Energy Efficiency

Energy efficiency (EE) is the first strategy to make the best use of the available energy resources. Increasing efficiency in the conversion, delivery, and utilization of energy should be an essential part of a comprehensive national energy policy. Through improved energy efficiency, India can improve balance of payments, strengthen national security, and mitigate the environmental impacts of energy use by reducing emission of both local air pollutants that impact public health,

and greenhouse gases that induce climate change. Increased energy efficiency will help to decrease our vulnerability to oil supply disruptions because of lower energy use and demand. It has been shown that India can reduce about 20 per cent of its energy use through EE improvements (Reddy and Balachandra 2003).

Clean Coal Technologies (CCT): If the government needs to do anything specific on the efficiency front, it has to be with coal as it is the most reliable source of energy for India. However, coal has the dubious distinction of being the most polluting fossil fuel (Massachusetts Institute of Technology [MIT] 2007). Clean coal technologies involve beneficiating coal and efficiency improvement of the existing plants and using advanced technologies like CHP, fluidized bed combustion (FBC), integrated gassification combined cycle (IGCC), and pressurized fluidized bed combustion (PFBC). CCTs are environmentally satisfactory and economically viable. These technologies address the dual crisis of energy poverty and climate change. Even if CCTs are yet to be commercialized with Indian coal, it will be still useful looking at the increasing share of imported coal in India in future.

Diversity of Supply

Under the alternative policy scenario for India, the non-fossil fuel–based energy demand has close to 30 per cent share in the primary energy mix. Renewables not only reduce import dependency and diversify the energy use, but also help abate climate change. The country is well endowed with renewable energy sources and has high technical potential (Table 14.7). The demand of other renewables, which

Table 14.7   Estimated Potential and Cumulative Achievement for Some of the Selected Renewable Energy Technologies

Renewable Technologies	Potential	Cumulative Achievement
Family Type Biogas Plants (in nos)	$120*10^5$	$39.4*10^5$
Solar Photovoltaic Programme (in MW)	50 (per sq. km)	110
Solar Water Heating Systems (in million sq. km)	140	2.15
Solar Cooker (in nos)		$6.17*10^5$
Biopower (Agro Residues & Plantations) (in MW)	16,881	605.8
Wind Power (MW)	45,195.	7,844.52
Small Hydro Power (up to 25 MW) (in MW)	15,000	2,045.61
Cogeneration-bagasse (in MW)	5,000	719.83
Waste to Energy (Urban & Industrial) (in MW)	2,700	55.25
Captive/CHP/Distributed Renewable Power		205.23

Source: Ministry of New and Renewable Energy (2008).

includes wind, solar, geothermal, tidal, and wave energy, is likely to increase at an annual growth rate of 15.8 per cent during 2005–30 (see Table 14.1). Barring a couple of exceptions like solar water heating and wind power, most of the renewable energy technologies in India have fallen inside the 'valley of death', where the cost of production is high and the scale of production is low. The failure is attributed to the fact that the technologies are promoted as one-time demonstration projects and not with the objective of commercialization (Balachandra et al. 2010).

Nuclear Energy: In the alternative policy scenario, nuclear energy experiences close to 10 per cent annual growth in demand. Being clean and not leading to global warming, nuclear energy is a preferred alternative to fossil fuels. As the ongoing bilateral nuclear deals get actualized, India would get imported uranium to expand its nuclear energy programme. Also, in parallel, India has uniquely been developing a nuclear fuel cycle to exploit its reserves of thorium.

GLOBAL CONNECTEDNESS

With less reserve of oil and gas, India has no other option except to import. India is enhancing its supply security by making its global footprint multifaceted through diversification of suppliers' portfolio. *Hydrocarbon Vision 2025* document (Ministry of Petroleum and Natural Gas 2010) promotes investment in equity oil abroad. India's oil and gas companies are aggressively bidding for assets in other countries to gain

access to resources that will help satisfy the needs during the coming decades. Also, India has been upgrading its new exploration and licensing policy, attracting growing interest from foreign companies. Regional cooperation too has been emerging as a solution to India's energy security problem.

Cross-border energy trade:[17] There are other countries in the Asia-Pacific region that share equal concern as India in terms of economic dynamism, environmental degradation, lack of human development, and energy insecurity. Cross-border energy trade can be considered as one of the answers to this. India's neighbouring countries have comparative advantages in certain energy endowments. Being mountainous countries, Bhutan and Nepal have high hydro potential, Pakistan has high gas reserves, and Bangladesh and Afghanistan have moderate to low gas capacity. For its excess demand, India can tap these resources, which can be transacted with low transportation cost. For example, India is tackling its huge power deficit with successful hydroelectricity imports from Bhutan and Nepal (UNDP 2007b). However, similar success is yet to be realized in natural gas pipeline projects.

DEMAND-SIDE ENABLERS

Producing adequate energy always does not ensure energy security. Modern energy services need to be made available to the consumers who should be in a position to accept and afford the same. Given the present resource constraints and the socio-economic disparity among the consumers, it remains a herculean task to provide all the consumers with modern energy services. India's urban–rural divide is apparent from the fact that in rural areas only 14 per cent of the households use LPG for cooking whereas 57 per cent use it in urban areas (NSSO 2007). Similarly, in rural India, 45.1 per cent of people do not have access to electricity, and the corresponding figure for urban areas is 7.7 per cent. Also, there is a strong positive relationship between income and household demand for commercial fuels (Reddy et al. 2009). The rich use energy for luxury whereas the poor remain deprived of basic services. Following are some of the enablers to attain demand-side energy security.

Technology Enablers

Technology sometimes has the answer to the question of empowering vulnerable sections of the society. Mobile

[17] Excess demand on one side and excess supply of energy at the other side of border opens up increased cooperation between neighbouring countries to trade in energy. Cross-border energy trade is carried out with the agenda of creating a win–win situation for both the countries through trade. It brings revenue to the exporting country and reduces the energy poverty of the importing country. It also reduces the energy inequality in the entire region.

communication is one such example. The revolution in this area has made the technology available and affordable to the poor. India's rural areas have abundant biomass resources and there is ample scope for technology innovation based on such resources. The traditional biomass consumption for household cooking and heating must give way to biomass to fuel power plants to produce biogas for cooking and to make biofuels for transport (IEA 2007a). Improvement in technologies of decentralized power generation system can make energy services accessible in remote areas. Research, development, and use of energy-efficient stoves, power-efficient bulbs, and fuel-efficient vehicles can accelerate the process of energy service universalization. The transmission and distribution (T&D) losses in India at 28.65 per cent are some of the highest in the world (CEA 2007). By bringing down the T&D losses to the level of China, electricity can be made available to more than half of the deprived households.

Infrastructure Enablers

Infrastructure is associated with energy access and, hence, security. In India, though close to 80 per cent of the villages are electrified (as on March 2006), only 55 per cent of the rural households have electricity connections (CEA 2006; NSSO 2007). This shows an absence of electricity connection infrastructure from village point to the household. Better infrastructure also betters energy trade. Literature shows that, despite gas reserves, projects in developing economies cannot be realized as they cannot afford expensive infrastructure involving foreign exchange (Energy Sector Management Assistance Programme [ESMAP] 2003). The momentum is gaining ground for investment in massive infrastructure projects. It is a step in the right direction.

Economic Enablers

India's energy service strategy must move from 'fossil fuel subsidy' to 'subsidy to energy-efficient and renewable technologies' (EERT). Once an electric connection is provided and a compact fluorescent lamp (CFL) is fixed in a household, supply of kerosene for rural lighting is no longer needed. It is interesting to note that kerosene is subsidized to promote the use of clean cooking fuel in rural areas. But only about 1.3 per cent of the rural households use kerosene as a cooking fuel, whereas as high as 44.4 per cent use it as lighting fuel (NSSO 2007). Kerosene provides poor lighting service and is a source of indoor air pollution. Also, half of the subsidized kerosene supplies are diverted to adulterate petrol because of the price differential (Gangopadhyay et al. 2005), and such use greatly contributes to air pollution (Shelar and Barahate 2007). Similarly for LPG, since the

subsidy is non-targeted, 50 per cent of the same goes to the top expenditure decile and quartile in rural and urban areas, respectively (Gangopadhyay et al. 2005; Misra et al. 2005). So, it is worthwhile to consider the diversion of these fossil fuel subsidies to EERT.

Political Enablers

A conducive political climate—both inside and outside—is a prerequisite for ensuring security on the energy front. The Iran–Pakistan–India natural gas pipeline is an example of how hostile relationship with the neighbouring countries can spoil energy projects. Though the project has been under negotiations for fifteen years, it could not take off because of lack of confidence owing to bitter relationships. Amiable political relationship promotes cross-border trade, which connects the usually inaccessible border areas to interior cities, stimulating economic activity in those areas and ensuring energy security.

Confederations[18] facilitate the institutional infrastructure for energy security. The European Union (EU) is an example where market-based reforms in the member countries led to a slow and steady development of a single energy market. Liberalization brought in a win–win situation for both the consumers and state by lowering price and increasing choices. Confederations like the Association of Southeast Asian Nations (ASEAN) are in the process of energy integration through cross-border power grid and gas trade. Also, ASEAN countries, after the 1973 oil crisis formed the Asian Council on Petroleum (ASCOPE) for cooperation among the member countries to navigate energy issues (Weerawat 2007). However, India-centric confederation, that is, the South Asian Association for Regional Cooperation (SAARC) has only 3 per cent intra-regional energy trade to its credit (Lahiri-Dutt 2006). All this is limited to Indo-Nepal, Indo-Bhutan, and Indo-Bangladesh electricity trade. A more responsible and mature SAARC can bring in the necessary energy policy integration in the region, which will not only increase supply options, but also enhance demand-side security through competitive pricing of fuels and access to energy services in remote border areas.

Socio-cultural Enablers

Rural households in India, at times, do not accept modern energy services based on renewable technologies because the same are considered 'inferior' compared to energy based on fossil fuels. At the same time, households ignore the fact that biomass fuels have high opportunity cost as gathering

[18] Confederation is a union of sovereign states for common action in relation to other states.

them involves back-breaking and time-consuming work for people, particularly women and girl children. The need to gather fuels may deprive the girl child from schooling. This 'hard-earned' energy is used very inefficiently (15 per cent conversion efficiency) and causes indoor air pollution, which again affects the health of women and the girl child more adversely as they spend more time indoors and are primarily responsible for cooking. The economic burden of traditional biomass-based fuels for time spent on gathering these and the loss due to sickness is estimated at around Rs 300 billion annually (Planning Commission 2008). A social change with gender consideration will call for right choice of energy technology and will promote EERTs, which, in turn, build energy security.

Environmental Enablers

Environmental enablers have two facets. One is bringing in environmental standards like enforcing efficiency standard for buildings, appliances, and vehicles. These compulsory provisions catalyse the demand-side security by aligning the energy demands towards appropriate technologies. Provision of solar water heaters for new buildings in Bengaluru is an example in this regard. The second facet of these enablers is about creating environmental awareness programme, for instance, to use public transport or shifting from incandescent bulb to CFL. These measures will reduce energy consumption and thereby increase the security.

POLICY PRESCRIPTIONS

Adequate supply of low-cost energy of quality and convenience is core to the energy security goal. For universalization of modern energy services like cooking (with gaseous fuels) and lighting (with electricity) to Indian households, the model proposed by Reddy et al. (2009), termed as EMPOWERS (Entrepreneurship-based Model for Provision of Wholesome Energy Related Basic Services) is a case in point. This actor-oriented model with entrepreneurs at the core also involves financial institutions, utilities, equipment manufacturers, and non-governmental organizations (NGOs), apart from government and consumers. This model encompasses both supply and demand side energy security strategies. A targeted programme-based access creation is proposed, which envisages multi-stakeholder responsibility and cost sharing. A desirable scenario is developed with base year as 2010–1 and 2030–1 as final target year, and the interim period is divided into four five-year plans. The annual investments for the four plan periods are estimated at Rs 93 billion, Rs 93 billion, Rs 102 billion, and Rs 87 billion, respectively. The cumulative CO_2 emissions reduction in the entire plan period is approximately 2,300 mt

(Table 14.8). Energy security becomes plausible with entrepreneurs as they act as interface and government is alleviated from targeting millions of 'end users'. If EMPOWERS becomes operational, it will be a win–win situation for all: consumers benefit through improved access to modern energy services, governments advance social and economic development objectives, and private enterprise and equipment manufactures expand business opportunities.

At the micro level, energy insecurity affects the efficiency of household activities and lessens the productive working hours. At the macro level, lack of energy affects a country's ability to engage in manufacturing and services and to support critical agricultural activities. The policy prescriptions need to distinguish between household energy security and national energy security. The energy policy must focus on the households that are the lowest in the economic ladder. The poor are in a Catch-22 situation: neither can they afford to have modern energy carriers nor can they come out of the poverty trap in the present state of energy starvation. Whereas the poor struggle for energy services for basic needs like cooking and lighting, the rich overuse energy for comfort and luxury. So, 'targeted' policies, not universal ones, are more effective for the energy sector as energy is a limited resource without having an upper limit for individual spending.

In a recent study by Ray (2009) on the Indian manufacturing sector, the author has concluded that structural change in the industry contributed to 70 per cent of the energy improvements, with the rest coming from technical change. This finding is also applicable to sectors other than industry. As the economy moves from high energy intensity to low energy intensity activities, the energy security improves. In the pursuit of climate improvement through energy management, India needs to follow the path of a 'Climate Realist'.[19] This middle path approach integrates climate policies with those of development priorities and stresses the need for using sustainable development as a framework for climate change policies.

THE FUTURE

The health of the economy in India depends on reliable, affordable, adequate, and environmentally sound supplies of energy. The rising cost of energy hurts consumers who must spend a greater percentage of their income on energy.

---

[19] 'Climate Realists' are the breed of analysts who are convinced of the climate change problem while remaining profoundly sceptical of the impacts and proposed solutions. They start from a sustainable development perspective, which prioritizes poverty reduction and equity and at the same time minimizes environmental impacts (Bradley et al. 2005; Reddy and Assenza 2009b).

Table 14.8   Energy Needs, Cost, and Investment Estimates of Providing Electric Lighting Services for Households (Rs billion)

Item	Year			
Cooking	2015	2020	2025	2030
Incremental Annual Energy Requirements (PJ)	236.6	310	382.6	205.2
Annual Capital Cost—Stoves	8.67	9.78	10.45	6.41
Annual Capital Cost—Biogas Plants	5.77	9.36	13.42	6.27
Annual Capital Cost—Distribution System	4.29	6.96	9.97	4.66
Annual Capital Cost—Total	18.74	26.12	33.85	17.35
Annual Recurring Cost	74.2	83.99	90.07	55.08
Annual Cost—Total	92.94	110.11	123.91	72.42
Initial Investment Required—Stoves	53.29	60.13	64.25	39.42
Initial Investment Required—Biogas Plant	50.99	81.07	116.1	54.29
Initial Investment Required—Distribution System	37.15	60.26	86.29	40.35
Total Investment Required	140.43	201.46	266.65	134.05
Lighting	2015	2020	2025	2030
Incremental Annual Energy Requirements for Lighting (GWh)	1411	1426	1580	1442
Annual Capital Cost—Supply	2.9	2.92	3.23	2.93
Annual Capital Cost—Generation	1.61	1.6	1.64	1.32
Annual Capital Cost—Transmission	0.85	0.86	0.96	0.89
Annual Capital Cost—Distribution	0.44	0.45	0.5	0.45
Annual Capital Cost—Final Connection	5.27	5.3	5.75	4.8
Annual Capital Cost—CFLs	4.38	4.43	4.91	4.48
Annual Capital Cost—Total	12.56	12.63	13.75	11.94
Annual Recurring Cost	1.81	1.82	2.01	1.81
Annual Cost—Total	14.36	14.45	15.76	13.77
Installed Capacity Required (MW)	308	311	344	312
Initial Investment Required—Supply	28.05	28.34	31.4	28.59
Initial Investment Required—Generation	14.14	14.27	15.76	14.19
Initial Investment Required—Transmission	8.99	9.1	10.12	9.4
Initial Investment Required—Distribution	4.93	4.98	5.5	5
Initial Investment Required—Final Connection	47.91	48.06	52.18	43.57
Initial Investment Required—CFLs	16.73	16.87	18.57	16.48
Total Investment Required	92.68	93.27	102.15	88.65

Source: Reddy et al. (2009).

Industries too suffer and their profits shrink due to rise in energy costs. India's increasing dependence on natural gas and petroleum fuels makes it vulnerable to supply disruptions and price spikes. Hence, the country should design strategies to secure supply sources and reduce energy demand. Diversification will remain the fundamental starting principle of energy security for fossil fuels. It also requires developing a new generation of 'clean coal' and low-carbon technologies, encouraging a growing role for a variety of renewable energy sources, including hydrogen fuel, as they become more competitive. A move towards more sustainable technologies and fuel types is needed to meet the future challenges. Investment in energy-efficient as well as renewable energy technologies and infrastructure will require conducive economic and environmental policies in place. In a world of increasing interdependence, energy security will depend much on how countries manage their relations with one another. That is why energy security will be one of the main challenges for Indian foreign policy in the years to come. The energy security policies of the country need to be oriented with sustainable development as the primary goal and climate mitigation as its by-product.

Energy being critical for MDGs, India must target in the next couple of decades for universalization of provision of energy services for all its citizens.

REFERENCES

Asian Development Bank (ADB) (2006), *Energy Efficiency and Climate Change Considerations for On-road Transport in Asia*. Manila: ADB.

Alhajji A.F. and James L. Williams (2003), 'Measures of Petroleum Dependence and Vulnerability in OECD Countries', *Middle East Economic Survey*, 46(16).

Asia Pacific Energy Research Centre (APERC) (2007), *A Quest for Energy Security in the 21st Century*. Institute of Energy Economics, Tokyo: APERC.

Balachandra P., Hippu Salk Kristle Nathan, and B. Sudhakara Reddy (2010), 'Commercialisation of Sustainable Energy Technologies', *Renewable Energy*, 35(8): 1842–51.

Belgrave, R., C.K. Ebinger, and H. Okino (eds) (1987), 'Introduction', in *Energy Security to 2000*. Boulder: Westview Press.

British Petroleum (BP) (2008), *Statistical Review of World Energy 2008*. London: BP.

——— (2009), *Statistical Review of World Energy 2009*. London: BP.

Bradley, R., K. Baumert, N. Dubash, J. Moreira, S. Mwakasonda, W. Ng, L. Noguiera, V. Parente, J. Pershing, L. Schipper, H. Winkler, and F. Cardoso (2005), 'Growing in the Greenhouse: Protecting the Climate by Putting Development First', *World Resources Institute*, XI.

Central Electricity Authority (CEA) (2006), 'Actual Power Supply Position (Revised)', April 2005–March 2006. Available at http://www.cea.nic.in/power sec-reports/executive summary/2006 04/22-23.pdf (accessed on 25 August 2009).

——— (2007), *All India Electricity Statistics General Review 2007*. New Delhi: CEA.

Clingendael International Energy Programme (CIEP) (2004), EU Energy Supply Security and Geopolitics (Tren/C1-06-2002), CIEP Study, Clingendael Institute, The Hague.

Coq C.L. and Elena Paltseva (2009), 'Measuring the Security of External Energy Supply in the European Union', *Energy Policy*, 37(11): 4474–81.

Energy Sector Management Assistance Programme (ESMAP) (2003), 'Cross Border Oil and Gas Pipeline, Problems and Prospects', Joint UNDP and World Bank initiative, ESMAP, Washington DC.

Foster J., J. Greer, and E. Thorbecke (1984), 'A Class of Decomposable Poverty Measures', *Econometrica*, 52(3): 761–6.

Gangopadhyay S., B. Ramaswami, and W. Wadhwa (2005), 'Reducing Subsidies on Household Fuels in India: How will it Affect the Poor?', *Energy Policy*, 33(18): 2326–36.

Grubb, M., L. Butler, and P. Twomey (2005), 'Diversity and Security in UK Electricity Generation: The Influence of Low-Carbon Objectives', *Energy Policy*, 34: 4050–62.

International Energy Agency (IEA) (2005), *World Energy Outlook*. Paris: OECD/IEA.

——— (2007a), *World Energy Outlook 2007, China and India Insights*. Paris: OECD/IEA.

——— (2007b), *Energy Security and Climate Policy, Assessing Interactions*. Paris: OECD/IEA.

Jansen J.C., W.G. Van Arkel, and M.G. Boots (2004), 'Designing Indicators of Long-term Energy Supply Security', Energy Research Centre of the Netherlands, Petten, the Netherlands.

Kruyt, Bert, D.P. vanVuuren, H.J.M. deVries, and H. Groenenberg (2009), 'Indicators for Energy Security', *Energy Policy*, 37(6): 2166–81.

Lahiri-Dutt, K. (2006), 'Energy Resources: Will They be the Last Frontier in South Asia?', Australia South Asia Research Centre (ASARC) Working Paper 2006/10, Australian National University.

Li, L.-D., Q. Wang, H. Liu, and Y. Song (2008), 'Calculation and Analysis of Diversity of Domestic Primary Energy Supply', *Journal of North-eastern University*, 29(4): 577–80.

Löschel Andreas, Ulf Moslener, and Dirk T.G. Rübbelke (2010a), 'Indicators of Energy Security in Industrialised Countries', *Energy Policy*, 38(4): 1607–8.

——— (2010b), 'Energy Security—Concepts and Indicators', *Energy Policy*, 38(4): 1665–71.

Ministry of Petroleum and Natural Gas (2010), *India Hydrocarbon Vision—2025*, Report, Government of India. Available at http://petroleum.nic.in/vision.doc (accessed on 10 August 2010).

Mishra, Srijit and Hippu Salk Kristle Nathan (2008), 'On a Class of Human Development Index Measures', Indira Gandhi Institute of Development Research (IGIDR), WP-2008-020, October. Available at http://www. igidr.ac.in/pdf/publication/WP-2008-020.pdf

Misra N., R. Chawla, L. Srivastava, and R.K. Pachauri (2005), *Petroleum Prices in India: Balancing Efficiency and Equity*. New Delhi: The Energy and Resources Institute (TERI).

Massachusetts Institute of Technology (MIT) (2007), *The Future of Coal: Options for a Carbon-Constrained World*. Cambridge, MA: Massachusetts Institute of Technology.

Modi V., S. Mc Dade, D. Lallement, and J. Sagir (2005), 'Energy Services for the Millennium Development Goals', Report, International Bank for Reconstruction and Development/The World Bank and the United Nations Development Programme.

National Sample Survey Organisation (NSSO) (2007), *Energy Used by Indian Households 2004/2005*, NSS 61st Round. New Delhi: Ministry of Statistics and Program Implementation, Government of India.

Nathan, H.S.K., S. Mishra, and S. Reddy (2008), 'An Alternative Approach to Measure HDI', Working Paper No. WP-2008-001, IGIDR. Available at http://www.igidr.ac.in/pdf/publication/WP-2008-001.pdf

Nathan, H.S.K. and S. Reddy (2010), 'Selection Criteria for Sustainable Development Indicators', Working Paper No. WP-2010-013, IGIDR. Available at http://www.igidr.ac.in/pdf/publication/WP-2010-013.pdf

Pachauri, S., A. Mueller, A. Kemmler, and D. Spreng (2004), 'On Measuring Energy Poverty in Indian Households', *World Development*, 32(12): 2083–104.

Planning Commission (2008), *Eleventh Five-Year Plan, 2007–12. Agriculture, Rural Development, Industry, Services and Physical Infrastructure*, Volume III. New Delhi: Planning Commission, Government of India.

Ray, Binay (2009), 'Energy Efficiency and Technology Management in Indian Industry', PhD Thesis, IGIDR, Mumbai.

Reddy, A.K.N. (2002), 'Energy Technologies and Policies for Rural Development', in T.B. Johansson and J. Goldemberg (eds), *Energy for Sustainable Development: A Policy Agenda*, pp. 115–36. New York: United Nations Development Programme.

Reddy, Sudhakara B. and Gaudenz B. Assenza (2009a), 'Climate Change: A Developing Country Perspective', *Current Science*, 97(1): 50–62.

——— (2009b), 'The Great Climate Debate', *Energy Policy*, 32(8): 2997–3008.

Reddy, Sudhakara B., P. Balachandra, and Hippu Salk Kristle Nathan (2009), 'Universalization of Access to Modern Energy Services in Indian Households—Economic and Policy Analysis', *Energy Policy*, 37(11): 4645–57.

Reddy, Sudhakara B. and P. Balachandra (2003), 'Integrated Energy–Environment Policy Analysis', *Utilities Policy*, 11(2): 59–73.

Ruijven, Bas van (2008), 'Energy and Development—A Modelling Approach', PhD Thesis, Department of Science, Technology and Society, Copernicus Institute for Sustainable Development and Innovation, Utrecht University.

Sauter R. and G. MacKerron (2008), 'The New Energy Challenge: Security and Sustainability', 7th BIEE Academic Conference, St. John's College, Oxford, 24–25 September.

Shelar, Mahesh and S.D. Barahate (2007), 'Energy Stamps to Discourage Inefficient Use of Kerosene and Reduce Emissions from Autorickshaws: A Case Study from Maharashtra, India', *Energy for Sustainable Development*, 11(4): 74–7.

Stirling, A. (1993), 'What Does Energy Security of Supply Mean?', in S. Thomas (ed.), *Energy Policy: An Agenda for the 1990s*. Brighton, UK: Science Policy Research Unit (SPRU).

Subramanian, S. (2004), 'A Re-scaled Version of the Foster–Greer–Thorbecke Poverty Indices based on an Association with the Minkowski Distance Function', Research Paper No. 2004/10, United Nations University–World Institute for Development Economics Research (UNU–WIDER), Helsinki.

The Energy and Resources Institute (TERI) (2006), *Teri Energy Data Directory and Year Book (TEDDY) 2004/05*. New Delhi: TERI.

United Nations Development Programme (UNDP) (2007a), *Human Development Report, 2007/2008*. New York: Oxford University Press.

——— (2007b), 'Policy Study on Cross-Border Energy Trade and Its Impact on the Poor', Technical Report, First Draft, Regional Energy Programme for Poverty Reduction (REP-PoR).

United Nations Framework Convention on Climate Change (UNFCCC) (2007), *Climate Change: Impacts, Vulnerabilities and Adaptation in Developing Countries*. Climate Change Secretariat, United Nations Framework Convention on Climate Change.

Weerawat, Chantankome (2007), 'SAARC Energy Trade Study', paper presented at Regional Policy Dialogue on Cross-border Energy Trade in Asia and the Pacific, 3–4 December, UNDP, Bangkok.

World Bank (2006), *A Decade of Measuring the Quality of Governance: Governance Matters 2006—Worldwide Governance Indicators*. Washington DC: The International Bank for Reconstruction and Development/The World Bank.

Zeleny, M.A. (1974), 'Concept of Compromise Solutions and Method of Displaced Ideal', *Computers and Operations Research*, 1(4): 479–96.

15

Disasters

Natural and Man-made

Nirmal Sengupta[*]

INTRODUCTION

What are disasters? Let us first brush up our memory of the recent past to understand what we are about to deal with in this chapter.

- In August 2008, the Kosi River changed its direction, bringing large parts of Bihar under unprecedented submergence. The flood deluge lasted for about two weeks. Half a million people remained stranded; over 3 million people were badly affected.
- On 26 July 2005, after receiving its highest rainfall in recorded history, Mumbai experienced its worst flood. The financial capital of India came to a standstill for over 48 hours. The General Insurance Corporation alone settled claims worth Rs 650 crore.
- A few months earlier, on 26 December 2004, a colossal tsunami ranging from 3 to 10 metres had struck over 2,260 km of east coast, killing more than 10,000 people and leaving behind a huge trail of destruction.
- On the morning of the Republic Day in 2001, a powerful earthquake hit Gujarat, killing more than 13,800

people and damaging 12 lakh houses. In the Latur earthquake of 1993, as many as 22,000 people were killed.
- On 25 October 1999, a super-cyclone with wind speed 260–300 km/hour hit the 140-km-long coast of Orissa and travelled more than 250 km inland. Lasting 36 hours, it killed about 10,000 people and ravaged 200 lakh hectares of land.
- In a three-week-long heat wave in May–June 1998, more than 2,500 people died of heatstroke, heat-induced diarrhoea, and vomiting. In the winter of 2002–3, in a month-long cold wave, more than 350 people died in north India.
- On 18 August 1998, a massive rockfall wiped out village Malpa of Uttarakhand. The landslide killed 210 people, including 60 pilgrims to Kailash-Mansarovar.
- In an avalanche in Jammu region in February 2005, over 240 people were dead and 300 missing.
- In late summer of 1995, the hills of Uttarakhand and Himachal Pradesh witnessed an extensive forest fire that gradually spread over several districts, affecting forest area of 6,777 sq km.
- In September 1994, Surat announced an epidemic of the dreaded disease plague. Within four days of the announcement, nearly 4 lakh people fled the city.

[*] The author gratefully acknowledges the help received from the EMDAT team at the Centre for Research on the Epidemiology of Disasters, Catholic University of Louvain, Brussels.

These are some of the past events that are difficult to forget. We have also not forgotten the series of famines that ravaged India again and again in the historical past. Even today we have droughts, just as bad as in the past. But the last time we heard of a famine situation in India was in connection with the 1965–7 drought. We have learnt how to avoid famines, one of the worst disasters in Indian history. We may succeed in developing strategies for dealing with other disasters. This is the motivation for undertaking systematic studies of disasters and disaster management.

Disasters are defined by the United Nations (UN) and the World Bank as 'a serious disruption of the functioning of society, causing widespread human, material or environmental losses which exceed the ability of affected society to cope on its own resources'. All crises or emergency situations are not 'disasters'. The larger ones causing serious disruptions requiring special measures are classified as a distinct category. Emergency Disasters Data Base (EMDAT) operationalizes the definition as: a disaster is an event that meets at least one of the following criteria:

- 10 or more people reported killed
- 100 people or more reported affected
- declaration of a state of emergency
- call for international assistance

Reinsurance companies (e.g., Swiss Re 2009) use somewhat stricter criteria like twenty or more dead or missing, along with cut-off points in terms of economic loss or insured loss. Recently, Munich Reinsurance has introduced a classification scheme based on the scale of an event. The National Disaster Management Division of India classified natural calamities as major and minor 'depending upon their potential to cause damage to human life and property'. Droughts, floods, earthquakes, cyclones, and tsunamis are major disasters; avalanches, landslides, forest fires, heat waves, and cold waves are minor.

Scientific and technical measures like the Richter scale cannot be used for defining or classification of events as disasters. 'Hydrologic floods are not necessarily associated with flood damages' (Pielke and Downton 2000). State governments declare droughts by considering fall in groundwater levels; drying of wells, rivers, and reservoirs; shortage of drinking water; and poor agricultural production. The Meteorological Department of India uses a standard, defined by overall rainfall deficiency. By this standard, 1965–7 had experienced only 'mild drought' (Sinha and Shewale 2001; De et al. 2005). In reality, this was the last visit of famine to India.

Apart from those due primarily to natural phenomena, there are also man-made disasters. EMDAT distinguishes two generic categories for disasters: natural and technological. The technological disasters comprise three groups: (a) industrial accidents, (b) transport accidents, and (c) miscellaneous accidents. Ever since the World Trade Centre attack, the disaster databases of reinsurance companies include property damages due to terrorism as well. Some of the major 'man-made disasters' that India went through were:

- The heinous terrorist attack in Mumbai during 26–29 November 2008 is one of the world's biggest disasters.
- In December 1995, during the annual prize ceremony of the local DAV School at Dabwali town on the Haryana–Punjab border, 442 people, mostly children between the ages of 5 and 17 years, were burnt to death in a devastating fire.
- One of the worst industrial disasters of all time occurred in Bhopal in December 1984. Highly poisonous methyl isocyanate (MIC) gas leaked out of the Union Carbide pesticide factory into the night air of Bhopal, exposing 500,000 people to severe toxicity. The official death toll was a conservative 3,598. Many of those who survived, lived lives worse than death.
- In 1975 at Chasnala, Jharkhand state, an explosion in the underground coal mine resulted in one of the worst mining disasters. Miners were first trapped under a mountain of debris when the roof caved in. When rescue operation was on full swing, water from an adjacent water body gushed into the mine, drowning the still-trapped miners. The official death toll was 372.
- In 1954, about 800 pilgrims died at the Kumbh Mela stampede in Allahabad. In India, stampedes leading to disasters are frequent. In August and September 2008, 162 and 224 people died in stampedes at Naina Devi temple in Himachal Pradesh and Chamunda Devi temple in Jodhpur, respectively. In January 2005, death toll rose to 258 in a stampede at Mandradevi shrine, Maharashtra.

Damages caused by mob violence and wars are not included in disaster studies.

NATURAL DISASTERS SINCE INDEPENDENCE

In general, disaster damage data is of a very poor quality. Since speed of action matters, the first estimates are made within a few hours from the event. These are then revised. But good data is costly, and rarely is there a reason to incur the cost for thorough revision. Besides, there are some inherent problems in defining damages. Even the 'number of deaths' data, the simplest quantitative information, needs revisions again and again, sometimes after months. There is no clear answer to whether deaths due to malnutrition, water-borne diseases, or other health problems following a disaster should be included. Estimates of economic losses are extremely poor. There is no standard methodology for calculations. Besides, the data collected by different agencies are not always comparable. Every database reflects the concerns of the data collecting agency. Insurance and reinsurance agencies are more concerned with economic valuation of loss. EMDAT, a collaborative effort of the World Health Organization (WHO) and Catholic University of Louvain, is concerned about the humanitarian damages more than the property losses. The national and state governments may have their own priorities and may use distinct set of criteria for defining damages. However, the data about India found in all three global databases—EMDAT, Swiss Re, and Munich Re—are quite in agreement (Guha-Sapir and Below 2002). Within India, different government departments concerned with specific type of resources and services, collect some data about one or the other type of disaster. In the past, the National Disaster Management Authority had made a feeble attempt at compilation (viz., Government of India 2004: 63). We have used whatever reliable data is available.

For flood damage data, there are two sources. EMDAT collects data primarily from UN agencies, supplementing it with information obtained from some reputed international non-governmental organizations (NGOs), research institutions, insurance institutions, and the press. In earlier years when this network was weak, EMDAT did not have any information for several events. For later years, when their coverage improved, the EMDAT reports for population affected, loss of homes, and deaths were almost always lower than the Central Water Commission (CWC) reports. For earthquakes, another international agency, National Geophysical Data Centre, collates information available from sources somewhat similar to that of the EMDAT. But at times, this source and the EMDAT data of earthquakes differ in coverage. Table 15.1 presents summary data from all these sources.

A comparison of columns (3) and (4) suggests that the frequency of each type of natural disaster increased in the latter half. This could not be because of incomplete coverage in the earlier years. If there were coverage problems, then EMDAT would have missed more of the smaller events in the earlier years. Later, when they were better organized, better coverage of smaller events along with the large ones would have resulted in lower numbers for people affected per event compared to the earlier years. This is certainly not the pattern when we compare columns (5) and (6). Therefore, we reckon that the coverage of EMDAT for natural disasters in India was not poor even in the 1950s; the increases in frequency of each type of natural disaster in the more recent period, as shown by columns (3) and (4), are real.

Comparison of the data in columns (5) and (6) shows that the average number of people affected per disaster event has decreased for cyclones and storms. For flood, drought, and epidemic disasters, there are some increases, but just

Table 15.1 Natural Disasters—Summary Table of Disaster Events

Type of Disaster		No. of Events		Average Size of Events Included in Database					
				No. of People Affected (lakh)		No. of Deaths (thousand))		No. of People Homeless (thousand)	
		1950–79	1980–2008	1950–79	1980–2008	1950–79	1980–2008	1950–79	1980–2008
(1)	(2)	(3)	(4)	(5)	(6)	(7)	(8)	(9)	(10)
Flood	EMDAT	50	171	23.41	39.32	0.41	0.23	148.78	48.23
	CWC*	27**	26**	256.65	403.31	1.36	1.83	918.98	1,528.35
Earthquakes and Tsunami	EMDAT	7	16	0.07	17.42	0.28	3.11	0.00	130.36
	NGDC	3	13	0.17	21.44	0.60	3.82		160.42
Drought		5	6	621.33	1,251.96	300.00	0.05	0.00	0.00
Cyclones and Storms		46	81	7.83	6.24	0.69	0.28	169.81	17.54
Landslides/Avalanches		7	31	0.01	1.24	0.21	0.09		516.65
Epidemics		7	55	0.03	0.07	0.78	0.27		
Heat and Cold Waves		9	35		0.00	0.26	0.31		
Others		3				0.00			

Sources: Flood: CWC—Central Water Commission data for floods. Houses damaged fully or partially in CWC data are included in category 'homeless'.
Earthquake: NGDC—National Geophysical Data Centre data for earthquakes.
The rest of the data is from *EMDAT*.

Notes: *CWC data is about annual averages. CWC does not show 'number of floods'.
** No. of years. Separate flood events are not available in CWC data.

about as much as the growth of general population. Only for geophysical disasters like earthquakes, tsunamis, landslides, mudslides, and avalanches, the increases in people affected per event are astronomical, far more than to be explained by population growth. The number of earthquakes of magnitude 6.0 and above in the first and the latter half were six and eight, respectively. It seems that in recent years these natural hazards have hit more of the densely populated areas. Later we will show that this is substantiated also by the economic loss data. Landslides and avalanches might have increased because of undue interference by human beings.

That the disaster management efforts have been paying dividends is corroborated also by the data about fatality and homelessness. Except for the geophysical disasters, the death per event has decreased uniformly over the period as per the EMDAT data. This is also true for the homelessness data for flood and cyclones. The CWC flood-related data tells a different story. But here too, the increase in average number of deaths is below the population growth during these periods. Also, the CWC data is about houses damaged fully or partially. Partial damages are not included in category 'homeless' by EMDAT.

Both the factors, population growth and increase in frequencies of disasters, would contribute to increases in the number of people affected by disasters each year. This is confirmed by columns (3) and (4) of Table 15.2; for each single type of natural disaster, the annual average of people affected has increased. Together, the natural disasters every year affected more than 5 per cent of total population of the country during 1980–2008, an increase from about 3 per cent during the first half after independence (1950–79). Indeed, this is the reality all over the world; we have to live in an increasingly hazardous natural environment and must learn to cope with this. Table 15.2 shows that in India the disaster management efforts have registered noticeable success in reducing the damages from certain types of disasters. Both death rate and damages to houses in cyclones and storms have decreased. Droughts do not damage houses. But fatality from droughts has been reduced to almost zero. This is in spite of increases in people affected by these disasters. One may feel uneasy about the accuracy of the EMDAT data for the number of deaths from 1965–7 drought. This cannot be exact. But nutritional databases confirm that this severe three-year drought had created endemic hunger and widespread malnutrition, which must have resulted in numerous deaths.

On the negative side, earthquakes and tsunamis, which had caused only nominal amount of damages in the earlier period, caused far greater damages in the recent past.

Table 15.2   Natural Disasters: Total Physical Damages

Type of Disaster		Annual Average for the Period					
		Population Affected (lakh)		No. of Deaths		Population Homeless (thousand)	
		1950–79	1980–2008	1950–79	1980–2008	1950–79	1980–2008
(1)	(2)	(3)	(4)	(5)	(6)	(7)	(8)
Flood	EMDAT	39.00 (25.23)	231.86 (44.64)	676 (1.3)	1,342 (27.69)	247.97 (48.78)	284.41 (53.66)
	CWC	256.67	403.31	1,359	1,831	918.98	1,528.35
Earthquakes and Tsunami	EMDAT	0.03 (0.01)	9.62 (1.85)	65 (0.13)	1,715 (35.37)	0.00 (0)	71.93 (13.57)
	NGDC	0.03	9.62	60	1,714	0.00	71.93
Drought		103.57 (66.98)	259.03 (49.87)	50,000 (95.94)	11 (0.23)	0.00	0.00
Cyclones and Storms		12.00 (7.77)	17.45 (3.36)	1,065 (2.04)	782 (16.13)	260.37 (51.22)	48.97 (9.24)
Landslides/ Avalanches		0.00 (0.00)	1.32 (0.25)	48 (0.09)	98 (2.02)	0.00 (0.00)	124.70 (23.53)
Epidemics		0.01 (0.01)	0.14 (0.03)	182 (0.35)	521 (10.75)		
Heat and Cold Waves				79 (0.15)	378 (7.80)		
Total (EMDAT only)		154.60 (100)	519.38 (100)	52,115 (100)	4,848 (100)	508.33 (100)	530.00 (100)

Note: The figures in parentheses are percentage distributions of EMDAT data.

Indeed, they accounted for more than a third of the total deaths in this period, being closely followed by flood. Even after improvement, cyclones and storms still accounted for a large share of total deaths, followed by epidemics, and heat waves and cold waves. Certain types of disasters do not damage houses. More than a half of damages on this front were caused by flood. For avalanches and landslides, the EMDAT data about homeless population seems to be highly exaggerated. On closer scrutiny of records we found that most of this was for just two events, 1986 landslides of Uttar Pradesh and Himachal Pradesh and Kulla landslide (1995) of Himachal Pradesh. Neither of these was as extensive as to create lakhs of homeless people.

Drought and flood are the two types of disasters that affect extensive area. Heat and cold waves too have similar nature. Others affect smaller areas, but may cause intensive damages. Flood occurs every year. India is the most flood-affected country in the world (Lin et al. 2007). The CWC also publishes the total area affected. It shows that between 1953 and 2005, on an average, as much as 7.35 million hectares was affected annually by floods. This is an area equal to a half of

Bangladesh. Each year about 33 million people, as much as the population of Canada, are affected by flood.

MAN-MADE DISASTERS IN RECENT PERIOD

Table 15.3 summarizes the data about man-made disasters during 1980–2008. In interpreting this data, one must not forget that these are about disaster events, not about accidents or fires or terrorist acts in general. Terrorism-related data is from the Global Terrorism Database (GTD). We have taken only those events with ten or more deaths. The GTD database runs till 2007. We have added the information for 2008 from newspapers, etc. The rest are EMDAT data of the broad group categorized as technological disasters.

Between 1980 and 2008, more than 32.5 thousand people have been killed in man-made disasters. This is about a fourth part of the deaths in natural disasters. Another 1.26 lakh people have been injured by individual events. The Bhopal gas leak dwarfs all other disasters. The number of people killed immediately was high. But far higher were the number injured, many of whom lived very painful existences

Table 15.3 Man-made Disasters: Physical Damages, 1980–2008

Disaster Subtype	No. of Events	Total Physical Damages (in '000)			
		No. of People Affected	No. of People Killed	No. of People Injured	Fatality Rate as % of People Involved
(1)	(2)	(3)	(4)	(5)	(6)
Industrial Disasters					
Hazardous Gas Leak and Chemical Spill	5	401.21	2.50	101.21	0.62
Air and Water Poisoning	14	1.75	0.98	1.64	35.99
Industrial and Miscellaneous Disasters					
Fire	40	175.88	1.72	1.28	0.97
Explosion of Buildings and Structures	33	3.00	0.92	0.89	23.50
Collapse of Buildings and Structures	39	0.66	1.25	0.66	64.85
Miscellaneous Other Accidents	27	6.05	1.73	4.05	22.29
Transport Disasters					
Air Accident	16	0.10	0.98	0.10	91.78
Rail Accident	100	5.70	4.30	5.70	43.40
Road Accident	232	3.25	7.89	3.25	70.40
Water Transport Accident	73	0.15	3.87	0.00	95.97
Terrorism Disasters					
Terrorist Acts	359	NA	7.04	7.90	47.11
Total	938	597.74	32.48	125.92	5.15

Sources: Terrorism data from GTD. Only those events with ten or above deaths have been considered here. The GTD database runs till 2007. The information for 2008 has been added from newspapers, etc.

Note: The rest of the data is from EMDAT.

for the rest of their lives. The maximum number of deaths, however, is accounted for by transport disasters. Fatality rates in gas leak, chemical spill, or fire are low. Those are high for transport disasters and in collapse of buildings and structures. Miscellaneous other accidents like major stampedes account for a high share of injuries though fatality rate is moderate.

Comparisons with other countries show that with 411 industrial and 95 miscellaneous accident disasters between 1990 and 2008, China tops the lists. India follows with 56 and 78, respectively. In transport disasters, India has the disgrace of being the leading country with 337 such disasters. China follows with 182. In terrorism-related disasters, as one would expect, India with 289 incidences, leads. At the other end, countries like Japan or France faced just six industrial disasters each, and only a few of other types. However, it is no wonder that the two largest countries face maximum numbers of disasters. Surprise springs up once we eliminate the size effect. In average annual damages per 1 crore of population (Figure 15.1), neither China nor India was leading in any category. But Japan and France were not shining anymore. Two mega-disasters—Sakai food poisoning (1996) and gas attack in Tokyo metro (1995)—made Japan the leading country in threat to population from industrial and terrorism-related disasters. This shows the need to be careful against misinterpretation of disaster data.

Even after several quiet years, just one very big disaster may cause severe damage. In industrial disasters, India's record is better because Bhopal disaster was not included within this period. One single terrorist attack made the US the leading country in deaths due to this category of disasters. Indeed, the data warns against lowering of guards at any time.

Figure 15.1 shows a few distinct patterns. In comparison to the developed countries, the less developed countries have higher fatality rate than injury. Though India faces numerous disasters of each type, its large size and relatively less occurrence of mega events during this period assign to the country moderate rankings in damages per population. As expected, disasters due to terrorist acts are one of the worst threats that India is facing in the recent years. Table 15.4 shows the changing scenario of disastrous terrorist violence in India. The damages per terrorist-inflicted disaster are increasing steadily.

ESTIMATES OF ECONOMIC LOSS

Different types of disasters damage in different ways. Earthquakes and landslides cause severe damage to house property or infrastructure. Drought and epidemics do not affect property. Death tolls may not be high in a major flood or a forest fire. But people affected and property loss

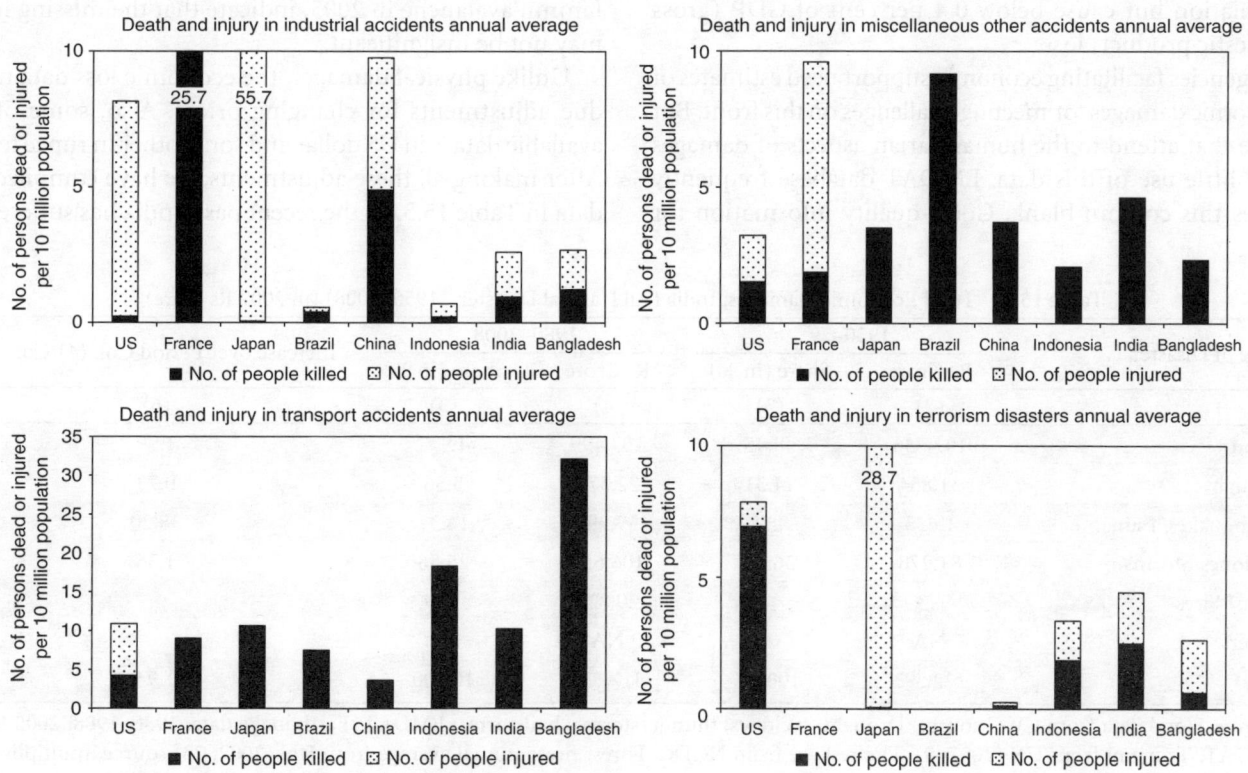

Figure 15.1 Physical Damages Caused by Man-made Disasters (Inter-country Comparison, 1991–2005)

Table 15.4   India: Disastrous Terrorist Acts, 1970–2008

Years	No. of Events	Average per Event		
		No. of People Killed	No. of People Injured	No. of Events with 50 or More Deaths
(1)	(2)	(3)	(4)	(5)
1970–9	0	0	0	0
1980–9	70	15.4	15.6	1
1990–9	174	18.9	13.7	7
2000–8	115	22.2	34.2	9
Total	359	19.6	22.0	17

Sources: GTD for events with deaths 10 or above. The information for 2008 has been added from newspapers, etc.

would be high. The after-effects of disasters extend to poorer health, disease, epidemic outbreak, anxiety, and trauma. Families are broken by death and disabilities. Social order may break down, leading to looting, rape, and murder. Business opportunities are lost. Transport and communications facilities are disrupted. Large-scale temporary and permanent migrations in search of livelihood are known features. Some disasters cause severe environmental damages and transform the local ecosystems. These are many different dimensions of damages caused by disasters, many of which do not admit economic valuations. Thus, every year, natural disasters affect above 5 per cent of Indian population but cause below 0.4 per cent of GDP (gross domestic product) loss.

Agencies facilitating economic support need estimates of economic damages for meeting challenges on this front. But those that attend to the humanitarian aspects of damages have little use of this data. EMDAT database frequently leaves this column blank. Good-quality information for the insured part of the economic damages is available from insurance companies. But most of the damages in India are not insured. The international donor agencies need careful estimates of economic damages, but only for larger disasters that draw their attention. For the rest, the economic loss data are either not available or are poor in quality.

We have relied on the CWC data for flood damages. The comparison of the cost of damage data shows that except for some recent years, the EMDAT data is either lower or marginally higher than that of CWC. For earthquake damages, two sources of data are available: National Geophysical Data Centre data for earthquakes and EMDAT. Although they collect information from similar set of agencies, and for most parts, provide identical data, the data gaps are not identical. We have, therefore, combined the two sources to obtain data of total losses from earthquakes. For droughts, cyclones, and storms, EMDAT is the only source of data for economic damage estimates. In a country-wide study in 1995, the Forest Survey of India estimated (UN 2002) that about 1.45 million hectares of forest were affected by fire annually and that average tangible annual loss due to forest fires in country is Rs 440 crore or about $100 million. Though it is for all forest fires, we have used this data. For the rest of the categories, little data is available. Stray information like economic loss of over $260 million in Surat plague (Pallipparambil 2005), Rs 50 crore Central grant to the state government for rebuilding the infrastructure damaged in Jammu avalanche in 2005, indicate that the missing items may not be insignificant.

Unlike physical damages, the economic loss data needs due adjustments for changing prices. Also, some of the available data is in US dollar and some other in rupee terms. After making all these adjustments, we have compiled the data in Table 15.5. In the recent past, India has suffered an

Table 15.5   Total Economic Damages: India (All Natural Disasters, 1950–2008) (in 2007 Rs crore)

Type of Disaster	1950–79		1980–2008		Increase over Period Col. (4)/Col. (2)
	Rs Crore	Share (in %)	Rs Crore	Share (in %)	
(1)	(2)	(3)	(4)	(5)	(6)
Flood	107,836	48.45	207,499	49.72	1.99
Drought	31,854	14.31	22,371	5.36	0.73
Earthquakes/Tsunami	1,625	0.73	59,990	14.37	38.20
Cyclones/Storms	81,278	36.51	106,655	25.56	1.36
Forest Fires	NA		20,824	4.99	
Others	NA		NA		
Total	222,593	100.00	417,338	100.00	1.94

Sources: Flood data from CWC source. Drought, cyclones, thunderstorms, hailstorms: EMDAT. Earthquake data: 1986, 1988, 2005 from EMDAT. Tsunami from UN (2007: 9). The rest are from NGDC. Forest fires: annual average from UN (2002: 23) source, multiplied by number of years.

Notes: No adjustment has been made for missing data. Conversion at the rate of Rs 40 per US$.

average economic loss of Rs 14,000 crore (US$ 3.6 billion) per annum. Floods account for about a half of economic loss due to natural disasters. The next in importance is loss caused by cyclones and storms. Earthquakes have become an important contributor in the recent period. Earthquake damages have increased enormously from the first three decades. Economic values of damages from other sources too have increased, though not as much. The losses from droughts have decreased in real term.

There are no standard methods for valuations of the physical losses in disaster. This leads to wide discrepancies. How are the valuations of Indian data? Here we list the averages of the imputed values (in 2007 prices) of crops, houses, and public property damages in the CWC flood-related data since 1953 till 2005.

Value of crop damaged per hectare of crop area	Rs 8,784
Value of unit of damaged house	Rs 7,144
Damage to public utilities per 1,000 persons affected	Rs 6.25 lakh

The valuations are on the lower side (see Box 15.1). Harvest prices of crops in India are about three to four times more than this. The careful estimates submitted three years after the tsunami (UN 2007) or the Asian Development Bank–World Bank estimates of the Gujarat earthquake loss (Lahiri et al. 2001) had imputed the average value of a damaged house at Rs 50,000. This too is conservative and the state government estimates were higher. It is true that the damages caused by earthquakes or tsunamis are near complete. Floods usually do not cause such havoc. Still, the rates for flood damage seem to be too low. A more serious problem is that the CWC estimates do not include loss of private property. To be fair, CWC clearly identifies the data as damages to 'total crops, houses and public utilities' without ever equating it to total loss. The unaccounted loss of private property in floods may be very high. Swiss Reinsurance (Swiss Re 2007: 17) sources indicate that only the insured losses in 2006 flood were Rs 1,800 crore. Their estimate of total damage was Rs 15,000 crore or $3.39 billion, a whooping 30 times the estimate (Rs 507.09 crore) of the CWC.

Table 15.6 shows the comparison with some other countries. In terms of total economic loss, India is among the leading countries in the world. But due to the large size of its economy, the impact on the economy gets thinned. This is true for the US, China, or Japan. Bangladesh suffers much less of economic loss in absolute terms but far greater adverse impact due to small size of its economy. In the world there are small countries for which disasters cost even a half of GDP. In that sense, India is not one amongst the worst sufferers of natural disasters. But it is not in the

Box 15.1   Flood—Undercutting Economic Loss

The June 2008 flood in the upper Mississippi River Basin is one of the two worst floods in the US history. About 11 million people were affected, 20 people were killed, and 5 million acres of agricultural land was inundated. The corresponding figures for *average annual* losses of Indian floods between 1953 and 2005 are uniformly higher: 33 million people affected, 1,589 people killed, and 8.74 million acres of crop area damaged. Economic loss from the June 2008 flood in the US is estimated at a whooping $10 billion, ten times higher than the Indian estimates of average annual losses from floods in India. The gigantic difference is because the US estimation methods (a) use higher valuation of each component of damage and (b) include damages to private property.

Source: Flood data for India taken from CWC and for US from Munich Re Group.

league of the more fortunate ones like Brazil or France, and a host of others not shown here.

For man-made disasters, insured losses are the most common sources of economic information. The problem is to separate according to scale, etc., so as to fit disasters alone. Only for some big disasters is specific data available. Thus, EMDAT records a total loss of Rs 2,200 crore in six technological disasters like Machhu dam collapse (1979), Charkhi Dadri midair collision (1996), HPCL Vizag Refinery fire (1997), and ONGC Bombay High fire (2005). After the terrorist attack in Mumbai in November 2008, the Associated Chambers of Commerce and Industry of India (ASSOCHAM) estimated that a minimum of Rs 1,000 crore per day was lost when hotels, shops, and all businesses remained closed for about four days.

Table 15.6   Total Economic Damages: Selected Countries (All Natural Disasters, 1990–2008) (in 2005 US$ billion)

Selected Countries	Total Economic Damage US$ Billion	% of GDP Lost
(1)	(2)	(3)
USA	487.71	0.19
China	299.02	0.48
Japan	203.83	0.25
India	39.41	0.17
France	25.27	0.05
Indonesia	20.79	0.25
Bangladesh	13.39	1.04
Brazil	4.33	0.02

Source: EMDAT.

All these are only the direct economic losses. The impacts include business and service opportunities lost for several years. Including secondary effects, the costs to economic development are substantial.

In 2008, in 137 natural catastrophes and 174 man-made disasters, the total economic loss was $269 billion, of which 85 per cent was due to natural disasters (Swiss Re 2009). Time series data suggest that disasters are increasing, so are the damages caused by them. This may be due partly to increase in population, climate change, or increasing violence. Rapid increase in economic loss, however, owes primarily to economic development. Developed countries accounted for only 0.63 per cent of fatalities but 38.65 per cent of overall loss in damages caused by natural disasters in 2008 (Munich Re 2009). A fast-growing country like India needs to take this in account.

DISASTER MANAGEMENT

Not so long ago disasters were seen as emergency situations. Responses were limited to emergency management, calamity relief, and at times, insurance provisions. With the realization that relief and rehabilitation yield only temporary result, there was a policy shift towards prevention and mitigation. In 1989, the UN General Assembly declared 1990–2000 as the International Decade for Natural Disaster Reduction. A four-dimensional strategy consisting of disaster prevention, mitigation, preparedness, and relief was put forth. The strategy emanates from current understanding of the disaster process. All natural hazards do not cause damages. A volcanic eruption in the barren island of Andaman was not a disaster. Only when a 'natural hazard' occurs in a well-settled area does it cause serious damages to vulnerable people and structures. Thus, disaster risk consists of three components:

- Hazard: physical effects of the threatening natural event
- Exposure: humans and the value of the various types of structures and lifeline systems, such as water supply, communications network, and transportation network, that are present in the location
- Vulnerability: lack of resistance of the exposed structures and systems to the hazardous force

One may write

Disaster Risk = Hazard × Exposure × Vulnerability

While earthquakes and tsunamis are 'natural hazards' that cannot be eliminated, it is possible to reduce vulnerability by careful steps. On the other hand, a hazard like chemical pollution needs to be managed primarily by containing the production of the hazardous substance. Thus, appropriate policies differ from case to case. Epidemics, for example, find immunization as the best strategy in some cases, and eradication for some others. Flood zoning policy is directed to reduce exposure. Fire damages are greatly reduced by reducing vulnerability through precautionary measures.

Although parts of this strategy had made humble beginning in India, the global thinking has led to systematization and concerted efforts. Some of the highlights of successful disaster management in India are multifarious drought management programmes that started quite early; introduction of early warning systems for cyclones and tsunamis; earthquake-resistant building designs; networks of cyclone shelters; or new building standards in seismic zones. These programmes have reduced both physical and economic damages. For better coordination, nodal agencies have been created at all levels. Further details of current disaster management programmes are beyond the purview of this chapter. We will conclude by introducing the financing methods.

FINANCING DISASTER MANAGEMENT

Rightful claims of compensations from negligent party responsible for causing a man-made accident face the severe hurdle of tedious litigations. Disasters bring many claimants together who may sustain the harrowing judicial process and ultimately make some difference, as were after Bhopal gas leak (1984) or Uphaar cinema hall fire (Delhi, 1997). But these cases have not brought any systematic change; volunteerism is still the major driving force for compensations. A disaster drawing wide public attention usually prompts the appropriate authority to show its concern by announcing compensations for death and injury. Several private groups and agencies too mobilize public contributions for relief. Prime Minister's National Relief Fund or similar funds managed by chief ministers of states consist entirely of public contributions. International assistance from the World Bank, Asian Development Bank, and similar agencies is an important source of finance after major disasters. India with forty-three loans tops the list of recipients of World Bank's disaster lending (World Bank 2006).

By far, the major source of financing is the government. In earlier years, when disasters were seen as emergency management works, financial supports by the government were in the form of ad hoc relief. Prevention and mitigation programmes like Drought Prone Areas Programme or departmental budgets for irrigation and flood control were met from the regular plan expenditures. The Ninth Finance Commission (1989–95), coinciding with the International Decade for Natural Disaster Reduction, introduced a Calamity Relief Fund (CRF) and simplified the procedures for grants and loans. The CRF has continued since then and has become the major source of finance for meeting relief expenses. Between 2000 and 2005, an average of Rs 2,200 crore was distributed from CRF each year. But it is an item of non-plan expenditure; systematization of expenses for restoration of infrastructure and other capital assets was awaited. The Eleventh Finance Commission (2000–5) went into this issue and recommended against using CRF for this end, suggesting that restoration expenses should be met from the plan funds on priority basis. Besides, most of the international donor agency assistances, like that of the World Bank, are given primarily for reconstruction. On the whole, funding required for restorations of public property and infrastructure is met regularly from one source or another. Not so is the case for damaged private properties. Part of this relief and rehabilitation grants is distributed as compensation for damaged houses. But apart from that, rarely is there any other assistance for restoration of private property. Direct economic losses are only a part of the story. Adverse economic impacts multiply if reconstructions are delayed and business and service opportunities are lost for several years.

Systematic restoration of damaged private property can be done through insurance. With increasing cost of damages and tightening fiscal positions of the governments, this is becoming the only available option. In general, insurance markets are not yet well developed in poorer countries, covering less than 2 per cent of the potential flood insurance market (World Bank 2006). The situation in India seems to be better. Swiss Re (2007: 17) sources show that in 2006 flood that affected many industries in Gujarat and Andhra Pradesh, about 12 per cent of total losses were insured. In many developed countries, private insurers are reluctant to cover disasters. The situation in India seems to be better. Both life and private property are insurable against all kinds of disasters, including terrorist act, though there are riders. For poorer sections, crop insurance schemes, covering losses due to natural calamities, were introduced in 1985. More recently, drought insurance programmes like Weather Index Insurance have been operated on a pilot basis. But these have not been of much help to the poor because of their faulty designs and extremely poor delivery.

Before concluding, let us note that disaster insurance is desirable but not an easy to implement proposition. Business models of insurance companies are based on predictable risk. Disasters unsettle them. Insurance markets respond to disasters by raising the price which sets a cyclical process, often leading to collapse of the market. In the past, the US private flood insurance market collapsed in this way and necessitated introduction of a Federal Flood Insurance programme in 1968. France has made its insurance programme for natural catastrophes (CatNat) mandatory. The frequent occurrences of mega-disasters in recent years have intensified this problem. Before 1989, there was not a single natural disaster in the US that cost the insurance industry $1 billion (Kunreuther 2006). Since then, more than 25 such mega-disasters have happened. Several insurance companies went bankrupt after the Katrina hurricane disaster. To save the market, new instruments like catastrophe bonds are being tried. Reinsurance mechanisms have been strengthened. Governments have extended their supports.

The insurance market in India has just started feeling the pinch. After the Mumbai flood in 2005, the General Insurance Corporation alone had settled claims worth Rs 650 crore. After the 2006 flood that hit several large industries at Vadodara, Hazira, and Bhadrachalam, insurance claims mounted to Rs 1,800 crore (Swiss Re 2007: 17). Following global practice, after World Trade Centre attack, India too had created its catastrophe insurance mechanism for damages caused by terrorist acts. Till recently, there was no claim from this terrorism pool. The first ever disbursement from this pool was made to Taj and Oberoi hotels after the 2008 Mumbai disaster. Insurance companies have raised the premium for terrorism cover.

REFERENCES

Central Water Commission (CWC) (2007), *Water Sector at a Glance*. New Delhi: CWC.

———— (various years), *Annual Report*. New Delhi: CWC.

De, U.S., R.K. Dube, and G.S. Prakasa Rao (2005), 'Extreme Weather Events Over India in the Last 100 Years', *Journal of the Indian Geophysical Union*, 9(3): 173–87.

Emergency Disasters Data Base (EMDAT) (2009), *EM-DAT: The OFDA/CRED International Disaster Database*, available at www.emdat.be, Université Catholique de Louvain, Brussels, Belgium, Data version: v12.07, 2009.

Global Terrorism Database (GTD), *Global Terrorism Database*, National Consortium for the Study of Terrorism and Responses to Terror (START). Available at http://www.start.umd.edu/start/

Government of India (2004), *Disaster Management in India: A Status Report, Version 1.0*. New Delhi: Ministry of Home Affairs, National Disaster Management Division.

Guha-Sapir, D. and R. Below (2002), *The Quality and Accuracy of Disaster Data—A Comparative Analyses of Three Global Data Sets*. Brussels: Center for Research on the Epidemiology of Disasters (CRED), WHO Centre for Research on the Epidemiology of Disasters, University of Louvain.

Kunreuther, Howard (2006), 'Reflections on U.S. Disaster Insurance Policy for the 21st Century', NBER Working Paper No. 12449.

Lahiri, Ashok K., T.K. Sen, P. Kavita Rao, and P.R. Jena (2001), 'Economic Consequences of the Gujarat Earthquake', National Institute of Public Finance and Policy, Working Paper No. 01/1.

Lin, T., Franklin D. De Guzman, and Maria Cita Cuevas (2007), 'Flood Insurance as a Flood Management Tool: An Economic Perspective', ERD Working Paper No. 99, Asian Development Bank, Manila.

Munich Re (2009), *Topics Geo-Natural Catastrophes 2008: Analyses, Assessments, Positions*, US version, Knowledge Series, Münchener Rückversicherungs-Gesellschaft, Munich.

National Geophysical Data Centre (NGDC) (2009), *Earthquake Data and Information*, Boulder, Colorado. Available at http://www.ngdc.noaa.gov/hazard/earthqk.shtml

Pallipparambil, G R. (2005), 'The Surat Plague and Its Aftermath', in *Essays on Yersinia pestis (the Plague)*, Montana State University, essays were written by graduate students. Available at http://entomology.montana.edu/historybug/yersiniaEssays/Introduction_to_essays.htm

Pielke, Jr. Roger A. and Mary W. Downton (2000), 'Precipitation and Damaging Floods: Trends in the United States, 1932–97', *Journal of Climate*, 13(20): 3625–37.

Sinha Ray, K. C. and M.P. Shewale (2001), 'Probability of Occurrence of Drought in Various Subdivisions', *Mausam*, July, 52(3), pp. 541–46.

Swiss Re (2007), *Natural Catastrophes and Man-made Disasters in 2006—Low Insured Losses*, Swiss Re Sigma No. 2/2007. Zurich: Swiss Reinsurance Co.

——— (2009), *Swiss Re Sigma Study: 2008 One of the Worst Years for Catastrophe Losses*. Zurich: Swiss Reinsurance Co.

UN Economic Commission for Europe, FAO (2002), *International Forest Fire News*, No. 26.

United Nations (UN) (2007), *Tsunami India—Three Years After, A Report by the United Nations, United Nations Team for Tsunami Recovery Support*, Chennai.

World Bank (2006), *Hazards of Nature, Risks to Development, An IEG Evaluation of World Bank Assistance for Natural Disasters*. Washington DC: World Bank.

16

India's Export Sophistication in a Comparative Perspective

C. Veeramani and Gordhan K. Saini

INTRODUCTION

Since the onset of the trade liberalization process in 1991, firms in India's domestic industries, which had been operating under protective umbrellas, have been forced to respond to competitive pressure from imports. In this scenario, domestic firms might respond by dropping their least sophisticated product lines and by moving up in the quality ladder. If this indeed happens, it will be reflected in the growing sophistication of India's export basket.

Using highly disaggregated trade data, this chapter attempts to analyse the relative sophistication of India's exports of manufactures during the pre- and post-liberalization periods. We also compare the Indian experience with that of other selected developing countries/regional groups. Following Schott (2008), we assume that the sophistication level of a country's exports improves as its export basket becomes more similar to that of the high-income OECD (Organisation for Economic Co-operation and Development) countries. This is consistent with the fact that richer countries generally hold comparative advantages in products that are highly sophisticated.

TRADE LIBERALIZATION AND EXPORT SOPHISTICATION: WHAT ARE THE CAUSAL LINKS?

In this section, drawing upon the existing literature, we elaborate on the causal mechanisms that may link trade liberalization to export sophistication. In the context of growing integration of national economies, a large number of empirical and theoretical studies address the question of how the domestic firms respond to trade liberalization and increased foreign competition. Empirical evidence from the developing countries confirms the positive effect of trade liberalization on aggregate productivity.[1] As noted by Tybout (2003), the productivity gains in these countries have been driven primarily by within-industry resource reallocation as opposed to across-industry reallocation emphasized by the old theories of comparative advantage.[2] Trade liberalization can lead to within-industry resource reallocation in two possible ways. First, market shares might be reallocated from the least productive to the most productive firms within a given industry (Melitz 2003). Second, firms are forced to focus on their 'core competencies' by dropping the product lines that are inconsistent with their comparative advantages (Bernard et al. 2006b).

An important outcome of these adjustment processes, apart from the productivity gains, is the potential improvement in the 'sophistication' level of the country's export

[1] See Tybout (2003) for a survey.
[2] The importance of within-industry resource reallocation is also evident from studies that establish significant growth of intra-industry trade in many countries after trade liberalization. See Veeramani (2002, 2009) for evidence from India and for references to other studies.

basket. This can happen for the following two reasons. First, within an industry, the relatively more productive firms may also be producing the relatively more sophisticated varieties. Thus, reallocation of market shares towards the more productive firms may imply an overall improvement in the sophistication level of the country's export basket. Second, heightened competition may induce the firms to 'move up' by reallocating resources within and across plants towards the manufacture of more sophisticated goods.

We may expect an improvement in the level of India's export sophistication for certain other reasons as well. First, accumulation of productive factors, such as human and physical capital, that characterizes economic growth, can bring about a dynamic process of changing comparative advantage. For example, the road to export success of the Newly Industrialized Countries (NICs) of Asia started with labour-intensive and low-technology manufactures. However, as investments in the physical and human capital rose and as labour costs increased with the accumulation of skills, relatively more sophisticated manufacturing activity expanded in these countries at the expense of labour-intensive manufactures. Second, trade and foreign direct investment (FDI) play an important role as a transmission channel for knowledge spillovers across countries (e.g., Keller 2004). Thus, India's export basket may become more sophisticated over time as a result of the positive spillover effects from her expanding trade and inward FDI. Finally, trade enables the use of better (Aghion and Howitt 1992) and larger (Romer 1987) variety of intermediate products and capital equipments, which can directly improve the sophistication level of a country's exports.

TRENDS AND PATTERNS OF MANUFACTURED EXPORTS

This section provides an overview of the trends and patterns of manufactured exports for India and other selected countries/regional groups. The selection of eighteen developing countries (including India) is based on the fulfilment of all the following three criteria: (i) the country should fall in the group of lower and middle-income countries (World Bank classification); (ii) the country's gross domestic product (GDP) (constant US$) in 2006 should be at least $21 billion (which is the GDP figure of Sri Lanka in 2006); and (iii) the average share of manufactured exports in the total exports of the country should be higher than 50 per cent during 2000–6 (India's average share during this period was 74 per cent).[3] Excluding India and China, the remaining sixteen of these

countries have been clubbed into five regional groups. These are Africa–3 (Morocco, South Africa, Tunisia); Central and South America–2 (Brazil, Mexico); South Asia–3 (Bangladesh, Pakistan, Sri Lanka); South-East Asia–4 (Indonesia, Malaysia, Philippines, Thailand); and Turkey and Eastern Europe–3 (Turkey, Hungary, Poland, Romania).

During 1990–2006, manufactured exports from India grew at a rate of 12 per cent per annum. During the same period, exports from China and Turkey and Eastern Europe–3 had recorded significantly higher growth rates of 19 per cent and 16 per cent respectively. However, India fares better than South Asia–3 (9 per cent growth rate) and high-income OECD (6 per cent growth rate). Exports from the remaining regional groups grew at rates roughly similar to that of India: that is, 13 per cent for both Africa–3 and Central and South America–2; and 11 per cent for South-East Asia–4 (estimated using United Nations COMTRADE Database, accessed through World Bank's WITS software).

Table 16.1 shows the composition of manufactured exports across the 1-digit level of Standard International Trade Classification (SITC). The composition of India's exports shows some changes away from the traditional labour-intensive sectors of 'manufactured materials' and 'miscellaneous manufactures' in favour of the relatively more capital-intensive 'chemicals' and 'machinery'. Yet, the traditional sectors account for about two-thirds India's manufactured exports in 2006, which is next to the South Asia–3 where they (mainly due to textiles) account for as much as 95 per cent of total manufactured exports. China shows a significant increase in the share of machinery, accounting for half of its total manufactured exports, a figure close to that of high-income OECD. Overall, at the highly aggregate 1-digit level of SITC, China's export basket exhibits greater degree of overlap with the high-income OECD compared to India's export overlap with the latter.

It may be instructive to look at the relative shares of differentiated and homogenous products in a country's total export. For, the variation in quality/sophistication matters more in differentiated products as compared to homogenous products. Rauch (1999) proposed a classification of 4-digit SITC categories into three classes: 'homogenous', 'differentiated', and an intermediate category called 'reference-priced'. Table 16.2 uses this classification scheme to show the changes in the shares of the three categories of products within the manufacturing sector.

As expected, differentiated products account for the major share in all countries/regional groups, except for Africa–3, which is specialized in homogenous products.[4]

---

[3] Twenty-one countries have satisfied all these criteria, but three of them (Slovakia, Croatia, and Ukraine) have been dropped due to non-availability of data.

[4] Within Africa-3, however, Morocco is specialized in differentiated products, while South Africa and Tunisia are specialized in homogenous products.

Table 16.1   Composition of Manufactured Exports (per cent)

Country and Region	Chemicals		Manufactured Materials		Machinery		Miscellaneous Manufacturing	
	1990	2006	1990	2006	1990	2006	1990	2006
India	*11*	*17*	*53*	*45*	*11*	*16*	*26*	*22*
China	8	5	28	19	24	50	39	26
Africa–3	28	12	17	43	10	29	44	16
Central and South America–2	12	7	37	17	42	64	9	12
South Asia–3	1	2	58	41	2	2	40	54
South-East Asia–4	4	8	27	16	39	61	30	14
Turkey and Eastern Europe–3	12	7	35	25	29	50	24	18
High-income OECD	12	17	20	18	53	53	15	13

Source: United Nations COMTRADE Database (accessed through World Bank's WITS software), available at http://wits.worldbank.org/wits/

Table 16.2   Export Profiles according to Rauch (1999) Classification (per cent)

Country and Region	Homogenous		Differentiated		Reference-priced	
	1990	2006	1990	2006	1990	2006
India	*0.1*	*0.5*	*50.5*	*67.6*	*49.5*	*31.9*
China	0.5	0.2	95.9	95.8	3.6	4.1
Africa–3	56.8	41.8	12.2	23.9	31.0	34.3
Central and South America–2	4.2	1.5	87.4	92.1	8.4	6.4
South Asia–3	0.0	1.4	94.3	96.1	5.7	2.5
South East Asia–4	1.1	0.2	93.0	95.6	6.0	4.2
Turkey and Eastern Europe–3	2.5	0.8	75.9	78.9	21.7	20.3
High-income OECD	2.3	2.5	85.8	83.4	11.9	14.1

Source: United Nations COMTRADE Database (accessed through World Bank's WITS software), available at http://wits.worldbank.org/wits/

The share of differentiated products in India's total manufactured exports increased from 50.5 per cent in 1990 to 67.6 per cent in 2006. To the extent higher product differentiation represents higher level of sophistication, the increase in the share of differentiated products is suggestive of the growing sophistication levels of India's export basket. China is highly specialized in differentiated products, accounting for 96 per cent of total manufactured exports, and so are South-East Asia–4 and South Asia–3. There is a large share of differentiated products in South Asia–3 because most of the 4-digit items under 'textiles' (the main export category of South Asia–3) are classified as differentiated products.

We now turn to a more direct measure of export sophistication proposed by Lall et al. (2006). The basic idea behind the sophistication index proposed by Lall et al. (2006) is that the products exported by the richer countries are more sophisticated than the products exported by the poor countries. Thus, sophistication scores are calculated for each product for 1990 and 2000 by taking the weighted average (the weight being each country's share of world

exports in the given product) of exporter incomes. The scores are then normalized to yield an index ranging from 0 to 100. The authors have grouped the 181 manufactured products (at the 3-digit level of SITC) into six sophistication levels by dividing the total number of products into sets of 30 each (31 for the last group) along the sophistication scale, where sophistication level 1 (SL1) is the most sophisticated group while sophistication level 6 (SL6) is the least sophisticated.

Table 16.3 shows the value shares (in total manufactured exports) of the six sophistication levels. It is clear that the share of the least sophisticated SL6 has declined substantially from 44 per cent to 26 per cent in India while the shares of all other sophistication groups have increased. The combined share of the most sophisticated groups (SL1 and SL2) has increased from 13 per cent to 15 per cent. Overall, Table 16.3 indicates a slow but definite increase in the sophistication level of India's export basket. The combined shares of the middle level SL3 and SL4 have registered significant increases from 12 per cent in 1990 to 21 per cent in 2006. Despite the overall improvement in

Table 16.3 Sophistication of Exports Using Lall et al. (2006) Methodology (Percentage Shares of Sophistication Levels in Total Manufactured Exports)

Country and Region	SL1		SL2		SL3		SL4		SL5		SL6	
	1990	2006	1990	2006	1990	2006	1990	2006	1990	2006	1990	2006
India	8	9	5	6	6	11	6	10	32	38	44	26
China	14	8	7	5	8	20	9	30	17	15	45	23
Africa–3	2	8	3	14	6	15	18	14	23	20	48	29
Central and South America–2	17	17	16	14	14	22	12	13	15	14	26	19
South Asia–3	3	2	1	1	1	2	3	3	12	8	81	85
South-East Asia–4	2	6	4	7	15	18	22	38	22	13	35	17
Turkey and Eastern Europe–3	12	15	8	15	10	17	18	16	21	19	31	18
High-income OECD	24	27	20	20	19	20	18	17	10	11	9	6

Source: United Nations COMTRADE Database (accessed through World Bank's WITS software), available at http://wits.worldbank.org/wits/

the sophistication level, it may be noted that the relatively less sophisticated SL5 and SL6 together still accounted for as much as two-thirds of India's manufactured exports in 2006. This is consistent with the earlier observation that the traditional groups 'manufactured materials' and 'miscellaneous manufactures' (most of which are grouped under SL5 and SL6) accounted for about two-thirds of India's exports in 2006 (see Table 16.1).

In China, the combined share of the least sophisticated SL5 and SL6 declined from 62 per cent in 1990 to 38 per cent in 2006, while the combined share of the middle level SL3 and SL4 increased substantially from 17 per cent to 50 per cent. However, the combined share of the most sophisticated SL1 and SL2 declined from 21 per cent to 13 per cent, while their share marginally increased in India from 13 per cent to 15 per cent. Thus, the entire increase in the sophistication level of China's exports is accounted for by the middle levels SL3 and SL4.

A general rise in the level of export sophistication can be seen in all the regional groups as well, except for South Asia–3. The shares of the least sophisticated SL5 and SL6 have declined in all the regional groups (with the exception of South Asia–3) while the shares of other sophistication levels have generally increased. Not surprisingly, high-income OECD is highly specialized in the most sophisticated SL1 and SL2 with a combined share of 47 per cent in 2006. As far as the middle-level categories (SL3 and SL4) are concerned, South-East Asia–4 ranks first with a combined share of 56 per cent, followed by China with a share of 50 per cent in 2006.

The preceding analysis uses data at a rather aggregate level of commodity classification, which may hide important heterogeneities within these commodity groups, for example, variation in the quality of the varieties within a commodity group. Use of finely disaggregated data

enables us to analyse the issue in greater detail. In particular, the unit values (value divided by quantity) calculated using finely disaggregated data are more accurate as they do not suffer from the aggregation biases. Thus, the analyses in the following sections are based on highly disaggregated (10-digit level) US bilateral import data for 1989 and 2006. These two years are selected since they are respectively the earliest and the latest years for which comparable data are available.[5] We use the US data since these are available at the most finer a level of disaggregation.

MARKET SHARES AND PRODUCT PENETRATION OF COUNTRIES/REGIONAL GROUPS IN THE US MARKET

This section provides an overview of the performance of India, China, and the different regional groups in the US market, in terms of their shares in total US import value and the extent of their product penetration (see Table 16.4). As expected, the high-income OECD countries dominate the US import market in all industry groups (SITC 1-digit), though less so over time. While the high-income OECD countries accounted for as high as 70 per cent of the US manufacturing imports in 1989, this share fell to 48 per cent by 2006. This decline in the OECD share is largely due to the phenomenal rise of China's share in the US imports and to a lesser extent due to the increase in the share of Mexico. Between 1989 and 2006, China's share in the US imports increased from 3 per cent to 21 per cent while Mexico's share increased from 5 per cent to 11 per cent. During the same

[5] The US data are accessed from Robert Feenstra's homepage (http://cid.econ.ucdavis.edu/).

Table 16.4   Market Share and Product Penetration in Manufacturing

Country/Region	Market Share		Product Penetration		Intensive Margin	Extensive Margin
	1989	2006	1989	2006		
India	*0.7*	*1.5*	*25*	*54*	*54.2*	*45.8*
China	3.0	21.1	44	85	30.2	69.8
Africa–3	0.4	0.5	11	25	56.2	43.8
Central and South America–2	6.4	11.8	51	63	41.1	58.9
South Asia–3	0.4	0.7	12	21	36.9	63.1
South-East Asia–4	3.1	5.3	34	52	15.9	84.1
Turkey and Eastern Europe–3	0.4	0.7	19	43	35.3	64.7
High-income OECD	69.6	47.8	98	97	49.7	50.3

Source: Authors' calculations using US Customs Service data (accessed from Robert Feenstra's homepage, http://cid.econ.ucdavis.edu/).

period, India's share increased from 0.7 per cent to 1.5 per cent. In both the years, India's share remained higher than that of South Asia–3, Turkey and Eastern Europe–3, and Africa–3 while the shares of South-East Asia–4 and Central and South America–2 remained significantly higher than that of India.

Among the eighteen developing countries, India ranks fourth with respect to the market share in 2006, just behind China, Mexico, and Malaysia. The market shares are highly correlated with the size of countries (measured by GDP), with the spearman rank correlation being 0.77 for 2006. This is consistent with the theories of international trade that predict that a larger economy will export more in absolute terms than a smaller economy (Hummels and Klenov 2005). Given that India is the second largest country among the eighteen countries, her market share (with a rank of 4) is less than what would be expected, given India's relative size.

Product penetration of a country/regional group will be 100 per cent if all varieties are exported and close to 0 per cent if very few varieties are exported. It is clear from Table 16.4 that product penetration by the OECD is nearly 100 per cent in both the years, while that by other countries/regional groups had increased significantly over time. While China shows the largest increase, it is noteworthy that India's product penetration rate of 54 per cent in 2006 is higher than that of other regional groups, excluding Central and South America–2.

Product penetration rates of the eighteen individual countries are highly correlated with their size (measured by GDP), with the spearman rank correlation being as high as 0.92 for 2006. This is consistent with the prediction of monopolistic competition model of trade that larger countries would export a wider array of varieties (Krugman 1981). Among the eighteen countries, India ranks third in terms of product penetration in 2006 and ranks second

in terms of the absolute change in product penetration between 1989 and 2006. Thus, India's product penetration rate is broadly consistent with her size.

A country's export can grow by increasing the export value of incumbent varieties (intensive margin) and/or by increasing the number of varieties exported (extensive margin). It is worthwhile to examine the relative importance of intensive margin and extensive margin by decomposing the export growth between 1989 and 2006. Intensive margin is defined as part of the growth that is attributable to continuously produced goods while extensive margin is the growth due to the net adding and dropping of products. Extensive margin accounts for about 46 per cent of India's export growth while it accounts for 70 per cent of China's export growth. Extensive margin is considerably more important than intensive margin in India's chemicals (89 per cent) and machinery (74 per cent) while intensive margin is more important in traditional labour-intensive export industries such as manufactured materials and miscellaneous manufacturing.[6] In the case of China's exports, extensive margins account for the major share in all industry groups (SITC 1-digit).

EXPORT SIMILARITY WITH THE HIGH-INCOME OECD COUNTRIES

The analysis in the third section, 'Trends and Patterns of Manufactured Exports', confirms that the high-income OECD countries specialize in the most sophisticated groups of products. This is as expected since the richer countries have a comparative advantage in knowledge-intensive

---

[6] Industry group-wise (SITC 1-digit) data are not reported in the table, but can be obtained from the author.

products. Thus, we assume that the sophistication level of a country's exports improves as its export basket becomes more similar to that of the high-income OECD countries. We compute an export similarity index (ESI), first suggested by Finger and Kreinin (1979) and used in Schott (2008). For any two US trading partners *a* and *b*, this index is just the sum of the two countries' minimum presence in each good.

$$ESI_t^{ab} = \sum_p \min\left(s_{pt}^a, s_{pt}^b\right)$$

where s_{pt}^a and s_{pt}^b are the shares of product *p* in the total manufactured exports of country *a* and country *b*, respectively, in year *t*. The index is bound by 0 and unity: it equals 0 if countries *a* and *b* have no products in common in year *t*, and it equals unity if their products are distributed identically across products.

The ESI values of each country/regional group with the high-income OECD are shown in Table 16.5 (column 2). The growing similarity of India's export bundle with that of the high-income OECD is evident from the significant increase of India's ESI from 0.07 in 1989 to 0.16 in 2006. Among the countries/regional groups shown Table 16.5, product mix overlap with the OECD is the highest for Central and South America–2, followed by Turkey and Eastern Europe–3 and China. As expected, values of the ESI are the lowest for South Asia–3 and Africa–3. Among the eighteen individual countries, India's rank with respect to the ESI has improved from seventh in 1989 to fourth in 2006 (just behind Mexico, China, and Brazil).[7] In terms of the absolute change of ESI between 1989 and 2006, India ranks second with an absolute change of 0.09 among the eighteen individual countries. Poland ranks first with an absolute change of 0.10.

In general, the smaller the difference in any two countries' level of per capita income, the greater will be the degree of similarity in their export basket. Thus, we may expect that the value of the ESI (with the high-income OECD) of the relatively richer developing country would be higher than that of the poor countries. The spearman correlation coefficient between the ESI (with the high-income OECD) and per capita GDP of the eighteen countries is 0.50 for 2006. However, both India and China are clear exceptions to the general positive relationship between ESI and per capita GDP. Among the eighteen countries, while India ranks sixteenth with respect to the level of per capita GDP, her rank with respect to the value of ESI is fourth. China's ranks with respect to per capita GDP and ESI are eleventh and second

respectively. Thus, exclusion of India and China leads to an increase of the spearman correlation coefficient from 0.50 to as high as 0.70, clearly suggesting that these two countries are outliers in the relationship between per capita GDP and ESI. In other words, India and China exhibit significantly greater overlap with the OECD than one would expect for a country with their levels of per capita GDP.

We have also computed the ESI of India with other countries/regional groups (not reported in Table 16.5). As expected, India's export basket is most similar to that of South Asia–3, though less so over time. India's ESI with South Asia–3 has declined from 0.23 in 1989 to 0.18 in 2006. In contrast, India's ESI with China and other regional groups increased in 2006 compared to 1989: from 0.13 to 0.16 with China; from 0.04 to 0.07 with Africa–3; from 0.06 to 0.13 with Central and South America–2; from 0.11 to 0.12 with South-East Asia–4; and from 0.15 to 0.16 with Turkey and Eastern Europe–3.

Export sophistication involves two dimensions—that is, *across* product sophistication and *within* product sophistication. For example, the rising ESI of India with the high-income OECD implies growing sophistication of India's exports in the across product dimension. The concern with within product sophistication arises mainly due to variation in the quality of the varieties (within a product) exported by different countries. Thus, while India's ESI with the high-income OECD is increasing over time, the latter may be exporting increasingly higher quality products compared to the former.

In order to gauge the changes in within product sophistication, we compute a quality overlap index (QOI) making use of the US import unit values, which are proxied for quality. The QOI compares the quality level of the high-income OECD export basket with that of the country/regional group under consideration. The index is defined only for the subsets of products for which both the high-income OECD and the country/regional group under consideration report positive export values for the given year. The index is defined as:

$$QOI_{pt}^a = 1 - \frac{\left|uv_{pt}^{oecd} - uv_{pt}^a\right|}{\left(uv_{pt}^{oecd} + uv_{pt}^a\right)}$$

where (uv_{pt}^{oecd}) is the unit value of US imports from the high-income OECD in product *p* and year *t*, and (uv_{pt}^a) is the unit value of US imports from country/regional group *a* in product *p* and year *t*. The value of this index ranges from 0 to unity. Higher the value of the index, the greater is the quality overlap between the high-income OECD and country/regional group *a* in product *p*. A value close to 0 indicates significant quality divergence between the high-income OECD and country/regional group *a* in product *p*.

---

[7] For India, we have computed the ESI for 1995 and 2001 as well. The values of the index are 0.8 and 0.11, respectively, for 1995 and 2001, indicating that the increase has been consistent over the years.

Table 16.5   Export Similarity Index, Quality Overlap Index, and Median Unit Value Ratios

Country/Region	ESI		QOI		Median of Log UVR_{pt}^{oecd}		Median of Log UVR_{pt}^{india}	
	1989	2006	1989	2006	1989	2006	1989	2006
India	*0.07*	*0.16*	*0.62*	*0.61*	*−0.18 (65)*	*−0.20 (66)*	*–*	*–*
China	0.14	0.20	0.53	0.45	−0.29 (78)	−0.35 (79)	−0.11 (62)	−0.14 (65)
Africa–3	0.06	0.08	0.86	0.82	0.01 (49)	0.07 (44)	0.12 (41)	0.35 (27)
Central and South America–2	0.32	0.26	0.58	0.56	−0.13 (67)	−0.12 (62)	−0.01 (51)	0.04 (47)
South Asia–3	0.03	0.03	0.57	0.55	−0.30 (79)	−0.44 (79)	−11 (65)	−0.10 (62)
South-East Asia–4	0.15	0.17	0.63	0.49	−0.13 (62)	−0.23 (71)	0.09 (40)	−0.02 (53)
Turkey and Eastern Europe–3	0.10	0.21	0.70	0.57	−0.17 (68)	−0.04 (53)	0.03 (46)	0.21 (34)

Source: Authors' calculations using US Customs Service data (accessed from Robert Feenstra's homepage, http://cid.econ.ucdavis.edu/).

Notes: The values in parentheses under column (4) are the percentage shares of the total number of products where the unit values are higher for OECD than the given country/regional group. The values in parentheses under column (5) are the percentage shares where the unit values are higher for India than the given country/region.

Table 16.5 (column 3) shows the weighted averages of the QOI, where the weights being the value share of product p in country/regional group a's exports to the US. What is immediately noticeable from the table is an across-the-board decline in the value of the QOI in 2006 over 1989. This indicates a growing divergence in the qualities of the products exported by the high-income OECD and other countries/regional groups. Further analysis later shows that, for the most part, this divergence is attributable to the faster quality growth of the high-income OECD export bundle compared to that of other countries/regional groups. Thus, while the export bundles of developing countries are becoming more similar to that of the high-income OECD, the latter is upgrading the quality of its products at a faster rate as a response to competition.[8]

Interestingly, values of the QOI for India are higher than that of China in both the years. Among the eighteen individual countries, India's rank with respect to the QOI improved from ninth in 1989 to sixth in 2006. China's rank remained very low at seventeenth in both the years, the only countries below China being Tunisia in 1989 and Hungary in 2006.

The results show relatively high values of QOI for Africa–3, which is mainly due to South Africa. It may, however, be noted that product penetration by Africa–3 is one of the smallest (Table 16.4) and that the QOI is defined only for this small subset of products.[9] Further, exports of Africa–3 mostly belong to the group of 'homogenous' products while other countries/regional groups mainly export differentiated products (Table 16.2). If quality variation is less pervasive in homogenous products compared to differentiated products, the relatively high quality overlap between Africa–3 and the high-income OECD (measured by QOI) may not be surprising.[10]

While it is expected that the high-income OECD countries would export higher quality products compared to other countries/regional groups, the QOI is not helpful in making this kind of comparison. We attempt to compare the high-income OECD unit values in each of the products with those of other countries/regional groups using the unit value ratios defined as:

$$UVR_{pt}^{oecd} = \frac{uv_{pt}^{a}}{uv_{pt}^{oecd}}$$

Value of the unit value ratio in product p and time $t(uvr_{pt}^{oecd})$ will be less (more) than unity if the unit value of country/regional group a in product p and time $t(uv_{pt}^{a})$ is lower (higher) than that of the high-income OECD (uv_{pt}^{oecd}). We took the log of the unit value ratios, and therefore any ratio less than 0 indicates that the quality of the product p imported from the high-income OECD is higher than that from country/regional group a, and vice-versa for any ratio greater than 0. As in the case of the QOI, unit value ratios are defined only for the subsets of products for which both

---

[8] Schott (2008) makes a similar observation.

[9] Product penetration by high-income OECD is nearly 100 per cent (Table 16.4), which implies that it has an export presence in almost all products. Thus, the number of products for which the QOI is defined for each country/regional group can easily be understood from the extent of their product penetration.

[10] Lall et al. (2006) reported a relatively high level of export sophistication for sub-Saharan Africa (with and without South Africa) and noted that this is 'not based on technological sophistication but the distribution of certain resource based products in richer countries' (p. 13). It is likely that these resource-based products are also what are termed as 'homogenous' products.

the high-income OECD and the country/regional group under consideration report positive export values for the given year.

The medians of log unit value ratios are reported in Table 16.5 (column 4). It is evident that the median ratios are negative for all countries/regional groups, except for Africa–3 where it is a small positive. Thus, as expected, the high-income OECD generally exports higher quality products as compared to other countries/regional groups. Percentage shares of the total number of products for which the OECD reports higher unit values than the given country/regional group are shown in parentheses under column (4) in Table 16.5.[11] It is again clear that in the majority of the cases, OECD products show higher levels of quality than other countries/regional groups (except for Africa–3). India reports higher unit values than high-income OECD in about 34 per cent of the total number of products in 2006. This compares better than China, which reports higher unit values than the high-income OECD in about 21 per cent of the total number of products in 2006.

Higher absolute values of the unit value ratios in 2006 compared to 1989 indicate faster quality upgrading in the high-income OECD. This is the case with India, China, South Asia–3, and South-East Asia–4. As noted by Schott (2008), the widening quality gaps between the high-income OECD and other countries/regional groups might indicate international product cycling, that is, the former seems to be specializing in even more sophisticated varieties as a response to globalization. These responses are consistent with more direct evidence of quality upgrading observed in firm-level data (e.g., Bernard et al. 2006).

Finally, we attempt to compare the Indian unit values with those of other countries/regional groups using the unit value ratios defined as:

$$UVR_{pt}^{india} = \frac{uv_{pt}^{a}}{uv_{pt}^{india}}$$

Log value of these ratios will be less than 0 if India's export unit values are higher than that of other countries/regions.[12] The median values of the ratios and the percentage shares of the total number of products for which India reports higher unit values than the given country/regional group are shown in column (5) of Table 16.5. It is evident

that in both the years, India's export unit values are distinctly higher than those of China and South Asia–3 and are marginally higher than South-East Asia–4 in 2006. India's export unit values are higher than that of China in as many as 65 per cent of the total number of products in 2006.

That India exports relatively higher quality products than China, despite the spectacular export performance of the latter, is intriguing. A plausible explanation for this may be found in the relatively high capital and skill intensity of exports and industrial output in India. Despite her comparative advantage in unskilled labour-intensive goods, the fast growing exports from India are either skilled labour-intensive or capital-intensive (Panagariya 2008). This outcome, according to Kochhar et al. (2006) and Panagariya (2008), is a consequence of distortionary policies in India, particularly those related to the firing and hiring of labour. Thus, if the unit value of a product variety increases with the capital and skill embodied in that variety, it may be argued that the relatively high export unit values of India are reflections of her distorted specialization in capital- and skill-intensive varieties/process.

CONCLUSION

Trade liberalization is expected to bring about an improvement in the sophistication level of a country's export basket. The present chapter, using highly disaggregated trade data, is an attempt to analyse the changes in the relative sophistication of India's exports of manufactures during the pre- and post-liberalization periods. We have also compared the Indian experience with the experiences of other selected developing countries/regional groups.

The rising share of differentiated products in India's export basket is suggestive of growing export sophistication. Analysis using a more direct measure of export sophistication proposed by Lall et al. (2006) has confirmed a slow but definite increase in the sophistication level of India's export basket in 2006 compared to 1990. This analysis was carried out using data at a rather aggregate level of commodity classification, that is, at the 3-digit level of SITC. Since the aggregate data may hide important heterogeneities within the commodity groups (for example, variation in quality), we have also made use of the highly disaggregated (10-digit level) US bilateral import data.

We assume that the sophistication level of a country's exports improves as its export basket becomes more similar to that of the high-income OECD countries. Growing similarity of India's export bundle with that of the high-income OECD is evident from the consistent and significant increase of the former's ESI with the latter over the years. Among the eighteen selected developing countries, India's rank with respect to the ESI has improved from seventh in

---

[11] Total number of products here represents the subsets of products for which both the high-income OECD and the country/regional group under consideration report positive export values for the given year.

[12] These ratios are defined only for the subsets of products for which both India and the country/regional group under consideration report positive export values for the given year.

1989 to fourth in 2006. In terms of the absolute change of ESI between 1989 and 2006, India ranks second among the eighteen countries.

The analyses using the US import unit values suggest that the high-income OECD generally exports higher quality products as compared to other countries/regional groups. While the ESI captures sophistication in the across product dimension, the QOI of the individual countries captures sophistication in the within product dimension. The analysis showed that while the export bundles of developing countries (including India) are becoming more similar to that of the high-income OECD, the latter is upgrading the quality of its products at a faster rate as a response to competition.

While China shows a higher level of sophistication than India in the across product dimension (as measured by ESI), India ranks above China with respect to sophistication in the within product dimension (measured by QOI). We have also compared the Indian unit values with those of other developing countries/regions using the unit value ratios. It is evident that India's export unit values are distinctly higher than those of China and South Asia–3. We have argued that this could be a consequence of distortionary policies in India that encourage specialization in capital- and skill-intensive varieties/process at the cost of unskilled labour-intensive activities where the country holds its true comparative advantage.

REFERENCES

Aghion, Philippe and Peter Howitt (1992), 'A Model of Growth Through Creative Destruction', *Econometrica*, 60(2): 323–51.

Bernard, Andrew, J. Bradford Jensen, and Peter K. Schott (2006a), 'Survival of the Best Fit: Exposure to Low-Wage Countries and the (Uneven) Growth of US Manufacturing Plants', *Journal of International Economic Studies*, 68: 219–37.

Bernard, Andrew, Stephen J. Redding, and Peter K. Schott (2006b), 'Multi-product Firms and Trade Liberalization', NBER Working Paper 12782, Cambridge, MA.

Finger, J.M. and M.E. Kreinin (1979), 'A Measure of "Export Similarity" and Its Possible Uses', *Economic Journal*, 89(356): 905–12.

Hummels, David and Peter Klenov (2005), 'The Variety and Quality of a Nation's Exports', *American Economic Review*, 95(3): 704–23.

Keller, Wolfgang (2004), 'International Technology Diffusion', *Journal of Economic Literature*, 42(3): 752–82.

Kochhar, Kalpana, Utsav Kumar, Raghuram Rajan, Arvind Subramanian, and Ioannis Tokatlidis (2006), 'India's Pattern of Development: What Happened, What Follows', NBER Working Paper 12023, Cambridge, MA.

Krugman, Paul R. (1981), 'Intraindustry Specialization and the Gains from Trade', *Journal of Political Economy*, 89(5): 959–73.

Lall, Sanjaya, John Weiss, and Jinkang Zhang (2006), 'The "Sophistication" of Exports: A New Trade Measure', *World Development*, 34(2): 222–37.

Melitz, Marc (2003), 'The Impact of Trade on Intra-industry Reallocations and Aggregate Industry Productivity', *Econometrica*, 71(6): 1695–725.

Panagariya, Arvind (2008), *India: The Emerging Giant*. New York: Oxford University Press.

Rauch, James E. (1999), 'Networks versus Markets in International Trade', *Journal of International Economics*, 48(1): 7–35.

Romer, Paul M. (1987), 'Growth Based on Increasing Returns Due to Specialization', *American Economic Review*, 77(2): 56–62.

Schott, Peter K. (2008), 'The Relative Sophistication of Chinese Exports', *Economic Policy*, 23(53): 5–49.

Tybout, James R. (2003), 'Plant and Firm Level Evidence on "New" Trade Theories', in E. Kwan Choi and James Harrigan (eds), *Handbook of International Trade*, pp. 545–64. Oxford, UK: Blackwell.

Veeramani, C. (2002), 'Intra-Industry Trade of India: Trends and Country-Specific Factors', *Weltwirtschaftliches Archiv/Review of World Economics*, 138(3): 509–33.

——— (2009), 'Trade Barriers, Multinational Involvement, and Intra-Industry Trade: Panel Data Evidence from India', *Applied Economics*, 41(20): 2541–53.

A STATISTICAL PROFILE
OF
INDIA'S DEVELOPMENT

A1 NATIONAL INCOME
Table A1.1 Key National Accounts Aggregates (at Constant Prices)

Note: Values are followed by percentage growth rates in parentheses where applicable.

Year	GDP at Factor Cost (2)	Net Factor Income from Abroad (3)	GNP at Factor Cost (2+3) (4)	Consumption of Fixed Capital (5)	NNP at Factor Cost (4–5) (6)	NDP at Factor Cost (2–5) (7)	Indirect Taxes Less Subsidies (9–2) (8)	GDP at Market Prices (2+8) (9)	NDP at Market Prices (7+8) (10)	GNP at Market Prices (4+8) (11)	NNP at Market Prices (6+8) (12)
1999–2000 Series											
1950–1	224786 (–)	−886	223899 (–)	18975	204924 (–)	205811	11281 (–)	236067 (–)	217092 (–)	235180 (–)	216205 (–)
1951–2	230034 (2.3)	−554	229480 (2.5)	19810	209669 (2.1)	210224	12961 (14.9)	242995 (2.9)	223185 (2.8)	242441 (3.1)	222631 (3.0)
1952–3	236562 (2.8)	−449	236113 (2.9)	20552	215561 (2.8)	216010	12824 (−1.1)	249386 (2.6)	228833 (2.5)	248937 (2.7)	228384 (2.6)
1953–4	250960 (6.1)	−371	250589 (6.1)	21299	229290 (6.3)	229661	13760 (7.3)	264720 (6.1)	243421 (6.4)	264349 (6.2)	243050 (6.4)
1954–5	261615 (4.2)	−566	261048 (4.2)	22144	238904 (4.3)	239470	15813 (14.9)	277428 (4.8)	255284 (4.9)	276862 (4.7)	254718 (4.8)
1955–6	268316 (2.6)	−211	268105 (2.7)	13693	254412 (6.3)	254623	18055 (14.2)	286370 (3.2)	272678 (6.8)	286160 (3.4)	272467 (7.0)
1956–7	283589 (5.7)	−328	283261 (5.7)	14900	268361 (5.5)	268689	18762 (3.9)	302352 (5.6)	287451 (5.4)	302024 (5.5)	287123 (5.4)
1957–8	280160 (−1.2)	−500	279660 (−1.3)	16099	263561 (−1.7)	264061	20903 (11.4)	301063 (−0.4)	284964 (−0.9)	300563 (−0.5)	284464 (−0.9)
1958–9	301422 (7.6)	−687	300735 (7.5)	17185	283549 (7.6)	284237	21902 (4.8)	323324 (7.4)	306139 (7.4)	322637 (7.3)	305452 (7.4)
1959–60	308018 (2.2)	−1214	306803 (2.0)	18417	288386 (1.9)	289601	23766 (8.5)	331784 (2.6)	313367 (2.4)	330570 (2.5)	312153 (2.2)
1960–1	329825 (7.1)	−1452	328373 (7.0)	19328	309045 (7.2)	310496	20292 (−14.6)	350117 (5.5)	330789 (5.6)	348665 (5.5)	329337 (5.5)
1961–2	340060 (3.1)	−1940	338120 (3.0)	20604	317516 (2.9)	319455	23050 (13.6)	363110 (3.7)	342506 (3.5)	361170 (3.6)	340566 (3.4)
1962–3	347253 (2.1)	−2229	345024 (2.0)	21928	323096 (1.8)	325326	26444 (14.7)	373698 (2.9)	351770 (2.7)	371468 (2.9)	349540 (2.6)
1963–4	364834 (5.1)	−2245	362589 (5.1)	21183	341406 (5.6)	343651	31200 (18.0)	396034 (6.0)	374851 (6.6)	393789 (6.0)	372606 (6.6)
1964–5	392503 (7.6)	−2878	389625 (7.5)	22907	366719 (7.5)	369596	33057 (6.0)	425560 (7.5)	402653 (7.4)	422682 (7.3)	399775 (7.3)
1965–6	378157 (−3.7)	−3060	375098 (−3.7)	24723	350374 (−4.4)	353434	36105 (9.2)	414263 (−2.7)	389540 (−3.3)	411203 (−2.7)	386480 (−3.3)
1966–7	382006 (1.0)	−2983	379023 (1.0)	26656	352367 (0.5)	355350	32109 (−11.1)	414115 (0.0)	387459 (−0.5)	411132 (0.0)	384476 (−0.5)
1967–8	413094 (8.1)	−3670	409423 (8.0)	28785	380638 (8.1)	384309	33454 (4.2)	446548 (7.8)	417763 (7.8)	442877 (7.7)	414092 (7.7)
1968–9	423874 (2.6)	−3498	420375 (2.7)	28115	392261 (3.0)	395759	37738 (12.8)	461612 (3.4)	433497 (3.8)	458113 (3.4)	429998 (3.8)
1969–70	451496 (6.5)	−3748	447747 (6.5)	30397	417351 (6.4)	421099	40302 (6.8)	491798 (6.5)	461401 (6.4)	488049 (6.5)	457653 (6.4)
1970–1	474131 (5.0)	−3877	470254 (5.0)	32534	437719 (4.9)	441597	43017 (6.7)	517148 (5.2)	484614 (5.0)	513270 (5.2)	480736 (5.0)
1971–2	478918 (1.0)	−3806	475112 (1.0)	34756	440356 (0.6)	444162	46666 (8.5)	525584 (1.6)	490829 (1.3)	521779 (1.7)	487023 (1.3)
1972–3	477392 (−0.3)	−3492	473901 (−0.3)	37141	436760 (−0.9)	440252	45306 (−2.9)	522698 (−0.5)	485558 (−1.1)	519207 (−0.5)	482066 (−1.0)
1973–4	499120 (4.6)	−3179	495941 (4.7)	39498	456444 (4.4)	459623	40924 (−9.7)	540045 (3.3)	500547 (3.1)	536865 (3.4)	497368 (3.2)
1974–5	504914 (1.2)	−2489	502425 (1.3)	41862	460563 (0.7)	463053	41529 (1.5)	546443 (1.2)	504582 (0.8)	543954 (1.3)	502092 (0.9)
1975–6	550379 (9.0)	−2147	548232 (9.1)	44093	504138 (9.3)	506285	46049 (10.9)	596428 (9.1)	552334 (9.5)	594281 (9.3)	550187 (9.6)
1976–7	557258 (1.2)	−1974	555284 (1.3)	46665	508619 (0.9)	510594	49043 (6.5)	606301 (1.7)	559636 (1.3)	604326 (1.7)	557662 (1.4)
1977–8	598885 (7.5)	−1648	597237 (7.6)	49548	547688 (7.6)	549336	51426 (4.9)	650311 (7.3)	600763 (7.3)	648663 (7.3)	599114 (7.4)
1978–9	631839 (5.5)	−1571	630268 (5.5)	52421	577847 (5.5)	579418	55596 (8.1)	687435 (5.7)	635014 (5.7)	685864 (5.7)	633443 (5.7)

(Continued)

Table A1.1 *Continued*

(1)	(2)		(3)	(4)		(5)	(6)	(7)		(8)		(9)		(10)		(11)		(12)	
1979–80	598974	-5.2	-293	598681	-5.0	55224	543457	543749	-6.2	52456	-5.6	651430	-5.2	596206	-6.1	651138	-5.1	595913	-5.9
1980–1	641921	7.2	-2	641919	7.2	58371	583548	583550	7.3	53440	1.9	695361	6.7	636990	6.8	695359	6.8	636988	6.9
1981–2	678033	5.6	-1039	676994	5.5	61478	615516	616554	5.7	59045	10.5	737078	6.0	675599	6.1	736039	5.9	674560	5.9
1982–3	697861	2.9	-3584	694277	2.6	64899	629378	632962	2.7	64761	9.7	762622	3.5	697723	3.3	759038	3.1	694139	2.9
1983–4	752669	7.9	-3975	748695	7.8	68432	680263	684238	8.1	65618	1.3	818288	7.3	749856	7.5	814313	7.3	745881	7.5
1984–5	782484	4.0	-5533	776951	3.8	72365	704586	710119	3.8	67089	2.2	849573	3.8	777208	3.6	844040	3.7	771675	3.5
1985–6	815049	4.2	-5529	809521	4.2	76491	733029	738558	4.0	78992	17.7	894041	5.2	817550	5.2	888512	5.3	812021	5.2
1986–7	850217	4.3	-6164	844053	4.3	80811	763242	769406	4.2	86454	9.4	936671	4.8	855860	4.7	930506	4.7	849696	4.6
1987–8	880267	3.5	-8277	871991	3.3	85730	786260	794537	3.3	93472	8.1	973739	4.0	888009	3.8	965462	3.8	879732	3.5
1988–9	969702	10.2	-11823	957879	9.8	90990	866889	878712	10.6	97880	4.7	1067582	9.6	976592	10.0	1055760	9.4	964770	9.7
1989–90	1029178	6.1	-12685	1016494	6.1	96868	919626	932311	6.1	101933	4.1	1131111	6.0	1034244	5.9	1118427	5.9	1021559	5.9
1990–1	1083572	5.3	-15878	1067694	5.0	99921	967773	983651	5.5	110078	8.0	1193650	5.5	1093729	5.8	1177772	5.3	1077851	5.5
1991–2	1099072	1.4	-16613	1082459	1.4	106140	976319	992932	0.9	107274	-2.5	1206346	1.1	1100206	0.6	1189732	1.0	1083592	0.5
1992–3	1158025	5.4	-16785	1141240	5.4	112597	1028643	1045428	5.3	114432	6.7	1272457	5.5	1159860	5.4	1255672	5.5	1143075	5.5
1993–4	1223816	5.7	-15270	1208545	5.9	119648	1088897	1104168	5.6	109307	-4.5	1333123	4.8	1213475	4.6	1317853	5.0	1198205	4.8
1994–5	1302076	6.4	-15483	1286594	6.5	127366	1159227	1174710	6.4	119755	9.6	1421831	6.7	1294464	6.7	1406348	6.7	1278982	6.7
1995–6	1396974	7.3	-16653	1380321	7.3	136598	1243724	1260376	7.3	132478	10.6	1529453	7.6	1392855	7.6	1512800	7.6	1376202	7.6
1996–7	1508378	8.0	-15972	1492406	8.1	146130	1346276	1362248	8.1	136660	3.2	1645037	7.6	1498907	7.6	1629066	7.7	1482936	7.8
1997–8	1573263	4.3	-13027	1560236	4.5	156218	1404018	1417045	4.0	138472	1.3	1711735	4.1	1555517	3.8	1698708	4.3	1542490	4.0
1998–9	1678410	6.7	-13840	1664570	6.7	167375	1497195	1511035	6.6	139342	0.6	1817752	6.2	1650377	6.1	1803912	6.2	1636537	6.1
1999–2000	1786526	6.4	-15431	1771095	6.4	181421	1589673	1605104	6.2	165510	18.8	1952036	7.4	1770614	7.3	1936605	7.4	1755183	7.2
2000–1	1864301	4.4	-22428	1841873	4.0	193855	1648018	1670446	4.1	166410	0.5	2030711	4.0	1836856	3.7	2008283	3.7	1814428	3.4
2001–2	1972606	5.8	-20139	1952467	6.0	208469	1743998	1764137	5.6	164045	-1.4	2136651	5.2	1928182	5.0	2116512	5.4	1908043	5.2
2002–3	2048286	3.8	-17867	2030419	4.0	223685	1806734	1824601	3.4	168847	2.9	2217133	3.8	1993448	3.4	2199266	3.9	1975581	3.5
2003–4	2222758	8.5	-19500	2203258	8.5	241441	1961817	1981317	8.6	179969	6.6	2402727	8.4	2161286	8.4	2383227	8.4	2141786	8.4
2004–5	2388768	7.5	-21085	2367683	7.5	262499	2105184	2126269	7.3	213297	18.5	2602065	8.3	2339556	8.2	2580980	8.3	2318481	8.2
2004–5 Series																			
2004–5	2967599	–	-22375	2945224	–	321229	2623995	2646370	–	271625	–	3239224	–	2917995	–	3216849	–	2895620	–
2005–6	3249130	9.5	-24944	3224186	9.5	351974	2872212	2897156	9.5	291429	7.3	3540559	9.3	3188585	9.3	3515615	9.3	3163641	9.3
2006–7	3564627	9.7	-26948	3537679	9.7	387767	3149912	3176860	9.7	310005	6.4	3874632	9.4	3486865	9.4	3847684	9.4	3459917	9.4
2007–8@	3893457	9.2	-17071	3876386	9.6	426416	3449970	3467041	9.1	354461	14.3	4224918	9.6	3821502	9.6	4230847	10.0	3804431	10.0
2008–9*	4154973	6.7	-16799	4138174	6.8	465982	3672192	3688991	6.4	310387	-12.4	4465360	5.1	3999378	4.7	4448561	5.1	3982579	4.7

Table A1.1 *Continued*

Year	GDP at Factor Cost — Public Sector (13)	Per cent of GDP	Private Sector (14)	Per Cent of GDP	Private Final Consumption Expenditure in Domestic Market (PFCE) (15)	%	Government Final Consumption Expenditure (GFCE) (16)	%	Gross Domestic Capital Formation (Adjusted) (17)	%	Net Domestic Capital Formation (Adjusted) (18)	%	Per Capita GNP at Factor Cost (19)	%	Per Capita NNP at Factor Cost (in Rupees) *** (20)	%	Per Capita NDP at Factor Cost (21)	%	Population (million) *** (22)	%
1999–2000 Series																				
1950–1	–	–	–	–	207559	–	14004	–	24643	–	5668	–	6237	–	5708	–	5733	–	359	–
1951–2	–	–	–	–	220752	6.4	14149	1.0	31265	26.9	11455	102.1	6287	0.8	5744	0.6	5760	0.5	365	1.7
1952–3	–	–	–	–	229660	4.0	14166	0.1	23030	–26.3	2478	–78.4	6347	1.0	5795	0.9	5807	0.8	372	1.9
1953–4	–	–	–	–	243467	6.0	14343	1.3	26312	14.2	5012	102.3	6612	4.2	6050	4.4	6060	4.4	379	1.9
1954–5	–	–	–	–	251454	3.3	14427	0.6	29508	12.1	7364	46.9	6763	2.3	6189	2.3	6204	2.4	386	1.8
1955–6	–	–	–	–	253858	1.0	14827	2.8	39798	34.9	26106	254.5	6822	0.9	6474	4.6	6479	4.4	393	1.8
1956–7	–	–	–	–	265088	4.4	15858	7.0	48223	21.2	33323	27.6	7064	3.5	6692	3.4	6700	3.4	401	2.0
1957–8	–	–	–	–	259851	–2.0	17858	12.6	44927	–6.8	28828	–13.5	6838	–3.2	6444	–3.7	6456	–3.6	409	2.0
1958–9	–	–	–	–	283706	9.2	18492	3.5	44633	–0.7	27448	–4.8	7195	5.2	6783	5.3	6800	5.3	418	2.2
1959–60	–	–	–	–	286933	1.1	18824	1.8	44355	–0.6	25938	–5.5	7202	0.1	6770	–0.2	6798	0.0	426	1.9
1960–1	27807	8.4	302017	91.6	303255	5.7	19840	5.4	52500	18.4	33172	27.9	7566	5.1	7121	5.2	7154	5.2	434	1.9
1961–2	31116	9.2	308943	90.8	308425	1.7	21353	7.6	51617	–1.7	31013	–6.5	7615	0.6	7151	0.4	7195	0.6	444	2.3
1962–3	36318	10.5	310935	89.5	312443	1.3	25763	20.7	58725	13.8	36797	18.7	7600	–0.2	7117	–0.5	7166	–0.4	454	2.3
1963–4	39874	10.9	324960	89.1	324066	3.7	31659	22.9	63651	8.4	42468	15.4	7814	2.8	7358	3.4	7406	3.4	464	2.2
1964–5	43414	11.1	349089	88.9	343425	6.0	33074	4.5	69412	9.1	46505	9.5	8220	5.2	7737	5.1	7797	5.3	474	2.2
1965–6	47532	12.6	330625	87.4	343729	0.1	36280	9.7	77792	12.1	53069	14.1	7734	–5.9	7224	–6.6	7287	–6.5	485	2.3
1966–7	50500	13.2	331506	86.8	348196	1.3	36903	1.7	84686	8.9	58030	9.3	7657	–1.0	7119	–1.5	7179	–1.5	495	2.1
1967–8	53825	13.0	359268	87.0	367895	5.7	37898	2.7	79229	–6.4	50444	–13.1	8091	5.7	7522	5.7	7595	5.8	506	2.2
1968–9	58339	13.8	365535	86.2	377559	2.6	39887	5.2	77235	–2.5	49120	–2.6	8115	0.3	7573	0.7	7640	0.6	518	2.4
1969–70	62991	14.0	388505	86.0	391582	3.7	43656	9.5	87852	13.7	57455	17.0	8464	4.3	7889	4.2	7960	4.2	529	2.1
1970–1	68645	14.5	405485	85.5	404880	3.4	47800	9.5	89870	2.3	57336	–0.2	8692	2.7	8091	2.6	8163	2.5	541	2.3
1971–2	72708	15.2	406210	84.8	412758	1.9	52485	9.8	94318	4.9	59562	3.9	8576	–1.3	7949	–1.8	8017	–1.8	554	2.4
1972–3	77376	16.2	400016	83.8	415523	0.7	52988	1.0	93933	–0.4	56792	–4.7	8358	–2.5	7703	–3.1	7765	–3.2	567	2.3
1973–4	85259	17.1	413861	82.9	425720	2.5	52914	–0.1	111567	18.8	72069	26.9	8551	2.3	7870	2.2	7925	2.1	580	2.3
1974–5	87197	17.3	417717	82.7	425399	–0.1	50937	–3.7	100075	–10.3	58214	–19.2	8473	–0.9	7767	–1.3	7809	–1.5	593	2.2
1975–6	94884	17.2	455495	82.8	449557	5.7	55857	9.7	103685	3.6	59592	2.4	9032	6.6	8305	6.9	8341	6.8	607	2.4
1976–7	104842	18.8	452416	81.2	458521	2.0	60038	7.5	117640	13.5	70976	19.1	8956	–0.8	8204	–1.2	8235	–1.3	620	2.1
1977–8	110188	18.4	488697	81.6	495910	8.2	62091	3.4	129808	10.3	80260	13.1	9420	5.2	8639	5.3	8665	5.2	634	2.3
1978–9	118225	18.7	513614	81.3	526219	6.1	66685	7.4	156955	20.9	104534	30.2	9726	3.3	8917	3.2	8942	3.2	648	2.2

(Continued)

Table A1.1 *Continued*

(1)	(13)		(14)		(15)		(16)		(17)		(18)		(19)		(20)		(21)		(22)	
1979–80	123313	*20.6*	475661	*79.4*	514416	*–2.2*	70858	*6.3*	141769	*–9.7*	86544	*–17.2*	9016	*–7.3*	8185	*–8.2*	8189	*–8.4*	664	*2.5*
1980–1	134410	*20.9*	507511	*79.1*	560718	*9.0*	74146	*4.6*	149728	*5.6*	91357	*5.6*	9454	*4.9*	8594	*5.0*	8594	*4.9*	679	*2.3*
1981–2	141421	*20.9*	536612	*79.1*	583839	*4.1*	77267	*4.2*	144196	*–3.7*	82718	*–9.5*	9783	*3.5*	8895	*3.5*	8910	*3.7*	692	*1.9*
1982–3	155445	*22.3*	542416	*77.7*	588909	*0.9*	84700	*9.6*	143958	*–0.2*	79059	*–4.4*	9806	*0.2*	8890	*–0.1*	8940	*0.3*	708	*2.3*
1983–4	165203	*21.9*	587467	*78.1*	635334	*7.9*	88490	*4.5*	151247	*5.1*	82815	*4.8*	10355	*5.6*	9409	*5.8*	9464	*5.9*	723	*2.1*
1984–5	177021	*22.6*	605464	*77.4*	651495	*2.5*	95069	*7.4*	163269	*7.9*	90904	*9.8*	10514	*1.5*	9534	*1.3*	9609	*1.5*	739	*2.2*
1985–6	192924	*23.7*	622125	*76.3*	680420	*4.4*	105089	*10.5*	178991	*9.6*	102499	*12.8*	10722	*2.0*	9709	*1.8*	9782	*1.8*	755	*2.2*
1986–7	207985	*24.5*	642232	*75.5*	698991	*2.7*	114969	*9.4*	179971	*0.5*	99161	*–3.3*	10948	*2.1*	9899	*2.0*	9979	*2.0*	771	*2.1*
1987–8	221517	*25.2*	658750	*74.8*	721499	*3.2*	124390	*8.2*	205216	*14.0*	119486	*20.5*	11066	*1.1*	9978	*0.8*	10083	*1.0*	788	*2.2*
1988–9	236618	*24.4*	733084	*75.6*	769480	*6.7*	131208	*5.5*	233728	*13.9*	142738	*19.5*	11899	*7.5*	10769	*7.9*	10916	*8.3*	805	*2.2*
1989–90	256978	*25.0*	772200	*75.0*	804428	*4.5*	138219	*5.3*	249711	*6.8*	152843	*7.1*	12366	*3.9*	11188	*3.9*	11342	*3.9*	822	*2.1*
1990–1	263002	*24.3*	820570	*75.7*	843556	*4.9*	142914	*3.4*	291611	*16.8*	191690	*25.4*	12726	*2.9*	11535	*3.1*	11724	*3.4*	839	*2.1*
1991–2	278197	*25.3*	820875	*74.7*	860869	*2.1*	142674	*–0.2*	246099	*–15.6*	139959	*–27.0*	12646	*–0.6*	11406	*–1.1*	11600	*–1.1*	856	*2.0*
1992–3	285618	*24.7*	872407	*75.3*	879689	*2.2*	147599	*3.5*	269647	*9.6*	157051	*12.2*	13088	*3.5*	11796	*3.4*	11989	*3.4*	872	*1.9*
1993–4	297804	*24.3*	926012	*75.7*	918944	*4.5*	156360	*5.9*	286305	*6.2*	166657	*6.1*	13549	*3.5*	12207	*3.5*	12379	*3.3*	892	*2.3*
1994–5	320493	*24.6*	981583	*75.4*	961346	*4.6*	158523	*1.4*	349266	*22.0*	221899	*33.1*	14138	*4.4*	12739	*4.4*	12909	*4.3*	910	*2.0*
1995–6	348736	*25.0*	1048239	*75.0*	1018423	*5.9*	170895	*7.8*	375888	*7.6*	239290	*7.8*	14874	*5.2*	13402	*5.2*	13582	*5.2*	928	*2.0*
1996–7	361505	*24.0*	1146873	*76.0*	1097390	*7.8*	178825	*4.6*	374006	*–0.5*	227876	*–4.8*	15776	*6.1*	14231	*6.2*	14400	*6.0*	946	*1.9*
1997–8	397073	*25.2*	1176189	*74.8*	1122195	*2.3*	198947	*11.3*	419378	*12.1*	263160	*15.5*	16185	*2.6*	14565	*2.3*	14700	*2.1*	964	*1.9*
1998–9	421219	*25.1*	1257191	*74.9*	1190267	*6.1*	223204	*12.2*	419885	*0.1*	252510	*–4.0*	16934	*4.6*	15231	*4.6*	15372	*4.6*	983	*2.0*
1999–2000	457006	*25.6*	1329520	*74.4*	1257541	*5.7*	252744	*13.2*	506244	*20.6*	324823	*28.6*	17693	*4.5*	15881	*4.3*	16035	*4.3*	1001	*1.8*
2000–1	463499	*24.9*	1400802	*75.1*	1303435	*3.6*	255087	*0.9*	488658	*–3.5*	294803	*–9.2*	18075	*2.2*	16173	*2.2*	16393	*2.2*	1019	*1.8*
2001–2	490976	*24.9*	1481630	*75.1*	1377919	*5.7*	260879	*2.3*	474449	*–2.9*	265980	*–9.8*	18774	*3.9*	16769	*3.7*	16963	*3.5*	1040	*2.1*
2002–3	518845	*25.3*	1529841	*74.7*	1417031	*2.8*	259960	*–0.4*	554044	*16.8*	330359	*24.2*	19227	*2.4*	17109	*2.0*	17278	*1.9*	1056	*1.5*
2003–4	536250	*24.1*	1686508	*75.9*	1501974	*6.0*	266599	*2.6*	651346	*17.6*	409905	*24.1*	20553	*6.9*	18301	*7.0*	18482	*7.0*	1072	*1.5*
2004–5	553629	*23.2*	1835139	*76.8*	1584690	*5.5*	276125	*3.6*	793545	*21.8*	531046	*29.6*	21742	*5.8*	19331	*5.6*	19525	*5.6*	1089	*1.6*
2004–5 Series																				
2004–5	–	–	–	–	1926858	*–*	356135	*–*	1057618	*–*	736389	*–*	27045	*–*	24095	*–*	24301	*–*	1089	*–*
2005–6	–	–	–	–	2091639	*8.6*	385599	*8.3*	1212585	*14.7*	860611	*16.9*	29152	*7.8*	25969	*7.8*	26195	*7.8*	1106	*1.6*
2006–7	–	–	–	–	2265665	*8.3*	400315	*3.8*	1388239	*14.5*	1000471	*16.3*	31530	*8.2*	28074	*8.1*	28314	*8.1*	1122	*1.4*
2007–8@	–	–	–	–	2483357	*9.6*	438976	*9.7*	1622226	*16.9*	1195810	*19.5*	34063	*8.0*	30316	*8.0*	30466	*8.0*	1138	*1.4*
2008–9★	–	–	–	–	2651786	*6.8*	512126	*16.7*	1557757	*–4.0*	1091775	*–8.7*	35859	*5.3*	31821	*5.0*	31967	*4.9*	1154	*1.4*

Source: Central Statistical Organisation (CSO).

Notes: @ Provisional; ★ Quick Estimates.

Figures in italics are percentage changes.

(Rupees crore)

Table A1.2 Gross and Net Domestic Savings by Sectors (at Current Prices)

Year	GDP at Current Market Prices	NDP at Current Market Prices	Domestic Savings GDS		CFC		NDS		Household Sector Savings Gross		CFC		Net		Private Corporate Sector Savings Gross		CFC		Net		Public Sector Savings Gross		CFC		Net	
(1)	(2)	(3)	(4)		(5)		(6)		(7)		(8)		(9)		(10)		(11)		(12)		(13)		(14)		(15)	
1999–2000 Series																										
1950–1	10085	9559	871	*8.6*	526	*5.2*	345	*3.6*	578	*5.7*	415	*4.1*	163	*1.7*	93	*0.9*	20	*0.2*	73	*0.8*	200	*2.0*	91	*0.9*	109	*1.1*
1951–2	10721	10130	969	*9.0*	591	*5.5*	378	*3.7*	546	*5.1*	456	*4.3*	90	*0.9*	136	*1.3*	26	*0.2*	110	*1.1*	287	*2.7*	109	*1.0*	178	*1.8*
1952–3	10522	9888	845	*8.0*	634	*6.0*	211	*2.1*	599	*5.7*	480	*4.6*	119	*1.2*	64	*0.6*	33	*0.3*	31	*0.3*	182	*1.7*	121	*1.1*	61	*0.6*
1953–4	11452	10805	875	*7.6*	647	*5.7*	228	*2.1*	616	*5.4*	486	*4.2*	130	*1.2*	90	*0.8*	34	*0.3*	56	*0.5*	169	*1.5*	127	*1.1*	42	*0.4*
1954–5	10834	10157	988	*9.1*	677	*6.2*	311	*3.1*	671	*6.2*	503	*4.6*	168	*1.7*	118	*1.1*	39	*0.4*	79	*0.8*	199	*1.8*	135	*1.2*	64	*0.6*
1955–6	11030	10548	1356	*12.3*	481	*4.4*	875	*8.3*	991	*9.0*	287	*2.6*	704	*6.7*	134	*1.2*	43	*0.4*	91	*0.9*	231	*2.1*	151	*1.4*	80	*0.8*
1956–7	13140	12594	1561	*11.9*	546	*4.2*	1015	*8.1*	1108	*8.4*	322	*2.5*	786	*6.2*	155	*1.2*	52	*0.4*	103	*0.8*	298	*2.3*	171	*1.3*	127	*1.0*
1957–8	13536	12914	1356	*10.0*	621	*4.6*	735	*5.7*	920	*6.8*	360	*2.7*	560	*4.3*	121	*0.9*	66	*0.5*	55	*0.4*	315	*2.3*	196	*1.4*	119	*0.9*
1958–9	15086	14401	1379	*9.1*	685	*4.5*	694	*4.8*	934	*6.2*	396	*2.6*	538	*3.7*	140	*0.9*	76	*0.5*	64	*0.4*	305	*2.0*	214	*1.4*	91	*0.6*
1959–60	15895	15130	1720	*10.8*	765	*4.8*	955	*6.3*	1205	*7.6*	431	*2.7*	774	*5.1*	185	*1.2*	87	*0.5*	98	*0.6*	330	*2.1*	247	*1.6*	83	*0.6*
1960–1	17407	16560	1952	*11.2*	847	*4.9*	1105	*6.7*	1136	*6.5*	457	*2.6*	679	*4.1*	281	*1.6*	103	*0.6*	178	*1.1*	535	*3.1*	286	*1.6*	249	*1.5*
1961–2	18445	17501	2074	*11.2*	945	*5.1*	1129	*6.5*	1143	*6.2*	493	*2.7*	650	*3.7*	320	*1.7*	126	*0.7*	194	*1.1*	611	*3.3*	325	*1.8*	286	*1.6*
1962–3	19826	18780	2440	*12.3*	1046	*5.3*	1394	*7.4*	1394	*7.0*	530	*2.7*	864	*4.6*	344	*1.7*	147	*0.7*	197	*1.0*	702	*3.5*	370	*1.9*	332	*1.8*
1963–4	22774	21725	2703	*11.9*	1049	*4.6*	1654	*7.6*	1439	*6.3*	476	*2.1*	963	*4.4*	394	*1.7*	153	*0.7*	241	*1.1*	870	*3.8*	420	*1.8*	450	*2.1*
1964–5	26563	25358	3077	*11.6*	1205	*4.5*	1872	*7.4*	1684	*6.3*	524	*2.0*	1160	*4.6*	389	*1.5*	184	*0.7*	205	*0.8*	1004	*3.8*	497	*1.9*	507	*2.0*
1965–6	28016	26612	3833	*13.7*	1404	*5.0*	2429	*9.1*	2409	*8.6*	606	*2.2*	1803	*6.8*	405	*1.4*	209	*0.7*	196	*0.7*	1019	*3.6*	589	*2.1*	430	*1.6*
1966–7	31711	30058	4328	*13.6*	1652	*5.2*	2676	*8.9*	3019	*9.5*	708	*2.2*	2311	*7.7*	424	*1.3*	244	*0.8*	180	*0.6*	885	*2.8*	700	*2.2*	185	*0.6*
1967–8	37133	35237	4293	*11.6*	1896	*5.1*	2397	*6.8*	2993	*8.1*	819	*2.2*	2174	*6.2*	410	*1.1*	276	*0.7*	134	*0.4*	890	*2.4*	801	*2.2*	89	*0.3*
1968–9	39324	37390	4657	*11.8*	1935	*4.9*	2722	*7.3*	3122	*7.9*	884	*2.2*	2238	*6.0*	439	*1.1*	300	*0.8*	139	*0.4*	1096	*2.8*	751	*1.9*	345	*0.9*
1969–70	43298	41081	6044	*14.0*	2218	*5.1*	3826	*9.3*	4211	*9.7*	1036	*2.4*	3175	*7.7*	549	*1.3*	327	*0.8*	222	*0.5*	1284	*3.0*	855	*2.0*	429	*1.0*
1970–1	46249	43687	6571	*14.2*	2562	*5.5*	4009	*9.2*	4371	*9.5*	1184	*2.6*	3187	*7.3*	672	*1.5*	380	*0.8*	292	*0.7*	1528	*3.3*	998	*2.2*	530	*1.2*
1971–2	49523	46603	7281	*14.7*	2919	*5.9*	4362	*9.4*	4917	*9.9*	1345	*2.7*	3572	*7.7*	769	*1.6*	433	*0.9*	336	*0.7*	1595	*3.2*	1142	*2.3*	453	*1.0*
1972–3	54591	51243	7788	*14.3*	3348	*6.1*	4440	*8.7*	5263	*9.6*	1532	*2.8*	3731	*7.3*	806	*1.5*	495	*0.9*	311	*0.6*	1719	*3.1*	1321	*2.4*	398	*0.8*
1973–4	66428	62370	10912	*16.4*	4059	*6.1*	6853	*11.0*	7590	*11.4*	1852	*2.8*	5738	*9.2*	1083	*1.6*	588	*0.9*	495	*0.8*	2239	*3.4*	1618	*2.4*	621	*1.0*
1974–5	78426	73149	12298	*15.7*	5276	*6.7*	7022	*9.6*	7668	*9.8*	2403	*3.1*	5265	*7.2*	1465	*1.9*	794	*1.0*	671	*0.9*	3165	*4.0*	2079	*2.7*	1086	*1.5*
1975–6	84221	78141	14196	*16.9*	6080	*7.2*	8116	*10.4*	9163	*10.9*	2708	*3.2*	6455	*8.3*	1083	*1.3*	936	*1.1*	147	*0.2*	3950	*4.7*	2435	*2.9*	1515	*1.9*
1976–7	90751	84196	17320	*19.1*	6554	*7.2*	10766	*12.8*	11223	*12.4*	2891	*3.2*	8332	*9.9*	1181	*1.3*	962	*1.1*	219	*0.3*	4916	*5.4*	2702	*3.0*	2214	*2.6*
1977–8	102796	95565	19995	*19.5*	7231	*7.0*	12764	*13.4*	13619	*13.2*	3158	*3.1*	10461	*10.9*	1413	*1.4*	1028	*1.0*	385	*0.4*	4963	*4.8*	3045	*3.0*	1918	*2.0*
1978–9	111371	103171	23601	*21.2*	8200	*7.4*	15401	*14.9*	16300	*14.6*	3599	*3.2*	12701	*12.3*	1652	*1.5*	1139	*1.0*	513	*0.5*	5649	*5.1*	3462	*3.1*	2187	*2.1*
1979–80	122155	112142	24213	*19.8*	10013	*8.2*	14200	*12.7*	15828	*13.0*	4380	*3.6*	11448	*10.2*	2398	*2.0*	1394	*1.1*	1004	*0.9*	5987	*4.9*	4239	*3.5*	1748	*1.6*
1980–1	145370	133634	26881	*18.5*	11736	*8.1*	15145	*11.3*	18724	*12.9*	5119	*3.5*	13605	*10.2*	2339	*1.6*	1679	*1.2*	660	*0.5*	5818	*4.0*	4937	*3.4*	881	*0.7*
1981–2	170805	156720	30896	*18.1*	14085	*8.2*	16811	*10.7*	19659	*11.5*	6033	*3.5*	13626	*8.7*	2560	*1.5*	2076	*1.5*	484	*0.3*	8677	*5.1*	5977	*3.5*	2700	*1.7*

(Continued)

Table A1.2 Continued

(1)	(2)	(3)	(4)		(5)		(6)		(7)		(8)		(9)		(10)		(11)		(12)		(13)		(14)		(15)	
1982–3	191059	174754	33787	*17.7*	16305	*8.5*	17482	*10.0*	21230	*11.1*	6788	*3.6*	14442	*8.3*	2980	*1.6*	2420	*1.3*	560	*0.3*	9577	*5.0*	7097	*3.7*	2480	*1.4*
1983–4	222485	203952	38091	*17.1*	18533	*8.3*	19558	*9.6*	26122	*11.7*	7624	*3.4*	18498	*9.1*	3254	*1.5*	2713	*1.2*	541	*0.3*	8715	*3.9*	8197	*3.7*	518	*0.3*
1984–5	249268	227870	45453	*18.2*	21397	*8.6*	24056	*10.6*	32689	*13.1*	8630	*3.5*	24059	*10.6*	4040	*1.6*	3167	*1.3*	873	*0.4*	8724	*3.5*	9601	*3.9*	–877	*–0.4*
1985–6	281330	256035	53389	*19.0*	25295	*9.0*	28094	*11.0*	36942	*13.1*	9936	*3.5*	27006	*10.5*	5426	*1.9*	3811	*1.4*	1615	*0.6*	11021	*3.9*	11548	*4.1*	–527	*–0.2*
1986–7	314816	285881	58036	*18.4*	28935	*9.2*	29101	*10.2*	41653	*13.2*	11202	*3.6*	30451	*10.2*	5336	*1.7*	4418	*1.4*	918	*0.3*	11047	*3.5*	13314	*4.2*	–2267	*–0.8*
1987–8	357861	324883	72264	*20.2*	32979	*9.2*	39285	*12.1*	55907	*15.6*	12814	*3.6*	43093	*13.3*	5932	*1.7*	4963	*1.4*	969	*0.3*	10425	*2.9*	15202	*4.2*	–4777	*–1.5*
1988–9	424531	385897	87166	*20.5*	38634	*9.1*	48532	*12.6*	66907	*15.8*	14796	*3.5*	52111	*13.5*	8486	*2.0*	5934	*1.4*	2552	*0.7*	11773	*2.8*	17904	*4.2*	–6131	*–1.6*
1989–90	487684	442117	106092	*21.8*	45567	*9.3*	60525	*13.7*	82765	*17.0*	17260	*3.5*	65505	*14.8*	11845	*2.4*	7049	*1.4*	4796	*1.1*	11482	*2.4*	21257	*4.4*	–9775	*–2.2*
1990–1	569624	518546	130010	*22.8*	51078	*9.0*	78932	*15.2*	104789	*18.4*	18298	*3.2*	86491	*16.7*	15164	*2.7*	8412	*1.5*	6752	*1.3*	10057	*1.8*	24367	*4.3*	–14310	*–2.8*
1991–2	654729	592759	141089	*21.5*	61971	*9.5*	79118	*13.3*	103495	*15.8*	21615	*3.3*	81880	*13.8*	20304	*3.1*	10918	*1.7*	9386	*1.6*	17290	*2.6*	29437	*4.5*	–12147	*–2.0*
1992–3	752591	680462	159682	*21.2*	72129	*9.6*	87553	*12.9*	123315	*16.4*	24656	*3.3*	98659	*14.5*	19968	*2.7*	13556	*1.8*	6412	*0.9*	16399	*2.2*	33916	*4.5*	–17517	*–2.6*
1993–4	865805	784923	189933	*21.9*	80882	*9.3*	109050	*13.9*	149534	*17.3*	27634	*3.2*	121900	*15.5*	29866	*3.4*	15943	*1.8*	13923	*1.8*	10533	*1.2*	37305	*4.3*	–26773	*–3.4*
1994–5	1015764	921942	247462	*24.4*	93822	*9.2*	153640	*16.7*	188790	*18.6*	31334	*3.1*	157457	*17.1*	35260	*3.5*	19293	*1.9*	15967	*1.7*	23412	*2.3*	43195	*4.3*	–19783	*–2.1*
1995–6	1191813	1080686	291002	*24.4*	111126	*9.3*	179876	*16.6*	201015	*16.9*	37071	*3.1*	163945	*15.2*	59153	*5.0*	24341	*2.0*	34812	*3.2*	30834	*2.6*	49714	*4.2*	–18880	*–1.7*
1996–7	1378617	1250226	313068	*22.7*	128391	*9.3*	184677	*14.8*	220973	*16.0*	41707	*3.0*	179266	*14.3*	62209	*4.5*	30025	*2.2*	32184	*2.6*	29886	*2.2*	56659	*4.1*	–26774	*–2.1*
1997–8	1527158	1383409	363506	*23.8*	143749	*9.4*	219757	*15.9*	270308	*17.7*	46445	*3.0*	223863	*16.2*	65769	*4.3*	34981	*2.3*	30788	*2.2*	27429	*1.8*	62323	*4.1*	–34894	*–2.5*
1998–9	1751199	1588997	389747	*22.3*	162202	*9.3*	227545	*14.3*	329760	*18.8*	53686	*3.1*	276074	*17.4*	68856	*3.9*	40145	*2.3*	28711	*1.8*	–8869	*–0.5*	68371	*3.9*	–77240	*–4.9*
1999–2000	1952036	1770614	484256	*24.8*	181421	*9.3*	302835	*17.1*	412516	*21.1*	61522	*3.2*	350994	*19.8*	87234	*4.5*	46198	*2.4*	41036	*2.3*	–15494	*–0.8*	73701	*3.8*	–89195	*–5.0*
2000–1	2102314	1900496	499033	*23.7*	201818	*9.6*	297215	*15.6*	454853	*21.6*	70080	*3.3*	384773	*20.2*	81062	*3.9*	54312	*2.6*	26750	*1.4*	–36882	*–1.8*	77426	*3.7*	–114308	*–6.0*
2001–2	2278952	2050655	534885	*23.5*	228297	*10.0*	306588	*15.0*	504165	*22.1*	81375	*3.6*	422790	*20.6*	76906	*3.4*	62555	*2.7*	14351	*0.7*	–46186	*–2.0*	84367	*3.7*	–130553	*–6.4*
2002–3	2454561	2204053	646521	*26.3*	250507	*10.2*	396014	*18.0*	563240	*22.9*	91972	*3.7*	471268	*21.4*	99217	*4.0*	68909	*2.8*	30308	*1.4*	–15936	*–0.6*	89626	*3.7*	–105562	*–4.8*
2003–4	2754620	2474572	820684	*29.8*	280048	*10.2*	540636	*21.8*	664064	*24.1*	105488	*3.8*	558576	*22.6*	127100	*4.6*	77802	*2.8*	49298	*2.0*	29521	*1.1*	96758	*3.5*	–67237	*–2.7*
2004–5	3149407	2820366	997874	*31.7*	329041	*10.4*	668833	*23.7*	716875	*22.8*	127283	*4.0*	589592	*20.9*	212048	*6.7*	92956	*3.0*	119092	*4.2*	68951	*2.2*	108802	*3.5*	–39851	*–1.4*
2004–5 Series																											
2004–5	3239224	2917995	1044280	*32.2*	321230	*9.9*	723050	*24.8*	755445	*23.3*	113846	*3.5*	641599	*22.0*	212812	*6.6*	96772	*3.0*	116040	*4.0*	76023	*2.3*	110612	*3.4*	–34589	*–1.2*
2005–6	3706473	3336742	1226044	*33.1*	369730	*10.0*	856314	*25.7*	858705	*23.2*	131142	*3.5*	727563	*21.8*	277493	*7.5*	116580	*3.1*	160913	*4.8*	89845	*2.4*	122008	*3.3*	–32163	*–1.0*
2006–7	4283979	3859064	1474788	*34.4*	424915	*9.9*	1049873	*27.2*	980195	*22.9*	148933	*3.5*	831262	*21.5*	342130	*8.0*	140269	*3.3*	201861	*5.2*	152463	*3.6*	135713	*3.2*	16750	*0.4*
2007–8@	4947857	4458639	1801469	*36.4*	489218	*9.9*	1312251	*29.4*	1120221	*22.6*	168187	*3.4*	952034	*21.4*	431588	*8.7*	172736	*3.5*	258852	*5.8*	249660	*5.0*	148295	*3.0*	101365	*2.3*
2008–9*	5574449	4999219	1811585	*32.5*	575229	*10.3*	1236356	*24.7*	1261332	*22.6*	201737	*3.6*	1059595	*21.2*	470256	*8.4*	205236	*3.7*	265020	*5.3*	79997	*1.4*	168256	*3.0*	–88259	*–1.8*

Source: Central Statistical Organisation (CSO).

Notes: @ Provisional Estimates; ⋆ Quick Estimates.

Consumption of fixed capital has been worked out from the estimated value of capital stock and the expected age of various types of assets.

Figures in italics are as percentages to GDP at current prices except those for net savings in cols(6), (9), (12), and (15), which are as percentages to NDP at current market prices.

(Rupees crore)

Table A1.3 Gross Capital Formation by Sectors at 1999–2000 Prices

Year	Gross Capital Formation (GCF)					Finances for Gross Capital Formation (derived)#	Errors and Omissions**	Gross Capital Formation Adjusted (2+8)		Con-sumption of Fixed Capital		Net Capital Formation (2−10)		Net Capital Formation Adjusted (8+11)	
	Aggregate GCF (3+4+5+6)		Public Sector	Private Corporate Sector	Household Sector	Valuables*										
(1)	(2)		(3)	(4)	(5)	(6)	(7)	(8)	(9)		(10)		(11)		(12)	
1999–2000 Series																
1950–1	30375	12.9	–	–	–	–	18912	−5731	24643	10.4	18975	8.0	11400	5.3	5668	2.6
1951–2	30902	12.7	–	–	–	–	31629	364	31265	12.9	19810	8.2	11091	5.0	11455	5.1
1952–3	25892	10.4	–	–	–	–	20169	−2861	23030	9.2	20552	8.2	5339	2.3	2478	1.1
1953–4	25263	9.5	–	–	–	–	27360	1048	26312	9.9	21299	8.0	3964	1.6	5012	2.1
1954–5	31088	11.2	–	–	–	–	27928	−1580	29508	10.6	22144	8.0	8943	3.5	7364	2.9
1955–6	38710	13.5	–	–	–	–	40887	1088	39798	13.9	13693	4.8	25017	9.2	26106	9.6
1956–7	47047	15.6	–	–	–	–	49399	1176	48223	15.9	14900	4.9	32147	11.2	33323	11.6
1957–8	48185	16.0	–	–	–	–	41668	−3259	44927	14.9	16099	5.3	32086	11.3	28828	10.1
1958–9	44119	13.6	–	–	–	–	45148	515	44633	13.8	17185	5.3	26934	8.8	27448	9.0
1959–60	47800	14.4	–	–	–	–	40911	−3445	44355	13.4	18417	5.6	29383	9.4	25938	8.3
1960–1	54245	15.5	–	–	–	–	50753	−1746	52500	15.0	19328	5.5	34917	10.6	33171	10.0
1961–2	58336	16.1	–	–	–	–	44899	−6719	51617	14.2	20604	5.7	37732	11.0	31013	9.1
1962–3	62647	16.8	–	–	–	–	54804	−3921	58725	15.7	21928	5.9	40719	11.6	36797	10.5
1963–4	70704	17.9	–	–	–	–	56599	−7053	63651	16.1	21183	5.3	49521	13.2	42468	11.3
1964–5	77277	18.2	–	–	–	–	61548	−7864	69412	16.3	22907	5.4	54370	13.5	46505	11.5
1965–6	79358	19.2	–	–	–	–	76225	−1567	77792	18.8	24723	6.0	54635	14.0	53068	13.6
1966–7	83699	20.2	–	–	–	–	85672	987	84686	20.4	26656	6.4	57043	14.7	58030	15.0
1967–8	86257	19.3	–	–	–	–	72201	−7028	79229	17.7	28785	6.4	57472	13.8	50444	12.1
1968–9	84844	18.4	–	–	–	–	69626	−7609	77235	16.7	28115	6.1	56729	13.1	49120	11.3
1969–70	91552	18.6	–	–	–	–	84151	−3701	87852	17.9	30397	6.2	61156	13.3	57455	12.5
1970–1	93138	18.0	–	–	–	–	86602	−3268	89870	17.4	32534	6.3	60604	12.5	57336	11.8
1971–2	100811	19.2	–	–	–	–	87824	−6494	94318	17.9	34756	6.6	66055	13.5	59562	12.1
1972–3	101376	19.4	–	–	–	–	86489	−7443	93933	18.0	37141	7.1	64235	13.2	56792	11.7
1973–4	107909	20.0	–	–	–	–	115225	3658	111567	20.7	39498	7.3	68411	13.7	72069	14.4
1974–5	110642	20.2	–	–	–	–	89507	−10568	100075	18.3	41862	7.7	68781	13.6	58213	11.5
1975–6	116845	19.6	–	–	–	–	90526	−13160	103685	17.4	44093	7.4	72752	13.2	59592	10.8
1976–7	126227	20.8	–	–	–	–	109053	−8587	117640	19.4	46665	7.7	79563	14.2	70976	12.7
1977–8	133046	20.5	–	–	–	–	126570	−3238	129808	20.0	49548	7.6	83497	13.9	80260	13.4
1978–9	151067	22.0	–	–	–	–	162843	5888	156955	22.8	52421	7.6	98646	15.5	104534	16.5
1979–80	148350	22.8	–	–	–	–	135188	−6581	141769	21.8	55224	8.5	93125	15.6	86544	14.5
1980–1	139351	20.0	–	–	–	–	160105	10377	149728	21.5	58371	8.4	80980	12.7	91357	14.3
1981–2	163945	22.2	–	–	–	–	124447	−19749	144196	19.6	61478	8.3	102467	15.2	82718	12.2
1982–3	162565	21.3	–	–	–	–	125350	−18608	143958	18.9	64899	8.5	97666	14.0	79058	11.3

(Continued)

Table A1.3 Continued

(1)	(2)	(3)	(4)	(5)	(6)	(7)	(8)	(9)	(10)	(11)	(12)
1983–4	161587 *19.7*	– –	– –	– –	–	140907	–10340	151247 *18.5*	68432 *8.4*	93155 *12.4*	82815 *11.0*
1984–5	178509 *21.0*	– –	– –	– –	–	148030	–15240	163269 *19.2*	72365 *8.5*	106144 *13.7*	90904 *11.7*
1985–6	198507 *22.2*	– –	– –	– –	–	159474	–19517	178991 *20.0*	76491 *8.6*	122016 *14.9*	102499 *12.5*
1986–7	202804 *21.7*	– –	– –	– –	–	157139	–22833	179971 *19.2*	80811 *8.6*	121993 *14.3*	99161 *11.6*
1987–8	204283 *21.0*	– –	– –	– –	–	206149	933	205216 *21.1*	85730 *8.8*	118553 *13.4*	119486 *13.5*
1988–9	235799 *22.1*	– –	– –	– –	–	231656	–2072	233728 *21.9*	90990 *8.5*	144809 *14.8*	142738 *14.6*
1989–90	244049 *21.6*	– –	– –	– –	–	255372	5661	249711 *22.1*	96868 *8.6*	147182 *14.2*	152842 *14.8*
1990–1	270707 *22.7*	– –	– –	– –	–	312515	20904	291611 *24.4*	99921 *8.4*	170786 *15.6*	191690 *17.5*
1991–2	245108 *20.3*	– –	– –	– –	–	247089	990	246099 *20.4*	106140 *8.8*	138969 *12.6*	139959 *12.7*
1992–3	278074 *21.9*	– –	– –	– –	–	261221	–8427	269647 *21.2*	112597 *8.8*	165478 *14.3*	157051 *13.5*
1993–4	270165 *20.3*	– –	– –	– –	–	302445	16140	286305 *21.5*	119648 *9.0*	150517 *12.4*	166657 *13.7*
1994–5	321731 *22.6*	– –	– –	– –	–	376800	27535	349266 *24.6*	127366 *9.0*	194364 *15.0*	221899 *17.1*
1995–6	382142 *25.0*	– –	– –	– –	–	369635	–6254	375888 *24.6*	136598 *8.9*	245544 *17.6*	239290 *17.2*
1996–7	344795 *21.0*	– –	– –	– –	–	403217	29211	374006 *22.7*	146130 *8.9*	198665 *13.3*	227876 *15.2*
1997–8	396774 *23.2*	– –	– –	– –	–	441981	22603	419378 *24.5*	156218 *9.1*	240556 *15.5*	263160 *16.9*
1998–9	407811 *22.4*	– –	– –	– –	–	431960	12075	419885 *23.1*	167375 *9.2*	240436 *14.6*	252510 *15.3*
1999–2000	509518 *26.1*	144610 *7.4*	143475 *7.4*	205914 *10.5*	15519	506244	–3274	506244 *25.9*	181421 *9.3*	328097 *18.5*	324823 *18.3*
2000–1	485049 *23.9*	140315 *6.9*	102912 *5.1*	227566 *11.2*	14256	488658	3609	488658 *24.1*	193855 *9.5*	291194 *15.9*	294803 *16.0*
2001–2	502116 *23.5*	144540 *6.8*	111726 *5.2*	232360 *10.9*	13489	474449	–27667	474449 *22.2*	208469 *9.8*	293647 *15.2*	265980 *13.8*
2002–3	554734 *25.0*	134468 *6.1*	130848 *5.9*	276489 *12.5*	12930	554044	–691	554044 *25.0*	223685 *10.1*	331049 *16.6*	330359 *16.6*
2003–4	633105 *26.3*	145578 *6.1*	163091 *6.8*	302895 *12.6*	21541	651346	18241	651346 *27.1*	241441 *10.0*	391664 *18.1*	409905 *19.0*
2004–5	781622 *30.0*	166989 *6.4*	274130 *10.5*	306630 *11.8*	33873	793545	11924	793545 *30.5*	262499 *10.1*	519123 *22.2*	531046 *22.7*
2005–6	930738 *32.7*	202935 *7.1*	373165 *13.1*	321498 *11.3*	33140	948480	17742	948480 *33.3*	287426 *10.1*	643312 *25.2*	661054 *25.8*
2006–7	1060108 *34.0*	232844 *7.5*	441866 *14.2*	347307 *11.1*	38091	1073783	13675	1073783 *34.4*	316406 *10.1*	743702 *26.5*	757377 *27.0*
2007–8	1220412 *35.9*	290032 *8.5*	513210 *15.1*	378052 *11.1*	39118	1231244	10832	1231244 *36.2*	350067 *10.3*	870345 *28.5*	881177 *28.9*
2004–5 Series											
2004–5	1051977 *32.5*	240755 *7.4*	332624 *10.3*	437544 *13.5*	41054	1057618	5641	1057618 *32.7*	321229 *9.9*	730748 *25.0*	736389 *25.2*
2005–6	1213232 *34.3*	278702 *7.9*	479163 *13.5*	415207 *11.7*	40160	1212585	–647	1212585 *34.2*	351974 *9.9*	861258 *27.0*	860611 *27.0*
2006–7	1408067 *36.3*	324342 *8.4*	575916 *14.9*	461627 *11.9*	46182	1388239	–19828	1388239 *35.8*	387768 *10.0*	1020299 *29.3*	1000471 *28.7*
2007–8@	1616464 *38.1*	379495 *8.9*	708487 *16.7*	481026 *11.3*	47456	1622226	5762	1622226 *38.2*	426416 *10.0*	1190048 *31.1*	1195810 *31.3*
2008–9★	1589646 *35.6*	414122 *9.3*	590642 *13.2*	526209 *11.8*	58673	1557758	–31888	1557757 *34.9*	465982 *10.4*	1123664 *28.1*	1091775 *27.3*

Source: Central Statistical Organisation (CSO).

Notes: @ Provisional Estimates; ★ Quick Estimates.

★ Excluding works of art and antiques (valuables are a new item in the 1999–2000 Series).

Data are not directly available in the NAS at constant prices, they are derived series.

★★ Errors and omissions at current prices have been deflated by the implicit price deflators of capital formation by the CSO.

Financing of Gross Capital Formation = Gross Saving + Net Foreign Capital Inflow

Figures in italics are as percentages to GDP at 1999–2000 prices, except for cols 10 and 11, which are as percentage to NDP at 1999–2000 prices.

– Not available.

(Rupees crore)

Table A1.4 Gross Capital Formation by Sectors at Current Prices

(1) Year	Gross Capital Formation (GCF)				(7) Gross Domestic Savings	(8) Net Foreign Capital Inflow (-) Outflow (+)	(9) Finances for Gross Capital Formation (7+8)	(10) Errors and Omissions (9−2)**	(11) GCF Adjusted (2+10)	(12) Consumption of Fixed Capital (CFC)	(13) Net Capital Formation (NCF) (2−12)	(14) NCF Adjusted (13+10)	Price Deflators (1999–2000=100)	
	(2) Aggregate (3+4+5+6)	(3) Public Sector	(4) Private Corporate Sector	(5) Household Sector	(6) Valuables*									(15) GDCF	(16) GDP at Market Prices (Unadjusted)
1999–2000 Series															
1950–1	1037 *10.3*	294 *2.9*	227 *2.2*	516 *5.1*	—	871	−21	850	−187	850 *8.4*	526	511 *5.3*	324 *3.4*	3.4	4.3
1951–2	1139 *10.6*	342 *3.2*	265 *2.5*	532 *5.0*	—	969	183	1152	13	1152 *10.7*	591	548 *5.4*	561 *5.5*	3.7	4.4
1952–3	912 *8.7*	296 *2.8*	88 *0.8*	527 *5.0*	—	845	−34	811	−101	811 *7.7*	634	278 *2.8*	177 *1.8*	3.5	4.2
1953–4	827 *7.2*	337 *2.9*	16 *0.1*	474 *4.1*	—	875	−13	862	35	862 *7.5*	647	180 *1.7*	215 *2.0*	3.3	4.3
1954–5	1057 *9.8*	508 *4.7*	161 *1.5*	389 *3.6*	—	988	16	1004	−53	1004 *9.3*	677	381 *3.7*	327 *3.2*	3.4	3.9
1955–6	1357 *12.3*	563 *5.1*	232 *2.1*	562 *5.1*	—	1356	39	1395	38	1395 *12.6*	481	876 *8.3*	914 *8.7*	3.5	3.9
1956–7	1876 *14.3*	738 *5.6*	363 *2.8*	775 *5.9*	—	1561	360	1921	45	1921 *14.6*	546	1330 *10.6*	1375 *10.9*	4.0	4.3
1957–8	1960 *14.5*	908 *6.7*	423 *3.1*	629 *4.6*	—	1356	473	1829	−131	1829 *13.5*	621	1338 *10.4*	1208 *9.4*	4.1	4.5
1958–9	1735 *11.5*	898 *6.0*	264 *1.8*	572 *3.8*	—	1379	376	1755	20	1755 *11.6*	685	1049 *7.3*	1070 *7.4*	3.9	4.7
1959–60	2097 *13.2*	1000 *6.3*	325 *2.0*	772 *4.9*	—	1720	230	1950	−147	1950 *12.3*	765	1333 *8.8*	1186 *7.8*	4.4	4.8
1960–1	2511 *14.4*	1259 *7.2*	572 *3.3*	680 *3.9*	—	1952	480	2432	−79	2433 *14.0*	847	1665 *10.1*	1586 *9.6*	4.6	5.0
1961–2	2720 *14.7*	1272 *6.9*	794 *4.3*	654 *3.5*	—	2074	345	2419	−301	2419 *13.1*	945	1776 *10.1*	1474 *8.4*	4.7	5.1
1962–3	3063 *15.5*	1590 *8.0*	579 *2.9*	895 *4.5*	—	2440	440	2880	−183	2880 *14.5*	1046	2017 *10.7*	1834 *9.8*	4.9	5.3
1963–4	3481 *15.3*	1852 *8.1*	933 *4.1*	696 *3.1*	—	2703	440	3143	−338	3143 *13.8*	1049	2432 *11.2*	2094 *9.6*	4.9	5.8
1964–5	4080 *15.4*	2146 *8.1*	964 *3.6*	970 *3.7*	—	3077	600	3677	−403	3677 *13.8*	1205	2875 *11.3*	2472 *9.7*	5.3	6.2
1965–6	4519 *16.1*	2438 *8.7*	745 *2.7*	1337 *4.8*	—	3833	599	4432	−87	4432 *15.8*	1404	3115 *11.7*	3028 *11.4*	5.7	6.8
1966–7	5192 *16.4*	2366 *7.5*	671 *2.1*	2155 *6.8*	—	4328	923	5251	59	5251 *16.6*	1652	3539 *11.8*	3599 *12.0*	6.2	7.7
1967–8	5572 *15.0*	2570 *6.9*	873 *2.4*	2128 *5.7*	—	4293	837	5130	−442	5130 *13.8*	1896	3676 *10.4*	3234 *9.2*	6.5	8.3
1968–9	5570 *14.2*	2422 *6.2*	821 *2.1*	2327 *5.9*	—	4657	416	5073	−497	5073 *12.9*	1935	3636 *9.7*	3138 *8.4*	6.6	8.5
1969–70	6543 *15.1*	2530 *5.8*	721 *1.7*	3292 *7.6*	—	6044	241	6285	−258	6285 *14.5*	2218	4326 *10.5*	4067 *9.9*	7.1	8.8
1970–1	7211 *15.6*	3104 *6.7*	1107 *2.4*	3000 *6.5*	—	6571	394	6965	−246	6965 *15.1*	2562	4648 *10.6*	4403 *10.1*	7.7	8.9
1971–2	8275 *16.7*	3631 *7.3*	1282 *2.6*	3362 *6.8*	—	7281	478	7759	−516	7759 *15.7*	2919	5355 *11.5*	4840 *10.4*	8.2	9.4
1972–3	8719 *16.0*	4152 *7.6*	1432 *2.6*	3135 *5.7*	—	7788	297	8085	−634	8085 *14.8*	3348	5371 *10.5*	4737 *9.2*	8.6	10.4
1973–4	10946 *16.5*	5212 *7.8*	1757 *2.6*	3978 *6.0*	—	10912	392	11304	358	11304 *17.0*	4059	6888 *11.0*	7245 *11.6*	10.1	12.3
1974–5	14225 *18.1*	6083 *7.8*	2848 *3.6*	5294 *6.8*	—	12298	653	12951	−1274	12951 *16.5*	5276	8949 *12.2*	7675 *10.5*	12.9	14.4
1975–6	15825 *18.8*	8236 *9.8*	2344 *2.8*	5245 *6.2*	—	14196	−117	14079	−1746	14079 *16.7*	6080	9745 *12.5*	7999 *10.2*	13.5	14.1
1976–7	17168 *18.9*	9360 *10.3*	1437 *1.6*	6371 *7.0*	—	17320	−1309	16011	−1157	16011 *17.6*	6554	10614 *12.6*	9457 *11.2*	13.6	15.0
1977–8	18985 *18.5*	8689 *8.5*	2530 *2.5*	7766 *7.6*	—	19995	−1465	18530	−455	18530 *18.0*	7231	11754 *12.3*	11299 *11.8*	14.3	15.8
1978–9	22850 *20.5*	10805 *9.7*	2403 *2.2*	9642 *8.7*	—	23601	128	23729	879	23729 *21.3*	8200	14650 *14.2*	15529 *15.1*	15.1	16.2
1979–80	25909 *21.2*	12898 *10.6*	3263 *2.7*	9747 *8.0*	—	24213	580	24793	−1116	24793 *20.3*	10013	15895 *14.2*	14780 *13.2*	17.5	18.8

(Continued)

Table A1.4 *Continued*

(1)	(2)	(3)	(4)	(5)	(6)	(7)	(8)	(9)	(10)	(11)	(12)	(13)	(14)	(15)	(16)
1980–1	26964 *18.5*	12994 *8.9*	3855 *2.7*	10114 *7.0*	— —	26881	2094	28975	2011	28975 *19.9*	11736	15228 *11.4*	17239 *12.9*	*19.3*	*20.9*
1981–2	37897 *22.2*	18092 *10.6*	9760 *5.7*	10045 *5.9*	— —	30896	2611	33507	−4390	33507 *19.6*	14085	23812 *15.2*	19422 *12.4*	*23.1*	*23.2*
1982–3	40932 *21.4*	21543 *11.3*	10898 *5.7*	8491 *4.4*	— —	33787	2566	36353	−4579	36353 *19.0*	16305	24627 *14.1*	20048 *11.5*	*25.2*	*25.1*
1983–4	43364 *19.5*	22810 *10.3*	7726 *3.5*	12828 *5.8*	— —	38091	2517	40608	−2756	40608 *18.3*	18533	24831 *12.2*	22075 *10.8*	*26.8*	*27.2*
1984–5	53225 *21.4*	27366 *11.0*	11048 *4.4*	14810 *5.9*	— —	45453	3292	48745	−4480	48745 *19.6*	21397	31827 *14.0*	27348 *12.0*	*29.8*	*29.3*
1985–6	66016 *23.5*	32063 *11.4*	15549 *5.5*	18404 *6.5*	— —	53389	6234	59623	−6393	59623 *21.2*	25295	40721 *15.9*	34328 *13.4*	*33.3*	*31.5*
1986–7	72493 *23.0*	37275 *11.8*	16901 *5.4*	18317 *5.8*	— —	58036	6355	64391	−8102	64391 *20.5*	28935	43558 *15.2*	35456 *12.4*	*35.7*	*33.6*
1987–8	78730 *22.0*	36361 *10.2*	13282 *3.7*	29087 *8.1*	— —	72264	6825	79089	359	79089 *22.1*	32979	45752 *14.1*	46110 *14.2*	*38.5*	*36.8*
1988–9	100348 *23.6*	43137 *10.2*	17487 *4.1*	39724 *9.4*	— —	87166	12304	99470	−878	99470 *23.4*	38634	61714 *16.0*	60836 *15.8*	*42.6*	*39.8*
1989–90	115689 *23.7*	49707 *10.2*	21215 *4.4*	44767 *9.2*	— —	106092	12279	118371	2682	118371 *24.3*	45567	70122 *15.9*	72804 *16.5*	*47.4*	*43.1*
1990–1	137598 *24.2*	56874 *10.0*	25575 *4.5*	55149 *9.7*	— —	130010	18196	148206	10608	148206 *26.0*	51078	86520 *16.7*	97128 *18.7*	*50.8*	*47.7*
1991–2	143885 *22.0*	62052 *9.5*	40439 *6.2*	41394 *6.3*	— —	141089	3377	144466	581	144466 *22.1*	61971	81914 *13.8*	82495 *13.9*	*58.7*	*54.3*
1992–3	178912 *23.8*	68533 *9.1*	52431 *7.0*	57948 *7.7*	— —	159682	13816	173498	−5414	173498 *23.1*	72129	106784 *15.7*	101369 *14.9*	*64.3*	*59.1*
1993–4	183727 *21.2*	75923 *8.8*	53008 *6.1*	54796 *6.3*	— —	189933	4791	194724	10997	194724 *22.5*	80882	102845 *13.1*	113842 *14.5*	*68.0*	*64.9*
1994–5	238971 *23.5*	94775 *9.3*	76139 *7.5*	68057 *6.7*	— —	247462	11893	259355	20384	259355 *25.5*	93822	145149 *15.7*	165533 *18.0*	*74.3*	*71.4*
1995–6	316944 *26.6*	97749 *8.2*	123899 *10.4*	95296 *8.0*	— —	291002	20780	311782	−5162	311782 *26.2*	111126	205818 *19.0*	200656 *18.6*	*82.9*	*77.9*
1996–7	304961 *22.1*	103159 *7.5*	122491 *8.9*	79312 *5.8*	— —	313068	17738	330806	25845	330806 *24.0*	128391	176570 *14.1*	202415 *16.2*	*88.4*	*83.8*
1997–8	365005 *23.9*	107830 *7.1*	134643 *8.8*	122531 *8.0*	— —	363506	22302	385808	20803	385808 *25.3*	143749	221256 *16.0*	242059 *17.5*	*92.0*	*89.2*
1998–9	396384 *22.6*	122849 *7.0*	124122 *7.1*	149414 *8.5*	— —	389747	18362	408109	11725	408109 *23.3*	162202	234183 *14.7*	245907 *15.5*	*97.2*	*96.3*
1999–2000	509518 *26.1*	144610 *7.4*	143475 *7.4*	205914 *10.5*	15519 *0.8*	484256	21988	506244	−3274	506244 *25.9*	181421	328097 *18.5*	324823 *18.3*	*100.0*	*100.0*
2000–1	508009 *24.2*	144638 *6.9*	109013 *5.2*	239634 *11.4*	14724 *0.7*	499033	12755	511788	3779	511788 *24.3*	201818	306191 *16.1*	309970 *16.3*	*104.7*	*103.5*
2001–2	551042 *24.2*	156537 *6.9*	123628 *5.4*	256689 *11.3*	14187 *0.6*	534885	−14229	520656	−30386	520656 *22.8*	228297	322745 *15.7*	292359 *14.3*	*109.7*	*106.7*
2002–3	618807 *25.2*	149399 *6.1*	145466 *5.9*	309985 *12.6*	13957 *0.6*	646521	−28486	618035	−772	618035 *25.2*	250507	368300 *16.7*	367528 *16.7*	*111.6*	*110.7*
2003–4	738221 *26.8*	174579 *6.3*	188266 *6.8*	350804 *12.7*	24572 *0.9*	820684	−61359	759325	21104	759325 *27.6*	280048	458173 *18.5*	479277 *19.4*	*116.6*	*114.6*
2004–5 Series															
2004–5	1051977 *32.5*	240755 *7.4*	332624 *10.3*	437544 *13.5*	41054 *1.3*	1044280	13338	1057618	5641	1057618 *32.7*	321230	730747 *25.0*	736388 *25.2*	*100.0*	*100.0*
2005–6	1271327 *34.3*	293188 *7.9*	499261 *13.5*	437486 *11.8*	41392 *1.1*	1226044	44604	1270648	−679	1270648 *34.3*	369730	901597 *27.0*	900918 *27.0*	*104.8*	*104.7*
2006–7	1542061 *36.0*	359778 *8.4*	621430 *14.5*	511144 *11.9*	49709 *1.2*	1474788	45524	1520312	−21749	1520312 *35.5*	424915	1117146 *28.9*	1095397 *28.4*	*109.5*	*110.6*
2007–8@	1859259 *37.6*	442177 *8.9*	795995 *16.1*	567496 *11.5*	53591 *1.1*	1801469	64430	1865899	6640	1865899 *37.7*	489218	1370041 *30.7*	1376681 *30.9*	*115.0*	*116.5*
2008–9*	1984178 *35.6*	524241 *9.4*	708377 *12.7*	679904 *12.2*	71656 *1.3*	1811585	132743	1944328	−39850	1944328 *34.9*	575229	1408949 *28.2*	1369099 *27.4*	*124.8*	*124.8*

Source: Central Statistical Organisation (CSO).

Notes: @ Provisional Estimates; * Quick Estimates.

** Errors and Omissions = (Domestic Savings + Net Capital Inflow – Domestic Capital Formation)

* Excluding works of art and antiques (valuables are a new item in the 1999–2000 Series).

Figures in italics are as percentage to GDP at current prices, except for Net Capital Formation in cols (13) and (14), which are as percentages to NDP at current market prices.

Table A1.5 Net Capital Stock By Sectors and Capital–Output Ratios

(Rupees crore)

End-March	Net Capital Stock				Net Fixed Capital Stock				Inventory				Average Capital–Output Ratio (ACOR)						Incremental Capital–Output Ratio (ICOR)	
				of which: House-hold Sector				of which: House-hold Sector				of which: House-hold Sector	Net Capital Stock to Output*			Net Fixed Capital Stock to Output*			NDCF to Output	NFCF to Output
	Total (3+4)	Public Sector	Private Sector		Total (7+8)	Public Sector	Private Sector		Total (11+12)	Public Sector	Private Sector		Total	Public Sector	Private Sector	Total	Public Sector	Private Sector		
(1)	(2)	(3)	(4)	(5)	(6)	(7)	(8)	(9)	(10)	(11)	(12)	(13)	(14)	(15)	(16)	(17)	(18)	(19)	(20)	(21)
1999–2000 Prices																				
1980–1	2129911	926853	1203058	1044511	1979055	871235	1107820	996156	150856	55618	95238	48355	–	–	–	–	–	–	2.28	1.98
1981–2	2233149	984615	1248535	1065206	2062509	922419	1140091	1014722	170640	62196	108444	50483	3.54	8.26	2.45	3.28	7.75	2.24	2.51	2.51
1982–3	2331613	1047206	1284408	1075553	2146258	981685	1164573	1022308	185356	65521	119835	53246	3.61	7.97	2.51	3.32	7.47	2.28	4.82	5.06
1983–4	2425595	1107050	1318545	1095337	2234479	1040615	1193864	1037910	191115	66435	124680	57427	3.48	7.97	2.37	3.20	7.49	2.15	1.62	1.70
1984–5	2532616	1171603	1361013	1116434	2327416	1100495	1226921	1055066	205201	71108	134093	61368	3.49	7.88	2.37	3.21	7.40	2.14	3.51	3.56
1985–6	2655583	1238646	1416937	1142658	2427496	1162633	1264863	1074999	228087	76013	152074	67659	3.51	7.62	2.39	3.22	7.16	2.15	3.60	3.49
1986–7	2778591	1311060	1467531	1163600	2533218	1233077	1300141	1089142	245373	77983	167390	74458	3.53	7.49	2.41	3.22	7.04	2.14	3.21	3.39
1987–8	2898208	1370895	1527312	1204717	2647176	1296983	1350193	1124887	251031	73912	177119	79830	3.57	7.40	2.44	3.26	6.98	2.16	4.75	4.49
1988–9	3045086	1435958	1609127	1262933	2774709	1363031	1411678	1170940	270377	72927	197450	91993	3.38	7.25	2.29	3.09	6.87	2.02	1.70	1.49
1989–90	3192958	1499733	1693225	1321112	2909727	1423128	1486599	1227607	283231	76605	206627	93506	3.35	6.95	2.29	3.05	6.60	2.01	2.85	2.51
1990–1	3364499	1567343	1797157	1396383	3068980	1486869	1582111	1298456	295519	80473	215046	97927	3.33	7.15	2.27	3.04	6.78	1.99	3.73	3.09
1991–2	3504384	1627710	1876674	1433209	3210023	1551045	1658979	1335249	294361	76665	217695	97960	3.46	7.05	2.40	3.16	6.70	2.11	15.08	15.10
1992–3	3670845	1685549	1985296	1489845	3361235	1604660	1756575	1389791	309610	80889	228722	100054	3.43	7.15	2.37	3.14	6.81	2.10	2.99	2.86
1993–4	3832354	1746182	2086172	1543896	3524687	1662426	1862261	1444560	307667	83755	223911	99336	3.40	7.11	2.36	3.12	6.77	2.10	2.84	2.60
1994–5	4028808	1820020	2208789	1598800	3702567	1736930	1965637	1493264	326242	83090	243151	105536	3.35	6.84	2.35	3.08	6.52	2.09	3.15	2.49
1995–6	4276330	1882847	2393484	1672943	3920712	1800789	2119922	1555886	355619	82057	273561	117056	3.29	6.47	2.36	3.02	6.19	2.10	2.79	2.52
1996–7	4476532	1938094	2538438	1720831	4136609	1854329	2282280	1611940	339923	83765	256158	108890	3.21	6.48	2.31	2.96	6.20	2.06	2.24	2.10
1997–8	4718789	1988441	2730348	1808156	4364242	1900973	2463269	1689115	354547	87468	267079	119041	3.24	5.98	2.42	3.00	5.72	2.18	4.80	4.12
1998–9	4964096	2045144	2918952	1911638	4612145	1955426	2656719	1794201	351951	89718	262233	117437	3.20	5.76	2.43	2.97	5.50	2.21	2.69	2.59
1999–2000	5284581	2116052	3168529	2065515	4890250	2011010	2879239	1935508	394332	105042	289290	130006	3.22	5.43	2.52	2.99	5.17	2.29	4.13	3.50
2000–1	5562273	2180525	3381747	2227150	5153528	2066974	3086553	2080809	408745	113551	295194	146340	3.29	5.53	2.60	3.05	5.25	2.37	5.05	4.50
2001–2	5842614	2247335	3595279	2385607	5435252	2125784	3309468	2242907	407362	121551	285811	142700	3.27	5.35	2.62	3.04	5.07	2.40	2.77	2.93
2002–3	6159028	2301268	3857760	2579004	5733172	2183512	3549660	2423276	425856	117756	308100	155728	3.32	5.19	2.72	3.09	4.91	2.51	5.27	4.78
2003–4	6525010	2363654	4161356	2787634	6082142	2253567	3828575	2620559	442868	110087	332781	167075	3.23	5.15	2.66	3.01	4.89	2.45	2.64	2.28
2004–5	7013887	2444597	4569291	2999480	6531681	2328758	4202922	2827646	482207	115838	366368	171834	3.22	5.14	2.67	3.00	4.90	2.45	3.70	3.10
2005–6	7632389	2557941	5074447	3217888	7082912	2429585	4653327	3038698	549477	128357	421120	179190	3.17	5.08	2.66	2.95	4.83	2.44	3.26	2.68

(Continued)

Table A1.5 *Continued*

(1)	(2)	(3)	(4)	(5)	(6)	(7)	(8)	(9)	(10)	(11)	(12)	(13)	(14)	(15)	(16)	(17)	(18)	(19)	(20)	(21)
2006–7	8351053	2697028	5654025	3456938	7731972	2563023	5168949	3268797	619081	134005	485076	188141	3.15	4.81	2.70	2.92	4.57	2.47	3.36	2.82
2007–8	9206589	2882247	6318342	3725984	8482009	2736126	5745882	3524983	724580	152121	572460	201001	3.18	4.78	2.75	2.93	4.53	2.50	3.81	3.14
At Current Prices																				
1980–1	392849	166975	225874	183224	352123	151389	200734	170985	40726	15586	25140	12239	–	–	–	–	–	–	0.87	0.75
1981–2	471586	200405	271181	216245	422058	181678	240380	202533	49528	18727	30801	13712	3.06	7.22	2.15	2.74	6.55	1.91	0.96	0.89
1982–3	549463	236644	312820	245934	493061	216043	277019	230770	56402	20601	35801	15164	3.25	6.98	2.32	2.91	6.35	2.06	1.26	1.26
1983–4	626765	271796	354970	279393	564693	249621	315073	261736	62072	22175	39897	17657	3.19	6.88	2.27	2.87	6.30	2.01	0.81	0.85
1984–5	720982	316484	404498	315702	649494	291177	358317	295313	71488	25307	46181	20389	3.27	6.98	2.31	2.94	6.42	2.05	1.24	1.22
1985–6	842334	376731	465603	357877	758191	348050	410141	333981	84143	28681	55462	23896	3.41	7.07	2.42	3.07	6.52	2.13	1.50	1.41
1986–7	960195	431218	528976	402527	865539	400376	465162	374900	94656	30842	63814	27627	3.54	6.95	2.53	3.19	6.43	2.23	1.38	1.44
1987–8	1086937	487627	599310	457185	983358	456269	527089	425566	103579	31358	72221	31619	3.55	6.80	2.55	3.20	6.34	2.24	1.36	1.28
1988–9	1248477	560820	687657	518628	1125666	527145	598521	477659	122811	33675	89136	40969	3.38	6.51	2.43	3.06	6.10	2.13	1.08	0.94
1989–90	1445748	651980	793768	593634	1303591	613556	690035	546828	142157	38424	103733	46806	3.40	6.49	2.44	3.06	6.11	2.13	1.42	1.24
1990–1	1661637	739053	922584	688653	1500724	695152	805572	635643	160913	43901	117012	53010	3.35	6.57	2.40	3.02	6.18	2.09	1.44	1.19
1991–2	1957812	875454	1082358	787685	1780441	828299	952142	730600	177371	47155	130216	57085	3.40	6.41	2.47	3.08	6.05	2.16	1.21	1.21
1992–3	2243329	998146	1245182	883117	2036322	943305	1093016	817833	207007	54841	152166	65284	3.45	6.53	2.50	3.13	6.18	2.19	1.31	1.25
1993–4	2505447	1100519	1404928	988041	2282924	1039304	1243620	917269	222523	61215	161308	70772	3.34	6.38	2.42	3.04	6.03	2.14	1.12	1.03
1994–5	2872672	1259442	1613230	1107149	2615461	1192282	1423179	1028989	257211	67160	190051	78160	3.23	6.15	2.36	2.95	5.82	2.08	1.38	1.09
1995–6	3409948	1445116	1964831	1318351	3108086	1373796	1734289	1226439	301862	71320	230542	91912	3.23	5.97	2.40	2.94	5.66	2.12	1.43	1.28
1996–7	3836686	1625708	2210978	1446902	3538078	1549822	1988256	1357846	298608	75886	222722	89056	3.20	6.26	2.35	2.93	5.96	2.10	1.26	1.19
1997–8	4260304	1784818	2475486	1600885	3938080	1703118	2234962	1498466	322224	81700	240524	102419	3.22	5.83	2.43	2.97	5.56	2.19	1.92	1.65
1998–9	4755685	1958568	2797116	1806455	4425120	1871206	2553913	1704282	330565	87362	243203	102173	3.10	5.54	2.36	2.88	5.29	2.14	1.26	1.21
1999–2000	5284581	2116052	3168529	2065515	4890250	2011010	2879239	1935508	394332	105042	289290	130006	3.13	5.32	2.44	2.90	5.06	2.22	2.15	1.82
2000–1	5792328	2247493	3544835	2326414	5362453	2126807	3235646	2171865	429875	120685	309190	154549	3.21	5.41	2.54	2.97	5.13	2.32	2.62	2.34
2001–2	6378203	2428479	3949724	2622112	5939423	2295368	3644054	2466478	438781	133111	305670	153635	3.26	5.32	2.62	3.02	5.03	2.41	2.00	2.12
2002–3	6885976	2566647	4319329	2900698	6415160	2434828	3980332	2727702	470816	131818	338997	172997	3.30	5.13	2.71	3.07	4.86	2.50	2.60	2.36
2003–4	7625229	2743527	4881702	3305597	7111895	2613736	4498160	3110809	513334	129791	383542	194788	3.21	5.13	2.64	3.00	4.88	2.43	1.94	1.65
2004–5	8885252	3055665	5829587	3905644	8295809	2909398	5386412	3692102	589442	146267	443175	213542	3.24	5.17	2.69	3.02	4.93	2.49	2.35	1.95
2005–6	10187719	3366815	6820904	4426808	9490879	3198261	6292618	4195336	696840	168554	528286	231472	3.29	5.40	2.74	3.06	5.13	2.53	2.52	2.07
2006–7	11732465	3729645	8002819	5010180	10902197	3543876	7358321	4754091	830268	185770	644498	256090	3.28	5.26	2.78	3.05	5.00	2.56	2.46	2.06
2007–8	13683123	4217745	9465378	5720362	12657710	3994908	8662802	5433015	1025414	222837	802576	287347	3.33	5.36	2.85	3.09	5.08	2.61	2.85	2.34

Source: CSO, National Accounts Statistics (various issues).

Notes: * Average of beginning and year-end capital stock as ratio of the year's Net Domestic Product (NDP) at factor cost. $ Based on increase in NDP at factor cost.
– Data are not available.

Table A1.6 Rank of States in Descending Order of Per Capita State Domestic Product in Real Terms (Arranged as per 2007–8 Per Capita)

(1)	Per Capita GSDP at 1980–1 prices					Per Capita GSDP at 1999–2000 prices					(12)	Per Capita NSDP at 1980–1 prices					Per Capita NSDP at 1999–2000 prices				
	1981–2	Rank	1990–1	Rank	CAGR 1990–1 over 1980–1	2000–1	Rank	2006–7	Rank	CAGR 2006–7 over 2000–1		1981–2	Rank	1990–1	Rank	CAGR 1990–1 over 1980–1	2000–1	Rank	2006–7	Rank	CAGR 2006–7 over 2000–1
(1)	(2)	(3)	(4)	(5)	(6)	(7)	(8)	(9)	(10)	(11)	(12)	(13)	(14)	(15)	(16)	(17)	(18)	(19)	(20)	(21)	(22)
Chandigarh	–	–	–	–	–	51977	1	76046	1	6.5	Chandigarh	–	–	–	–	–	47756	1	70674	1	6.8
Goa	3895	2	5597	2	4.1	46202	2	65579	2	6.0	Goa	3083	2	4665	2	4.7	40208	2	56152	2	5.7
Delhi	4600	1	6146	1	3.3	42164	3	59350	3	5.9	Delhi	4229	1	5644	1	3.3	38971	3	54632	3	5.8
Puducherry	3097	4	3416	7	1.1	37342	4	53348	4	6.1	Puducherry	2817	4	3100	7	1.1	33502	4	46989	4	5.8
Haryana	2705	6	3784	4	3.8	26544	7	39967	5	7.1	Haryana	2419	7	3420	5	3.9	24413	6	36695	5	7.0
Maharashtra	2695	7	3776	5	3.8	25754	8	36057	6	5.8	Maharashtra	2452	6	3432	4	3.8	22387	8	30989	6	5.6
Gujarat	2280	8	2953	8	2.9	21761	12	34627	7	8.0	Kerala	1487	18	1782	18	2.0	19976	10	30521	7	7.3
Kerala	1683	17	2076	17	2.4	22680	10	34448	8	7.2	A & N Islands	2544	5	2532	10	-0.1	23844	7	30310	8	4.1
Himachal Pradesh	1888	10	2483	11	3.1	24591	9	33887	9	5.5	Punjab	2818	3	3762	3	3.3	25870	5	29989	9	2.5
A & N Islands	2759	5	2916	10	0.6	26741	6	33850	10	4.0	Himachal Pradesh	1718	11	3762	3	9.1	21724	9	28890	10	4.9
Punjab	3174	3	4216	3	3.2	28589	5	33801	11	2.8	Gujarat	2011	8	2235	11	1.2	18097	12	28795	11	8.0
Tamil Nadu	1743	14	2482	12	4.0	22306	11	31368	12	5.8	Tamil Nadu	1555	15	2200	12	3.9	19833	11	27774	12	5.8
Karnataka	1739	16	2376	13	3.5	19641	13	27511	13	5.8	Karnataka	1563	14	2119	14	3.4	17419	13	24111	13	5.6
Andhra Pradesh	1673	18	2293	15	3.6	18121	16	26649	14	6.6	Andhra Pradesh	1504	17	2069	15	3.6	16404	16	23940	14	6.5
Sikkim	1757	13	3621	6	8.4	18131	15	25962	15	6.2	Sikkim	1644	13	3327	6	8.1	15383	18	22140	15	6.3
Uttranchal	–	–	–	–	–	16476	21	24893	16	7.1	Tripura	1298	24	1620	23	2.5	15333	19	21908	16	6.1
West Bengal	1871	11	2369	14	2.7	17820	17	23795	17	4.9	Uttranchal	–	–	–	–	–	14604	22	21837	17	6.9
Tripura	1411	25	1804	23	2.8	16574	19	23482	18	6.0	West Bengal	1727	10	2166	13	2.5	16452	15	21731	18	4.7
Arunachal Pradesh	1850	12	2929	9	5.2	16290	22	22384	19	5.4	Meghalaya	1367	22	1698	21	2.4	14928	21	20217	19	5.2
Meghalaya	1529	21	1808	22	1.9	16526	20	22299	20	5.1	Arunachal Pradesh	1692	12	2695	8	5.3	15170	20	20073	20	4.8
Mizoram	–	–	–	–	–	18604	14	21520	21	2.5	Mizoram	–	–	–	–	–	16774	14	19031	21	2.1
Jammu & Kashmir	2019	9	–	–	–	16065	23	19680	22	3.4	Nagaland	1553	16	1990	16	2.8	15481	17	17068	22	1.6

(Continued)

Table A1.6 Continued

(1)	(2)	(3)	(4)	(5)	(6)	(7)	(8)	(9)	(10)	(11)	(12)	(13)	(14)	(15)	(16)	(17)	(18)	(19)	(20)	(21)	(22)
Chhattisgarh	–	–	–	–	–	13257	27	19259	23	6.4	Rajasthan	1261	26	1804	17	4.1	13464	24	16938	23	3.9
Rajasthan	1416	24	2028	18	4.1	15119	24	19190	24	4.1	Chhattisgarh	–	–	–	–	–	11546	28	16841	24	6.5
Nagaland	1742	15	2184	16	2.5	16585	18	18371	25	1.7	Jammu & Kashmir	1777	9	1764	19	-0.1	13820	23	16831	25	3.3
Orissa	1371	26	1708	24	2.5	11870	30	17430	26	6.6	Orissa	1265	25	1537	26	2.2	10493	30	15211	26	6.4
Manipur	1586	19	1976	19	2.5	14029	25	16839	27	3.1	Manipur	1443	19	1756	20	2.2	12686	25	15090	27	2.9
Assam	1485	22	1702	25	1.5	13515	26	16492	28	3.4	Assam	1374	20	1545	25	1.3	12419	26	14946	28	3.1
Jharkhand	–	–	–	–	–	12270	29	16215	29	4.8	Jharkhand	–	–	–	–	–	10660	29	14169	29	4.9
Madhya Pradesh	1529	20	1839	20	2.1	13067	28	14688	30	2.0	Madhya Pradesh	1369	21	1586	24	1.6	11750	27	12916	30	1.6
Uttar Pradesh	1449	23	1816	21	2.5	10874	31	12822	31	2.8	Uttar Pradesh	1299	23	1624	22	2.5	9714	31	11343	31	2.6
Bihar	1080	27	1315	26	2.2	6662	32	8611	32	4.4	Bihar	933	27	1139	27	2.2	6111	32	7863	32	4.3

Sources: CSO and individual states relevant ministry department.

Notes: ' – ' not relevant/not available.

CAGR: Compounded annual growth rate.

Data for 1981–2 is annual averages for 1980–1 to 1982–3.

Data for 1990–1 is annual averages for 1989–90 to 1991–2.

Data for 2000–1 is annual averages for 1999–2000 to 2001–2.

Data for 2006–7 is annual averages for 2005–6 to 2007–8.

Table A2 PRODUCTION
Table A2.1   Production Trends in Major Agricultural Crops

(Million tonne)

Year	Rice	Wheat	Coarse Cereals	Cereals	Pulses	Food Grains	Oil-seeds	Cotton (Lint)@	Jute & Mesta*	Tobacco	Sugarcane	Tea* (Jan-Dec) Mn kg	Coffee*
(1)	(2)	(3)	(4)	(5)	(6)	(7)	(8)	(9)	(10)	(11)	(12)	(13)	(14)
1950–1	20.58	6.46	15.38	42.42	8.41	50.83	5.16	3.04	3.31	0.26	57.05	279.00	24.00
1951–2	21.30	6.18	16.09	43.57	8.42	51.99	5.03	3.28	4.72	0.21	61.63	291.00	24.00
1952–3	22.90	7.50	19.61	50.01	9.19	59.20	4.73	3.34	5.32	0.25	51.00	306.00	21.00
1953–4	28.21	8.02	22.97	59.20	10.62	69.82	5.37	4.13	3.77	0.27	44.41	267.00	25.00
1954–5	25.22	9.04	22.82	57.08	10.95	68.03	6.40	4.45	3.86	0.26	58.74	293.00	26.00
1955–6	27.56	8.76	19.49	55.81	11.05	66.85	5.73	4.18	5.39	0.30	60.54	308.00	35.00
1956–7	29.04	9.40	19.87	58.31	11.55	69.86	6.36	4.92	5.81	0.31	69.05	309.00	43.00
1957–8	25.53	7.99	21.23	54.75	9.56	64.31	6.35	4.96	5.33	0.24	71.16	311.00	44.00
1958–9	30.85	9.96	23.18	63.99	13.15	77.14	7.30	4.88	6.91	0.32	73.36	325.00	47.00
1959–60	31.68	10.32	22.87	64.87	11.80	76.67	6.56	3.68	5.69	0.29	77.82	326.00	50.00
1960–1	34.57	11.00	23.74	69.31	12.70	82.02	6.98	5.60	5.26	0.31	110.00	321.00	68.00
1961–2	35.66	12.07	23.22	70.95	11.76	82.71	7.28	4.85	8.24	0.34	103.97	354.00	46.00
1962–3	33.21	10.78	24.63	68.62	11.53	80.15	7.39	5.54	7.19	0.34	91.91	347.00	56.00
1963–4	37.00	9.85	23.72	70.57	10.07	80.64	7.13	5.75	7.98	0.36	104.23	346.00	69.00
1964–5	39.31	12.26	25.37	76.94	12.42	89.36	8.56	6.01	7.66	0.36	121.91	372.00	61.00
1965–6	30.59	10.40	21.42	62.41	9.94	72.35	6.40	4.85	5.78	0.29	123.99	366.00	64.00
1966–7	30.44	11.39	24.05	65.88	8.35	74.23	6.43	5.27	6.58	0.35	92.83	376.00	78.00
1967–8	37.61	16.54	28.80	82.95	12.10	95.05	8.30	5.78	7.59	0.37	95.50	385.00	71.00
1968–9	39.76	18.65	25.18	83.59	10.42	94.01	6.85	5.45	3.84	0.36	124.68	402.00	73.00
1969–70	40.43	20.09	27.29	87.81	11.69	99.50	7.73	5.56	6.79	0.34	135.02	396.00	63.00
1970–1	42.22	23.83	30.55	96.60	11.82	108.42	9.63	4.76	6.19	0.36	126.37	419.00	110.20
1971–2	43.07	26.41	24.60	94.08	11.09	105.17	9.08	6.95	6.84	0.42	113.57	435.00	68.90
1972–3	39.24	24.74	23.14	87.12	9.91	97.03	7.14	5.74	6.09	0.37	124.87	456.00	91.10
1973–4	44.05	21.78	28.83	94.66	10.01	104.67	9.39	6.31	7.68	0.46	140.81	472.00	86.40
1974–5	39.58	24.10	26.13	89.81	10.02	99.83	9.15	7.16	5.83	0.36	144.29	489.00	92.50
1975–6	48.74	28.84	30.41	107.99	13.04	121.03	10.61	5.95	5.91	0.35	140.60	487.00	84.00
1976–7	41.92	29.01	28.88	99.81	11.36	111.17	8.43	5.84	7.10	0.42	153.01	512.00	102.20
1977–8	52.67	31.75	30.02	114.44	11.97	126.41	9.66	7.24	7.15	0.49	176.97	556.00	125.10
1978–9	53.77	35.51	30.44	119.72	12.18	131.90	10.10	7.96	8.33	0.45	151.66	564.00	110.50
1979–80	42.33	31.83	26.97	101.13	8.57	109.70	8.74	7.65	7.96	0.44	128.83	544.00	149.80
1980–1	53.63	36.31	29.02	118.96	10.63	129.59	9.37	7.01	8.16	0.48	154.25	569.60	118.60
1981–2	53.25	37.45	31.09	121.79	11.51	133.30	12.08	7.88	8.37	0.52	186.36	560.40	150.00
1982–3	47.12	42.79	27.75	117.66	11.86	129.52	10.00	7.53	7.17	0.58	189.51	560.70	130.00
1983–4	60.10	45.48	33.90	139.48	12.89	152.37	12.69	6.39	7.72	0.49	174.08	581.50	105.00
1984–5	58.34	44.07	31.17	133.58	11.96	145.54	12.95	8.51	7.79	0.49	170.32	639.90	195.10
1985–6	63.83	47.05	26.20	137.08	13.36	150.44	10.83	8.73	12.65	0.44	170.65	656.20	122.30
1986–7	60.56	44.32	26.83	131.71	11.71	143.42	11.27	6.91	8.62	0.46	186.09	624.60	192.30
1987–8	56.86	46.17	26.36	129.39	10.96	140.35	12.65	6.38	6.78	0.37	196.74	674.30	123.00

(Continued)

Table A2.1 *Continued*

(1)	(2)	(3)	(4)	(5)	(6)	(7)	(8)	(9)	(10)	(11)	(12)	(13)	(14)
1988–9	70.49	54.11	31.47	156.07	13.85	169.92	18.03	8.74	7.86	0.49	203.04	701.10	215.00
1989–90	73.57	49.85	34.76	158.18	12.86	171.04	16.92	11.42	8.29	0.55	225.57	684.10	180.00
1990–1	74.29	55.14	32.70	162.13	14.26	176.39	18.61	9.84	9.23	0.56	241.05	720.34	170.00
1991–2	74.68	55.69	25.99	156.36	12.02	168.38	18.60	9.71	10.29	0.58	254.00	754.19	208.00
1992–3	72.86	57.21	36.59	166.66	12.82	179.48	20.11	11.40	8.59	0.60	228.03	703.93	169.40
1993–4	80.30	59.84	30.81	170.95	13.31	184.26	21.50	10.74	8.42	0.56	229.66	760.83	208.00
1994–5	81.81	65.77	29.88	177.46	14.04	191.50	21.34	11.89	9.08	0.57	275.54	752.90	180.00
1995–6	76.98	62.10	29.03	168.11	12.31	180.42	22.10	12.86	8.81	0.54	281.10	756.02	223.00
1996–7	81.73	69.35	34.11	185.19	14.25	199.44	24.38	14.23	11.13	0.62	277.56	780.14	205.00
1997–8	82.54	66.35	30.40	179.29	12.97	192.26	21.32	10.85	11.02	0.64	279.54	835.60	228.30
1998–9	86.08	71.29	31.33	188.70	14.91	203.61	24.75	12.29	9.81	0.74	288.72	855.20	265.00
1999–2000	89.68	76.37	30.34	196.39	13.41	209.80	20.71	11.53	10.55	0.52	299.32	836.80	292.00
2000–1	84.98	69.68	31.08	185.74	11.07	196.81	18.44	9.52	10.56	0.34	295.96	848.40	301.00
2001–2	93.34	72.77	33.37	199.48	13.37	212.85	20.66	10.00	11.68	0.55	297.21	847.40	301.00
2002–3	71.82	65.76	26.07	163.65	11.13	174.77	14.84	8.62	11.28	0.49	287.38	846.00	275.00
2003–4	88.53	72.15	37.60	198.28	14.91	213.19	25.19	13.73	11.17	0.55	233.86	850.50	270.00
2004–5	83.13	68.64	33.46	185.23	13.13	198.36	24.35	16.43	10.27	0.55	237.09	906.84	281.90
2005–6	91.79	69.35	34.06	195.20	13.39	208.60	27.98	18.50	10.84	0.55	281.17	1000.00	300.00
2006–7	93.35	75.81	33.92	203.08	14.20	217.28	24.29	22.63	11.27	0.52	355.52	900.00	300.00
2007–8	96.69	78.57	40.76	216.02	14.76	230.78	29.76	25.88	11.21	0.49	348.19	na	na
2008–9	99.18	80.68	40.03	219.90	14.57	234.47	27.72	22.28	10.37	na	285.03	na	na
2009–10A	87.56	80.28	34.27	202.11	14.74	216.85	26.32	22.32	10.36	na	251.27	na	na
Decadal Growth Rates in per cent per Annum													
1950–1 to 1959–60	4.34	4.93	2.51	3.75	3.51	3.72	4.11	3.98	4.82	2.81	6.98	1.73	11.96
1960–1 to 1969–70	1.92	9.46	1.92	3.35	−0.22	2.89	1.47	0.21	−2.60	0.91	2.29	2.21	4.16
1970–1 to 1979–80	2.58	5.02	1.56	2.98	0.12	2.72	1.53	2.85	2.90	2.43	2.59	2.99	5.98
1980–1 to 1989–90	4.03	3.29	0.43	2.97	1.27	2.83	6.10	3.50	0.91	−0.10	3.31	2.84	4.44
1990–1 to 1999–2000	2.00	3.12	−0.10	2.08	0.14	1.90	0.81	0.35	2.35	−0.86	2.75	1.99	5.79
2000–1 to 2009–10	2.39	2.15	3.41	2.34	2.67	2.49	6.50	15.56	−0.56	2.04	2.30	2.83	0.18

Sources: GOI (2005), *Agricultural Statistics at a Glance*, Ministry of Agriculture and GOI (2006), *Economic Survey 2005–06*, Ministry of Finance and various earlier issues.

Notes: Decadal growth rates is worked out on three-year moving averages. It indicates compound growth rate in the production data calculated for the specified period using the semi-log model ln Y = a+bt, where t = time, Y = production, and the compound growth is obtained by taking antilog of 'b', deducting one from it and multiplying it with 100.

A: Second advance estimate. na: Not available.

* Production in million bales of 180 kg each.

@ Production in million bales of 170 kg each.

Total of nine oilseeds out of eleven.

Table A2.2   Trends in Yields of Major Crops

(kg per hectare)

Year	Rice	Wheat	Coarse Cereals	Cereals	Pulses	Food Grains	Total Oilseeds #	Sugar-cane	Tea	Coffee	Cotton (Lint)	Jute & Mesta	Tobacco
(1)	(2)	(3)	(4)	(5)	(6)	(7)	(8)	(9)	(10)	(11)	(12)	(13)	(14)
1950–1	668	663	408	542	441	522	481	33422	na	na	88	1043	731
1951–2	714	653	414	557	448	536	430	31786	na	na	85	1074	723
1952–3	764	763	462	607	463	580	424	29495	na	na	89	1028	675
1953–4	902	750	506	678	489	640	488	31497	na	na	100	992	737
1954–5	820	803	520	664	500	631	511	36303	na	na	100	1021	737
1955–6	874	708	449	639	476	605	474	32779	na	na	88	1038	739
1956–7	900	695	473	664	495	629	509	33683	na	na	104	977	728
1957–8	790	682	495	630	424	587	502	34325	na	na	105	944	669
1958–9	930	789	519	707	541	672	561	37658	na	na	104	1130	836
1959–60	937	772	522	713	475	662	470	36414	971	448	86	1049	716
1960–1	1013	851	528	753	539	710	507	45549	na	na	125	1049	766
1961–2	1028	890	519	763	485	706	493	42349	na	na	103	1104	811
1962–3	931	793	556	733	475	680	482	40996	na	na	122	1041	842
1963–4	1033	730	540	757	416	687	481	46353	na	na	119	1130	817
1964–5	1078	913	514	817	520	757	561	46838	na	na	122	1136	876
1965–6	862	827	483	676	438	629	419	43717	na	na	104	936	778
1966–7	863	887	533	707	377	644	428	40336	na	na	114	1058	834
1967–8	1032	1103	608	840	534	783	530	40665	na	na	123	1137	871
1968–9	1076	1169	545	843	490	781	473	49236	na	na	122	855	821
1969–70	1073	1208	578	865	531	805	522	49121	na	na	122	1120	770
1970–1	1123	1307	665	949	524	872	579	48322	1182	816	106	1032	810
1971–2	1141	1380	564	936	501	858	526	47511	1221	499	151	1107	914
1972–3	1070	1271	548	886	474	813	452	50933	1271	620	127	1104	837
1973–4	1151	1172	623	918	427	827	555	51163	1311	554	142	1188	1001
1974–5	1045	1338	606	907	455	824	529	49855	1353	593	161	1068	954
1975–6	1235	1410	694	1041	533	944	627	50903	1341	488	138	1164	950
1976–7	1089	1387	689	985	494	894	512	53383	1407	544	144	1173	969
1977–8	1308	1480	710	1100	510	991	563	56160	1519	652	157	1108	979
1978–9	1328	1568	721	1136	515	1022	570	49114	1528	564	167	1186	1109
1979–80	1074	1436	652	982	385	876	516	49358	1455	749	160	1177	1031
1980–1	1336	1630	695	1142	473	1023	532	57844	1491	624	152	1130	1065
1981–2	1308	1691	733	1157	483	1032	639	58359	1461	691	166	1311	1172
1982–3	1231	1816	685	1150	519	1035	563	56441	1422	573	163	1265	1157
1983–4	1457	1843	813	1296	548	1162	679	55978	1468	453	141	1320	1120
1984–5	1417	1870	795	1285	526	1149	684	57673	1606	830	196	1242	1113
1985–6	1552	2046	664	1323	547	1175	570	59889	1641	507	197	1524	1111
1986–7	1471	1916	675	1266	506	1128	605	60444	1508	791	169	1454	1187
1987–8	1465	2002	721	1315	515	1173	629	60006	1628	508	168	1274	1155
1988–9	1689	2244	814	1493	598	1331	824	60992	1693	878	202	1540	1307
1989–90	1745	2121	922	1530	549	1349	742	65612	1652	478	252	1646	1335

(Continued)

Table A2.2 *Continued*

(1)	(2)	(3)	(4)	(5)	(6)	(7)	(8)	(9)	(10)	(11)	(12)	(13)	(14)
1990–1	1740	2281	900	1571	578	1380	771	65395	1794	732	225	1634	1353
1991–2	1751	2394	778	1574	533	1382	719	66069	1800	746	216	1662	1369
1992–3	1744	2327	1063	1654	573	1457	797	63843	1664	582	257	1658	1425
1993–4	1888	2380	939	1701	598	1501	799	67120	1796	712	249	1713	1463
1994–5	1911	2559	929	1760	610	1546	843	71254	1767	614	257	1760	1486
1995–6	1797	2483	940	1703	552	1491	851	67787	1770	731	242	1712	1356
1996–7	1882	2679	1072	1831	635	1614	926	66496	1809	675	265	1818	1444
1997–8	1900	2485	986	1775	567	1552	816	71134	1865	746	208	1792	1394
1998–9	1921	2590	1068	1856	634	1627	944	71203	1803	877	224	1722	1451
1999–2000	1986	2778	1034	1926	635	1704	853	70935	1702	947	225	1836	1211
2000–1	1901	2708	1027	1844	544	1626	810	68577	1673	959	190	1867	1318
2001–2	2079	2762	1131	1980	607	1734	913	67370	1800	937	186	2007	1565
2002–3	1744	2610	966	1753	543	1535	691	63576	1800	839	191	1960	1506
2003–4	2077	2713	1221	1987	635	1727	1064	59380	1800	1000	307	2008	1486
2004–5	1984	2602	1153	1918	577	1652	885	64752	1800	1000	318	2019	1498
2005–6	2102	2619	1172	1968	598	1715	1004	66928	1500	1000	362	2173	1481
2006–7	2131	2708	1182	2021	612	1756	916	69022	1667	1000	421	2170	1409
2007–8	2202	2802	1431	2151	625	1860	1115	68877	1500	1000	467	2101	1417
2008–9	2186	2891	1429	2284	655	1898	1026	62321	na	na	419	2052	na

Source: GOI (2009), *Agricultural Statistics at a Glance*.

Note: na: Not available.

Table A2.3 Horticulture and Livestock Production

(000 tonne)

	2008–9	2007–8	2006–7	2005–6	2004–5	2003–4	2002–3	2001–2	2000–1	1999–00	1998–9	1997–8	1996–7	1995–6	1994–5	1993–4	1992–3	1991–2
Horticulture Production																		
Total	220484	212842	191832	178100	164100	152000	144400	146500	143806	149187	146020	128611	128482	125483	118394	114616	107388	96562
Fruits	69453	65602	59563	57600	53100	49200	45200	43100	45370	45496	44042	43263	40458	41507	38603	37255	32955	28632
Apple	1985	2001	1624	1755.6	1739	1522	1348	1158	1227	1047	1380	1321	1308	1215	1183	1298	1168	1148
Banana	27119	23861	20998	18702	16328	13857	13304	14210	14137	16814	15073	13340	12440	13095	13168	11901	10460	7790
Citrus Fruit	8528	8038	7145	6326	5933	5787	5677	4789	4386	4651	4575	4311	4456	3798	3701	3912	2979	2822
Lemon				1786	1033	1493	1440	1414	1377	1492	1260	1101	1048	920	970	924	na	na
Mosambi				2122	2079	2019	785	1210	1160	1017	773	882	844	880	887	825	na	na
Orange				1313	1236	1244	1137	1660	1414	1658	1674	1472	1720	1162	709	1058	na	na
Grapes	1764	1733	1685	1631	1565	1475	1248	1184	1057	1138	1083	969	1135	604	673	703	653	668
Guava	2330	1981	1831	1823	1683	1831	1793	1716	1632	1711	1801	1614	1601	1501	1388	1273	1204	1095
Litchi	433	418	403	381	369	479	476	356	412	433	429	455	378	365	333	313	261	244
Mango	12831	13997	13734	12538	11830	11490	12733	10020	10057	10504	9782	10234	9981	10811	10993	10113	9223	8716
Papaya	3641	2904	2482	2317	2535	1692	2147	2590	1796	1666	1582	1619	1299	1330	1373	1266	804	805
Pineapple	1354	1247	1362	1353	1279	1234	1172	1182	1211	1025	1006	937	925	1071	1055	1007	859	769
Sapota	1309	1258	1216	1117	1077	921	913	594	741	635	668	644	589	570	496	481	423	396
Vegetables	133071	129261	115010	99400	91600	84800	84800	88600	93920	90831	87536	72683	75074	71594	67286	65787	63806	58532
Brinjal	10420	9703	9453	9136	8601	8477	8001	8348	7652	8117	7882	7735	6586	6443	6232	4612	na	na
Cabbage	6805	5909	5589	5922	6114	5595	5392	5678	5507	5909	5624	5324	3613	3862	3906	3593	3237	2771
Cauliflower	6566	5972	5579	5260	4515	4940	4444	4891	4696	4718	4691	4471	3419	2474	3244	2873	3612	2998
Okra	4524	4189	4070	3684	3512	3631	3245	3325	3352	3419	3380	3211	3040	4032	3989	3029	2738	1887
Onion	13972	14244	10847	9248	7761	6268	4210	5252	4721	4900	5330	3620	4180	4080	4040	4006	3490	3580
Peas	2914	2561	2402	2299	1945	1901	2062	2038	3008	2712	2706	2422	2339	2341	2306	1528	1492	852
Tomato	11328	10463	10055	9362	8825	8126	7617	7462	7242	7427	8272	6184	5788	5442	5261	4934	4550	4243
Potato	36284	34673	28599	29094	28788	27926	23161	24456	22243	25000	22495	17652	24216	18843	17401	17392	18479	18195
Sweet Potato	1121	1096	1067	1149	1179	1179	1130	1130	1007	1007	1152	1048	1102	1138	1166	1221	1216	1131
Tapioca	9623	9056	8232	7925	7463	5950	5426	6516	6768	6014	5830	6682	5663	5443	5857	6029	5413	5833
Coconuts*	10894	14744	15840	14811	12833	12178	12535	12963	12597	12129	126	12717	13061	12952	13300	11975	11241	10050
Cashewnut	695	770	765	579	544	535	460	460	450	520	460	360	430	418	322	348	349	305
Flowers	989	868	880	694	659	580	735	535	556	509	419	366	367	334	261	233	na	na
Plantation Crops	12082	12059	12007	11263	9835	13161	9697	9697	9458	9278	11063	9449	9730	9630	9767	8866	8347	7498
Spices	4145	4357	3953	5108	4001	5113	3765	3765	3023	3023	3091	2801	2805	2410	2477	2470	2280	1900
Livestock Production																		
Milk	109	105	101	97	91	88	86	84	81	78	75	72	69	66	64	61	58	56
Fish (000 tonne)	7608	7127	6869	6572	6304	6399	6200	5956	5656	5675	5298	5388	5348	4949	4789	4644	4365	4157
Eggs (billion)	56	54	51	46	45	40	40	39	37	30	30	29	28	27	26	24	23	22

Sources: National Horticulture Board, Ministry of Agriculture, Government of India, *Indian Horticulture Data Base—2001* and *Economic Survey 2005–06.*

Notes: Coconut production is in number of nuts in thousands (1453.24 nuts = 1 tonne). na: Not available.

Table A2.4   Value of Output from Agriculture, Horticulture, and Livestock

At Constant (1999–2000) Prices

	Agriculture, Horticulture, and Livestock	Agriculture (4 to 11)	Cereals	Pulses	Oilseeds	Sugars	Fibres	Drugs and Narcotics	Condiments and Spices	Others	Horticulture# (Fruits and Vegetables)	Livestock
(1)	(2)	(3)	(4)	(5)	(6)	(7)	(8)	(9)	(10)	(11)	(12)	(13)
1950–1	114288	81834	30342	11506	8242	4156	3856	2397	3308	18029	15269	32454
	(100.0)	(71.6)	(26.5)	(10.1)	(7.2)	(3.6)	(3.4)	(2.1)	(2.9)	(15.8)	(13.4)	(28.4)
1955–6	131255.758	97145	38660	14542	9370	5103	5155	2738	3615	17963	14284	34111
	(100.0)	(74.0)	(29.5)	(11.1)	(7.1)	(3.9)	(3.9)	(2.1)	(2.8)	(13.7)	(10.9)	(26.0)
1960–1	150683.078	112933	48004	16140	11082	6820	6543	2879	4164	17301	16286	37750
	(100.0)	(74.9)	(31.9)	(10.7)	(7.4)	(4.5)	(4.3)	(1.9)	(2.8)	(11.5)	(10.8)	(25.1)
1965–6	142745.255	104853	42806	12736	10466.997	8146	5530	3137	4047	17984	20113	37893
	(100.0)	(73.5)	(30.0)	(8.9)	(7.3)	(5.7)	(3.9)	(2.2)	(2.8)	(12.6)	(14.1)	(26.5)
1970–1	178061.059	137394	65096	15204	15023	8040	6066	3994	5491	18479	32064	40667
	(100.0)	(77.2)	(36.6)	(8.5)	(8.4)	(4.5)	(3.4)	(2.2)	(3.1)	(10.4)	(18.0)	(22.8)
1975–6	198834.058	151065	73311	16992	15702	9220	6547	4365	5668	19261	36383	47769
	(100.0)	(76.0)	(36.9)	(8.5)	(7.9)	(4.6)	(3.3)	(2.2)	(2.9)	(9.7)	(18.3)	(24.0)
1980–1	217184.637	158845	81070	14339	14469	9611	8028	5134	6877	19316	42003	58339
	(100.0)	(73.1)	(37.3)	(6.6)	(6.7)	(4.4)	(3.7)	(2.4)	(3.2)	(8.9)	(19.3)	(26.9)
1985–6	256809.669	179269	93326	17202	16267	10226	10652	5703	8672	17222	48268	77540
	(100.0)	(69.8)	(36.3)	(6.7)	(6.3)	(4.0)	(4.1)	(2.2)	(3.4)	(6.7)	(18.8)	(30.2)
1990–1	311709.225	218761	110632	19042	26828	14252	11244	6889	10230	19644	54299	92949
	(100.0)	(70.2)	(35.5)	(6.1)	(8.6)	(4.6)	(3.6)	(2.2)	(3.3)	(6.3)	(17.4)	(29.8)
1991–2	307365.367	211309	107007	15914	26739	15184	11267	7150	9863	18184	53401	96056
	(100.0)	(68.7)	(34.8)	(5.2)	(8.7)	(4.9)	(3.7)	(2.3)	(3.2)	(5.9)	(17.4)	(31.3)
1992–3	324203.455	223278	112932	17378	28753	13413	12736	6688	11408	19970	58365	100925
	(100.0)	(68.9)	(34.8)	(5.4)	(8.9)	(4.1)	(3.9)	(2.1)	(3.5)	(6.2)	(18.0)	(31.1)
1993–4	334774	229088	117026	17918	29960	13673	12183	7489	12010	18829	60670	105686
	(100.0)	(68.4)	(35.0)	(5.4)	(8.9)	(4.1)	(3.6)	(2.2)	(3.6)	(5.6)	(18.1)	(31.6)
1994–5	349934	240065	121714	18200	31095	15821	13542	7299	12278	20115	63620	109870
	(100.0)	(68.6)	(34.8)	(5.2)	(8.9)	(4.5)	(3.9)	(2.1)	(3.5)	(5.7)	(18.2)	(31.4)
1995–6	345152	231521	114805.041	16387	31227	16018	14578	7407	11957	19141	67337	113631
	(100.0)	(67.1)	(33.3)	(4.7)	(9.0)	(4.6)	(4.2)	(2.1)	(3.5)	(5.5)	(19.5)	(32.9)
1996–7	371946	254335	126197	19216	34597	16101	16234	9025	13325	19639	76864	117612
	(100.0)	(68.4)	(33.9)	(5.2)	(9.3)	(4.3)	(4.4)	(2.4)	(3.6)	(5.3)	(20.7)	(31.6)
1997–8	362742	241889	122973	17432	30681	16093	12785	8841	13255	19830	77849	120853
	(100.0)	(66.7)	(33.9)	(4.8)	(8.5)	(4.4)	(3.5)	(2.4)	(3.7)	(5.5)	(21.5)	(33.3)
1998–9	387159	261325	129346	20243	34509	18806	14383	9517	15704	18817	84982	125834
	(100.0)	(67.5)	(33.4)	(5.2)	(8.9)	(4.9)	(3.7)	(2.5)	(4.1)	(4.9)	(22.0)	(32.5)
1999–2000	398044	268514	134096	18153	28625	24669	13373	10752	15447	23397	86155	129531
	(100.0)	(67.5)	(33.7)	(4.6)	(7.2)	(6.2)	(3.4)	(2.7)	(3.9)	(5.9)	(21.6)	(32.5)
2000–1	387120	253424	125540.974	15669	26637	24640	10792	9950	15907	24287	91786	133696
	(100.0)	(65.5)	(32.4)	(4.0)	(6.9)	(6.4)	(2.8)	(2.6)	(4.1)	(6.3)	(23.7)	(34.5)
2001–2	416580	276721	135003.979	18576	29550	24576	11527	10093	17393	30002	93809	139860
	(100.0)	(66.4)	(32.4)	(4.5)	(7.1)	(5.9)	(2.8)	(2.4)	(4.2)	(7.2)	(22.5)	(33.6)
2002–3	380277	236627	110732	15698	22612	23591	10324	10120	16442	27109	94090	143649
	(100.0)	(62.2)	(29.1)	(4.1)	(5.9)	(6.2)	(2.7)	(2.7)	(4.3)	(7.1)	(24.7)	(37.8)
2003–4	431612	284284	132338	20762	34841	19635	15097	9509	18644	33459	90392	147328
	(100.0)	(65.9)	(30.7)	(4.8)	(8.1)	(4.5)	(3.5)	(2.2)	(4.3)	(7.8)	(20.9)	(34.1)
2004–5	430812	276567	125257	17868	33898	19994	18130	10985	19014	31422	94500	154245
	(100.0)	(64.2)	(29.1)	(4.1)	(7.9)	(4.6)	(4.2)	(2.5)	(4.4)	(7.3)	(21.9)	(35.8)
2005–6	454452	293857	132879	18435	38208	22527	19502	11466	19446	31393	102594	160595
	(100.0)	(64.7)	(29.2)	(4.1)	(8.4)	(5.0)	(4.3)	(2.5)	(4.3)	(6.9)	(22.6)	(35.3)
2006–7	472921	305857	137544	19622	33439	27832	23678	12093	20305	31343	107537	167064
	(100.0)	(64.7)	(29.1)	(4.1)	(7.1)	(5.9)	(5.0)	(2.6)	(4.3)	(6.6)	(22.7)	(35.3)
2007–8	497887	324023	146429	20407	39481	27258	26820	11730	20519	31377	113734	173864
	(100.0)	(65.1)	(29.4)	(4.1)	(7.9)	(5.5)	(5.4)	(2.4)	(4.1)	(6.3)	(22.8)	(34.9)

(Continued)

Table A2.4 *Continued*

(1)	Agriculture, Horticulture, and Livestock (14)	Agriculture (16 to 23) (15)	Cereals (16)	Pulses (17)	Oilseeds (18)	Sugars (19)	Fibres (20)	Drugs and Narcotics (21)	Condiments and Spices (22)	Others (23)	Horticulture[#] (Fruits and Vegetables) (24)	Livestock (25)
1950–1	5581	4502	2013	333	442	184	227	150	157	996	406	1079
	(100.0)	(80.7)	(36.1)	(6.0)	(7.9)	(3.3)	(4.1)	(2.7)	(2.8)	(17.8)	(7.3)	(19.3)
1955–6	4889	3830	1808	238	298	219	268	139	97	762	582	1060
	(100.0)	(78.3)	(37.0)	(4.9)	(6.1)	(4.5)	(5.5)	(2.8)	(2.0)	(15.6)	(11.9)	(21.7)
1960–1	7455	5993	3114	459	594	325	400	192	192	717	770	1462
	(100.0)	(80.4)	(41.8)	(6.2)	(8.0)	(4.4)	(5.4)	(2.6)	(2.6)	(9.6)	(10.3)	(19.6)
1965–6	10920	8901	4787	702	958	531	452	276	260	933	1399	2019
	(100.0)	(81.5)	(43.8)	(6.4)	(8.8)	(4.9)	(4.1)	(2.5)	(2.4)	(8.5)	(12.8)	(18.5)
1970–1	17864	14600	7975	990	1779	781	907	427	448	1292	2715	3264
	(100.0)	(81.7)	(44.6)	(5.5)	(10.0)	(4.4)	(5.1)	(2.4)	(2.5)	(7.2)	(15.2)	(18.3)
1975–6	29208	22957	12917	1580	2259	1488	1086	726	772	2129	4274	6251
	(100.0)	(78.6)	(44.2)	(5.4)	(7.7)	(5.1)	(3.7)	(2.5)	(2.6)	(7.3)	(14.6)	(21.4)
1980–1	46568	36073	18393	3168	4168	2983	2021	1088	964	3288	7886	10494
	(100.0)	(77.5)	(39.5)	(6.8)	(9.0)	(6.4)	(4.3)	(2.3)	(2.1)	(7.1)	(16.9)	(22.5)
1985–6	74590	52816	27805	4939	5621	3448	2842	1783	1988	4390	14474	21774
	(100.0)	(70.8)	(37.3)	(6.6)	(7.5)	(4.6)	(3.8)	(2.4)	(2.7)	(5.9)	(19.4)	(29.2)
1990–1	142473	100766	47167	9280	17738	6899	5810	3165	3528	7180	23450	41707
	(100.0)	(70.7)	(33.1)	(6.5)	(12.5)	(4.8)	(4.1)	(2.2)	(2.5)	(5.0)	(16.5)	(29.3)
1991–2	169581	119017	58776	8209	19995	7604	7272	3484	5152	8526	27018	50564
	(100.0)	(70.2)	(34.7)	(4.8)	(11.8)	(4.5)	(4.3)	(2.1)	(3.0)	(5.0)	(15.9)	(29.8)
1992–3	186080	128208	64315	9588	19740	8411	6808	3590	5887	9869	31364	57873
	(100.0)	(68.9)	(34.6)	(5.2)	(10.6)	(4.5)	(3.7)	(1.9)	(3.2)	(5.3)	(16.9)	(31.1)
1993–4	214623	147921	71910	12216	23098	10670	9535	4397	6010	10086	35723	66702
	(100.0)	(68.9)	(33.5)	(5.7)	(10.8)	(5.0)	(4.4)	(2.0)	(2.8)	(4.7)	(16.6)	(31.1)
1994–5	247830	171977	82034	13518	25789	13048	13851	4300	7342	12094	40435	75853
	(100.0)	(69.4)	(33.1)	(5.5)	(10.4)	(5.3)	(5.6)	(1.7)	(3.0)	(4.9)	(16.3)	(30.6)
1995–6	265922	180310	83992	13896	27641	13043	14198	5688	7906	13944	49475	85611
	(100.0)	(67.8)	(31.6)	(5.2)	(10.4)	(4.9)	(5.3)	(2.1)	(3.0)	(5.2)	(18.6)	(32.2)
1996–7	312401	215596	103982	17091	33091	14022	15338	7000	9464	15607	57870	96806
	(100.0)	(69.0)	(33.3)	(5.5)	(10.6)	(4.5)	(4.9)	(2.2)	(3.0)	(5.0)	(18.5)	(31.0)
1997–8	316883	210082	102639	15079	28988	15899	13038	8607	9866	15966	75309	106801
	(100.0)	(66.3)	(32.4)	(4.8)	(9.1)	(5.0)	(4.1)	(2.7)	(3.1)	(5.0)	(23.8)	(33.7)
1998–9	369041	251158	124114	19475	35312	18643	14536	9094	13254	16729	83367	117882
	(100.0)	(68.1)	(33.6)	(5.3)	(9.6)	(5.1)	(3.9)	(2.5)	(3.6)	(4.5)	(22.6)	(31.9)
1999–2000	398044	268514	134096	18153	28625	24669	13373	10752	15447	23397	86155	129531
	(100.0)	(67.5)	(33.7)	(4.6)	(7.2)	(6.2)	(3.4)	(2.7)	(3.9)	(5.9)	(21.6)	(32.5)
2000–1	390235	251179	122687	16995	25860	27151	11093	10949	13394	23051	94893	139057
	(100.0)	(64.4)	(31.4)	(4.4)	(6.6)	(7.0)	(2.8)	(2.8)	(3.4)	(5.9)	(24.3)	(35.6)
2001–2	422293	275113	133744	20220	30081	27049	11144	10620	13955	28299	102959	147180
	(100.0)	(65.1)	(31.7)	(4.8)	(7.1)	(6.4)	(2.6)	(2.5)	(3.3)	(6.7)	(24.4)	(34.9)
2002–3	407479	253350	116165	17583	28815	25270	11001	11454	13469	29593	106633	154129
	(100.0)	(62.2)	(28.5)	(4.3)	(7.1)	(6.2)	(2.7)	(2.8)	(3.3)	(7.3)	(26.2)	(37.8)
2003–4	476748	313778	139522	22063	47723	22867	17853	11394	15686	36669	108522	162970
	(100.0)	(65.8)	(29.3)	(4.6)	(10.0)	(4.8)	(3.7)	(2.4)	(3.3)	(7.7)	(22.8)	(34.2)
2004–5	495137	314906	137669	19843	46024	27992	18517	12868	15598	36396	114225	180231
	(100.0)	(63.6)	(27.8)	(4.0)	(9.3)	(5.7)	(3.7)	(2.6)	(3.2)	(7.4)	(23.1)	(36.4)
2005–6	553433	357041	155830	24283	49684	34621	20320	14320	17383	40600	137894	196392
	(100.0)	(64.5)	(28.2)	(4.4)	(9.0)	(6.3)	(3.7)	(2.6)	(3.1)	(7.3)	(24.9)	(35.5)
2006–7	613137	399153	173810	30297	47556	39558	26205	16085	21670	43971	145008	213984
	(100.0)	(65.1)	(28.3)	(4.9)	(7.8)	(6.5)	(4.3)	(2.6)	(3.5)	(7.2)	(23.7)	(34.9)
2007–8	691650	451049	195755	30824	69155	39019	34216	15924	23278	42877	168518	240601
	(100.0)	(65.2)	(28.3)	(4.5)	(10.0)	(5.6)	(4.9)	(2.3)	(3.4)	(6.2)	(24.4)	(34.8)

Source: CSO (2009), National Accounts Statistics (various issues).

Note: Horticulture includes floriculture.

Table A2.5 Structural Changes in Indian Industry and Decadal Growth

Sector Group	Weight as per Index Numbers					Growth Rates per cent per Annum					
	1956=100	1960=100	1970=100	1980–1=100	1993–4=100	1970–1 to 1980–1	1980–1 to 1990–1	1990–1 to 1993–4	1993–4 to 2003–4	2004–5 to 2008–9	1993–4 to 2008–9
Mining and Quarrying	7.47	9.72	9.69	11.5	10.47	4.6	7.6	1.4	3.1	8.1	6.6
Manufacturing	88.85	84.91	81.08	77.1	79.36	4.7	7.7	2.4	6.6	3.8	3.4
Electricity	3.68	5.37	9.23	11.4	10.17	4.2	9.1	6.8	5.5	8.8	7.1
General Index	100	100	100	100	100	7.6	7.9	2.9	6.1	5.6	5.3
Use-based Category											
Basic Goods	22.33	25.11	32.28	39.42	35.57	6.0	7.9	5.8	4.9	7.0	5.3
Capital Goods	4.71	11.76	15.25	16.43	9.26	5.6	11.3	–3.9	6.7	15.4	9.1
Intermediate Goods	24.59	25.88	20.95	20.51	26.51	3.5	6.3	4.9	7.1	6.1	6.3
Consumer Goods	48.37	37.25	31.52	23.65	28.66	3.4	6.5	2.2	6.6	8.1	7.5
Consumer Durables	2.21	5.68	3.41	2.55	5.37	4.6	14.8	0.7	9.9	5.3	9.3
Consumer Non-durables	46.16	31.57	28.11	21.1	23.3	3.3	5.1	2.6	5.6	8.7	6.9

Source: (i) Economic and Political Weekly Research Foundation (EPWRF) (2002), *Annual Survey of Industries 1993–4 to 1997–8: A Data Base on the Industrial Sector in India* and (ii) as in Table A2.6.

Note: Growth indicates compound growth rate in index numbers of industrial production for groups and general index calculated for the specified period using the semi-log model lnY = a+bt, where t = time, Y + index value and the compound growth is obtained by taking antilog of 'b', deducting one from it and mutiplying it with 100.

Table A2.6 Index of Industrial Production with Major Groups and Sub-groups

Major Groups	Weights	Annual Average Growth 1993–4 to 2008–9	1980–1 to 1992–3	Full Fiscal Year Averages based on 1993–4 = 100 2008–9	2007–8	2006–7	2005–6	2004–5	2003–4	2002–3	2001–2	2000–1	1999–2000	1998–9	1997–8	1996–7	1995–6	1994–5
(1)	(2)	(3)	(4)	(5)	(6)	(7)	(8)	(9)	(10)	(11)	(12)	(13)	(14)	(15)	(16)	(17)	(18)	(19)
General Index	100.00	7.0	6.8	275.4 (2.8)	268.0 (8.5)	247.1 (11.6)	221.5 (8.2)	204.8 (8.4)	189.0 (7.0)	176.6 (5.7)	167.0 (2.7)	162.6 (5.0)	154.9 (6.7)	145.2 (4.1)	139.5 (6.7)	130.8 (6.1)	123.3 (13.0)	109.1 (9.1)
Mining and Quarrying	10.47	3.9	7.0	176.0 (2.6)	171.6 (5.1)	163.2 (5.4)	154.9 (1.0)	153.4 (4.4)	146.9 (5.2)	139.6 (5.8)	131.9 (1.2)	130.3 (2.8)	126.7 (1.0)	125.4 (−0.8)	126.4 (−6.9)	118.2 (−1.9)	120.5 (9.7)	109.8 (9.8)
Manufacturing	79.36	7.5	6.5	295.1 (2.8)	287.2 (9.0)	263.5 (12.5)	234.2 (9.1)	214.6 (9.2)	196.6 (7.4)	183.1 (6.0)	172.7 (2.9)	167.9 (5.3)	159.4 (7.1)	148.8 (4.4)	142.5 (6.7)	133.6 (7.3)	124.5 (14.1)	109.1 (9.1)
Electricity	10.17	5.5	8.6	223.7 (2.8)	217.7 (6.4)	204.7 (7.2)	190.9 (5.2)	181.5 (5.2)	172.6 (5.1)	164.3 (3.2)	159.2 (3.1)	154.4 (4.0)	148.5 (7.3)	138.4 (6.5)	130.0 (6.6)	122.0 (4.0)	117.3 (8.1)	108.5 (8.5)
Use-based Classification																		
Basic Goods	35.57	5.7	7.3	229.6 (2.5)	223.9 (6.8)	209.7 (10.6)	189.6 (6.6)	177.9 (5.5)	168.6 (5.4)	159.9 (4.9)	152.5 (2.6)	148.7 (3.8)	143.3 (5.5)	135.8 (1.6)	133.6 (6.9)	125.0 (3.0)	121.4 (10.8)	109.6 (9.6)
Capital Goods	9.26	9.8	8.8	396.8 (7.0)	370.8 (18.0)	314.2 (18.5)	265.1 (15.5)	229.6 (13.9)	201.5 (13.6)	177.4 (10.5)	160.6 (−3.0)	165.6 (1.4)	163.3 (6.9)	152.7 (12.6)	135.6 (5.8)	128.2 (11.5)	115.0 (5.3)	109.2 (9.2)
Intermediate Goods	26.51	6.6	5.2	256.6 (−2.8)	264.1 (9.0)	242.4 (12.3)	215.9 (2.3)	211.1 (6.1)	199.0 (6.4)	187.1 (3.9)	180.1 (1.6)	177.2 (4.5)	169.5 (8.8)	155.8 (6.1)	146.8 (8.0)	135.9 (8.1)	125.7 (19.4)	105.3 (5.3)
Consumer Goods	28.66	7.8	5.8	306.6 (4.4)	293.6 (6.1)	276.8 (10.2)	251.2 (11.9)	224.4 (11.7)	200.9 (7.1)	187.5 (7.1)	175.1 (6.1)	165.1 (7.9)	153.0 (5.7)	144.8 (2.2)	141.7 (5.5)	134.3 (6.2)	126.5 (12.8)	112.1 (12.1)
Consumer Durables	5.36	9.5	10.6	376.2 (−0.5)	378.0 (−1.0)	382.0 (9.8)	347.9 (14.6)	303.5 (14.4)	265.4 (11.6)	237.8 (−6.3)	253.7 (12.0)	226.5 (14.0)	198.7 (14.1)	174.1 (5.6)	164.9 (7.8)	152.9 (4.6)	146.2 (25.8)	116.2 (16.2)
Consumer Non-durables	23.30	7.3	5.1	286.3 (4.4)	274.2 (8.6)	252.6 (10.4)	228.9 (11.0)	206.2 (10.8)	186.1 (5.8)	175.9 (12.0)	157.0 (4.0)	151.0 (6.0)	142.5 (3.2)	138.1 (1.2)	136.5 (4.8)	130.2 (6.6)	122.1 (9.8)	111.2 (11.2)
Group-wise Index Number of Industrial Production																		
Food Products	9.08*	4.2	5.0	178.9 (−9.7)	198.2 (7.0)	185.2 (8.6)	170.6 (2.0)	167.3 (−0.4)	167.9 (−0.5)	168.7 (11.0)	152.0 (−1.6)	154.5 (10.1)	140.3 (4.2)	134.7 (0.7)	133.8 (−0.4)	134.3 (3.5)	129.8 (6.7)	121.6 (21.6)
Beverages, Tobacco, and Related Products	2.38	12.6	1.4	578.5 (16.2)	498.0 (12.0)	444.5 (11.0)	400.3 (15.7)	345.9 (10.8)	312.1 (8.5)	287.6 (27.9)	224.8 (12.2)	200.4 (4.3)	192.1 (7.6)	178.5 (12.9)	158.1 (19.4)	132.4 (13.5)	116.7 (13.3)	103.0 (3.0)
Cotton Textiles	5.52	3.4	3.7	160.9 (−1.9)	164.0 (4.3)	157.3 (14.8)	137.0 (8.5)	126.3 (7.6)	117.4 (−3.1)	121.2 (−2.7)	124.5 (−2.2)	127.3 (2.9)	123.7 (6.7)	115.9 (−7.7)	125.6 (2.4)	122.7 (12.1)	109.5 (10.5)	99.1 (−0.9)
Wool, Silk, and Man-made Fibre Textiles	2.26	7.3	−0.6	281.2 (0.0)	281.2 (4.8)	268.4 (7.8)	248.9 (−0.0)	249.0 (3.5)	240.5 (6.8)	225.1 (3.0)	218.5 (4.4)	209.3 (5.8)	197.8 (11.9)	176.8 (2.8)	172.0 (18.5)	145.1 (10.5)	131.3 (14.7)	114.5 (14.5)

(Continued)

Table A2.6 Continued

(1)	(2)	(3)	(4)	(5)	(6)	(7)	(8)	(9)	(10)	(11)	(12)	(13)	(14)	(15)	(16)	(17)	(18)	(19)
Jute and Other Vegetable Fibre Textiles	0.59	1.2	−0.3	108.6	120.7	90.7	107.7	107.2	103.4	107.9	99.6	105.8	105.0	106.0	114.3	97.8	102.4	95.1
				(−10.0)	(33.1)	(−15.8)	(0.5)	(3.7)	(−4.2)	(8.3)	(−5.9)	(0.8)	(−0.9)	(−7.3)	(−16.9)	(−4.5)	(7.7)	(−4.9)
Textile Products (including Wearing Apparel)	2.54	8.3	7.4	312.5	295.5	285.0	255.5	219.6	184.3	190.3	166.3	162.4	156.1	153.1	158.7	146.3	133.7	98.5
				(5.8)	(3.7)	(11.5)	(16.3)	(19.2)	(−3.2)	(−14.4)	(2.4)	(4.0)	(2.0)	(−3.5)	(8.5)	(9.4)	(35.7)	(−1.5)
Wood and Wood Products, Furniture, and Fixtures	2.70	2.2	6.6	115.6	127.9	91.0	70.5	74.8	81.7	76.5	92.8	104.3	101.4	121.0	128.5	131.9	123.2	99.3
				(−9.6)	(−40.5)	(29.1)	(−5.7)	(−8.4)	(6.8)	(−17.6)	(−11.0)	(2.9)	(−16.2)	(−5.8)	(−2.6)	(7.1)	(24.1)	(−0.7)
Paper and Paper Products and Printing, Publishing, and Allied Industries	2.65	6.8	6.2	260.0	255.3	248.6	228.6	230.7	208.7	180.5	169.0	164.0	180.5	169.8	146.4	136.9	125.5	108.6
				(1.8)	(2.7)	(8.7)	(−0.9)	(10.5)	(15.6)	(6.8)	(3.0)	(−9.1)	(6.3)	(16.0)	(6.9)	(9.1)	(15.6)	(8.6)
Leather, Leather Products, and Fur Products	1.14	3.3	4.9	156.3	167.8	150.2	149.3	156.9	147.0	152.9	158.0	150.0	135.5	119.1	110.2	107.8	98.5	86.6
				(−6.9)	(11.7)	(0.6)	(−4.8)	(6.7)	(−3.9)	(−3.2)	(5.3)	(10.7)	(13.8)	(8.1)	(2.2)	(9.4)	(13.7)	(−13.4)
Basic Chemicals and Chemical Products (except products of petroleum and coal)	14.00	8.3	9.0	326.3	313.4	283.4	258.5	238.6	208.4	191.8	185.0	176.6	164.6	149.7	140.4	122.7	117.1	105.3
				(4.1)	(10.6)	(9.6)	(8.3)	(14.5)	(8.7)	(3.7)	(4.8)	(7.3)	(10.0)	(6.6)	(14.4)	(4.8)	(11.2)	(5.3)
Rubber, Plastic, Petroleum, and Coal Products	5.73	6.2	6.6	242.6	246.4	226.3	200.5	192.2	187.7	179.7	170.4	153.4	137.2	138.7	124.6	118.4	116.1	107.7
				(−1.5)	(8.9)	(12.9)	(4.3)	(2.4)	(4.5)	(5.5)	(11.1)	(11.8)	(−1.1)	(11.3)	(5.2)	(2.0)	(7.8)	(7.7)
Non-metallic Mineral Products	4.40	8.5	4.6	327.0	323.2	305.8	271.1	244.3	240.6	232.0	220.7	218.2	220.8	177.5	163.9	144.5	133.9	108.3
				(1.2)	(5.7)	(12.8)	(11.0)	(1.5)	(3.7)	(5.1)	(1.1)	(−1.2)	(24.4)	(8.3)	(13.4)	(7.9)	(23.6)	(8.3)
Basic Metal and Alloy Industries	7.45	8.4	2.1	325.1	312.7	278.9	227.0	196.1	186.0	170.4	156.0	149.6	146.9	139.9	143.5	139.8	131.0	113.1
				(4.0)	(12.1)	(22.9)	(15.8)	(5.4)	(9.2)	(9.2)	(4.3)	(1.8)	(5.0)	(−2.5)	(2.6)	(6.7)	(15.8)	(13.1)
Metal Products and Parts except Machinery and Equipment	2.81	3.7	5.2	165.9	172.9	183.2	164.4	166.3	157.3	151.7	142.6	158.5	137.8	139.5	119.2	110.5	100.7	105.6
				(−4.0)	(−5.6)	(11.4)	(−1.1)	(5.7)	(3.7)	(6.4)	(−10.0)	(15.0)	(−1.2)	(17.0)	(7.9)	(9.7)	(−4.6)	(5.6)
Machinery and Equipment other than Transport Equipment	9.57	10.4	15.0	429.1	394.4	357.1	312.8	279.4	233.3	201.4	198.3	195.8	182.5	155.0	152.7	144.3	137.4	115.8
				(8.8)	(10.4)	(14.2)	(12.0)	(19.8)	(15.8)	(1.6)	(1.3)	(7.3)	(17.7)	(1.5)	(5.8)	(5.0)	(18.7)	(15.8)
Transport Equipment and Parts	3.98	9.7	6.0	387.9	378.4	367.7	319.7	283.7	272.6	232.9	203.3	190.3	194.1	183.6	152.9	149.1	132.5	112.9
				(2.5)	(2.9)	(15.0)	(12.7)	(4.1)	(17.0)	(14.6)	(6.8)	(−2.0)	(5.7)	(20.1)	(2.5)	(12.5)	(17.4)	(12.9)
Other Manufacturing Industries	2.56	9.5	11.5	358.9	357.4	298.4	276.9	221.2	186.6	173.3	173.2	159.1	142.5	169.7	168.0	170.2	136.5	108.5
				(0.4)	(19.8)	(7.8)	(25.2)	(18.5)	(7.7)	(0.1)	(8.9)	(11.6)	(16.0)	(1.0)	(−1.3)	(24.7)	(25.8)	(8.5)

Source: Central Statistical Organisation (CSO), GOI, Ministry of Statistics and Programme Implementation.

Notes: Figures in brackets are percentage variations over the previous year. (QE = Quick Estimate)

A3 BUDGETARY TRANSACTIONS

Table A3.1 Budgetary Position of Government of India

(Rupees crore)

Budget Heads	2010–11 Budget	2009–10 Revised	2009–10 Budget	2008–9 Actuals	2007–8 Actuals	2006–7 Actuals	2005–6 Actuals	2004–5 Actuals	2003–4 Actuals	2002–3 Actuals	2001–2 Actuals
(1)	(2)	(3)	(4)	(5)	(6)	(7)	(8)	(9)	(10)	(11)	(12)
(1) Revenue Receipts	682212	577294	614497	540259	541864	434387	347077	305991	263813	230834	201306
(a) Tax Revenue (net to centre)	534094	465103	474218	443319	439547	351182	270264	224798	186982	158544	133532
(b) Non-tax Revenue	148118	112191	140279	96940	102317	83205	76813	81193	76831	72290	67774
(2) Capital Receipts	426538	444252	406341	343697	170807	149000	158661	192264	207390	182414	161004
(a) Non-debt Capital Receipts of which:	45129	30212	5345	6705	43895	6427	12226	66467	84118	37342	20049
(a.1) Recovery of Loans	5129	4254	4225	6139	5100	5893	10645	62043	67165	34191	16403
(a.2) Other Receipts of which:	40000	25958	1120	566	38795	534	1581	4424	16953	3151	3646
(a.2.1) Disinvestment of Equity of PSEs	40000	25958	1120	566	38795	534	1581	4424	16953	3151	3646
(b) Borrowings and Other Liabilities	381409	414040	400996	336992	126912	142573	146435	125797	123272	145072	140955
(3) Total Receipts	1108750	1021546	1020838	883956	712671	583387	505738	498255	471203	413248	362310
	(8.5)	(15.6)	(15.5)	(24.0)	(22.2)	(15.4)	(1.5)	(5.7)	(14.0)	(14.1)	(11.3)
	[16.0]	[16.6]	[16.6]	[15.9]	[14.4]	[13.6]	[13.6]	[15.4]	[17.1]	[16.8]	[15.9]
(4) Non-plan Expenditure	735657	706371	695689	843495	681161	555945	476958	453454	348989	302708	261259
(a) On Revenue Account of which:	643599	641944	618834	793798	594433	514609	439376	384329	283502	268074	239954
(a.1) Interest Payment	248664	219500	225511	192204	171030	150272	132630	126934	124088	117804	107460
(b) On Capital Account	92058	64427	76855	49697	86728	41336	37582	69125	65487	34634	21305
(5) Plan Expenditure	373092	315176	325149	275235	205082	169860	140638	132293	122280	111470	101194
(a) On Revenue Account	315125	264411	278398	234774	173572	142418	111858	87495	78638	71569	61657
(b) On Capital Account	57967	50765	46751	40461	31510	27442	28780	44798	43642	39901	39537
(6) Total Expenditure (4 + 5)	1108749	1021547	1020838	1118730	886243	725805	617596	585747	471269	414178	362453
	(8.5)	(−8.7)	(−8.8)	(26.2)	(22.1)	(17.5)	(5.4)	(24.3)	(13.8)	(14.3)	(11.3)
(7) Revenue Deficit	276512	329061	282735	253539	52569	80222	92300	78338	98261	107879	100162
	[4.0]	[5.3]	[4.6]	[4.5]	[1.1]	[1.9]	[2.5]	[2.4]	[3.6]	[4.4]	[4.4]
(8) Fiscal Deficit	381408	414041	400996	336992	126912	142573	146435	125794	123273	145072	140955
	[5.5]	[6.7]	[6.5]	[6.0]	[2.6]	[3.3]	[4.0]	[3.9]	[4.5]	[5.9]	[6.2]
(9) Primary Deficit	132744	194541	175485	144788	−44118	−7699	13805	−1140	−815	27268	33495
	[1.9]	[3.2]	[2.8]	[2.6]	[−0.9]	[−0.2]	[0.4]	[0.0]	[0.0]	[1.1]	[1.5]

(Continued)

Table A3.1 Continued

Budget Heads	2000–1 Actuals	1999–2000 Actuals	1998–9 Actuals	1997–8 Actuals	1996–7 Actuals	1995–6 Actuals	1994–5 Actuals	1993–4 Actuals	1992–3 Actuals	1991–2 Actuals	1990–1 Actuals
(1)	(13)	(14)	(15)	(16)	(17)	(18)	(19)	(20)	(21)	(22)	(23)
(1) Revenue Receipts	192605	181482	149485	133886	126279	110130	91083	75453	74128	66030	54954
(a) Tax Revenue (net to centre)	136658	128271	104652	95672	93701	81939	67454	53449	54044	50069	42978
(b) Non-tax Revenue	55947	53211	44833	38214	32578	28191	23629	22004	20084	15961	11976
(2) Capital Receipts	132987	116571	129856	98167	74728	68145	69655	66400	48490	45384	50344
(a) Non-debt Capital Receipts of which:	14171	11854	16507	9230	7995	7902	11952	6143	8317	9059	5712
(a.1) Recovery of Loans	12046	10131	10633	8318	7540	6505	6345	6191	6356	6021	5712
(a.2) Other Receipts of which:	2125	1723	5874	912	455	1397	5607	–48	1961	3038	0
(a.2.1) Disinvestment of Equity of PSEs	2125	1724	5874	912	380	362	5078	–48	1961	3038	0
(b) Borrowings and Other Liabilities	118816	104717	113349	88937	66733	60243	57703	60257	40173	36325	44632
(3) Total Receipts	325592	298053	279341	232053	201007	178275	160738	141853	122618	111414	105298
	(9.2)	(6.7)	(20.4)	(15.4)	(12.8)	(10.9)	(13.3)	(15.7)	(10.1)	(5.8)	
	[15.5]	[15.3]	[16.0]	[15.2]	[14.6]	[15.0]	[15.8]	[16.4]	[16.3]	[17.0]	[18.5]
(4) Non-plan Expenditure	242942	221902	212548	172991	147473	131901	113361	98998	85958	80469	76198
(a) On Revenue Account of which:	226782	202309	176900	145176	127298	110839	93847	83545	72925	67234	60850
(a.1) Interest Payment	99314	90249	77882	65637	59478	50031	44049	36695	31035	26563	21471
(b) On Capital Account	16160	19593	35648	27815	20175	21062	19514	15453	13033	13235	15348
(5) Plan Expenditure	82669	76182	66818	59077	53534	46374	47378	42855	36660	30961	29118
(a) On Revenue Account	51076	46800	40519	35174	31635	29021	28265	24624	19777	15074	12666
(b) On Capital Account	31593	29382	26299	23903	21899	17353	19113	18231	16883	15887	16452
(6) Total Expenditure (4 + 5)	325611	298084	279366	232068	201007	178275	160739	141853	122618	111430	105316
	(9.2)	(6.7)	(20.4)	(15.5)	(12.8)	(10.9)	(13.3)	(15.7)	(10.0)	(5.8)	
	[15.5]	[15.3]	[16.0]	[15.5]	[12.8]	[10.9]	[13.3]	[15.7]	[10.0]	[5.8]	
(7) Revenue Deficit	85234	67596	67909	46449	32654	29730	31029	32716	18574	16261	18562
	[4.1]	[3.5]	[3.9]	[3.0]	[2.4]	[2.5]	[3.1]	[3.8]	[2.5]	[2.5]	[3.3]
(8) Fiscal Deficit	118816	104717	113349	88937	66733	60243	57703	60257	40173	36325	44650
	[5.7]	[5.4]	[6.5]	[5.8]	[4.8]	[5.1]	[5.7]	[7.0]	[5.3]	[5.5]	[7.8]
(9) Primary Deficit	19502	14468	35467	23300	7255	10212	13655	23562	9138	9762	23134
	[0.9]	[0.7]	[2.0]	[1.5]	[0.5]	[0.9]	[1.3]	[2.7]	[1.2]	[1.5]	[4.1]

Source: Budget at a Glance and Expenditure Budget, Ministry of Finance, GOI.

Notes: (1) Figures in round brackets are variations over the previous year in percentages.

(2) Figures in square brackets are percentages to GDP at current market prices.

(3) GDP data is as per the revised series from 2004–5 and it is at 1999–2000 series before 2004–5. GDP is estimated at 12.5 per cent growth from previous year for 2010–11.

Table A3.2 Consolidated Budgetary Position of State Government at a Glance

Year	2000–1	2001–2	2002–3	2003–4	2004–5	2005–6	2006–7	2007–8	2008–9	2008–9	2009–10
Total Revenue Receipts	232509	249422	273674	309187	363512	431021	530556	623748	719835	737865	804943
% Change over the Year	(14.6)	(7.3)	(9.7)	(13.0)	(17.6)	(18.6)	(23.1)	(17.6)	(15.4)	(2.5)	(9.1)
% to GDP	10.2	10.2	9.9	9.5	9.8	10.1	10.7	11.2	11.7	12.0	11.6
Revenue Expenditure	287825	309819	330853	372594	402670	438034	505699	580805	691409	727165	837238
% Change over the Year	(11.8)	(7.6)	(6.8)	(12.6)	(8.1)	(8.8)	(15.4)	(14.9)	(19.0)	(5.2)	(15.1)
% to GDP	12.6	12.6	12.0	11.5	10.9	10.2	10.2	10.4	11.2	11.8	12.1
Surplus (+)/Deficit (−)	−55316	−60397	−57179	−63407	−39158	−7013	24857	42943	28426	10700	−32295
Total Capital Receipts	109705	115714	140866	205641	200148	164607	142802	141987	175306	186201	225114
% Change over the Year	(7.6)	(5.5)	(21.7)	(46.0)	(−2.7)	(−17.8)	(−13.2)	(−0.6)	(23.5)	(6.2)	(20.9)
% to GDP	4.8	4.7	5.1	6.3	5.4	3.8	2.9	2.5	2.8	3.0	3.2
Capital Expenditure	52010	58861	79396	141709	150758	123648	151585	171520	201374	213259	218540
% Change over the Year	(3.0)	(13.2)	(34.9)	(78.5)	(6.4)	(−18.0)	(22.6)	(13.2)	(17.4)	(5.9)	(2.5)
% to GDP	2.3	2.4	2.9	4.4	4.1	2.9	3.1	3.1	3.3	3.5	3.2
Surplus (+)/Deficit (−)	57695	56853	61470	63932	49390	40959	−8783	−29533	−26068	−27058	6574
Total Receipts	342214	365136	414539	514828	563660	595628	673358	765735	895141	924066	1030057
% Change over the Year	(12.3)	(6.7)	(13.5)	(24.2)	(9.5)	(5.7)	(13.1)	(13.7)	(16.9)	(3.2)	(11.5)
% to GDP	15.0	14.9	15.0	15.9	15.2	13.9	13.6	13.7	14.5	15.0	14.9
Total Expenditure	339835	368680	410249	514302	553428	561682	657280	752324	892783	940423	1055778
% Change over the Year	(10.3)	(8.5)	(11.3)	(25.4)	(7.6)	(1.5)	(17.0)	(14.5)	(18.7)	(5.3)	(12.3)
% to GDP	14.9	15.0	14.9	15.9	14.9	13.1	13.3	13.5	14.5	15.3	15.2
Overall Surplus (+)/Deficit (−)	2379	−3544	4290	526	10232	33946	16078	13411	2358	−16357	−25721
Fiscal Deficit	87923	94260	99726	120631	107774	90084	77509	75455	112653	146349	199510
% to GDP	3.9	3.8	3.6	3.7	2.9	2.1	1.6	1.4	1.8	2.4	2.9
Revenue Deficit	55316	60398	57179	63407	39158	7013	−24857	−42943	−28426	−10701	32295
% to GDP	2.4	2.5	2.1	2.0	1.1	0.2	−0.5	−0.8	−0.5	−0.2	0.5
Net RBI Credit	−1092	3451	−3100	293	−2705	2425	640	1140	0	602	0

(Continued)

Table A3.2 *Continued*

Year	1990–1	1991–2	1992–3	1993–4	1994–5	1995–6	1996–7	1997–8	1998–9	1999–2000
Total Revenue Receipts	66467	80536	91090	104997	120303	134507	150041	166820	172787	202927
% Change over the Year	(17.6)	(21.2)	(13.1)	(15.3)	(14.6)	(11.8)	(11.5)	(11.2)	(3.6)	(17.4)
% to GDP	10.2	10.7	10.5	10.3	10.1	9.8	9.8	9.5	8.9	9.7
Revenue Expenditure	71776	86186	96205	108868	127009	143127	166919	184312	217249	257475
% Change over the Year	(19.2)	(20.1)	(11.6)	(13.2)	(16.7)	(12.7)	(16.6)	(10.4)	(17.9)	(18.5)
% to GDP	11.0	11.5	11.1	10.7	10.7	10.4	10.9	10.5	11.1	12.2
Surplus (+)/Deficit (−)	−5309	−5650	−5115	−3871	−6706	−8620	−16878	−17492	−44462	−54548
Total Capital Receipts	24693	27238	30073	28489	43190	42805	42011	58907	85363	101925
% Change over the Year	(22.9)	(10.3)	(10.4)	(−5.3)	(51.6)	(−0.9)	(−1.9)	(40.2)	(44.9)	(19.4)
% to GDP	3.8	3.6	3.5	2.8	3.6	3.1	2.8	3.4	4.4	4.8
Capital Expenditure	19312	21743	23129	24980	32138	31506	32335	39612	44169	50501
% Change over the Year	(16.6)	(12.6)	(6.4)	(8.0)	(28.7)	(−2.0)	(2.6)	(22.5)	(11.5)	(14.3)
% to GDP	2.9	2.9	2.7	2.5	2.7	2.3	2.1	2.3	2.3	2.4
Surplus (+)/Deficit (−)	5381	5495	6944	3509	11052	11299	9676	19295	41194	51424
Total Receipts	91160	107773	121163	133486	163493	177312	192051	225727	258151	304852
% Change over the Year	(19.0)	(18.2)	(12.4)	(10.2)	(22.5)	(8.5)	(8.3)	(17.5)	(14.4)	(18.1)
% to GDP	13.9	14.3	14.0	13.1	13.7	12.9	12.6	12.9	13.2	14.5
Total Expenditure	91088	107929	119335	133849	159147	174632	199254	223924	261419	307977
% Change over the Year	(18.6)	(18.5)	(10.6)	(12.2)	(18.9)	(9.7)	(14.1)	(12.4)	(16.7)	(17.8)
% to GDP	13.9	14.3	13.8	13.2	13.4	12.7	13.0	12.8	13.4	14.6
Overall Surplus (+)/Deficit (−)	72	−156	1828	−363	4346	2680	−7203	1803	−3268	−3125
Fiscal Deficit	18787	18900	20891	20364	27308	30870	36561	43474	73295	90099
% to GDP	2.9	2.5	2.4	2.0	2.3	2.2	2.4	2.5	3.8	4.3
Revenue Deficit	5309	5651	5114	3872	6706	8620	16878	17492	44462	54549
% to GDP	0.8	0.8	0.6	0.4	0.6	0.6	1.1	1.0	2.3	2.6
Net RBI Credit	420	−340	176	591	48	16	898	1543	5579	1312

Source: Budget at a Glance and Expenditure Budget, Vol.1, Ministry of Finance, GOI (2010–11 and earlier budgets).

Note: GDP data is as per the revised series from 2004–5 and it is at 1999–2000 series before 2004–5. GDP is estimated at 12.5 per cent growth from previous year for 2010–11.

A4 MONEY AND BANKING
Table A 4.1 Money Stock Measures

(Rupees crore)

31 March	Currency in Circulation	Cash with Banks	Currency with the Public	'Other' Deposits with the RBI	Bankers' Deposits with RBI	Demand Deposits	Time Deposits	Reserve Money (3+4+5+6)	Money Supply (M3)	Net Bank Credit to Government	Net RBI Credit to Central Government	Bank Credit to Commercial Sector	Net Foreign Exchange Assets of Banking Sector	Government's Currency Liabilities to Public	Net Non-Monetary Liabilities of Bkg Sector	Net Non-monetary Liabilities of RBI	RBI's Gross Claims on Banks
(1)	(2)	(3)	(4=2−3)	(5)	(6)	(7)	(8)	(9)	(11)	(12)	(13)	(14)	(15)	(16)	(17)	(18)	(19)
1950–1	.	.	1405	24	59	591	331	1494	2352	808	–	588	860	241	145	68	–
1951–2	1292	43	1249	18	47	545	325	1357 (−9.2)	2137 (−9.1)	–	–	–	–	–	–	–	–
1952–3	1273	45	1228	14	47	521	357	1334 (−1.7)	2121 (−0.7)	–	–	–	–	–	–	–	–
1953–4	1330	41	1289	12	42	527	372	1385 (3.8)	2200 (3.7)	–	–	–	–	–	–	–	–
1954–5	1417	40	1377	7	48	571	424	1472 (6.3)	2379 (8.1)	–	–	–	–	–	–	–	–
1955–6	1614	43	1571	9	53	637	466	1676 (13.9)	2683 (12.8)	1105	–	829	764	189	204	88	–
1956–7	1668	45	1623	8	58	711	527	1734 (3.5)	2869 (6.9)	–	–	–	–	–	–	–	–
1957–8	1720	46	1674	16	68	723	750	1804 (4.0)	3164 (10.3)	–	–	–	–	–	–	–	–
1958–9	1846	54	1792	15	68	719	950	1929 (6.9)	3476 (9.9)	–	–	–	–	–	–	–	–
1959–60	2001	70	1931	17	93	772	1163	2111 (9.4)	3883 (11.7)	–	–	–	–	–	–	–	–
1960–1	2154	56	2098	13	71	757	1095	2239 (6.1)	3964 (2.1)	2489	–	1503	178	206	413	250	–
1961–2	2256	54	2202	23	73	824	1198	2352 (5.0)	4247 (7.1)	2691	–	1643	121	227	435	247	–
1962–3	2439	60	2379	30	77	908	1243	2546 (8.2)	4560 (7.4)	2893	–	1860	79	236	507	278	–
1963–4	2670	64	2606	32	79	1115	1285	2781 (9.2)	5037 (10.5)	3135	–	2119	114	256	586	304	–
1964–5	2841	72	2769	22	99	1289	1418	2962 (6.5)	5498 (9.2)	3342	–	2369	95	275	583	340	–
1965–6	3112	78	3034	17	104	1478	1605	3233 (9.1)	6134 (11.6)	3809	–	2656	71	287	689	360	–
1966–7	3289	90	3199	41	134	1711	1867	3464 (7.1)	6817 (11.1)	4008	–	3142	149	310	792	434	–
1967–8	3468	92	3376	56	137	1918	2110	3662 (5.7)	7460 (9.4)	4254	–	3564	161	317	836	422	–
1968–9	3794	112	3682	81	194	2016	2527	4069 (11.1)	8306 (11.3)	4697	–	4072	326	341	1130	590	–
1969–70	4160	165	3995	58	173	2483	3103	4390 (7.9)	9639 (16.0)	4752	3291	5407	584	360	1464	630	642
1970–1	4557	186	4371	60	205	2943	3646	4822 (9.8)	11020 (14.3)	5455	3667	6522	551	384	1892	866	531
1971–2	5006	205	4801	80	296	3442	4370	5382 (11.6)	12693 (15.2)	6625	4249	7363	619	412	2325	1271	480
1972–3	5680	242	5438	58	295	4204	5313	6033 (12.1)	15013 (18.3)	7976	5461	8762	583	457	2765	1435	731
1973–4	6595	274	6321	53	625	4826	6424	7273 (20.6)	17624 (17.4)	8939	6092	10791	663	502	3271	1641	981
1974–5	6701	354	6347	75	828	5553	7574	7604 (4.6)	19549 (10.9)	9999	6620	12730	414	531	4125	2061	1315
1975–6	7053	348	6705	77	678	6543	9155	7808 (2.7)	22480 (15.0)	10629	6331	15614	939	556	5257	2645	1404
1976–7	8288	415	7873	121	1389	8030	11757	9798 (25.5)	27781 (23.6)	11804	7147	18851	2529	568	5971	3433	926
1977–8	9152	521	8631	70	1719	5687	18518	10941 (11.7)	32906 (18.4)	13727	6887	21222	4445	593	7081	3708	1117
1978–9	10835	604	10231	166	3081	6895	22820	14082 (28.7)	40112 (21.9)	15930	9077	25532	5338	603	7292	3735	1200
1979–80	12382	728	11654	391	3800	7955	27226	16573 (17.7)	47226 (17.7)	20014	11727	31011	5343	592	9734	4558	

(Continued)

Table A 4.1 *Continued*

31 March	Components of Money Supply									Money Supply (M3)	Sources of Change in Money Supply (M3)							
	Currency in Circulation	Cash with Banks	Currency with the Public	'Other' Deposits with the RBI	Bankers' Deposits with RBI	Demand Deposits	Time Deposits	Reserve Money (3+4+5+6)			Net Bank Credit to Government	Net RBI Credit to Central Government	Bank Credit to Commercial Sector	Net Foreign Exchange Assets of Banking Sector	Government's Currency Liabilities to Public	Net Non-Monetary Liabilities of Bkg Sector	Net Non-monetary Liabilities of RBI	RBI's Gross Claims on Banks
(1)	(2)	(3)	(4=2-3)	(5)	(6)	(7)	(8)	(9)		(11)	(12)	(13)	(14)	(15)	(16)	(17)	(18)	(19)
1980–1	14307	881	13426	411	4734	9587	32350	19452	(17.4)	55774 (18.1)	25718	15278	36641	4730	618	11934	5360	1276
1981–2	15411	937	14474	168	5419	10295	37815	20998	(7.9)	62752 (12.5)	30633	18486	43462	2768	657	14768	6522	1673
1982–3	17639	980	16659	186	5285	11690	44649	23110	(10.1)	73184 (16.6)	35257	21853	51162	1828	682	15745	6074	2025
1983–4	20643	1040	19603	291	8060	13504	53127	28994	(25.5)	86525 (18.2)	40642	25802	60726	1646	720	17208	5311	2771
1984–5	23875	1203	22672	595	10746	16648	63018	35216	(21.5)	102933 (19.0)	50343	31857	70953	3134	778	22274	8737	3174
1985–6	26524	1465	25059	289	11352	18747	75299	38165	(8.4)	119394 (16.0)	58321	38047	82803	3872	939	26542	10707	2462
1986–7	29913	1531	28382	309	14586	22825	90116	44808	(17.4)	141632 (18.6)	72020	45138	94741	4815	1192	31136	13444	2760
1987–8	35122	1563	33559	397	17970	24599	105720	53489	(19.4)	164275 (16.0)	84370	51697	107487	5672	1380	34634	14225	4441
1988–9	40119	1790	38329	694	22145	27763	126707	62958	(17.7)	193493 (17.8)	96475	58200	127882	6800	1475	39139	16936	7079
1989–90	48286	1986	46300	598	28707	34162	149890	77591	(23.2)	230950 (19.4)	117151	72013	151704	6818	1555	46278	17536	7472
1990–1	55282	2234	53048	674	31823	39170	172936	87779	(13.1)	265828 (15.1)	140193	86758	171769	10581	1621	58336	27022	10007
1991–2	63738	2640	61098	885	34882	52423	202643	99505	(13.4)	317049 (19.3)	158263	92266	187993	21226	1704	52137	27415	5102
1992–3	71326	3053	68273	1313	38140	54480	239950	110779	(11.3)	364016 (14.8)	176238	96523	220135	24443	1824	58624	28246	9885
1993–4	85396	3095	82301	2525	50751	65952	280306	138672	(25.2)	431084 (18.4)	203918	96783	237774	54612	1990	67210	26037	5552
1994–5	104681	4000	100681	3383	61218	88193	335338	169283	(22.1)	527596 (22.4)	222419	98913	292723	79032	2379	68958	29358	13470
1995–6	122569	4311	118258	3344	68544	93233	384356	194457	(14.9)	599191 (13.6)	257778	118768	344648	82141	2503	87880	32297	21955
1996–7	137217	5130	132087	3194	59574	105334	455397	199985	(2.8)	696012 (16.2)	288620	120702	376307	105496	2918	77330	35184	7005
1997–8	151056	5477	145579	3541	71806	118725	553488	226402	(13.2)	821332 (18.0)	330597	133617	433310	138095	3352	84022	43282	7096
1998–9	175846	6902	168944	3736	79703	136388	671892	259286	(14.5)	980960 (19.4)	386677	145416	495990	177853	3846	83406	60540	13262
1999–2000	197061	7979	189082	3034	80460	149681	782378	280555	(8.2)	1124174 (14.6)	441378	139829	586564	205648	4578	113994	70222	16785
2000–1	218205	8654	209550	3630	81477	166270	933771	303311	(8.1)	1313220 (16.8)	511955	146534	679218	249820	5354	133126	79345	12965
2001–2	250974	10179	240794	2850	84147	179199	1075512	337970	(11.4)	1498355 (14.1)	589565	141384	759647	311035	6366	168258	101220	10748
2002–3	282473	10892	271581	3242	83346	198757	1244379	369061	(9.2)	1717960 (14.7)	676523	112985	898981	393715	7071	258330	127141	7160
2003–4	327028	12057	314971	5119	104365	258626	1426960	436512	(18.3)	2005676 (16.7)	742904	36920	1016151	526586	7296	287261	107585	5419
2004–5	368661	12347	356314	6478	113996	286998	1595887	489135	(12.1)	2245677 (12.0)	752436	−23258	1275912	649255	7448	439374	119776	5258
2005–6	429578	17454	412124	6869	135511	407423	1893104	571958	(16.9)	2719519 (21.1)	759416	5160	1688681	726194	7656	462429	122463	5795
2006–7	504099	21244	482854	7496	197295	477604	2342113	708890	(23.9)	3310068 (21.7)	827626	2136	2128862	913179	8161	567761	177019	7635
2007–8	590801	22390	568410	9054	328447	578372	2862046	928302	(31.0)	4017882 (21.4)	899518	−114636	2578990	1295131	9224	764980	210221	4590
2008–9	691153	24790	666364	5573	291275	581247	3510835	988001	(6.4)	4764019 (18.6)	1277199	61761	3013337	1352184	10054	888754	387927	10357

Source: RBI Handbook on Statistics on the Indian Economy.

Note: 1 Figures in brackets are percentage change over the year.

(Rupees crore)

Table A4.2 Selected Indicators of Scheduled Commercial Bank Operations (Year-end) (Outstandings)

Year	Aggregate Deposits	Demand Deposits	Time Deposits	Bank Credit	C/D Ratio	Food Credit	Non-food Credit	Investments	I/D Ratio	Govt Securities	Other Approved Securities	Cash in Hand	Balances with RBI	Borrowings from RBI
(1)	(2)	(3)	(4)	(5)	(6)	(7)	(8)	(9)	(10)	(11)	(12)	(13)	(14)	(15)
1950–1	882	593	290	547	62.0	–	–	–	–	–	–	35	58	12
1951–2	852 (−3.4)	566 (−4.6)	286 (−1.4)	522 (−4.6)	61.3	–	–	–	–	296	–	35	46	56
1952–3	832 (−2.3)	522 (−7.8)	310 (8.4)	529 (1.3)	63.6	–	–	–	–	303	–	32	43	19
1953–4	848 (1.9)	522 (0.0)	326 (5.2)	538 (1.7)	63.4	–	–	–	–	319	–	32	41	31
1954–5	943 (11.2)	567 (8.6)	375 (15.0)	623 (15.8)	66.1	–	–	–	–	344	–	32	46	37
1955–6	1043 (10.6)	631 (11.3)	412 (9.9)	761 (22.2)	73.0	–	–	–	–	360	–	36	49	65
1956–7	1175 (12.7)	704 (11.6)	472 (14.6)	900 (18.3)	76.6	–	–	–	–	347	–	34	54	103
1957–8	1452 (23.6)	731 (3.8)	721 (52.8)	963 (7.0)	66.3	–	–	–	–	440	–	37	68	42
1958–9	1635 (12.6)	722 (−1.2)	913 (26.6)	1014 (5.3)	62.0	–	–	–	–	613	–	43	64	62
1959–60	1902 (16.3)	781 (8.2)	1121 (22.8)	1128 (11.2)	59.3	–	–	–	–	715	–	62	91	79
1960–1	1736 (−8.7)	710 (−9.1)	1026 (−8.5)	1336 (18.4)	77.0	–	–	–	–	559	–	46	71	95
1961–2	1917 (10.4)	786 (10.7)	1131 (10.2)	1408 (5.4)	73.4	–	–	–	–	601	–	49	75	53
1962–3	2042 (6.5)	867 (10.3)	1175 (3.9)	1588 (12.8)	77.8	–	–	–	–	593	–	52	74	71
1963–4	2285 (11.9)	1071 (23.5)	1214 (3.3)	1817 (14.4)	79.5	–	–	–	–	640	–	58	89	84
1964–5	2583 (13.0)	1239 (15.7)	1344 (10.7)	2035 (12.0)	78.8	–	–	–	–	718	–	67	96	153
1965–6	2950 (14.2)	1427 (15.2)	1523 (13.3)	2287 (12.4)	77.5	–	–	–	–	811	–	73	97	74
1966–7	3425 (16.1)	1649 (15.6)	1776 (16.6)	2692 (17.7)	78.6	–	–	–	–	893	–	87	129	140
1967–8	3856 (12.6)	1845 (11.9)	2011 (13.2)	3032 (12.6)	78.6	–	–	–	–	967	–	89	132	104
1968–9	4338 (12.5)	1934 (4.8)	2404 (19.5)	3396 (12.0)	78.3	–	–	–	–	1055	–	109	166	106
1969–70	5028 (15.9)	2235 (15.6)	2793 (16.2)	3971 (16.9)	79.0	56	3915	1481	29.5	1167	314	146	176	238
1970–1	5906 (17.5)	2626 (17.5)	3280 (17.4)	4684 (18.0)	79.3	214	4469	1772	30.0	1362	410	167	197	368
1971–2	7106 (20.3)	3127 (19.1)	3979 (21.3)	5263 (12.4)	74.1	345	4918	2190	30.8	1650	539	181	267	208
1972–3	8643 (21.6)	3794 (21.3)	4849 (21.9)	6115 (16.2)	70.8	340	5775	2897	33.5	2161	736	221	279	139
1973–4	10139 (17.3)	4336 (14.3)	5803 (19.7)	7399 (21.0)	73.0	367	7032	3286	32.4	2362	924	246	610	409
1974–5	11827 (16.6)	4963 (14.5)	6865 (18.3)	8762 (18.4)	74.1	613	8149	3915	33.1	2826	1088	296	612	473
1975–6	14155 (19.7)	5817 (17.2)	8338 (21.5)	10877 (24.1)	76.8	1521	9356	4607	32.5	3283	1324	305	608	798
1976–7	17566 (24.1)	6943 (19.4)	10623 (27.4)	13173 (21.1)	75.0	2191	10982	5536	31.5	3930	1606	354	1146	967
1977–8	22211 (26.4)	4872 (−29.8)	17340 (63.2)	14939 (13.4)	67.3	1984	12955	7897	35.6	5907	1990	469	1674	331
1978–9	27016 (21.6)	5826 (19.6)	21190 (22.2)	18285 (22.4)	67.7	2210	16075	9109	33.7	6622	2488	557	2634	546
1979–80	31759 (17.6)	6643 (14.0)	25116 (18.5)	21537 (17.8)	67.8	2100	19437	10624	33.5	7444	3181	616	3634	739

(Continued)

Table A 4.2 *Continued*

Year	Aggregate Deposits		Demand Deposits		Time Deposits		Bank Credit		C/D Ratio	Food Credit	Non-food Credit	Investments	I/D Ratio	Govt Securities	Other Approved Securities	Cash in Hand	Balances with RBI	Borrowings from RBI
(1)	(2)		(3)		(4)		(5)		(6)	(7)	(8)	(9)	(10)	(11)	(12)	(13)	(14)	(15)
1980–1	37988	(19.6)	7798	(17.4)	30190	(20.2)	25371	(17.8)	66.8	1759	23612	13186	34.7	9219	3967	766	4092	589
1981–2	43733	(15.1)	8383	(7.5)	35350	(17.1)	29682	(17.0)	67.9	2127	27555	15141	34.6	10157	4984	788	4883	831
1982–3	51358	(17.4)	9984	(19.1)	41374	(17.0)	35493	(19.6)	69.1	2965	32528	18334	35.7	12078	6257	878	5208	815
1983–4	60596	(18.0)	11312	(13.3)	49284	(19.1)	41294	(16.3)	68.1	4022	37272	21246	35.1	13473	7772	928	7783	1336
1984–5	72244	(19.2)	14132	(24.9)	58113	(17.9)	48953	(18.5)	67.8	5665	43287	28138	38.9	18697	9441	1044	6884	1558
1985–6	85404	(18.2)	15612	(10.5)	69792	(20.1)	56067	(14.5)	65.6	5535	50533	30553	35.8	19045	11509	1127	11053	954
1986–7	102724	(20.3)	19227	(23.2)	83496	(19.6)	63308	(12.9)	61.6	5104	58204	38582	37.6	24847	13735	1174	14381	1293
1987–8	118045	(14.9)	20247	(5.3)	97798	(17.1)	70536	(11.4)	59.8	2190	68346	46504	39.4	30517	15987	1306	17656	1753
1988–9	140150	(18.7)	23342	(15.3)	116808	(19.4)	84719	(20.1)	60.4	769	83950	54662	39.0	35815	18847	1444	21376	3527
1989–90	166959	(19.1)	28856	(23.6)	138103	(18.2)	101453	(19.8)	60.8	2006	99446	64369	38.6	42292	22078	1649	23463	2399
1990–1	192541	(15.3)	33192	(15.0)	159349	(15.0)	116301	(14.6)	60.4	4506	111795	75065	39.0	49998	25067	1804	23861	3468
1991–2	230758	(19.8)	45088	(35.8)	185670	(16.5)	125592	(8.0)	54.4	4670	120922	90196	39.1	62727	27469	2008	34179	577
1992–3	268572	(16.4)	46461	(3.0)	222111	(19.6)	151982	(21.0)	56.6	6743	145239	105656	39.3	75945	29711	2293	28535	1619
1993–4	315132	(17.3)	56572	(21.8)	258560	(16.4)	164418	(8.2)	52.2	10907	153510	132523	42.1	101202	31321	2283	47760	1813
1994–5	386859	(22.8)	76903	(35.9)	309956	(19.9)	211560	(28.7)	54.7	12275	199286	149253	38.6	117685	31568	2972	60029	7415
1995–6	433819	(12.1)	80614	(4.8)	353205	(14.0)	254015	(20.1)	58.6	9791	244224	164782	38.0	132227	32555	3113	50667	4847
1996–7	505599	(16.5)	90610	(12.4)	414989	(17.5)	278401	(9.6)	55.1	7597	270805	190514	37.7	158890	31624	3347	49848	560
1997–8	598485	(18.4)	102513	(13.1)	495972	(19.5)	324079	(16.4)	54.1	12485	311594	218705	36.5	186957	31748	3608	57698	395
1998–9	714025	(19.3)	117423	(14.5)	596602	(20.3)	368837	(13.8)	51.7	16816	352021	254595	35.7	223217	31377	4362	63548	2894
1999–2000	813345	(13.9)	127366	(8.5)	685978	(15.0)	435958	(18.2)	53.6	25691	410267	308944	38.0	278456	30488	5330	57419	6491
2000–1	962618	(18.4)	142552	(11.9)	820066	(19.5)	511434	(17.3)	53.1	39991	471443	370159	38.5	340035	30125	5658	59544	3896
2001–2	1103360	(14.6)	153048	(7.4)	950312	(15.9)	589723	(15.3)	53.4	53978	535745	438269	39.7	411176	27093	6245	62402	3616
2002–3	1280853	(16.1)	170289	(11.3)	1110564	(16.9)	729215	(23.7)	56.9	49479	679736	547546	42.7	523417	24129	7567	58335	79
2003–4	1504416	(17.5)	225022	(32.1)	1279394	(15.2)	840785	(15.3)	55.9	35961	804824	677588	45.0	654758	22830	7898	68997	0
2004–5	1700198	(13.0)	248028	(10.2)	1452171	(13.5)	1100428	(30.9)	64.7	41121	1059308	739154	43.5	718982	20172	8472	88105	50
2005–6	2109049	(24.0)	364640	(47.0)	1744409	(20.1)	1507077	(37.0)	71.5	40691	1466386	717454	34.0	700742	16712	13046	127061	1488
2006–7	2611933	(23.8)	429731	(17.9)	2182203	(25.1)	1931189	(28.1)	73.9	46521	1884669	791516	30.3	776058	15458	16139	180222	6245
2007–8	3196939	(22.4)	524310	(22.0)	2672630	(22.5)	2361914	(22.3)	73.9	44399	2317515	971715	30.4	958661	13053	18044	257122	4000
2008–9	3834110	(19.9)	523085	(-0.2)	3311025	(23.9)	2775549	(17.5)	72.4	46211	2729338	1166410	30.4	1155786	10624	20281	238195	11728

Source: RBI *Handbook on Statistics on the Indian Economy*.

Notes: Data in brackets are pecentage change over the year.

Data relate to amount outstanding as on last Friday of March up to 1984–5 and last reporting Friday of March thereafter.

Table A4.3 Trends in State-wise Bank Deposits and Credit and Credit–Deposit Ratios
(For Scheduled Commercial Banks)

(Amount in rupees lakh) (C–D ratio in per cent)

		A. Credit as per Sanction								
	Name of the State	All-India								
		2008			1998			1988		
Sr. No.		Deposits	Credit	C–D Ratio	Deposits	Credit	C–D Ratio	Deposits	Credit	C–D Ratio
	(1)	(2)	(3)	(4)	(5)	(6)	(7)	(8)	(9)	(10)
	Northern Region	**74321282**	**50335537**	**67.7**	**13423982**	**6547156**	**48.8**	**2843318**	**1241332**	**43.7**
1	Haryana	7447260	4475199	60.1	1227304	526951	42.9	250445	143758	57.4
2	Himachal Pradesh	1920032	832767	43.4	441860	94697	21.4	90458	30812	34.1
3	Jammu & Kashmir	2512588	1415925	56.4	579352	218270	37.7	122230	41172	34.1
4	Punjab	10011096	6725819	67.2	2784956	1017076	36.5	687541	273463	33.7
5	Rajasthan	7278779	5994229	82.4	1722040	813075	47.2	338820	184868	39.8
6	Chandigarh	2327048	2239631	96.2	492805	285229	57.9	96684	55908	57.8
7	Delhi	42824479	28651967	66.9	6175666	3591858	58.2	1257140	511351	40.7
	North-Eastern Region	**4847770**	**1972961**	**40.7**	**948313**	**287949**	**30.4**	**227557**	**114601**	**50.4**
8	Arunachal Pradesh	257520	81686	31.7	41807	5562	13.3	8927	2489	27.9
9	Assam	3105073	1315034	42.4	611116	205320	33.6	148793	81939	55.1
10	Manipur	178472	86453	48.4	28117	16373	58.2	6982	4873	69.8
11	Meghalaya	451162	149732	33.2	103999	15996	15.4	24874	6429	25.8
12	Mizoram	137562	86510	62.9	21469	4975	23.2	5913	2339	39.6
13	Nagaland	254429	86419	34.0	55543	10577	19.0	14893	5034	33.8
14	Tripura	463551	167127	36.1	86262	29147	33.8	17175	11498	66.9
	Eastern Region	**35916780**	**18510834**	**51.5**	**7906529**	**3234440**	**40.9**	**2032273**	**946526**	**46.6**
15	Bihar	6792436	1915634	28.2	2579491	730809	28.3	622168	199688	32.1
16	Jharkhand	4329118	1529962	35.3						
17	Orissa	5387782	3031898	56.3	870907	414353	47.6	161244	153248	95.0
18	Sikkim	210577	98608	46.8	28058	5971	21.3	7842	1576	20.1
19	West Bengal	19083465	11899905	62.4	4404758	2079786	47.2	1237808	591083	47.8
20	Andaman & Nicobar Isl.	113402	34827	30.7	23315	3522	15.1	3211	931	29.0
	Central Region	**36385719**	**16779180**	**46.1**	**8220810**	**2940761**	**35.8**	**1831496**	**788623**	**43.1**
21	Chhattisgarh	3099196	1544444	49.8						
22	Madhya Pradesh	8138161	4894541	60.1	2221640	1173112	52.8	480844	287319	59.8
23	Uttar Pradesh	21477764	9379366	43.7	5999170	1767648	29.5	1350652	501304	37.1
24	Uttarakhand	3670599	960830	26.2						
	Western Region	**103352380**	**91597114**	**88.6**	**15890075**	**10564598**	**66.5**	**3168542**	**1943445**	**61.3**
25	Goa	1853997	545950	29.4	468194	115755	24.7	102056	31100	30.5
26	Gujarat	15059276	10019545	66.5	3480451	1706783	49.0	777566	395692	50.9
27	Maharashtra	86266872	81000250	93.9	11906361	8734470	73.4	2284989	1515482	66.3
28	Dadra & Nagar Haveli	62465	14901	23.9	10805	2423	22.4	698	485	69.5
29	Daman & Diu	109771	16469	15.0	24264	5168	21.3	3234	687	21.2
	Southern Region	**70170686**	**62505024**	**89.1**	**13257151**	**9419540**	**71.1**	**2656080**	**2134790**	**80.4**
30	Andhra Pradesh	17864726	16155255	90.4	3203384	2277271	71.1	716719	529233	73.8
31	Karnataka	20960885	16378855	78.1	3190019	2183409	68.4	619696	534640	86.3
32	Kerala	10991919	6968932	63.4	2764978	1221821	44.2	500287	332374	66.4
33	Tamil Nadu	19855422	22768632	114.7	3997529	3701151	92.6	798155	727350	91.1
34	Lakshadweep	32885	2467	7.5	3831	299	7.8	448	121	27.0
35	Pondicherry	464850	230883	49.7	97410	35588	36.5	20774	11072	53.3
	All-India Total	**324994617**	**241700652**	**74.4**	**59646860**	**32994444**	**55.3**	**12759267**	**7169317**	**56.2**

(Continued)

Table A4.3   *Continued*

B. Credit as per Utilization*

Sr. No.	Name of the State	All-India								
		2008			1998			1988		
		Deposits	Credit	C–D Ratio	Deposits	Credit	C–D Ratio	Deposits	Credit	C–D Ratio
	(1)	(2)	(3)	(4)	(5)	(6)	(7)	(8)	(9)	(10)
	Northern Region	**74321282**	**52110179**	**70.1**	**13423982**	**6380254**	**47.5**	**2843318**	**1220380**	**42.9**
1	Haryana	7447260	5003818	67.2	1227304	676686	55.1	250445	184921	73.8
2	Himachal Pradesh	1920032	985180	51.3	441860	112010	25.3	90458	32689	36.1
3	Jammu & Kashmir	2512588	1414285	56.3	579352	206655	35.7	122230	42335	34.6
4	Punjab	10011096	7620156	76.1	2784956	1084364	38.9	687541	283727	41.3
5	Rajasthan	7278779	7281854	100.0	1722040	890819	51.7	338820	194868	57.5
6	Chandigarh	2327048	2229172	95.8	492805	276855	56.2	96684	35147	36.4
7	Delhi	42824479	27575713	64.4	6175666	3132865	50.7	1257140	446693	35.5
	North-Eastern Region	**4847770**	**2343372**	**48.3**	**948313**	**317992**	**33.5**	**227557**	**139592**	**61.3**
8	Arunachal Pradesh	257520	148642	57.7	41807	7011	16.8	8927	2830	31.7
9	Assam	3105073	1546989	49.8	611116	230726	37.8	148793	102503	68.9
10	Manipur	178472	89701	50.3	28117	16486	58.6	6982	4907	70.3
11	Meghalaya	451162	185442	41.1	103999	16314	15.7	24874	7717	31.0
12	Mizoram	137562	90145	65.5	21469	5420	25.2	5913	4132	69.9
13	Nagaland	254429	111638	43.9	55543	11792	21.2	14893	5792	38.9
14	Tripura	463551	170814	36.8	86262	30242	35.1	17175	11711	68.2
	Eastern Region	35916780	20904902	58.2	7906529	3193959	40.4	2032273	923257	45.4
15	Bihar	6792436	3054865	45.0	2579491	741334	28.7	622168	205515	33.0
16	Jharkhand	4329118	1738310	40.2						
17	Orissa	5387782	3362388	62.4	870907	430208	49.4	161244	159268	98.8
18	Sikkim	210577	113178	53.7	28058	5038	18.0	7842	2725	34.7
19	West Bengal	19083465	12551150	65.8	4404758	2013533	45.7	1237808	554560	44.8
20	Andaman & Nicobar Isl.	113402	85012	75.0	23315	3845	16.5	3211	1189	37.0
	Central Region	**36385719**	**19859983**	**54.6**	**8220810**	**3223348**	**39.2**	**1831496**	**823987**	**45.0**
21	Chhattisgarh	3099196	2045902	66.0						
22	Madhya Pradesh	8138161	5365398	65.9	2221640	1259703	56.7	480844	293832	61.1
23	Uttar Pradesh	21477764	11290206	52.6	5999170	1963645	32.7	1350652	530155	39.3
24	Uttarakhand	3670599	1158477	31.6						
	Western Region	**103352380**	**78581584**	**76.0**	**15890075**	**10331382**	**65.0**	**3168542**	**1906603**	**60.2**
25	Goa	1853997	622393	33.6	468194	120076	25.6	102056	31953	31.3
26	Gujarat	15059276	14728157	97.8	3480451	1870774	53.8	777566	432480	55.6
27	Maharashtra	86266872	63090991	73.1	11906361	8309778	69.8	2284989	1439938	63.0
28	Dadra & Nagar Haveli	62465	76172	121.9	10805	13788	127.6	698	1222	175.1
29	Daman & Diu	109771	63871	58.2	24264	16965	69.9	3234	1009	31.2
	Southern Region	**70170686**	**67900631**	**96.8**	**13257151**	**9547509**	**72.0**	**2656080**	**2155497**	**81.2**
30	Andhra Pradesh	17864726	17367932	97.2	3203384	2318581	72.4	716719	538778	75.2
31	Karnataka	20960885	19763025	94.3	3190019	2241691	70.3	619696	544634	87.9
32	Kerala	10991919	7294462	66.4	2764978	1236187	44.7	500287	336748	67.3
33	Tamil Nadu	19855422	23237430	117.0	3997529	3703607	92.6	798155	723161	90.6
34	Lakshadweep	32885	4901	14.9	3831	374	9.8	448	127	28.3
35	Pondicherry	464850	232881	50.1	97410	47069	48.3	20774	12049	58.0
	All-India Total	**324994617**	**241700652**	**74.4**	**59646860**	**32994444**	**55.3**	**12759267**	**7169317**	**56.2**

Source: Reserve Bank of India, *Basic Statistical Returns of Scheduled Commercial Banks in India* (various issues).

Notes: * Use of bank credit in another place from the place of *sanction* captures *utilization* of bank credit and C–D ratio as per *utilisation*.

Data for 1998 and 2008 relate to end-March and those for 1988, to end-June.

Table A4.4 Distribution of Outstanding Credit of Scheduled Commercial Banks according to Occupation

(Amount in rupees crore)

Occupation	March 2008			March 2005			March 2000		
	No. of Accounts	Credit Limit Amount	Amount Outstanding	No. of Accounts	Credit Limit Amount	Amount Outstanding	No. of Accounts	Credit Limit Amount	Amount Outstanding
I. Agriculture (Direct+Indirect)	38205178	321418	274141 (11.3)	26656308	149143	124385 (10.8)	20532891	53554	45638 (9.9)
II. Industry	4065753	1308392	928536 (38.4)	3716669	714005	446825 (38.8)	5354140	271867	213779 (46.5)
1. Mining and Quarrying	23189	43416	30363 (1.3)	18141	31760	15817 (1.4)	6611	6377	4852 (1.1)
2. Food Manufacturing and Processing	376198	81127	58500 (2.4)	232424	66490	31050 (2.7)	108750	22804	17624 (3.8)
3. Textiles	462797	154049	108310 (4.5)	225788	91265	52407 (4.5)	186917	38887	30586 (6.6)
4. Paper Paper Products and Printing	68817	23707	17668 (0.7)	47359	15948	10615 (0.9)	45509	6033	4907 (1.1)
5. Leather and Leather Products	62243	11441	8884 (0.4)	25988	6221	4148 (0.4)	19693	3607	2731 (0.6)
6. Rubber and Rubber Products	59306	24697	17221 (0.7)	45811	15272	8986 (0.8)	14395	3687	2767 (0.6)
7. Chemicals and Chemical Products	223384	97367	66523 (2.8)	97054	70565	39233 (3.4)	94993	35783	26758 (5.8)
8. Basic Metals and Metal Products	378269	167956	115234 (4.8)	133686	85590	53855 (4.7)	93764	29842	24792 (5.4)
9. Engineering	674025	97675	68579 (2.8)	229269	60410	40415 (3.5)	112711	33734	25138 (5.5)
10. Vehicles Vehicle Parts and Transport Equipments	56188	73995	35413 (1.5)	40873	29420	18897 (1.6)	41942	11713	8056 (1.8)
11. Other Industries	1287392	101056	74331 (3.1)	2313243	78474	52691 (4.6)	4546356	36708	30609 (6.7)
12. Electricity Gas and Water	6923	107707	80749 (3.3)	5140	50744	36317 (3.2)	2686	11296	8574 (1.9)
13. Construction	340594	234274	180785 (7.5)	282672	76442	58376 (5.1)	63972	6616	5599 (1.2)
III. Transport Operations	734179	57078	44696 (1.8)	577543	17762	13721 (1.2)	974401	10524	8075 (1.8)
IV. Professional and Other Services	5764136	249071	187268 (7.7)	1469713	80093	55266 (4.8)	1831185	18422	14653 (3.2)
V. Personal Loans	44024161	687741	485416 (20.1)	32835257	347598	255982 (22.2)	14420051	61077	51639 (11.2)
(i) Loans for Purchase of Consumer Durables	992246	8704	7147 (0.3)	1510200	8057	6349 (0.6)	1187325	3426	2781 (0.6)
(ii) Loans for Housing	5214331	291825	248435 (10.3)	3666450	145034	126797 (11.0)	2253390	21001	18525 (4.0)
(iii) Rest of the Personal Loans	37817584	387211	229834 (9.5)	27658607	194507	122836 (10.7)	10979336	36650	30332 (6.6)
VI. Trade	6455472	285896	212556 (8.8)	6091108	173357	129646 (11.2)	7072533	85882	71618 (15.6)
1. Retail Trade	6018572	151821	107405 (4.4)	5591844	78494	56127 (4.9)	6595516	31197	25662 (5.6)
VII. Finance	197730	228486	170554 (7.1)	107968	91440	73277 (6.4)	70485	30166	21873 (4.8)
VIII. All Others	7543571	146009	113840 (4.7)	5696228	72867	53368 (4.6)	4114711	37604	32806 (7.1)
Total Bank Credit	106990180	3284091	2417007 (100)	77150794	1646266	1152468 (100)	54370397	569096	460081 (100)
Of which: 1. Artisans and Village Industries				1288321	7904	6149 (0.5)	2013171	3016	2677 (0.6)
2. Other Small-scale Industries				939186	62853	47076 (4.1)	2126150	43600	35070 (7.6)

(Continued)

Table A4.4 *Continued*

Occupation	March 1990				December 1980		December 1975	
I. Agriculture (Direct + Indirect)	24520595	10339615	19313	16626 (15.9)	4920	3722 (15.7)	1493	1071 (10.7)
II. Industry	4125322	837313	59762	50846 (48.7)	17124	11555 (48.8)	9009	5777 (57.7)
1. Mining and Quarrying	8858	3987	982	877 (0.8)	267	191 (0.8)	188	132 (1.3)
2. Food Manufacturing and Processing	94534	37993	5454	4288 (4.1)	1737	955 (4.0)	877	379 (3.8)
3. Textiles	87634	54963	8611	7495 (7.2)	2943	1983 (8.4)	1619	1056 (10.5)
4. Paper-Paper Products and Printing	36906	20952	1860	1623 (1.6)	550	417 (1.8)	255	178 (1.8)
5. Leather and Leather Products	11173	5117	1093	1004 (1.0)	234	169 (0.7)	91	71 (0.7)
6. Rubber and Rubber Products	11853	6458	1002	887 (0.9)	320	245 (1.0)	145	104 (1.0)
7. Chemicals and Chemical Products	64825	43149	7493	6352 (6.1)	2176	1410 (6.0)	933	590 (5.9)
8. Basic Metals and Metal Products	74936	45392	6166	5398 (5.2)	1962	1324 (5.6)	1070	755 (7.5)
9. Engineering	88135	54149	10613	8926 (8.6)	3454	2389 (10.1)	1868	1231 (12.3)
10. Vehicles, Vehicle Parts, and Transport Equipments	25597	13991	2667	2306 (2.2)	855	550 (2.3)	433	311 (3.1)
11. Other Industries	3577835	529390	8740	7384 (7.1)	1065	767 (3.2)	829	547 (5.5)
12. Electricity, Gas, and Water	2773	702	1121	843 (0.8)	291	125 (0.5)	174	106 (1.1)
13. Construction	23431	12638	1566	1438 (1.4)	230	180 (0.8)	90	70 (0.7)
III. Transport Operations	1240476	378273	4146	3286 (3.2)	1324	1078 (4.6)	328	259 (2.6)
IV. Personal Loans and Professional Other Services	8125421	3612241	11200	9791 (9.4)	1574	1336 (5.6)	636	496 (5.0)
1. Professional Services	1592015	187091	1129	967 (0.9)	115	93 (0.4)	38	30 (0.3)
2. Other Services	1664209	701956	2413	2126 (2.0)	437	366 (1.5)	204	150 (1.5)
3. Personal Loan	4869197	2267767	7,658	6698 (6.4)	937	810 (3.4)	394	317 (3.2)
(i) Loans for Purchase of Consumer Durables	420095	191480	507	443 (0.4)	43	35 (0.1)	20	12 (0.1)
(ii) Loans for Housing	547114	205250	2908	2536 (2.4)	293	252 (1.1)	108	93 (0.9)
(iii) Rest of the Personal Loans	3901988	1871037	4243	3719 (3.6)	601	524 (2.2)	266	211 (2.1)
V. Trade	8837621	1886767	17121	14486 (13.9)	7224	4653 (19.7)	3252	1820 (18.2)
1. Retail Trade	8438399	1735156	6319	5560 (5.3)	1050	801 (3.4)	385	263 (2.6)
VI. Financial Institutions	14122	8633	2708	2234 (2.1)	368	228 (1.0)	315	151 (1.5)
1. Leasing/Hire Purchase and Finance Units	3801	–	920	771 (0.7)	–	–	–	–
2. Housing Finance Companies/Corporations	186	–	144	134 (0.1)	–	–	–	–
VII. Miscellaneous	6987129	3185453	7405	7042 (6.8)	1335	1100 (4.6)	670	442 (4.4)
Total Bank Credit	53850686	20248295	121654	104312 (100)	33868	23673 (100)	15703	10015 (100)
Of which: 1. Artisans and Village Industries	2151263	–	1061	926 (0.9)	–	–	–	–
2. Other Small-scale Industries	1606146	668570	14098	11986 (11.5)	3709	2844 (12.0)	1773	1178 (11.8)

Source: RBI Banking Statistics: *Basic Statistical Returns of Scheduled Commercial Banks in India.*

Notes: – not available. Figures in brackets are percentages to total bank credit.

A5 CAPITAL MARKET

Table A5.1 Resource Mobilization from the Primary Market

(Rupees crore)

Year	Total		Category-wise				Issue Type				Instrument-wise									
			Public		Right		Listed		IPOs		Equities				CCPS		Bonds		Others	
											At Par		At Premium							
	Number	Amount	Number	Amount	Number	Amount	Number	Amount	Number	Amount	Number	Amount	Number	Amount	Number	Amount	Number	Amount	Number	Amount
(1)	(2)	(3)	(4)	(5)	(6)	(7)	(8)	(9)	(10)	(11)	(12)	(13)	(14)	(15)	(16)	(17)	(18)	(19)	(20)	(21)
2009–10																				
Mar-10																				
Feb-10																				
Jan-10	8	2466	8	2466	0	0	1	35	7	2432	0	0	8	2466	0	0	0	0	0	0
Dec-09	5	3701	3	3553	2	148	2	148	3	3553	0	0	5	3701	0	0	0	0	0	0
Nov-09	3	978	2	713	1	265	1	265	2	713	0	0	3	978	0	0	0	0	0	0
Oct-09	4	2023	3	1983	1	40	1	40	3	1983	0	0	4	2023	0	0	0	0	0	0
Sep-09	14	5839	4	3388	10	2451	10	2451	4	3388	0	0	13	5659	1	180	0	0	0	0
Aug-09	6	7405	4	7207	2	198	2	198	3	6207	1	9	4	6396	0	0	1	1000	0	0
Jul-09	4	4179	4	4179	0	0	0	0	3	3179	0	0	3	3179	0	0	1	1000	0	0
Jun-09	4	328	2	308	2	20	3	50	1	278	0	0	4	328	0	0	0	0	0	0
May-09	1	9	0	0	1	9	1	9	0	0	0	0	1	9	0	0	0	0	0	0
Apr-09	0	0	0	0	0	0	0	0	0	0	0	0	0	0	0	0	0	0	0	0
2008-9	47	16220	22	3582	25	12637	25	12637	21	2082	5	96	40	14176	1	448	1	1500	0	0
2007-8	124	87029	92	54511	32	32518	39	44434	85	42595	7	387	113	79352	2	5687	2	1603	0	0
2006-7	124	33508	85	29796	39	3710	47	5002	77	28504	2	12	119	32889	0	0	2	356	1	249
2005-6	139	27382	103	23294	36	4088	60	16446	79	10936	10	372	128	27000	0	0	0	0	1	10
2004-5	60	28256	34	24640	26	3616	37	14507	23	13749	6	420	49	23968	0	0	5	3867	0	0
2003-4	57	23273	35	22265	22	1007	36	19838	21	3434	14	360	37	18589	0	0	6	4324	0	0
2002-3	27	4070	14	3639	12	431	20	3032	6	1038	6	143	11	1314	0	0	8	2600	2	13
2001-2	35	7543	20	6502	15	1041	28	6341	7	1202	7	151	8	1121	0	0	16	5601	4	670
2000-1	151	6108	124	5379	27	729	37	3386	114	2722	84	818	54	2408	2	142	10	2704	1	36
1999-2000	94	7817	65	6257	28	1560	42	5098	51	2719	30	786	52	3780	0	0	10	3200	2	51
1998-9	59	5587	32	5019	26	568	40	5182	18	405	20	197	20	660	3	78	10	4450	6	202
1997-8	114	4569	62	2862	49	1708	59	3522	52	1048	64	271	33	1610	3	10	4	1550	10	1128
1996-7	889	14277	751	11557	131	2719	167	8326	717	5950	697	3433	148	4412	5	75	10	5400	29	957
1995-6	1738	20804	1426	14240	299	6564	368	9880	1357	10924	1181	4958	480	9727	8	145	6	2086	63	3888
1994-5	1735	27632	1342	21045	350	6588	453	11061	1239	16572	942	5529	651	12441	7	124	0	0	135	9538
1993-4	1143	24372	773	15449	370	8923	451	16508	692	7864	608	3808	383	9220	1	2	9	1991	142	9351

Source: SEBI (2006), *Handbook of Statistics on the Indian Securities Market 2005* and *SEBI Bulletin* (various issues).

Note: Instrument-wise break up may not tally with the total number of issues, as for one issue there could be more than one instrument.

Table A5.2 Trends in Resource Mobilization by Mutual Funds (Sector-wise)

(Rupees crore)

Year	Gross Mobilization				Redemption*				Net Inflow				Assets at the End of Period
	Private Sector	Public Sector	UTI	Total	Private Sector	Public Sector	UTI	Total	Private Sector	Public Sector	UTI	Total	
(1)	(2)	(3)	(4)	(5)	(6)	(7)	(8)	(9)	(10)	(11)	(12)	(13)	(14)
2009–10	7698483	1438688	881851	10019022	7643555	1426189	866198	9935942	54928	12499	15653	83080	613979
Mar-10	718987	145154	106344	970485	846854	162670	118111	1127635	–127867	–17516	–11767	–157150	613979
Feb-10	608193	90957	87822	786972	601413	90982	60402	752798	6780	–26	27420	34174	766869
Jan-10	656236	140089	88413	884738	588375	125061	74061	787497	67861	15028	14352	97241	758712
Dec-09	578134	143322	55356	776812	694959	166117	72940	934015	–116825	–22795	–17584	–157204	665146
Nov-09	660871	120522	61116	842509	626749	111799	58836	797385	34122	8723	2280	45124	821659
Oct-09	820703	142658	86835	1050196	713694	125404	69805	908903	107009	17254	17030	141292	774796
Sep-09	611919	119339	65886	797144	724705	135712	81055	941472	–112786	–16373	–15169	–144328	627999
Aug-09	719368	118634	80658	918660	694615	115969	75403	885987	24753	2665	5255	32672	756638
Jul-09	714369	130666	83891	928926	623928	110045	71274	805247	90441	20621	12617	123680	721886
Jun-09	550023	104874	64151	719048	610089	116913	75981	802984	–60066	–12039	–11830	–83937	582679
May-09	520943	87214	59722	667879	497234	83588	56908	637731	23709	3626	2814	30148	664450
Apr-09	538754	100262	69465	708481	420940	81298	51422	554289	117814	18964	18043	154191	593516
2008–9	4292751	710472	423131	5426354 (97.3)	4326768	701092	426790	5454650	–34018	9380	–3658	–28296	417300
2007–8	3780753	346126	337498	4464377 (90.2)	3647449	335448	327678	4310575	133304	10677	9820	153802	505152
2006–7	1599873	196340	142280	1938493 (45.2)	1520836	188719	134954	1844508	79038	7621	7326	93985	326292
2005–6	914703	110319	73127	1098149 (29.6)	871727	103940	69704	1045370	42977	6379	3424	52779	231862
2004–5	736463	56589	46656	839708 (25.9)	728864	59266	49378	837508	7599	–2677	–2722	2200	149600
2003–4	534649	31548	23992	590189 (21.4)	492105	28951	22326	543382	42544	2597	1666	46807	139616
2002–3	284096	23515	7096	314707 (12.8)	272026	21954	16530	310510	12070	1561	–9434	4197	109299
2001–2	147798	12082	4643	164523 (7.2)	134748	10673	11927	157348	13050	1409	–7284	7175	100594
2000–1	75009	5535	12413	92957 (4.4)	65160	6580	12090	83830	9849	–1045	323	9127	90586
1999–2000	43726	3817	13698	61241 (3.1)	28559	4562	9150	42271	15167	–745	4548	18970	107946
1998–9	7847	1671	13193	22711 (1.3)	6394	1336	15930	23660	1453	335	–2737	–949	68193
1997–8	1974	332	9100	11406 (0.7)	na	na	na	na	na	na	na	na	na
1996–7	346	151	4280	4777 (0.3)	na	na	na	na	na	na	na	na	na
1995–6	312	296	5900	6508 (0.5)	na	na	na	na	na	na	na	na	na
1994–5	2084	2143	9500	13727 (1.4)	na	na	na	na	na	na	na	na	na
1993–4	1549	9527	51000	62076 (7.2)	na	na	na	na	na	na	na	na	na

Source: Securities and Exchange Board of India.

Notes: * Includes repurchases as well as redemption. na: Not available.

1. Figures in brackets are percentages to GDP at current market prices (GDP data are as per revised series from 2004–5 series and as per 1999–2000 series before 2004–5).

2. IDBI principal has now become principal MF, a private sector mutual fund.

3. Erstwhile UTI has been divided into UTI mutual fund (registered with SEBI) and the specified undertaking of UTI (not registered with SEBI). Above data contain information only of UTI mutual fund.

4. Net assets pertaining to funds of funds schemes is not included in the above data.

Table A5.3   Trends in Resource Mobilization by Mutual Funds (Institution-wise)

(Rupees crore)

Year	UTI	Bank-sponsored MFs			Institution-sponsored MFs	Private Sector MFs					Grand Total (2 + 3 + 6 + 7)
		Total (4 + 5)	Joint Ventures Predominantly Indian	Others		Total (8 to 11)	Indian	Foreign	Joint Ventures Predominantly Indian	Joint Ventures Predominantly Foreign	
(1)	(2)	(3)	(4)	(5)	(6)	(7)	(8)	(9)	(10)	(11)	(12)
Sales: All Schemes											
2009–10	na	1427990	451533	976457	987155	7603878	3687355	*229299*	3400912	286312	10019023
2008–9	na	773728	347405	426323	363066	4289559	1782552	*257363*	1875872	373772	5426353
2007–8	na	489594	143324	346270	194030	3780752	1369180	*182305*	1392729	836538	4464376
2006–7	na	214013	52512	161501	124607	1599972	479754		621899	498319	1938592
2005–6	na	137226	48167	89059	46220	914703	256752		346518	311433	1098149
2004–5	na	90446	30995	59451	12800	736462	242428		156925	337109	839708
2003–4	na	46661	na	na	21897	521632	143050		140545	238037	590190
2002–3	7062	11090	na	na	17535	278986	83351		71513	124122	314673
2001–2	4643	4242	na	na	9371	146267	33634		48396	64237	164523
2000–1	12413	2181	na	na	4011	74352	19901		20796	33655	92957
1999–2000	13536	1828	na	na	2211	42164	6688		15539	19937	59739
Redemptions: All Schemes											
2009–10	na	1403421	443905	959516	982284	7550237	3662271	*227502*	3367105	293349	9935942
2008–9	na	773407	343980	429427	357112	4324131	1806550	*263674*	1865948	387959	5454650
2007–8	na	471274	135645	335629	191851	3647450	1311006	*175937*	1341120	819387	4310575
2006–7	na	203293	48942	154351	120381	1520838	450447		591457	478934	1844512
2005–6	na	129535	43973	85562	44108	871727	238053		329429	304245	1045370
2004–5	na	92460	29970	62490	16183	728865	237060		156198	335607	837508
2003–4	na	43183	na	na	19796	480402	133131		127280	219991	543381
2002–3	7246	10536	na	na	16121	267322	79341		68333	119648	301225
2001–2	11927	3329	na	na	8550	133542	31181		43239	59122	157348
2000–1	12090	4125	na	na	3147	64467	17576		18353	28538	83829
1999–2000	9663	1744	na	na	1864	27933	5718		10641	11574	41204
Net Sales											
2009–10	na	24569	7628	16941	4871	53641	25084	*1797*	33807	−7037	83081
2008–9	na	321	3425	−3104	5954	−34572	−23998	*−6311*	9924	−14187	−28297
2007–8	na	18320	7679	10641	2179	133302	58174	*6368*	51609	17151	153801
2006–7	na	10720	3570	7150	4226	79134	29307		30442	19385	94080
2005–6	na	7691	4194	3497	2112	42976	18699		17089	7188	52779
2004–5	na	−2014	1025	−3039	−3383	7597	5368		727	1502	2200
2003–4	na	3478	na	na	2101	41230	9919		13265	18046	46809
2002–3	−184	554	na	na	1414	11664	4010		3180	4474	13448
2001–2	−7284	913	na	na	821	12725	2453		5157	5115	7175
2000–1	323	−1944	na	na	864	9885	2325		2443	5117	9128
1999–2000	3873	84	na	na	347	14231	970		4898	8363	18535
Assets under Management											
2009–10	na	130429	46637	83792	42304	574792	235585	*50253*	267481	21473	747525
2008–9	na	81013	31127	49886	23092	389180	153432	*32728*	180163	22857	493285
2007–8	na	81229	32174	49055	14337	442942	166104	*31168*	165790	79880	538508
2006–7	na	54570	16807	37763	9643	262175	80157		104779	77239	326388
2005–6	na	45119	13186	31933	5229	181514	50602		74144	56768	231862
2004–5	na	29103	6595	22508	3010	117487	30750		30885	55852	149600
2003–4	na	28085	na	na	6539	108625	19885		33143	51964	143249
2002–3	13516	4491	na	na	5935	55522	10180		15459	29883	79464
2001–2	51434	3970	na	na	4234	40956	5177		15502	20277	100594
2000–1	58017	3333	na	na	3507	25730	3370		8620	13740	90587
1999–2000	76547	7842	na	na	3570	25046	2331		9724	12991	113005

Source: Association of Mutual Funds in India (AMFI) (available at www.amfiindia.com).

Notes: na: Not available.

Figures in square brackets are percentages to GDP at current market prices (new series).

Table A5.4   Trends in FII Investments

Year	Gross Purchases (Rs crore)	Gross Sales (Rs crore)		Net Investment			Net Investment (US $ mn)	Cumulative Net Investment (US$ mn)
				Total (Rs crore)	Equity	Debt		
(1)	(2)	(3)		(4)	(5)	(6)	(7)	(8)
2009–10								
Mar-10								
Feb-10								
Jan-10	78812	70399	89.3	8413	10.7	−500	8913	1849	81922
Dec-09	57394	48683	84.8	8711	15.2	10233	−1522	1873	80073
Nov-09	63633	57452	90.3	6181	9.7	5497	684	1330	78200
Oct-09	83353	67380	80.8	15973	19.2	9077	6896	3428	76870
Sep-09	78952	58379	73.9	20573	26.1	18344	2228	4263	73442
Aug-09	60674	56151	92.5	4523	7.5	4903	−379	945	69179
Jul-09	80212	67030	83.6	13182	16.4	11066	2115	2727	68235
Jun-09	76073	71174	93.6	4898	6.4	3830	1068	1059	65508
May-09	81266	63861	78.6	17406	21.4	20117	−2711	3577	64449
Apr-09	49715	40716	81.9	8999	18.1	6508	2490	1791	60872
2008–9	614579	660389	107.5	−45811	−7.5	−47706	1895	−9837	59081
2007–8	948018	881839	93.0	66179	7.0	53403	12776	16442	68919
2006–7	520506	489665	94.1	30841	5.9	25237	5607	6821	52477
2005–6	346976	305509	88.0	41467	12.0	48801	−7334	9363	45657
2004–5	216951	171071	78.9	45880	21.1	44123	1759	10352	36293
2003–4	144855	99091	68.4	45764	31.6	39960	5805	10005	25942
2002–3	47062	44372	94.3	2689	5.7	2528	162	566	15936
2001–2	50071	41308	82.5	8763	17.5	8067	685	1839	15371
2000–1	74051	64118	86.6	9933	13.4	10124	−46	2160	13531
1999–2000	56857	46735	82.2	10122	17.8	na	na	2474	11372
1998–9	16116	17699	109.8	−1584	−9.8	na	na	−386	8899
1997–8	18695	12737	68.1	5958	31.9	na	na	1650	9285
1996–7	15554	6980	44.9	8575	55.1	na	na	2432	7635
1995–6	9694	2752	28.4	6942	71.6	na	na	2036	5202
1994–5	7631	2835	37.2	4796	62.8	na	na	1528	3167
1993–4	5593	467	8.3	5127	91.7	na	na	1634	1638
1992–3	17	4	23.5	13	76.5	na	na	4	4

Source: Securities and Exchange Board of India (SEBI) (available at www.sebi.gov.in).

Notes: na: Not available.

Net Investment in US$ mn at monthly exchange rate.

Table A5.5 Business Growth of Capital Market Segment of National Stock Exchange (NSE)

Month/ Year	No. of Companies Listed *	No. of Companies Permitted to Trade $	No. of Companies Available for Trading *@	No. of Trading Days	No. of Companies/ Securities Traded	No. of Trades (million)	Traded Quantity (million)	Turnover (Rs crore)	Average Daily Turnover (Rs crore)	Average Trade Size (Rs)	Demat Securities Traded (million)	Demat Turnover (Rs crore)	Market Capitalization (Rs crore)*	% to GDP
(1)	(2)	(3)	(4)	(5)	(6)	(7)	(8)	(9)	(10)	(11)	(12)	(13)	(14)	(15)
2009–10	1470	37	1359	244	1371	1683	221553	4138024	16959		221553	4138025	6009173	(97.5)
Mar-10	1470	37	1359	21	1371	124	13797	286246	13631	23184	13797	286246	6009173	
Feb-10	1461	31	1342	20	1328	113	12354	245143	12257	21645	12354	245143	5755305	
Jan-10	1457	31	1338	19	1320	140	18042	338443	17813	24124	18042	338443	5782965	
Dec-09	1453	10	1303	21	1297	126	15038	292900	13948	23324	15038	292900	5699637	
Nov-09	1443	10	1292	20	1286	132	15740	324477	16224	24630	15740	324477	5430088	
Oct-09	1439	0	1291	20	1365	135	16848	362969	18148	26953	16848	362969	5024830	
Sep-09	1434	0	1287	20	1376	139	19651	365063	18253	26320	19651	365063	5353880	
Aug-09	1431	0	1288	21	1608	148	19443	364969	17379	24741	19443	364969	4975800	
Jul-09	1426	0	1282	23	1326	171	21936	426143	18528	24929	21936	426143	4816459	
Jun-09	1426	0	1282	22	1535	180	27485	482414	21928	26807	27485	482414	4432596	
May-09	1425	0	1280	20	1390	148	22903	382561	19128	25791	22903	382561	4564572	
Apr-09	1470	0	1279	17	1372	127	18316	266696	15688	20980	18316	266697	3375025	
2008–9	1432	0	1291	243	1327	1365	142636	2752023	11325	20161	142636	2752023	2896194	(52.0)
2007–8	1381	0	1236	251	1264	1173	149847	3551038	14148	30280	149847	3551038	4858122	(98.2)
2006–7	1228	0	1084	249	1191	785	85546	1945285	7812	24790	85546	1945287	3367350	(78.6)
2005–6	1069	0	929	251	956	609	84449	1569556	6253	25777	84449	1569558	2813201	(75.9)
2004–5	970	1	839	253	870	451	79769	1140071	4471	25283	79769	1140072	1585585	(48.9)
2003–4	909	18	787	254	804	378	71330	1099535	4329	29090	71330	1099534	1120976	(40.7)
2002–3	818	107	788	251	899	240	36407	617989	2462	25776	36405	617984	537133	(21.9)
2001–2	793	197	890	247	1019	175	27841	513167	2078	29270	27772	512866	636861	(27.9)
2000–1	785	320	1029	251	1201	168	32954	1339510	5337	86980	30722	1264337	657847	(31.3)
1999–2000	720	479	1152	254	na	98	24270	839052	3303	85244	15377	711706	1020426	(52.3)
1998–9	648	609	1254	251	na	55	16533	414474	1651	75954	854	23818	491175	(28.0)
1997–8	612	745	1357	244	na	38	13569	370193	1520	97054			481503	(31.5)
1996–7	550	934	1484	250	na	26	13556	294503	1176	112086			419367	(30.4)
1995–6	422	847	1269	246	na	7	3991	67287	276	101505			401459	(33.7)
1994–5 (Nov–Mar)	135	543	678	102	na	0.3	139	1805	17	56310			363350	(35.8)

Source: NSE News (various issues).

Notes: Figures in brackets are percentages to GDP at current market prices. GDP data are as per revised series from 2004–5 and as per 1999–2000 series before 2004–5. na: Not available.

* Data relates to period end. @ Excludes suspended companies. $ Includes companies listed on Madras Stock Exchange and BSE, which have been permitted on the NSE.

Table A5.6   Settlement Statistics of Capital Market Segment of NSE of India

	No. of trades (million)	Traded Quantity (number)	Number of Shares (Deliver-able)	Per cent of Shares Delivered to Total Trade	Trading Value (Rs crore)	Value of Shares Deliverable (Rs crore)	Percentage of Delivered to Value of Shares Traded	Securities Pay-in (Rs crore)	Short Delivery (million)	Per cent of Short Delivery to Total Delivery	Funds Pay in (Rs crore)
(1)	(2)	(3)	(4)	(5)	(6)	(7)	(8)	(9)	(10)	(11)	(12)
2009–10											
Mar-10											
Feb-10	115	12591	2536	22.52	253467	58767	23.19		8	0.18	18354
Jan-10	136	17572	4428	25.20	324584	85206	26.25		8	0.18	25887
Dec-09	127	15073	3429	22.75	298215	68853	23.09	68748	7	0.19	17995
Nov-09	133	16104	3559	22.10	332248	74650	22.47	74565	5	0.14	22913
Oct-09	140	17321	4022	23.22	373953	89940	24.05	89834	7	0.17	26965
Sep-09	134	19160	4344	22.67	349940	82209	23.49	82124	6	0.14	24853
Aug-09	148	19171	3961	20.66	371474	78662	21.18	78561	7	0.18	23751
Jul-09	169	21682	3976	18.34	419077	80194	19.14	80078	6	0.15	25433
Jun-09	182	28112	5311	18.89	496589	98889	19.91	98761	8	0.15	29632
May-09	144	21907	4555	20.79	357932	74436	20.80	74317	11	0.25	25219
Apr-09	126	17934	3441	19.19	261310	48149	18.43	48072	7	0.20	16269
2008–9	1364	141893	30393	21.42	2749450	611535	22.44	610498	63	0.21	220704
2007–8	1165	148123	36797	24.84	3519919	972803	27.64	970618	100	0.27	309543
2006–7	786	85051	23907	28.11	1940094	544435	28.06	543950	77	0.32	173188
2005–6	600	81844	22724	27.77	1516839	409353	26.99	407976	89	0.39	131426
2004–5	449	78800	20228	25.67	1140969	277101	24.29	276120	87	0.43	97241
2003–4	375	70453	17555	24.92	1090632	221364	20.30	220341	101	0.58	81588
2002–3	240	36541	8235	22.54	621569	87956	14.15	87447	47	0.57	34092
2001–2	172	27470	5930	21.59	508121	71766	14.12	64353	36	0.61	28048
2000–1	161	30420	5020	16.50	1263898	106277	8.41	94962	34	0.68	45937
1999–2000	96	23861	4871	20.42	803050	82607	10.29	79783	63	1.3	27992
1998–9	55	16531	2799	16.93	413573	66204	16.01	30755	31	1.09	12175
1997–8	38	13522	2205	16.31	370010	59775	16.15	21713	33	1.51	10827
1996–7	26	13432	1645	12.25	292314	32640	11.17	13790	38	2.32	7212
1995–6	6	3901	726	18.62	65742	11775	17.91	5805	18	2.46	3258
1994–5	0.3	133	69	51.74	1728	898	51.98	611	1	0.85	300
(Nov-Mar)											

Source: *NSE News* (various issues).

Table A5.7 Business Growth of Futures and Options Market Segment, NSE

Month/ Year	Index Futures		Stock Futures		Interest Rate Futures		Index Options		Stock Options		Total		Average Daily Turn-over (Rs crore)	Open Interest at End Period	
	Number of Contracts Traded	Turnover (Rs crore)	Num-ber of Contracts Traded	Turnover (Rs crore)	Number of Con-tracts Traded	Turnover (Rs crore)	Number of Contracts Traded	National Turnover (Rs crore)	Number of Con-tracts Traded	National Turnover (Rs crore)	Num-ber of Contracts Traded	National Turnover (Rs crore)		No. of Contracts	Trading Value (Rs crore)
(1)	(2)	(3)	(4)	(5)	(6)	(7)	(8)	(9)	(10)	(11)	(12)	(13)	(14)	(15)	(16)
2009–10															
Mar-10															
Feb-10	13891843	326871	10725789	354485	0	0	34588704	847236	1223627	41285	60429963	1569877	78494		
Jan-10	12056359	298849	12546679	444134	0	0	27084605	695860	1414178	51454	53101821	1490297	78436		
Dec-09	13337833	329496	11307332	395954	0	0	29525940	756677	1252898	42855	55424003	1524982	72618	2756002	77760
Nov-09	15178552	363523	13260546	438220	0	0	32965274	816408	1360703	43666	62765075	1661817	83091	3390368	91419
Oct-09	13615447	329610	14044526	465829	0	0	26671252	669591	1378569	45387	55709794	1510417	75521	3336784	83327
Sep-09	13032242	302425	13157621	434119	0	0	25074041	609076	1237428	42758	52501332	1388378	69419	3239338	88791
Aug-09	16892217	366312	13113118	412363	0	0	28535857	658757	1129195	36214	59670387	1473646	70174	2955633	75134
Jul-09	18271805	382924	15500535	450632	0	0	31786743	701247	1268003	38706	66827086	1573509	68413	2467693	62474
Jun-09	16207959	346934	11127649	589657	0	0	24189642	545644	882947	49745	52408197	1531980	69635	2527295	58987
May-09	16617516	317415	9528178	448155	0	0	21495541	430515	644280	31168	134285515	1227253	61363	2305330	64823
Apr-09	18662382	301764	9858642	356383	0	0	27374936	480300	807323	31427	56703283	1169874	67257	2753069	57076
2008–9	210428103	3570111	221577980	3479642	0	0	212088444	3731501	13295970	229227	657390497	11010481	45311	3227759	57705
2007–8	156598579	3820667	203587952	7548563	0	0	55366038	1362111	9460631	359136	425013200	13090477	52153	2282671	48900
2006–7	81487424	2539576	104955401	3830972	0	0	25157438	791912	5283310	480995	216883573	7643455	29543	1791549	38670
2005–6	58537886	1513791	80905493	2791721	0	0	12935116	338469	5240776	508930	157619271	5152911	19220	1028003	38469
2004–5	21635449	772174	47043066	1484067	0	0	3293558	121954	5045112	168858	77017185	2547053	10107	592646	21052
2003–4	17192274	554463	32485160	1305949	1013	20	1732414	52823	5583071	217212	56993932	2130467	8288	235792	7188
2002–3	2126763	43952	10675786	286532	-	-	442241	9248	3523062	100133	16768909	439862	1752	97025	2194
2001–2	1025588	21482	1957856	51516	-	-	175900	3766	1037529	25163	4196873	101926	410	93917	2150
2000–1 (Jun–Mar)	90580	2365	-	-	-	-	-	-	-	-	90580	2365	11	na	na

Source: NSE News (various issues).

Notes: National Turnover = (Strike price + Premium) * Quantity

(–) Means the period when derivative trade was not operational.

Table A5.8 Settlement Statistics in Futures and Options Segment, NSE

(Rupees crore)

Year	Index/Stock Futures		Index/Stock Options		Total
	MTM Settlement	Final Settlement	Premium Settlement	Exercise Settlement	
(1)	(2)	(3)	(4)	(5)	(6)
2009–10					
Mar-10					
Feb-10					
Jan-10					
Dec-09	3955	59	955	333	5301
Nov-09	5313	149	870	174	6506
Oct-09	4706	180	697	141	5724
Sep-09	3243	66	848	214	4371
Aug-09	5022	37	894	125	6078
Jul-09	6109	109	1066	218	7501
Jun-09	6961	158	916	573	8607
May-09	7818	141	1289	1069	10317
Apr-09	4856	274	945	495	6568
2008–9	75194	1498	10960	4188	91840
2007–8	144655	1312	6760	3792	156519
2006–7	61314	798	3194	1189	66494
2005–6	25586	598	1521	818	28523
2004–5	13024	228	941	456	14649
2003–4	10822	139	859	476	12296
2002–3	1738	46	331	196	2311
2001–2	505	22	165	94	786
2000–1	84	2	0	0	86

Source: National Stock Exchange, *NSE News* (various issues).

Table A5.9 Business Growth on the WDM Segment, NSE

(Rupees crore)

Year	Number of Trades	Trading Value (Rs crore)	Average Daily Trading Value (Rs crore)	Average Trade Size (Rs crore)	Market Capitalization
(1)	(2)	(3)	(4)	(5)	(6)
2009–10					
Mar-10					
Feb-10	1455	34800	1832	23.9	3153360
Jan-10	1957	57036	2852	29.1	3138177
Dec-09	1735	37567	1789	21.7	3129747
Nov-09	2564	64999	3250	25.4	3099214
Oct-09	1875	43731	2302	23.3	3072733
Sep-09	2301	58674	3088	25.5	3024417
Aug-09	1583	38232	1912	24.2	2970459
Jul-09	2582	51222	2227	19.8	3117776
Jun-09	1948	44568	2026	22.9	3075905
May-09	2089	40266	2013	19.3	3008407
Apr-09	2408	45653	2853	19.0	2988333
2009–10	22497	516748	2360	23.0	3153360
2008–9	16129	335952	1412	20.8	2848315
2007–8	16179	282317	1138	17.5	2123346
2006–7	19575	219106	898	11.2	1784801
2005–6	61891	475524	1755	7.7	1567574
2004–5	124308	887294	3039	7.1	1461734
2003–4	189518	1316096	4477	6.9	1215864
2002–3	167778	1068701	3598	6.4	864481
2001–2	144851	947191	3278	6.5	756794
2000–1	64470	428582	1483	6.6	580835
1999–2000	46987	304216	1035	6.5	494033
1998–9	16092	105469	365	6.6	411470
1997–8	16821	111263	385	6.6	343191
1996–7	7804	42278	145	5.4	292772
1995–6	2991	11868	41	4.0	207783
1994–5	1021	6781	35	6.6	158181
(Jun–Mar)					

Source: *NSE News* (various issues).

Table A5.10   Business Growth and Settlement of Capital Market Segments, Bombay Stock Exchange (BSE)

Month/ Year	No. of Companies/ Listed *	No. of Trading Days	No. of Trades (lakh)	Total Shares Traded (crore)	Total Turnover (Rs crore)	Total Average Daily Turnover (Rs crore)	Market Capitalization (Rs crore)	% to GDP	Number of Shares	Total Deliveries Per cent of Total Shares Traded	Value (Rs crore)	Per cent of Total Turnover
(1)	(2)	(3)	(4)	(5)	(6)	(7)	(8)	(9)	(10)	(11)	(12)	(13)
2009–10	4977	244	6056	11356	1378809	5651	6164157		3763	33.1	311192	22.6
Mar-10	4977	21	436	814	99779	4751	6164517		310	38.1	26357	26.4
Feb-10	4970	20	398	664	82509	4125	5903514		238	35.8	19985	24.2
Jan-10	4962	19	528	1071	117084	6162	5924340		388	36.2	30923	26.4
Dec-09	4955	21	452	827	98082	4671	6079892		287	34.7	23577	24.0
Nov-09	4951	20	455	778	105142	5257	4878200		254	32.6	24587	23.4
Oct-09	4951	20	471	902	114007	5700	5374559		318	35.3	26862	23.6
Sep-09	4946	20	511	1067	124220	6211	5708338		356	33.4	30166	24.3
Aug-09	4942	21	534	959	122319	5825	5285658		286	29.8	25300	20.7
Jul-09	4937	23	595	968	138986	6043	5139943		262	27.1	26125	18.8
Jun-09	4934	22	656	1279	159195	7236	4749935		356	27.8	32659	20.5
May-09	4928	20	552	1181	128542	6427	4865046		369	31.2	30146	23.5
Apr-09	4930	17	469	846	88943	5232	3586979		217	25.7	14505	16.3
2008–9	4929	243	5408	7396	1100074	4527	3086076	55.4	1966	26.7	230881	21.0
2007–8	4887	251	5303	9860	1578856	6290	5138015	103.8	3616	36.9	478034	30.3
2006–7	4821	249	3462	5608	956185	3840	3545041	82.8	2297	41.1	298885	31.3
2005–6	4781	251	2639	6644	816073	3251	3022191	81.5	3007	47.6	320111	39.2
2004–5	4731	253	2374	4772	518715	2050	1698428	52.4	1875	39.3	140056	27.0
2003–4	5528	254	2028	3904	503053	1981	1201207	43.6	1332	34.1	107153	21.3
2002–3	5650	251	1413	2214	314073	1251	572197	23.3	699	31.6	48741	15.5
2001–2	5782	247	1277	1822	307292	1244	612224	26.9	577	31.7	59980	19.5
2000–1	5869	251	1428	2585	1000032	3984	571553	27.2	867	33.5	166941	16.7
1999–2000	5815	251	740	2086	686428	2735	912842	46.8	943	45.2	174740	25.3
1998–9	5849	243	354	1293	310750	1279	619532	35.4	506	39.1	85617	27.6
1997–8	5853	244	196	859	207113	849	630221	41.3	244	28.4	22512	10.9
1996–7	5832	240	155	809	124190	517	505137	36.6	212	26.2	10993	8.9
1995–6	5603	232	171	772	50064	216	563748	47.3	268	34.7	11527	23.0
1994–5	4702	231	196	1072	67749	293	468837	46.2	447	41.7	26641	39.3
1993–4	3585	218	123	758	84536	388	368071	42.5	na		15861	18.8

Source: BSE—Key Statistics.

Note: * Data relates to period end.

Table A 5.11 Working of Clearing Corporation of India Limited (CCIL)

	Outright				Repo				Forex*				CBLO**			
	Number of Trades	Average Trades	Volume	Average Volume	Number. of Trades	Average Trades	Volume	Average Volume	Number of Trades	Average Trades	Volume	Average Volume	Number of Trades	Average Trades	Volume	Average Volume
2009–10	316956	1332	2913890	12243	28651	101	6072829	21308	883949	3980	2988971	3843	142052	498	1541378	54531
Mar-10	19330	967	165761	8288	2253	94	459604	19150	79603	3843	303237	3980	13879	578	1440135	60006
Feb-10	21120	1112	181384	9547	1919	87	436071	19821	78977	4388	273009	15167	11680	531	1400191	63645
Jan-10	25116	1256	234273	11714	1830	73	364133	14565	80396	4466	260266	14459	11417	457	1264283	50571
Dec-09	26957	1284	245506	11691	2304	92	512490	20500	75273	3584	243251	11583	13109	524	1383447	55338
Nov-09	32717	1636	300252	15013	2250	98	518162	22529	78570	4365	220689	12260	11557	502	1262123	54875
Oct-09	25080	1320	236008	12421	2295	100	539220	23444	75320	4184	224261	12459	12211	531	1341206	58313
Sep-09	29401	1547	282082	14846	2722	118	643526	27979	67627	3757	221282	12293	12038	523	1434930	62388
Aug-09	18692	935	170489	8524	2480	103	559289	23304	65665	3283	211395	10570	11911	496	1370384	57099
Jul-09	34807	1582	304703	13850	2664	102	526597	20254	77755	3534	248295	11286	11756	452	1209015	46501
Jun-09	27453	1248	249716	11351	2839	109	564049	21694	73731	3351	263942	11997	12211	470	1392384	53553
May-09	26516	1326	259205	12960	2865	119	538788	22449	71963	3788	271612	14295	11422	476	1164123	48505
Apr-09	29767	1860	284512	17782	2230	112	410899	20545	59069	3692	247731	15483	8861	443	879158	43958
2008–9	245964	1047	2160233	9192	24280	85	4094286	14266	837520	3657	3758904	16414	118941	414	8824784	30748
2007–8	188843	765	1653851	6696	26612	91	3948751	13523	757074	3181	3133665	13167	113277	385	8110828	27588
2006–7	137100	562	1021536	4187	29008	99	2556501	8755	606808	2550	1776981	7466	85881	292	4732271	16096
2005–6	125509	467	864751	3215	25673	88	1694509	5803	489649	2084	1179688	5020	67463	229	2953134	10045
2004–5	160682	550	1134222	3884	24364	83	1557907	5335	466327	1976	899782	3813	29351	101	976757	3345
2003–4	243585	820	1575133	5303	20927	71	943189	3208	330517	1425	501342	2161	3060	10	76851	262
2002–3	191843	646	1076147	3623	11672	39	468229	1577	100232	1101	136102	1496	159	3	852	16

Source: Rakshitra, CCIL.

Notes: * Commenced operations from 12 November 2002; cash and tom settlement is with effect from 5 February 2004.

** Commenced operation from 20 January 2003.

A6 INVESTMENT

Table A6.1 Trends in Total Investment

(Rupees crore)

Non-financial	Mar-96	Mar-97	Mar-98	Mar-99	Mar-00	Mar-01	Mar-02	Mar-03	Mar-04	Mar-05	Mar-06	Mar-07	Mar-08	Mar-09	Mar-10
	1150015	1213028	1268426	1334840	1398879	1503488	1510055	1503896	1651338	2047397	2819309	4406062	6127290	8649871	10184646
Manufacturing	514740	495129	475927	425567	385355	325773	275902	298409	338730	564601	909655	1305220	1703434	2145121	2465761
Food & Beverages	17091	15600	13428	10590	12074	10479	13023	14585	15418	16652	21524	33884	38366	57631	57552
Food Products	14385	13640	11850	9088	10793	9535	11636	12848	13278	14367	19083	30567	35119	53774	53373
Textiles	34026	25107	19160	14906	10407	11161	8380	10518	13222	17797	29153	48913	53300	49085	47332
Cotton Textiles	12335	8935	6761	5007	2939	3032	3012	4006	3714	5923	10723	14738	14620	13162	10218
Chemicals	232398	231132	251513	267752	246081	209935	167344	164961	171737	202997	304667	375907	516206	551821	597268
Fertilizers	23371	25083	29646	30903	38843	31963	12782	4115	6641	6841	11201	14260	26058	27824	40307
Organic Chemicals	69389	73316	89766	103184	78537	63161	54340	34956	39141	45470	62663	86657	85158	123633	115559
Petroleum Products	96735	102903	108176	114925	110191	96274	81308	102037	97598	120144	187503	217803	332857	299388	313938
Non-metallic Mineral Products	31193	32712	23996	19604	20477	17099	15247	13673	15948	23918	29233	66630	105743	162379	161235
Cement	24217	26825	18899	15981	17274	14529	12589	11180	11315	17261	22735	57467	93619	138249	138656
Metals & Metal Products	144656	124703	106117	71266	54873	37242	34731	59752	90574	255172	461712	642349	785005	1008274	1292003
Ferrous Metals	128520	110022	86468	54443	46432	29582	26242	43780	73301	216183	423869	588508	705568	893524	1181592
Non-ferrous Metals	16137	14681	19649	16823	8441	7660	8489	15972	17273	38988	37843	53841	79436	114750	110411
Machinery	15228	18733	15178	12526	14414	14830	14814	12603	11422	19774	21732	46164	90766	186289	183734
Non-electrical Machinery	3316	5199	5599	4653	4172	3158	3386	2881	3466	5499	5747	15809	20968	44459	44149
Electrical Machinery	4910	4681	3909	3280	4304	5437	4914	4061	3655	4712	5287	7413	7971	17992	9427
Electronics	7001	8853	5670	4592	5939	6235	6515	5661	4302	9563	10699	22941	61827	123838	130158
Transport Equipment	16360	27776	28658	16980	19757	18716	16395	18084	14761	17299	24257	62534	81694	96152	91420
Automobile	14588	24397	24682	13452	15898	16137	14051	15881	11848	14037	19671	57268	67803	82112	76789
Miscellaneous Manufacturing	23789	19364	17877	11943	7272	6313	5969	4232	5650	10992	17376	28839	32354	33489	35217
Paper & Paper Products	18596	14032	14143	8524	5446	5029	4277	2252	3820	9136	14399	20832	23457	21323	21368
Mining	59018	43903	52187	68042	77644	90961	86427	79643	90357	97435	129583	150157	179045	335360	356880
Electricity	475437	498990	506626	528665	576816	577905	556530	528399	570477	665803	916128	1480693	2043120	3059622	3584225
Electricity Generation	468058	488565	496638	515925	565773	567832	542854	513987	553355	640713	892258	1451727	2009244	3001823	3503557

(Continued)

Table A6.1 *Continued*

Non-financial	Mar-96	Mar-97	Mar-98	Mar-99	Mar-00	Mar-01	Mar-02	Mar-03	Mar-04	Mar-05	Mar-06	Mar-07	Mar-08	Mar-09	Mar-10
	1150015	1213028	1268426	1334840	1398879	1503488	1510055	1503896	1651338	2047397	2819309	4406062	6127290	8649871	10184646
Electricity Distribution	7379	10424	9988	12740	11043	10073	13676	14412	17122	25090	23870	28967	33876	57798	80668
Services (other than financial)	88472	163310	222520	287703	330958	462643	522736	529645	586831	644665	740642	1023782	1481268	2156452	2727093
Hotels & Tourism	6220	10782	11223	12061	11930	20387	21267	22266	15185	16055	20953	28878	40898	56857	74767
Recreational Services	708	802	1036	991	915	3339	3266	5779	8068	7505	15145	26491	30889	39333	58857
Health Services	901	908	1123	2409	2801	3356	4172	6891	8180	11116	12169	15230	20491	36075	43332
Transport Services	46867	103332	135573	164267	174275	216872	259395	290317	335858	371930	450334	574648	828196	1258553	1671501
Communication Services	9791	14889	30875	43951	54460	93796	104551	78994	72920	72191	62009	62164	136582	204451	201164
Information Technology	3103	4411	5056	5163	7494	25213	32315	32240	36148	36688	47040	89458	137056	168705	185566
Storage & Distribution	20881	28185	36781	58009	76744	95271	91652	84860	99138	115465	108287	137300	151511	191398	231843
Construction	12348	11696	11166	24862	28106	46205	68459	67801	64942	74892	123300	446211	720423	953316	1050687
Financial Services	1150015	1213028	1268426	1334840	1398879	1334	275	0	35	35	49	2035	2260	2260	2260
Irrigation	86633	103389	108138	118014	117461	120875	119003	120600	123751	141098	157236	173291	181489	227560	284315
All Industries	1236648	1316417	1376564	1452853	1516340	1625697	1629333	1624497	1775124	2188530	2976594	4581388	6311039	8879691	10471221

Source: CMIE, Monthly Review of Investment Projects, CapEX.

Note: Total Investment covers projects announced and proposed and those under implementation.

Table A6.2 Investment under Implementation in Total Investment

(Rupees crore)

	Mar-96	Mar-97	Mar-98	Mar-99	Mar-00	Mar-01	Mar-02	Mar-03	Mar-04	Mar-05	Mar-06	Mar-07	Mar-08	Mar-09	Mar-10
Non-financial	588737	736416	726355	774830	820759	968937	1074286	980818	991307	1209333	1430479	1987687	2467789	3328484	4774817
Manufacturing	266727	318097	284627	256761	215211	200922	182839	175216	174370	270397	391881	572446	682882	852346	1091263
Food & Beverages	10561	9001	6913	5924	8190	8055	6578	6664	7223	8136	10382	12123	14787	14321	25244
Food Products	9165	7557	5675	4756	6968	7258	5879	6058	6376	7148	9561	10764	13860	13325	22826
Textiles	19580	17326	10105	7357	4655	4731	3826	4903	5733	10032	14927	26468	30628	19814	23516
Cotton Textiles	7443	6020	4276	3082	1410	1986	1809	2220	1629	3746	5912	8011	7551	6397	4912
Chemicals	122961	129516	131524	153243	135578	123138	116508	99840	91922	122506	199894	241285	245381	285923	307316
Fertilizers	13275	15203	15183	15734	9864	8359	4125	2526	2136	4673	6894	8188	11618	8195	11760
Organic Chemicals	38338	41461	39481	40729	39958	35122	34647	25049	23942	23733	28714	46555	43586	56062	44215
Petroleum Products	46181	53526	61824	86817	72832	69803	67668	64054	55407	76642	136096	147137	150108	166781	168197
Non-metallic Mineral Products	20724	20933	14339	11921	13214	11737	9826	6161	7273	12819	14425	21504	34195	41407	72292
Cement	16849	17350	10883	9526	10678	9924	8014	4367	4624	8726	10487	17577	31398	37470	66189
Metals & Metal Products	62307	92297	78174	50298	33580	29349	23255	36315	45103	94907	122202	216476	286512	418238	497507
Ferrous Metals	54316	81313	60641	35265	27068	22856	16141	25014	32382	74676	102156	166927	235422	349946	422121
Non-ferrous Metals	7992	10984	17533	15033	6511	6494	7114	11301	12721	20231	20045	49549	51090	68292	75386
Machinery	6786	13442	9606	7964	9766	10071	9910	8579	7423	10791	10662	20617	30860	22564	79948
Non-electrical Machinery	1513	3293	3919	2753	2637	2020	1633	1478	2082	3810	3390	9400	10174	14052	22409
Electrical Machinery	2200	3214	2601	2325	3631	3347	4148	3449	2435	2951	2613	1340	2349	2123	4460
Electronics	3073	6934	3087	2887	3497	4703	4129	3652	2906	4029	4659	9876	18337	6388	53079
Transport Equipment	11424	23488	25372	14267	7565	10892	9813	10321	6013	6658	9671	24136	32321	41246	66616
Automobile	10164	20918	22293	11858	5073	8906	8085	8743	4424	5036	8455	22464	28576	33936	56385
Miscellaneous Manufacturing	12383	12094	8593	5787	2663	2948	3124	2433	3680	4548	9719	9836	8197	8834	18825
Paper & Paper Products	8229	7869	5849	3584	1607	1857	1897	1322	3040	3691	8858	8637	6916	6394	11237
Mining	29936	34791	32884	44735	46811	63492	64153	57207	61857	68258	72631	73403	68811	117934	194285
Electricity	233853	285161	286211	312077	356427	388419	420791	312718	325649	398920	451031	588387	714651	925626	1311556
Electricity Generation	228074	276337	278957	301399	348418	380451	408949	303076	314306	380306	432736	571801	696938	904922	1280790
Electricity Distribution	5779	8824	7255	10678	8009	7968	11842	9642	11343	18614	18295	16586	17713	20704	32765
Services (other than financial)	56484	96992	118943	142716	179339	275910	349788	373820	374658	411930	448866	522315	649777	947986	1499651

(Continued)

Table A6.2 *Continued*

Non-financial	Mar-96	Mar-97	Mar-98	Mar-99	Mar-00	Mar-01	Mar-02	Mar-03	Mar-04	Mar-05	Mar-06	Mar-07	Mar-08	Mar-09	Mar-10
	588737	736416	726355	774830	820759	968937	1074286	980818	991307	1209333	1430479	1987687	2467789	3328484	4774817
Hotels & Tourism	3719	5818	6593	8512	8801	16707	17396	17265	8154	8760	9378	12934	18438	26328	44543
Recreational Services	502	282	48	613	805	2929	2553	4287	5655	5179	5075	10550	12746	14882	38591
Health Services	464	457	517	952	1230	1900	3581	5130	5519	5098	5273	6812	8754	9996	30713
Transport Services	30619	57653	66168	77187	88586	115697	163375	194288	211203	240191	285539	326418	395302	532903	847182
Communication Services	5100	12705	25570	32446	40158	77688	89676	67960	60498	59378	52209	44754	61130	139464	138502
Information Technology	2091	3969	4455	3129	4935	21081	24202	26932	25380	26518	28960	43561	64672	84451	113047
Storage & Distribution	13987	16108	15592	19878	33756	37460	45787	52642	51325	59992	51132	50666	51770	63893	132672
Construction	1737	1376	3690	18540	22971	40194	56715	61858	54772	59828	66070	231136	351669	484593	678063
Financial Services	588737	736416	726355	774830	820759	1334	275	0	0	0	14	0	0	0	0
Irrigation	76390	93129	99205	100917	100548	105044	103368	101908	107287	120631	126924	139404	130790	188668	260300
All Industries	665127	829545	825560	875747	921307	1075316	1177929	1082726	1098593	1329964	1557417	2127091	2598579	3517153	5035118

Source: CMIE, Monthly Review of Investment Projects, CapEX.

Table A6.3 Rate of Implementation (Investments under Implementation Expressed as per cent of Total Investment)

	Mar-96	Mar-97	Mar-98	Mar-99	Mar-00	Mar-01	Mar-02	Mar-03	Mar-04	Mar-05	Mar-06	Mar-07	Mar-08	Mar-09	Mar-10
Non-financial	51.2	60.7	57.3	58.0	58.7	64.4	71.1	65.2	60.0	59.1	50.7	45.1	40.3	38.5	46.9
Manufacturing	51.8	64.2	59.8	60.3	55.8	61.7	66.3	58.7	51.5	47.9	43.1	43.9	40.1	39.7	44.3
Food & Beverages	61.8	57.7	51.5	55.9	67.8	76.9	50.5	45.7	46.8	48.9	48.2	35.8	38.5	24.8	43.9
Food Products	63.7	55.4	47.9	52.3	64.6	76.1	50.5	47.2	48.0	49.8	50.1	35.2	39.5	24.8	42.8
Textiles	57.5	69.0	52.7	49.4	44.7	42.4	45.7	46.6	43.4	56.4	51.2	54.1	57.5	40.4	49.7
Cotton Textiles	60.3	67.4	63.3	61.6	48.0	65.5	60.1	55.4	43.9	63.2	55.1	54.4	51.6	48.6	48.1
Chemicals	52.9	56.0	52.3	57.2	55.1	58.7	69.6	60.5	53.5	60.3	65.6	64.2	47.5	51.8	51.5
Fertilizers	56.8	60.6	51.2	50.9	25.4	26.2	32.3	61.4	32.2	68.3	61.5	57.4	44.6	29.5	29.2
Organic Chemicals	55.3	56.6	44.0	39.5	50.9	55.6	63.8	71.7	61.2	52.2	45.8	53.7	51.2	45.3	38.3
Petroleum Products	47.7	52.0	57.2	75.5	66.1	72.5	83.2	62.8	56.8	63.8	72.6	67.6	45.1	55.7	53.6
Non-metallic Mineral Products	66.4	64.0	59.8	60.8	64.5	68.6	64.4	45.1	45.6	53.6	49.3	32.3	32.3	25.5	44.8
Cement	69.6	64.7	57.6	59.6	61.8	68.3	63.7	39.1	40.9	50.6	46.1	30.6	33.5	27.1	47.7
Metals & Metal Products	43.1	74.0	73.7	70.6	61.2	78.8	67.0	60.8	49.8	37.2	26.5	33.7	36.5	41.5	38.5
Ferrous Metals	42.3	73.9	70.1	64.8	58.3	77.3	61.5	57.1	44.2	34.5	24.1	28.4	33.4	39.2	35.7
Non-ferrous Metals	49.5	74.8	89.2	89.4	77.1	84.8	83.8	70.8	73.6	51.9	53.0	92.0	64.3	59.5	68.3
Machinery	44.6	71.8	63.3	63.6	67.8	67.9	66.9	68.1	65.0	54.6	49.1	44.7	34.0	12.1	43.5
Non-electrical Machinery	45.6	63.3	70.0	59.2	63.2	64.0	48.2	51.3	60.1	69.3	59.0	59.5	48.5	31.6	50.8
Electrical Machinery	44.8	68.7	66.5	70.9	84.4	61.6	84.4	84.9	66.6	62.6	49.4	18.1	29.5	11.8	47.3
Electronics	43.9	78.3	54.4	62.9	58.9	75.4	63.4	64.5	67.6	42.1	43.5	43.1	29.7	5.2	40.8
Transport Equipment	69.8	84.6	88.5	84.0	38.3	58.2	59.9	57.1	40.7	38.5	39.9	38.6	39.6	42.9	72.9
Automobile	69.7	85.7	90.3	88.1	31.9	55.2	57.5	55.1	37.3	35.9	43.0	39.2	42.1	41.3	73.4
Miscellaneous Manufacturing	52.1	62.5	48.1	48.5	36.6	46.7	52.3	57.5	65.1	41.4	55.9	34.1	25.3	26.4	53.5
Paper & Paper Products	44.2	56.1	41.4	42.0	29.5	36.9	44.4	58.7	79.6	40.4	61.5	41.5	29.5	30.0	52.6
Mining	50.7	79.2	63.0	65.7	60.3	69.8	74.2	71.8	68.5	70.1	56.0	48.9	38.4	35.2	54.4
Electricity	49.2	57.1	56.5	59.0	61.8	67.2	75.6	59.2	57.1	59.9	49.2	39.7	35.0	30.3	36.6
Electricity Generation	48.7	56.6	56.2	58.4	61.6	67.0	75.3	59.0	56.8	59.4	48.5	39.4	34.7	30.1	36.6
Electricity Distribution	78.3	84.7	72.6	83.8	72.5	79.1	86.6	66.9	66.2	74.2	76.6	57.3	52.3	35.8	40.6
Services (other than financial)	63.8	59.4	53.5	49.6	54.2	59.6	66.9	70.6	63.8	63.9	60.6	51.0	43.9	44.0	54.9
Hotels & Tourism	59.8	54.0	58.7	70.6	73.8	81.9	81.8	77.5	53.7	54.6	44.8	44.8	45.1	46.3	59.6
Recreational Services	71.0	35.1	4.6	61.8	87.9	87.7	78.1	74.2	70.1	69.0	33.5	39.8	41.3	37.8	65.6
Health Services	51.5	50.3	46.0	39.5	43.9	56.6	85.8	74.4	67.5	45.9	43.3	44.7	42.7	27.7	70.9
Transport Services	65.3	55.8	48.8	47.0	50.8	53.3	63.0	66.9	62.9	64.6	63.4	56.8	47.7	42.3	50.7
Communication Services	52.1	85.3	82.8	73.8	73.7	82.8	85.8	86.0	83.0	82.3	84.2	72.0	44.8	68.2	68.9
Information Technology	67.4	90.0	88.1	60.6	65.8	83.6	74.9	83.5	70.2	72.3	61.6	48.7	47.2	50.1	60.9
Storage & Distribution	67.0	57.2	42.4	34.3	44.0	39.3	50.0	62.0	51.8	52.0	47.2	36.9	34.2	33.4	57.2
Construction	14.1	11.8	33.0	74.6	81.7	87.0	82.8	91.2	84.3	79.9	53.6	51.8	48.8	50.8	64.5
Financial Services	51.2	60.7	57.3	58.0	58.7	100.0	100.0	0.0	0.0	0.0	28.6	0.0	0.0	0.0	0.0
Irrigation	88.2	90.1	91.7	85.5	85.6	86.9	86.9	84.5	86.7	85.5	80.7	80.4	72.1	82.9	91.6
All Industries	**53.8**	**63.0**	**60.0**	**60.3**	**60.8**	**66.1**	**72.3**	**66.6**	**61.9**	**60.8**	**52.3**	**46.4**	**41.2**	**39.6**	**48.1**

Source: CMIE, Monthly Review of Investment Projects, CapEX.

(*Rupees crore*)

Table A6.4 Trends in Total Investment by States and Union Territories

	Mar-96	Mar-97	Mar-98	Mar-99	Mar-00	Mar-01	Mar-02	Mar-03	Mar-04	Mar-05	Mar-06	Mar-07	Mar-08	Mar-09	Mar-10
Andhra Pradesh	97831	105294	117137	121404	152186	162926	130515	138977	152259	189311	249526	370088	538796	697997	809765
Arunachal Pradesh	3976	4078	4142	5342	5777	4310	2878	2852	11352	11205	11692	53088	92210	103929	111879
Assam	14063	18034	17321	16026	13894	11393	13081	13828	13746	15877	24844	40547	39160	41311	52952
Bihar	10550	19611	12539	13817	16827	10959	26174	26088	28146	29524	35849	46074	66586	103006	112588
Chhattisgarh	19311	20252	19326	21024	29748	22839	29399	41845	47815	65928	101135	157115	282438	360698	415128
Delhi	8696	9921	13584	15035	15573	13346	23902	25513	25486	30034	39150	55248	94904	112660	114470
Goa	6394	6044	8106	9744	8800	8380	8555	8493	6345	3093	2840	2959	2468	5493	8914
Gujarat	127687	129711	137617	157888	146943	172421	156981	139790	159726	176555	253974	439076	542206	1057465	1201815
Haryana	22251	19844	19789	17396	22636	24000	24379	28679	32203	38764	97524	234520	287250	313950	313573
Himachal Pradesh	23469	26492	24544	26096	27565	29023	27072	30757	36746	42118	48921	53254	56570	73261	78231
Jammu & Kashmir	9147	10480	14615	13780	14041	13720	18845	18313	22050	25252	30885	30558	43498	60320	80069
Jharkhand	21593	17232	23124	16844	29670	26367	25237	27106	40020	65924	228630	327091	363165	451486	531472
Karnataka	105423	133278	125530	119447	112601	136490	129720	127092	134021	163398	219348	255383	363179	490114	733375
Kerala	33665	44221	53353	60726	56425	47379	50699	68733	68399	75482	84412	92698	114650	160592	210340
Madhya Pradesh	90844	60263	54214	54125	49054	47241	50148	52812	53734	60731	97410	142690	228209	310666	371087
Maharashtra	123473	145670	159048	191111	185058	208653	211789	214377	218834	233834	288987	524693	662373	847750	1037644
Manipur	599	725	851	955	1108	1125	1234	6235	6308	6873	6968	9497	9697	14459	19320
Meghalaya	364	490	675	375	740	1033	827	740	924	888	1498	7857	9282	10577	11255
Mizoram	1412	1522	1522	1594	1506	2037	1831	1939	2633	2633	2633	2565	1486	1486	1851
Nagaland	389	497	670	650	887	217	278	274	314	240	243	754	754	1944	3704
Orissa	113354	121647	131069	127319	126738	113765	98116	61822	90334	229122	301527	480017	633744	917993	993029
Punjab	24555	30694	26644	28310	28373	33335	33339	32711	35253	34351	42662	61410	86997	149005	172226
Rajasthan	36727	37616	38593	42908	35693	38522	43137	42090	37720	42611	53287	70703	97068	189648	246815
Sikkim	4296	472	462	462	3186	6822	8182	7763	8416	15303	16663	22997	19927	19223	22321
Tamil Nadu	98565	125162	147247	171035	187846	181022	179553	176009	159608	172754	186901	262947	400894	574839	664101
Tripura	769	461	543	253	3453	5651	5379	5092	4642	8601	9630	10991	10087	10773	11910
Uttar Pradesh	74338	62449	61345	54318	53331	55517	58141	63370	64177	86375	92013	123583	207647	291723	410161
Uttarakhand	19490	16668	17424	17543	19450	19827	17316	22018	25007	33164	47402	55577	56702	96744	94038
West Bengal	67090	65211	62589	64484	64959	59600	61537	75499	89996	115215	130471	282310	460976	550283	579479
Union Territories	*1572*	*1337*	*1487*	*1460*	*1121*	*1805*	*2425*	*3219*	*2156*	*2320*	*1959*	*5315*	*29841*	*33214*	*29575*
Andaman & Nicobar	73	80	80	65	77	77	69	32	32	17	17	17	17	596	1046
Chandigarh	82	129	116	214	454	670	1275	1684	882	916	880	4443	25923	25657	24954
Dadra & Nagar Haveli	1251	852	1049	999	413	857	1013	1394	1146	1145	734	483	1564	4405	1285
Daman & Diu	167	275	241	178	175	177	44	88	72	215	301	346	2331	2550	2273
Lakshadweep				4	4	24	24	21	24	27	27	27	6	6	18
Puducherry	2332	2125	2970	1136	1168	1463	2183	2095	2579	2481	4756	4719	4380	4483	11658
Unallocated	27172	9927	8451	3928	3748	7003	6529	6032	16765	7380	18864	20119	35813	45397	64060
Multi-states	45252	68991	70033	76319	96236	157508	179954	152335	177410	201191	243992	334944	468079	777202	952416
India	1236648	1316417	1376564	1452853	1516340	1625697	1629333	1624497	1775124	2188530	2976594	4581388	6311039	8879691	10471221

Source: CMIE, Monthly Review of Investment Projects, CapEX.

Note: Total Investment covers projects announced and proposed and those under implementation.

Table A6.5 Trends in Investments under Implementation by States and Union Territories

(Rupees crore)

	Mar-96	Mar-97	Mar-98	Mar-99	Mar-00	Mar-01	Mar-02	Mar-03	Mar-04	Mar-05	Mar-06	Mar-07	Mar-08	Mar-09	Mar-10
Andhra Pradesh	51654	71520	74530	69024	73207	80785	90475	85294	84985	103324	136358	168441	193537	336609	467113
Arunachal Pradesh	2476	2479	2556	3702	3905	4042	2792	2816	2803	2656	2656	2656	34557	30985	47532
Assam	12062	16191	16138	13284	10428	10579	11840	12866	12769	12883	18285	26683	25007	27201	35882
Bihar	4651	6369	7197	9013	8795	8988	25604	25272	27128	28515	27681	30291	31202	36337	55581
Chhattisgarh	12829	18361	15470	16754	25718	19066	21707	27882	29021	33559	38566	43838	59321	108532	172332
Delhi	7569	6151	6400	7109	7747	9764	20847	22347	21334	25917	26964	30871	67047	82244	69792
Goa	2554	2441	1170	2086	1780	1714	1662	1864	1947	1111	848	1107	955	1590	2641
Gujarat	84188	94572	90521	101650	98730	113419	115905	90772	95966	114619	147501	209703	240602	318692	484428
Haryana	14897	11100	12568	14598	18763	17624	16631	21508	23066	32574	47459	165720	183605	204795	227492
Himachal Pradesh	17236	21757	20182	23664	22685	24751	25004	27388	27597	28405	30710	30242	32974	44093	44185
Jammu & Kashmir	6770	7332	12178	11347	11576	13090	17549	15168	18804	20631	25206	20886	18918	25612	40741
Jharkhand	9567	8403	13404	6553	16999	20864	21195	19754	21499	32163	55045	90611	120352	140535	172751
Karnataka	55377	89291	90511	80743	69274	98996	101187	88378	86820	96775	100760	157975	188000	200942	254255
Kerala	15766	21936	27864	21847	29808	28046	25486	33713	33055	45273	49355	52609	63196	71149	95532
Madhya Pradesh	40365	46802	43249	50429	41343	45361	45734	43652	45651	41011	45235	80719	88739	117839	165983
Maharashtra	68373	87009	102938	126549	129006	143145	148098	143459	137705	152387	170294	189758	253934	315895	626989
Manipur	599	710	710	814	967	1110	1211	5559	5559	6821	6821	9297	9397	14133	18865
Meghalaya	329	155	315	302	665	707	672	677	877	852	1208	2073	2318	3180	7450
Mizoram	1412	1522	1517	1594	1506	1053	1281	1389	2084	1617	1617	298	228	228	228
Nagaland	365	419	607	612	813	94	129	129	41	88	88	3	3	555	565
Orissa	34976	66333	54983	55161	47833	64613	56903	42447	52199	115365	130106	197866	228483	295286	430457
Punjab	10605	11620	9236	23288	23197	25688	25962	21136	19886	20303	27930	41077	45639	80635	115184
Rajasthan	23980	27202	23756	24088	26443	23973	30317	24530	24834	22911	35227	40819	46416	71412	94212
Sikkim	296	472	462	462	3186	6822	6882	6246	6599	12943	13961	17396	14448	13826	14054
Tamil Nadu	54649	56076	60557	78311	104364	111555	129044	91983	75150	85802	94611	123500	139856	229793	308496
Tripura	367	355	365	121	116	2292	2132	1916	1234	1693	1847	7895	8036	8165	8934
Uttar Pradesh	43050	47287	35077	31735	34770	38344	39451	43332	44124	64066	63481	75640	93141	149835	199157
Uttarakhand	12911	11532	12936	13279	16661	16522	17304	17036	20858	24807	30583	28184	30080	29693	32902
West Bengal	40194	37183	36315	32784	33683	34007	38996	42294	46078	48562	62989	108474	175326	215932	277610
Union Territories	*3262*	*3105*	*3031*	*1154*	*848*	*1246*	*2773*	*3632*	*2849*	*2927*	*3770*	*3791*	*20162*	*22750*	*32160*
Andaman & Nicobar	73	65	65	65	77	77	69	32	32	17	0	17	17	96	96
Chandigarh	72	129	79	79	264	260	865	1422	568	702	602	1351	17923	20412	23294
Dadra & Nagar Haveli	1042	781	660	798	271	521	817	1198	941	1010	618	195	68	99	610
Daman & Diu	106	163	133	74	7	6	12	62	40	33	240	206	215	206	144
Lakshadweep				4	4	24	24	21	24	24	24	3	3	3	18
Puducherry	1970	1967	2094	135	226	359	986	898	1244	1141	2287	2019	1937	1935	7998
Multi-states	31802	53859	48816	53687	56492	107045	133147	118267	126051	149384	160220	168416	182847	318646	529282
Unallocated	0	0	0	0	0	9	9	18	18	18	33	253	253	33	2333
India	665127	829545	825560	875747	921307	1075316	1177929	1082726	1098593	1329964	1557417	2127091	2598579	3517153	5035118

Source: CMIE, Monthly Review of Investment Projects, CapEX.

Table A6.6 Rate of Implementation (Investments under Implementation Represented as per cent of Total Investment)

(Rupees crore)

	Mar-96	Mar-97	Mar-98	Mar-99	Mar-00	Mar-01	Mar-02	Mar-03	Mar-04	Mar-05	Mar-06	Mar-07	Mar-08	Mar-09	Mar-10
Andhra Pradesh	52.8	67.9	63.6	56.9	48.1	49.6	69.3	61.4	55.8	54.6	54.6	45.5	35.9	48.2	57.7
Arunachal Pradesh	62.3	60.8	61.7	69.3	67.6	93.8	97.0	98.7	24.7	23.7	22.7	5.0	37.5	29.8	42.5
Assam	85.8	89.8	93.2	82.9	75.1	92.9	90.5	93.0	92.9	81.1	73.6	65.8	63.9	65.8	67.8
Bihar	44.1	32.5	57.4	65.2	52.3	82.0	97.8	96.9	96.4	96.6	77.2	65.7	46.9	35.3	49.4
Chhattisgarh	66.4	90.7	80.0	79.7	86.5	83.5	73.8	66.6	60.7	50.9	38.1	27.9	21.0	30.1	41.5
Delhi	87.0	62.0	47.1	47.3	49.7	73.2	87.2	87.6	83.7	86.3	68.9	55.9	70.6	73.0	61.0
Goa	39.9	40.4	14.4	21.4	20.2	20.5	19.4	21.9	30.7	35.9	29.8	37.4	38.7	28.9	29.6
Gujarat	65.9	72.9	65.8	64.4	67.2	65.8	73.8	64.9	60.1	64.9	58.1	47.8	44.4	30.1	40.3
Haryana	66.9	55.9	63.5	83.9	82.9	73.4	68.2	75.0	71.6	84.0	48.7	70.7	63.9	65.2	72.5
Himachal Pradesh	73.4	82.1	82.2	90.7	82.3	85.3	92.4	89.0	75.1	67.4	62.8	56.8	58.3	60.2	56.5
Jammu & Kashmir	74.0	70.0	83.3	82.3	82.4	95.4	93.1	82.8	85.3	81.7	81.6	68.4	43.5	42.5	50.9
Jharkhand	44.3	48.8	58.0	38.9	57.3	79.1	84.0	72.9	53.7	48.8	24.1	27.7	33.1	31.1	32.5
Karnataka	52.5	67.0	72.1	67.6	61.5	72.5	78.0	69.5	64.8	59.2	45.9	61.9	51.8	41.0	34.7
Kerala	46.8	49.6	52.2	36.0	52.8	59.2	50.3	49.1	48.3	60.0	58.5	56.8	55.1	44.3	45.4
Madhya Pradesh	44.4	77.7	79.8	93.2	84.3	96.0	91.2	82.7	85.0	67.5	46.4	56.6	38.9	37.9	44.7
Maharashtra	55.4	59.7	64.7	66.2	69.7	68.6	69.9	66.9	62.9	65.2	58.9	36.2	38.3	37.3	60.4
Manipur	100.0	97.9	83.4	85.2	87.3	98.7	98.1	89.2	88.1	99.2	97.9	97.9	96.9	97.7	97.6
Meghalaya	90.4	31.7	46.7	80.5	89.9	68.4	81.3	91.5	94.9	95.9	80.6	26.4	25.0	30.1	66.2
Mizoram	100.0	100.0	99.7	100.0	100.0	51.7	70.0	71.7	79.1	61.4	61.4	11.6	15.3	15.3	12.3
Nagaland	93.9	84.3	90.6	94.2	91.7	43.5	46.4	47.2	13.1	36.7	36.2	0.4	0.4	28.6	15.3
Orissa	30.9	54.5	41.9	43.3	37.7	56.8	58.0	68.7	57.8	50.4	43.1	41.2	36.1	32.2	43.3
Punjab	43.2	37.9	34.7	82.3	81.8	77.1	77.9	64.6	56.4	59.1	65.5	66.9	52.5	54.1	66.9
Rajasthan	65.3	72.3	61.6	56.1	74.1	62.2	70.3	58.3	65.8	53.8	66.1	57.7	47.8	37.7	38.2
Sikkim	6.9	100.0	100.0	100.0	100.0	100.0	84.1	80.5	78.4	84.6	83.8	75.6	72.5	71.9	63.0
Tamil Nadu	55.4	44.8	41.1	45.8	55.6	61.6	71.9	52.3	47.1	49.7	50.6	47.0	34.9	40.0	46.5
Tripura	47.8	77.0	67.2	47.8	3.3	40.6	39.6	37.6	26.6	19.7	19.2	71.8	79.7	75.8	75.0
Uttar Pradesh	57.9	75.7	57.2	58.4	65.2	69.1	67.9	68.4	68.8	74.2	69.0	61.2	44.9	51.4	48.6
Uttarakhand	66.2	69.2	74.2	75.7	85.7	83.3	99.9	77.4	83.4	74.8	64.5	50.7	53.0	30.7	35.0
West Bengal	59.9	57.0	58.0	50.8	51.9	57.1	63.4	56.0	51.2	42.1	48.3	38.4	38.0	39.2	47.9
Union Territories	**83.5**	**89.7**	**68.0**	**44.5**	**37.0**	**38.1**	**60.2**	**68.4**	**60.2**	**61.0**	**56.1**	**37.8**	**58.9**	**60.3**	**78.0**
Andaman & Nicobar	100.0	81.3	81.3	100.0	100.0	100.0	100.0	100.0	100.0	100.0	0.0	100.0	100.0	16.0	9.1
Chandigarh	87.8	100.0	67.8	36.8	58.1	38.8	67.8	84.4	64.4	76.7	68.3	30.4	69.1	79.6	93.3
Dadra & Nagar Haveli	83.3	91.6	62.9	79.9	65.8	60.8	80.6	85.9	82.1	88.2	84.2	40.3	4.3	2.2	47.5
Daman & Diu	63.4	59.1	55.4	41.3	3.8	3.2	26.4	70.5	55.7	15.2	79.7	59.6	9.2	8.1	6.4
Lakshadweep				100.0	100.0	100.0	100.0	100.0	100.0	87.2	87.2	9.2	41.7	41.7	100.0
Puducherry	84.5	92.6	70.5	11.9	19.4	24.5	45.2	42.9	48.2	46.0	48.1	42.8	44.2	43.2	68.6
Multi-states	70.3	78.1	69.7	70.3	58.7	68.0	74.0	77.6	71.1	74.2	65.7	50.3	39.1	41.0	55.6
Unallocated	0.0	0.0	0.0	0.0	0.0	0.1	0.1	0.3	0.1	0.2	0.2	1.3	0.7	0.1	3.6
India	**53.8**	**63.0**	**60.0**	**60.3**	**60.8**	**66.1**	**72.3**	**66.6**	**61.9**	**60.8**	**52.3**	**46.4**	**41.2**	**39.6**	**48.1**

Source: CMIE, Monthly Review of Investment Projects, CapEX.

A7 PRICES

Table A7.1 Wholesale Price Index: Point-to-Point and Average Annual Changes

Year	Point-to-point (Mar–Mar)				Average			
	All Commodities	Annual Change (per cent)	Food Index	Annual Change (per cent)	All Commodities	Annual Change (per cent)	Food Index	Annual Change (per cent)
Base Year 1993–4 = 100								
2009–10								
2008–9	228.2	1.2	233.5	8.1	233.9	8.3	226.8	8.8
2007–8	225.5	7.5	216.0	7.1	215.9	4.7	208.4	5.0
2006–7	209.8	6.6	201.7	8.2	206.2	5.4	198.5	5.9
2005–6	196.8	3.9	186.5	3.6	195.6	4.4	187.4	3.3
2004–5	189.4	5.3	180.1	3.0	187.3	6.5	181.4	3.5
2003–4	179.8	4.8	174.9	3.6	175.9	5.5	175.2	4.3
2002–3	171.6	6.0	168.8	3.7	166.8	3.4	167.9	2.9
2001–2	161.9	1.8	162.7	3.1	161.3	3.6	163.2	4.1
2000–1	159.1	6.4	157.8	−1.7	155.7	7.2	156.7	0.6
1999–00	149.5	5.6	160.6	4.4	145.3	3.2	155.7	1.0
1998–9	141.6	5.4	153.8	9.6	140.7	6.0	154.2	11.9
1997–8	134.4	4.3	140.3	3.9	132.8	4.3	137.8	4.1
1996–7	128.8	5.4	135.0	12.2	127.2	4.7	132.4	7.8
1995–6	122.2	4.5	120.3	5.4	121.6	7.8	122.8	6.5
1994–5	116.9	16.9	114.1	14.1	112.8	12.8	115.3	15.3
Base Year 1981–2 = 100								
1994–5	284.9	10.6	298.9	10.7	274.7	10.9	297.2	9.9
1993–4	257.6	10.5	270.0	5.2	247.8	8.4	270.5	6.6
1992–3	233.1	7.1	256.8	7.3	228.6	10.0	253.7	10.9
1991–2	217.7	13.6	239.4	17.3	207.8	13.7	228.8	18.2
1990–1	191.7	12.7	204.0	17.9	182.7	10.3	193.6	11.2
1989–90	170.1	8.6	173.1	5.1	165.7	7.4	174.1	4.7
1988–9	156.6	5.5	164.7	4.4	154.3	7.5	166.3	8.3
1987–8	148.5	10.7	157.7	13.9	143.6	8.2	153.5	8.9
1986–7	134.2	5.3	138.6	7.8	132.7	5.8	140.9	10.2
1985–6	127.4	5.1	128.5	5.2	125.4	4.4	127.9	2.2
1984–5	121.2	5.6	122.2	2.3	120.1	6.5	125.2	4.5
1983–4	114.8	7.2	119.4	9.5	112.8	7.5	119.8	12.2
1982–3	107.1	7.1	109.0	9.0	104.9	4.9	106.8	6.8
Base Year 1970–1 = 100								
1982–3	294.3	6.5	257.8	7.9	288.7	2.6	252.3	−1.0
1981–2	276.4	2.6	238.8	−2.6	281.3	9.3	254.8	6.5
1980–1	269.5	15.9	245.1	16.9	257.3	18.2	239.2	22.3
1979–80	232.6	23.1	209.7	27.2	217.6	17.1	195.6	16.9
1978–9	189.0	3.3	164.9	−1.9	185.8	0.0	167.4	−5.5
1977–8	182.9	0.0	168.1	−2.5	185.8	5.2	177.1	7.0
1976–7	182.9	12.5	172.4	18.6	176.6	2.1	165.5	−2.2

(*Continued*)

Table A 7.1 *Continued*

Year	Point-to-point (Mar–Mar)				Average			
	All Commodities	Annual Change (per cent)	Food Index	Annual Change (per cent)	All Commodities	Annual Change (per cent)	Food Index	Annual Change (per cent)
1975–6	162.6	−6.9	145.4	−15.9	173.0	−1.1	169.3	−4.2
1974–5	174.6	10.9	172.9	11.7	174.9	25.2	176.6	19.7
1973–4	157.5	29.2	154.8	20.8	139.7	20.2	147.5	19.9
1972–3	121.9	12.8	128.2	16.4	116.2	10.0	123.0	15.8
1971–2	108.1	8.2	110.1	10.1	105.6	5.6	106.3	6.3
Base Year 1961–2 = 100								
1971–2	192.2	5.8	216.2	7.3	188.4	4.0	210.0	2.9
1970–1	181.6	3.2	201.4	0.8	181.1	5.5	204.0	3.6
1969–70	175.9	6.7	199.8	7.3	171.6	3.7	197.0	0.0
1968–9	164.8	3.2	186.2	−3.5	165.4	−1.1	197.0	−5.3
1967–8	159.7	0.2	192.9	2.3	167.3	11.6	208.0	21.6
1966–7	159.4	16.5	188.6	26.5	149.9	13.9	171.0	17.9
1965–6	136.8	11.6	149.1	12.3	131.6	7.6	145.0	8.9
1964–5	122.6	8.2	132.8	10.5	122.3	11.0	133.1	16.9
1963–4	113.3	8.5	120.2	15.4	110.2	6.2	113.9	8.5
1962–3	104.4	4.4	104.2	4.2	103.8	3.8	105.0	5.0
Base Year 1952–3 = 100								
1962–3	127.1	2.9	123.4	3.6	127.9	2.2	126.1	5.0
1961–2	123.5	−3.1	119.1	1.4	125.1	0.2	120.1	0.1
1960–1	127.5	7.2	117.5	0.4	124.9	6.7	120.0	0.6
1959–60	118.9	5.8	117.0	2.8	117.1	3.7	119.3	3.6
1958–9	112.4	6.6	113.8	11.2	112.9	4.2	115.2	8.3
1957–8	105.4	−0.2	102.3	0.0	108.4	2.9	106.4	4.0
1956–7	105.6	7.6	102.3	10.2	105.3	13.8	102.3	18.5
1955–6	98.1	8.0	92.8	11.9	92.5	3.2	86.3	5.1
1954–5	90.8	−9.5	82.9	−15.9	89.6	−11.5	82.1	−18.0
1953–4	100.3	0.3	98.6	0.3	101.2	1.2	100.1	0.1
Base Year August 1939 = 100								
1952–3	385.2		365.0		380.6	−12.4	351.3	−11.8
1951–2					434.6	6.1	398.3	−4.3
1950–1					409.7	-	416.4	-

Source: Office of the Economic Adviser, Ministry of Commerce and Industry, GOI.

Note: With effect from 17 October 2009 Office of the Economic Adviser discontinued dessimination of price data on a weekly basis and started giving monthly data from September. Hence in this table point-to-point basis has been worked out by using March data instead of end-March data for all the years.

Table A7.2   Cost of Living Indices

(A) Consumer Price Index for Industrial Workers

Year	Annual Average				Point-to-Point			
	Total Index	Annual Change (per cent)	Food Index	Annual Change (per cent)	Total Index	Annual Change (per cent)	Food Index	Annual Change (per cent)
(1)	(2)	(3)	(4)	(5)	(6)	(7)	(8)	(9)
Base Year 2001 = 100								
2008–9	145	9.0	153	12.5	148	8.0	156	10.6
2007–8	133	6.4	136	7.9	137	7.9	141	9.3
2006–7	125	6.7	126	na	127	6.7	129	na
2005–6	117	4.3	na	na	119	5.3	na	na
2004–5	112	3.9	na	na	113	3.7	na	na
Base Year 1982 = 100								
2004–5	520	3.9	506	2.2	525	4.2	502	1.6
2003–4	500	3.8	495	3.8	504	3.5	494	3.1
2002–3	482	4.1	477	7.0	487	4.1	479	3.7
2001–2	463	4.3	446	−1.5	468	5.2	462	3.6
2000–1	444	3.7	453	1.6	445	2.5	446	0.0
1999–00	428	3.4	446	0.2	434	4.8	446	0.2
1998–99	414	13.1	445	14.7	414	8.9	445	11.0
1997–8	366	7.0	388	5.1	380	8.3	401	7.5
1996–7	342	9.3	369	9.5	351	10.0	373	10.0
1995–6	313	12.2	337	13.5	319	8.9	339	9.0
1994–5	279	8.1	297	9.2	293	9.7	311	10.7
1993–4	258	7.5	272	7.1	267	9.9	281	11.1
1992–3	240	9.6	254	10.4	243	6.1	253	5.0
1991–2	219	13.5	230	15.6	229	13.9	241	16.4
1990–1	193	11.6	199	12.4	201	13.6	207	16.3
1989–00	173	6.1	177	4.7	177	8.6	178	5.3
1988–9	163	9.4	169	11.2	163	6.5	169	8.3
1987–8	149	8.8	152	7.8	153	10.9	156	9.9
1986–7	137	8.7	141	10.2	138	6.2	142	7.6
1985–6	126	6.8	128	4.9	130	8.3	132	10.0
1984–5	118	6.3	122	4.3	120	5.3	120	2.6
1983–4	111	11.0	117	17.0	114	14.0	117	17.0
Base Year 1960 =100								
1983–4	547	12.6	581	14.4	558	11.2	583	11.7
1982–3	486	7.8	508	6.7	502	9.8	522	9.9
1981–2	451	12.5	476	13.6	457	8.8	475	8.7
1980–1	401	11.4	419	12.3	420	12.6	437	13.5
1979–80	360	8.8	373	7.8	373	12.3	385	12.9
1978–9	331	2.2	346	0.3	332	3.4	341	1.5
1977–8	324	7.6	345	8.8	321	2.9	336	1.2
1976–7	301	−3.8	317	−7.3	312	9.1	332	12.2
1975–6	313	−1.3	342	−4.5	286	−10.9	296	−17.5

(*Continued*)

Table A7.2 *Continued*

(A) Consumer Price Index for Industrial Workers

Year	Annual Average				Point-to-Point			
	Total Index	Annual Change (per cent)	Food Index	Annual Change (per cent)	Total Index	Annual Change (per cent)	Food Index	Annual Change (per cent)
(1)	(2)	(3)	(4)	(5)	(6)	(7)	(8)	(9)
1974–5	317	26.8	358	28.3	321	16.7	359	17.7
1973–4	250	20.8	279	25.1	275	27.3	305	29.2
1972–3	207	7.8	223	8.8	216	11.3	236	15.1
1971–2	192	3.2	205	1.5	194	5.4	205	5.1
1970–1	186	5.1	202	4.7	184	2.8	195	0.5
1969–70	177	1.7	193	0.5	179	5.3	194	6.0
1968–9	174	−18.3	192	−15.8	170		183	
Base Year 1949 = 100								
1968–9	212	−0.5	223	−2.2	207	−2.8	212	−6.2
1967–8	213	11.5	228	15.2	213	6.5	226	7.6
1966–7	191	13.0	198	13.8	200	14.9	210	18.6
1965–6	169	7.6	174	7.4	174	9.4	177	9.3
1964–5	157	14.6	162	17.4	159	11.2	162	13.3
1963–4	137	4.6	138	5.3	143	6.7	143	5.9
1962–3	131	3.1	131	4.0	134	2.3	135	3.8
1961–2	127	2.4	126	0.0	131	4.0	130	3.2
1960–1	124	0.8	126	0.8	126	1.6	126	0.0
1959–60	123	4.2	125	5.9	124	2.5	126	0.8
1958–9	118	5.4	118	5.4	121	4.3	125	5.9
1957–8	112	4.7	112	6.7	116	4.5	118	5.4
1956–7	107	11.5	105	14.1	111	5.7	112	6.7
1955–6	96	−3.0	92	−8.9	105	9.4	105	14.1
1954–5	99	−6.6	101	−7.3	96	−5.0	92	−8.9
1953–4	106	1.9	109	na	101	−2.9	101	−3.8
1952–3	104	−1.0	na	na	104	6.1	105	na
1951–2	105	4.0	na	na	98	−4.9	na	na
1950–1	101	na	na	na	103	na	na	na

Source: Various Issues of *Economic Survey* (GOI), *RBI Bulletin*, and *Indian Labour Journal*.

Note: na: Not available.

Table A7.2 *Continued*

	(B) Consumer Price Index for Urban Non-manual Employees				(C) Consumer Price Index for Agricultural Laboureres								
	Annual Average		Point-to-Point			Annual Average*				Point-to-Point**			
	Total Index	Annual change (per cent)	Total Index	Annual change (per cent)		Total Index	Annual Change (per cent)	Food Index	Annual Change (per cent)	Total Index	Annual Change (per cent)	Food Index	Annual Change (per cent)
	(10)	(11)	(12)	(13)	(14)	(15)	(16)	(17)	(18)	(19)	(20)	(21)	(22)
	Base Year 1984–85 = 100					Base Year 1986–87 = 100							
2008–9	561.0	8.9	577.0	9.3	2008–9	450.0	10.0	451.8	11.2	463.0	9.5	463.0	9.7
2007–8	515.0	6.0	528.0	6.0	2007–8	409.0	7.6	406.4	8.2	423.0	7.9	422.0	8.5
2006–7	486.0	6.5	498.0	7.6	2006–7	380.0	6.1	375.6	7.0	392.0	5.9	389.0	6.9
2005–6	456.3	4.8	463.0	4.8	2005–6	358.1	4.7	351.1	4.9	370.0	7.2	364.0	8.3
2004–5	435.6	3.7	441.0	3.7	2004–5	341.9	2.9	334.7	2.8	345.0	2.7	336.0	2.1
2003–4	420.3	3.7	424.0	3.7	2003–4	332.3	3.0	325.6	3.0	336.0	1.8	329.0	1.5
2002–3	405.0	3.8	410.0	3.8	2002–3	322.6	3.8	316.2	4.0	330.0	5.1	324.0	5.9
2001–2	390.0	5.1	395.0	4.8	2001–2	310.8	2.2	304.0	1.6	314.0	2.6	306.0	2.3
2000–1	371.0	5.4	377.0	5.6	2000–1	304.0	−1.7	299.1	−4.7	306.0	−1.3	299.0	−3.5
1999–2000	352.0	3.5	357.0	5.9	1999–2000	309.2	3.5	313.8	2.8	310.0	3.0	310.0	1.3
1998–99	340.0	12.6	337.0	8.0	1998–9	298.7	11.1	305.2	13.3	301.0	6.7	306.0	7.0
1997–8	302.0	6.7	312.0	7.2	1997–8	268.8	3.5	269.3	2.1	282.0	8.9	286.0	10.9
1996–7	283.0	9.3	291.0	10.2	1996–7	259.8	8.6	263.7	9.3	259.0	4.9	258.0	3.2
1995–6	259.0	11.6	264.0	8.2	1995–6	239.3	na	241.3	na	247.0	na	250.0	na
1994–5	232.0	7.4	244.0	9.9		Base Year 1960 = 100							
1993–4	216.0	6.9	222.0	8.3	1995–6	1381.0	7.6	na	na	1337.0	0.0	na	na
1992–3	202.0	10.4	205.0	6.8	1994–5	1283.0	11.9	na	na	1337.0	12.4	na	na
1991–2	183.0	13.7	192.0	13.6	1993–4	1147.0	6.9	na	na	1189.0	12.5	na	na
1990–1	161.0	11.0	169.0	13.4	1992–3	1073.0	6.6	na	na	1057.0	−1.0	na	na
1989–90	145.0	6.6	149.0	8.0	1991–2	1007.0	21.3	na	na	1068.0	21.9	na	na
1988–9	136.0	7.9	138.0	7.0	1990–1	830.0	10.4	na	na	876.0	15.4	na	na
1987–8	126.0	9.6	129.0	10.3	1989–90	752.0	3.9	na	na	759.0	3.1	na	na
1986–7	115.0	7.5	117.0	6.4	1988–9	724.0	11.4	na	na	736.0	9.7	na	na
1985–6	107.0	7.0	110.0	10.0	1987–8	650.0	12.5	na	na	671.0	14.1	na	na
	Base Year 1960 = 100				1986–7	578.0	4.1	na	na	588.0	4.8	na	na
1985–6	568.0	6.8	584.0	8.1	1985–6	555.0	5.7	na	na	561.0	5.8	na	na
1984–5	532.0	8.1	540.0	6.9	1984–5	525.0	0.4	na	na	530.0	3.7	na	na
1983–4	492.0	10.3	505.0	9.3	1983–4	523.0	8.7	na	na	511.0	0.4	na	na
1982–3	446.0	8.0	462.0	9.2	1982–3	481.0	7.4	na	na	509.0	14.9	na	na
1981–2	413.0	11.9	423.0	9.9	1981–2	448.0	9.5	na	na	443.0	3.3	na	na
1980–1	369.0	11.8	385.0	12.2	1980–1	409.0	13.6	na	na	429.0	14.1	na	na
1979–80	330.0	7.8	343.0	11.4	1979–80	360.0	13.6	na	na	376.0	18.2	na	na
1978–9	306.0	3.4	308.0	3.7	1978–9	317.0	−1.9	na	na	318.0	1.9	na	na
1977–8	296.0	6.9	297.0	4.2	1977–8	323.0	7.0	na	na	312.0	−2.2	na	na
1976–7	277.0	0.0	285.0	7.5	1976–7	302.0	−4.7	na	na	319.0	13.9	na	na
1975–6	277.0	2.6	265.0	−4.3	1975–6	317.0	−13.9	na	na	280.0	−25.3	na	na
1974–5	270.0	22.2	277.0	16.4	1974–5	368.0	30.0	na	na	375.0	16.8	na	na
1973–4	221.0	15.1	238.0	19.6	1973–4	283.0	25.8	na	na	321.0	32.6	na	na
1972–3	192.0	6.7	199.0	8.2	1972–3	225.0	12.5	na	na	242.0	18.6	na	na
1971–2	180.0	3.4	184.0	5.7	1971–2	200.0	4.2	na	na	204.0	7.9	na	na
1970–1	174.0	4.2	174.0	2.4	1970–1	192.0	−0.5	na	na	189.0	−3.6	na	na
1969–70	167.0	3.7	170.0	5.6	1969–70	193.0	4.3	na	na	196.0	5.4	na	na
1968–9	161.0	1.3	161.0	1.3	1968–9	185.0	−10.2	na	na	186.0	−2.6	na	na
1967–8	159.0	8.9	159.0	5.3	1967–8	206.0	8.4	na	na	191.0	−7.7	na	na
1966–7	146.0	10.6	151.0	11.9	1966–7	190.0	24.2	na	na	207.0	32.7	na	na
1965–6	132.0	6.5	135.0		1965–6	153.0	7.0	na	na	156.0		na	na
1964–5	124.0				1964–5	143.0		na	na	na		na	na

Notes: Current series with base 1984–5 = 100 was introduced w.e.f. November 1987.

The conversion factor from the new to the old series is 5.32.

* Averages based on agricultural year, i.e., July–June of every year; ** June over June. na: Not available.

The base is revised to 1986–7 w.e.f. November 1995.

Though the base of the series is 1960–1, the indices are available from September 1964 only.

A8 BALANCE OF PAYMENTS

Table A8.1 Foreign Exchange Reserves (End Period)

End of	SDRs			Gold		Foreign Currency Assets		Reserve Tranche Position in IMF		Total	
	In million SDRs	Rupees crore	In million US$	Rupees crore	In million US$	Rupees crore	In million US$	Rupees crore	In million US$	Rupees crore	In million US$
(1)	(2)	(3)	(4)	(5)	(6)	(7)	(8)	(9)	(10)	(11)	(12)
2009–10											
Mar-10											
Feb-10	3297	23360	5053	82845	17920	1174202	253991	6441	1393	1286848	278357
Jan-10	3297	23762	5124	83724	18056	1188753	256362	6554	1413	1302793	280955
Dec-09	3297	24128	5169	85387	18292	1207065	258583	6655	1426	1323235	283470
Nov-09	3297	24676	5309	84508	18162	1223313	263191	6806	1464	1339303	288146
Oct-09	3297	24618	5242	50718	10800	1252740	266768	6557	1581	1335502	284391
Sep-09	3297	25096	4828	49556	10316	1270049	264373	6595	1365	1351258	281278
Aug-09	3083	23597	4821	48041	9828	1276976	261247	6444	1349	1355209	277245
July-09	0	3	1	46576	9671	1255197	260631	5974	1338	1308220	271641
June-09	0	2	1	46914	9800	1216345	254093	5886	1248	1269235	265142
May-09	0	2	1	45417	9604	1189136	251456	4938	1245	1240441	262306
April-09	1	6	1	46357	9231	1212747	241487	5000	983	1264048	251702
2008–9(p)	1	6	1	48793	9577	1228792	241476	5000	981	1282591	251735
2007–8	11	74	18	40124	10039	1196023	299230	1744	436	1237965	309723
2006–7	1	8	2	29573	6784	836597	191924	2044	469	868222	199179
2005–6	2	12	3	25674	5755	647327	145108	3374	756	676387	151622
2004–5	3	20	5	19686	4500	593121	135571	6289	1438	619116	141514
2003–4	2	10	2	18216	4198	466215	107448	5688	1311	490129	112959
2002–3	3	19	4	16785	3534	341476	71890	3190	672	361470	76100
2001–2	8	50	10	14868	3047	249118	51049			264036	54106
2000–1	2	11	2	12711	2725	184482	39554			197204	42281
1999–2000	3	16	4	12973	2974	152924	35058			165913	38036
1998–9	6	34	8	12559	2960	125412	29522			138005	32490
1997–8	1	4	1	13394	3391	102507	25975			115905	29367
1996–7	1	7	2	14557	4054	80368	22367			94932	26423
1995–6	56	280	82	15658	4561	58446	17044			74384	21687
1994–5	5	23	7	13752	4370	66006	20809			79781	25186
1993–4	76	339	108	12794	4078	47287	15068			60420	19254
1992–3	13	55	18	10549	3380	20140	6434			30744	9832
1991–2	66	233	90	9039	3499	14578	5631			23850	9220
1990–1	76	200	102	6828	3496	4388	2236			11416	5834

Source: RBI, *Monthly Bulletin* (various issues).

Notes:
1. Gold was valued at Rs 84.39 per 10 grams till 16 October 1990. It has been valued close to international market price with effect from 17 October 1990.
2. Conversion of SDRs into US dollar is done at exchange rates released by the IMF.
3. With effect from 1 April 1991 the conversion of foreign currency assets into US dollar is done at weekend rates for weekend data and or month-end rate for month-end data based on New York closing exchange rates. Prior to that it was done by using representative exchange rate released by the IMF.
4. Since March 1993, foreign exchange holdings are converted into rupees at rupee–US dollar market exchange rates.
5. Reserve tranche position has been reported as part of reserves since 2002–3.

Table A8.2 Balance of Payments, 1990–1 to 2008–9

(US$ million)

Item	2008–9 (P)			2007–8 (PR)			2006–7			2005–6		
	Credit	Debt	Net	Credit	Debt	Net	Credit	Debt	Net	Credit	Debt	Net
(1)	(2)	(3)	(4)	(5)	(6)	(7)	(8)	(9)	(10)	(11)	(12)	(13)
A. Current Account												
1. Merchandise	175184	294587	–119403	166163	257789	–91626	128888	190670	–61782	105152	157056	–51904
2. Invisibles	162556	72970	89586	148604	74012	74592	114558	62341	52217	89687	47685	42002
a. Services	101224	51406	49818	90077	52512	37565	73780	44311	29469	57659	34489	23170
a1. Travel	10894	9432	1462	11349	9254	2095	9123	6684	2439	7853	6638	1215
a2. Transportation	11066	12777	–1711	10014	11514	–1500	7974	8068	–94	6325	8337	–2012
a3. Insurance	1409	1131	278	1639	1044	595	1195	642	553	1062	1116	–54
a4. G.n.i.e.	389	791	–402	330	376	–46	253	403	–150	314	529	–215
a5. Miscellaneous	77466	27275	50191	66745	30324	36421	55235	28514	26721	42105	17869	24236
of which: Software Services	47000	2814	44186	40300	3058	37242	31300	2267	29033	23600	1338	22262
Business Services	16251	15269	982	16771	16715	56	14544	15866	–1322	9307	7748	1559
Financial Services	3939	2961	978	3217	3138	79	3106	2991	115	1209	965	244
Communication Services	2170	996	1174	2408	859	1549	2262	796	1466	1575	289	1286
b. Transfers	47025	2746	44279	44259	2315	41944	31470	1391	30079	25620	933	24687
b1. Official	645	413	232	753	514	239	635	381	254	669	475	194
b2. Private	46380	2333	44047	43506	1801	41705	30835	1010	29825	24951	458	24493
c. Income	14307	18818	–4511	14268	19185	–4917	9308	16639	–7331	6408	12263	–5855
c1. Investment Income	13482	17499	–4017	13808	18089	–4281	8926	15688	–6762	6229	11491	–5262
c2. Compensation to Employees	825	1319	–494	460	1096	–636	382	951	–569	179	772	–593
Total Current Account (1+2)	337740	367557	–29817	314767	331801	–17034	243446	253011	–9565	194839	204741	–9902
B. Capital Account												
1. Foreign Investment (a+b)	164909	161447	3462	272762	227805	44957	133210	118457	14753	77298	61770	15528
a. In India	163659	142532	21127	270049	206419	63630	132360	102617	29743	77082	55687	21395
a1. Direct	35148	166	34982	34361	125	34236	22826	87	22739	8962	61	8901
a2. Portfolio	128511	142366	–13855	235688	206294	29394	109534	102530	7004	68120	55626	12494
b. Abroad	1250	18915	–17665	2713	21386	–18673	850	15840	–14990	216	6083	–5867
2. Loans (a+b+c)	60158	55157	5001	83528	41598	41930	54642	30152	24490	39479	31570	7909
a. External Assistance	5042	2404	2638	4241	2127	2114	3767	1992	1775	3631	1929	1702
a1. By India	24	32	–8	24	28	–4	20	32	–12	24	88	–64
a2. To India	5018	2372	2646	4217	2099	2118	3747	1960	1787	3607	1841	1766

(Continued)

Table A8.2 *Continued*

Item	2008–9 (P)			2007–8 (PR)			2006–7			2005–6		
	Credit	Debt	Net	Credit	Debt	Net	Credit	Debt	Net	Credit	Debt	Net
(1)	(2)	(3)	(4)	(5)	(6)	(7)	(8)	(9)	(10)	(11)	(12)	(13)
b. Commercial Borrowings(MT and LT)	15382	7224	8158	30376	7743	22633	20883	4780	16103	14343	11835	2508
b1. By India	2005	785	1220	1592	1624	−32	626	966	−340	0	251	−251
b2. To India	13377	6439	6938	28784	6119	22665	20257	3814	16443	14343	11584	2759
c. Short-term (to India)	39734	45529	−5795	48911	31728	17183	29992	23380	6612	21505	17806	3699
3. Banking Capital (a+b)	64998	68395	−3397	55813	44056	11757	37209	35296	1913	21658	20285	1373
a. Commercial Banks	64885	67810	−2925	55734	43624	12110	36799	35218	1581	20586	20144	442
a1. Assets	25673	28726	−3053	19562	12668	6894	14466	17960	−3494	772	3947	−3175
a2. Liabilities	39212	39084	128	36172	30956	5216	22333	17258	5075	19814	16197	3617
of which: Non-resident deposits	37089	32799	4290	29401	29222	179	19914	15593	4321	17835	15046	2789
b. Others	113	585	−472	79	432	−353	410	78	332	1072	141	931
4. Rupee Debt Service	0	101	−101	0	121	−121	0	162	−162	0	572	−572
5. Other Capital	12391	8210	4181	20904	11434	9470	8230	4021	4209	5941	4709	1232
Total Capital Account (1 to 5)	302456	293310	9146	433007	325014	107993	233291	188088	45203	144376	118906	25470
C. Errors and Omissions	591	0	591	1205	0	1205	968	0	968	0	516	−516
D. Overall Balance (A+B+C)	640787	660867	−20080	748979	656815	92164	477705	441099	36606	339215	324163	15052
E. Monetary Movements (1+2)	20080	0	20080	0	92164	−92164	0	36606	−36606	0	15052	−15052
1. IMF	0	0	0	0	0	0	0	0	0	0	0	0
2. Foreign Exchange Reserves	20080	0	20080	0	92164	−92164	0	36606	−36606	0	15052	−15052

(Continued)

Table A8.2 *Continued*

Item	2004–5			2003–4			2002–3			2001–2		
	Credit	Debt	Net	Credit	Debt	Net	Credit	Debt	Net	Credit	Debt	Net
(1)	(14)	(15)	(16)	(17)	(18)	(19)	(20)	(21)	(22)	(23)	(24)	(25)
A. Current Account												
1. Merchandise	85206	118908	–33702	66285	80003	–13718	53774	64464	–10690	44703	56277	–11574
2. Invisibles	69533	38301	31232	53508	25707	27801	41925	24890	17035	36737	21763	14974
a. Services	43249	27823	15426	26868	16724	10144	20763	17120	3643	17140	13816	3324
a1. Travel	6666	5249	1417	5037	3602	1435	3312	3341	–29	3137	3014	123
a2. Transportation	4683	4539	144	3207	2328	879	2536	3272	–736	2161	3467	–1306
a3. Insurance	870	722	148	419	363	56	369	350	19	288	280	8
a4. G.n.i.e.	401	411	–10	240	212	28	293	228	65	518	283	235
a5. Miscellaneous	30629	16902	13727	17965	10219	7746	14253	9929	4324	11036	6772	4264
of which: Software Services	17700	800	16900	12800	476	12324	9600	737	8863	7556	672	6884
Business Services												
Financial Services												
Communication Services												
b. Transfers	21691	906	20785	22736	574	22162	17640	802	16838	16218	362	15856
b1. Official	616	356	260	554	0	554	451	0	451	458	0	458
b2. Private	21075	550	20525	22182	574	21608	17189	802	16387	15760	362	15398
c. Income	4593	9572	–4979	3904	8409	–4505	3522	6968	–3446	3379	7585	–4206
c1. Investment Income	4124	8219	–4095	3774	7531	–3757	3405	6949	–3544	3254	7098	–3844
c2. Compensation to Employees	469	1353	–884	130	878	–748	117	19	98	125	487	–362
Total Current Account (1+2)	154739	157209	–2470	119793	105710	14083	95699	89354	6345	81440	78040	3400
B. Capital Account												
1. Foreign Investment (a+b)	46934	33934	13000	32682	18938	13744	14001	9840	4161	15488	8802	6686
a. In India	46899	31601	15298	32540	16862	15678	13928	7913	6015	15389	7243	8146
a1. Direct	6052	65	5987	4322	0	4322	5095	59	5036	6130	5	6125
a2. Portfolio	40847	31536	9311	28218	16862	11356	8833	7854	979	9259	7238	2021
b. Abroad	35	2333	–2298	142	2076	–1934	73	1927	–1854	99	1559	–1460
2. Loans (a+b+c)	30287	19378	10909	19667	24031	–4364	11568	15418	–3850	11601	12862	–1261
a. External Assistance	3809	1886	1923	3350	6208	–2858	2878	6006	–3128	3352	2235	1117
a1. By India	24	128	–104	24	128	–104	0	32	–32	0	87	–87
a2. To India	3785	1758	2027	3326	6080	–2754	2878	5974	–3096	3352	2148	1204

(*Continued*)

Table A8.2 Continued

Item	2004–5			2003–4			2002–3			2001–2		
	Credit	Debt	Net	Credit	Debt	Net	Credit	Debt	Net	Credit	Debt	Net
(1)	(14)	(15)	(16)	(17)	(18)	(19)	(20)	(21)	(22)	(23)	(24)	(25)
b. Commercial Borrowings (MT and LT)	9084	3890	5194	5228	8153	−2925	3514	5206	−1692	2687	4272	−1585
b1. By India	0	232	−232	3	0	3	9	0	9	3	0	3
b2. To India	9084	3658	5426	5225	8153	−2928	3505	5206	−1701	2684	4272	−1588
c. Short-term (to India)	17394	13602	3792	11089	9670	1419	5176	4206	970	5562	6355	−793
3. Banking Capital (a+b)	14581	10707	3874	19222	13189	6033	18958	8533	10425	13870	11006	2864
a. Commercial Banks	14304	10325	3979	18887	12386	6501	18422	8287	10135	13385	10725	2660
a1. Assets	505	552	−47	950	161	789	6089	976	5113	1267	1711	−444
a2. Liabilities	13799	9773	4026	17937	12225	5712	12333	7311	5022	12118	9014	3104
of which: Non-resident Deposits	8071	9035	−964	14281	10639	3642	10214	7236	2978	11435	8681	2754
b. Others	277	382	−105	335	803	−468	536	246	290	485	281	204
4. Rupee Debt Service	0	417	−417	0	376	−376	0	474	−474	0	519	−519
5. Other Capital	6737	6081	656	4314	2615	1699	1841	1263	578	2298	1517	781
Total Capital Account (1 to 5)	98539	70517	28022	75885	59149	16736	46368	35528	10840	43257	34706	8551
C. Errors and Omissions	607	0	607	602	0	602	0	200	−200	0	194	−194
D. Overall Balance (A+B+C)	253885	227726	26159	196280	164859	31421	142067	125082	16985	124697	112940	11757
E. Monetary Movements (1+2)	0	26159	−26159	0	31421	−31421	0	16985	−16985	0	11757	−11757
1. IMF	0	0	0	0	0	0	0	0	0	0	0	0
2. Foreign Exchange Reserves	0	26159	−26159	0	31421	−31421	0	16985	−16985	0	11757	−11757

(Continued)

Table A8.2 *Continued*

Item	2000–1			1999–2000			1998–9			1997–8		
	Credit	Debt	Net	Credit	Debt	Net	Credit	Debt	Net	Credit	Debt	Net
(1)	(26)	(27)	(28)	(29)	(30)	(31)	(32)	(33)	(34)	(35)	(36)	(37)
A. Current Account												
1. Merchandise	45452	57912	−12460	37542	55383	−17841	34298	47544	−13246	35680	51187	−15507
2. Invisibles	32267	22473	9794	30312	17169	13143	25770	16562	9208	23244	13237	10007
a. Services	16268	14576	1692	15709	11645	4064	13186	11021	2165	9429	8110	1319
a1. Travel	3497	2804	693	3036	2139	897	2993	1743	1250	2914	1437	1477
a2. Transportation	2046	3558	−1512	1707	2410	−703	1925	2680	−755	1836	2522	−686
a3. Insurance	270	223	47	231	122	109	224	112	112	240	183	57
a4. G.n.i.e.	651	319	332	582	270	312	597	325	272	276	160	116
a5. Miscellaneous	9804	7672	2132	10153	6704	3449	7447	6161	1286	4163	3808	355
of which: Software Services	6341	591	5750									
Business Services												
Financial Services												
Communication Services												
b. Transfers	13317	211	13106	12672	34	12638	10649	62	10587	12254	45	12209
b1. Official	252	0	252	382	0	382	308	1	307	379	0	379
b2. Private	13065	211	12854	12290	34	12256	10341	61	10280	11875	45	11830
c. Income	2682	7686	−5004	1931	5490	−3559	1935	5479	−3544	1561	5082	−3521
c1. Investment Income	2554	7218	−4664	1783	5478	−3695	1893	5462	−3569	1561	5020	−3459
c2. Compensation to Employees	128	468	−340	148	12	136	42	17	25	0	62	−62
Total Current Account (1+2)	77719	80385	−2666	67854	72552	−4698	60068	64106	−4038	58924	64424	−5500
B. Capital Account												
1. Foreign Investment (a+b)	17720	11858	5862	12240	7123	5117	5892	3580	2312	9266	3913	5353
a. In India	17650	10859	6791	12121	6930	5191	5743	3331	2412	9169	3779	5390
a1. Direct	4031	0	4031	2170	3	2167	2518	38	2480	3596	34	3562
a2. Portfolio	13619	10859	2760	9951	6927	3024	3225	3293	−68	5573	3745	1828
b. Abroad	70	999	−929	119	193	−74	149	249	−100	97	134	−37
2. Loans (a+b+c)	23806	18542	5264	13060	11459	1601	14771	10353	4418	17301	12502	4799
a. External Assistance	2941	2531	410	3074	2183	891	2726	1927	799	2885	2000	885
a1. By India	0	17	−17	0	10	−10	0	21	−21	0	22	−22
a2. To India	2941	2514	427	3074	2173	901	2726	1906	820	2885	1978	907

(Continued)

Table A8.2 Continued

Item	2000–1			1999–2000			1998–9			1997–8		
	Credit	Debt	Net	Credit	Debt	Net	Credit	Debt	Net	Credit	Debt	Net
(1)	(26)	(27)	(28)	(29)	(30)	(31)	(32)	(33)	(34)	(35)	(36)	(37)
b. Commercial Borrowings (MT and LT)	9621	5318	4303	3207	2874	333	7231	2864	4367	7382	3372	4010
b1. By India	0	5	–5	20	0	20	5	—	5	11	0	11
b2. To India	9621	5313	4308	3187	2874	313	7226	2864	4362	7371	3372	3999
c. Short-term (to India)	11244	10693	551	6779	6402	377	4814	5562	–748	7034	7130	–96
3. Banking Capital (a+b)	9744	11705	–1961	10659	8532	2127	8897	8199	698	8910	9803	–893
a. Commercial Banks	9423	11305	–1882	10259	7955	2304	7468	7916	–448	8164	9424	–1260
a1. Assets	206	4380	–4174	2653	1863	790	1344	2741	–1397	580	2775	–2195
a2. Liabilities	9217	6925	2292	7606	6092	1514	6124	5175	949	7584	6649	935
of which: Non-resident Deposits	8988	6672	2316	7405	5865	1540	6000	5040	960	7532	6407	1125
b. Others	321	400	–79	400	577	–177	1429	283	1146	746	379	367
4. Rupee Debt Service	0	617	–617	0	711	–711	0	802	–802	0	767	–767
5. Other Capital	2856	2564	292	4572	2262	2310	4610	2801	1809	3815	2463	1352
Total Capital Account (1 to 5)	54126	45286	8840	40531	30087	10444	34170	25735	8435	39292	29448	9844
C. Errors and Omissions	0	305	–305	656	0	656	0	175	–175	167	0	167
D. Overall Balance (A+B+C)	131845	125976	5869	109041	102639	6402	94238	90016	4222	98383	93872	4511
E. Monetary Movements (1+2)	1448	7316	–5868	0	6402	–6402	0	4222	–4222	0	4511	–4511
1. IMF	0	26	–26	0	260	–260	0	393	–393	0	618	–618
2. Foreign Exchange Reserves	1448	7290	–5842	0	6142	–6142	0	3829	–3829	0	3893	–3893

(Continued)

Table A8.2 *Continued*

Item	1996–7 Credit (38)	1996–7 Debt (39)	1996–7 Net (40)	1995–6 Credit (41)	1995–6 Debt (42)	1995–6 Net (43)	1994–5 Credit (44)	1994–5 Debt (45)	1994–5 Net (46)	1993–4 Credit (47)	1993–4 Debt (48)	1993–4 Net (49)
(1)												
A. Current Account												
1. Merchandise	34133	48948	–14815	32311	43670	–11359	26855	35904	–9049	22683	26739	–4056
2. Invisibles	21405	11209	10196	17676	12216	5460	15554	9874	5680	11319	8421	2898
a. Services	7474	6748	726	7342	7542	–186	6135	5533	602	5264	4729	535
a1. Travel	2878	858	2020	2711	1167	1544	2365	818	1547	2222	497	1725
a2. Transportation	1953	2394	–441	2010	2169	–159	1696	1863	–167	1433	1765	–332
a3. Insurance	217	153	64	178	142	36	152	181	–29	124	195	–71
a4. G.n.i.e.	72	178	–106	13	218	–205	10	165	–155	30	153	–123
a5. Miscellaneous	2354	3165	–811	2430	3846	–1416	1912	2506	–594	1455	2119	–664
of which: Software Services									0			
Business Services												
Financial Services												
Communication Services												
b. Transfers	12858	81	12777	8890	39	8851	8533	24	8509	5660	27	5633
b1. Official	423	13	410	351	6	345	421	5	416	373	5	368
b2. Private	12435	68	12367	8540	33	8507	8112	19	8093	5287	22	5265
c. Income	1073	4380	–3307	1429	4634	–3205	886	4317	–3431	395	3665	–3270
c1. Investment Income	1073	4380	–3307	1429	4633	–3204	886	4317	–3431	395	3665	–3270
c2. Compensation to Employees												
Total Current Account (1+2)	55538	60157	–4619	49987	55886	–5899	42409	45778	–3369	34002	35160	–1158
B. Capital Account												
1. Foreign Investment (a+b)	7824	1861	5963	5632	1028	4604	5763	956	4807	4611	376	4235
a. In India	7816	1663	6153	5618	824	4794	5753	831	4922	4611	376	4235
a1. Direct	2863	22	2841	2162	29	2133	1351	8	1343	651	65	586
a2. Portfolio	4953	1641	3312	3456	795	2661	4402	823	3579	3960	311	3649
b. Abroad	8	198	–190	14	204	–190	10	125	–115	0	0	0
2. Loans (a+b+c)	17720	12925	4795	11332	9131	2201	10930	7895	3035	9971	8159	1812
a. External Assistance	3056	1955	1101	2933	2066	867	3193	1675	1518	3476	1580	1896
a1. By India	0	8	–8	0	16	–16	2	10	–8	0	5	–5
a2. To India	3056	1947	1109	2933	2050	883	3191	1665	1526	3476	1575	1901

(Continued)

Table A8.2 *Continued*

Item	1996–7			1995–6			1994–5			1993–4		
	Credit	Debt	Net	Credit	Debt	Net	Credit	Debt	Net	Credit	Debt	Net
(1)	(38)	(39)	(40)	(41)	(42)	(43)	(44)	(45)	(46)	(47)	(48)	(49)
b. Commercial												
Borrowings (MT and LT)	7579	4723	2856	4262	2977	1285	4249	3125	1124	3015	2330	685
b1. By India	8	0	8	10	0	10	97	3	94	102	24	78
b2. To India	7571	4723	2848	4252	2977	1275	4152	3122	1030	2913	2306	607
c. Short-term (to India)	7085	6247	838	4137	4088	49	3488	3095	393	3480	4249	−769
3. Banking Capital (a+b)	8018	5789	2229	6453	5691	762	7020	7354	−334	11500	9237	2263
a. Commercial Banks	7632	5407	2225	6172	5235	937	6449	7075	−626	10614	8956	1658
a1. Assets	755	1625	−870	867	1251	−384	241	1203	−962	276	1120	−844
a2. Liabilities	6877	3782	3095	5305	3984	1321	6208	5872	336	10338	7836	2502
of which: Non-resident Deposits	6775	3425	3350	4929	3826	1103	5805	5633	172	8850	7645	1205
b. Others	386	382	4	281	456	−175	571	279	292	886	281	605
4. Rupee Debt Service	0	727	−727	0	952	−952	0	983	−983	0	1053	−1053
5. Other Capital	2629	2883	−254	748	3285	−2537	2201	224	1977	2873	1235	1638
Total Capital Account (1 to 5)	36191	24185	11881	24165	20087	4078	25914	17412	8502	28955	20060	8895
C. Errors and Omissions	0	594	−594	600	0	600	654	0	654	800	0	800
D. Overall Balance (A+B+C)	91729	84936	6793	74752	75973	−1221	68977	63190	5787	63757	55220	8537
E. Monetary Movements (1+2)	0	6793	−6793	2936	1715	1221	0	5787	−5787	321	8858	−8537
1. IMF	0	975	−975	0	1715	−1715	0	1143	−1143	321	134	187
2. Foreign Exchange Reserves	0	5818	−5818	2936	0	2936	0	4644	−4644	0	8724	−8724

(*Continued*)

Table A8.2 *Continued*

(1)	1992–3 Credit (50)	1992–3 Debt (51)	1992–3 Net (52)	1991–2 Credit (53)	1991–2 Debt (54)	1991–2 Net (55)	1990–1 Credit (56)	1990–1 Debt (57)	1990–1 Net (58)
A. Current Account									
1. Merchandise	18869	24316	−5447	18266	21064	−2798	18477	27915	−9438
2. Invisibles	9334	7413	1921	9502	7882	1620	7464	7706	−242
a. Services	4730	3601	1129	5022	3815	1207	4551	3571	980
a1. Travel	2098	385	1713	1977	465	1512	1456	392	1064
a2. Transportation	982	1485	−503	939	1289	−350	983	1093	−110
a3. Insurance	158	146	12	108	126	−18	111	88	23
a4. G.n.i.e.	75	100	−25	17	119	−102	15	173	−158
a5. Miscellaneous	1417	1485	−68	1981	1816	165	1986	1825	161
of which: Software Services									
Business Services									
Financial Services									
Communication Services									
b. Transfers	4228	13	4215	4259	16	4243	2545	15	2530
b1. Official	364	1	363	461	1	460	462	1	461
b2. Private	3864	12	3852	3798	15	3783	2083	14	2069
c. Income	376	3799	−3423	221	4051	−3830	368	4120	−3752
c1. Investment income	376	3799	−3423	221	4051	−3830	368	4120	−3752
c2. Compensation to Employees									
Total Current Account (1+2)	28203	31729	−3526	27768	28946	−1178	25941	35621	−9680
B. Capital Account									
1. Foreign Investment (a+b)	589	32	557	151	18	133	113	10	103
a. In India	589	32	557	151	18	133	113	10	103
a1. Direct	345	30	315	147	18	129	107	10	97
a2. Portfolio	244	2	242	4	0	4	6	0	6
b. Abroad	0	0	0	0	0	0	0	0	0
2. Loans (a+b+c)	8671	8260	411	9416	5437	3979	9431	3898	5533
a. External Assistance	3302	1446	1856	4366	1335	3031	3397	1193	2204
a1. By India	0	3	−3	0	6	−6	0	6	−6
a2. To India	3302	1443	1859	4366	1329	3037	3397	1187	2210

(Continued)

Table A8.2 *Continued*

(1)	1992–3 Credit (50)	1992–3 Debt (51)	1992–3 Net (52)	1991–2 Credit (53)	1991–2 Debt (54)	1991–2 Net (55)	1990–1 Credit (56)	1990–1 Debt (57)	1990–1 Net (58)
b. Commercial	1179	1545	–366	3152	1689	1463	4282	2028	2254
Borrowings (MT and LT)									
b1. By India	12	20	–8	19	12	7	30	24	6
b2. To India	1167	1525	–358	3133	1677	1456	4252	2004	2248
c. Short-term (to India)	4190	5269	–1079	1898	2413	–515	1752	677	1075
3. Banking Capital (a+b)	11998	8172	3826	10958	10394	564	10105	9423	682
a. Commercial Banks	10653	7723	2930	9065	8929	136	7959	7055	904
a1. Assets	1234	161	1073	1335	1107	228	426	789	–363
a2. Liabilities	9419	7562	1857	7730	7822	–92	7533	6266	1267
of which: Non-resident Deposits	9188	7187	2001	7695	7405	290	7347	5811	1536
b. Others	1345	449	896	1893	1465	428	2146	2368	–222
4. Rupee Debt Service	0	878	–878	0	1240	–1240	0	1193	–1193
5. Other Capital	1359	1399	–40	2809	2335	474	3117	1186	1931
Total Capital Account (1 to 5)	22617	18741	3876	23334	19424	3910	22766	15710	7056
C. Errors and Omissions	0	940	–940	0	133	–133	132	0	132
D. Overall Balance (A+B+C)	50820	51410	–590	51102	48503	2599	48839	51331	–2492
E. Monetary Movements (1+2)	1623	1033	590	1245	3844	–2599	3136	644	2492
1. IMF	1623	335	1288	1245	459	786	1858	644	1214
2. Foreign Exchange Reserves	0	698	–698	0	3385	–3385	1278	0	1278

Source: RBI, *Monthly Bulletin* (various issues).

Notes: Increase (–ve)/Decrease (+ve)

PR: Partially Revised; P: Preliminary.

Table A8.3 Invisibles in India's Balance of Payments (By Category: Receipts and Payments)

(US$ million)

Invisibles: Receipts

	Invisibles	% to current account receipts	Services	*of which:* Travel	*of which:* Transportation	*of which:* Insurance	G.n.i.e	Misc.	*of which:* Software Services	Transfers	*of which:* Private Transfers	*of which:* Workers Remittances	Income
1990–1	7464	28.8	4551	1456	983	111	15	1986		2545	2083		368
1991–2	9502	34.2	5022	1977	939	108	17	1981		4258	3798		222
1992–3	9334	33.1	4730	2098	982	158	75	1417		4228	3864		376
1993–4	11319	33.3	5264	2222	1433	124	30	1455		5660	5286		395
1994–5	15554	36.7	6135	2365	1696	152	10	1912		8533	8112		886
1995–6	17664	35.3	7344	2712	2011	179	13	2430	754	8891	8540		1430
1996–7	21405	38.5	7474	2878	1953	217	72	2354		12858	12435		1073
1997–8	23244	39.4	9429	2914	1836	240	276	4163		12254	11875		1561
1998–9	25770	42.9	13186	2993	1925	224	597	7447		10649	10341		1935
1999–2000	30312	44.7	15709	3036	1707	231	582	10153	3962	12672	12290	7423	1931
2000–1	32267	41.5	16268	3497	2046	270	651	9804	6341	13317	13065	7747	2682
2001–2	36737	45.1	17140	3137	2161	288	518	11036	7556	16218	15760	6578	3379
2002–3	41925	43.8	20763	3312	2536	369	293	14253	9600	17640	17189	9914	3522
2003–4	53508	44.7	26868	5037	3207	419	240	17965	12800	22736	22182	10379	3904
2004–5	69533	44.9	43249	6666	4683	870	401	30629	17700	21691	21075	9973	4593
2005–6	89687	46.0	57659	7853	6325	1062	314	42105	23600	25620	24951	10455	6408
2006–7	114558	47.1	73780	9123	7974	1195	253	55235	31300	31470	30835	14740	9308
2007–8	148875	47.3	90342	11349	10014	1639	331	67010	40300	44261	43508	21922	24272
2008–9	163534	46.4	101678	10894	11286	1419	389	77691	46300	47547	46903	23886	14309

Invisibles: Payments

	Invisibles	% to current account receipts	Services	Travel	Transportation	Insurance	G.n.i.e	Misc.	Software Services	Transfers	Private Transfers	Workers Remittances	Income
1990–1	7706	21.6	3571	392	1093	88	173	1825		15	14		4120
1991–2	7882	27.2	3815	465	1288	126	120	1816		16	15		4051
1992–3	7413	23.4	3601	385	1485	146	100	1485		13	12		3799
1993–4	8422	24.0	4730	497	1765	196	153	2119		27	22		3665
1994–5	9874	21.6	5533	818	1863	181	165	2506		24	19		4317
1995–6	12217	21.9	7544	1168	2169	143	218	3847		38	32		4634
1996–7	11209	18.6	6748	858	2394	153	178	3165		81	68		4380
1997–8	13236	20.5	8110	1437	2522	183	160	3808		45	45		5081
1998–9	16562	25.8	11021	1743	2680	112	325	6161		62	61		5479
1999–2000	17169	23.7	11645	2139	2410	122	270	6704	138	34	34	29	5490
2000–1	22473	28.0	14576	2804	3558	223	319	7672	591	211	211	124	7686
2001–2	21763	27.9	13816	3014	3467	280	283	6772	672	362	362	292	7585
2002–3	24890	27.9	17120	3341	3272	350	228	9929	737	802	802	757	6968
2003–4	25707	24.3	16724	3602	2328	363	212	10219	476	574	574	522	8409
2004–5	38301	24.4	27823	5249	4539	722	411	16902	800	906	550	421	9572
2005–6	47685	23.3	34489	6638	8337	1116	529	17869	1338	933	458	354	12263
2006–7	62341	24.6	44311	6684	8068	642	403	28514	2267	1391	1010	823	16639
2007–8	74012	22.4	51490	9258	11514	1044	376	29298	3358	2316	1802	1585	19339
2008–9	72970	19.1	52047	9425	12820	1130	793	27879	2814	2749	2336	1928	18816

Source: RBI Bulletin (various issues).

A9 EXCHANGE RATE

Table A9.1 Exchange Rate for the Indian Rupee vis-à-vis Some Select Currencies

(Indian Rupee per Currency, per cent appreciation (+), depreciation (−))

Countries	Currency	2001–1 to 2008–9	1992–3 to 2000–1	2008–9	2007–8	2006–7	2005–6	2004–5	2003–4	2002–3	2001–2	2000–1	1999–2000	1998–9	1997–8	1996–7	1995–6	1994–5	1993–4	1992–3
(1)	(2)	(3)	(4)	(5)	(6)	(7)	(8)	(9)	(10)	(11)	(12)	(13)	(14)	(15)	(16)	(17)	(18)	(19)	(20)	(21)
Developing Countries																				
Argentina	Pesos	222.2	−41.8	14.18	12.95	14.78	15.08	15.34	16.16	14.39	38.85	45.71	43.36	42.08	37.18	35.52	33.47	31.43	31.47	26.61
Bangladesh	Taka	29.0	−21.6	0.67	0.59	0.65	0.68	0.74	0.79	0.84	0.84	0.86	0.87	0.89	0.83	0.84	0.83	0.78	0.79	0.68
Brazil	Reais	3.5	62.6	23.26	21.71	21.01	19.06	15.67	15.69	15.13	19.77	24.08	23.87	31.83	33.86	34.72	35.30	39.15	na	na
China	Yuan	−17.6	−14.4	6.70	5.40	5.73	5.44	5.43	5.55	5.85	5.76	5.52	5.23	5.08	4.48	4.27	4.02	3.67	4.83	4.73
Colombia	Pesos	−3.5	59.2	0.02	0.02	0.02	0.02	0.02	0.02	0.02	0.02	0.02	0.02	0.03	0.03	0.03	0.04	0.04	0.04	0.03
Hong Kong	Hong Kong Dollar	−0.9	−26.2	5.91	5.16	5.82	5.70	5.77	5.91	6.21	6.12	5.86	5.58	5.43	4.80	4.59	4.33	na	na	na
Indonesia	Rupiah for Rs 100	11236.8	155.0	0.45	0.44	0.50	0.46	0.49	0.54	0.54	0.46	0.51	0.58	0.43	0.80	1.50	1.47	1.44	1.49	1.29
Israel	New Sheqalim	−10.4	−7.9	12.44	10.17	10.42	9.70	10.08	10.30	10.11	11.02	11.15	10.47	10.73	10.57	10.94	11.01	10.41	10.90	10.27
Iran	Rials	438.7	957.9	0.00	0.00	0.00	0.00	0.01	0.01	0.01	0.02	0.03	0.02	0.02	0.02	0.02	0.02	0.02	0.02	0.27
Kenya	Shillings	−7.6	29.6	0.64	0.60	0.63	0.59	0.57	0.61	0.62	0.61	0.59	0.60	0.67	0.62	0.63	0.61	0.62	0.48	0.76
Korea	Won	3.5	−14.3	0.04	0.04	0.05	0.04	0.04	0.04	0.04	0.04	0.04	0.04	0.03	0.03	0.03	0.04	0.04	0.04	0.03
Kuwait	Dinar	−11.6	−40.3	168.43	143.86	156.32	151.59	152.82	154.81	160.35	155.45	148.83	142.07	138.26	122.22	118.22	112.00	105.50	104.76	88.89
Malaysia	Ringgit	−10.2	−13.7	13.39	11.95	12.53	11.74	11.82	12.09	12.74	12.55	12.02	11.40	10.85	11.65	14.20	13.37	12.17	12.05	10.38
Mexico	Pesos	25.3	77.4	3.83	3.70	4.11	4.12	3.96	4.24	4.80	5.19	4.79	4.60	4.42	4.61	4.62	4.91	7.71	10.02	8.51
Mynammar	Kyats	−17.4	−37.7	8.39	7.34	7.88	7.58	7.87	7.72	7.53	7.02	6.93	6.86	6.68	5.90	5.92	5.88	5.35	5.11	4.32
Nigeria	Naira	19.8	205.4	0.37	0.33	0.35	0.34	0.34	0.35	0.39	0.42	0.44	0.45	1.11	1.70	1.62	1.53	1.43	1.43	1.34
Pakistan	Rupees	33.9	26.4	0.61	0.66	0.75	0.74	0.77	0.80	0.82	0.77	0.82	na	0.92	0.89	0.95	1.03	1.02	1.08	1.04
Philippines	Pesos	−1.0	5.9	1.00	0.91	0.90	0.81	0.81	0.84	0.93	0.93	0.99	1.10	1.04	1.12	1.35	1.29	1.22	1.13	1.04
Qatar	Riyals	−0.7	−42.2	12.64	11.06	12.43	12.16	12.34	12.62	13.30	13.10	12.55	11.90	11.56	10.21	9.75	9.19	8.63	8.62	7.26
Russia	Rubles	−3.7	308.9	1.69	1.61	1.69	1.56	1.57	1.53	1.53	1.60	1.62	1.67	3.02	6.32	6.64	na	na	na	na
Saudi Arabia	Riyals	−0.5	−42.2	12.27	10.74	12.08	11.82	11.98	12.27	12.93	12.74	12.20	11.57	11.23	9.92	9.48	8.94	8.38	8.38	7.05
Singapore	Singapore Dollar	−17.6	−38.4	31.93	27.27	28.91	26.61	26.82	26.57	27.37	26.31	26.30	25.59	25.03	23.99	25.15	23.73	21.06	19.58	16.20
South Africa	Rand	20.8	45.0	5.16	5.65	6.42	6.93	7.18	6.40	4.97	5.00	6.24	7.03	7.24	7.88	7.92	9.10	8.76	9.38	9.05

(Continued)

Table A9.1 *Continued*

(1)	(2) Currency	(3) 2001–1 to 2008–9	(4) 1992–3 to 2000–1	(5) 2008–9	(6) 2007–8	(7) 2006–7	(8) 2005–6	(9) 2004–5	(10) 2003–4	(11) 2002–3	(12) 2001–2	(13) 2000–1	(14) 1999–0	(15) 1998–9	(16) 1997–8	(17) 1996–7	(18) 1995–6	(19) 1994–5	(20) 1993–4	(21) 1992–3
Sri Lanka	Rupees	36.2	2.9	0.42	0.36	0.43	0.44	0.44	0.47	0.50	0.52	0.57	0.61	0.63	0.62	0.63	0.64	0.63	0.64	0.59
Thailand	Baht	−18.5	−5.6	1.35	1.19	1.22	1.09	1.12	1.13	1.13	1.07	1.10	1.14	1.08	1.01	1.39	1.34	1.25	1.24	1.04
UAE	Dirhams	−0.7	−42.2	12.52	10.96	12.32	12.05	12.23	12.51	13.18	12.99	12.44	11.80	11.45	10.12	9.67	9.12	8.55	8.54	7.19
Industrialized Countries																				
Australia	Australian Dollar	−28.4	−25.4	35.57	46.35	59.15	33.46	33.23	31.94	27.23	24.52	25.46	27.95	26.13	26.60	27.99	25.17	23.30	21.49	18.99
Canada	Canadian Dollar	−25.4	−29.3	40.74	39.00	39.75	37.10	35.14	33.96	31.27	30.47	30.38	29.45	27.97	26.49	26.09	24.55	22.76	23.94	21.48
Denmark	Kroner	−36.1	−21.3	8.70	7.65	7.78	7.22	7.59	7.24	6.45	5.66	5.56	6.01	6.35	5.46	5.96	6.02	5.11	4.76	4.37
Egypt@	Pounds	30.4	−22.9	9.30	7.20	7.62	7.70	7.56	7.04	8.34	10.80	12.13	12.78	12.50	10.18	10.60	10.12	9.28	9.28	9.35
Japan	Yen	−9.7	−48.8	0.46	0.35	0.39	0.39	0.42	0.41	0.40	0.38	0.41	0.39	0.33	0.30	0.32	0.35	0.32	0.29	0.21
Sweden	Kroner	−25.1	−12.3	6.46	6.12	6.30	5.76	6.20	5.90	5.23	4.54	4.84	5.15	5.30	4.77	5.18	4.79	4.15	3.97	4.24
Switzerland	Swiss Francs	−35.3	−30.8	41.61	34.75	36.54	34.75	36.70	34.85	32.70	28.18	26.92	27.90	29.27	25.43	27.36	28.62	23.87	21.42	18.62
USA	Dollar	−0.7	−42.2	45.99	40.21	45.25	44.26	44.93	45.95	48.41	47.69	45.69	43.33	42.06	37.16	35.50	33.47	31.40	31.36	26.41
UK	Pound	−14.4	−33.9	78.97	80.83	85.66	79.08	82.90	77.81	74.82	68.28	67.57	69.84	69.55	60.99	56.33	52.40	48.84	47.19	44.66
Euro*		−36.2		64.97	56.97	58.02	53.85	56.48	53.87	47.92	42.14	41.42	44.71							
Belgium	Franc		−30.1											1.17	1.02	1.11	1.14	0.98	0.82	0.82
France	Franc		−30.9											7.21	6.23	6.75	6.75	5.84	5.46	4.98
Germany	Deutsche Mark		−30.2											24.18	20.94	22.87	23.40	20.10	18.72	16.87
Italy	Lire		−18.0											0.02	0.02	0.02	0.02	0.02	0.02	0.02
Netherlands	Guidars		−30.1											21.44	18.60	20.39	20.89	17.92	16.68	14.98

Source: International Financial Statistics, IMF (various issues).

Notes: * Consisting of Currencies of Belgium, France, Germany, Netherlands, and Italy Euro currency came into existence with effect from 1 January 1998; in their cases per cent appreciation or depreciation worked out is for the period 1992–3 to 1998–9 and 2000–1 to 2008–9 for the purpose of comparability.

@ Data for Egypt is as at the end of the period.

The liberalized exchange rate management system (LERMS) was instituted in March 1992 in conjunction with other measures of liberalization in the areas of trade, industry, foreign investment, and the import of gold. The ultimate convergence of the dual rates was made effective as of 1 March 1993.

Table A9.2 Indices of Real Effective Exchange Rate (REER) and Nominal Effective Exchange Rate (NEER) of the Indian Rupee (new series)

Year/Month	36-Currency - Export and Trade Based Weights				6-Currency Trade Based Weights			
	Trade Based Base 1993–4 = 100		Export Based Base 1993–4 = 100		Base 1993–4 = 100 (April–March)		Base 2007–8 = 100 (April–March)	
	REER	NEER	REER	NEER	NEER	REER	NEER	REER
(1)	(2)	(3)	(4)	(5)	(6)	(7)	(8)	(9)
2009–10								
Mar-10								
Feb-10								
Jan-10	96.26 (2.8)	86.29 (1.8)	95.76 (2.9)	83.56 (2.0)	64.30 (2.4)	108.86 (2.4)	86.01 (2.4)	95.29 (2.4)
Dec-09	93.62 (0.1)	84.73 (0.5)	93.03 (0.1)	81.95 (0.6)	62.79 (0.8)	106.26 (0.4)	83.99 (0.8)	93.02 (0.4)
Nov-09	93.56 (1.6)	84.27 (–0.0)	92.90 (1.7)	81.50 (–0.0)	62.30 (–0.2)	105.81 (1.8)	83.34 (–0.2)	92.63 (1.8)
Oct-09	92.06 (2.3)	84.31 (2.6)	91.36 (2.4)	81.53 (2.7)	62.40 (3.0)	103.97 (2.7)	83.47 (2.9)	91.01 (2.7)
Sep-09	90.01 (–0.3)	82.18 (–1.1)	89.25 (–0.3)	79.36 (–1.1)	60.61 (–1.0)	101.25 (–0.3)	81.08 (–1.0)	88.63 (–0.3)
Aug-09	90.26 (0.6)	83.13 (–0.3)	89.54 (0.6)	80.21 (–0.3)	61.22 (–0.2)	101.52 (0.9)	81.90 (–0.2)	88.87 (0.9)
Jul-09	89.71 (–0.6)	83.40 (–1.6)	89.03 (–0.6)	80.48 (–1.7)	61.36 (–1.7)	100.64 (–0.5)	82.08 (–1.7)	88.10 (–0.5)
Jun-09	90.21 (0.6)	84.78 (0.4)	89.53 (0.5)	81.86 (0.3)	62.43 (0.2)	101.11 (–0.3)	83.51 (0.2)	88.51 (–0.3)
May-09	89.70 (2.4)	84.43 (1.0)	89.07 (2.3)	81.59 (1.1)	62.31 (1.3)	101.37 (2.8)	83.35 (1.3)	88.74 (2.8)
Apr-09	87.62	83.61	87.10	80.73	61.49	98.58	82.25	86.30
2008–9	94.32 (–10.0)	84.67 (–9.8)	94.12 (–9.6)	84.67 (–11.2)	64.87 (–13.2)	104.47 (–8.5)	86.78 (–13.2)	91.45 (–8.5)
2007–8	104.81 (6.4)	93.91 (9.3)	104.12 (6.9)	95.30 (9.0)	74.76 (7.6)	114.23 (8.2)	100.00 (7.6)	100.00 (8.2)
2006–7	98.48 (–3.8)	85.89 (–4.4)	97.42 (–3.1)	87.46 (–4.1)	69.49 (–3.9)	105.57 (–1.6)	92.96 (–3.9)	92.41 (–1.6)
2005–6	102.35 (2.3)	89.85 (2.9)	100.54 (2.3)	91.17 (3.1)	72.28 (3.9)	107.30 (5.4)	96.69 (3.9)	93.93 (5.4)
2004–5	100.09 (0.5)	87.31 (0.2)	98.30 (–0.8)	88.41 (0.6)	69.58 (–0.6)	101.78 (2.6)	93.07 (–0.6)	89.10 (2.6)
2003–4	99.56 (1.4)	87.14 (–2.2)	99.07 (3.2)	87.89 (1.0)	69.97 (–1.8)	99.17 (1.5)	93.59 (–1.8)	86.81 (1.5)
2002–3	98.18 (–2.7)	89.12 (–2.7)	95.99 (–2.6)	87.01 (–2.3)	71.27 (–6.3)	97.68 (–4.9)	95.33 (–6.3)	85.51 (–4.9)
2001–2	100.86 (0.8)	91.58 (–0.6)	98.59 (–0.1)	89.08 (–1.2)	76.04 (–1.8)	102.71 (–0.1)	101.72 (–1.8)	89.91 (–0.1)
2000–1	100.09 (4.3)	92.12 (1.2)	98.67 (3.6)	90.12 (–0.3)	77.43 (0.3)	102.82 (5.3)	103.57 (0.3)	90.01 (5.3)
1999–2000	95.99 (3.2)	91.02 (2.2)	95.28 (1.0)	90.42 (0.1)	77.16 (–0.4)	97.69 (1.6)	103.21 (0.2)	85.51 (1.6)
1998–9	93.04 (–7.7)	89.05 (–3.2)	94.34 (–8.5)	90.34 (–1.8)	77.49 (–11.9)	96.14 (–7.9)	103.05 (–12.4)	84.16 (–7.9)
1997–8	100.77 (4.1)	92.04 (3.1)	103.07 (4.2)	91.97 (3.3)	87.94 (1.3)	104.41 (3.3)	117.63 (1.3)	91.40 (3.3)
1996–7	96.83 (–1.4)	89.27 (–2.5)	98.95 (–1.1)	89.03 (–2.1)	86.85 (–1.9)	101.11 (–0.2)	116.17 (–1.9)	88.51 (–0.2)
1995–6	98.19 (–5.9)	91.54 (–7.5)	100.10 (–4.6)	90.94 (–7.4)	88.56 (–8.7)	101.27 (–4.3)	118.46 (–8.7)	88.65 (–4.3)
1994–5	104.32 (4.3)	98.91 (–1.1)	104.88 (4.9)	98.18 (–1.8)	96.96 (–3.0)	105.82 (5.8)	129.69 (–3.1)	92.63 (5.8)
1993–4	100.00	100.00	100.00	100.00	100.00	100.00	133.82	87.58

Source: RBI Bulletin.

Notes: Figures in brackets represent annual appreciation (+) or depreciation (–) of the rupee as per the respective NEER and REER Indices. RBI has revised the existing 36 currency indices of NEER and REER with the new series of NEER and REER and published this in the December 2005 *RBI Bulletin*. Six country indices includes Euro, Japaneese yen, UK pound, USA dollar, Hong Kong dollar, and Chinese yuan.

A10 FOREIGN TRADE

Table A10.1 India's Foreign Trade

(US$ million)

Year	Exports		Total	Imports		Total	Trade Balance		Total
	Oil	Non-oil		Oil	Non-oil		Oil	Non-oil	
(1)	(2)	(3)	(4)	(5)	(6)	(7)	(8)	(9)	(10)
1970–1	11.3	2020.0	2031.3	179.8	1982.5	2162.3	−168.5	37.5	−131.0
1971–2	14.1	2137.8	2151.9	259.8	2181.7	2441.5	−245.7	−43.9	−289.6
1972–3	37.7	2531.0	2568.7	265.9	2167.2	2433.1	−228.2	363.8	135.6
1973–4	15.7	3222.6	3238.3	719.0	3073.6	3792.6	−703.3	149.0	−554.3
1974–5	17.2	4174.9	4192.1	1457.0	4233.6	5690.6	−1439.8	−58.7	−1498.5
1975–6	21.7	4627.0	4648.7	1411.7	4652.0	6063.7	−1390.0	−25.0	−1415.0
1976–7	20.8	5707.6	5728.4	1574.3	4077.4	5651.7	−1553.5	1630.2	76.7
1977–8	18.3	6280.3	6298.6	1806.4	5205.4	7011.8	−1788.1	1074.9	−713.2
1978–9	17.2	6943.1	6960.3	2038.2	6240.5	8278.7	−2021.0	702.6	−1318.4
1979–80	23.3	7903.1	7926.4	4034.7	7255.9	11290.6	−4011.4	647.2	−3364.2
1980–1	31.5	8453.2	8484.7	6654.9	9211.6	15866.5	−6623.4	−758.4	−7381.8
1981–2	246.3	8457.6	8703.9	5786.2	9386.7	15172.9	−5539.9	−929.1	−6469.0
1982–3	1278.0	7829.6	9107.6	5816.2	8970.4	14786.6	−4538.2	−1140.8	−5679.0
1983–4	1535.8	7913.6	9449.4	4673.1	10637.8	15310.9	−3137.3	−2724.2	−5861.5
1984–5	1529.4	8348.7	9878.1	4549.8	9862.5	14412.3	−3020.4	−1513.8	−4534.2
1985–6	527.0	8377.5	8904.5	4078.0	11988.9	16066.9	−3551.0	−3611.4	−7162.4
1986–7	321.8	9422.9	9744.7	2199.5	13527.2	15726.7	−1877.7	−4104.3	−5982.0
1987–8	500.4	11588.1	12088.5	3118.1	14037.6	17155.7	−2617.7	−2449.5	−5067.2
1988–9	348.7	13621.7	13970.4	3009.0	16488.2	19497.2	−2660.3	−2866.5	−5526.8
1989–90	418.4	16194.1	16612.5	3767.5	17451.7	21219.2	−3349.1	−1257.6	−4606.7
1990–1	522.7	17622.5	18145.2	6028.1	18044.4	24072.5	−5505.4	−421.9	−5927.3
1991–2	414.7	17450.7	17865.4	5324.8	14085.7	19410.5	−4910.1	3365.0	−1545.1
1992–3	476.2	18061.0	18537.2	6100.0	15781.6	21881.6	−5623.8	2279.4	−3344.4
1993–4	397.8	21840.5	22238.3	5753.5	17552.7	23306.2	−5355.7	4287.8	−1067.9
1994–5	416.9	25913.6	26330.5	5927.8	22726.5	28654.4	−5510.9	3187.1	−2323.8
1995–6	453.7	31341.2	31794.9	7525.8	29149.5	36675.3	−7072.0	2191.7	−4880.4
1996–7	481.8	32987.9	33469.7	10036.2	29096.2	39132.4	−9554.4	3891.7	−5662.7
1997–8	352.8	34653.7	35006.4	8164.0	33320.5	41484.5	−7811.2	1333.1	−6478.1
1998–9	89.4	33129.3	33218.7	6398.6	35990.1	42388.7	−6309.2	−2860.8	−9170.0
1999–2000	38.9	36783.5	36822.4	12611.4	37059.3	49670.7	−12572.5	−275.8	−12848.3
2000–1	1869.7	42690.6	44560.3	15650.1	34886.4	50536.5	−13780.4	7804.2	−5976.2
2001–2	2119.1	41707.6	43826.7	14000.3	37413.0	51413.3	−11881.2	4294.6	−7586.6
2002–3	2576.5	50142.9	52719.4	17639.5	43772.6	61412.1	−15063.0	6370.3	−8692.7
2003–4	3568.4	60274.1	63842.6	20569.5	57579.6	78149.1	−17001.1	2694.5	−14306.5
2004–5	6989.3	76546.6	83535.9	29844.1	81673.3	111517.4	−22854.8	−5126.7	−27981.5
2005–6	11639.6	91450.9	103090.5	43963.1	105202.6	149165.7	−32323.5	−13751.7	−46075.2
2006–7	18634.6	107779.5	126414.1	56945.3	128790.0	185735.2	−38310.7	−21010.5	−59321.2
2007–8	26903.8	136228.3	163132.2	79715.0	171939.0	251654.0	−52811.2	−35710.6	−88521.8
2008–9			168704.0	93176.0	194583.4	287759.4	.	.	−119055.2

Source: RBI (2009), *Handbook of Statistics on Indian Economy*.

Table A 10.2   Changing Scenerio in Foreign Trade
Exports

(US$ million)

Year	Gems and Jewellery	Chemicals and Products	Textile and Textile Products	Petroleum Products	Machinery and Instruments	Transport Equipment	Manufacture of Metals	Iron Ore	Iron & Steel	Electronic Goods	Top Ten commodities/groups	Total Exports
1987–8	2015.1	791.6	3013.8	500.4	397.0	195.2	222.3	427.7	21.6	154.1	7738.8	12088.5
	(16.7)	(6.5)	(24.9)	(4.1)	(3.3)	(1.6)	(1.8)	(3.5)	(0.2)	(1.3)	(64.0)	(100.0)
1988–9	3032.8	1090.5	3037.7	348.7	509.5	250.7	305.1	464.8	52.1	200.5	9292.4	13970.4
	(21.7)	(7.8)	(21.7)	(2.5)	(3.6)	(1.8)	(2.2)	(3.3)	(0.4)	(1.4)	(66.5)	(100.0)
1989–90	3180.7	1553.8	3746.5	418.4	603.9	316.0	445.7	557.1	98.9	302.7	11223.7	16612.5
	(19.1)	(9.4)	(22.6)	(2.5)	(3.6)	(1.9)	(2.7)	(3.4)	(0.6)	(1.8)	(67.6)	(100.0)
1990–1	2924.1	1728.0	4342.6	522.7	696.2	400.6	456.3	584.7	161.1	232.4	12048.7	18145.2
	(16.1)	(9.5)	(23.9)	(2.9)	(3.8)	(2.2)	(2.5)	(3.2)	(0.9)	(1.3)	(66.4)	(100.0)
1991–2	2738.2	1868.8	4693.1	414.7	581.4	496.4	484.2	582.3	153.5	265.2	12277.8	17865.4
	(15.3)	(10.5)	(26.3)	(2.3)	(3.3)	(2.8)	(2.7)	(3.3)	(0.9)	(1.5)	(68.7)	(100.0)
1992–3	3071.7	1786.1	5007.4	476.2	541.6	533.7	560.2	381.2	306.1	212.3	12876.5	18537.2
	(16.6)	(9.6)	(27.0)	(2.6)	(2.9)	(2.9)	(3.0)	(2.1)	(1.7)	(1.1)	(69.5)	(100.0)
1993–4	3995.8	2377.2	5472.3	397.8	638.9	591.9	663.2	438.0	568.4	303.6	15447.1	22238.3
	(18.0)	(10.7)	(24.6)	(1.8)	(2.9)	(2.7)	(3.0)	(2.0)	(2.6)	(1.4)	(69.5)	(100.0)
1994–5	4500.4	3066.8	7117.7	416.9	726.7	771.3	706.2	413.1	528.4	412.2	18659.7	26330.5
	(17.1)	(11.6)	(27.0)	(1.6)	(2.8)	(2.9)	(2.7)	(1.6)	(2.0)	(1.6)	(70.9)	(100.0)
1995–6	5274.8	3597.0	8031.6	453.7	829.8	924.9	826.4	514.5	696.7	670.1	21819.5	31794.9
	(16.6)	(11.3)	(25.3)	(1.4)	(2.6)	(2.9)	(2.6)	(1.6)	(2.2)	(2.1)	(68.6)	(100.0)
1996–7	4752.7	3912.8	8635.8	481.8	1057.1	968.7	913.5	480.7	769.8	783.7	22756.6	33469.7
	(14.2)	(11.7)	(25.8)	(1.4)	(3.2)	(2.9)	(2.7)	(1.4)	(2.3)	(2.3)	(68.0)	(100.0)
1997–8	5345.5	4396.3	9050.4	352.8	1195.7	929.1	1023.2	476.2	874.7	759.6	24403.5	35006.4
	(15.3)	(12.6)	(25.9)	(1.0)	(3.4)	(2.7)	(2.9)	(1.4)	(2.5)	(2.2)	(69.7)	(100.0)
1998–9	5929.3	4009.2	8866.3	89.4	1154.8	761.8	1040.0	384.0	579.1	502.8	23316.7	33218.7
	(17.8)	(12.1)	(26.7)	(0.3)	(3.5)	(2.3)	(3.1)	(1.2)	(1.7)	(1.5)	(70.2)	(100.0)
1999–2000	7502.3	4706.5	9822.1	38.9	1183.2	810.2	1225.6	271.2	833.0	681.0	27074.0	36822.4
	(20.4)	(12.8)	(26.7)	(0.1)	(3.2)	(2.2)	(3.3)	(0.7)	(2.3)	(1.8)	(73.5)	(100.0)
2000–1	7384.0	5885.9	11285.0	1869.7	1580.1	991.9	1577.7	357.6	1028.3	1051.5	33011.7	44560.3
	(16.6)	(13.2)	(25.3)	(4.2)	(3.5)	(2.2)	(3.5)	(0.8)	(2.3)	(2.4)	(74.1)	(100.0)
2001–2	7306.3	6051.8	10206.5	2119.1	1734.1	1020.9	1604.0	426.4	898.1	1171.3	32538.5	43826.7
	(16.7)	(13.8)	(23.3)	(4.8)	(4.0)	(2.3)	(3.7)	(1.0)	(2.0)	(2.7)	(74.2)	(100.0)
2002–3	9029.9	7455.3	11617.0	2576.5	2008.4	1333.9	1847.6	867.9	1856.0	1252.7	39845.2	52719.4
	(17.1)	(14.1)	(22.0)	(4.9)	(3.8)	(2.5)	(3.5)	(1.6)	(3.5)	(2.4)	(75.6)	(100.0)
2003–4	10573.3	9445.9	12791.5	3568.4	2776.3	1956.0	2426.5	1125.8	2477.8	1728.3	48869.8	63842.6
	(16.6)	(14.8)	(20.0)	(5.6)	(4.3)	(3.1)	(3.8)	(1.8)	(3.9)	(2.7)	(76.5)	(100.0)
2004–5	13761.8	12443.7	13555.3	6989.3	3719.4	2829.7	3401.5	3277.3	3921.0	1831.8	65730.8	83535.9
	(16.5)	(14.9)	(16.2)	(8.4)	(4.5)	(3.4)	(4.1)	(3.9)	(4.7)	(2.2)	(78.7)	(100.0)
2005–6	15529.1	14769.5	16402.1	11639.6	5077.5	4323.0	4233.2	3801.1	3548.3	2173.1	81496.5	103090.5
	(15.1)	(14.3)	(15.9)	(11.3)	(4.9)	(4.2)	(4.1)	(3.7)	(3.4)	(2.1)	(79.1)	(100.0)
2006–7	15977.0	17335.5	17373.2	18678.7	6722.8	4949.9	5081.2	3902.0	5238.6	2854.0	98112.9	126414.1
	(12.6)	(13.7)	(13.7)	(14.8)	(5.3)	(3.9)	(4.0)	(3.1)	(4.1)	(2.3)	(77.6)	(100.0)
2007–8	19688.3	22375.2	20691.5	28377.0	9132.6	7028.2	7054.8	5814.9	5449.2	3511.7	129123.2	162983.9
	(12.1)	(13.7)	(12.7)	(17.4)	(5.6)	(4.3)	(4.3)	(3.6)	(3.3)	(2.2)	(79.2)	(100.0)
2008–9	27704.98	23827.96	19864.68	26829.56	10953.0	11142.1	7550.8	4723.6	5822.5	7127.5	145546.7	182630.5
	(15.2)	(13.0)	(10.9)	(14.7)	(6.0)	(6.1)	(4.1)	(2.6)	(3.2)	(3.9)	(79.7)	(100.0)

Source: RBI(2009), *Handbook of Statistics on Indian Economy.*

(Continued)

Table A 10.2 *Continued*
Imports

(US$ million)

Year	Petroleum, Crude, and Products	Electronic Goods	Gold and Silver	Machinery	Pearls, & Precious Stones	Organic and In-organic Chemicals	Iron and Steel	Transport Equipment	Fertilizers	Edible Oils	Top 10 commodities	Total Imports/All Commodities
1987–8	3118.1	0.0	0.0	2016.5	1556.7	834.4	1017.8	586.1	391.8	747.2	10268.6	17155.7
	(18.2)	(0.0)	(0.0)	(11.8)	(9.1)	(4.9)	(5.9)	(3.4)	(2.3)	(4.4)	(59.9)	(100.0)
1988–9	3009.0	0.0	0.0	1809.5	2192.8	1307.9	1335.0	519.8	644.7	503.9	11322.6	19497.2
	(15.4)	(0.0)	(0.0)	(9.3)	(11.2)	(6.7)	(6.8)	(2.7)	(3.3)	(2.6)	(58.1)	(100.0)
1989–90	3767.5	0.0	0.0	1929.9	2554.6	1153.8	1352.4	889.3	1082.9	125.4	12855.8	21219.2
	(17.8)	(0.0)	(0.0)	(9.1)	(12.0)	(5.4)	(6.4)	(4.2)	(5.1)	(0.6)	(60.6)	(100.0)
1990–1	6028.1	0.0	0.0	2100.0	2083.1	1275.6	1177.6	930.5	984.3	181.6	14760.8	42217.7
	(14.3)	(0.0)	(0.0)	(5.0)	(4.9)	(3.0)	(2.8)	(2.2)	(2.3)	(0.4)	(35.0)	(100.0)
1991–2	5324.8	0.0	0.0	1457.5	1957.1	1378.7	798.9	371.2	954.2	100.5	12342.9	19410.5
	(27.4)	(0.0)	(0.0)	(7.5)	(10.1)	(7.1)	(4.1)	(1.9)	(4.9)	(0.5)	(63.6)	(100.0)
1992–3	6100.0	0.0	0.0	1652.6	2442.1	1427.5	778.6	461.8	977.7	57.6	13897.9	21881.6
	(27.9)	(0.0)	(0.0)	(7.6)	(11.2)	(6.5)	(3.6)	(2.1)	(4.5)	(0.3)	(63.5)	(100.0)
1993–4	5753.5	912.4	0.0	1881.9	2634.5	1370.7	795.0	1270.4	825.9	53.1	15497.4	23306.2
	(24.7)	(3.9)	(0.0)	(8.1)	(11.3)	(5.9)	(3.4)	(5.5)	(3.5)	(0.2)	(66.5)	(100.0)
1994–5	5927.8	1228.1	712.6	2727.8	1629.7	2137.1	1163.6	1113.6	1052.4	198.8	17891.5	28654.4
	(20.7)	(4.3)	(2.5)	(9.5)	(5.7)	(7.5)	(4.1)	(3.9)	(3.7)	(0.7)	(62.4)	(100.0)
1995–6	7525.8	1752.3	867.1	3924.4	2106.0	2565.5	1446.2	1105.1	1682.7	676.2	23651.3	36675.3
	(20.5)	(4.8)	(2.4)	(10.7)	(5.7)	(7.0)	(3.9)	(3.0)	(4.6)	(1.8)	(64.5)	(100.0)
1996–7	10036.2	1423.8	991.5	3644.3	2925.0	2660.9	1370.6	1484.3	911.2	825.1	26272.9	39132.4
	(25.6)	(3.6)	(2.5)	(9.3)	(7.5)	(6.8)	(3.5)	(3.8)	(2.3)	(2.1)	(67.1)	(100.0)
1997–8	8164.0	2087.8	3169.3	3621.9	3342.1	2956.1	1421.1	1051.3	1116.6	743.9	27674.1	41484.5
	(19.7)	(5.0)	(7.6)	(8.7)	(8.1)	(7.1)	(3.4)	(2.5)	(2.7)	(1.8)	(66.7)	(100.0)
1998–9	6398.6	2223.0	5072.1	3044.5	3760.3	2683.7	1063.5	798.2	1076.4	1803.9	27924.2	42388.7
	(15.1)	(5.2)	(12.0)	(7.2)	(8.9)	(6.3)	(2.5)	(1.9)	(2.5)	(4.3)	(65.9)	(100.0)
1999–2000	12611.4	2796.6	4706.1	2745.0	5436.0	2866.3	951.7	1136.6	1399.1	1856.8	36505.6	49670.7
	(25.4)	(5.6)	(9.5)	(5.5)	(10.9)	(5.8)	(1.9)	(2.3)	(2.8)	(3.7)	(73.5)	(100.0)
2000–1	15650.1	3508.5	4638.0	2708.8	4807.7	2443.9	777.8	700.3	751.8	1308.2	37295.1	50536.5
	(31.0)	(6.9)	(9.2)	(5.4)	(9.5)	(4.8)	(1.5)	(1.4)	(1.5)	(2.6)	(73.8)	(100.0)
2001–2	14000.3	3782.0	4582.3	2970.8	4622.6	2799.6	833.7	1149.4	679.0	1355.6	36775.3	51413.3
	(27.2)	(7.4)	(8.9)	(5.8)	(9.0)	(5.4)	(1.6)	(2.2)	(1.3)	(2.6)	(71.5)	(100.0)
2002–3	17639.5	5599.4	4288.3	3565.6	6062.8	3025.2	943.7	1897.4	625.8	1814.2	45461.9	61412.1
	(28.7)	(9.1)	(7.0)	(5.8)	(9.9)	(4.9)	(1.5)	(3.1)	(1.0)	(3.0)	(74.0)	(100.0)
2003–4	20569.5	7506.1	6856.4	4743.6	7128.7	4031.9	1506.1	3227.9	720.8	2542.5	58833.5	78149.1
	(26.3)	(9.6)	(8.8)	(6.1)	(9.1)	(5.2)	(1.9)	(4.1)	(0.9)	(3.3)	(75.3)	(100.0)
2004–5	29844.1	9993.2	11150.0	6817.8	9422.7	5699.9	2669.7	4327.4	1377.1	2465.3	83767.2	111517.4
	(26.8)	(9.0)	(10.0)	(6.1)	(8.4)	(5.1)	(2.4)	(3.9)	(1.2)	(2.2)	(75.1)	(100.0)
2005–6	43963.1	13241.7	11317.7	10009.8	9134.4	6984.1	4572.2	8838.5	2127.0	2024.0	112212.6	149165.7
	(29.5)	(8.9)	(7.6)	(6.7)	(6.1)	(4.7)	(3.1)	(5.9)	(1.4)	(1.4)	(75.2)	(100.0)
2006–7	57143.6	15972.6	14646.0	13850.4	7487.5	7830.7	6424.7	9438.6	3144.1	2108.3	138046.5	185735.2
	(30.8)	(8.6)	(7.9)	(7.5)	(4.0)	(4.2)	(3.5)	(5.1)	(1.7)	(1.1)	(74.3)	(100.0)
2007–8	79683.5	20219.8	17875.7	19870.1	7975.5	9901.5	8692.8	20121.5	5408.6	2559.9	192308.8	251562.3
	(31.7)	(8.0)	(7.1)	(7.9)	(3.2)	(3.9)	(3.5)	(8.0)	(2.2)	(1.0)	(76.4)	(100.0)
2008–9	91291.2	23149.3	18682.6	20914.5	14439.1	12157.7	9363.7	13022.9	13577.4	3438.5	220036.9	291474.56
	(31.3)	(7.9)	(6.4)	(7.2)	(5.0)	(4.2)	(3.2)	(4.5)	(4.7)	(1.2)	(75.5)	(100.0)

Source: RBI(2009), *Handbook of Statistics on Indian Economy.*

Table A10.3 Foreign Trade with Major Trading Partners

(US$ million)

(1)	China (2)		Germany (3)		Australia (4)		USA (5)		Switzerland (6)		UK (7)		Singapore (8)		UAE (9)		Japan (10)		Italy (11)		Hong Kong (12)		Total (13)	
	Export	Import	Export	Import	Export	Import	Export	Import	Export	Import	Export	Import	Export	Import	Export	Import	Export	Import	Export	Import	Export	Import	Export	Import
2008–9	9354	32497	6389	12006	1439	11099	21150	18561	769	11870	6650	5872	8450	7655	24477	23791	3026	7886	3825	4428	6655	6452	185295	303696
	(5.0)	(10.7)	(3.4)	(4.0)	(0.8)	(3.7)	(11.4)	(6.1)	(0.4)	(3.9)	(3.6)	(1.9)	(4.6)	(2.5)	(13.2)	(7.8)	(1.6)	(2.6)	(2.1)	(1.5)	(3.6)	(2.1)	(100.0)	(100.0)
2007–8	10871	27146	5122	9885	1152	7815	20731	21067	614	9758	6706	4954	7379	8123	15637	13483	3858	6326	3914	3907	6313	2698	163132	251654
	(6.7)	(10.8)	(3.1)	(3.9)	(0.7)	(3.1)	(12.7)	(8.4)	(0.4)	(3.9)	(4.1)	(2.0)	(4.5)	(3.2)	(9.6)	(5.4)	(2.4)	(2.5)	(2.4)	(1.6)	(3.9)	(1.1)	(100.0)	(100.0)
2006–7	8294	17461	3980	7546	925	7008	18866	11736	467	9124	5618	4175	6069	5490	12032	8658	2863	4596	3583	2674	4681	2484	126414	185735
	(6.6)	(9.4)	(3.1)	(4.1)	(0.7)	(3.8)	(14.9)	(6.3)	(0.4)	(4.9)	(4.4)	(2.2)	(4.8)	(3.0)	(9.5)	(4.7)	(2.3)	(2.5)	(2.8)	(1.4)	(3.7)	(1.3)	(100.0)	(100.0)
2005–6	6759	10868	3586	6024	821	4947	17353	9455	480	6556	5059	3930	5425	3354	8592	4354	2481	4061	2519	1856	4471	2207	103091	149166
	(6.6)	(7.3)	(3.5)	(4.0)	(0.8)	(3.3)	(16.8)	(6.3)	(0.5)	(4.4)	(4.9)	(2.6)	(5.3)	(2.2)	(8.3)	(2.9)	(2.4)	(2.7)	(2.4)	(1.2)	(4.3)	(1.5)	(100.0)	(100.0)
2004–5	5616	7098	2826	4015	720	3825	13766	7001	541	5940	3681	3566	4006	2651	7348	4641	2128	3235	2286	1373	3692	1730	83536	111517
	(6.7)	(6.4)	(3.4)	(3.6)	(0.9)	(3.4)	(16.5)	(6.3)	(0.6)	(5.3)	(4.4)	(3.2)	(4.8)	(2.4)	(8.8)	(4.2)	(2.5)	(2.9)	(2.7)	(1.2)	(4.4)	(1.6)	(100.0)	(100.0)
2003–4	2955	4053	2545	2919	584	2649	11490	5035	450	3313	3023	3234	2125	2085	5126	2060	1709	2668	1729	1071	3262	1493	63843	78149
	(4.6)	(5.2)	(4.0)	(3.7)	(0.9)	(3.4)	(18.0)	(6.4)	(0.7)	(4.2)	(4.7)	(4.1)	(3.3)	(2.7)	(8.0)	(2.6)	(2.7)	(3.4)	(2.7)	(1.4)	(5.1)	(1.9)	(100.0)	(100.0)
2002–3	1976	2792	2107	2405	504	1337	10896	4444	383	2330	2496	2777	1422	1435	3328	957	1864	1836	1357	812	2613	973	52719	61412
	(3.7)	(4.5)	(4.0)	(3.9)	(1.0)	(2.2)	(20.7)	(7.2)	(0.7)	(3.8)	(4.7)	(4.5)	(2.7)	(2.3)	(6.3)	(1.6)	(3.5)	(3.0)	(2.6)	(1.3)	(5.0)	(1.6)	(100.0)	(100.0)
2001–2	952	2036	1788	2028	418	1306	8513	3150	409	2871	2161	2563	972	1304	2492	915	1510	2146	1207	705	2366	729	43827	51413
	(2.2)	(4.0)	(4.1)	(3.9)	(1.0)	(2.5)	(19.4)	(6.1)	(0.9)	(5.6)	(4.9)	(5.0)	(2.2)	(2.5)	(5.7)	(1.8)	(3.4)	(4.2)	(2.8)	(1.4)	(5.4)	(1.4)	(100.0)	(100.0)
2000–1	831	1502	1908	1760	406	1063	9305	3015	438	3160	2299	3168	877	1464	2598	659	1795	1842	1309	724	2641	852	44560	50537
	(1.9)	(3.0)	(4.3)	(3.5)	(0.9)	(2.1)	(20.9)	(6.0)	(1.0)	(6.3)	(5.2)	(6.3)	(2.0)	(2.9)	(5.8)	(1.3)	(4.0)	(3.6)	(2.9)	(1.4)	(5.9)	(1.7)	(100.0)	(100.0)
1999–2000	539	1287	1738	1842	403	1082	8396	3564	354	2598	2035	2707	673	1534	2083	2334	1685	2536	1120	735	2511	818	36822	49671
	(1.5)	(2.6)	(4.7)	(3.7)	(1.1)	(2.2)	(22.8)	(7.2)	(1.0)	(5.2)	(5.5)	(5.4)	(1.8)	(3.1)	(5.7)	(4.7)	(4.6)	(5.1)	(3.0)	(1.5)	(6.8)	(1.6)	(100.0)	(100.0)
1998–9	427	1097	1852	2141	387	1445	7200	3640	319	2942	1855	2621	518	1384	1868	1721	1652	2466	1055	1088	1881	449	33219	42389
	(1.3)	(2.6)	(5.6)	(5.1)	(1.2)	(3.4)	(21.7)	(8.6)	(1.0)	(6.9)	(5.6)	(6.2)	(1.6)	(3.3)	(5.6)	(4.1)	(5.0)	(5.8)	(3.2)	(2.6)	(5.7)	(1.1)	(100.0)	(100.0)
1997–8	718	1119	1924	2529	438	1486	6803	3717	368	2641	2141	2444	780	1198	1692	1780	1899	2145	1115	922	1932	316	35006	41485
	(2.1)	(2.7)	(5.5)	(6.1)	(1.3)	(3.6)	(19.4)	(9.0)	(1.0)	(6.4)	(6.1)	(5.9)	(2.2)	(2.9)	(4.8)	(4.3)	(5.4)	(5.2)	(3.2)	(2.2)	(5.5)	(0.8)	(100.0)	(100.0)
1996–7	615	757	1893	2831	385	1317	6555	3686	300	1127	2047	2135	978	1063	1476	1736	2006	2187	934	987	1863	319	33470	39132
	(1.8)	(1.9)	(5.7)	(7.2)	(1.2)	(3.4)	(19.6)	(9.4)	(0.9)	(2.9)	(6.1)	(5.5)	(2.9)	(2.7)	(4.4)	(4.4)	(6.0)	(5.6)	(2.8)	(2.5)	(5.6)	(0.8)	(100.0)	(100.0)
1995–6	333	812	1977	3145	376	1022	5520	3861	282	1021	2011	1918	902	1092	1428	1607	2216	2468	1014	1064	1821	388	31795	36675
	(1.0)	(2.2)	(6.2)	(8.6)	(1.2)	(2.8)	(17.4)	(10.5)	(0.9)	(2.8)	(6.3)	(5.2)	(2.8)	(3.0)	(4.5)	(4.4)	(7.0)	(6.7)	(3.2)	(2.9)	(5.7)	(1.1)	(100.0)	(100.0)

(Continued)

Table A10.3 *Continued*

(1)	China (2)		Germany (3)		Australia (4)		USA (5)		Switzerland (6)		UK (7)		Singapore (8)		UAE (9)		Japan (10)		Italy (11)		Hong Kong (12)		Total (13)	
	Export	Import	Export	Import	Export	Import	Export	Import	Export	Import	Export	Import	Export	Import	Export	Import	Export	Import	Export	Import	Export	Import	Export	Import
1994–5	254	761	1748	2187	346	915	5021	2906	247	824	1690	1559	770	900	1266	1533	2027	2040	858	741	1517	287	26331	28654
	(1.0)	(2.7)	(6.6)	(7.6)	(1.3)	(3.2)	(19.1)	(10.1)	(0.9)	(2.9)	(6.4)	(5.4)	(2.9)	(3.1)	(4.8)	(5.4)	(7.7)	(7.1)	(3.3)	(2.6)	(5.8)	(1.0)	(100.0)	(100.0)
1993–4	279	302	1539	1790	245	659	3999	2737	221	506	1379	1536	752	627	1158	1003	1741	1522	604	538	1250	189	22238	23306
	(1.3)	(1.3)	(6.9)	(7.7)	(1.1)	(2.8)	(18.0)	(11.7)	(1.0)	(2.2)	(6.2)	(6.6)	(3.4)	(2.7)	(5.2)	(4.3)	(7.8)	(6.5)	(2.7)	(2.3)	(5.6)	(0.8)	(100.0)	(100.0)
1992–3	141	126	1427	1657	223	838	3516	2147	199	378	1213	1417	589	632	814	1112	1437	1428	622	524	765	170	18537	21882
	(0.8)	(0.6)	(7.7)	(7.6)	(1.2)	(3.8)	(19.0)	(9.8)	(1.1)	(1.7)	(6.5)	(6.5)	(3.2)	(2.9)	(4.4)	(5.1)	(7.7)	(6.5)	(3.4)	(2.4)	(4.1)	(0.8)	(100.0)	(100.0)
1991–2	48	21	1270	1559	203	586	2921	1995	219	151	1138	1202	389	695	739	1248	1652	1369	580	448	614	106	17865	19411
	(0.3)	(0.1)	(7.1)	(8.0)	(1.1)	(3.0)	(16.4)	(10.3)	(1.2)	(0.8)	(6.4)	(6.2)	(2.2)	(3.6)	(4.1)	(6.4)	(9.2)	(7.1)	(3.2)	(2.3)	(3.4)	(0.5)	(100.0)	(100.0)
1990–1	18	31	1421	1936	179	816	2673	2923	224	268	1186	1613	379	796	439	1059	1694	1808	558	608	597	166	18145	24073
	(0.1)	(0.1)	(7.8)	(8.0)	(1.0)	(3.4)	(14.7)	(12.1)	(1.2)	(1.1)	(6.5)	(6.7)	(2.1)	(3.3)	(2.4)	(4.4)	(9.3)	(7.5)	(3.1)	(2.5)	(3.3)	(0.7)	(100.0)	(100.0)
1989–90	24	40	1064	1674	201	539	2686	2561	219	219	961	1783	280	540	427	857	1639	1692	457	464	537	149	16613	21219
	(0.1)	(0.2)	(6.4)	(7.9)	(1.2)	(2.5)	(16.2)	(12.1)	(1.3)	(1.0)	(5.8)	(8.4)	(1.7)	(2.5)	(2.6)	(4.0)	(9.9)	(8.0)	(2.7)	(2.2)	(3.2)	(0.7)	(100.0)	(100.0)
1988–9	91	98	854	1697	183	488	2574	2237	188	194	796	1656	223	429	293	602	1488	1817	373	347	565	121	13970	19497
	(0.7)	(0.5)	(6.1)	(8.7)	(1.3)	(2.5)	(18.4)	(11.5)	(1.3)	(1.0)	(5.7)	(8.5)	(1.6)	(2.2)	(2.1)	(3.1)	(10.6)	(9.3)	(2.7)	(1.8)	(4.0)	(0.6)	(100.0)	(100.0)
1987–8	15	119	817	1665	139	388	2252	1544	157	182	783	1410	211	323	239	588	1245	1640	384	395	344	93	12089	17156
	(0.1)	(0.7)	(6.8)	(9.7)	(1.1)	(2.3)	(18.6)	(9.0)	(1.3)	(1.1)	(6.5)	(8.2)	(1.7)	(1.9)	(2.0)	(3.4)	(10.3)	(9.6)	(3.2)	(2.3)	(2.8)	(0.5)	(100.0)	(100.0)

Source: Directorate General of Commercial Intelligence and Statistics (DGCI&S).

Notes: Figures in brackets are percentages to total export/import. The countries are selected as per the the following criteria. USA, UAE, and China are top in both import and export in 2008–9. UK, Singapore, UAE, and Germany are top destination of exports in 2008–9. Australia and Switzerland are two top import destinations to India in 2008–9. Japan, Italy, and Hong Kong are another three partners in trade where both export and imports are above $1000 million.

A11 FOREIGN INVESTMENT AND NRI DEPOSITS
Table A11.1 Foreign Investment Inflows

(US$ million)

Year	Direct Investment (I + II + III)	I. Equity (a + b + c + d + e)	a. Government (SIA/FIPB)	b. RBI	c. NRI	d. Acquisition of Shares*	e. Equity Capital of Unincorporated Bodies #	II. Reinvested Earnings +	III. Other Capital ++	Portfolio Investment (a + b + c)	a. GDRs/ADRs ##	b. FIIs **	c. Offshore Funds and Others	Total (A + B)
1990–1	97	0	0	0	0	0	0	0	0	6	0	0	6	103
1991–2	129	129	66	0	63	0	0	0	0	4	0	0	4	133
1992–3	315	315	222	42	51	0	0	0	0	244	240	1	3	559
1993–4	586	586	280	89	217	0	0	0	0	3567	1520	1665	382	4153
1994–5	1314	1314	701	171	442	0	0	0	0	3824	2082	1503	239	5138
1995–6	2144	2144	1249	169	715	11	0	0	0	2748	683	2009	56	4892
1996–7	2821	2821	1922	135	639	125	0	0	0	3312	1366	1926	20	6133
1997–8	3557	3557	2754	202	241	360	0	0	0	1828	645	979	204	5385
1998–9	2462	2462	1821	179	62	400	0	0	0	–61	270	–390	59	2401
1999–2000	2155	2155	1410	171	84	490	0	0	0	3026	768	2135	123	5181
2000–1	4029	2400	1456	454	67	362	61	1350	279	2760	831	1847	82	6789
2001–2	6130	4095	2221	767	35	881	191	1645	390	2021	477	1505	39	8151
2002–3	5035	2764	919	739	–	916	190	1833	438	979	600	377	2	6014
2003–4	4322	2229	928	534	–	735	32	1460	633	11377	459	10918	–	15699
2004–5	6051	3778	1062	1258	–	930	528	1904	369	9315	613	8686	16	15366
2005–6	8961	5975	1126	2233	–	2181	435	2760	226	12492	2552	9926	14	21453
2006–7	22826	16481	2156	7151	–	6278	896	5828	517	7003	3776	3225	2	29829
2007–8	34835	26864	2298	17127	–	5148	2291	7679	292	27271	6645	20328	298	62106
2008–9	35180	27995	4699	17998	–	4632	666	6428	757	–13,855	1162	–15,017	–	21325

Source: RBI Bulletin.

Table A11.2   NRI Deposits: Outstandings

(US$ million)

End-March	FCNR(A)	FCNR(B)	NR(E)RA	NR(NR)RD	NRO	Total
2010						
Mar						
Feb	0	14352	25797	0	7139	47288
Jan	0	14539	25744	0	7060	47343
Dec	0	14665	25905	0	6920	47490
Nov	0	14698	26079	0	6962	47739
Oct	0	14625	25715	0	6652	46992
Sep	0	14188	25434	0	6350	45972
Aug	0	14053	24931	0	6003	44987
Jul	0	14156	25369	0	5971	45496
Jun	0	14014	24952	0	5613	44579
May	0	14017	25418	0	5613	45048
Apr	0	13384	23935	0	5063	42382
2009	0	13211	23570	0	4773	41554
2008	0	14168	26716	0	2788	43672
2007	0	15129	24495	0	1616	41240
2006	0	13064	22070	0	1148	36282
2005	0	11452	21291	232	0	32975
2004	0	10961	20559	1746	0	33266
2003	0	10199	14923	3407	0	28529
2002	0	9673	8449	7052	0	25174
2001	0	9076	7147	6849	0	23072
2000	0	8172	6758	6754	0	21684
1999	0	7835	6045	6618	0	20498
1998	1	8467	5637	6262	0	20367
1997	2306	7496	4983	5604	0	20389
1996	4255	5720	3916	3542	0	17433
1995	7051	3063	4556	2486	0	17156
1994	9300	1108	3523	1754	0	15685
1993	10617	0	2740	621	0	13978
1992	9792	0	3025	0	0	12817
1991	10103	0	3618	0	0	13721

Source: *RBI Bulletin* (various issues).

Notes: All figures are inclusive of interest. FCNR(A): foreign currency non-resident (account); NR(NR)RD: non-resident (non-repatriable) rupee deposits (introduced in June 2002; FCNR(A): foreign currency non-resident (accounts) (introduced in May 2003); NR(E)RA: non-resident (external) rupee accounts; and NRO: non-resident ordinary account.

Table A11.3 FDI Inflows: Year-wise, Route-wise, and Sector-wise Break-up (August 1991 to November 2009)

Actual Inflows of FDI/NRI: Year-wise and Route-wise

	Rs crore								US$ million							
	Govt's Approval (FIPB, SIA route)	RBI's Automatic Approval	Amount of Inflows on Acquisition of Shares	RBI's Various NRI Scheme	Total	Stock Swapped	Closing Balance of Advance	Grand Total	Govt's Approval (FIPB, SIA route)	RBI's Automatic Approval	Amount of Inflows on Acquisition of Shares	RBI's Various NRI Scheme	Total	Stock Swapped	Closing Balance of Advance	Grand Total
(1)	(2)	(3)	(4)	(5)	(6)	(7)	(8)	(9)	(10)	(11)	(12)	(13)	(14)	(15)	(16)	(17)
1991 (Aug–Dec)	1912	–	–	1623	3535	–	–	3535	78	0		66	144			144
1992	4907	475	–	1530	6912	–	–	6912	188	18		59	264			264
1993	10414	2411	–	5794	18620	–	–	18620	340	79		189	608			608
1994	16044	3626	–	11453	31122	–	–	31122	511	116		365	992			992
1995	39674	5302	–	19878	64854	–	–	64854	1264	169		633	2065			2065
1996	57667	6196	3038	20621	87522	–	–	87522	1677	180	88	600	2545			2545
1997	101284	8677	9540	10396	129898	–	–	129898	2824	242	266	290	3621			3621
1998	82397	6107	40594	3595	132692	–	–	132692	2086	155	1028	91	3359			3359
1999	61895	7608	19608	3488	92599	–	9068	101667	1474	181	467	83	2205		216	2421
2000	63368	16975	20581	3488	104411	–	19126	123537	1474	395	479	81	2429		445	2873
2001	96386	32411	29622	2293	160711	–	7066	167778	2142	720	658	51	3571		157	3728
2002	69580	39030	52623	111	161344	840	19771	181956	1450	813	1096	2	3361	18	412	3791
2003	42956	23400	29284	–	95639	1725	18808	116172	934	509	637		2079	38	409	2526
2004	48517	54221	45076	–	147814	-	24852	172665	1055	1179	980		3213		540	3754
2005	49728	68687	74292	–	192707	284	–	192991	1136	1558	1661		4355	6		4361
2006	69683	321758	112131	–	503572	-	–	503572	1534	7121	750		11120			11120
2007	107873	361001	186075	–	654950	142406	–	797357	2586	8889	4447		15921	3325		19156
2008	135588	1004681	256986	–	1397255	212	–	1397467	3209	23651	6187		33029	5		33034
2009 (Jan–Nov)	227355	862373	148217	–	1237945	2581	–	1240527	4630	17824	3050		25504	54		25558
Total	1275189	2740504	1011383	84270	5111275	147426	98690	5470842	30483	62639	23427	2510	119059	3342	2179	125919

(30 Nov 2009)

Source: www.Dipp.nic.in (*SIA Newsletter*).

A12 POPULATION

Table A12.1 State-wise Population, 1951–2001

(in million)

State/UTs	2001	Decadal Growth (%) (1991–2001)	1991	Decadal Growth (%) (1981–91)	1981	Decadal Growth (%) (1971–81)	1971	Decadal Growth (%) (1961–71)	1961	Decadal Growth (%) (1951–61)	1951	Decadal Growth (%) (1941–51)
(1)	(2)	(3)	(4)	(5)	(6)	(7)	(8)	(9)	(10)	(11)	(12)	(13)
India	1028.61	21.5	846.39	23.9	683.33	24.7	548.16	24.8	439.23	21.6	361.09	13.3
Andhra Pradesh	76.21	14.6	66.51	24.2	53.55	23.1	43.50	20.9	35.98	15.6	31.12	14.0
Arunachal Pradesh	1.10	27.2	0.87	36.9	0.63	35.0	0.47	38.9	0.34	–	–	–
Assam	26.66	18.9	22.41	24.2	18.04	23.4	14.63	35.0	10.84	35.0	8.03	19.9
Bihar	83.00	28.6	64.53	-7.7	69.92	24.1	56.35	21.3	46.45	19.8	38.78	10.3
Goa	1.35	15.4	1.17	16.2	1.01	26.7	0.80	34.7	0.59	7.9	0.55	1.1
Gujarat	50.67	22.7	41.31	21.2	34.09	27.7	26.70	29.4	20.63	26.9	16.26	18.7
Haryana	21.14	28.4	16.46	27.4	12.92	28.8	10.04	32.2	7.59	33.8	5.67	7.6
Himachal Pradesh	6.08	17.6	5.17	20.8	4.28	23.7	3.46	23.0	2.81	17.9	2.39	5.4
Jammu & Kashmir	10.14	29.9	7.80	30.3	5.99	29.7	4.62	29.7	3.56	9.4	3.25	10.4
Karnataka	52.85	17.5	44.98	21.1	37.14	26.7	29.30	24.2	23.59	21.6	19.40	19.4
Kerala	31.84	9.4	29.10	14.3	25.45	19.2	21.35	26.3	16.90	24.8	13.55	22.8
Madhya Pradesh	60.35	24.3	48.57	-8.0	52.79	26.7	41.65	28.7	32.37	24.2	26.07	8.7
Maharashtra	96.88	22.7	78.94	25.7	62.78	24.5	50.41	27.5	39.55	23.6	32.00	19.3
Manipur	2.17	18.1	1.84	29.3	1.42	32.4	1.07	37.6	0.78	34.9	0.58	12.9
Meghalaya	2.32	30.7	1.78	32.9	1.34	32.0	1.01	31.6	0.77	26.9	0.61	9.0
Mizoram	0.89	29.0	0.69	39.7	0.49	48.8	0.33	24.8	0.27	35.7	0.20	28.1
Nagaland	1.99	64.5	1.21	56.1	0.78	50.2	0.52	39.8	0.37	73.2	0.21	12.1
Orissa	36.80	16.2	31.66	20.1	26.37	20.2	21.95	25.0	17.55	19.8	14.65	6.4
Punjab	24.36	20.1	20.28	20.8	16.79	23.9	13.55	21.7	11.14	21.5	9.16	-4.6
Rajasthan	56.51	28.4	44.01	28.4	34.26	33.0	25.77	27.8	20.16	26.2	15.97	15.2
Sikkim	0.54	33.0	0.41	28.5	0.32	50.5	0.21	29.6	0.16	17.4	0.14	13.1
Tamil Nadu	62.41	11.7	55.86	15.4	48.41	17.5	41.20	22.3	33.69	11.8	30.12	14.7
Tripura	3.20	16.1	2.76	34.2	2.06	31.7	1.56	36.6	1.14	78.7	0.64	24.6
Uttar Pradesh	166.20	25.9	132.00	19.1	110.86	25.5	88.34	19.8	73.76	16.7	63.22	11.8
West Bengal	80.18	16.5	68.80	26.1	54.58	23.2	44.31	26.9	34.93	32.8	26.30	13.2
Uttranchal	8.49	19.4	7.11	–	–	–	–	–	–	–	–	–
Jharkhand	26.95	23.4	21.84	–	–	–	–	–	–	–	–	–
Chhattisgarh	20.83	18.3	17.62	–	–	–	–	–	–	–	–	–
Union Territories												
Andaman & Nicobar	0.36	28.1	0.28	48.7	0.19	64.3	0.12	-82.0	0.64	106.5	0.31	-8.8
Chandigarh	0.90	40.2	0.64	42.0	0.45	75.9	0.26	114.2	0.12	-50.0	0.24	4.3
Dadra & Nagar Haveli	0.22	59.4	0.14	32.7	0.10	40.5	0.07	27.6	0.06	38.1	0.04	5.0
Daman and Diu	0.16	54.9	0.10	29.1	0.08	25.4	0.06	70.3	0.04	-24.5	0.05	14.0
Delhi	13.85	47.0	9.42	51.5	6.22	55.2	4.01	50.7	2.66	52.5	1.74	90.0
Lakshadweep	0.06	15.4	0.05	30.0	0.04	25.0	0.03	33.3	0.02	14.3	0.02	16.7
Pondicherry	0.97	20.5	0.81	33.8	0.60	28.0	0.47	27.9	0.37	16.4	0.32	11.2

Source: Census of India (2001), Primary Census Abstract and Census of India (1991), Final Population Totals: Paper 1 of 1992, Vol. II.

Table 12.2 State-wise: Rural and Urban Population of India, 1951–2001

(in million)

State/UTs	2001 Rural	2001 Urban	1991 Rural	1991 Urban	1981 Rural	1981 Urban	1971 Rural	1971 Urban	1961 Rural	1961 Urban	1951 Rural	1951 Urban
India	741.66	285.36 (27.7)	628.69	217.61 (25.7)	523.87	159.46 (23.3)	439.05	109.11 (19.9)	360.30	78.94 (18.0)	298.64	62.44 (17.3)
Andhra Pradesh	55.22	20.50 (26.9)	48.62	17.89 (26.9)	41.06	12.49 (23.3)	35.10	8.40 (19.3)	29.71	6.28 (17.4)	25.69	5.42 (17.4)
Arunachal Pradesh	0.48	0.06 (5.5)	0.75	0.11 (12.8)	0.59	0.04 (6.5)	0.45	0.02 (3.6)	0.34	–	–	–
Assam	23.25	3.39 (12.7)	19.93	2.49 (11.1)	16.26	1.78 (9.9)	13.34	1.29 (8.8)	10.06	0.78 (7.2)	7.68	0.35 (4.3)
Bihar	74.20	8.68 (10.5)	75.02	11.35 (17.6)	61.20	8.72 (12.5)	50.72	5.63 (10.0)	42.53	3.91 (8.4)	36.16	2.63 (6.8)
Goa	0.68	0.67 (49.6)	0.69	0.48 (41.0)	0.69	0.32 (32.1)	0.59	0.20 (25.5)	0.50	0.09 (14.7)	0.48	0.07 (13.0)
Gujarat	31.70	18.90 (37.3)	27.06	14.25 (34.5)	23.48	10.60 (31.1)	19.20	7.50 (28.1)	15.32	5.32 (25.8)	11.84	4.43 (27.2)
Haryana	14.97	6.11 (28.9)	12.41	4.06 (24.6)	10.10	2.83 (21.9)	8.26	1.77 (17.7)	6.28	1.31 (17.2)	4.71	0.97 (17.1)
Himachal Pradesh	5.48	0.60 (9.8)	4.72	0.45 (8.7)	3.96	0.33 (7.6)	3.22	0.24 (7.0)	2.63	0.18 (6.3)	2.23	0.15 (6.5)
Jammu & Kashmir	7.57	2.51 (24.7)	5.88	1.84 (23.6)	4.73	1.26 (21.0)	3.76	0.86 (18.6)	2.97	0.59 (16.7)	2.80	0.46 (14.0)
Karnataka	34.81	17.92 (33.9)	31.07	13.91 (30.9)	26.41	10.73 (28.9)	22.18	7.12 (24.3)	18.32	5.27 (22.3)	14.95	4.45 (23.0)
Kerala	23.57	8.27 (26.0)	21.42	7.68 (26.4)	20.68	4.77 (18.7)	17.81	3.47 (16.2)	14.35	2.55 (15.1)	11.72	1.83 (13.5)
Madhya Pradesh	44.28	16.10 (26.7)	50.84	15.34 (23.2)	41.59	10.59 (20.1)	34.87	6.79 (16.3)	27.75	4.63 (14.3)	22.94	3.13 (12.0)
Maharashtra	55.73	41.02 (42.3)	48.40	30.54 (38.7)	40.79	21.99 (35.0)	34.70	15.71 (31.2)	28.39	11.16 (28.2)	22.80	9.20 (28.8)
Manipur	1.82	0.57 (26.3)	1.33	0.51 (27.5)	1.05	0.38 (26.4)	0.93	0.14 (13.1)	0.71	0.07 (8.7)	0.58	0.03 (4.8)
Meghalaya	1.85	0.45 (19.5)	1.45	0.33 (18.6)	1.09	0.24 (18.0)	0.87	0.15 (14.5)	0.65	0.12 (15.2)	0.55	0.06 (9.9)
Mizoram	0.45	0.44 (49.6)	0.37	0.32 (46.1)	0.37	0.12 (24.7)	0.30	0.04 (11.4)	0.25	0.01 (5.3)	0.19	0.01 (3.6)
Nagaland	1.64	0.35 (17.7)	1.00	0.21 (17.2)	0.66	0.12 (15.5)	0.47	0.05 (9.9)	0.35	0.02 (5.1)	0.21	0.00 (0.9)
Orissa	31.21	5.50 (14.9)	27.43	4.24 (13.4)	23.26	3.11 (11.8)	20.10	1.85 (8.4)	16.44	1.11 (6.3)	14.05	0.59 (4.1)
Punjab	16.04	8.25 (33.9)	14.29	5.99 (29.5)	12.14	4.65 (27.7)	10.34	3.22 (23.7)	8.57	2.57 (23.1)	7.17	1.99 (21.7)
Rajasthan	43.27	13.21 (23.4)	33.94	10.07 (22.9)	27.05	7.21 (21.0)	21.22	4.54 (17.6)	16.87	3.28 (16.3)	13.02	2.96 (18.5)
Sikkim	0.48	0.06 (11.1)	0.37	0.04 (9.1)	0.27	0.05 (16.1)	0.19	0.02 (9.5)	0.16	0.07 (43.2)	0.14	0.03 (21.7)
Tamil Nadu	34.87	27.24 (43.7)	36.78	19.08 (34.2)	32.46	15.95 (33.0)	28.73	12.47 (30.3)	24.70	8.99 (26.7)	22.79	7.33 (24.4)
Tripura	2.65	0.54 (17.0)	2.34	0.42 (15.3)	1.83	0.23 (11.0)	1.39	0.16 (10.4)	1.04	0.10 (9.0)	0.60	0.04 (6.8)
Uttar Pradesh	131.54	34.51 (20.8)	111.51	27.61 (20.9)	90.96	19.90 (17.9)	75.95	12.39 (14.0)	64.28	9.48 (12.9)	54.59	8.63 (13.6)
West Bengal	57.74	22.49 (28.0)	49.37	18.71 (27.2)	40.13	14.45 (26.5)	33.35	10.97 (24.7)	26.39	8.54 (24.5)	20.02	6.28 (23.9)
Uttranchal	6.31	2.17 (25.6)	–	–	–	–	–	–	–	–	–	–
Jharkhand	20.92	5.99 (22.2)	–	–	–	–	–	–	–	–	–	–
Chhattisgarh	16.62	4.18 (20.0)	–	–	–	–	–	–	–	–	–	–
Union Territories												
Andaman & Nicobar	0.24	0.12 (32.2)	0.21	0.08 (26.7)	0.14	0.05 (23.8)	0.09	0.03 (22.6)	0.05	0.01 (2.2)	0.02	0.01 (2.6)
Chandigarh	0.09	0.81 (89.9)	0.07	0.58 (89.7)	0.03	0.42 (93.6)	0.02	0.23 (90.7)	0.02	0.10 (82.5)	0.02	0.00 (0.0)
Dadra & Nagar Haveli	0.17	0.05 (22.7)	0.13	0.01 (8.7)	0.10	0.01 (6.7)	0.07	0.00 (0.0)	0.06	0.00 (0.0)	0.04	0.00 (0.0)
Daman and Diu	0.10	0.06 (36.1)	0.05	0.05 (47.1)	0.05	0.03 (36.7)	0.04	0.02 (38.1)	0.02	0.01 (35.1)	0.03	0.02 (36.7)
Delhi	0.96	12.82 (92.6)	0.92	8.47 (89.9)	0.45	5.77 (92.7)	0.42	3.66 (91.5)	0.30	2.36 (88.7)	0.31	1.44 (82.4)
Lakshadweep	0.03	0.03 (45.0)	0.02	0.03 (55.8)	0.02	0.02 (47.5)	0.03	0.00 (0.0)	0.02	0.00 (0.0)	0.02	0.00 (0.0)
Pondicherry	0.33	0.65 (66.5)	0.30	0.52 (64.0)	0.29	0.32 (52.3)	0.27	0.20 (42.3)	0.28	0.09 (24.4)	0.32	0.00 (0.0)

Source: Census of India (2001), *Provisional Population Totals*, Part 1 of 2001 and Census of India (1991), *Final Population Totals, Paper–1 of 1992, Vol. II.*

Note: Figures within brackets represents urban share in total population in percentages.

Table A12.3   State-wise: Sex Ratio (females per 1000 males)

State/UTs	2001	1991	1981	1971	1961	1951	1941	1931	1921	1911	1901
(1)	(2)	(3)	(4)	(5)	(6)	(7)	(8)	(9)	(10)	(11)	(12)
India	933	927	934	930	941	946	945	950	955	964	972
Andhra Pradesh	978	972	975	977	981	986	980	987	993	992	985
Arunachal Pradesh	893	859	862	861	894	na	na	na	na	na	na
Assam	935	923	910	896	869	868	875	874	896	915	919
Bihar	919	907	948	957	1005	1000	1002	995	1020	1051	1061
Goa	961	967	975	981	1066	1128	1084	1088	1120	1108	1091
Gujarat	920	934	942	934	940	952	941	945	944	946	954
Haryana	861	865	870	867	868	871	869	844	844	835	867
Himachal Pradesh	968	976	973	958	938	912	890	897	890	889	884
Jammu & Kashmir	892	896	892	878	878	873	869	865	870	876	882
Karnataka	965	960	963	957	959	966	960	965	969	981	983
Kerala	1058	1036	1032	1016	1022	1028	1027	1022	1011	1008	1004
Madhya Pradesh	919	912	921	920	932	945	946	947	949	967	972
Maharashtra	922	934	937	930	936	941	949	947	950	966	978
Manipur	978	958	971	980	1015	1036	1055	1065	1041	1029	1037
Meghalaya	972	955	954	942	937	949	966	971	1000	1013	1036
Mizoram	935	921	919	946	1009	1041	1069	1102	1109	1120	1113
Nagaland	900	886	863	871	933	999	1021	997	992	993	973
Orissa	972	971	981	988	1001	1022	1053	1067	1086	1056	1037
Punjab	876	882	879	865	854	844	836	815	799	780	832
Rajasthan	921	910	919	911	908	921	906	907	896	908	905
Sikkim	875	878	835	863	904	907	920	967	970	951	916
Tamil Nadu	987	974	977	978	992	1007	1012	1027	1029	1042	1044
Tripura	948	945	946	943	932	904	886	885	885	885	874
Uttar Pradesh	898	876	882	876	907	908	907	903	908	916	938
West Bengal	934	917	911	891	878	865	852	890	905	925	945
Uttranchal	962	936	936	940	947	940	907	913	916	907	918
Jharkhand	941	922	940	945	960	961	978	989	1002	1021	1032
Chhattisgarh	989	985	996	998	1008	1024	1032	1043	1041	1039	1046
Union Territories											
Andaman & Nicobar	846	818	760	644	617	625	574	495	303	352	318
Chandigarh	777	790	769	749	652	781	763	751	743	720	771
Dadra & Nagar Haveli	812	952	974	1007	963	946	925	911	940	967	960
Daman and Diu	710	969	1062	1099	1169	1125	1080	1088	1143	1040	995
Delhi	821	827	808	801	785	768	715	722	733	793	862
Lakshadweep	948	943	975	978	1020	1043	1018	994	1027	987	1063
Pondicherry	1001	979	985	989	1013	1030	na	na	1053	1058	na

Source: Census of India (2001), *Provisional Population Totals*, Part 1 of 2001.

Note: Excludes Mao-Maram, Paomata, and Purul sub-divisions of Senapati district of Manipur.

Table A12.4 State-Wise Literacy Rate, 1951–2001

(in percentage of population)

State/UTs	2001			1991			1981			1971			1961			1951		
	Persons	Male	Female	Persons	Male	Female	Persons	Male	Female	Persons	Male	Female	Persons	Male	Female	Persons	Male	Female
(1)	(2)	(3)	(4)	(5)	(6)	(7)	(8)	(9)	(10)	(11)	(12)	(13)	(14)	(15)	(16)	(17)	(18)	(19)
India	64.8	75.3	53.7	52.2	64.1	39.3	43.6	56.4	29.8	34.5	39.5	18.7	28.3	34.40	12.9	18.3	24.9	7.9
Male–Female Gap	(21.6)			(24.8)			(26.6)			(24.0)			(25.1)			(18.3)		
Andhra Pradesh	60.5	70.3	50.4	44.1	55.1	32.7	35.7	46.8	24.2	24.6	33.1	15.8	21.2	30.20	12.0	13.2	19.7	6.5
Arunachal Pradesh	54.3	63.8	43.5	41.6	51.5	29.7	25.5	35.1	14.0	11.3	17.8	3.7	47.9	na	na	na	na	na
Assam	63.3	71.3	54.6	52.9	61.9	43.0	na	na	na	28.7	na	na	33.0	37.30	16.0	18.3	27.4	7.9
Bihar	47.0	59.7	33.1	38.5	52.5	22.9	32.0	46.6	16.5	19.9	30.6	8.7	21.8	29.80	6.9	12.2	20.5	3.8
Goa	82.0	88.4	75.4	75.5	83.6	67.1	64.7	76.0	55.2	na	54.3	35.1	36.2	na	na	23.0	na	na
Gujarat	69.1	79.7	57.8	61.3	73.1	48.6	52.2	65.1	38.5	35.8	46.1	24.8	30.5	41.10	19.1	23.1	32.3	13.5
Haryana	67.9	78.5	55.7	55.9	69.1	40.5	43.9	58.5	26.9	26.9	37.2	14.9	24.1	na	na	na	na	na
Himachal Pradesh	76.5	85.3	67.4	63.9	75.4	52.1	51.2	64.3	37.7	32.0	43.1	20.2	24.9	27.20	6.2	7.7	12.6	2.4
Jammu and Kashmir	55.5	66.6	43.0	na	na	na	32.7	44.2	19.6	18.6	na	na	13.0	17.00	4.3	na	na	na
Karnataka	66.6	76.1	56.9	56.0	67.3	44.3	46.2	58.7	33.2	31.5	48.6	27.8	29.8	36.10	14.2	19.3	29.1	9.2
Kerala	90.9	94.2	87.7	89.8	93.6	86.2	81.6	87.7	75.7	60.4	74.0	64.5	55.1	55.00	38.9	40.7	50.2	31.5
Madhya Pradesh	63.7	76.1	50.3	44.2	58.4	28.9	34.2	48.4	19.0	22.1	32.7	10.9	20.5	27.00	6.7	9.8	16.2	3.2
Maharashtra	76.9	86.0	67.0	64.9	76.6	52.3	55.8	69.7	41.0	39.2	51.0	26.4	35.1	42.00	16.8	20.9	31.4	9.7
Manipur	70.5	80.3	60.5	59.9	71.6	47.6	49.6	64.1	34.6	32.9	46.0	19.5	36.0	45.10	15.9	11.4	20.8	2.4
Meghalaya	62.6	65.4	59.6	49.1	53.1	44.9	42.0	46.6	37.2	29.5	34.1	24.6	na	na	na	na	na	na
Mizoram	88.8	90.7	86.7	82.3	85.6	78.6	74.3	79.4	68.6	na	60.5	46.7	na	na	na	na	na	na
Nagaland	66.6	71.2	61.5	61.6	67.6	54.8	50.2	58.5	40.3	27.4	35.0	18.7	20.4	24.00	11.3	10.4	15.0	5.7
Orissa	63.1	75.3	50.5	49.1	63.1	34.7	41.0	56.5	25.1	26.2	38.3	13.9	25.2	34.70	8.6	15.8	27.3	4.5
Punjab	69.7	75.2	63.4	58.5	65.7	50.4	48.1	55.5	39.6	33.7	40.4	25.9	31.5	33.00	14.1	15.2	21.0	8.5
Rajasthan	60.4	75.7	43.9	38.6	55.0	20.4	30.1	44.8	14.0	19.1	28.7	8.5	18.1	23.70	5.8	8.9	14.4	3.0
Sikkim	68.8	76.0	60.4	56.9	65.7	46.7	41.6	53.0	27.4	17.7	na	na	14.2	19.60	4.3	7.3	12.8	1.3
Tamil Nadu	73.5	82.4	64.4	62.7	73.8	51.3	54.4	68.1	40.4	39.5	51.8	26.9	36.4	44.50	18.2	20.8	31.7	10.0
Tripura	73.2	81.0	64.9	60.4	70.6	49.7	50.1	61.5	38.0	31.0	40.2	21.2	24.3	29.60	10.2	15.5	22.3	8.0
Uttar Pradesh	56.3	68.8	42.2	41.6	55.7	25.3	33.3	47.4	17.2	21.7	31.5	10.6	20.7	27.30	7.0	10.8	17.4	3.6
West Bengal	68.6	77.0	59.6	57.7	67.8	46.6	48.6	59.9	36.1	33.2	42.8	22.4	34.5	40.10	17.0	24.0	34.2	12.2
Uttranchal	71.6	83.3	59.6	na	na	na	na	na	na	na	na	na	na	na	na	na	na	na
Jharkhand	53.6	67.3	38.9	na	na	na	na	na	na	na	na	na	na	na	na	na	na	na
Chhattisgarh	64.7	77.4	51.9	na	na	na	na	na	na	na	na	na	na	na	na	na	na	na
Union Territories																		
Andaman & Nicobar	81.3	86.3	75.2	73.0	79.0	65.5	63.2	70.3	53.2	43.6	na	na	40.1	42.40	19.4	25.8	34.2	12.3
Chandigarh	81.9	86.1	76.5	77.8	82.0	72.3	74.8	78.9	69.3	61.6	na	na	55.1	na	na	na	na	na
Dadra & Nagar Haveli	57.6	71.2	40.2	40.7	53.6	27.0	32.7	44.7	20.4	15.0	na	na	11.6	14.70	4.1	4.0	na	na
Daman and Diu	78.2	86.8	65.6	71.2	82.7	59.4	59.9	74.5	46.5	44.8	na	na	34.9	na	na	22.9	na	na
Delhi	81.7	87.3	74.7	75.3	82.0	67.0	71.9	79.3	62.6	56.6	na	na	62.0	60.80	42.5	38.4	43.0	32.3
Lakshadweep	86.7	92.5	80.5	81.8	90.2	72.9	68.4	81.2	55.3	43.7	na	na	27.2	35.80	11.0	15.2	25.6	5.3
Pondicherry	81.2	88.6	73.9	74.7	83.7	65.6	65.1	77.1	53.0	46.0	na	na	43.7	50.40	24.6	na	na	na

Source: Office of the Registrar General of India, Ministry of Home Affairs.

Note: Excludes Mao-Maram, Paomata, and Purul sub-divisions of Senapati district of Manipur.

Table A12.5 State-wise Infant Mortality Rate, 1961, 1981, 1991, 2001, and 2008

(Number per thousand)

State/Uts	2008			2001			1991			1981			1961		
	Persons	Male	Female	Persons	Male	Female	Persons	Male	Female	Persons	Male	Female	Persons	Male	Female
(1)	(2)	(3)	(4)	(5)	(6)	(7)	(8)	(9)	(10)	(11)	(12)	(13)	(14)	(15)	(16)
India	53	58	36	71	na	na	77	79	74	115	122	108	115	122	108
Andhra Pradesh	52	58	36	66	na	na	55	67	51	91	100	82	91	100	82
Arunachal Pradesh	32	34	19	44	na	na	91	111	103	126	141	111	126	141	111
Assam	64	66	39	78	na	na	92	96	87	–	–	–	–	–	–
Bihar	56	57	42	67	na	na	75	62	89	94	95	94	94	95	94
Goa	10	10	11	36	na	na	51	56	48	90	87	93	57	60	56
Gujarat	50	58	35	64	na	na	78	74	82	115	120	110	84	81	84
Haryana	54	58	43	69	na	na	52	57	54	126	132	119	94	87	119
Himachal Pradesh	44	45	27	64	na	na	82	84	81	143	160	126	92	101	89
Jammu & Kashmir	49	51	37	45	na	na	na	na	na	108	115	99	78	78	78
Karnataka	45	50	33	58	na	na	74	81	53	81	87	74	77	74	79
Kerala	12	12	10	16	na	na	42	45	41	54	61	48	52	55	48
Madhya Pradesh	70	75	48	97	na	na	133	131	136	150	158	140	150	158	140
Maharashtra	33	40	23	49	na	na	74	72	76	119	131	106	92	96	89
Manipur	14	16	8	25	na	na	28	29	27	32	31	33	32	31	33
Meghalaya	58	60	43	52	na	na	80	79	82	79	81	76	79	81	76
Mizoram	37	45	24	23	na	na	53	51	56	83	94	70	69	73	65
Nagaland	26	25	28	na	na	na	51	51	52	68	76	58	68	76	58
Orissa	69	71	49	98	na	na	125	129	111	163	172	153	115	119	111
Punjab	41	45	33	54	na	na	74	81	53	127	138	114	77	74	79
Rajasthan	63	69	38	83	na	na	87	94	79	141	146	135	114	114	114
Sikkim	33	35	19	52	na	na	60	58	62	127	135	118	96	105	87
Tamil Nadu	31	34	28	53	na	na	54	55	51	104	114	93	86	89	82
Tripura	34	36	26	49	na	na	82	81	84	130	143	116	111	106	116
Uttar Pradesh	67	70	49	85	na	na	99	98	104	130	131	128	130	131	128
West Bengal	35	37	29	53	na	na	62	75	51	95	103	57	95	103	57
Chhattisgarh	57	59	48	na	na	na	na	na	na	na	na	na	na	na	na
Jharkhand	46	49	32	na	na	na	na	na	na	na	na	na	na	na	na
Uttarakhand	44	48	24	na	na	na	na	na	na	na	na	na	na	na	na
Union Territories															
Andaman & Nicobar	31	35	23	30	na	na	69	71	61	95	114	76	77	78	66
Chandigarh	28	22	29	32	na	na	48	50	47	118	141	96	53	53	53
Dadra & Nagar Haveli	34	38	20	61	na	na	81	84	73	117	149	82	98	102	93
Daman and Diu	31	29	36	na	na	na	56	61	50	90	87	93	57	60	56
Delhi	35	40	34	51	na	na	54	55	51	100	108	92	67	66	70
Lakshadweep	31	28	35	30	na	na	91	100	78	132	170	88	118	124	88
Pondicherry	25	31	22	21	na	na	34	32	35	84	100	68	73	77	68

Source: Economic Survey 2009–10, Economic Survey 2002–03, and National Human Development Report 2001, Planning Commission

Note: na: Not applicable or not relevant.

A13 SOCIAL SECTOR

Table A13.1 Human Development Index for India by State, 1981, 1991, and 2001

State/UTs	HDI 1981								HDI 1991								HDI 2001	
	Rural		Urban		Combined		Gender Disparity Index		Rural		Urban		Combined		Gender Disparity Index		Combined	
	Value	Rank	Value	Rank	Value	Rank	Value	Rank	Value	Rank	Value	Rank	Value	Rank	Value	Rank	Value	Rank
(1)	(2)	(3)	(4)	(5)	(6)	(7)	(8)	(9)	(10)	(11)	(12)	(13)	(14)	(15)	(16)	(17)	(18)	(19)
India	0.263		0.442		0.302		0.620		0.340		0.511		0.381		0.676		0.472	
Andhra Pradesh	0.262	25	0.425	23	0.298	23	0.744	10	0.344	23	0.473	29	0.377	23	0.801	23	0.416	10
Arunachal Pradesh	0.228	28	0.419	24	0.242	31	0.537	28	0.300	28	0.572	15	0.328	29	0.776	28	*	
Assam	0.261	26	0.380	28	0.272	26	0.462	32	0.326	26	0.555	19	0.348	26	0.575	30	0.386	14
Bihar	0.220	30	0.378	29	0.237	32	0.471	30	0.286	30	0.460	31	0.308	32	0.469	32	0.367	15
Goa	0.422	5	0.517	10	0.445	5	0.785	2	0.534	3	0.658	3	0.575	4	0.775	13	*	
Gujarat	0.315	14	0.458	18	0.360	14	0.723	6	0.380	18	0.532	23	0.431	17	0.714	22	0.479	6
Haryana	0.332	13	0.465	17	0.360	15	0.536	24	0.409	15	0.562	17	0.443	16	0.714	17	0.509	5
Himachal Pradesh	0.374	10	0.600	1	0.398	10	0.783	4	0.442	12	0.700	1	0.469	13	0.858	4	*	
Jammu & Kashmir	0.301	17	0.468	16	0.337	19	0.584	19	0.364	22	0.575	14	0.402	21	0.740	25	*	
Karnataka	0.295	18	0.489	14	0.346	16	0.707	20	0.367	21	0.523	24	0.412	19	0.753	11	0.478	7
Kerala	0.491	1	0.544	6	0.500	2	0.872	1	0.576	1	0.628	9	0.591	3	0.825	2	0.638	1
Madhya Pradesh	0.209	32	0.395	26	0.245	30	0.664	25	0.282	32	0.491	28	0.328	30	0.662	28	0.394	12
Maharashtra	0.306	15	0.489	15	0.363	13	0.740	15	0.403	16	0.548	21	0.452	15	0.793	15	0.523	4
Manipur	0.440	2	0.553	5	0.461	4	0.802	7	0.503	7	0.618	12	0.536	9	0.815	3	*	
Meghalaya	0.293	20	0.442	21	0.317	21	0.799	12	0.332	24	0.624	10	0.365	24	0.807	12	*	
Mizoram	0.381	9	0.558	4	0.411	8	0.502	18	0.464	10	0.648	5	0.548	7	0.770	6	*	
Nagaland	0.295	19	0.519	8	0.328	20	0.783	16	0.442	13	0.633	7	0.486	11	0.729	21	*	
Orissa	0.252	27	0.368	31	0.267	27	0.547	27	0.328	25	0.469	30	0.345	28	0.639	27	0.404	11
Punjab	0.386	8	0.494	13	0.411	9	0.688	14	0.447	11	0.566	16	0.475	12	0.710	19	0.537	2
Rajasthan	0.216	31	0.386	27	0.256	28	0.650	17	0.298	29	0.492	27	0.347	27	0.692	16	0.424	9
Sikkim	0.302	16	0.515	11	0.342	18	0.643	23	0.398	17	0.618	11	0.425	18	0.647	20	*	
Tamil Nadu	0.289	21	0.445	19	0.343	17	0.710	9	0.421	14	0.560	18	0.466	14	0.813	9	0.531	3
Tripura	0.264	23	0.498	12	0.287	24	0.422	31	0.368	20	0.551	20	0.389	22	0.531	29	*	
Uttar Pradesh	0.227	29	0.398	25	0.255	29	0.447	29	0.284	31	0.444	32	0.314	31	0.520	31	0.388	13
West Bengal	0.264	24	0.427	22	0.305	22	0.556	26	0.370	19	0.511	26	0.404	20	0.631	26	0.472	8
Andaman & Nicobar	0.335	12	0.575	2	0.394	11	0.645	21	0.528	5	0.653	4	0.574	5	0.857	1	*	
Chandigarh	0.437	4	0.565	3	0.550	1	0.719	7	0.501	8	0.694	2	0.674	1	0.764	7	*	
Dadra & Nagar Haveli	0.269	22	0.268	32	0.276	25	0.888	11	0.310	27	0.519	25	0.361	25	0.832	14	*	
Daman and Diu	0.409	6	0.518	9	0.438	6	0.760	5	0.492	9	0.629	8	0.544	8	0.714	8	*	
Delhi	0.439	3	0.531	7	0.495	3	0.595	22	0.530	4	0.635	6	0.624	6	0.690	10	*	
Lakshadweep	0.395	7	0.371	30	0.434	7	0.688	8	0.520	6	0.545	10	0.532	10	0.680	24	*	
Pondicherry	0.338	11	0.443	20	0.386	12	0.753	13	0.556	2	0.591	13	0.571	6	0.783	5	*	

Source: Planning Commission (2002), *National Human Development Report, 2001,* March.

Notes: * Not available for the year 2001.

The HDI is a composite of variables capturing attainments in three dimensions of human development *viz.* economic, educational, and health. This has been worked out by a combination of measures: per capita monthly expenditures adjusted for inequality; a combination of literacy rate and intensity of formal education, and a combination of life expectancy at age 1 and infant mortality rate. For details see the technical note in the source for the estimation methodology.

Table A 13.2 Number and per cent of Population below Poverty Line and Poverty Line

State	1973-4								1983-4								1993-4							
	Rural			Urban			Combined		Rural			Urban			Combined		Rural			Urban			Combined	
	No. of Persons (Lakh)	% of Persons	Poverty Line (Rs)	No. of Persons (Lakh)	% of Persons	Poverty Line (Rs)	No. of Persons (Lakh)	% of Persons	No. of Persons (Lakh)	% of Persons	Poverty Line (Rs)	No. of Persons (Lakh)	% of Persons	Poverty Line (Rs)	No. of Persons (Lakh)	% of Persons	No. of Persons (Lakh)	% of Persons	Poverty Line (Rs)	No. of Persons (Lakh)	% of Persons	Poverty Line (Rs)	No. of Persons (Lakh)	% of Persons
Andhra Pradesh	178.21	48.41	41.71	47.48	50.61	53.96	225.69	48.86	114.34	26.53	72.66	50.24	36.30	106.43	164.58	28.91	74.49	15.92	163.02	74.47	38.33	278.14	153.97	22.19
Arunachal Pradesh	2.57	52.67	49.82	0.09	36.92	50.26	2.66	51.93	2.70	42.60	98.32	0.12	21.73	97.51	2.82	40.88	3.62	45.01	232.05	0.11	7.73	212.42	3.73	39.35
Assam	76.37	52.67	49.82	5.46	36.92	50.26	81.83	51.21	73.43	42.60	98.32	4.26	21.73	97.51	77.69	40.47	94.33	45.01	232.05	2.03	7.73	212.42	96.36	40.86
Bihar	336.52	62.99	57.68	34.05	52.96	61.27	370.57	61.91	417.70	64.37	97.48	44.35	47.33	111.80	462.05	62.22	450.86	58.21	212.16	42.49	34.50	238.49	493.35	54.96
Goa	3.16	46.85	50.47	1.00	37.69	59.48	4.16	44.26	1.16	14.81	88.24	1.07	27.00	126.47	2.23	18.90	0.38	5.34	194.94	1.53	27.03	328.56	1.91	14.92
Gujarat	94.61	46.35	47.10	43.81	52.57	62.17	138.42	48.15	72.88	29.80	83.29	45.04	39.14	123.22	117.92	32.79	62.16	22.18	202.11	43.02	27.89	297.22	105.19	24.21
Haryana	30.08	34.23	49.95	8.24	40.18	52.42	38.32	35.36	22.03	20.56	88.57	7.57	24.15	103.48	29.60	21.37	36.56	28.02	233.79	7.31	16.38	258.23	43.88	25.05
Himachal Pradesh	9.38	27.42	49.95	0.35	13.17	51.93	9.73	26.39	7.07	17.00	88.57	0.34	9.43	102.26	7.41	16.40	15.40	30.34	233.79	0.46	9.18	253.61	15.86	28.44
Jammu & Kashmir	18.41	45.51	46.59	2.07	21.32	37.17	20.48	40.83	13.11	26.04	91.75	2.49	17.76	99.62	15.60	24.24	19.05	30.34	233.79	1.86	9.18	253.61	20.92	25.17
Karnataka	128.40	55.14	47.24	42.27	52.53	58.22	170.67	54.47	100.50	36.33	83.31	49.31	42.82	120.19	149.81	38.24	95.99	29.88	186.63	60.46	40.14	302.89	156.46	33.16
Kerala	111.36	59.19	51.68	24.16	62.74	62.78	135.52	59.79	81.62	39.03	99.35	25.15	45.68	122.64	106.77	40.42	55.95	25.76	243.84	20.46	24.55	280.54	76.41	25.43
Madhya Pradesh	231.21	62.66	50.20	45.09	57.65	63.02	276.30	61.78	215.48	48.90	83.59	62.49	53.06	122.82	277.97	49.78	216.19	40.64	193.10	82.33	48.38	317.16	298.52	42.52
Maharashtra	210.84	57.71	50.47	76.58	43.87	59.48	287.42	53.24	193.75	45.23	88.24	97.14	40.26	126.47	290.89	43.44	193.33	37.93	194.94	111.90	35.15	328.56	305.22	36.86
Manipur	5.11	52.67	49.82	0.75	36.92	50.26	5.86	49.96	4.76	42.60	98.32	0.89	21.73	97.51	5.65	37.02	6.33	45.01	232.05	0.47	7.73	212.42	6.80	33.78
Meghalaya	4.88	52.67	49.82	0.64	36.92	50.26	5.52	50.20	5.04	42.60	98.32	0.57	21.73	97.51	5.62	38.81	7.09	45.01	232.05	0.29	7.73	212.42	7.38	37.92
Mizoram	1.62	52.67	49.82	0.20	36.92	50.26	1.82	50.32	1.58	42.60	98.32	0.37	21.73	97.51	1.96	36.00	1.64	45.01	232.05	0.30	7.73	212.42	1.94	25.66
Nagaland	2.65	52.67	49.82	0.25	36.92	50.26	2.90	50.81	3.19	42.60	98.32	0.31	21.73	97.51	3.50	39.25	4.85	45.01	232.05	0.20	7.73	212.42	5.05	37.92
Orissa	142.24	67.28	46.87	12.23	55.62	59.34	154.47	66.18	164.65	67.53	106.28	16.66	49.15	124.81	181.31	65.29	140.90	49.72	194.03	19.70	41.64	298.22	160.60	48.56
Punjab	30.47	28.21	49.95	10.02	27.96	51.93	40.49	28.15	16.79	13.20	88.57	11.85	23.79	101.03	28.64	16.18	17.76	11.95	233.79	7.35	11.35	253.61	25.11	11.77
Rajasthan	101.41	44.76	50.96	27.10	52.13	59.99	128.51	46.14	96.77	33.50	80.24	30.06	37.94	113.55	126.83	34.46	94.68	26.46	215.89	33.82	30.49	280.85	128.50	27.41
Sikkim	1.09	52.67	49.82	0.10	36.92	50.26	1.19	50.86	1.24	42.60	98.32	0.10	21.73	97.51	1.35	39.71	1.81	45.01	232.05	0.03	7.73	212.42	1.84	41.43
Tamil Nadu	172.60	57.43	45.09	66.92	49.40	51.54	239.52	54.94	181.61	53.99	96.15	78.46	46.96	120.30	260.07	51.66	121.70	32.48	196.53	80.40	39.77	296.63	202.10	35.03
Tripura	7.88	52.67	49.82	0.66	36.92	50.26	8.54	51.00	8.35	42.60	98.32	0.60	21.73	97.51	8.95	40.03	11.41	45.01	232.05	0.38	7.73	212.42	11.79	39.01
Uttar Pradesh	449.99	56.53	48.92	85.74	60.09	57.37	535.73	57.07	448.03	46.45	83.85	108.71	49.82	110.23	556.74	47.07	496.17	42.28	213.01	108.28	35.39	258.65	604.46	40.85
West Bengal	257.96	73.16	54.49	41.34	34.67	54.81	299.30	63.43	268.60	63.05	105.55	50.09	32.32	105.91	318.69	54.85	209.90	40.80	220.74	44.66	22.41	247.53	254.56	35.66
All India	2612.90	56.44	49.63	600.46	49.01	56.64	3213.36	54.88	2519.57	45.65	89.50	709.40	40.79	115.65	3228.97	44.48	2440.31	37.27	205.84	763.37	32.36	281.35	3203.67	35.97

Source: Planning Commission.

(*Continued*)

Table A 13.2 *Continued*

State	1999–2000 (30-day Recall Period)								2004–5 (Based on MRP Consumption)								2004–5 (Based on URP Consumption)							
	Rural			Urban			Combined		Rural			Urban			Combined		Rural			Urban			Combined	
	No. of Persons (Lakh)	% of Persons	Poverty Line (Rs)	No. of Persons (Lakh)	% of Persons	Poverty Line (Rs)	No. of Persons (Lakh)	% of Persons	No. of Persons (Lakh)	% of Persons	Poverty Line (Rs)	No. of Persons (Lakh)	% of Persons	Poverty Line (Rs)	No. of Persons (Lakh)	% of Persons	No. of Persons (Lakh)	% of Persons	Poverty Line (Rs)	No. of Persons (Lakh)	% of Persons	Poverty Line (Rs)	No. of Persons (Lakh)	% of Persons
Andhra Pradesh	58.13	11.05	262.94	60.88	26.63	457.40	119.01	15.77	43.21	7.50	292.95	45.50	20.70	542.89	88.71	11.10	64.70	11.20	292.95	61.40	28.00	542.89	126.10	15.80
Arunachal Pradesh	3.80	40.04	365.43	0.18	7.47	343.99	3.98	33.47	1.47	17.00	387.64	0.07	2.40	378.84	1.54	13.40	1.94	22.30	387.64	0.09	3.30	378.84	2.03	17.60
Assam	92.17	40.04	365.43	2.38	7.47	343.99	94.55	36.09	41.46	17.00	387.64	0.93	2.40	378.84	42.39	15.00	54.50	22.30	387.64	1.28	3.30	378.84	55.77	19.70
Bihar	376.51	44.30	333.07	49.13	32.91	379.78	425.64	42.60	262.92	32.90	354.36	27.09	28.90	435.00	290.01	32.50	336.72	42.10	354.36	32.42	34.60	435.00	369.15	41.40
Goa	0.11	1.35	318.63	0.59	7.52	539.71	0.70	4.40	54.72	31.20	322.41	16.39	34.70	560.00	71.11	32.00	71.50	40.80	322.41	19.47	41.20	560.00	90.96	40.90
Gujarat	39.80	13.17	318.94	28.09	15.59	474.41	67.89	14.07	0.13	1.90	362.25	1.62	20.90	665.90	1.74	12.00	0.36	5.40	362.25	1.64	21.30	665.90	2.01	13.80
Haryana	11.94	8.27	362.81	5.39	9.99	420.20	17.34	8.74	46.25	13.90	353.93	21.18	10.10	541.16	67.43	12.50	63.49	19.10	353.93	27.19	13.00	541.16	90.69	16.80
Himachal Pradesh	4.84	7.94	367.45	0.29	4.63	420.20	5.12	7.63	14.57	9.20	414.76	7.99	11.30	504.49	22.56	9.90	21.49	13.60	414.76	10.60	15.10	504.49	32.10	14.00
Jammu & Kashmir	2.97	3.97	367.45	0.49	1.98	420.20	3.46	3.48	4.10	7.20	394.28	0.17	2.60	504.49	4.27	6.70	6.14	10.70	394.28	0.22	3.40	504.49	6.36	10.00
Karnataka	59.91	17.38	309.59	44.49	25.25	511.44	104.40	20.04	2.20	2.70	391.26	2.34	8.50	553.77	4.54	4.20	3.66	4.60	391.26	2.19	7.90	553.77	5.85	5.40
Kerala	20.97	9.38	374.79	20.07	20.27	477.06	41.04	12.72	89.76	40.20	366.56	10.63	16.30	451.24	100.39	34.80	103.19	46.30	366.56	13.20	20.20	451.24	116.39	40.30
Madhya Pradesh	217.32	37.06	311.34	81.22	38.44	481.65	298.54	37.43	43.33	12.00	324.17	53.28	27.20	599.66	96.60	17.40	75.05	20.80	324.17	63.83	32.60	599.66	138.89	25.00
Maharashtra	125.12	23.72	318.63	102.87	26.81	539.71	227.99	25.02	23.59	9.60	430.12	13.92	16.40	559.39	37.51	11.40	32.43	13.20	430.12	17.17	20.20	559.39	49.60	15.00
Manipur	6.53	40.04	365.43	0.66	7.47	343.99	7.19	28.54	141.99	29.80	327.78	66.97	39.30	570.15	210.97	32.40	175.65	36.90	327.78	74.03	42.10	570.15	249.68	38.30
Meghalaya	7.89	40.04	365.43	0.34	7.47	343.99	8.23	33.87	128.43	22.20	362.25	131.40	29.00	665.90	259.83	25.20	171.13	29.60	362.25	146.25	32.20	665.90	317.38	30.70
Mizoram	1.40	40.04	365.43	0.45	7.47	343.99	1.85	19.47	2.86	17.00	387.64	0.14	2.40	378.84	3.00	13.20	3.76	22.30	387.64	0.20	3.30	378.84	3.95	17.30
Nagaland	5.21	40.04	365.43	0.28	7.47	343.99	5.49	32.67	3.32	17.00	387.64	0.12	2.40	378.84	3.43	14.10	4.36	22.30	387.64	0.16	3.30	378.84	4.52	18.50
Orissa	143.69	48.01	323.92	25.40	42.83	473.12	169.09	47.15	0.78	17.00	387.64	0.11	2.40	378.84	0.89	9.50	1.02	22.30	387.64	0.16	3.30	378.84	1.18	12.60
Punjab	10.20	6.35	362.68	4.29	5.75	388.15	14.49	6.16	2.94	17.00	387.64	0.09	2.40	378.84	3.03	14.50	3.87	22.30	387.64	0.12	3.30	378.84	3.99	19.00
Rajasthan	55.06	13.74	344.03	26.78	19.85	465.92	81.83	15.28	129.29	39.80	325.79	24.30	40.30	528.49	153.59	39.90	151.75	46.80	325.79	26.74	44.30	528.49	178.49	46.40
Sikkim	2.00	40.04	365.43	0.04	7.47	343.99	2.05	36.55	9.78	5.90	410.38	3.52	3.80	466.16	13.30	5.20	15.12	9.10	410.38	6.50	7.10	466.16	21.63	8.40
Tamil Nadu	80.51	20.55	307.64	49.97	22.11	475.60	130.48	21.12	66.69	14.30	374.57	40.50	28.10	559.63	107.18	17.50	87.38	18.70	374.57	47.51	32.90	559.63	134.89	22.10
Tripura	12.53	40.04	365.43	0.49	7.47	343.99	13.02	34.44	0.85	17.00	387.64	0.02	2.40	378.84	0.87	15.20	1.12	22.30	387.64	0.02	3.30	378.84	1.14	20.10
Uttar Pradesh	412.01	31.22	336.88	117.88	30.89	416.29	529.89	31.15	56.51	16.90	351.86	58.59	18.80	547.42	115.10	17.80	76.50	22.80	351.86	69.13	22.20	547.42	145.62	22.50
West Bengal	180.11	31.85	350.17	33.38	14.86	409.22	213.49	27.02	4.70	17.00	387.64	0.14	2.40	378.84	4.85	14.40	6.18	22.30	387.64	0.20	3.30	378.84	6.38	18.90
All India	1932.43	27.09	327.56	670.07	23.62	454.11	2602.50	26.10	357.68	25.30	365.84	100.47	26.30	483.26	458.15	25.50	473.00	33.40	365.84	117.03	30.60	483.26	590.03	32.80

Source: Planning Commission.

Table A13.3 Education Statistics

Year	Number of Educational Institutions						Enrolment by Stages in School			Drop-out Rates of All Student			Pupil–Teacher Ratio		
	Primary	Upper Primary	High/Hr Sec./Inter/Pre. Jr Colleges	Colleges for General Education	Colleges for Professional Education	Universities/Deemed Univ., etc.	Primary	Middle/Upper primary	High/Hr Sec./Inter/Pre. Jr. Colleges	I–V	I–VIII	I–X	Primary	Middle/Upper primary	High/Hr Sec./Inter/Pre. Jr Colleges
1950–1	209671	13596	7416	370	208	27	19.2	3.1	1.5				24	20	21
1955–6	278135	21730	10838	466	218	31	24.6	4.8	2.6						
1960–1	330399	49663	17329	967	852	45	35.0	6.7	3.4	64.9	78.3		36	31	25
1965–6	391064	75798	27614	1536	770	64	50.5	10.5	5.7						
1970–1	408378	90621	37051	2285	992	82	57.0	13.3	7.6	67	77.9		39	32	25
1975–6	454270	106571	43054	3667	3276	101	65.6	16.0	8.9						
1980–1	494503	118555	51573	3421	3542	110	73.8	20.7	11.0	58.7	72.7	82.5	38	33	27
1985–6	528872	134846	65837	4067	1533	126	87.4	27.1	16.5						
1990–1	560935	151456	79796	4862	886	184	97.4	34.0	19.1	42.6	60.9	71.3	43	37	31
1991–2	566744	155926	82576	5058	950	196	100.9	35.6	20.4						
1992–3	571248	158498	84608	5334	989	207	99.6	34.1	20.5	45	61.1	72.9			
1993–4	570455	162804	89226	5639	1125	213	97.0	34.1	20.7						
1994–5	586810	168772	94946	6089	1230	219	105.1	36.4	22.1						
1995–6	593410	174145	99274	6569	1354	226	107.1	37.5	22.9	42.1	58.8	69.6	43	37	32
1996–7	603646	180293	103241	6759	1770	228	108.2	38.1	24.0	40.2	56.5	70.0			
1997–8	619222	185961	107140	7199	2075	229	110.3	39.5	25.4	39.2	56.1	69.3			
1998–9	628994	193093	112050	7494	2113	237	111.7	40.4	26.7	41.5	56.3	66.7			
1999–2000	641695	198004	116820	7782	2124	244	113.6	41.3	28.0	40.3	55.1	67.0			
2000–1	638738	206269	126047	7929	2223	254	113.8	42.8	27.6	40.7	53.7	68.6	43	38.0	32.0
2001–2	664041	219626	133492	8737	2409	272	113.9	44.8	30.5	39	54.6	66.0	43	34.0	34.0
2002–3	651382	245274	137207	9166	2610	304	122.4	46.9	33.2	34.9	52.8	62.6	42	34.0	33.0
2003–4	712239	262286	145962	9427	2751	304	128.3	48.7	35.0	31.5	52.3	62.7	45	35.0	33.0
2004–5	767520	274731	152049	10377	3201	407	130.8	51.2	37.1	29	50.8	61.9	46	35.0	33.0
2005–6	771082	288199	154032	11549	4991	350	132.1	52.2	38.4	25.7	48.8	61.6	46	34.0	33.0
2006–7	784852	305584	169568	11458	7024	368	133.7	54.5	22.8						

Source: Department of Education.

Table 13.4 Health Statistics

| Year | Central Sector Expenditure on Health (Rs crore) | | | Allopathic Medicine | | Ayush (Indian System of Medicine) | | | | | | | | |
| | Family Welfare | Central Sector Health | ISM&H/ AYUSH | No. of Medical College | No. of Admission | Total Ayush Hospitals | | | | No. of Dispensaries | | AYUSH Practitioners | |
						No.	No. per Crore Population	No. of Beds	No. of Beds/Hospitals	Dispensaries	No. per Crore Population	Practitioners	No. per Crore Population
1991–2	na	na	na	146	12199	2723	315	37826	13.9	20879	2417	562016	6506
1992–3	1000	291	11	146	11241	2777	315	38661	13.9	21120	2396	568486	6448
1993–4	1270	462	21	146	10400	2807	312	42043	15.0	21221	2359	573226	6373
1994–5	1430	552	26	152	12249	2845	310	42831	15.1	21496	2343	581703	6341
1995–6	1581	646	24	165	7039	2848	304	48484	17.0	20904	2235	586998	6275
1996–7	1535	792	23	165	3568	2856	300	51328	18.0	19464	2041	591510	6203
1997–8	1822	706	33	165	3949	2930	302	52088	17.8	19762	2033	602036	6194
1998–9	2343	818	50	147	11733	3045	308	55421	18.2	20075	2027	609404	6154
1999–2000	3100	930	49	147	10104	3880	385	74611	19.2	20707	2053	681124	6753
2000–1	3090	1095	79	189	18168	3943	383	69476	17.6	20627	2005	688802	6696
2001–2	3614	1290	82	na	na	3909	374	69049	17.7	20239	1936	691470	6613
2002–3	3917	1360	90	na	na	3224	304	70336	21.8	20974	1974	695024	6542
2003–4	4409	1326	134	na	na	3136	291	63816	20.3	21246	1969	699883	6486
2004–5	4862	1772	199	229	24690	3158	288	64869	20.5	21138	1929	706586	6449
2005–6	5673	2254	291	242	26449	3340	300	66125	19.8	21476	1928	713684	6405
2006–7	7487	1982	317	262	28928	3360	297	68155	20.3	21769	1925	725568	6415
2007–8	10380	2100	488	266	30290	na	na	na	na	na	na	na	na
2008–9	11930	3650	534	289	32815	na	na	na	na	na	na	na	na
2009–10	11930	3650	na	na	na	na	na	na	na	na	na	na	na

Source: National Health Profile 2008 and Ministry of Health.

A14 EMPLOYMENT

Table A14.1 Total Population, Workers, and Non-workers as per Population Censuses

(Number in million)

Year	Total Population			Workers			Non-workers		
	Persons	Males	Females	Persons	Males	Females	Persons	Males	Females
(1)	(3)	(4)	(5)	(6)	(7)	(8)	(9)	(10)	(11)
2001	1028.6	532.2	496.4	402.2	275.0	127.2	626.4	257.1	369.2
	(100.0)	(100.0)	(100.0)	(39.1)	(51.7)	(25.6)	(60.9)	(48.3)	(74.4)
1991	846.3	439.2	407.1	306.0	218.6	87.4	510.1	205.0	305.2
	(100.0)	(100.0)	(100.0)	(36.2)	(49.8)	(21.5)	(60.3)	(46.7)	(75.0)
1981	683.3	353.3	330.0	244.6	181.0	63.6	420.7	162.9	257.8
	(100.0)	(100.0)	(100.0)	(35.8)	(51.2)	(19.3)	(61.6)	(46.1)	(78.1)
1971	548.2	284.0	264.1	180.7	144.4	36.3	367.5	134.8	232.7
	(100.0)	(100.0)	(100.0)	(33.0)	(50.8)	(13.7)	(67.0)	(47.5)	(88.1)
1961	439.2	226.3	212.9	188.4	129.0	59.4	249.9	96.8	153.1
	(100.0)	(100.0)	(100.0)	(42.9)	(57.0)	(27.9)	(56.9)	(42.8)	(71.9)
1951	361.1	185.6	175.5	139.5	99.1	40.4	217.4	84.2	133.1
	(100.0)	(100.0)	(100.0)	(38.6)	(53.4)	(23.0)	(60.2)	(45.4)	(75.8)
1941	318.7	163.8	154.8	na	na	na	na	na	na
	(100.0)	(100.0)	(100.0)						
1931	279.0	143.1	135.9	120.6	83.0	37.6	157.9	59.5	98.5
	(100.0)	(100.0)	(100.0)	(43.2)	(58.0)	(27.7)	(56.6)	(41.6)	(72.5)
1921	251.3	128.6	122.8	117.9	77.8	40.1	133.4	50.7	82.7
	(100.0)	(100.0)	(100.0)	(46.9)	(60.5)	(32.7)	(53.1)	(39.4)	(67.3)
1911	252.1	128.4	123.7	121.4	79.6	41.8	131.1	49.0	82.1
	(100.0)	(100.0)	(100.0)	(48.1)	(62.0)	(33.8)	(52.0)	(38.2)	(66.4)
1901	238.4	120.9	117.5	111.4	74.1	37.3	127.6	47.1	80.5
	(100.0)	(100.0)	(100.0)	(46.7)	(61.3)	(31.7)	(53.5)	(39.0)	(68.5)

Source: Census document: 2001 and 1961. (In the 1961 census document a note on the working force estimates 1901–61 by B.R. Kalra is available.)

Notes: Figures in brackets are percentages to respective totals. The 1981 data include interpolated data for Assam and 1991 figures include projected data for Jammu & Kashmir. The 2001 data include estimated total for Kachch district, Morvi, Maliya-Miyana and Wankaner talukas of Rajkot district, Jodiya taluka of Jamnagar district of Gujarat state, and entire Kinnaur district of HP where census was not conducted due to natural calamities.

Table A14.2 Number of Persons Employed per 1000 Persons according to Usual Status and Current Weekly Status Approaches Worker Population Ratios (WPRs) also called Work Force Participation Rates (WFPRs)

			WPRs: Male								WPRs: Female							
			Usual Status				Current Weekly Status		Current Daily Status		Usual Status				Current Weekly Status		Current Daily Status	
			ps		All (ps + ss)						ps		All (ps + ss)					
Round No.	Survey Month	Period Year	Rural	Urban	Rural	Urban	Rural	Urban	Rural	Urban	Rural	Urban	Rural	Urban	Rural	Urban	Rural	Urban
(1)	(2)	(3)	(4)	(5)	(6)	(7)	(8)	(9)	(10)	(11)	(12)	(13)	(14)	(15)	(16)	(17)	(18)	(19)
62	Jul–Jun	2005–6	537	534	549	540	524	529	491	513	224	121	310	143	257	132	203	118
61	Jul–Jun	2004–5	535	541	546	549	524	534	488	519	242	135	327	166	275	152	216	133
60	Jan–Jun	2004	527	531	542	540	511	525	471	504	228	121	315	150	245	136	190	118
59	Jan–Dec	2003	536	535	547	541	525	528			235	119	311	146	236	121		
58	Jul–Dec	2002	537	530	546	534	529	523			214	118	281	140	219	118		
57	Jul–Jun	2001–2	531	547	546	553	523	542			241	110	314	139	241	111		
56	Jul–Jun	2000–1	532	525	544	531	525	519			221	116	287	140	217	117		
55	Jul–Jun	1999–2000	522	513	531	518	510	509	478	490	231	117	299	139	253	128	204	111
54	Jan–Jun	1998	530	506	539	509	524	504			207	99	263	114	202	99		
53	Jan–Dec	1997	541	516	550	521	535	513			222	111	291	131	222	114		
52	Jul–Jun	1995–6	542	522	551	525	538	520			234	107	295	124	233	109		
51	Jul–Jun	1994–5	547	514	560	519	541	511			237	112	317	136	241	117		
50	Jul–Jun	1993–4	538	513	553	521	531	511	504	496	234	121	328	155	267	139	219	120
49	Jan–Jun	1993	532	506	545	509	527	504			243	113	311	130	232	109		
48	Jan–Dec	1992	541	502	556	507	536	501			250	125	313	146	244	122		
47	Jul–Dec	1991	538	511	546	516	534	509			244	120	294	132	238	117		
46	Jul–Jun	1990–1	542	508	553	513	535	506			242	123	292	143	230	124		
45	Jul–Jun	1989–90	537	501	548	512	528	503			252	124	319	146	230	121		
43	Jul–Jun	1987–8	517	496	539	506	504	492	501	477	245	118	323	152	220	119	207	110
38	Jan–Dec	1983	528	500	547	512	511	492	482	473	248	120	340	151	227	118	198	106
32	Jul–Jun	1977–8	537	497	552	508	519	490			248	123	331	156	232	125		
27	Oct–Sep	1972–3	na	na	565	533	549	521			na	na	330	143	287	131		

Source: NSS 62nd Round (Jul–Jun 2005–6), Report No. 522: *Employment and Unemployment Situation in India* and earlier NSS Reports.

Notes: (i) Dark lines represent regular Quinquennial Surveys; others are thin sample surveys.

(ii) Worker population rations (WPRs) represent the ratio of worker population in total population in the respective categories.

Table A14.3 Per 1000 Distribution of the Usually Employed by Status of Employment for All (Principal and Subsidiary Status Workers)

Round No.	Survey Month	Period Year	WPRs: Male						WPRs: Female					
			Rural			Urban			Rural			Urban		
			Self-Employed	Regular Wage/Salaried	Casual Labour	Self-Employed	Regular Wage/Salaried	Casual Labour	Self-Employed	Regular Wage/Salaried	Casual Labour	Self-Employed	Regular Wage/Salaried	Casual Labour
(1)	(2)	(3)	(4)	(5)	(6)	(7)	(8)	(9)	(10)	(11)	(12)	(13)	(14)	(15)
62	Jul–Jun	2005–6	567	100	333	424	420	157	622	39	339	438	397	165
61	Jul–Jun	2004–5	581	90	329	448	406	146	637	37	326	477	356	167
60	Jan–Jun	2004	572	93	335	441	406	153	615	38	347	446	362	192
59	Jan–Dec	2003	578	87	335	429	415	156	616	33	351	454	339	207
58	Jul–Dec	2002	569	88	344	443	407	150	558	36	406	459	308	233
57	Jul–Jun	2001–2	580	81	339	430	415	154	589	29	382	441	298	261
56	Jul–Jun	2000–1	589	95	316	414	411	175	593	32	375	444	315	241
55	Jul–Jun	1999–2000	550	88	362	415	407	168	573	31	396	453	333	214
54	Jan–Jun	1998	553	70	377	425	395	181	534	25	442	384	327	288
53	Jan–Dec	1997	594	73	333	400	415	185	570	21	409	397	313	290
52	Jul–Jun	1995–6	590	77	333	410	425	165	564	24	412	400	332	268
51	Jul–Jun	1994–5	604	68	328	404	431	165	570	22	408	426	301	273
50	Jul–Jun	1993–4	577	85	338	417	420	163	586	27	387	458	284	258
49	Jan–Jun	1993	591	79	330	389	395	216	585	23	392	407	262	331
48	Jan–Dec	1992	608	83	309	412	394	193	591	32	377	425	288	287
47	Jul–Dec	1991	595	92	313	489	399	172	568	31	401	470	280	250
46	Jul–Jun	1990–1	557	128	315	407	442	151	586	38	376	490	259	251
45	Jul–Jun	1989–90	597	98	305	423	413	164	609	28	363	486	292	222
43	Jul–Jun	1987–8	586	100	314	417	437	146	608	37	355	471	275	254
38	Jan–Dec	1983	605	103	292	409	437	154	619	28	353	458	258	284
32	Jul–Jun	1977–8	628	106	266	404	464	132	321	28	351	495	249	256
27	Oct–Sep	1972–3	659	121	220	392	507	101	645	41	314	484	279	237

Source: NSS 62 Round (Jul–Jun 2005–6), Report No. 522: *Employment and Unemployment Situation in India* and earlier NSS Reports.

Notes: (i) Dark lines represent regular Quinquennial Surveys; others are thin sample surveys.

(ii) Worker population rations (WPRs) represent the ratio of worker population in total population in the respective categories.

Table A14.4 Unemployment Rate (Number of Persons Unemployed Per 1000 Persons in the Labour Force)

Round No.	Survey Month	Period Year	Male Rural — Usual Status	Usual Adjusted	Current Weekly Status	Current Daily Status	Male Urban — Usual Status	Usual Adjusted	Current Weekly Status	Current Daily Status	Female Rural — Usual Status	Usual Adjusted	Current Weekly Status	Current Daily Status	Female Urban — Usual Status	Usual Adjusted	Current Weekly Status	Current Daily Status
(1)	(2)	(3)	(4)	(5)	(6)	(7)	(8)	(9)	(10)	(11)	(12)	(13)	(14)	(15)	(16)	(17)	(18)	(19)
62	July–Jun	2005–6	25 (14)	20 (11)	43 (24)	83 (44)	48 (27)	45 (25)	58 (32)	79 (44)	22 (5)	12 (4)	33 (9)	75 (16)	79 (10)	63 (10)	77 (11)	101 (13)
61	July–Jun	2004–5	21 (12)	16 (9)	38 (21)	80 (42)	44 (25)	38 (22)	52 (30)	75 (42)	31 (8)	18 (6)	42 (12)	87 (21)	91 (14)	69 (12)	90 (15)	116 (18)
60	Jan–Jun	2004	24 (13)	18 (10)	47 (25)	90 (47)	46 (25)	40 (22)	57 (32)	81 (45)	22 (5)	13 (4)	45 (12)	93 (19)	89 (12)	67 (11)	90 (14)	117 (16)
59	Jan–Dec	2003	19 (10)	15 (9)	28 (15)	–	43 (24)	40 (23)	51 (28)	–	10 (2)	6 (2)	16 (4)	–	44 (5)	35 (5)	49 (6)	–
58	Jul–Dec	2002	18 (10)	15 (8)	28 (15)	–	47 (26)	45 (25)	55 (31)	–	10 (2)	6 (2)	16 (4)	–	61 (8)	47 (7)	57 (7)	–
57	Jul–Jun	2001–2	14 (7)	11 (6)	26 (14)	–	42 (24)	39 (22)	46 (26)	–	20 (5)	14 (5)	26 (7)	–	49 (6)	38 (5)	48 (6)	–
56	Jul–Jun	2000–1	16 (9)	14 (8)	23 (12)	–	42 (23)	39 (22)	48 (26)	–	6 (1)	4 (1)	18 (4)	–	38 (5)	29 (4)	39 (5)	–
55	Jul–Jun	1999–2000	21 (11)	17 (9)	39 (21)	72 (37)	48 (26)	45 (24)	56 (30)	73 (38)	15 (4)	10 (3)	37 (10)	70 (15)	71 (9)	57 (8)	73 (10)	94 (12)
54	Jan–Jun	1998	24 (13)	21 (11)	29 (15)	–	53 (28)	51 (27)	54 (29)	–	20 (4)	15 (4)	27 (6)	–	81 (9)	68 (8)	78 (8)	–
53	Jan–Dec	1997	16 (9)	12 (7)	20 (11)	–	37 (21)	39 (21)	43 (23)	–	9 (2)	7 (2)	18 (4)	–	51 (6)	44 (6)	58 (7)	–
52	Jul–Jun	1995–6	15 (8)	13 (7)	18 (10)	–	40 (22)	38 (21)	41 (22)	–	8 (2)	7 (2)	9 (2)	–	36 (4)	31 (4)	35 (4)	–
51	Jul–Jun	1994–5	12 (7)	10 (6)	18 (10)	–	37 (20)	34 (18)	39 (21)	–	5 (1)	4 (1)	12 (3)	–	41 (5)	34 (5)	40 (5)	–
50	Jul–Jun	1993–4	20 (11)	14 (8)	31 (17)	56 (30)	45 (24)	41 (22)	52 (28)	67 (36)	14 (3)	8 (3)	30 (8)	56 (13)	83 (11)	61 (10)	79 (12)	104 (14)
49	Jan–Jun	1993	16	–	–	–	38	–	–	–	10	–	–	–	43	–	–	–
48	Jan–Dec	1992	16	–	–	–	46	–	–	–	12	–	–	–	67	–	–	–
47	Jul–Dec	1991	20	16	22	–	43	39	45	–	18	7	12	–	56	51	50	–
46	Jul–Jun	1990–1	13	–	–	–	45	–	–	–	4	–	–	–	54	–	–	–
45	Jul–Jun	1989–90	16	13	26	–	44	39	45	–	8	6	21	–	39	27	40	–
43	Jul–Jun	1987–8	28	18	42	46	61	52	66	88	35	24	44	67	85	62	92	120
38	Jan–Dec	1983	21	14	37	75	59	51	67	92	14	7	43	90	69	49	75	110
32	Jul–Jun	1977–8	22	13	36	71	65	54	71	94	55	20	41	92	178	124	109	145
27	Oct–Sep	1972–3	–	12	30	38	–	48	60	80	–	5	55	112	–	60	90	137

Source: NSS 62nd Round Report and earlier NSS Reports.

Notes: (i) Dark lines represent regular Quinquennial Surveys; others are thin sample surveys.

(ii) Worker population rations (WPRs) represent the ratio of worker population in total population in the respective categories.

(iii) Figures in brackets indicate the proportion of unemployed per 1000 persons (person–day).

Table A14.5 State-wise Sectoral Distribution of Usual (Principal + Subsidiary) Status Workers, 1983 to 2004–5

(per cent)

State	Year	Agriculture			Non-agriculture			of which: Manufacturing		
		Rural	Urban	Total	Rural	Urban	Total	Rural	Urban	Total
(1)	(2)	(3)	(4)	(5)	(6)	(7)	(8)	(9)	(10)	(11)
Andhra Pradesh	2004–5	71.8	10.0		28.2	90.0		8.6	19.5	
	1999–2000	78.8	9.6	65.5	21.2	90.4	34.5	6.2	22.0	9.2
	1993–4	79.2	16.5	67.1	20.8	83.5	32.9	7.6	22.0	10.1
	1983	80.1	15.7	69.3	19.9	84.3	30.7	7.9	25.0	10.7
Assam	2004–5	74.3	4.8		25.7	95.2		3.1	9.8	
	1999–2000	67.6	5.9	60.2	32.4	94.1	39.8	5.4	12.9	6.3
	1993–4	78.9	3.0	70.5	21.1	97.0	29.5	5.5	13.8	6.4
	1983	79.3	7.4	72.3	20.7	92.6	27.7	4.4	16.2	5.6
Bihar	2004–5	77.9	20.5		22.1	79.5		5.7	11.6	
	1999–2000	80.6	11.1	73.1	19.4	88.9	26.9	6.4	21.2	8.0
	1993–4	84.2	11.9	76.6	15.8	88.1	23.4	4.1	21.5	6.0
	1983	83.5	14.3	76.5	16.5	85.7	23.5	6.3	24.8	8.1
Gujarat	2004–5	77.3	6.2		22.7	93.8		7.8	37.2	
	1999–2000	80.0	9.8	59.7	20.0	90.2	40.3	7.0	27.3	12.8
	1993–4	78.8	8.0	58.9	21.2	92.0	41.1	9.5	34.8	16.6
	1983	85.0	18.0	68.7	15.0	82.0	31.3	5.7	35.0	12.9
Haryana	2004–5	64.1	11.2		35.9	88.8		8.9	26.6	
	1999–2000	68.4	10.6	53.0	31.6	89.4	47.0	8.3	23.9	12.5
	1993–4	71.7	11.6	56.9	28.3	88.4	43.1	4.8	28.3	10.6
	1983	77.1	16.0	64.1	22.9	84.0	35.9	6.4	26.1	10.6
Himachal Pradesh	2004–5	69.6	8.5		30.4	91.5		4.9	14.0	
	1999–2000	73.8	10.4	69.6	26.2	89.6	30.4	4.7	9.5	5.0
	1993–4	79.6	17.8	75.9	20.4	82.2	24.1	3.6	4.6	3.7
	1983	87.0	12.4	82.8	13.0	87.6	17.2	3.4	12.0	3.9
Jammu & Kashmir	2004–5	63.9	14.1		36.1	85.9		9.8	22.7	
	1999–2000	73.7	12.8	62.9	26.3	87.2	37.1	5.6	10.5	6.5
	1993–4	75.1	13.8	63.9	24.9	86.2	36.1	4.2	12.9	5.8
	1983	79.7	16.1	68.9	20.3	83.9	31.1	4.7	28.7	8.8
Karnataka	2004–5	81.0	8.2		19.0	91.8		6.2	21.7	
	1999–2000	84.4	19.9	69.6	15.6	80.1	30.4	6.0	28.9	11.3
	1993–4	81.9	16.6	65.7	18.1	83.4	34.3	6.7	26.9	11.7
	1999–2000	82.1	10.9	62.5	17.9	89.1	37.5	5.9	27.1	11.8
Kerala	2004–5	42.0	15.7		58.0	84.3		13.7	16.6	
	1999–2000	48.5	9.6	38.7	51.5	90.4	61.3	14.3	23.5	16.6
	1993–4	56.0	25.4	48.1	44.0	74.6	51.9	13.5	21.4	15.5
	1983	92.8	27.7	56.3	37.2	72.3	43.7	14.7	22.5	16.1
Madhya Pradesh	2004–5	82.5	12.1		17.5	87.9		5.0	20.1	
	1999–2000	87.2	15.5	73.9	12.8	84.5	26.1	4.2	21.7	7.4
	1993–4	89.9	16.4	77.7	10.1	83.6	22.3	3.5	20.5	6.3
	1983	90.3	15.4	79.5	9.7	84.6	20.5	3.9	25.9	7.1

(Continued)

Table A14.5   *Continued*

State	Year	Agriculture			Non-agriculture			of which: Manufacturing		
		Rural	Urban	Total	Rural	Urban	Total	Rural	Urban	Total
(1)	(2)	(3)	(4)	(5)	(6)	(7)	(8)	(9)	(10)	(11)
Maharashtra	2004–5	80.0	6.8		20.0	93.2		5.6	24.2	
	1999–2000	82.7	5.7	56.4	17.3	94.3	43.6	5.2	28.1	13.1
	1993–4	82.6	9.2	59.4	17.4	90.8	40.6	5.3	27.5	12.3
	1983	85.8	12.6	66.2	14.2	87.4	33.8	5.0	31.7	12.1
Orissa	2004–5	69.0	13.9		31.0	86.1		11.1	14.0	
	1999–2000	78.5	13.3	71.0	21.5	86.7	29.0	8.5	21.7	10.0
	1993–4	81.0	15.8	73.8	19.0	84.2	26.2	6.8	19.9	8.2
	1983	79.2	16.2	73.3	20.8	83.8	26.7	8.7	24.0	10.1
Punjab	2004–5	66.9	5.9		33.1	94.1		7.4	26.5	
	1999–2000	72.5	8.9	53.4	27.5	91.1	46.6	7.8	26.8	13.5
	1993–4	74.5	9.2	56.4	25.5	90.8	43.6	5.9	28.5	12.2
	1983	82.5	14.0	66.8	17.5	86.0	33.2	6.4	30.1	11.8
Rajasthan	2004–5	72.9	13.9		27.1	86.1		5.8	22.8	
	1999–2000	77.6	13.1	65.9	22.4	86.9	34.1	4.9	24.3	8.4
	1993–4	79.8	16.3	69.2	20.2	83.7	30.8	4.6	21.7	7.4
	1983	86.7	27.3	77.6	13.3	72.7	22.4	4.3	23.0	7.2
Tamil Nadu	2004–5	65.4	8.3		34.6	91.7		14.0	30.9	
	1999–2000	68.3	9.0	46.8	31.7	91.0	53.2	14.4	33.4	21.3
	1993–4	70.2	11.9	52.5	29.8	88.1	47.5	13.6	32.2	19.3
	1983	74.3	15.4	58.9	25.7	84.6	41.1	11.4	34.8	17.5
Uttar Pradesh	2004–5	72.8	10.5		27.2	89.5		8.9	28.4	
	1999–2000	76.1	9.4	63.6	23.9	90.6	36.4	8.6	29.2	12.5
	1993–4	80.0	15.0	69.0	20.0	85.0	31.0	7.1	27.1	10.5
	1983	82.0	12.2	71.7	18.0	87.8	28.3	7.4	29.2	10.6
West Bengal	2004–5	62.7	2.8		37.3	97.2		13.5	27.6	
	1999–2000	63.0	3.0	46.1	37.0	97.0	53.9	17.7	31.1	21.4
	1993–4	63.6	5.7	48.1	36.4	94.3	51.9	17.0	31.8	21.0
	1983	73.6	4.8	56.4	26.4	95.2	43.6	11.2	36.4	17.5

Source: NSSO, *Employment and Unemployment Situation in India.*

A15 HOUSEHOLD INDEBTEDNESS
Table A15.1 Household Indebtedness in India: A Profile

1. Amount of Debt by Occupational Categories of Households (Rs crore)

Year	Rural Households			Urban Households			All Households (4+7)
	Cultivator	Non-cultivator	All	Self-Employed	Others	All	
(1)	(2)	(3)	(4)	(5)	(6)	(7)	(8)
2002	81709	29759	111468	24341	40977	65327	176795
1991	17668	4543	22211	6306	8805	15232	37443
1981	5737	456	6193	1406	1617	3023	9216
1971	3374	474	3848	na	na	na	na

2. Proportion of Households Reporting Debt

Year	Rural Households			Urban Households		
	Cultivator	Non-cultivator	All	Self-Employed	Others	All
	(2)	(3)	(4)	(5)	(6)	(7)
2002	29.7	21.8	26.5	17.9	17.8	17.8
1991	34.6	26.8	32.0	28.5	25.9	26.9
1981	21.7	12.0	19.4	16.6	17.4	17.2
1971	44.4	33.3	41.3	na	na	na

3. Percentage Share of Outstanding Debt According to Credit Agency: Rural and Urban

	Rural						Urban		
	2002	1991	1981	1971	1961	1951	2002	1991	1981
A. Institutional	57.1	56.6	61.2	29.2	17.3	7.2	75.1	64.3	59.9
Government	2.3	5.7	4.0	6.7	6.6	3.7	7.6	9.3	14.6
Co-op. Society/Banks	27.3	18.6	28.6	20.1	10.4	3.5	20.5	14.2	17.5
Commercial Banks	24.5	29.0	28.0	2.2	0.3	0.0	29.7	17.7	22.5
Insurance	0.3	0.5	0.3	0.1	0.0	0.0	3.5	1.4	2.1
Provident Fund	0.3	0.9	0.3	0.1	0.0	0.0	2.0	3.3	3.2
Other Institutions	2.4	1.9	0.0	0.0	0.0	0.0	11.9	18.5	0.0
B. Non-institutional	42.9	39.6	38.8	70.8	82.7	92.8	24.9	32.0	40.1
Landlords	1.0	4.0	4.0	8.6	1.1	3.5	0.2	0.8	1.0
Agrl Moneylenders	10.0	6.3	8.6	23.1	47.0	25.2	0.9	1.2	3.6
Proff. Moneylenders	19.6	9.4	8.3	13.8	13.8	46.4	13.2	7.9	8.9
Traders	2.6	6.7	3.4	8.7	7.5	5.1	1.0	5.8	4.8
Relatives/Friends	7.1	6.7	9.0	13.8	5.8	11.5	7.6	10.4	15.2
Others	2.6	9.9	5.5	2.8	7.5	1.1	1.9	5.9	6.6
C. Not Specified	0.0	3.8	0.0	0.0	0.0	0.0	0.0	3.6	0.0

4. Cash Debt of Households Classified by Purpose of Loan (per cent)

	Rural Households								
	Cultivators			Non-cultivators			All Households		
	2002	1991	1981	2002	1991	1981	2002	1991	1981
1. Farm Business									
Capital Expenditure	34.3	14.4	45.3	6.3	2.4	8.4	26.8	12.0	42.4
Current Expenditure	18.2	3.2	18.5	3.0	0.7	5.9	14.2	2.7	17.6
2. Non-farm Business									
Capital Expenditure	7.4	4.7	6.3	14.2	9.8	18.8	9.2	5.8	7.2
Current Expenditure	2.0	1.5	1.5	4.8	3.8	4.5	2.8	2.0	1.7
3. Households									
Capital Expenditure in Residential Bldg	27.7	5.1	20.0	55.0	11.8	51.0	35.0	6.5	22.4
Current Expenditure	na	0.5	na	na	0.4	na	na	0.5	na
4. Productive Purposes (1+2+3)*	89.6	28.9	91.6	83.3	28.5	88.6	88.0	29.0	91.3
	(61.9)	(23.8)	(71.6)	(28.3)	(16.7)	(37.6)	(53.0)	(22.5)	(68.9)

(Continued)

Table A15.1 *Continued*

Rural Households

	Cultivators			Non-cultivators			All Households		
	2002	1991	1981	2002	1991	1981	2002	1991	1981
5. Other Purposes	10.4	45.4	8.1	16.4	57.6	11.4	12.0	48.0	8.5
Repayment of Debt	1.5	na	0.8	1.3	na	1.5	1.4	na	0.8
Expend. on Litigation	0.3	na	0.1	0.2	na	0.0	0.3	na	0.2
Fin. Investment Expend.	0.6	na	1.0	1.0	na	0.5	0.7	na	0.9
Other Purposes	8.0	na	6.2	13.9	na	9.4	9.6	na	6.6
6. Unspecified	0.0	25.2	0.3	0.3	13.5	0.0	0.1	22.8	0.2

Urban Households

	Self-Employed			Others			All Households		
	2002	1991	1981	2002	1991	1981	2002	1991	1981
1. Farm Business									
Capital Expenditure	7.3	5.7	7.2	0.9	0.3	4.3	3.3	2.5	5.6
Current Expenditure	4.4	0.2	8.1	0.4	0.1	1.1	1.9	0.1	4.4
2. Non-farm Business									
Capital Expenditure	36.1	21.1	41.6	4.8	3.3	7.3	16.5	10.8	23.2
Current Expenditure	7.5	8.1	15.0	0.7	1.0	2.5	3.2	4.0	8.3
3. Households									
Capital Expenditure in Residential Bldg	32.8	28.7	13.1	72.1	44.6	54.3	57.5	37.9	35.0
Current Expenditure	na	0.1	na	na	2.5	na	na	1.5	na
4. Productive Purposes (1+2+3)*	88.1	63.9	85.0	78.9	51.8	69.5	82.4	56.8	76.5
	(55.3)	(35.1)	(71.9)	(6.8)	(4.7)	(15.2)	(24.9)	(17.4)	(41.5)
5. Other Purposes	11.9	33.9	14.7	21.1	46.6	30.4	17.6	41.4	23.2
6. Unspecified	0.0	2.2	0.3	0.1	1.4	0.2	0.0	1.8	0.2

5. Amount of Cash Borrowing and Repayments by Occupational Category of Households

Year	Round	Amount of Borrowings in Rs Cr			Amount of Repayment in Rs Cr			Share of Cultivator Hhs (%)		Per cent of Repayments to Borrowings	
		Cultivator	Non-cultivator	All Hhs	Cultivator	Non-cultivator	All Hhs (incl. n.r)	Total Borrowings	Total Repayment	All Hhs	Cultivator
Rural											
2002–03	59	39294	15825	55119	17729	7154	24883	71.3	71.3	45.1	45.1
1991–92	48	10636	2862	13498	4070	1133	5203	78.8	78.3	38.5	38.3
1981–82	37	3757	427	4185	1899	193	2091	89.8	90.9	50.0	50.5
1971–72	26	1155	190	1345	1009	146	1155	85.9	87.4	85.9	87.4

Year	Round	Self-Employed	Others	All Hhs (incl. n.r)	Self-Employed	Others	All Hhs (incl. n.r)	Share of Self-Employed (%) Total Borrowings	Total Repayment	All Hhs	Self-Emp.
Urban											
2002–03	59	12215	21965	34181	6679	11768	18447	35.7	36.2	54.0	54.7
1991–92	48	2815	5098	7918	1513	3027	4540	35.7	33.3	57.3	53.7
1981–82	37	830	1156	1986	536	653	1189	41.8	45.1	59.9	64.6

Source: NSSO (2005), Household Indebtedness in India as on 30-6-2002, AIDIS Report No. 501 (59/18.2/2), December. NSSO (2006), Household Borrowing and Repayments in India during 1.7.2002 to 30.6.2003, AIDIS Report No. 502 (59/18.2/3), January.

Notes: * Figures in brackets relate to those given by NSSO for productive purposes (1 + 2).

na: Details are not available. n.r.: Not reported.

A16 ECONOMIC CENSUS

Table A16.1 Trends in Employment in Agricultural (excluding crop production and plantation) and Non-agricultural Enterprises, 1980–2005

Total Employment (in thousand)   Annual Growth Rate: Employment (per cent)

State	5th Economic Census 2005			4th Economic Census 1998			3rd Economic Census 1990			2nd Economic Census 1980			1998–2005			1990–8			1980–90		
	Rural	Urban	Combined	Rural	Urban	Combined	Rural	Urban	Combined	Rural	Urban	Combined	Rural	Urban	Combined	Rural	Urban	Combined	Rural	Urban	Combined
All-India	**50185**	**48782**	**98968**	**39901**	**43399**	**83299**	**33296**	**38780**	**72076**	**24474**	**29194**	**53668**	**(3.33)**	**(1.68)**	**(2.49)**	**(2.15)**	**(1.34)**	**(1.71)**	**(2.88)**	**(2.81)**	**(2.84)**
1 Andhra Pradesh	5718	3152	8871	4635	2877	7512	4082	2652	6734	2658	2054	4712	(3.05)	(1.32)	(2.40)	(1.60)	(1.02)	(1.38)	(4.38)	(2.59)	(3.64)
2 Arunachal Pradesh	64	43	107	52	28	81	62	31	93	32	13	44	(3.07)	(6.02)	(4.17)	(−2.13)	(−1.23)	(−1.82)	(6.97)	(9.65)	(7.80)
3 Assam	1792	943	2735	1551	644	2195	1120	570	1689	Census not conducted			(2.08)	(5.61)	(3.19)	(4.15)	(1.54)	(3.32)	Not available		
4 Bihar	1383	893	2276	1775	1654	3429	1743	1710	3454	1532	1245	2777	(1.79)	(−1.77)	(0.27)	(−0.95)	(−0.42)	(−0.68)	(−1.30)	(3.23)	(2.20)
5 Chhattisgarh	1014	597	1610	Included in Madhya Pradesh			Included in Madhya Pradesh			Included in Madhya Pradesh			(3.82)	(1.19)	(2.78)	Not available			Not available		
6 Goa	120	125	246	98	118	216	98	121	219	136	116	252	(2.99)	(0.88)	(1.87)	(0.04)	(−0.34)	(−0.17)	Not available		
7 Gujarat	2569	3245	5814	2351	2929	5280	2022	2704	4726	1528	2124	3652	(1.27)	(1.48)	(1.39)	(1.90)	(1.01)	(1.40)	(2.84)	(2.44)	(2.61)
8 Haryana	1074	1138	2212	595	964	1559	524	829	1353	370	604	974	(8.80)	(2.40)	(5.12)	(1.60)	(1.90)	(1.79)	(3.56)	(3.21)	(3.34)
9 Himachal Pradesh	462	205	667	387	189	577	312	156	469	236	108	344	(2.54)	(1.13)	(2.09)	(2.73)	(2.43)	(2.63)	(2.85)	(3.73)	(3.13)
10 Jammu & Kashmir	364	387	752	217	256	474	Census not conducted			247	242	489	(7.65)	(6.08)	(6.82)	Not available			Not available		
11 Jharkhand	580	589	1169	Included in Bihar			Included in Bihar			Included in Bihar			(−0.66)	(−1.21)	(−0.32)	Not available			Not available		
12 Karnataka	3320	2659	5978	2757	2496	5253	2588	2495	5083	2003	1863	3866	(2.69)	(0.91)	(1.86)	(0.79)	(0.01)	(0.41)	(2.60)	(2.96)	(2.77)
13 Kerala	3684	1876	5559	2760	1089	3849	1889	1400	3289	1603	849	2452	(4.21)	(8.08)	(5.39)	(4.85)	(−3.09)	(1.99)	(1.66)	(5.13)	(2.98)
14 Madhya Pradesh	1868	2352	4220	2441	2815	5256	2363	2522	4886	1601	1689	3290	(1.69)	(0.54)	(1.04)	(0.41)	(1.38)	(0.92)	(3.97)	(4.09)	(4.03)
15 Maharashtra	4625	7201	11827	3688	6756	10445	2847	6113	8960	2145	4605	6750	(3.29)	(0.91)	(1.79)	(3.29)	(1.26)	(1.93)	(2.87)	(2.87)	(2.87)
16 Manipur	121	114	235	97	104	201	77	80	157	46	59	105	(3.24)	(1.28)	(2.25)	(2.85)	(3.32)	(3.09)	(5.26)	(3.16)	(4.13)
17 Meghalaya	137	107	245	97	87	184	85	85	170	49	59	109	(5.05)	(3.02)	(4.12)	(1.76)	(0.26)	(1.03)	(5.55)	(3.71)	(4.58)
18 Mizoram	32	69	101	23	54	77	21	51	72	18	27	46	(4.96)	(3.45)	(3.91)	(1.15)	(0.74)	(0.86)	(1.27)	(6.51)	(4.67)
19 Nagaland	73	111	184	64	111	175	50	80	130	39	36	75	(1.95)	(0.02)	(0.75)	(3.27)	(4.08)	(3.78)	(2.44)	(8.46)	(5.70)
20 Orissa	2572	1004	3575	2158	937	3095	1716	896	2612	1250	699	1949	(2.54)	(0.99)	(2.08)	(2.90)	(0.56)	(2.14)	(3.22)	(2.51)	(2.97)
21 Punjab	1059	1628	2688	743	1357	2100	580	1190	1770	415	921	1336	(5.19)	(2.64)	(3.59)	(3.15)	(1.65)	(2.16)	(3.40)	(2.60)	(2.85)
22 Rajasthan	2271	1969	4240	1793	1749	3542	1318	1520	2838	1138	1179	2317	(3.44)	(1.71)	(2.60)	(3.92)	(1.77)	(2.81)	(1.48)	(2.57)	(2.05)
23 Sikkim	41	28	69	27	21	48	28	19	47	15	15	31	(6.41)	(4.32)	(5.52)	(−0.81)	(1.33)	(0.08)	(6.36)	(2.22)	(4.48)
24 Tamil Nadu	5188	4678	9867	3583	3608	7191	2882	3354	6236	2305	2841	5146	(5.43)	(3.78)	(4.62)	(2.76)	(0.91)	(1.80)	(2.26)	(1.68)	(1.94)
25 Tripura	249	130	379	168	101	268	132	89	220	83	52	134	(5.84)	(3.71)	(5.07)	(3.05)	(1.60)	(2.48)	(4.80)	(5.50)	(5.07)
26 Uttar Pradesh	4196	4344	8540	3232	4248	7480	2949	3959	6909	2621	3122	5743	(4.98)	(1.40)	(3.03)	(1.76)	(0.88)	(1.27)	(1.19)	(2.40)	(1.87)
27 Uttranchal	396	353	749	Included in Uttar Pradesh			Included in Uttar Pradesh			Included in Uttar Pradesh			(7.06)	(2.04)	(4.45)	Not available			Not available		
28 West Bengal	4921	4397	9318	4374	4397	8771	3636	3811	7448	2242	3101	5343	(1.70)	(−0.00)	(0.87)	(2.34)	(1.80)	(2.07)	(4.95)	(2.09)	(3.38)
Chandigarh	13	239	252	6	212	218	8	195	203	4	117	121	(12.11)	(1.71)	(2.07)	(−4.30)	(1.07)	(0.89)	(6.94)	(5.25)	(5.31)
Delhi	73	4007	4080	86	3415	3501	73	2012	2085	96	1375	1471	(−2.26)	(2.31)	(2.21)	(2.12)	(6.84)	(6.70)	(−2.81)	(3.88)	(3.55)
Pondicherry	64	129	193	49	132	182	30	90	120	26	55	81	(3.83)	(−0.37)	(0.88)	(6.21)	(5.00)	(5.31)	(1.66)	(4.93)	(3.99)
A & N Islands	28	36	64	37	25	63	31	21	52	21	17	38	(−3.90)	(5.15)	(0.35)	(2.25)	(2.26)	(2.25)	(4.02)	(2.39)	(3.33)
D & N Haveli	47	18	65	28	5	33	11	3	14	5	2	7	(7.56)	(22.03)	(10.33)	(11.82)	(5.85)	(10.81)	(8.28)	(3.86)	(7.23)
Daman and Diu	57	10	68	21	11	32	11	10	21	Included in Goa			(15.32)	(−0.06)	(11.49)	(9.01)	(0.60)	(5.50)	Not available		
Lakshadweep	7	5	12	5	11	16	6	10	16	8	6	14	(3.53)	(−9.60)	(−4.00)	(−2.17)	(−0.91)	(−0.20)	(−2.99)	(5.89)	(1.40)

Source: GOI (2006), press note dated 12 June on Fifth Economic Census 2005 and earlier Economic Census Reports.

Notes: (i) Annual growth rate for All-India between 1990 and 2005 is worked out after excluding Jammu & Kashmir as Economic Census for 1990 was not conducted.

(ii) Annual growth rate for Bihar, Madhya Pradesh and Uttar Pradesh for 1990 to 2005 are worked out after including Jharkhand, Chhattisgarh, and Uttranchal, respectively.

(iii) Similarly growth rate between 1980–90 and 1990–98 for all-India excludes Assam and Jammu and Kashmir as Economic Census of Assam was not conducted in 1980 and that of J&K in 1990.

Table A16.2   Trends in Number of Agricultural (excluding crop production and plantation) and Non-agricultural Enterprises:

Number of Enterprises (in Thousand) — columns under 5th Economic Census 2005, 4th Economic Census 1998, 3rd Economic Census 1990, 2nd Economic Census 1980. Annual Growth Rate: Number of Enterprises (per cent) — columns under 1998–2005, 1990–8, 1980–90. Each group divided into Rural (R), Urban (U), Combined (C).

No.	State/UT	5th 2005 R	5th 2005 U	5th 2005 C	4th 1998 R	4th 1998 U	4th 1998 C	3rd 1990 R	3rd 1990 U	3rd 1990 C	2nd 1980 R	2nd 1980 U	2nd 1980 C	98–05 R	98–05 U	98–05 C	90–8 R	90–8 U	90–8 C	80–90 R	80–90 U	80–90 C
	All-India	25809	16314	42124	17707	12641	30349	14722	10280	25002	11141	7220	18362	(5.53)	(3.71)	(4.80)	(2.27)	(2.50)	(2.36)	(2.83)	(3.60)	(3.14)
1	Andhra Pradesh	2896	1128	4023	2007	895	2903	1737	749	2487	1152	462	1614	(5.37)	(3.35)	(4.78)	(1.82)	(2.25)	(1.95)	(4.19)	(4.96)	(4.42)
2	Arunachal Pradesh	19	10	29	15	6	21	16	5	21	9	2	11	(3.65)	(7.08)	(4.74)	(−1.14)	(2.96)	(−0.07)	(5.72)	(10.25)	(6.61)
3	Assam	633	293	926	404	189	593	353	143	495	Census not conducted			(6.62)	(6.46)	(6.57)	(1.72)	(3.58)	(2.28)	Not available		
4	Bihar	872	418	1290	872	571	1443	783	445	1228	713	331	1045	(4.50)	(0.50)	(3.07)	(1.35)	(3.15)	(2.03)	(0.94)	(3.00)	(1.63)
5	Chhattisgarh	454	202	656	Included in Madhya Pradesh									(3.24)	(2.64)	(3.06)	Not available			Not available		
6	Goa	43	38	81	38	34	72	34	27	61	32	21	53	(1.75)	(1.75)	(1.75)	(1.46)	(2.85)	(2.09)	Not available		
7	Gujarat	1343	1075	2419	1084	830	1915	842	656	1498	699	490	1188	(3.11)	(3.77)	(3.40)	(3.22)	(2.99)	(3.12)	(1.88)	(2.96)	(2.34)
8	Haryana	453	375	828	237	295	533	209	248	457	159	161	320	(9.68)	(3.46)	(6.50)	(1.62)	(2.19)	(1.93)	(2.78)	(4.43)	(3.64)
9	Himachal Pradesh	219	52	272	182	44	225	148	35	183	115	24	139	(2.73)	(2.60)	(2.71)	(2.63)	(2.70)	(2.64)	(2.49)	(4.00)	(2.76)
10	Jammu & Kashmir	185	139	324	111	105	216	Census not conducted			125	71	197	(7.64)	(4.06)	(5.99)	Not available			Not available		
11	Jharkhand	294	197	491	Included in Bihar									(3.44)	(2.41)	(3.02)	Not available			Not available		
12	Karnataka	1598	902	2500	1152	760	1912	1033	661	1694	883	492	1375	(4.78)	(2.49)	(3.91)	(1.37)	(1.76)	(1.52)	(1.59)	(2.98)	(2.11)
13	Kerala	2117	731	2848	1241	324	1565	827	402	1229	659	213	872	(7.93)	(12.33)	(8.93)	(5.21)	(−2.66)	(3.07)	(2.29)	(6.56)	(3.49)
14	Madhya Pradesh	953	826	1778	1207	917	2124	1154	720	1873	867	474	1341	(1.74)	(1.40)	(1.58)	(0.57)	(3.07)	(1.58)	(2.90)	(4.27)	(3.40)
15	Maharashtra	2262	2113	4375	1613	1621	3234	1308	1315	2624	965	874	1839	(4.95)	(3.86)	(4.41)	(2.65)	(2.65)	(2.65)	(3.09)	(4.17)	(3.61)
16	Manipur	58	46	104	43	37	80	34	27	61	19	16	35	(4.46)	(2.92)	(3.76)	(3.05)	(3.97)	(3.47)	(6.01)	(5.62)	(5.84)
17	Meghalaya	56	28	85	36	20	56	32	18	50	21	12	33	(6.48)	(5.05)	(5.98)	(1.54)	(1.56)	(1.55)	(4.44)	(4.43)	(4.24)
18	Mizoram	18	29	47	10	15	25	10	13	23	8	6	13	(8.40)	(10.39)	(9.60)	(0.91)	(0.98)	(0.95)	(2.23)	(8.77)	(5.53)
19	Nagaland	21	17	38	14	16	30	13	11	24	9	7	16	(6.05)	(1.22)	(3.64)	(1.02)	(4.51)	(2.75)	(3.91)	(4.64)	(4.24)
20	Orissa	1425	367	1791	1157	293	1450	853	240	1094	629	174	804	(3.02)	(3.26)	(3.07)	(3.88)	(2.51)	(3.59)	(3.09)	(3.25)	(3.13)
21	Punjab	497	576	1072	303	415	717	254	345	599	202	261	463	(7.34)	(4.80)	(5.91)	(2.19)	(2.33)	(2.27)	(2.35)	(2.81)	(2.61)
22	Rajasthan	1210	746	1957	911	620	1531	689	481	1169	606	357	964	(4.15)	(2.69)	(3.57)	(3.55)	(3.24)	(3.42)	(1.28)	(3.01)	(1.95)
23	Sikkim	14	6	19	8	5	13	7	3	11	5	3	8	(8.39)	(1.16)	(5.83)	(0.74)	(5.89)	(2.54)	(3.40)	(1.08)	(2.62)
24	Tamil Nadu	2737	1710	4447	1408	1106	2514	1167	944	2111	981	787	1767	(9.96)	(6.43)	(8.49)	(2.38)	(2.00)	(2.21)	(1.75)	(1.84)	(1.79)
25	Tripura	136	52	188	70	34	104	61	25	85	39	14	54	(9.85)	(6.37)	(8.79)	(1.87)	(4.05)	(2.53)	(4.41)	(5.72)	(4.77)
26	Uttar Pradesh	2194	1822	4016	1479	1564	3043	1291	1342	2633	1151	1015	2166	(7.07)	(3.14)	(5.14)	(1.71)	(1.93)	(1.83)	(1.15)	(2.83)	(1.97)
27	Uttranchal	200	128	329	Included in Uttar Pradesh									(7.72)	(4.16)	(6.21)	Not available			Not available		
28	West Bengal	2831	1455	4286	2044	1191	3234	1818	932	2750	1044	659	1704	(4.77)	(2.90)	(4.10)	(1.48)	(3.11)	(2.05)	(5.70)	(3.52)	(4.90)
	Chandigarh	8	58	66	3	37	40	5	29	33	1	15	16	(15.57)	(6.67)	(7.46)	(−6.01)	(3.22)	(2.25)	(15.16)	(6.92)	(7.72)
	Delhi	28	726	754	30	656	686	23	432	455	28	262	290	(−0.91)	(1.45)	(1.36)	(3.07)	(5.38)	(5.27)	(−1.84)	(5.12)	(4.60)
	Pondicherry	17	33	50	13	29	43	10	21	31	10	13	23	(3.37)	(1.67)	(2.22)	(3.99)	(4.47)	(4.32)	(−0.31)	(4.99)	(2.94)
	A & N Islands	6	7	12	9	5	14	8	3	12	5	2	7	(−6.16)	(4.92)	(−1.36)	(0.82)	(3.86)	(1.78)	(4.70)	(5.08)	(4.81)
	D & N Haveli	5	4	9	3	1	4	2	1	3	1	0	2	(8.65)	(20.98)	(12.31)	(3.69)	(4.82)	(3.94)	(4.14)	(2.29)	(3.71)
	Daman and Diu	7	4	11	3	3	6	2	3	5	Included in Goa			(13.64)	(1.39)	(7.85)	(2.49)	(0.66)	(1.42)	Not available		
	Lakshadweep	2	1	3	2	3	5	2	3	5	3	1	5	(1.80)	(−11.31)	(−5.02)	(−1.30)	(0.94)	(0.02)	(−4.73)	(5.77)	(−0.25)

Source: Economic Census.

A17 International Comparison

Table A17.1 Human Development Characteristics of Some Selected Countries

Countries	HDI Rank	Human Development Index		Life Expectancy at Birth (years)			Adult Literacy Rate (% aged 15 & above)			Combined Gross Enrolment Ratio in Education (%)			GDP per Capita (PPP US$)	Gender Related Development Index		Total Population (million)		Total Fertility Rate (birth per woman)	
		1990	2007	Person 2007	Female 2007	Male 2007	Person 1999–2007	Female 1999–2007	Male 1999–2007	Person 2007	Female 2007	Male 2007	2007	Rank 2007	Value 2007	1990	2007	1990–5	2005–10
(1)	(2)	(3)	(4)	(5)	(6)	(7)	(8)	(9)	(10)	(11)	(12)	(13)	(14)	(15)	(16)	(17)	(18)	(19)	(20)
Australia	2	0.902	0.970	81.4	83.7	79.1	99.0	99.0	99.0	114.2	115.7	112.8	34923	1	0.966	17.1	20.9	1.9	1.8
Canada	4	0.933	0.966	80.6	82.9	78.2	99.0	99.0	99.0	99.3	101.0	97.6	35812	4	0.959	27.7	32.9	1.7	1.6
Netherlands	6	0.917	0.964	79.8	81.9	77.6	99.0	99.0	99.0	97.5	97.1	97.9	38694	7	0.954	15.0	16.5	1.6	1.7
France	8	0.909	0.961	81.0	84.5	77.4	99.0	99.0	99.0	95.4	97.4	93.5	33674	6	0.956	56.8	61.7	1.7	1.9
Japan	10	0.918	0.960	82.7	86.2	79.0	99.0	99.0	99.0	86.6	85.4	87.7	33632	14	0.945	123.2	127.4	1.5	1.3
United States	13	0.923	0.956	79.1	81.3	76.7	99.0	99.0	99.0	92.4	96.9	88.1	45592	19	0.942	254.9	308.7	2.0	2.1
Spain	15	0.896	0.955	80.7	84.0	77.5	97.9	97.3	98.6	96.5	99.9	93.3	31560	9	0.949	38.8	44.1	1.3	1.4
Italy	18	0.889	0.951	81.1	84.0	78.1	98.9	98.6	99.1	91.8	94.7	89.1	30353	15	0.945	57.0	59.3	1.3	1.4
New Zealand	20	0.884	0.950	80.1	82.1	78.1	99.0	99.0	99.0	107.5	113.4	102.0	27336	18	0.943	3.4	4.2	2.1	2.0
UK	21	0.891	0.947	79.3	81.5	77.1	99.0	99.0	99.0	89.2	92.8	85.9	35130	17	0.943	57.2	60.9	1.8	1.8
Germany	22	0.896	0.947	79.8	82.3	77.0	99.0	99.0	99.0	88.1	87.5	88.6	34401	20	0.939	79.4	82.3	1.3	1.3
Singapore	23	0.851	0.944	80.2	82.6	77.8	94.4	91.6	97.3	85.0			49704			3.0	4.5	1.8	1.3
Hong Kong	24		0.944	82.2	85.1	79.3	94.6	94.6	94.6	74.4	73.4	75.4	42306	22	0.934	5.7	6.9	1.3	1.0
Korea Rep.	26	0.802	0.937	79.2	82.4	75.8	99.0	99.0	99.0	98.5	90.6	105.8	24801	25	0.926	43.0	48.0	1.7	1.2
Kuwait	31		0.916	77.5	79.8	76.0	94.5	93.1	95.2	72.6	77.8	67.8	47812	34	0.892	2.1	2.9	3.2	2.2
UAR	35	0.834	0.903	77.3	78.7	76.6	90.0	91.5	89.5	71.4	78.7	65.4	54626	38	0.878	1.9	4.4	3.9	1.9
Chile	44	0.795	0.878	78.5	81.6	75.5	96.5	96.5	96.6	82.5	82.0	83.0	13880	41	0.871	13.2	16.6	2.6	1.9
Argentina	49	0.804	0.866	75.2	79.0	71.5	97.6	97.7	97.6	88.6	93.3	84.0	13238	46	0.862	32.5	39.5	2.9	2.3
Mexico	53	0.782	0.854	76.0	78.5	73.6	92.8	91.4	94.4	80.2	79.0	81.5	14104	48	0.847	83.4	107.5	3.2	2.2
Saudi Arabia	59	0.744	0.843	72.7	75.1	70.8	85.0	79.4	89.1	78.5	78.0	79.1	22935	60	0.816	16.3	24.7	5.4	3.2
Malaysia	66	0.737	0.829	74.1	76.6	71.9	91.9	89.6	94.2	71.5	73.1	69.8	13518	58	0.823	18.1	26.6	3.5	2.6
Russia	71	0.821	0.817	66.2	72.9	59.9	99.5	99.4	99.7	81.9	86.1	78.0	14690	59	0.816	148.1	141.9	1.5	1.4
Brazil	75	0.710	0.813	72.2	75.9	68.6	90.0	90.2	89.8	87.2	89.4	85.1	9567	63	0.810	149.6	190.1	2.6	1.9
Colombia	77	0.715	0.807	72.7	76.5	69.1	92.7	92.8	92.4	79.0	80.9	77.2	8587	64	0.806	33.2	44.4	3.0	2.5
Turkey	79	0.705	0.806	71.7	74.2	69.4	88.7	81.3	96.2	71.1	66.3	75.7	12955	70	0.788	56.1	73.0	2.9	2.1
Thailand	87	0.706	0.783	68.7	72.1	65.4	94.1	92.6	95.9	78.0	79.6	76.6	8135	72	0.782	56.7	67.0	2.1	1.8
China	92	0.608	0.772	72.9	74.7	71.3	93.3	90.0	96.5	68.7	68.5	68.9	5383	75	0.770	1142.1	1329.1	2.0	1.8
Jamaica	100		0.766	71.7	75.1	68.3	86.0	91.1	80.5	78.1	82.0	74.3	6079	81	0.762	2.4	2.7	2.8	2.4
Sri Lanka	102	0.683	0.759	74.0	77.9	70.3	90.8	89.1	92.7	68.7	69.9	67.5	4243	83	0.756	17.3	19.9	2.5	2.3
Phillippines	105	0.697	0.751	71.6	73.9	69.4	93.4	93.7	93.1	79.6	81.6	77.8	3406	86	0.748	62.4	88.7	4.1	3.1
Indonesia	111	0.624	0.734	70.5	72.5	68.5	92.0	88.8	95.2	68.2	66.8	69.5	3712	93	0.726	177.4	224.7	2.9	2.2
Egypt	123	0.580	0.703	69.9	71.7	68.2	66.4	57.8	74.6	76.4	77.3	76.3	5349			57.8	80.1	3.9	2.9
South Africa	129	0.698	0.683	51.5	53.2	49.8	88.0	87.2	88.9	76.8	77.3	76.3	9757	109	0.680	36.7	49.2	3.3	2.6
India	134	0.489	0.612	63.4	64.9	62.0	66.0	54.5	76.9	61.0	57.4	64.3	2753	114	0.594	862.2	1164.7	3.9	2.8
Myanmar	138	0.487	0.586	61.2	63.4	59.0	89.9	86.4	93.9	56.3			904			40.8	49.1	3.1	2.3
Pakistan	141	0.449	0.572	66.2	66.5	65.9	54.2	39.6	67.7	39.3	34.4	43.9	2496	124	0.532	115.8	173.2	5.7	4.0
Nepal	144	0.407	0.553	66.3	66.9	65.6	56.5	43.6	70.3	60.8	58.1	63.4	1049	119	0.545	19.1	28.3	4.9	2.9
Bangladesh	146	0.389	0.543	65.7	66.7	64.7	53.5	48.0	58.7	52.1	52.5	51.8	1241	123	0.536	115.6	157.8	4.0	2.4

Source: Human Development Report 2009, UNDP.